Lecture Notes in Computer Science 7155

Commenced Publication in 1973
Founding and Former Series Editors:
Gerhard Goos, Juris Hartmanis, and Jan van Leeuwen

Editorial Board

Michael Alexander   Pasqua D'Ambra
Adam Belloum   George Bosilca
Mario Cannataro   Marco Danelutto
Beniamino Di Martino   Michael Gerndt
Emmanuel Jeannot   Raymond Namyst
Jean Roman   Stephen L. Scott
Jesper Larsson Traff   Geoffroy Vallée
Josef Weidendorfer (Eds.)

Euro-Par 2011: Parallel Processing Workshops

CCPI, CGWS, HeteroPar, HiBB, HPCVirt, HPPC,
HPSS, MDGS, ProPer, Resilience, UCHPC, VHPC
Bordeaux, France, August 29 – September 2, 2011
Revised Selected Papers, Part I

 Springer

Volume Editors

Michael Alexander, E-mail: malexander@scilytics.com
Pasqua D'Ambra, E-mail: pasqua.dambra@na.icar.cnr.it
Adam Belloum, E-mail: a.s.z.belloum@uva.nl
George Bosilca, E-mail: bosilca@eecs.utk.edu
Mario Cannataro, E-mail: cannataro@unicz.it
Marco Danelutto, E-mail: marcod@di.unipi.it
Beniamino Di Martino, E-mail: beniamino.dimartino@unina.it
Michael Gerndt, E-mail: michael.gerndt@in.tum.de
Emmanuel Jeannot, E-mail: emmanuel.jeannot@inria.fr
Raymond Namyst, E-mail: raymond.namyst@labri.fr
Jean Roman, E-mail: jean.roman@inria.fr
Stephen L. Scott, E-mail: scottsl@ornl.gov
Jesper Larsson Traff, E-mail: traff@par.univie.ac.at
Geoffroy Vallée, E-mail: valleegr@ornl.gov
Josef Weidendorfer, E-mail: josef.weidendorfer@in.tum.de

ISSN 0302-9743   e-ISSN 1611-3349
ISBN 978-3-642-29736-6   e-ISBN 978-3-642-29737-3
DOI 10.1007/978-3-642-29737-3
Springer Heidelberg Dordrecht London New York

Library of Congress Control Number: 2012935785

CR Subject Classification (1998): C.4, D.2, C.2, D.4, C.2.4, C.3

LNCS Sublibrary: SL 1 – Theoretical Computer Science and General Issues

Typesetting: Camera-ready by author, data conversion by Scientific Publishing Services, Chennai, India

Printed on acid-free paper

Springer is part of Springer Science+Business Media (www.springer.com)

Preface

Euro-Par is an annual series of international conferences dedicated to the promotion and advancement of all aspects of parallel and distributed computing. Euro-Par 2011 was the 17th edition in this conference series. Euro-Par covers a wide spectrum of topics from algorithms and theory to software technology and hardware-related issues, with application areas ranging from scientific to mobile and cloud computing. Euro-Par provides a forum for the introduction, presentation and discussion of the latest scientific and technical advances, extending the frontier of both the state of the art and the state of the practice.

Since 2006, Euro-Par conferences provide a platform for a number of accompanying, technical workshops. This is a great opportunity for small and emerging communities to meet and discuss focussed research topics. This 2011 edition established a new record: 12 workshops were organized. Among these workshops, we had the pleasure of welcoming 4 newcomers: HPCVirt (previously held in conjunction with EuroSys), HPSS (first edition), MDGS (first edition) and Resilience (previously held in conjunction with CCgrid). It was also great to see the CCPI, HiBB and UCHPC workshops attracting a broad audience for their second edition. Here is the complete list of workshops that were held in 2011:

1. Cloud Computing Projects and Initiatives (CCPI)
2. CoreGRID/ERCIM Workshop on Grids, Clouds and P2P Computing (CGWS)
3. Algorithms, Models and Tools for Parallel Computing on Heterogeneous Platforms (HeteroPar)
4. High-Performance Bioinformatics and Biomedicine (HiBB)
5. System-Level Virtualization for High-Performance Computing (HPCVirt)
6. Highly Parallel Processing on a Chip (HPPC)
7. Algorithms and Programming Tools for Next-Generation High-Performance Scientific Software (HPSS)
8. Managing and Delivering Grid Services (MDGS)
9. Productivity and Performance (Proper)
10. Resiliency in High-Performance Computing (Resilience) in Clusters, Clouds, and Grids
11. UnConventional High-Performance Computing 2011 (UCHPC)
12. Virtualization in High-Performance Cloud Computing (VHPC).

The present volume includes the proceedings of all workshops. Each workshop had their own paper-reviewing process. Special thanks are due to the authors of all the submitted papers, the members of the Program Committees, all the reviewers and the workshop organizers. They all contributed to the success of this edition.

We are also grateful to the members of the Euro-Par Steering Committee for their support, in particular Luc Bougé and Christian Lengauer for all their advices regarding the coordination of workshops. We thank Domenico Talia,

Pasqua D'Ambra and Mario Rosario Guarracino of the organization of Euro-Par 2010 for sharing their experience with us.

A number of institutional and industrial sponsors contributed toward the organization of the conference. Their names and logos appear on the Euro-Par 2011 website http://europar2011.bordeaux.inria.fr/

It was our pleasure and honor to organize and host the Euro-Par 2011 workshops in Bordeaux. We hope all the participants enjoyed the technical program and the social events organized during the conference.

January 2011   Emmanuel Jeannot
                                                 Raymond Namyst
                                                    Jean Roman

Organization

Euro-Par Steering Committee

Chair

Chris Lengauer   University of Passau, Germany

Vice-Chair

Luc Bougé   ENS Cachan, France

European Respresentatives

José Cunha   New University of Lisbon, Portugal
Marco Danelutto   University of Pisa, Italy
Emmanuel Jeannot   INRIA, France
Paul Kelly   Imperial College, UK
Harald Kosch   University of Passau, Germany
Thomas Ludwig   University of Heidelberg, Germany
Emilio Luque   University Autonoma of Barcelona, Spain
Tomàs Margalef   University Autonoma of Barcelona, Spain
Wolfgang Nagel   Dresden University of Technology, Germany
Rizos Sakellariou   University of Manchester, UK
Henk Sips   Delft University of Technology,
                              The Netherlands
Domenico Talia   University of Calabria, Italy

Honorary Members

Ron Perrott   Queen's University Belfast, UK
Karl Dieter Reinartz   University of Erlangen-Nuremberg, Germany

Euro-Par 2011 Organization

Conference Co-chairs

Emmanuel Jeannot   INRIA, France
Raymond Namyst   University of Bordeaux, France
Jean Roman   INRIA, University of Bordeaux, France

Local Organizing Committee

Olivier Aumage   INRIA, France
Emmanuel Agullo   INRIA, France
Alexandre Denis   INRIA, France

Nathalie Furmento	CNRS, France
Laetitia Grimaldi	INRIA, France
Nicole Lun	LaBRI, France
Guillaume Mercier	University of Bordeaux, France
Elia Meyre	LaBRI, France

Euro-Par 2011 Workshops

Chair

Raymond Namyst   University of Bordeaux, France

Workshop on Cloud Computing Projects and Initiatives (CCPI)

Program Chairs

Beniamino Di Martino	Second University of Naples, Italy
Dana Petcu	West University of Timisoara, Romania
Antonio Puliafito	University of Messina, Italy

Program Committee

Pasquale Cantiello	Second University of Naples, Italy
Maria Fazio	University of Messina, Italy
Florin Fortis	West University of Timisoara, Romania
Francesco Moscato	Second University of Naples, Italy
Viorel Negru	West University of Timisoara, Romania
Massimo Villari	University of Messina, Italy

CoreGRID/ERCIM Workshop on Grids, Clouds and P2P Computing – CGWS2011

Program Chairs

M. Danelutto	University of Pisa, Italy
F. Desprez	INRIA and ENS Lyon, France
V. Getov	University of Westminster, UK
W. Ziegler	SCAI, Germany

Program Committee

Artur Andrzejak	Institute For Infocomm Research (I2R), Singapore
Marco Aldinucci	University of Torin, Italy
Alvaro Arenas	IE Business School, Madrid, Spain
Rosa M. Badia	Technical University of Catalonia, Spain
Alessandro Bassi	HIT ACHI, France

Augusto Ciuffoletti   University of Pisa, Italy
Marco Danelutto   University of Pisa, Italy
Marios Dikaiakos   University of Cyprus, Cyprus
Dick H.J. Epema   Delft University of Technology,
                                   The Netherlands
Thomas Fahringer   University of Innsbruck, Austria
Gilles Fedak   INRIA, France
Paraskevi Fragopoulou   FORTH-ICS, Greece
J. Gabarro   Technical University of Catalonia, Spain
Vladimir Getov   University of Westminster, UK
Sergei Gorlatch   University of Münster, Germany
T. Harmer   Belfast e-Science Center, UK
Ruben S. Montero   Complutense University of Madrid, Spain
Peter Kacsuk   MT A SZT AKI, Hungary
Thilo Kielmann   Vrije Universiteit, The Netherlands
Derrick Kondo   INRIA, France
Philippe Massonet   CETIC, Belgium
Carlo Mastroianni   ICAR-CNR, Italy
Norbert Meyer   Poznan Supercomputing and Networking
                                   Center, Poland
Ignacio M. Llorente   Complutense University of Madrid, Spain
Christian Pérez   INRIA/IRISA, France
Ron Perrott   Queen's University of Belfast, UK
Thierry Priol   INRIA, France
Omer Rana   Cardiff University, UK
Rizos Sakellariou   University of Manchester, UK
Alan Stewart   Queen's University of Belfast, UK
Junichi Suzuki   University of Massachusetts, Boston, USA
Domenico Talia   University of Calabria, Italy
Ian Taylor   Cardiff University, UK
Jordi Torres   Technical University of Catalonia - BSC, Spain
Paolo Trunfio   University of Calabria, Italy
Ramin Yahyapour   University of Dortmund, Germany
Demetrios Zeinalipour-Yazti   University of Cyprus, Cyprus
Wolfgang Ziegler   Fraunhofer Institute SCAI, Germany

5th Workshop on System-Level Virtualization for High-Performance Computing (HPCVirt 2011)

Program Chairs

Stephen L. Scott   Oak Ridge National Laboratory, USA
Geoffroy Vallée   Oak Ridge National Laboratory, USA
Thomas Naughton   Tennessee Tech University, USA

Program Committee

Patrick Bridges	UNM, USA
Thierry Delaitre	The University of Westminster, UK
Christian Engelmann	ORNL, USA
Douglas Fuller	ORNL, USA
Ada Gavrilovska	Georgia Tech, USA
Jack Lange	University of Pittsburgh, USA
Adrien Lebre	Ecole des Mines de Nantes, France
Laurent Lefevre	INRIA, University of Lyon, France
Jean-Marc Menaud	Ecole des Mines de Nantes, France
Christine Morin	INRIA, France
Thomas Naughton	ORNL, USA
Dimitrios Nikolopoulos	University of Crete, Greece
Josh Simons	VMWare, USA
Samuel Thibault	LaBRI, France

HPPC 2011: 5th Workshop on Highly Parallel Processing on a Chip

Program Chairs

Martti Forsell	VTT, Finland
Jesper Larsson Träff	University of Vienna, Austria

Program Committee

David Bader	Georgia Institute of Technology, USA
Martti Forsell	VTT, Finland
Jim Held	Intel, USA
Peter Hofstee	IBM, USA
Magnus Jahre	NTNU, Norway
Chris Jesshope	University of Amsterdam, The Netherlands
Ben Juurlink	Technical University of Berlin, Germany
Jörg Keller	University of Hagen, Germany
Christoph Kessler	University of Linköping, Sweden
Avi Mendelson	Microsoft, Israel
Vitaly Osipov	Karlsruhe Institute of Technology, Germany
Martti Penttonen	University of Eastern Finland, Finland
Sven-Bodo Scholz	University of Hertfordshire, UK
Jesper Larsson Träff	University of Vienna, Austria
Theo Ungerer	University of Augsburg, Germany
Uzi Vishkin	University of Maryland, USA

Sponsors

VTT, Finland	http://www.vtt.fi
University of Vienna	http://www.univie.ac.at
Euro-Par	http://www.euro-par.org

Algorithms and Programming Tools for Next-Generation High-Performance Scientific Software (HPSS 2011)

Program Chairs

Stefania Corsaro	University of Naples Parthenope and ICAR-CNR, Italy
Pasqua D'Ambra	ICAR-CNR, Naples, Italy
Francesca Perla	University of Naples Parthenope and ICAR-CNR, Italy

Program Committee

Patrick Amnestoy	University of Toulouse, France
Peter Arbenz	ETH Zurich, Switzerland
Rob Bisseling	Utrecht University, The Netherlands
Daniela di Serafino	Second University of Naples and ICAR-CNR, Italy
Jack Dongarra	University of Tennesse, USA
Salvatore Filippone	University of Rome Tor Vergata, Italy
Laura Grigori	INRIA, France
Andreas Grothey	University of Edinburgh, UK
Mario Rosario Guarracino	ICAR-CNR, Italy
Sven Hammarling	University of Manchester and NAG Ltd., UK
Mike Heroux	Sandia National Laboratories, USA
Gerardo Toraldo	University of Naples Federico II and ICAR-CNR, Italy
Bora Ucar	CNRS, France
Rich Vuduc	Georgia Tech, USA
Ulrike Meier Yang	Lawrence Livermore National Laboratory, USA

HeteroPar 2011: Algorithms, Models and Tools for Parallel Computing on Heterogeneous Platforms

Program Chairs

George Bosilca	ICL, University of Tennessee, Knoxville, USA

Program Committee

Jacques Bahi	University of Franche-Comté, France
Jorge Barbosa	FEUP, Portugal
George Bosilca	Innovative Computing Laboratory - University of Tennessee, Knoxville, USA
Andrea Clematis	IMATI CNR, Italy
Michel Dayde	IRIT - INPT / ENSEEIHT, France
Frederic Desprez	INRIA, France
Pierre-Francois Dutot	Laboratoire LIG, France
Alfredo Goldman	University of São Paulo - USP, Brasil

Thomas Herault	Innovative Computing Laboratory - University of Tennessee, Knoxville, USA
Shuichi Ichikawa	Toyohashi University of Technology, Japan
Emmanuel Jeannot	LaBRI, INRIA Bordeaux Sud-Ouest, France
Helen Karatza	Aristotle University of Thessaloniki, Greece
Zhiling Lan	Illinois Institute of Technology, USA
Pierre Manneback	University of Mons, Belgium
Kiminori Matsuzaki	Kochi University of Technology, Japan
Wahid Nasri	Higher School of Sciences and Techniques of Tunis, Tunisia
Dana Petcu	West University of Timisoara, Romania
Serge Petiton	Université des Sciences et Technologies de Lille, France
Casiano Rodriguez-Leon	Universidad de La Laguna, Spain
Franciszek Seredynski	Polish Academy of Sciences, Poland
Howard J. Siegel	CSU, USA
Antonio M. Vidal	Universidad Politécnica de Valencia, Spain
Ramin Yahyapour	TU University Dortmund, Germany

HiBB 2011: Second Workshop on High-Performance Bioinformatics and Biomedicine

Program Chairs

Mario Cannataro	University Magna Græcia of Catanzaro, Italy

Program Committee

Pratul K. Agarwal	Oak Ridge National Laboratory, USA
David A. Bader	College of Computing, Georgia University of Technology, USA
Ignacio Blanquer	Universidad Politécnica de Valencia, Valencia, Spain
Daniela Calvetti	Case Western Reserve University, USA
Werner Dubitzky	University of Ulster, UK
Ananth Y. Grama	Purdue University, USA
Concettina Guerra	University of Padova, Italy
Vicente Hernández	Universitad Politécnica de Valencia, Spain
Salvatore Orlando	University of Venice, Italy
Omer F. Rana	Cardiff University, UK
Richard Sinnott	National e-Science Centre, University of Glasgow, Glasgow, UK
Fabrizio Silvestri	ISTI-CNR, Italy
Erkki Somersalo	Case Western Reserve University, USA
Paolo Trunfio	University of Calabria, Italy
Albert Zomaya	University of Sydney, Australia

Managing and Delivering Grid Services 2011 (MDGS2011)

Program Chairs

Thomas Schaaf	Ludwig-Maximiians-Universität, Munich, Germany
Owen Appleton	Emergence Tech Limited, London, UK
Adam S.Z. Belloum	University of Amsterdam, The Netherlands
Joan Serrat-Fernández	Universitat Politècnica de Catalunya, Barcelona, Spain
Tomasz Szepieniec	AGH University of Science and Technology, Krakow, Poland

Program Committee

Nazim Agulmine	University of Evry, France
Michael Brenner	Leibniz Supercomputing Centre, Germany
Ewa Deelman	University of Southern California, USA
Karim Djemame	University of Leeds, UK
Thomas Fahringer	University of Innsbruck, Austria
Alex Galis	University College London, UK
Dieter Kranzlmüller	Ludwig-Maximilians-Universität, Germany
Laurent Lefebre	INRIA, France
Edgar Magana	CISCO research labs, USA
Patricia Marcu	Leibniz Supercomputing Centre, Germany
Carlos Merida	Barcelona Supercomputing Center, Spain
Steven Newhouse	European Grid Initiative, The Netherlands
Omer F. Rana	Cardiff University, UK
Stefan Wesner	High Performance Computing Center Stuttgart, Germany
Philipp Wieder	Technische Universität Dortmund, Germany
Ramin Yahyapour	Technische Universität Dortmund, Germany

4th Workshop on Productivity and Performance Tools for HPC Application Development (PROPER 2011)

Program Chairs

Michael Gerndt	TU München, Germany

Program Committee

Andreas Knüpfer	TU Dresden, Germany
Dieter an Mey	RWTH Aachen, Germany
Jens Doleschal	TU Dresden, Germany
Karl Fürlinger	University of California at Berkeley, USA
Michael Gerndt	TU München, Germany
Allen Malony	University of Oregon, USA

Shirley Moore	University of Tennessee, USA
Matthias Müller	TU Dresden, Germany
Martin Schulz	Lawrence Livermore National Lab, USA
Felix Wolf	German Research School for Simulation Sciences, Germany
Josef Weidendorfer	TU München, Germany
Shajulin Benedict	St. Xavier's College, India
Beniamino Di Martino	Seconda Università di Napoli, Italy
Torsten Höfler	University of Illinois, USA

Workshop on Resiliency in High-Performance Computing (Resilience) in Clusters, Clouds, and Grids

Program Chairs

Stephen L. Scott	Oak Ridge National Laboratory, USA
Chokchai (Box) Leangsuksun	Louisiana Tech University, USA

Program Committee

Vassil Alexandrov	Barcelona Supercomputing Center, Spain
David E. Bernholdt	Oak Ridge National Laboratory, USA
George Bosilca	University of Tennessee, USA
Jim Brandt	Sandia National Laboratories, USA
Patrick G. Bridges	University of New Mexico, USA
Greg Bronevetsky	Lawrence Livermore National Laboratory, USA
Franck Cappello	INRIA/UIUC, France/USA
Kasidit Chanchio	Thammasat University, Thailand
Zizhong Chen	Colorado School of Mines, USA
Nathan DeBardeleben	Los Alamos National Laboratory, USA
Jack Dongarra	University of Tennessee, USA
Christian Engelmann	Oak Ridge National Laboratory, USA
Yung-Chin Fang	Dell, USA
Kurt B. Ferreira	Sandia National Laboratories, USA
Ann Gentile	Sandia National Laboratories, USA
Cecile Germain	University Paris-Sud, France
Rinku Gupta	Argonne National Laboratory, USA
Paul Hargrove	Lawrence Berkeley National Laboratory, USA
Xubin He	Virginia Commonwealth University, USA
Larry Kaplan	Cray, USA
Daniel S. Katz	University of Chicago, USA
Thilo Kielmann	Vrije Universiteit Amsterdam, The Netherlands
Dieter Kranzlmueller	LMU/LRZ Munich, Germany
Zhiling Lan	Illinois Institute of Technology, USA
Chokchai (Box) Leangsuksun	Louisiana Tech University, USA
Xiaosong Ma	North Carolina State University, USA
Celso Mendes	University of Illinois at Urbana Champaign, USA

Christine Morin	INRIA Rennes, France
Thomas Naughton	Oak Ridge National Laboratory, USA
George Ostrouchov	Oak Ridge National Laboratory, USA
DK Panda	The Ohio State University, USA
Mihaela Paun	Louisiana Tech University, USA
Alexander Reinefeld	Zuse Institute Berlin, Germany
Rolf Riesen	IBM Research, Ireland
Eric Roman	Lawrence Berkeley National Laboratory, USA
Stephen L. Scott	Oak Ridge National Laboratory, USA
Jon Stearley	Sandia National Laboratories, USA
Gregory M. Thorson	SGI, USA
Geoffroy Vallee	Oak Ridge National Laboratory, USA
Sudharshan Vazhkudai	Oak Ridge National Laboratory, USA

UCHPC 2011: Fourth Workshop on UnConventional High-Performance Computing

Program Chairs

Anders Hast	University of Gävle, Sweden
Josef Weidendorfer	Technische Universität München, Germany
Jan-Philipp Weiss	Karlsruhe Institute of Technology, Germany

Steering Committee

Lars Bengtsson	Chalmers University, Sweden
Ren Wu	HP Labs, Palo Alto, USA

Program Committee

David A. Bader	Georgia Tech, USA
Michael Bader	Universität Stuttgart, Germany
Denis Barthou	Université de Bordeaux, France
Lars Bengtsson	Chalmers, Sweden
Karl Fürlinger	LMU, Munich, Germany
Dominik Göddeke	TU Dortmund, Germany
Georg Hager	University of Erlangen-Nuremberg, Germany
Anders Hast	University of Gävle, Sweden
Ben Juurlink	TU Berlin, Germany
Rainer Keller	HLRS Stuttgart, Germany
Gaurav Khanna	University of Massachusetts Dartmouth, USA
Harald Köstler	University of Erlangen-Nuremberg, Germany
Dominique Lavenier	INRIA, France
Manfred Mücke	University of Vienna, Austria
Andy Nisbet	Manchester Metropolitan University, UK
Ioannis Papaefstathiou	Technical University of Crete, Greece
Franz-Josef Pfreundt	Fraunhofer ITWM, Germany

Bertil Schmidt	Johannes Gutenberg University Mainz, Germany
Thomas Steinke	Zuse Institute, Berlin, Germany
Robert Strzodka	Max Planck Center for Computer Science, Germany
Carsten Trinitis	Technische Universität München, Germany
Josef Weidendorfer	Technische Universität München, Germany
Jan-Philipp Weiss	KIT, Germany
Gerhard Wellein	University of Erlangen-Nuremberg, Germany
Stephan Wong	Delft University of Technology, The Netherlands
Ren Wu	HP Labs, Palo Alto, USA
Peter Zinterhof Jr.	University of Salzburg, Austria
Yunquan Zhang	Chinese Academy of Sciences, Beijing, China

Additional Reviewers

Antony Brandon	Delft University of Technology, The Netherlands
Roel Seedorf	Delft University of Technology, The Netherlands

VHPC 2011: Sixth Workshop on Virtualization in High-Performance Cloud Computing

Program Chairs

Michael Alexander	scaledinfra technologies GmbH, Vienna, Austria
Gianluigi Zanetti	CRS4, Italy

Program Committee

Padmashree Apparao	Intel Corp., USA
Hassan Barada	Khalifa University, UAE
Volker Buege	University of Karlsruhe, Germany
Isabel Campos	IFCA, Spain
Stephen Childs	Trinity College Dublin, Ireland
William Gardner	University of Guelph, Canada
Derek Groen	UVA, The Netherlands
Ahmad Hammad	FZK, Germany
Sverre Jarp	CERN, Switzerland
Xuxian Jiang	NC State, USA
Kenji Kaneda	Google, Japan
Krishna Kant	Intel, USA
Yves Kemp	DESY Hamburg, Germany
Marcel Kunze	Karlsruhe Institute of Technology, Germany

Naoya Maruyama	Tokyo Institute of Technology, Japan
Jean-Marc Menaud	Ecole des Mines de Nantes, France
Oliver Oberst	Karlsruhe Institute of Technology, Germany
Jose Renato Santos	HP Labs, USA
Deepak Singh	Amazon Webservices, USA
Yoshio Turner	HP Labs, USA
Andreas Unterkirchner	CERN, Switzerland
Lizhe Wang	Rochester Institute of Technology, USA

Table of Contents – Part I

CCPI 2011: Workshop on Cloud Computing Projects and Initiatives

CoreGRID/ERCIM Workshop on Grids, Clouds and P2P Computing – CGWS2011

5th Workshop on System-Level Virtualization for High-Performance Computing (HPCVirt 2011)

HPPC 2010: 5th Workshop on Highly Parallel Processing on a Chip

Algorithms and Programming Tools for Next-Generation High-Performance Scientific Software HPSS 2011

Algorithms, Models and Tools for Parallel Computing on Heterogeneous Platforms (HeteroPar 2011)

Table of Contents – Part II

HiBB 2011: 2nd Workshop on High-Performance Bioinformatics and Biomedicine

Managing and Delivering Grid Services (MDGS)

PROPER 2011: Fourth Workshop on Productivity and Performance: Tools for HPC Application Development

Workshop on Resiliency in High-Performance Computing (Resilience) in Clusters, Clouds, and Grids

UCHPC 2011: Fourth Workshop on UnConventional High-Performance Computing

VHPC 2011: 6th Workshop on Virtualization in High-Performance Cloud Computing

CCPI 2011: Workshop on Cloud Computing Projects and Initiatives

Beniamino Di Martino[1] and Dana Petcu[2]

[1] Second University of Naples, Italy
[2] Institute e-Austria and West University of Timisoara, Romania

Foreword

Cloud computing is a recent computing paradigm for enabling convenient, on-demand network access to a shared pool of configurable computing resources (e.g. networks, servers, storage, applications, and services) that can be rapidly provisioned and released with minimal management effort or service provider interaction. Clouds are currently used mainly in commercial settings and focus on on-demand provision of IT infrastructure. Cloud computing can play a significant role in a variety of areas including innovations, virtual worlds, ebusiness, social networks, or search engines. But currently, it is still in its early stages, with consistent experimentation to come.

The *Workshop on Cloud Computing Projects and Initiatives* (CCPI), organized by the European FP7-ICT Project mOSAIC (http://www.mosaic-cloud.eu) - within the objectives of DG-INFSO - Internet of Services, Software and Virtualization Unit[1], gathered together scientists, engineers, computer users both from industry and academia to exchange and share experiences, new ideas, and research results from collaborative international and national projects and initiatives on Cloud Computing. A number of key projects funded by the European Commission and by National Government and Research Agencies, addressing several aspects of the Cloud Computing arena, were presented at the workshop, and now in the following post-workshop proceeding papers.

The paper *Towards Cross-Platform Cloud Computing*, by Magdalena Slawinska, Jaroslaw Slawinski, Vaidy Sunderam attempts to analyze the commonalities and differences between cloud offerings with a view to determining the extent to which they may be unified. They propose the concept of dynamic adapters supported by runtime systems for environment preconditioning, that help facilitate cross platform deployment of cloud applications. In this vision paper, they outline the issues involved, and present preliminary ideas for enhancing the executability of legacy applications on various cloud platforms.

The paper *QoS Monitoring in a Cloud Services Environment: the SRT-15 Aprroach* by Giuseppe Cicotti, Luigi Coppolino, Rosario Cristaldi, Salvatore D'Antonio and Luigi Romano presents a innovative Quality of Service monitoring facility, named QoSMONaaS, built on top of the SRT-15, a Cloud-oriented platform being developed in the context of the homonymous FP7 EU project.

---

[1] We wish to thank the Project Officer Maria Tsakali for her support.

In particular the authors present the main components of QoSMONaaS and its internal operation with respect to a case study of an Internet of Thing (IoT) application.

The paper *Enabling e-Science applications on the Cloud with COMPSs* from Daniele Lezzi, Roger Rafanell, Abel Carrion, Ignacio Blanquer Espert, Vicente Hernandez and Rosa M. Badia presents the implementation of scientific workflows through the COMPSs framework and their deployment and execution on the VENUS-C platform.

The paper *OPTIMIS and VISION Cloud: How to manage data in Clouds*, by Spyridon V. Gogouvitis, George Kousiouris, George Vafiadis, Hillel Kolodner and Dimosthenis Kyriazis presents two EU funded FP7 projects, namely OPTIMIS and VISION Cloud, that deal with data management in Cloud environments. The paper portrays the key value-add characteristics of their designs that improve the state of the art towards providing more advanced features for Cloud-based storage services. The similarities and differences between the approaches taken by the two projects in issues such as ease of management, data mobility and federation, coupling storage with computing power and guaranteeing QoS are presented and discussed.

The paper *Integrated Monitoring of Infrastructures and Applications in Cloud Environments* by Roberto Palmieri, Pierangelo di Sanzo, Francesco Quaglia, Paolo Romano, Sebastiano Peluso, and Diego Didona, illustrates some of the achievements of the Cloud-TM FP7 project. In particular, it presents the approach that has been taken while designing and implementing a monitoring subsystem, which represents a building block for the realization of a self-adapting, Cloud based middleware platform providing transactional data access to generic customer applications.

The paper *Towards Collaborative Data Management in the VPH-Share Project* by Siegfried Benkner, Jesus Bisbal, Gerhard Engelbrecht, Rod D. Hose, Yuriy Kaniovskyi, Martin Koehler, Carlos Pedrinaci, and Steven Wood outlines the vision of the European project VPH-Share in providing an organisational fabric (called infostructure) for the health care domain. The infostructure will be realised as a set of services on top of Cloud technologies for exposing and managing data, information and tools, and for enabling the composition of advanced workflows within the scope of the Virtual Physiological Human Initiative

The paper *SLM and SDM challenges in federated infrastructures* was produced by members of the EC funded gSLM project. It draws on experiences in service level management in e-Infrastructures such as Grids to set out the challenges in managing multi-cloud services. These include the weakness of service level agreements offered by commercial cloud providers, the complex relationship structures seen in multi-clouds, the difficulty in assigning responsibility in federated environments and the limited options for enforcement and penalisation these factors entail.

The paper *Rapid Prototyping of Architectures on the Cloud Using Semantic Resource Description* by Houssam Haitof attempts to present a framework for rapid instantiations of service representations of resources from their semantic description. The idea is to allow the rapid prototyping of resources and resource relationships to be used in Cloud infrastructure environments. A semantic model is presented as well as the managed resource framework used to generate service representations with a management interface.

The paper *Cloud Patterns for mOSAIC-enabled Scientific Applications* from T.F. Fortis ,G.E. Lopez, I.P. Cruz, G. Ferschl and T. Mahr illustrates the current achievements of the mOSAIC project related identification and description of a set of reusable cloud patterns and cloud use cases for scientific applications, extending existing results in order to address the specific requirements, as identified via the mOSAIC project.

The paper *Enhancing an autonomic cloud architecture with mobile agents* from Umberto Villano, Massimiliano Rak, Antonio Cuomo, Salvatore Venticinque presents an interesting application of mobile agents technology to support resource monitoring in clouds, grids and hybrid architectures. The proposal is integrated into a larger framework which supports autonomic management of distributed applications. A case study is shown in the context of Cloud@Home, a cloud environment built on top of voluntereed resources, currently under development as a project funded by the Italian research initiative PRIN 2008.

The paper *Mapping Application Requirements to Cloud Resources*, from Yih Leong Sun, Terence Harmer, Alan Stewart, and Peter Wright, proposes a constraints - based model for discovering Cloud resources in a multi-provider environment. This paper studies a financial use case scenario and suggests the use of a provider-agnostic approach which hides the complex implementation details of selecting Cloud resources.

Towards Cross-Platform Cloud Computing*

Magdalena Slawinska, Jaroslaw Slawinski, and Vaidy Sunderam

Department of Mathematics and Computer Science,
Emory University, Atlanta, Georgia, USA
{magg,jaross}@mathcs.emory.edu, vss@emory.edu

Abstract. Cloud computing is becoming increasingly popular and prevalent in many domains. However, there is high variability in the programming models, access methods, and operational aspects of different clouds, diminishing the viability of cloud computing as a true utility. Our ADAPAS project attempts to analyze the commonalities and differences between cloud offerings with a view to determining the extent to which they may be unified. We propose the concept of dynamic adapters supported by runtime systems for environment preconditioning, that help facilitate cross platform deployment of cloud applications. This vision paper outlines the issues involved, and presents preliminary ideas for enhancing the executability of applications on different cloud platforms.

1 Introduction

The past few years have witnessed rapidly growing interest in cloud computing. However, while instant, affordable, access to computing and data resources at dynamically variable levels is valuable, *usability* of clouds for legacy applications and software written in different programming models is low. Moreover, *heterogeneity* in cloud computing platforms often implies inflexibility in the ability to switch between providers, e.g., executing the same application on Microsoft's Windows Azure [7], Google App Engine [18], Amazon EC2 [21], Open Cirrus [5], etc is a formidable challenge.

In this paper we describe our proposed approach to enhance executability of applications on a variety of platforms, in particular, on multiple current and emerging clouds. We outline our project, titled <u>*Adaptive Application Platform Executive System*</u> (ADAPAS) that proposes abstractions for the *dynamic adaptability* of computing paradigms to specific resources. The goals of our project are: (1) *increasing flexibility* in user's choices with respect to target cloud platforms, and (2) *facilitating development* of cloud-aware applications by unifying interfaces and provisioning runtime support.

We believe that at least for certain classes of applications and target platforms, defining a unified capability interface, and subsequent application-to-platform mapping is possible, and that such flexibility will be of value. We note that the

---

* This work is partially supported by US National Science Foundation grants CNS-0720761 and OCI-1124418.

M. Alexander et al. (Eds.): Euro-Par 2011 Workshops, Part I, LNCS 7155, pp. 5–14, 2012.

eventual goal of *completely portable executability* may prove intractable, or at least be susceptible to some performance degradation. Nevertheless, these efforts will help evolve cloud computing frameworks, identify opportunities for unification, and may result in minimizing the porting effort across cloud platforms.

2   Background and Context

The rapid growth of cloud computing and *aaS resources has been accompanied by increased heterogeneity in platform types and resource access methods. The vision of "computing as another utility" is subsequently both expanded and diminished – the former as users scale out applications beyond on-premises resources and the latter as they try to reconcile programming paradigms with specific cloud facilities. Several projects have attempted to address these issues in different ways.

In order to scale an application out, one method is to provide homogenization at the access level and application paradigm level. There are several efforts to approach access homogenization by formal and informal standardization efforts such as Simple Cloud API [4], EUCALYPTUS [15], Nimbus [11], AppScale [8]. In order to support homogenization at the paradigm level, (1) resource providers offer specialized cloud services such as Amazon Elastic MapReduce [1], Tashi [13], or (2) users may adapt an resource to a required specialization level via conditioning, i.e., installing relevant middleware layers, e.g., ElasticWolf [19], Unibus [20], Nimbus [11].

Another aspect of application deployment is providing missing dependencies. This may be achieved by providing environments with encapsulated application's dependencies, e.g., statically linked executables, creating application bundles with all dependencies (PortableApps [2]), or preparing specialized images with preinstalled software dependencies (rPath, rBuild [3]). There are also projects that, instead of the homogenization approach, propose new application frameworks that provide their own programming models (e.g., CometCloud [12], Aneka [22]). In our project, we propose a novel approach based on (1) the *virtualized execution model* and (2) providing application's dependencies via an *adapter* layer.

3   Proposed Abstractions

As presented in Figure 1, ADAPAS aims to enhance the *executability* of applications to allow their execution on different back-ends, without the need for explicit porting effort. Initially, we intend to concentrate on scientific applications at the application side, and PaaS and IaaS cloud resources with primary focus on PaaS, specifically the Azure platform and GAE, as back-ends. Our approach, however, is intended to be applicable to any other classes of resources including grids and multiple cloud offerings. In the following paragraphs, we present the initial design of the ADAPAS framework.

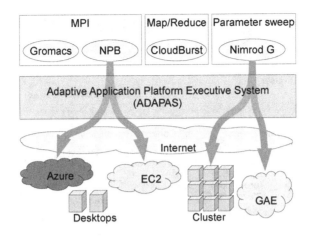

Fig. 1. The Adaptive Application Platform Executive System (ADAPAS) idea

3.1 ADAPAS Overview

Figure 2 depicts a system overview of ADAPAS. The core component of the system is a *Virtual Execution Platform* (VEP). The VEP contains a context layer that comprises *contexts* corresponding to execution environments for a given application, e.g., the MPI context corresponds to MPI applications. In order to execute an application, the VEP provides *adapters* on the application side, and *environment conditioners* on the resource side to provide the required matching.

3.2 Application Model

We assume that an application consists of one or more *programs* which are basic execution units. For instance, an MPI application may consist of one program that is instantiated in many copies. The user may have access to the application's source codes or/and precompiled binary files. The application may have *dependencies* such as binary compatible specific software packages, preinstalled runtimes, dynamically linked libraries, third-party services, etc. In the proposed approach, applications should not require modifications at the source code level in order to execute on specific computational back-ends. Initially, we focus on scientific applications based on established programming paradigms (e.g. SPMD message passing codes, parameter sweep applications, partitioned global address space applications, and workflows) as well as selected libraries and frameworks (e.g., MPICH2 [10], Co-Array Fortran [16], and HADOOP Map/Reduce [23]).

3.3 Resource Model

We model computational resources as *resource chunks* and *computing chunks*, as shown in Figure 3. Resource chunks are the smallest resource allocation units

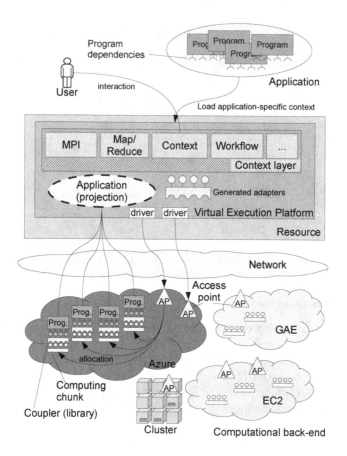

Fig. 2. The ADAPAS system overview

that can be *allocated* to perform the user's computational task on a given computational resource, e.g., cluster nodes on a local cluster, Amazon EC2 quad-core instances, a pluglet container in H2O [14]. A computing chunk is the smallest logical processing unit on the provided resource chunk that is capable of hosting an execution unit. For instance, an executing program, manifested as a process is a computing chunk in a typical timeshared Unix system. On Windows Azure, a computing chunk is a role (worker or web) since a role has the capability to run a program. Programs can be executed only if their dependencies can be expressed in terms of computing chunk capabilities, e.g., the x86 instruction set, a mathematic library, a connection to a database, supported services, etc.

3.4   Application Execution Model

ADAPAS provides a toolkit, called a *Virtual Execution Platform* (VEP), to manage application execution. VEP provides a unified execution model, specialized on-demand by dedicated and pluggable "execution contexts." Contexts support

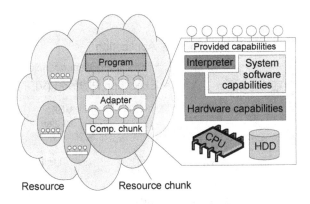

Fig. 3. Resources, resource chunks, and computing chunks

the user with a familiar, specific application-oriented execution environment (e.g., MPI, Map/Reduce, parameter sweep applications, workflow). Contexts will be loaded for a single application run and unloaded when the execution finishes.

The VEP is responsible for all execution stages: (1) obtaining an application (source codes, or binaries) from the client site or a repository, (2) program compilation against target-specific back-end resources (if application source codes are available), (3) resource chunk allocation to enable instantiation of computing chunks, (4) preparing and adaptation of the appropriate libraries required by the program to execute on a particular computing chunk, (5) staging-in the program with all adapted dependencies to the computing chunks, (6) coordinating all programs in order to execute the application, (7) presenting the application status to the application's current context, and (8) releasing resource chunks at the end of execution.

4   ADAPAS Design Approach

Since the goal of ADAPAS is to enhance executability of any unmodified application on any resource, the VEP needs to provide a unifying abstraction, capable of expressing computing capabilities for any computational back-end. To address this, we propose a Virtually Unified Capabilities (VUC) interface that will define common capabilities needed to execute a program. Second, resource capabilities need to meet program dependencies. We approach this through Dependency-Capability objects (DC objects), adapter middleware (adapters), and the VEP engine. The VEP engine will (1) identify program dependencies and discover resource capabilities, and (2) match requested dependencies with offered capabilities via the adapter and DC objects. Third, there is a need for mechanisms to provide missing program dependencies on a computing chunk to enable program execution. This is addressed by the VEP engine and DC objects with *callbacks*.

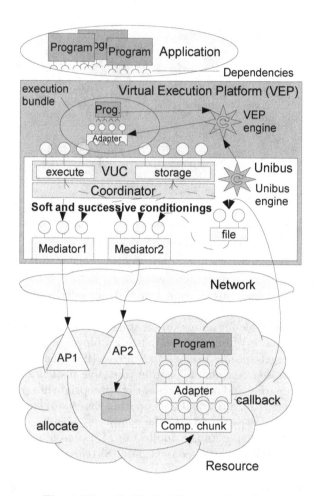

Fig. 4. Virtually Unified Resource Interface

Fourth, is the matter of providing a familiar interface to the user. We address this by proposing VEP-pluggable contexts that are specific for execution environments (e.g., MPI, Hadoop). These aspects are explored below in more detail.

4.1   Virtually Unified Capabilities

VUC capabilities are divided into two interfaces: *execution* and *storage*. The execution interface provides methods related to program execution: (1) sending an *execution bundle* to an assigned computing chunk, (2) starting the program, and (3) monitoring program execution. The execution bundle (bundle) is a complete set of files that are *necessary and sufficient* to execute the program: binary files and program dependencies. Storage interface methods are related to data management: staging-in and retrieving data.

As shown in Figure 4, VUC interfaces are built upon the *coordination layer* (*coordinator*). The coordinator is responsible for four coordination tasks: (1) resource chunk allocation, (2) assigning computing chunks to resource chunks, (3) releasing resource chunks, and (4) managing data transfer routes. For instance, in order to utilize computational power in a more efficient manner, the coordinator may assign four computing chunks to a quad-core CPU resource chunk. To improve network bandwidth, the coordinator may create a resource-local cache to reduce data transfer over the Internet. The coordinator may also aggregate different resources in order to (1) enhance offered capabilities (e.g., combining computing and storage resources to obtain computing *and* storage interfaces), or (2) provide specific features (e.g., fault-tolerant mechanisms, addressing security issues).

4.2   Dependency-Capability Objects

In order to enable the execution of a program, all program dependencies needs to be met on a target computing chunk. In a few cases the only dependency is a binary-compatible program executable. Usually, the program requires a middleware layer that allows the program to run on selected resources. Typically, a resource can be specialized to a required specialization level by soft conditioning (installing missing software dependencies). For a new class of resources such as *aaS, a resource specialization process needs to be augmented; we intend to do this via *dependency-capability objects* (DC objects).

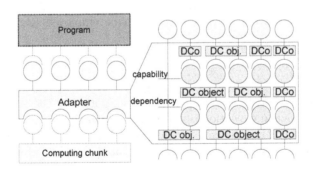

Fig. 5. DC objects create the adapter middleware

DC objects can be characterized as *software functions* or *transformations* that utilize underlying capabilities in order to provide new, more abstract capabilities that will satisfy program dependencies. Every DC object also has its own well defined dependencies as well as capabilities it offers, as presented in Figure 5. A DC object can invoke chunk capabilities, or other DC object capabilities.

We envision that DC objects may be *stateful* and *semantically-aware*. For instance, a DC object implementing the file interface may need to store handles to files as well as the file content. A semantically-aware DC object will be able to parse the passed parameters and accordingly specialize the invocation. For instance, if a program attempts to connect to a specific port, a DC object implementing the "connect" operation may infer that, in fact, the program requires a connection to a database. The connect operation may involve a series of operations such as re-routing the connection, connecting to a database, or translating queries (if the query is incompatible with the queried database), etc.

4.3 Adapters

We use adapters to address the problem of missing dependencies on a particular computing chunk for a specific application. The adapter, dynamically created or downloaded from a repository by the VEP, serves as a situation-specific middleware layer between application requirements, and a concrete computing chunk. In order to start an application program, the VEP will dynamically create the relevant adapter, attach it to the program bundle and deploy the bundle on a computing chunk.

We implement adapters as libraries containing DC objects that will provide functionally equivalent replacements invoked by original programs. Programs can be distributed as dynamically linked executable files or source codes. In the latter case, equivalent function replacement can be directly incorporated to the programs via static linking at the build stage. From a practical point of view, there are a few options to investigate on how to apply an adapter to a program. Static linking is the easiest method to "inject" dependencies into the program executables. Providing dynamic libraries may be possible by the DLL injection technique (LD_PRELOAD, LD_LIBRARY_PATH, ld.so.conf, *.local, etc). When appropriate, interception of system calls can be employed (e.g., UMview [9], ptrace [17], process monitors).

4.4 Contexts

Contexts are user interfaces to applications executed by the ADAPAS. They will support particular execution environments rather than a particular program. Technically, contexts may be implemented as VEP plugins that are automatically loaded for a particular application run. An example scenario of a context usage is presented below:

```
user@comp> vep target=azure app=npb.tar.gz ctx=mpi
VEP 1.0
mpi context loaded
vep:mpi_ctx>>> mpiexec -np 16 MG.B.16 > results.out
```

In the scenario above, the user starts the VEP and specifies, as input parameters, a target platform, an application to run, and an execution context. Next, the VEP loads the application to be executed, and also the specified execution context. This enables the user to interact with the application execution environment in a familiar manner. In the presented scenario, the context provides the mpiexec command that executes the MG benchmark [6]. The context command cooperates with the VEP in order to transparently compile and start a program and deliver output results. ADAPAS plans to provide a several standard contexts such as MPI, Map/Reduce, etc.

5 Summary

Cloud computing has been under a growing spotlight as a viable solution for providing a flexible, on-demand computing infrastructure. We propose an adaptive virtual platform to enable "completely portable executability" across different applications programming paradigms and resources, specifically cloud computational back-ends. We approach this by proposing the Virtual Execution Platform that will provide mechanisms to automatically and dynamically adapt programming paradigms to resources or resources to programming paradigms. We also propose the Virtually Unified Capabilities interface that will facilitate development of cloud-aware applications and interoperability across platforms.

References

1. Amazon Elastic MapReduce (2011), http://aws.amazon.com/elasticmapreduce/
2. PortableApps.com web page (2011), http://portableapps.com/
3. rPath Documentation (2011), http://docs.rpath.com/
4. The Simple Cloud API (2011), http://www.simplecloudapi.org/
5. Avetisyan, A.I., Campbell, R., Gupta, I., Heath, M.T., Ko, S.Y., Ganger, G.R., Kozuch, M.A., O'Hallaron, D., Kunze, M., Kwan, T.T., Lai, K., Lyons, M., Milojicic, D.S., Lee, H.Y., Soh, Y.C., Ming, N.K., Luke, J.-Y., Namgoong, H.: Open Cirrus: A Global Cloud Computing Testbed. Computer 43, 35–43 (2010)
6. Bailey, D., Barszcz, E., Barton, J., Browning, D., Carter, R., Dagum, L., Fatoohi, R., Frederickson, P., Lasinski, T., Schreiber, R., et al.: The NAS Parallel Benchmarks. International Journal of HPC Apps 5(3), 63 (1991)
7. Chappell, D.: Introducing Windows Azure. DavidChappell & Associates (December 2009), Sponsored by Microsoft Corporation
8. Chohan, N., Bunch, C., Pang, S., Krintz, C., Mostafa, N., Soman, S., Wolski, R.: AppScale Design and Implementation. Technical report, UCSB Technical Report Number 2009 (2009)
9. Gardenghi, L., Goldweber, M., Davoli, R.: View-OS: A New Unifying Approach Against the Global View Assumption. In: Bubak, M., van Albada, G.D., Dongarra, J., Sloot, P.M.A. (eds.) ICCS 2008, Part I. LNCS, vol. 5101, pp. 287–296. Springer, Heidelberg (2008)
10. Gropp, W.D.: MPICH2: A New Start for MPI Implementations. In: Kranzlmüller, D., Kacsuk, P., Dongarra, J., Volkert, J. (eds.) PVM/MPI 2002. LNCS, vol. 2474, p. 7. Springer, Heidelberg (2002)
11. Keahey, K., Figueiredo, R., Fortes, J., Freeman, T., Tsugawa, M.: Science Clouds: Early Experiences in Cloud Computing for Scientific Applications. In: Cloud Computing and Its Application (CCA 2008) (October 2008)
12. Kim, H., el Khamra, Y., Jha, S., Parashar, M.: An autonomic approach to integrated hpc grid and cloud usage. In: Fifth IEEE International Conference on e-Science 2009, pp. 366–373. IEEE (2009)

13. Kozuch, M., Ryan, M., Gass, R., Schlosser, S., O'Hallaron, D., Cipar, J., Krevat, E., López, J., Stroucken, M., Ganger, G.: Tashi: location-aware cluster management. In: Proceedings of the 1st Workshop on Automated Control for Datacenters and Clouds, pp. 43–48. ACM (2009)
14. Kurzyniec, D., Sunderam, V.: Combining FT-MPI with H2O: Fault-tolerant MPI across administrative boundaries. In: Proceedings of 19th IEEE International Parallel and Distributed Processing Symposium, pp. 120a–120a (2005)
15. Nurmi, D., Wolski, R., Grzegorczyk, C., Obertelli, G., Soman, S., Youseff, L., Zagorodnov, D.: The Eucalyptus Open-source Cloud-computing System. In: 9th IEEE International Symposium on Cluster Computing and the Grid, Shanghai, China (2009)
16. Reid, J., Numrich, R.W.: Co-arrays in the next Fortran Standard. Sci. Program 15(1), 9–26 (2007)
17. Rochkind, M.J.: Advanced UNIX programming. Prentice-Hall, Inc., Upper Saddle River (1985)
18. Severance, C.: Using Google App Engine. O'Reilly Media (May 2009)
19. Skomoroch, P.: MPI Cluster Programming with Python and Amazon EC2. In: PyCon 2008, Chicago (2008)
20. Slawinski, J., Slawinska, M., Sunderam, V.: The Unibus Approach to Provisioning Software Applications on Diverse Computing Resources. In: International Conference On High Performance Computing, 3rd International Workshop on Service Oriented Computing (December 2009)
21. Varia, J.: Cloud architectures. Technical report, Amazon Web Services, White Paper (2008)
22. Vecchiola, C., Pandey, S., Buyya, R.: High-performance cloud computing: A view of scientific applications. In: 10th International Symposium on Pervasive Systems, Algorithms, and Networks, pp. 4–16. IEEE (2009)
23. White, T.: Hadoop: The Definitive Guide. O'Reilly Media (May 2009)

QoS Monitoring in a Cloud Services Environment: The SRT-15 Approach

Giuseppe Cicotti, Luigi Coppolino, Rosario Cristaldi,
Salvatore D'Antonio, and Luigi Romano

Epsilon srl, Naples, Italy

Abstract. The evolution of Cloud Computing environments has resulted in a new impulse to the service oriented computing, with hardware
resources, whole applications and entire business processes provided as
services in the so called "as a service" paradigm. In such a paradigm the
resulting interactions should involve actors (users and providers of services) belonging to different entities and possibly to different companies,
hence the success of such a new vision of the IT world is strictly tied
to the possibility of guaranteed high quality levels in the provisioning
of resources and services. In this paper we present QoSMONaaS (Quality of Service MONitoring as a Service), a QoS monitoring facility built
on top of the SRT-15, a Cloud-oriented and CEP-based platform being
developed in the context of the homonymous EU funded project. In particular we present the main components of QoSMONaaS and illustrate
QoSMONaaS operation and internals with respect to a substantial case
study of an Internet of Thing (IoT) application.

Keywords: Quality of Service, Cloud Computing, Complex Event
Processing.

1 Introduction

Quality of Service (QoS) monitoring is key for a company's success, since assessing the actual quality of what service users are paying for has become a
mission-critical business practice requirement, and it will be even more so in the
future. The ever increasing complexity of individual components and interconnection among them has impaired our ability to measure the Key Performance
Indicators (KPIs) of the service which is to be monitored. Emerging development
paradigms, together with the amazing increase of the scale, have made this task
even more challenging in upcoming Future Internet (FI) scenarios, since individual business processes - whose internals are completely unknown - are being
integrated to quickly implement and cheaply deploy semantically richer business
processes. Evidence is demonstrating that QoS monitoring is a very much needed
facility in the current cloud computing scenario, and it will be even more so in the
future. In particular, in [1] authors emphasize that, due to the dynamic nature
of cloud computing environments, continuous monitoring of Quality of Service
(QoS) attributes is needed to enforce Service Level Agreements (SLAs). In [2],

M. Alexander et al. (Eds.): Euro-Par 2011 Workshops, Part I, LNCS 7155, pp. 15–24, 2012.

authors state that "An independent tool for monitoring/validating performance of a heterogeneous set of applications" is one of the capabilities which are most needed in the cloud. The availability of a dependable (i.e. reliable and timely) QoS monitoring facility would make it possible for organizations to understand if any failure and/or performance issue which they experience is caused by their cloud service providers, network infrastructure, or the design of the application itself. This would play a key role in the real take up of cloud computing technology, since, by allowing them to receive the full value of cloud computing services, it would increase the level of trust they would place in the cloud paradigm.

From a technical perspective, cloud computing makes QoS monitoring extremely challenging, for a number of reasons, and in particular:

- Business applications currently run (mostly) on privately owned service infrastructures, whose technology is - to a large extent - known. In a cloud computing context, they run on infrastructures which are: (i) shared, and (ii) virtualized. This also applies to the QoS monitor itself.
- It has to cope with dynamic composition of services, meaning that it must be able to track the evolution of services and it must be able to provide continuous QoS monitoring, i.e., even while changes are taking place.

We claim that QoS monitoring should be made available to all cloud users in a seamless way. To this end, the "as a service" model stands out as the ideal solution. Thus, we decided to implement a QoS monitoring facility, called QoSMON-aaS (Quality of Service MONitoring as a Service) which is provided according to this paradigm.

QoSMONaaS is realized as a pilot application into an SRT-15 project, a new cloud-based Platform as a Service (PaaS) on top of which it is possible to build/compose every software as a services (SaaS). The goal of the SRT-15 project (Subscription Racing Technology for 2015) [3] is to build a scalable platform for connecting FI business applications and services. The platform will enable the discovery and integration of dynamic enterprise services on the Internet. SRT-15 will allow for dependable and scalable cloud-based processing of data coming to and from a variety of heterogeneous enterprise services spread across multiple distributed locations. In order to be able to embrace the change in the enterprise information processing landscape, SRT-15 relies on technologies that support rapid change: cloud computing, content-based routing [4] and complex event processing [5]. Privacy issues, concerning to the anonymity of services (i.e without an exchanged event reveal the identity of sender) or content hiding, is also taken into account by SRT-15.

It is worth emphasizing that the approach we propose for a QoS monitoring is innovative with respect to several aspects which are briefly discussed in the following:

- most existing products only focus on resources monitoring (or on an homogeneous environment), while QoSMONaaS focuses on the performance delivered at the Business Process level into an heterogeneous environment such as Cloud Computing, which is what cloud users really care for.

- current solutions (including big player, e.g. IBM [6]) gather data at predefined interval time and analyze them in batch or streaming way merely reporting violation. On the contrary, QoSMONaaS efficiently can collect data in an asynchronous way processing it just when predetermined condition are met (e.g. when some KPI values go beyond their thresholds it forwards queries to get more information about the service) attempting to prevent violation condition via statistical and/or logical inference.
- the assumption of Trusted Third Party, usually accepted on QoS monitor, in our solution is released: the QoSMONaaS is a "peer among peers", which will be trusted by design thanks to the privacy functionality provided by SRT-15.
- by using Complex Event Processing (CEP) capabilities provided by the underlying SRT-15 platform, in place of getting single data, QoSMONaaS can extract sequences of events by means of queries built on purpose to discover particular patters so that to prevent and/or detect violation condition.

This work shows our novel approach to QoS monitoring, which has been conceived to perfectly suit a cloud computing context. The proposed methodology is based on a model description of the service to be monitored and a formal specification of the related SLAs. Based on this information QoSMONaaS is able to generate specific queries to be performed by a CEP in order to get events or sequences of events (patterns) allowing to recognize violations both ongoing or already happended.

The rest of the paper is organized as follows. Section 2 presents the novel approach that we propose for monitoring QoS in a cloud environment. The key idea is to provide QoS monitoring according to the "as a service" model. As such, the approach is implemented in a pilot application named QoSMONaaS, i.e. "QoS MONitoring as a Service". Section 3 illustrates how QoSMONaaS is implemented by using the SRT-15 platform key features, mainly Complex Event Processing (CEP). Section 4 presents how QoSMONaaS is being validated with respect to Smart Meters, a substantial case study of an Internet of Things (IoT) application developed by SAP for implementing remote monitoring of power consumption in a Smart Grid environment. Section 5 concludes the paper with lessons learned and directions of future research.

2 QoSMONaaS: Quality of Service MONitoring as a Service

QoSMONaaS implements a dependable QoS monitoring facility, which is made available to all applications running on top of the SRT-15 platform. A Conceptual view of the interaction model among the individual parties involved in the monitoring process is given in fig. 1.

SRT-15 Requirements: The underlying platform will have to guarantee:

- that internal SRT-15 information (log data), which are of interest for QoS monitoring, be made available to the QoSMONaaS application. This is made possible via the Extended Interface.
- that effective processing capabilities - i.e. relational algebra operators (or equivalent ones) - be made available, which allow QoSMONaaS to extract and process QoS-related data streams in real time. This is provided by the CEP facilities of the SRT-15 platform via the Basic Interface.
- that the real identity of parties being monitored is not revealed to the monitoring application. This is achieved by having SRT-15 facilities be mediated by the Anonymization System.
- that all facilities be reliable and timely.

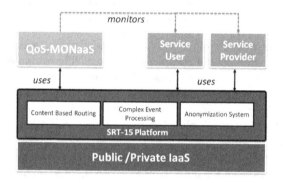

Fig. 1. SRT-15 and QoSMONaaS interaction overview

For more details about CEP facility of the SRT-15 platform, please refer to section 3, and to [3] and [7]. We explicitly emphasize that by introducing an Anonymization System (see fig. 1) in the loop, we avoid that the real identity of monitored parties be revealed to the monitoring application. This is essential for guaranteeing the aforementioned "trusted by design" and "peer among peers" characteristics of the QoSMONaaS application. The basic idea is that since the monitor ignores the real identities of parties, it cannot cheat. In the current implementation, we use a simple scheme, which is in all respects similar to those used in many social network applications [8] (basically, we rely on the simple technique of anonymizing graphs, by which we replace the identifying information of the parties with random ids). We are also exploring more sophisticated schemes, which will be the subject of a different paper.

3   QoSMONaaS Internals

QoSMONaaS main components and their operations are illustrated in fig. 2 and briefly described (additional details are provided in [9]).

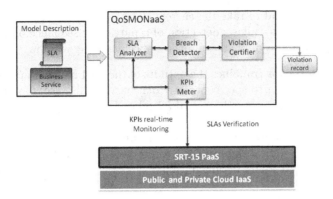

Fig. 2. QoSMONaaS Architecture

Model Description: In order for QoSMONaaS to be able to monitor the actual QoS delivered by the service provider, it is necessary to supply:

- a formal description of the specific business process (entities, relations and KPIs)
- a formal description of the SLA to be garanteed, that is a set of constraints that must be respected.

From a QoSMONaaS perspective, it is sufficient a service-centered model description that specify "what" rather than "how" the business process should do. To this scope, we are interested in a declarative specification of the main services involved in (used by) business process, relations among them, defined in term of exchanged events, and KPIs to keep under control.

The **SLA Analyzer** deals with two macro-functionalities: on the one hand read and processes (parsing) SLAs and model description provided as input, generating queries to pass through the KPI Meter. Furthermore, the SLA Analyzer collects all the information received by KPI Meter so as *analyze* them and *infer* new knowledge to be turned into fresh rules (CPE queries) to give again to the KPI Meter. Into QoSMONaaS application this component plays the role of decision maker allowing to have some advantages:

- adapting the monitoring (variable frequency of submitting queries) so as to minimize the downstream from SRT-15
- selecting just events and KPIs of interest and/or necessary to the analysis/monitoring process.
- efficiently submitting queries to CEP: just in case KPIs values raise a warning, the Engine triggers the Breach Detector sending it the SLA queries it must verify and the frequency of querying (e.g. check every 10 minutes).

The **KPI Meter** continuously monitors the actual value of the KPIs of interest by means of queries to submit to the CEP SRT-15's component. All the submitted queries can be distinguished on the basis of their result:

- Event Data - useful to take the current data value of interest
- Sequence of events - allows detection of a particular sequence of events (absent, if empty) in a data stream over a specified time window.

The **Breach Detector** combines the outputs of the KPI monitor and conditions from the SLA Analyzer to spot contract violations. In this case, report violation back to the SLA Analyzer and forward all related information to the Violation Certifier.

The **Violation Certifier** enriches the output of the Breach Detector with a timestamp and a digital signature, so to produce unforgeable evidence usable for forensic purposes (more details in [9]).

4   Case Study

The implementation of QoSMONaaS is being validated with respect to a substantial case study of an Internet of Things (IoT) application developed by SAP. The application, which is called Smart Meters, implements remote monitoring of power consumption in a Smart Grid environment.

Smart Meters use the SRT-15 platform for distribution and real-time processing of measurements related to energy consumption and production. This application is the ideal candidate to showcase the applicability of the proposed QoS monitoring approach to a realistic Future Internet (FI) scenario. The figure 3 shows an overview of the actors involved in this real Smart Meter application.

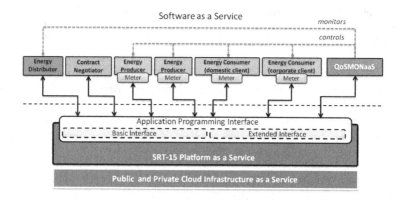

Fig. 3. Case Study: Smart Meter Application

The Energy Distributor (ED) sells energy power to Energy Consumers (ECs), based on a set of pre-defined SLAs. To do so, it buys energy from Energy Producers (EPs), also based on a set of others pre-defined SLAs. EPs and ECs are each one equipped with a Smart Meter which make measurements in (soft) real-time readily made available through the SRT-15 platform to the ED. In our case study EPs and ECs are directly attached to the Cloud through SRT-15. The ED uses SRT-15 as well, gathering data on power consumption, and processes it in an attempt to predict the energy demand for the next time frame. The ED's objective is to efficiently manage the unstable production of renewable energy and balance supply and demand. Based on the result of the prediction process, the ED knows that it needs to either contact additional EPs and add them to its pool or it may spare some of it (in case of surplus production). Contracts between parties are handled by the Contract Negotiator. The above mentioned actors (namely: Energy Distributor, Energy Consumers, Energy Producer, and Contract Negotiator) altogether form the Smart Meter application.

In our case study we use labels EP1, EP2, EC1, EC2 and ED for respectively referring to Energy Producers, Energy Consumers and Energy Distributor services all made available (published) on the SRT-15 platform. From the point of view of the ED service, that we need to monitor, it is linked to (uses) both Producer and Consumer services by means of events of measurement, called SmartMeterMeasureEvent, coming from their Smart Meter devices. However, there could be many other type of relations like, for example, DeviceStateEvent event, that conveys information details on consumption of each single device, appliance and/or complex system (e.g. machinery, networks, plant, etc.) installed at ECs so to remotely control any individual electrical device. An example of model description for an ED business process could be as follows:

```
1   Service Model:
2       complexType Services  = {Producers, Consumers};
3       complexType Producers = {EP1, EP2};
4       complexType Consumers = {EC1, EC2};
5       ED: Producers.SmartMeterMeasureEvent
6       ED: EC1.SmartMeterMeasureEvent
7       ED: EC2.*
8       ED: Services.SmartMeterInfoEvent
9       EC2: ED.RemoteControlEvent
10  KPI definition:
11      <define simple/complex KPI>
12  Constraints:
13      <conditions to be satisfied>
```

Rows 2 to 5 define the structure of the process, specifically they show the dependence of ED (row 5) from Producers, that is EP1 and EP2; rows 6 to 9 define the interest of some entities (ED and EC2) in specific events. The '*' symbol in row 7 represent the interest of ED in all the events produced by EC2.

In the Constraints section we can define some kind of special properties that must be satisfied over a whole (possibly endless) runtime execution of the service[1], whereas within KPI definition section all the KPIs concerning the business service are defined. In the case study under consideration we have two

---

[1] Typical properties considered on dynamic systems are those of safety, liveness, fairness, etc.

composite KPIs, Consumption and Production, respectively indicating the energy consumed by all ECs and the energy produced by all EPs (i.e. they are aggregated data). For the sake of simplicity we consider the real energy power put into distribution network by ED equal to the energy bought from all EPs; thus we can constrain the model with a safety property that Consumption < Production is always true in every state of the service model. Finally, we can identify the KPIs of interest for the process as follows:

```
1   KPI definition:
2     compositeKPI Consumption = \
          forall C in Consumers \
          select sum(measure) from C.SmartMeterMeasureEvent;
3     compositeKPI Production  = \
          forall P in Producers \
          select sum(measure) from P.SmartMeterMeasureEvent;
4     simpleKPI : EC2_PCnet = \
          select state from EC2.DeviceStateEvent;
5   Constraints:
6     Consumption < Production
```

Row 2 provides the relationship between the derived KPI Consumption and the basic event generated by each consumer. At the same way, the row 3 specifies a similar relation between the KPI Production and basic event produced by every producer.

The service level to be monitored is specified by a Service Level Agreement (SLA) between service provider and service user. An SLA is defined in WS-Agreement, a formal xml-based definition language written with the goal to provide a great flexibility for future extensions and customizations. In particular, we can decide the appropriate language useful to specify the quality conditions to be verified.

The choice on such a language should consider its ability of capturing:

- the KPI value conveyed by a single event
- a specified pattern of events into an ordered sequence of events.

Our choice was to use an Interval Temporal Logic (ITL), a language that combines first order and temporal operators. For the sake of brevity we will not introduce ITL, refer to [10] for a detail description of its syntax and semantics.

For our SLA some simple clauses could be:

1. between ED and each EP: the energy supplied by an EP, we say it p, is never less than a predefined threshold, t, for no longer than an I interval time.
2. between ED and EC1: the "availability" of energy power must be of 95% along 24h (about 1 hour per day of power outage)
3. between ED and EC2:
    - SLO 1: the "availability" of energy power must be of 99% along 24h during weekday

- SLO 2: the "availability" of energy power must be of 95% along 24h during weekend and holydays

Once the SLA has been provided with an ITL-like expression, the SLA Analyzer is able to interpret and translate it into queries executable by a CEP. For instance, clause 1) can be formalized through the following ITL-like expressions:

```
EP1.SmartMeasureEvent.measure > t over [15 min]
```

where I is sets to 15 minutes.

The SLA Analyzer parses this expression and, then, extracts the internal KPI, `measure` in this case, generating the two following CEP queries:

```
- select measure from EP1.SmartMeterMeasureEvent
  where measure > t
- select sequence(measure) as Seq
  from EP1.SmartMeterMeasureEvent
  where time.interval(15min) and Seq.forall(measure > t)
```

On the one hand, the first query is used by QoSMONaaS for continuously monitoring a possible "symptom" of the SLA violation and is forwarded to the KPI Meter. On the other hand, based on anomalous values and statistics of history data, the SLA Analyzer can decide to submit the second query to the CEP for detecting an SLA violation (see fig. 4). In this way the SLA Analyzer optimizes the number of requests submitted to the CEP. Clause 2) represents a more

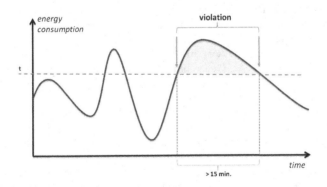

Fig. 4. QoSMONaaS Violation Detection

complex case as it requires the correlation of two events; in particular, we need to verify that the "absorbed power" field of each `SmartMeterMeasureEvent` has a value equal to the one of the "supplied power" in the `SmartMeterInfoEvent`. As for clause 3), breaches can be detected looking for periods of 1, 2 h out of 24 h without data events intended. Such an anomalous behavior can be the result of a power outage elapsed over the 5% of a day.

5 Conclusions and Directions of Future Work

QoS monitoring is an essential aspect to take under control SLAs contracted among business partners. Into a Cloud Computing context, which is based on the "as a service" paradigm, a continuous control of QoS attributes is a primary issue that the current state of the art products still have difficulties to deal with.

In this paper we have discussed the implementation of a new monitoring facility within the context of the SRT-15 project. The paper makes three important contributions. First, it proposes an innovative approach to QoS monitoring, which perfectly suits the cloud computing context. Second, it shows how such an approach can be efficiently implemented in a cloud computing platform which provides advanced features, specifically Complex Event Processing (CEP). Third, it demonstrates the advantages brought by the developed QoS monitoring facility to a realistic Future Internet (FI) application.

For the future we have been studying the possibility to combine the potential of statistical and logical reasoning to both estimate (in a probabilistic way) and predict violations. Furthermore, we will focus our attention on the performance of a "root cause analysis" in an SRT-15-based Cloud environment, for finding and linking together causes (anomalous states) and effects (violations).

References

1. Pankesh Patel, A.S., Ranabahu, A.: Service level agreement in cloud computing. In: UKPEW (2009)
2. Four keys for monitoring cloud services. White Paper from ManageEngine, http://www.manageengine.com/products/applications_manager/four-keys-for-monitoring-cloud-services.pdf
3. White Paper (2010), http://www.srt-15.eu/
4. Eugster, P.T., Felber, P.A., Guerraoui, R., Kermarrec, A.-M.: The many faces of publish/subscribe. ACM Computing Surveys 35, 114–131 (2003)
5. http://www.complexevents.com/event-processing/
6. IBM, Service Level Agreement Monitoring with IBM cognos now (2010)
7. Martin, A., Knauth, T., de Brum, D.B., Weigert, S., Creutz, S., Brito, A., Fetzer, C.: Low-overhead fault tolerance for high-throughput data processing systems. In: ICDCS (2011)
8. Ying, X., Pan, K., Wu, X., Guo, L.: Comparisons of randomization and k-degree anonymization schemes for privacy preserving social network publishing. In: SNA-KDD (2009)
9. Romano, L., Mari, D.D., Jerzak, Z., Fetzer, C.: A novel approach to qos monitoring in the cloud. In: 1st International Conference on Data Compression, Communication and Processing. IEEE Computer Society Press (June 2011)
10. Cau, A., Moszkowski, B.: Interval temporal logic (March 2010)

Enabling e-Science Applications on the Cloud with COMPSs

Daniele Lezzi[1,2,*], Roger Rafanell[1], Abel Carrión[4],
Ignacio Blanquer Espert[4], Vicente Hernández[4], and Rosa M. Badia[1,3]

[1] Barcelona Supercomputing Center, Centro Nacional de Supercomputación
(BSC-CNS)
[2] Universitat Politècnica de Catalunya (UPC)
[3] Artificial Intelligence Research Institute (IIIA),
Spanish Council for Scientific Research (CSIC)
{daniele.lezzi,roger.rafanell,rosa.m.badia}@bsc.es
[4] Instituto de Instrumentación para Imagen Molecular (I3M),
Centro mixto CSIC, Universitat Politècnica de València, CIEMAT
iblanque@dsic.upv.es, {abcarcol,vhernand}@i3m.upv.es

Abstract. COMP Superscalar (COMPSs) is a programming framework that provides an easy-to-use programming model and a runtime to ease the development of applications for distributed environments. Thanks to its modular architecture COMPSs can use a wide range of computational infrastructures providing a uniform interface for job submission and file transfer operations through adapters for different middlewares. In the context of the VENUS-C project the COMPSs framework has been extended through the development of a programming model enactment service that allows researcher to transparently port and execute scientific applications in the Cloud.

This paper presents the implementation of a bioinformatics workflow (using BLAST as core program), the porting to the COMPSs framework and its deployment on the VENUS-C platform. The proposed approach has been evaluated on a Cloud testbed using virtual machines managed by EMOTIVE Cloud and compared to a similar approach on the Azure platform and to other implementations on HPC infrastructures.

1 Introduction

The design of a framework that allows the porting and execution of scientific applications on top of virtualized infrastructures is currently a common topic in the distributed computing community. Programming frameworks are not currently aligned to highly scalable applications and thus do not exploit the capabilities of Clouds. These technologies are mainly based on virtualization and service orientation combined to provide elastic computing service and storage in a pay-per-use model.

---

* Corresponding author.

M. Alexander et al. (Eds.): Euro-Par 2011 Workshops, Part I, LNCS 7155, pp. 25–34, 2012.

The first issue to be solved is the existence of multiple Cloud solutions that are not interoperable. One of the most pressing problem with respect to Cloud computing is the current difference between the individual vendor approaches, and the implicit lack of interoperability. This problem has to be solved inside the runtime of the programming framework, developing the appropriate interfaces to interact with the several Cloud middlewares thus allowing the applications to run on federated infrastructures without having to adapt the applications.

An important property of Cloud computing that poses another requirement in the design of the runtime, is infinite scaling and elasticity, i.e. the capability to provision (and de-provision) resources on demand, and to scale up or down the number of available resources as needed by the users and the application. The runtime should be able to request the provision of additional virtual resources from the underlying Cloud infrastructure. Furthermore, automated decisions could be performed based on observations of dynamic properties and system behaviors.

The COMPSs[1] framework has been recently extended in the context of the VENUS-C project, an European funded initiative whose aim is to support researchers to leverage modern Cloud computing for their existing e-Science applications. The COMPSs Enactment Service[2] provides the users of VENUS-C platform with those interoperability and transparency features with regarding to the computational infrastructure, providing dynamic scaling of resources and keeping a straightforward programming model for enabling applications in the Cloud.

This paper presents the porting of a bioinformatics application to COMPSs in the VENUS-C platform. The rest of the paper is structured as follows: section 2 briefly describes COMPSs in the VENUS-C platform, section 3 contains the description of porting a bioinformatics application to COMPSs, section 4 analyzes the performance of the ported application and section 5 concludes the paper.

2   COMPSs and the VENUS-C Platform

VENUS-C develops and deploys an industrial-quality service-oriented Cloud computing platform based on virtualization technologies, to serve to the research and industrial user communities by taking advantage of previous experiences and knowledge on Grids and Supercomputing environments. The ultimate goal is to eliminate the obstacles to the wider adoption of Cloud computing technologies by designing and developing a shared data and computing resource infrastructure that is less challenging to implement and less costly to operate.

The programming models are a major contribution of the VENUS-C project to the scientific community. In conjunction with the data access mechanisms, these programming models provide researchers with a suitable abstraction for scientific computing on top of plain virtual resources that enable them with a scientific Platform-as-a-Service.

In order to shield the researcher from the intricacies of the concrete implementation of different programming models, each one is enacted behind a specific enactment service that researchers can use to submit jobs and manage their scientific workload. Each VENUS-C supported programming model exposes its functionality through an OGF BES/JSDL[3][4] compliant web service interface. COMPSs and the Microsoft Generic Worker[5] are the available frameworks to enable applications in the infrastructure. The Generic Worker allows the execution of binaries on the Windows Azure platform while COMPSs provides a programming framework for the definition of complex workflows.

Fig. 1 depicts a high level view of the VENUS-C job management middleware architecture.

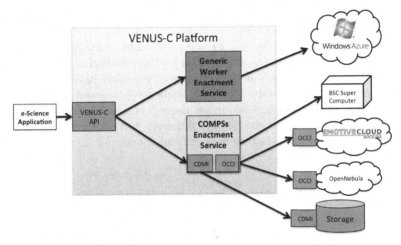

Fig. 1. The architecture of the VENUS-C Job Management Middleware

In VENUS-C, an e-Science application is separated in two parts: the core algorithmic part is ported to the Cloud through the programming models while the user interacts with the platform through a specific client, usually a graphical user interface (GUI), to prepare and modify data, visualize results, and start the scientific computation.

Each enactment service enables a specific instance of an application on the underlying computational infrastructure that includes Windows Azure and Unix virtual machines made available through several open source Cloud middlewares such OpenNebula[6] and EMOTIVE Cloud[7]. Interoperability with these providers is achieved through the use of an OCCI[8] connector and OVF[9] format to describe the Cloud resource capabilities. Moreover, COMPSs is also used to dispatch classical HPC workloads into a Supercomputing infrastructure allowing them to be provided as a service to the VENUS-C consumer.

The VENUS-C data management SDK supports the Cloud Data Management Interface (CDMI)[10] specification, pushed forward by the Storage Networking

Industry Association (SNIA). This interface includes both a deployable web service which exposes the CDMI interface, and the support libraries for different language bindings, that ease the call of the CDMI Service. The COMPSs enactment service implements a CDMI client that allows the access to different Cloud storage implementations through the same interface. This allows the user of the enactment service to run applications using data already available on a site thus avoiding him to be locked to a specific storage technology.

3   Evaluation of an e-Science Application

In order to validate the described framework a bioinformatics application has been adapted to run in a Cloud environment through the COMPSs enactment service. The aim is twofold: first, evaluating the complexity of porting the application to COMPSs in the VENUS-C platform; second, comparing the performance of the proposed solution to MPI and cloud implementations.

BLAST[11] is a widely-used bioinformatics tool for comparing primary biological sequence information, such as the amino-acid sequences of different proteins or the nucleotides of DNA sequences with sequence databases, identifying sequences that resemble the query sequence above a certain threshold. The work performed by BLAST is computationally intensive and embarassingly parallel, which makes it a good candidate to benefit from Cloud.

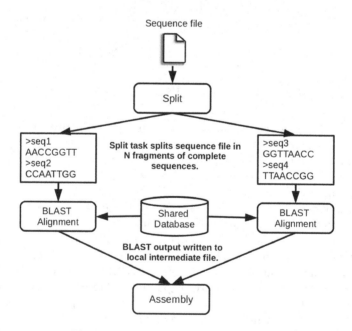

Fig. 2. The COMPSs BLAST Workflow

The BLAST workflow contains three blocks as depicted in Fig. 2:

- **Split:** the query sequences file is splitted in N fragments.
- **Alignment:** each sequence fragment is compared against the database by the blast binary.
- **Assembly:** assembly process combines all intermediate files into a single result file.

3.1   Porting of the Application

The porting of an application to COMPSs includes two steps; in the first step an interface file has to be provided by the programmer to select which methods, called from the application, will be executed remotely. The second step involves the preparation of the user code that implements these methods; in VENUS-C the interface file, the application code and the BLAST binary are assembled in a package that is stored into an application repository and deployed by the COMPSs enactment service when an execution is requested. This relieves the user of taking care of manual deployment of the binaries on the infrastructure and allows different versions of the same application to be available.

3.2   The COMPSs Application Interface

The interface declares the methods of the user application that have to be managed by the COMPSs runtime to be executed remotely; information about the method and its parameters is provided through the use of Java annotations; such metadata includes the name of the class that implements the method(s) and, for each parameter, its type (primitive, file, ...) and direction (in, out or in/out). The user can also express capabilities that a resource must fulfill to run a certain method (CPU number and type, memory, disk size, etc...).

```java
public interface BlastItf {
  @Method(declaringClass = "blast.worker.BlastImpl")
  @Constraints(storageElemSize = 0.3f, processorCPUCount = 4)
  void alignment(
    @Parameter(type = Type.STRING, direction = Direction.IN)
    String db,
    @Parameter(type = Type.FILE, direction = Direction.IN)
    String fragment,
    @Parameter(type = Type.FILE, direction = Direction.OUT)
    String resFile,
    @Parameter(type = Type.STRING, direction = Direction.IN)
    String blastBinary,
    @Parameter(type = Type.STRING, direction = Direction.IN)
    String cmdArgs);
}
```

3.3   Application Implementation

In the BLAST porting, the main application code splits the input sequences file in a number of fragments specified by the user. For each fragment, the *alignment* method is called. Each generated output is assembled by the *assemblyPartitions* method.

```
public static void main(String args[]) throws Exception {
    sequences[] = split(inputFile, nFrags);
    for (fragment: sequences)
    {
        output = "resFile" + index + ".txt";
        BlastImpl.alignment(db, fragment, output, ..., cmdArgs);
        seqOutputs.add(output);
        index++;
    }
    assemblyPartitions(seqOutputs, resultFile, tempDir, nFrags);
}
```

The *alignment* method is implemented in *BlastImpl* class and simply invokes the *blastx* binary, a BLAST suite algorithm that allows six-frame conceptual translation products of a nucleotide query sequence against a protein sequence database.

```
public void alignment(String db, String fragment,
                      String resFile, ..., String cmdArgs){

    String cmd = blastBinary+ " " +"-p blastx -d " + db +
                 " -i " +fragment+ " -o "+resFile+" "+cmdArgs;

    Process simProc = Runtime.getRuntime().exec(cmd);
    ...
}
```

4   Performance Analysis

In order to evaluate the described approach, a set of experiments has been conducted comparing the COMPSs BLAST implementation to another Cloud solution using the Azure Platform and to a parallel version of BLAST, mpiBLAST [12], on a parallel cluster. This tests aimed at measuring the scalability and the overall performance of the COMPSs BLAST porting using different numbers of processors and sequence fragments of the input sequence and at evaluating the Cloud overhead which involves the creation and the destruction of virtual resources on demand.

All the BLAST tests have been performed using the same use case of alignment of DNA sequences from the Sargasso Sea species against the non-redundant (NR) GenBank database with only prokaryote organisms. The input query file contains 398 sequences and the database contains 7 million of sequences with a total volume of 1 MB and 840 MB respectively.

The COMPSs porting of BLAST has been executed using the EMOTIVE Cloud middleware to manage a testbed that included two Intel Xeon Quad Core nodes at 3 GHz and 2.66 GHz respectively with 6 GB of memory, 250 GB of storage and an internal Gigabit Ethernet network. On each node a quad core VM instance has been deployed thus allowing COMPSs to execute up to 4 tasks in parallel in a single node. The input and output files are stored on a separate storage host and a network shared disk is mounted by the virtual machines. The enactment services takes care of copying data from the storage to the Cloud and moving back the result data at the end of execution.

The implementation of BLAST to the Windows Azure platform is also developed in the context of the VENUS-C project; the test used 1.6 GHz single core small Azure virtual machines instances, with 1.75 GB of memory, 225 GB of disk space and a 100 Mbps network.

The mpiBLAST version has been executed on the Tirant Supercomputer available at UPV. Tirant comprises 256 JS20 blades with IBM Power4 dual core processors at 2.0 GHz, 4 GB of memory and 36 GB of local storage. All the nodes are interconnected through Myrinet and Gigabit Network.

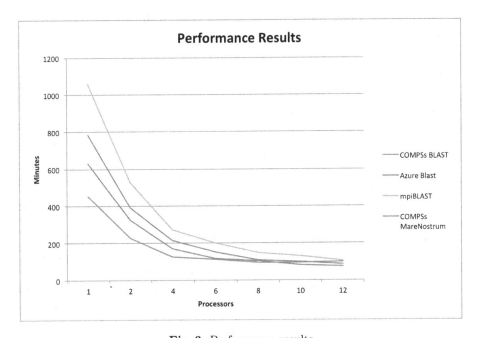

Fig. 3. Performance results

Another test has been conducted executing the COMPSs BLAST workflow on the MareNostrum Supercomputer available at BSC where the COMPSs runtime is used in production. MareNostrum comprises 2560 JS21 blades with two IBM PowerPC 970MP dual core processors at 2.3 GHz, 8 GB of memory and 36 GB of local storage. All the nodes are interconnected through Myrinet and Gigabit Network.

The results are summarized in Fig. 3. The COMPSs BLAST executed on the VENUS-C testbed using virtual resources shows better overall performance than the mpiBLAST implementation and than COMPSs BLAST executed in MareNostrum. It also performs better than the Azure execution up to 8 processors. This is due to the fact that only 2 physical nodes have been used in the tests allowing COMPSs to schedule only 8 tasks in parallel on the 8 available cores. Tests with 10 and 12 processors on the same testbed were performed deploying more virtual machines on the same host. In this case the Cloud overhead is bigger than the performance achieved through the parallel tasks scheduling. The Azure test was instead executed with an unlimited number of available resources. Nevertheless, it is worth noting that even in the worst case of limited resources, the COMPSs performance doesn't deteriorate and remains constant.

The total overhead of the COMPSs enactment service sums up to about 600 seconds on each execution; this value includes the virtual machines creation (about 200 seconds) and all the file transfers. These values can be improved using a more I/O efficient testbed than the one used for the experiments. The deployment overhead in Azure on the other side is of about 900 seconds but even removing the virtualization overhead the COMPSs BLAST implementation performs better.

5   Conclusions

This paper presented an approach for the porting and execution of scientific applications to Cloud environments through the COMPSs enactment service of the VENUS-C platform. A bioinformatics workflow based on the BLAST alignment tool has been ported to COMPSs and executed on a Cloud testbed with virtual resources managed by the EMOTIVE Cloud middleware.

The implementation of the COMPSs workflow required minimum intervention by the user who only had to provide the sequential application and an annotated interface for selecting the tasks. He interacts with the enactment service through a client that provides job and data management functionalities. It is worth noting that this implementation is not specific to the VENUS-C platform but can be used for other execution environments like clusters and grids. The same workflow for example has been also deployed on the MareNostrum supercomputer where the COMPSs framework is already offered to users to execute several scientific workflows.

The COMPSs BLAST on the VENUS-C testbed exhibited better performance than the mpiBLAST and Azure implementations considered. Even if the tests were conducted on a limited number of resources, the results are promising and show that despite few limitations introduced by the specific Cloud infrastructure, COMPSs keeps the scalability of the application and the overall performance of its runtime while offering the researcher useful Cloud features like optimized usage of resources and an easy programming and execution framework.

A similar approach, CloudBLAST[13], implements the workflow using the MapReduce[14] paradigm to parallelize the Blast execution and a networking middleware to interconnect VMs deployed in different sites. This approach requires the user to explicitly write the map and reduce functions whereas with COMPSs there is no need to change the existing user code. Also, COMPSs runtime is able to use machines from different cloud providers without the need of deploying virtual networks thanks to the interoperability with different cloud middlewares.

Future work includes the complete interoperability of COMPSs with all the infrastructures provided in the VENUS-C. A specific adaptor for the Generic Worker Role will be developed in order to provide COMPSs with the capability of executing the tasks on the Azure Platform. Also better scheduling policies will be introduced in the COMPSs runtime in order to optimize the selection of the resources. In the same way, scaling and elasticity mechanisms will be adopted to enhance the programming model with capabilities for scaling up or down the number of resources based on user-defined or policy driven criteria.

Acknowledgements. This work has been supported by the Spanish Ministry of Science and Innovation (contracts TIN2007-60625, CSD2007-00050 and CAC2007-00052), by Generalitat de Catalunya (contract 2009-SGR-980) and the European Commission (VENUS-C project, Grant Agreement Number: 261565).

References

1. Tejedor, E., Badia, R.M.: COMP Superscalar: Bringing GRID superscalar and GCM Together. In: 8th IEEE International Symposium on Cluster Computing and the Grid (May 2008)
2. Lezzi, D., Rafanell, R., Badia, R.M., Lordan, F., Tejedor, E.: COMPSs in the VENUS-C Platform: enabling e-Science applications on the Cloud. In: Proc. of the IBERGRID 2011 Conf., Santander (June 2011)
3. Foster, I., et al.: OGSA Basic Execution Service Version 1.0. Grid Forum Document GFD-RP. 108 (August 8, 2007)
4. Savva, A. (ed.): Job Submission Description Language (JSDL) Specification, Version 1.0. Grid Forum Document GFD-R.056 (November 7, 2005)
5. Simmhan, Y., van Ingen, C.: Bridging the Gap between Desktop and the Cloud for eScience Applications, Microsoft Research, U.S. (2010),
   http://research.microsoft.com/pubs/118329/
   Simmhan2010CloudSciencePlatform.pdf
6. Open Nebula, http://opennebula.org
7. Goiri, I., Guitart, J., Torres, J.: Elastic Management of Tasks in Virtualized Environments. In: XX Jornadas de Paralelismo, JP 2009, A Corua, Spain, September 16-18, pp. 671–676 (2009)

8. Open Cloud Computing Interface Working Group, http://www.occi-wg.org
9. Distributed Management Task Force Inc., Open Virtualization Format Specification v1.1, DMTF Standard DSP0243 (2010)
10. SNIA CDMI,
    http://www.snia.org/tech_activities/standards/curr_standards/cdmi/
11. Altschul, S.F., Gish, W., Miller, W., Myers, E.W., Lipman, D.J.: Basic Local Alignment Search Tool. Journal of Molecular Biology 215(3), 403–410 (1990), doi:10.1006/jmbi.1990.9999
12. Darling, A., Carey, L., Feng, W.: The Design, Implementation, and Evaluation of mpiBLAST. In: Proc. of the 4th Intl. Conf. on Linux Clusters (2003)
13. Matsunaga, A., Tsugawa, M., Fortes, J.: CloudBLAST: Combining MapReduce and Virtualization on Distributed Resources for Bioinformatics Applications. In: IEEE Fourth International Conference on eScience (2008)
14. Dean, J., Ghemawat, S.: MapReduce: Simplified Data Processing on Large Clusters. In: Proc. of the 6th Symp. on Operating Systems Design & Implementation, pp.137–150 (2004)

OPTIMIS and VISION Cloud:
How to Manage Data in Clouds

Spyridon V. Gogouvitis[1], George Kousiouris[1], George Vafiadis[1],
Elliot K. Kolodner[2], and Dimosthenis Kyriazis[1]

[1] National Technical University of Athens, Iroon Polytechniou 9, Athens, Greece
[2] IBM Haifa Research Labs, Haifa University, Mt. Carmel, Haifa, Israel
{spyrosg,gkousiou}@mail.ntua.gr, gvaf@iccs.gr,
kolodner@il.ibm.com, dimos@mail.ntua.gr

Abstract. In the rapidly evolving Cloud market, the amount of data being generated is growing continuously and as a consequence storage as a service plays an increasingly important role. In this paper, we describe and compare two new approaches, deriving from the EU funded FP7 projects OPTIMIS and VISION Cloud respectively, to filling existing gaps in Cloud storage offerings. We portray the key value-add characteristics of their designs that improve the state of the art for Cloud computing towards providing more advanced features for Cloud-based storage services.

Keywords: Cloud computing, Storage, Data Management.

1   Introduction

An important aspect of the Future Internet is the ever growing amount of data that is generated and stored in the Cloud. Be it user-generated data, such as multimedia content uploaded to social networking environments, or data coming from companies moving to the Cloud to take advantage of the cost savings it has to offer, generated data is growing faster than we can store it.

Storage Cloud solutions, by which storage is virtualized and offered on demand, promise to address the proliferation of data. Key concepts of Cloud Computing, such as the pay-as-you-go model, essentially unlimited scalability and capacity, lower costs and ease of use and management, are also prominent in Storage Clouds.

Nevertheless, issues such as Quality of Service assurances, mobility, interoperability and federation, security and compliance, energy efficiency and others still need to be addressed to enable the provision of data-intensive storage Cloud services. Furthermore, increasing legal requirements with regard to data storage locations is preventing storage providers from fully utilizing their infrastructures according to internal optimization capabilities, e.g., load balancing techniques. In this paper we describe two different approaches to achieving better management of data in Cloud environments, as realized by the OPTIMIS [1] and VISION Cloud [2] EU Projects.

M. Alexander et al. (Eds.): Euro-Par 2011 Workshops, Part I, LNCS 7155, pp. 35–44, 2012.

The remainder of this paper is structured as follows: Section 2 surveys current Cloud Storage offerings while Section 3 presents the physical model that is considered throughout the paper. Section 4 discusses the OPTIMIS approach to data management in Clouds and in Section 5 presents the VISION Cloud project. In Section 6 compares the approaches of the two projects. Finally, Section 6 concludes the paper.

2   Related Work

There are various approaches with regard to Cloud infrastructures that aim at providing storage services. Possibly the most well-known Cloud storage service today is the Amazon Simple Storage Service (S3) [3]. Amazon has not made public details of S3's design, though stating that it is "intentionally built with a minimal feature set". S3 allows writing, reading and deleting an unlimited amount of objects that are stored in buckets. It provides an SLA that guarantees service availability of 99.9%. S3 replicates objects in multiple locations to achieve a durability of 99.999999999%, although the service is not held accountable for any data loss. Amazon S3 buckets in most regions (US West, EU and Asia Pacific) provide read-after-write consistency for PUTS of new objects and eventual consistency for overwrite PUTS and DELETES. Buckets in the US Standard Region provide eventual consistency.

Another commercial solution is Windows Azure [4], which is mainly a PaaS offering that provides four different storage services, namely the Binary Large Object (BLOB) Service for storing text and binary data, the Table service, for structured storage that can be queried, the Queue service for persistent messaging between services and the Windows Azure Drive that allows Windows Azure applications to mount a Page Blob, which is single volume NTFS VHD. All data is stored in 3 replicas. The storage services may be accessed from within a service running in Windows Azure or directly over the Internet using a REST API. The BLOB service offers the following three resources: the storage account, containers, and blobs. Within one's storage account, containers provide a way to organize sets of blobs, which can be either block blobs optimized for streaming or page blobs optimized for random read/write operations and which provide the ability to write to a range of bytes in a blob.

EMC Atmos [5] is another Cloud storage solution with an API similar to Amazon S3. Some of the key differences include objects that are re-writable and user metadata that can be updated, richer geo-dispersion capabilities, two data models, namely a flat object interface and a namespace interface that similar to a file system with folders, and a richer account model that is more suitable for enterprise customers.

Google Storage for Developers [6] is a RESTful online storage web service using Google's infrastructure. It provides strong read-after-write data consistency and eventual consistency on list operations. It uses the notions of buckets, and the user is able to specify the geographic location of each bucket.

Nevertheless, the approaches described in this section do not meet the new challenges of data-intensive services. Starting from the data models, they are basic. Amazon S3, Google Storage, and the Windows Azure Blob Service allow associating user metadata in the form of key value pairs with objects and blobs, but they simply store the metadata and pass it back. EMC Atmos has a slightly richer model; it allows some of keys (called tags by Atmos) to be listable; this enables retrieving the objects that have a specific tag. The support for federation does not exist or is limited and requires homogeneity. Amazon S3, Google Storage and the Windows Azure Blob Service do not have any support for federation. EMC Atmos allows federating data in an Atmos system in a customer data center with the customer's data in a Cloud, provided it is also implemented with Atmos. No current Cloud storage offering provides computational abilities as an integral part of the Cloud storage system to the best of our knowledge. Access to an object is solely through its name with Amazon S3, Google Storage and the Windows Azure Blob Service. As mentioned above, EMCS Atmos has a slight richer access capability through its listable tags. But no current Cloud storage system has a rich flexible access to storage based on its content and relationships. Finally, the QoS mechanisms and SLAs provided by current offerings are very basic. In our approach, models, requirements and SLA schemas are expressed not only on storage resources and services, but also on the content descriptions for the underlying storage objects, in support of content centric storage.

3   Infrastructure Model

The physical model of the infrastructure is a network of data centers that can span over a large geographic area, connected by a dedicated network. Each data center is composed of one or multiple *storage clusters* containing physical compute, storage and networking resources.

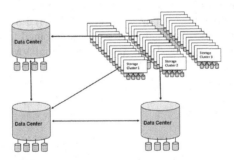

Fig. 1. Physical Model of a Storage Cloud consisting of multiple interconnected Data Centers

A *storage cluster* is composed of storage rich nodes constructed from commodity hardware and connected by commodity interconnect. The idea is to build the storage Cloud from low cost components, ensuring reliability in the software, and building advanced functionality on top of this foundation. For example, given today's hardware, the initial hardware configuration for the nodes could be 4 or 8 way multiprocessors (taking multicore into account) with 12 to 16 GB of RAM. Each node could have 12 to 24 high capacity direct attached disks (e.g., 2TB SATA drives). The architecture, design and implementation should support a system with hundreds of storage clusters, where each storage cluster can have several hundred nodes and the storage clusters are spread out over dozens of data centers.

4   The OPTIMIS Approach

The main goal of the OPTIMIS project is to enable a Cloud toolkit that will be able to accommodate management of a Cloud environment in configurable terms with regard to various factors such as Trust, Risk, Ecology and Cost (TREC). This is done for cases where multiple locations are envisioned to contain data centers, either belonging to one entity or different ones, through various deployment scenarios like federated, hybrid and multi-cloud cases. A more detailed analysis of the project goals and architecture appears in [8].

The OPTIMIS Data Management architecture is portrayed in Fig. 2. It is based on the distributed file system architecture (HDFS [7]) offered by the Hadoop framework. This consists of a central NameNode, which acts like the inode of the system, and a series of DataNodes, which act as the actual storage and processing nodes of the Hadoop cluster. Each file is divided into a number of blocks (with configurable size per file) and distributed over the DataNodes. Different blocks of the same file may belong to different DataNodes. This creates a very flexible framework for managing files, in order to optimize their processing and management actions (e.g. cluster balancing). Suitable RESTful interfaces have been added on top of the HDFS NameNode, in order to offer its functionality as a service. Furthermore, due to the multi-tenant environment, security features have been added in order to encrypt communication between the NameNode and the DataNodes, between the DataNodes themselves but also between the service VMs that utilize the account on the HDFS and the HDFS components. In cases when the storage space is running out, one or more DataNode VMs can be added from an external location. This location may be the same provider, or a different Cloud, through utilizing their available APIs for launching a VM instance of the OPTIMIS version of the HDFS DataNode. As soon as these VMs are launched, they are registered in the distributed file system that runs in the internal IP and can be managed like any other internal VM resource. The HDFS utilizes the storage space of these VMs as part of the file system offered to the services.

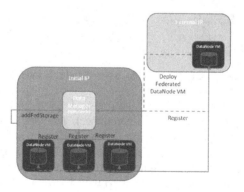

Fig. 2. OPTIMIS Data Manager Architecture

In order to offer data management or storage services as a Cloud Provider, the OPTIMIS solution encapsulates the HDFS and offers account creation for the end users of the OPTIMIS platform. Thus, each user that raises his/her Virtual Machines on the OPTIMIS Cloud is granted access on the HDFS through his/her own personal account. This appears as a directory. Through this form, the service data may be managed through the distributed file system in an efficient way, enabling parallel processing and access from numerous service VMs.

Another major aim of the OPTIMIS data management solution is to be able to capture and apply user requirements with regard to data location constraints. Extensive analysis on the legal requirements has indicated a series of actions that need to be undertaken by the Cloud provider in order to be compliant with the according legislation ([9]). For this reason, rack awareness features of HDFS along with block location information are utilized for monitoring purposes of the data location. An extension is also in progress in order to regulate the block placement policies according to each service's needs. This includes capabilities for processing the SLA in which these needs are expressed and act upon them, making sure that no blocks of data of a specific service are located on servers outside the user's identified geographical region.

Taking under consideration that OPTIMIS scenarios include multiple locations of data centers, that cooperate in distributing the load, what is necessary for a single location is to identify the fittest services that can be transferred to external data centers from a data activity point of view. Due to the fact that in general this load balancing may be performed on the fly and for a specific period of time (to meet for example a peak in demand), the optimal service VMs must be chosen. This is why the OPTIMIS data management module provides interfaces for ranking existing services with regard to their data activity. Through logging mechanisms added internally to the interfaces that are used by the service VM to access the distributed file system, each user action on the data is logged. These extensive logs are temporarily stored for a specific interval. After this interval they are preprocessed as a Map-Reduce task, in order to be transformed in a format suitable for incorporation in the time series prediction framework (Federation Candidate Selector-FCS) but also to reduce the storage space needed for the logs. The FCS component is responsible for processing the concentrated statistical results and create a model that is able to predict the expected user activity with regard to the HDFS (e.g. expected number of bytes read/written) for the forthcoming time period. Thus for example, it can recommend to the Cloud provider to choose a service VM to migrate that has the least activity in the near future. This estimation can also be used for other purposes, such as regulating the replication factor of a service's data on the HDFS. If a peak in read operations is expected for example, by having more replicas of a data block on the distributed data nodes the requestors of these operations will have more sources to choose from and thus balance the load.

Furthermore, in order to have multiple policies with regard to the different TREC factors, the OPTIMIS Data Manager exposes suitable interfaces that enable the Cloud provider to set predefined levels of specific metrics, like eco-efficiency. Each such level corresponds to a set of actions/policies in order to control for example the energy consumption of the infrastructure for which the DM is responsible for. For example, the number of DataNodes can be regulated through these interfaces.

High eco-efficiency may lead to decommissioning of a number of nodes that are used for storage in order to reduce carbon emissions. On the other hand, when performance is needed, extra nodes may be added on the fly in order to improve the system response times.

5   The VISION Cloud Approach

The main aim of VISION Cloud is to provide efficient support for data-intensive applications by taking a content-centric view of storage services. To this end five areas of innovation have been identified and are driving the VISION Cloud platform: i) content is managed through data objects associated with a rich metadata model, ii) avoidance of data lock-in by enabling the migration of data across administrative domains, iii) avoiding costly data transfers by moving computations close to the data through programming agents called *storlets*, iv) enabling efficient retrieval of objects based on their content, properties and the relationships among them and v) providing strong QoS guarantees, security and compliance with international regulations. More details on the aims and architecture can be found in [10] and [11]. A key element to achieve these aims is a data model with rich metadata, which is described in the following paragraphs.

5.1   Data and Account Model

In VISION Cloud the unit of storage is a *data object*. A data object contains data of arbitrary type and size, has a unique identifier that can be used to access it and has *metadata* associated with it. Each data object resides within the context of a single *container*. Containers are the unit of placement, reducing not only the frequency of making global placement decisions, but also the size of the location information that has to be stored globally. *Metadata* can be associated with both data objects as well as containers. We distinguish between two categories of metadata, namely *user* and *system* metadata. While the semantics of the former are transparent to VISION Cloud, the platform provides the facilities needed to create, update and make queries on it. System metadata, on the other hand, has concrete meaning to the Cloud storage system. It either directs the system how to deal with the object (e.g., access control, reliability, performance requirements, etc.), or provides system information about the object (e.g., size, creation time, last access time, etc) to the user.

The account model of VISION Cloud consists of tenants, sub-tenants and users. A *tenant* is an organization that subscribes to the platform's services. A tenant may represent a commercial firm, a governmental organization, or any other organization, including any group of one or more individual persons. It is the entity that negotiates Service Level Agreements (SLAs) with VISION Cloud and is billed accordingly. A tenant may also define *subtenants*. Subtenants can be viewed as different departments of the same organization. A firm consisting of an R&D Department and HR Department could therefore constitute different subtenants of the same tenant. This allows for different service levels to be set according to the requirements of each department, while also providing for isolation where needed. Thus, a commercial firm is able to "map" its business structure directly on the underlying storage. A *user* is the entity that actually consumes the storage services provided. For auditing, billing and security reasons every operation needs to be associated with a user.

5.2   Data Management

The architecture of VISION Cloud is logically divided into two facets, one concerned with data operations, such as creating and retrieving data objects, and one handling management operations, such as SLA negotiation and placement decisions of containers. The architectural separation between the data and management services is inspired by the unique service model of the storage Cloud. In compute Clouds, the management service is used to provision and manage compute resources, which interact with external entities as defined by the service provider. The storage Cloud is different - once the storage resources are provisioned, they may be used by different, independent service consumers through Cloud storage APIs, with different characteristics and requirements on latency, throughput, availability, reliability, consistency, etc. The data service and the management service are designed to be separate and independent in order to facilitate this differentiation and provide the flexibility required to enable the innovations mentioned earlier.

Most management decisions stem from the SLA under which a container is created. SLAs in VISION Cloud are dynamic, in the sense that a tenant is able to negotiate its terms, cost and penalties with the platform. Through SLAs the tenant is able to define various requirements to the platform, such as:

- Performance requirements, such latency and throughput
- Durability level, by which the probability of data loss is defined
- Availability, by which the probability that the data is available when requested is defined
- Geographic preference, by which a tenant asks that the data is stored within a specific geographic region
- Geographic exclusion, by which a tenant asks that the data is not stored within a geographic region
- Security, such as encryption of data with a specific algorithm
- Data dispersion, which defines the minimum geographic distance that datacenters holding replicas of the data should have.

These SLA requirements are automatically transformed to system requirements. For example a durability of 99.999% can be translated to creating 3 replicas of a given container. The management directives are thereafter added as metadata to containers during their creation process and are used for optimizing their placement.

In order to efficiently make placement decisions a clear and coherent global view of the system is needed. For this reason, VISION Cloud makes use of a monitoring mechanism that is able to collect, aggregate, analyze and distribute monitoring information across the collaborating clusters and data centers. Information from different sources can be collected, such as low-level hardware metrics and high-level software calls. For example every request to read an object can be monitored and logged. The purpose of this is two-fold. On one hand this information is needed for accounting and billing purposes, as a tenant will be able to bill customers based on the number of requests they execute on the platform. On the other hand this information can be collected for the system itself with the intention to analyze them and derive knowledge that could further enhance the way the system makes management decisions. For example, seeing that a certain container is accessed frequently from a specific geographic location could lead to it being moved closer to that location.

The coupling of management metadata with an advanced monitoring framework also allows for proactive SLA violation detection schemes to be developed. Building on the knowledge that is accumulated though the analysis of monitored parameters, the system is able to proactively detect conditions that could lead to degradation of the QoS delivered and take necessary management actions to avoid a possible SLA violation.

The programming model of VISION Cloud provides storlets, which also use the metadata associated with containers and objects to effectively perform computations on the stored data. Not only can storlets be directed to execute on specific objects based on their metadata, but they are also triggered due to changes in object metadata. The results of these computations can be further used to annotate objects with additional metadata, thereby correlating the knowledge gained with the data.

The rich data model of VISION Cloud enables applications to access data objects based on their content rather than their physical or logical location, though an API that supports queries based on the metadata associated with containers and objects, realizing a content-centric access to storage.

6   Comparison

Both projects recognize the importance of providing storage as a service in the emerging era of the Future Internet but follow different approaches in realizing this vision. In the next paragraphs we summarize the similarities and differences of the two projects regarding the challenges identified by both.

Abstraction Level. A main difference is in the level of implementation. OPTIMIS follows a regular file system approach, while VISION Cloud follows an object-based storage approach with a rich data model.

Data Mobility and Federation. Data mobility and federation is considered by both projects as an important factor. OPTIMIS achieves flexibility based on the storage VM concept that allows for one-step interoperable federation and easier commission and decommission to be used for TREC-based management. VISION Cloud approaches the problem by building upon a high-level abstraction of platforms and devices, enabled by the definition of an object-based data model and its metadata mechanism.

Computations. The coupling of storage with computation is another concern of both projects. OPTIMIS makes use of storage Virtual Machines that can be started on any available computational resource that is part of the Cloud. This approach offers computational power that is in par with traditional Cloud offerings. The combination of the placement of service VMs and storage VMs can lead to improved locality of data. VISION Cloud proposes storlets, a novel programming model for computational agents, by which computations can be injected into the Cloud and activated by events, such as creation of new data objects or changes in metadata of existing ones. These storlets run on compute resources on the storage servers where their object parameters reside.

Access Semantics to Storage. From a semantics point of view, OPTIMIS does not offer any data semantics but provides distributed storage to the end user in a transparent way. This storage, whether it is in the internal or external provider, is independent of the underlying storage implementation of traditional providers, thus reducing data lock-in. VISION Cloud enables applications to associate rich metadata with data objects, and thereby access the data objects through information about their content, rather than their location or their path in a hierarchical structure.

Placement of Data. Both projects focus on the optimal placement of data but at a different level. OPTIMIS focuses on recommending the suitable service VMs that when federated will have the least overhead with relation to the in-house distributed storage system. VISION Cloud automatically places container replicas based on the resources available in each cluster and data center, geographical constraints, and availability, resiliency and performance goals.

Legal Requirements. Finally, both approaches cover the need for user defined geographical location of data, in order to be in compliance with the legal requirements especially within the European Union area.

	OPTIMIS	VISION Cloud
Abstraction Level	Regular File System	Object-based storage
Data Mobility and Federation	Through storage VMs	Object-based data model with integrated metadata
Computations	Service VMs	Storlets
Access to storage	Hierarchical file system	Content-centric access
Optimal placement of data	Analysis of access patterns and legal constraints	Through SLAs and metadata
Legal Requirements	Control of geographical placement of data	Control of geographical placement of data

Fig. 3. Comparison of OPTIMIS and VISION Cloud

7   Conclusion

Providing storage as a service is an important aspect of the emerging Cloud ecosystem. Issues such as ease of management, data mobility and federation, coupling storage with computing power and guaranteeing QoS need to be researched to address the increasing volumes of data that are being produced and need to be processed and stored. In this paper we presented the contrasting approaches that two EU funded projects, OPTIMIS and VISION Cloud, take to data management and discussed their differences and similarities.

Acknowledgments. The research leading to these results is partially supported by the European Community's Seventh Framework Programme (FP7/2007-2013) under grant agreement n° 257019, in the context of the VISION Cloud Project and grant agreement n° 257115 , in the context of the OPTIMIS project.

References

1. OPTIMIS, http://www.optimis-project.eu/
2. VISION Cloud, http://www.visioncloud.eu/
3. Amazon simple storage service (Amazon S3), http://aws.amazon.com/s3
4. Microsoft Windows Azure Platform, http://www.microsoft.com/azure/default.mspx
5. EMC Atmos storage service, http://www.emccis.com/
6. Google Storage for Developers, http://code.google.com/apis/storage/
7. Hadoop, http://hadoop.apache.org/hdfs/
8. Ferrer, A.J., Hernández, F., Tordsson, J., Elmroth, E., Zsigri, C., Sirvent, R., Guitart, J., Badia, J.R., Djemame, K., Ziegler, W., Dimitrakos, T., Nair, S.K., Kousiouris, G., Konstanteli, K., Varvarigou, T., Hudzia, B., Kipp, A., Wesner, S., Corrales, M., Forgó, N., Sharif, T., Sheridan, C.: OPTIMIS: a Holistic Approach to Cloud Service Provisioning. In: First International Conference on Utility and Cloud Computing (UCC 2010), Chennai, India, December 14-16 (2010)
9. Barnitzke, B., Ziegler, W., Vafiadis, G., Nair, S., Kousiouris, G., Corrales, M., Wäldrich, O., Forgó N., Varvarigou, T.: Legal Restraints and Security Requirements on Personal Data and Their Technical Implementation in Clouds. To Appear in Workshop for E-contracting for Clouds, eChallenges 2011, Florence, Italy (2011)
10. Kolodner, E.K., Naor, D., Tal, S., Koutsoutos, S., Mavrogeorgi, N., Gogouvitis, S., Kyriazis, D., Salant, E.: Data-intensive Storage Services on Clouds: Limitations, Challenges and Enablers. To Appear in eChallenges 2011, Florence, Italy (2011)
11. Kolodner, E.K., Shulman-Peleg, A., Naor, D., Brand, P., Dao, M., Eckert, A., Gogouvitis, S.V., Harnik, D., Jaeger, M.C., Kyriazis, D.P., Lorenz, M., Messina, A., Shribmann, A., Tal, S., Voulodimos, A.S., Wolfsthal, Y.: Data-intensive Storage Services on Clouds: Limitations, Challenges and Enablers. In: Petcu, D., Poletti, J.L.V. (eds.) European Research Activities in Cloud Computing. Expected Date of Publication (to appear, March 2012)

Integrated Monitoring of Infrastructures and Applications in Cloud Environments

Roberto Palmieri[1], Pierangelo di Sanzo[1], Francesco Quaglia[1],
Paolo Romano[2], Sebastiano Peluso[2], and Diego Didona[2]

[1] Dipartimento di Informatica e Sistemistica, Sapienza Rome University, Italy
[2] Distributed Systems Group, INESC-ID, Lisbon, Portugal

Abstract. One approach to fully exploit the potential of Cloud technologies consists in leveraging on the Autonomic Computing paradigm. It could be exploited in order to put in place reconfiguration strategies spanning the whole protocol stack, starting from the infrastructure and then going up to platform/application level protocols. On the other hand, the very base for the design and development of Cloud oriented Autonomic Managers is represented by monitoring sub-systems, able to provide audit data related to any layer within the stack. In this article we present the approach that has been taken while designing and implementing the monitoring sub-system for the Cloud-TM FP7 project, which is aimed at realizing a self-adapting, Cloud based middleware platform providing transactional data access to generic customer applications.

1 Introduction

As well known, Cloud based technologies are making a revolutionary change in the way systems and applications are built, configured and run. In particular, the ability to acquire computational power and storage on-the-fly has opened the possibility to massively put in place Autonomic Management schemes aimed at optimizing performance/availability indexes vs specific cost metrics.

A relevant reflection of such a revolutionary change is in that several projects targeting Cloud oriented software platforms and applications aim at designing/ integrating multi-modal operating modes. In particular, the target is to make differentiated protocols coexist within both the platform and the application layer in order to dynamically select the best suited protocol (and well suited parameter settings for it) depending on specific environmental conditions, such as the current workload profile. Consequently, the need arises for defining/implementing frameworks and systems supporting audit and monitoring functionalities spanning the whole set of differentiated layers within the Cloud based system.

At current date, several proposals exist in the context of monitoring the usage of infrastructure level resources (e.g. CPU and RAM) [1]. These are mostly suited for Infrastructure-as-a-Service (IaaS) customers, to whom the possibility to trigger infrastructure level reconfigurations either automatically or on demand, based on the monitoring outcomes, is provided. On the other hand, Cloud providers offer the possibility to monitor the level of performance provided by

M. Alexander et al. (Eds.): Euro-Par 2011 Workshops, Part I, LNCS 7155, pp. 45–53, 2012.

specific, supported platforms [4], such as Web based platforms, in order to enable, e.g., auto-scale facilities aimed at dynamically resizing the offered computational platform. This is suited for Platform-as-a-Service (PaaS) customers, who aim at delivering specific performance levels, while relying on facilities already offered by their reference Cloud providers.

In this paper we describe the approach we have taken in the design/ development of a Workload and Performance Monitor (WPM) that provides audit data for both infrastructure resources and platform (or application) level components in an integrated manner. The main distinguishing feature of our solution is that it does not target any specific platform or application. Instead, it is flexible and adaptable so to allow integration with differentiated platform/application types. On the technological side, our design comes from the integration of the Lattice framework (natively oriented to infrastructure monitoring), which has been largely exploited in the context of the RESERVOIR project [2], and the JMX JAVA oriented framework (suited for the audit of JAVA based components). The whole design/implementation has been tailored for integration within the platform targeted by the Cloud-TM FP7 project [3]. This project aims at designing/developing a self-adaptive middleware level platform, based on the Infinispan in-memory data management layer [6], providing transactional data access services (according to agreed upon QoS vs cost constraints) to the overlying customer applications.

2   Technological Background

2.1   The Lattice Framework

Lattice relies on a reduced number of interacting components, each one devoted (and encapsulating) a specific task in relation to distributed data-gathering activities. In terms of interaction abstraction, the Lattice framework is based on the producer-consumer scheme, where both the producer and consumer components are, in their turn, formed by sub-components, whose instantiation ultimately determines the functionalities of the implemented monitoring system. A producer contains data sources which, in turn, contain one or more probes. Probes read data values to be monitored, encapsulate measures within measurement messages and put them into message queues. Data values can be read by probes periodically, or as a consequence of some event. A message queue is shared by the data source and the contained probes. When a measurement message is available within some queue, the data source sends it to the consumer, which makes it available to reporter components. Overall, the producer component injects data that are delivered to the consumer. Also, producer and consumer have the capability to interact in order to internally (re)configure their operating mode.

Three logical channels are defined for the interaction between the two components, named

- data plane;
- info plane;
- control plane.

The data plane is used to transfer data-messages, whose payload is a set of measures, each kept within a proper message-field. The structure of the message (in terms of amount of fields, and meaning of each field) is predetermined. Hence, message-fields do not need to be explicitly tagged so that only data-values are really transmitted, together with a concise header tagging the message with very basic information, mostly related to source identification and timestamping. Such a structure can be anyway dynamically reconfigured via interactions supported by the info plane. This is a very relevant feature of Lattice since it allows minimal message footprint for (frequently) exchanged data-messages, while still enabling maximal flexibility, in terms of on-the-fly (infrequent) reconfiguration of the monitoring-information structure exchanged across the distributed components within the monitoring architecture.

Finally, the control plane can be used for triggering reconfiguration of the producer component, e.g., by inducing a change of the rate at which measurements need to be taken. Notably, the actual transport mechanism supporting the planes is decoupled from the internal architecture of producer/consumer components. Specifically, data are disseminated across these components through configurable distribution mechanisms ranging from IP multicast to publish/subscribe systems, which can be selected on the basis of the actual deployment and which can even be changed over time without affecting other components, in term of their internal configuration. The framework is designed to support multiple producers and multiple consumers, providing the chance to dynamically manage data source configuration, probe-activation/deactivation, data sending rate, redundancy and so on.

2.2   Portability Issues

The Lattice framework is based on JAVA technology, so that producer/ consumer components encapsulate sub-components that are mapped onto a set of JAVA threads, each one taking care of specific activities. Some of these threads, such as the data-source or the data-consumer, constitute the general purpose backbone of the skeleton provided by Lattice. Other threads, most notably the probe-thread and the reporter-thread, implement the actual logic for taking/reporting measurement samples. The implementation of these threads can be seen as the ad-hoc portion of the whole monitoring infrastructure, which performs activities tailored to specific measurements to be taken, in relation to the context where the monitoring system operates.

By the reliance on JAVA, portability issues are mostly limited to the implementation of the ad-hoc components. As an example, a probe-thread based on direct access to the "proc" file system for gathering CPU/memory usage information is portable only across (virtualized) operating systems supporting that type of file system (e.g. LINUX). However, widening portability across general platforms would only entail reprogramming the internal logic of this probe, which in some cases can even be done by exploiting, e.g., pre-existing JAVA packages providing platform-transparent access to physical resource usage.

The aforementioned portability considerations also apply to reporter-threads, which can implement differentiated, portable logics for exposing data to back-end applications (e.g. by implementing logics that store the data within a conventional database).

3   Architectural Organization

Figure 1 shows the general architectural organization we have devised for WPM. It has been defined according to the need for supporting the following two main functionalities:

- statistical data gathering (SDG);
- statistical data logging (SDL).

The SDG functionality maps onto an instantiation of the Lattice framework. In our instantiation, the elements belonging to the monitored infrastructure, such as Virtual Machines (VMs), can be logically grouped, and each group will entail per-machine probes targeting two types of resources: (A) hardware/virtualized and (B) logical. Statistics for the first kind of resources are directly collected over the Operating System (OS), or via OS decoupled libraries, while statistics related to logical resources (e.g. the data-platform) are collected at the application level by relying on the JMX framework for JAVA components.

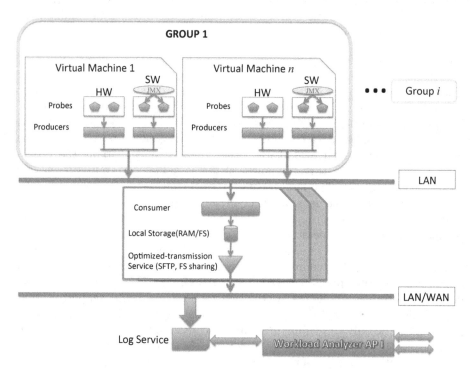

Fig. 1. WPM Architectural Organization

The data collected by the probes are sent to the producer component via the facilities natively offered by the Lattice framework. Each producer is coupled with one or many probes and it is responsible of managing them. The consumer is the Lattice component that receives the data from the producers, via differentiated messaging implementations, which could be selected on the basis of the specific system deployment. We envisage a LAN based clustering scheme such that the consumer is in charge of handling one or multiple groups of machines belonging to the same LAN. Anyway, in our architectural organization, the number of consumers is not meant to be fixed, instead it can be scaled up/down depending on the amount of instantiated probes/producers. Overall, the consumer can be instantiated as a centralized or a distributed process. Beyond collecting data from the producers, the consumer is also in charge of performing a local elaboration aimed at producing a suited stream representation to be provided as the input to the Log Service, which is in turn in charge of supporting the SDL functionality.

We decided to exploit the file system locally available at the consumer side to temporarily keep the stream instances to be sent towards the Log Service. The functional block which is responsible for the interaction between SDG and SDL is the so called *optimized-transmission service*. This can rely on top of differentiated solutions depending on whether the instance of SDL is co-located with the consumer or resides on a remote network. Generally speaking, with our organization we can exploit, e.g., SFTP or a locally shared File System. Also, stream compression schemes can be actuated to optimize both latency and storage occupancy.

The *Log Service* is the logical component responsible for storing and managing all the gathered data. It must support queries from any external application so to expose the statistical data for subsequent processing/analysis. The Log Service could be implemented in several manners, in terms of both the underlying data storage technology and the selected deployment (centralized vs distributed). As for the first aspect, different solutions could be envisaged in order to optimize access operations depending on, e.g. suited tradeoffs between performance and access flexibility. This is also related with the data model ultimately supported by the Log Service, which might be a traditional relational model or, alternatively, a <key,value> model. Further, the Log Service could maintain the data onto a stable storage support or within volatile memory, for performance vs reliability tradeoffs. The above aspects could depend on the the functionality/architecture of the application that is responsible for analyzing statistical data, which could be designed to be implemented as a geographically distributed process in order to better fit the WPM deployment (hence taking advantage from data partitioning and distributed processing).

3.1   Implementation of Infrastructure Oriented Probes

In this section we provide some technical specification for the probes developed in WPM. The design and the implementation of the infrastructure oriented probes has been tailored to the acquisition of statistical data in relation to (virtualized) hardware resources with no binding on a specific Operating System. This has been done by implementing the JAVA code associated with the probe on top of the SIGAR cross-platform JAVA based library (version 1.6.4) [5]. Infrastructure oriented probes are in charge of gathering statistical data on

1) CPU (per core): %user, %system, %idle.
2) RAM: kB free memory, kB used memory.
3) Network interfaces: total incoming data bytes, total outgoing data bytes, inbound bandwidth usage, outbound bandwidth usage.
4) Disks: %Free space (kB), %Used space (kB), mountPoint or Volume.

For all of the above four resources, the associated sampling process can be configured with differentiated timeouts whose values can be selected on the basis of the time-granularity according to which the sampled statistical process is expected to exhibit non-negligible changes.

3.2   Implementation of Data Platform Oriented Probes

The implementation of the data platform oriented probes has been extensively based on the JMX framework [7], which is explicitly oriented to support audit functionalities for JAVA based components. Essentially, each data platform oriented probe implements a JMX client, which can connect towards the JMX server running within the process where the monitored component resides. Then, via the JMX standard API, the probe retrieves the audit information internally produced by the monitored JAVA component in relation to its own activities. Anyway, the adoption of JMX Framework as a reference technology for implementing application level probes is not necessarily tied to a JAVA component. This is because a generic JMX probe can retrieve data form a JAVA component that wraps any possible monitored application, also written using any programming language.

As an instantiation of application level probes, in our implementation we developed a data platform probe that accesses the internal audit system of single Infinispan [6] caches (¹), in order to sample some parameters such as the Number of Commit, Number of Rollback, the Commit latency, etc.

3.3   Startup and Base Message Tagging Rules

Particular care has been taken in the design of the startup phase of WPM components, in relation to the fact that each probe could be deployed within a highly dynamic environment, where the set of monitored components (either belonging to the infrastructure or to the data platform) and the related instances can vary over time.

As pointed out, WPM will be a part of the Autonomic Manager of the Cloud-TM platform, which will rely on a Repository of Tunable Components where an XML description for each component currently taking part to the Cloud-TM

---

[1] We recall that Infinispan has been selected as the data layer within the Cloud-TM project, for which WPM constitutes one of the building blocks.

platform is recorded at component startup time. In the design of the WPM we rely on this repository, by exploiting it as a registry, where each probe can automatically retrieve information allowing it to univocally tag each measurement message sent to the Lattice consumer with the identity of the corresponding monitored component instance, as currently maintained by the registry. This will allow supporting a perfect matching between the measurement message and the associated instance of component, as seen by the overall infrastructure at any time instant. Such a process has been supported by embedding within Lattice probes a sensing functionality, allowing the retrieval of basic information related to the environment where the probe is activated (e.g. the IP number of the VM hosting that instance of the probe), which has been coupled with a matching functionality vs the registry in order to both

(a) retrieve the ID of the currently monitored component instance;
(b) retrieve information needed to correctly carry out the monitoring task, in relation to the target component instance.

Such a behavior is shown in Figure 2, where the interaction with the registry is actuated as a query over specific component types, depending on the type of probe issuing the query (an infrastructure oriented probe will query the registry for extracting records associated with VM instances, while a data platform oriented probe will query the registry for extracting records related to the specific component it is in charge of).

As for point (b), data platform probes rely on the use of JMX servers exposed by monitored components. Hence, the information requested to correctly support the statistical data gathering process entails the address (e.g. the port number) associated with the JMX server instance to be contacted. The information associated with point (b) is a "don't care" for infrastructure oriented probes since they do not operate via any intermediary (e.g. JMX server) entity.

3.4   Implementation of the Optimized-Transmission Service

In the current implementation, the optimized-transmission service has been implemented by relying on the use of zip and SSL-based file transfer functionalities. Each data stream portion assembled by the Lattice consumer is locally logged within a file, which is then zipped and sent towards the Log Service front-end via SSL. Exactly-once transmission semantic has been guaranteed via well known retransmission/filtering schemes, which have been based on a univocally determined name for each transmitted zipped file. Specifically, each Lattice consumer is univocally identified via a *consumer_ID*, which has been used to generate unique file names in the form

$$consumer\_ID + start\_timestamp + end\_timestamp$$

where start and end timestamp values within the file name identify the time interval during which the statistical data have been gathered by the consumer. These timestamp values are determined by exploiting the local clock accessible at the consumer side via the System.currentTimeMillis() service.

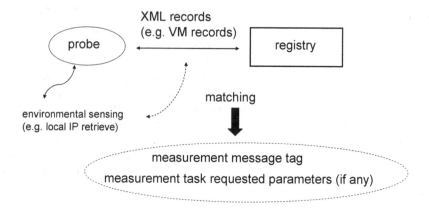

Fig. 2. Interaction between the Probes and the Registry

3.5 Implementation of the Log Service

As for the Cloud-TM data layer, the Log Service has been implemented by still relying on Infinispan [6], specifically by instantiating it as an Infinispan application that parses the input streams received from the Lattice consumer, and performs put operations on top of an Infinispan cache instance. The keys used for put operations correspond to message tags, as defined by the Lattice producer and its hosted probes. In particular, as explained above, each probe tags measurement messages with the unique ID associated with the monitored component. This ID has been used in our implementation to determine a unique key, to be used for a put operation, formed by:

$$component\_ID + type\_of\_measure + measure\_timestamp$$

where the *type_of_measure* identifies the specific measure carried out for that component (e.g. CPU vs RAM usage in case of a VM component), and the value expressed by *measure_timestamp* is again generated via the local clock accessible by the probe instance producing the message. Currently, the Log Service exposes to the external applications the Infinispan native <key,value> API, which does not prevent the possibility of supporting a different API in future releases.

4 Summary

In this article we have presented the architecture and the implementation of a Workload and Performance Monitor to be integrated within the architectural design of the Cloud-TM FP7 project platform. Our monitoring system provides integrated supports for gathering samples related to both hardware/virtualized resources and logical resources. It relies on the integration between the Lattice framework and JMX.

References

1. Clayman, S., Galis, A., Chapman, C., Toffetti, G., Rodero-Merino, L., Vaquero, L.M., Nagin, K., Rochwerger, B.: Monitoring Service Clouds in the Future Internet. IOS Press (2010)
2. http://www.reservoir-fp7.eu/index.php?page=open-source-code
3. http://www.cloudtm.eu/
4. http://aws.amazon.com/ec2/
5. http://www.hyperic.com/products/sigar
6. http://www.jboss.org/infinispan
7. Java Management Extensions (JMX) Technology,
   http://www.oracle.com/technetwork/java/javase/tech/javamanagement-140525.html

Towards Collaborative Data Management in the VPH-Share Project

Siegfried Benkner[1], Jesus Bisbal[2], Gerhard Engelbrecht[2], Rod D. Hose[3],
Yuriy Kaniovskyi[1], Martin Koehler[1], Carlos Pedrinaci[4], and Steven Wood[5]

[1] Faculty of Computer Science, University of Vienna, Austria
[2] Center for Computational Imaging & Simulation Technologies in Biomedicine,
Universitat Pompeu Fabra, Barcelona, Spain
[3] Department of Cardiovascular Science, Medical Physics Group,
University of Sheffield
[4] Knowledge Media Institute, The Open University, Milton Keynes, UK
[5] Dept. Medical Physics, Royal Hallamshire Hospital, Sheffield, UK

Abstract. The goal of the Virtual Physiological Human Initiative is to provide a systematic framework for understanding physiological processes in the human body in terms of anatomical structure and biophysical mechanisms across multiple length and time scales. In the long term it will transform the delivery of European healthcare into a more personalised, predictive, and integrative process, with significant impact on healthcare and on disease prevention. This paper outlines how the recently funded project VPH-Share contributes to this vision. The project is motivated by the needs of the whole VPH community to harness ICT technology to improve health services for the individual. VPH-Share will provide the organisational fabric (the infostructure), realised as a series of services, offered in an integrated framework, to expose and to manage data, information and tools, to enable the composition and operation of new VPH workflows and to facilitate collaborations between the members of the VPH community.

Keywords: virtual physiological human, healthcare infrastructure.

1 Introduction

The Virtual Physiological Human Initiative (VPH-I) from the European Commission aims to provide a systematic framework for understanding physiological processes in the human body in terms of anatomical structure and biophysical mechanisms at multiple length and time scales. Multiple projects are funded and try to meet specific objectives addressing data integration and knowledge extraction systems or patient specific computational modeling and simulation. To achieve these objectives a combined data/compute infrastructure will need to be developed.

M. Alexander et al. (Eds.): Euro-Par 2011 Workshops, Part I, LNCS 7155, pp. 54–63, 2012.

The VPH-Share project[1] has been funded within the VPH initiative and will provide a systematic framework for the understanding of physiological processes in the human body. A long term objective is to transform the European healthcare into a more personalised, predictive, and integrative process with significant impact on healthcare and on disease prevention. The project will provide an integrated framework, realised as set of services, to expose and manage data, information and tools, to enable the composition and operation of new VPH workflows and to facilitate collaborations between the members of the VPH community. The project consortium comprises 21 partners from the European Union and New Zealand including data providers, providing data sources from individual patients (medical images and biomedical signals), research institutes, universities, and industry.

The project addresses four flagship workflows from European projects which provide existing data, tools, and models driving the development of the infostructure and pilot the applications. The flagship workflow include a workflow' from the @neurIST project[2], dealing with the management of unruptered cerebral aneurysms and associated research into risk factors. The euHeart[3] workflow supports integrated cardiac care using patient-specific cardiovascular modeling and the VPHOP workflow[4] is in the domain of osteoporotic research. The fourth flagship workflow, Virolab[5], drives a virtual laboratory for decision support for the treatment of viral diseases. By covering these workflows the VPH-Share project aims at the provisioning of a generic data management and computational infrastructure for supporting generic VPH workflows.

The main focus of the project is the provisioning of a patient avatar which can be defined as a coherent digital representation of a patient. The provisioning of a patient avatar will rely on the DIKW hierarchy[6] promoted by the ARGOS Observatory [1]. On the lowest layer, the DIKW pyramid, proposes data including instantiations of measurements. By utilizing data as input to diagnosis it becomes information which can be cognitively processed by means of knowledge. If knowledge becomes confirmed and accepted, it is called wisdom. By following these paradigm new data sources need to be established and made widely available through an appropriate infrastructure, including a data management platform, which we call data infostructure.

In the following, we clarify some terminology used in the rest of this paper. By the term 'infrastructure', we mean the raw data, and the tools and services that operate on them (for example to access, to transfer, to store) without any

---

[1] VPH-Share: https://www.biomedtown.org/biomed_town/vphshare/reception/website/
[2] @neurIST: Integrated biomedical informatics for the management of cerebral aneurysms, http://cilab2.upf.edu/aneurist1
[3] EuHeart: Integrated cardiac care using patient-specific cardiovascular modeling, http://www.euheart.eu
[4] VPHOP: the Osteoporotic Virtual Physiological Human, http://www.vphop.eu
[5] ViroLab: a virtual laboratory for decision support in viral diseases treatment, http://www.virolab.org
[6] DIKW hierarchy: http://en.wikipedia.org/wiki/DIKW

understanding of the content of the data, and the hardware resources that are used in all data and modelling operations. We use 'infostructure' to describe the systems and services that VPH-Share will develop to transform data into information and thence into knowledge.

2   VPH-Share Infostructure

The DIKW hierarchy described in the previous section inspired the vision for the infostructure the VPH-Share project aims to build. The main components of this infostructure are presented in Figure 1 as a layered architecture. It illustrates the generation of new (medical) wisdom and the respective tools and services to be developed/used for this - from data to knowledge, through the VPH-Share enabled infrastructure. New, validated VPH models will thus be developed and integrated into so-called 'patient-centred computational workflows' (detailed in Section 2.2).

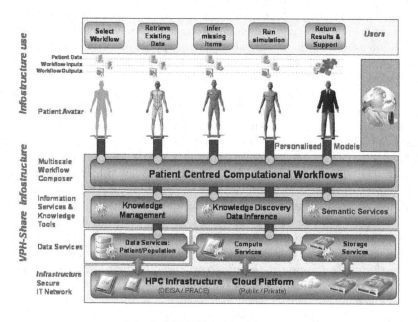

Fig. 1. VPH-Share Architecture

More specifically, starting at the bottom of Figure 1, the architecture includes the lowest level of services that provide access to computational infrastructure and manage execution of VPH-Share operations. It is foreseen that both, the Cloud computing paradigm as well as high performance computing services, will be available in order to address the wide diversity of challenges in the VPH. From the data management perspective, this first layer is mainly aimed at the management of large files. More structured (e.g. relational, xml) data is managed by a set of specific data services to contribute, access, distribute, and annotate these type of data sets.

On top of these services, advanced semantic services are added to facilitate the sharing and re-use of these datasets. In addition, data inference strategies and engines are also added, in order to exploit the wealth of knowledge hidden within the vast amounts of data that will be stored within this infostructure. In that respect, it must be noted that biomedical datasets are inevitably incomplete, thus these services will generate (or, rather, 'infer') this input from other relevant data which is available.

The architecture also provides a unified, but modular, user interface to all available services.

Concrete realisation of the vision is effected in four patient-centred computational workflows, as defined in Section 2.2. This ensures that all advances, tools and services developed within the project are at all times fit for purpose and meaningful to the biomedical researcher.

2.1   Patient Avatar

The VPH-Share project has introduced a central concept, referred to as the *Patient Avatar*. This is an evolving concept which has received different names since its initial conception. For example, it was called the Virtual Patient Metaphor, in the @neurIST project [3], and more recently in the Network of Excellence (NoE) is called the *Digital Me* [2]. Following the strategic vision defined by the NoE, the patient avatar is described as: "a coherent digital representation of each patient that is used as an integrative framework for the consolidation within the European research system of fundamental and translational Integrative Biomedical Research and the provision to European Citizens of an affordable Personalised, Predictive, and Integrative Medicine".

For a concrete realisation of the patient avatar the project provides the means to be specific about which information it must contain to be relevant to specific contexts, a concept that will be explicitly and directly tested within each of our VPH-Share workflows. At the least personalised level this avatar will contain population averages, or even best guesses, for all information items. The progression from the silhouette to the clothed man in Figure 1 illustrates the personalisation of the avatar as the VPH-Share data inference services operate on the information that is available about the individual to refine the estimates of those data items (and their likely ranges) that have not been measured or recorded.

2.2   VPH-Share Workflows

The concepts associated with the construction of an infostructure can become very abstract, and the project recognised the danger of trying to impose on the community a solution that might be conceptually elegant, computationally efficient, and even robust, but which may ultimately be very difficult to use by typical VPH researchers. To address this issue we have selected four driving patient-centred computational workflows, which we would suggest represent some of the best from completed or running ICT projects in the 6th and 7th

Framework Programmes, namely @neurIST, euHeart, VPHOP and Virolab, to serve as the empirical basis and benchmarks for the support structure to be developed by this proposal. It can be claimed that together they encapsulate the breadth of challenges presented to the VPH researcher.

Our use of the flagship workflows to guide the development of the infostructure, and to pilot its application, is consistent with the VPH NoE Vision document's recommendation that "all progress in the VPH must be driven and motivated through associated complex clinical workflows" [2]. In spite of the variety of problems the VPH as a whole addresses, there is a relative small number of possible workflows that are being developed to address the general problem of producing personalised, quantitative, and predictive models. This observation creates an opportunity for standardisation of methods and tools, which must constitute the backbone of this infostructure. Its construction is the ultimate goal of the VPH-Share project.

2.3   VPH-Share Cloud Infrastructure

The VPH-Share project will provide a Cloud infrastructure facilitating access to data and compute resources needed for data hosting and the execution of applications. On top of the Cloud infrastructure, VPH-Share services including data, semantic, and compute services, as well as workflows, will be hosted on demand. On the data side, a key requirement is to enable data hosting locally at the data provider's site, as this is the key requirement of many clinical institutions. Since some compute services and workflows have demanding compute requirements, access to HPC e-infrastructures will be integrated too.

On top of these requirements, there is a need for public and private Cloud environments, as well as access to HPC resources. The main goal is not to implement low-level Cloud middleware services, but rather to built a flexible Software as a Service (SaaS) environment on top of existing Infrastructure as a Service (IaaS) solutions. The infrastructure will provide easy deployment and execution of scientific applications and on-demand Cloud resource management. The Cloud infrastructure will include a policy driven security framework which ensures that the information exchange between VPH users and the services and data stored in the Cloud is secure and reliable.

3   VPH-Share Data Infrastructure

The VPH-Share data infrastructure aims at creating a unified data management platform supporting the efficient management and sharing of biomedical information consented for research. The platform comprises generic services and protocols to enable data holders to manage, provide, and share the information. The design of the data management platform follows an incremental Extract-Transform-Load (ETL) process that allows the provisioning of an evolving platform that can be extended as new information sources become available. Using semantic data integration technologies, the platform supports on-demand customised views on the available information [4].

The data infrastructure provides different types of services supporting access and integration of federated data sources. The focus of the infrastructure is the provisioning of relational data sources that are available in the form of relational databases or as files following a relational schema (e.g. CSV files). The services support querying of the data sources via relational as well as semantic concepts and provide a consistent interface to the other software components involved in the project. The services are exposed on top of the VPH-Share Cloud-based resource infrastructure.

The data infrastructure provides a uniform data management platform on top of services achieving the following objectives:

3.1   VPH-Share Data Sources

The VPH-Share project identified multiple VPH-relevant data sources which will be supported and Cloud-enabled by the data infrastructure. These data sources include clinical, research and simulation data sources, accessible via the data management platform. The VPH-Share project will discuss the requirements for different data sources, design patterns, as well as data schemes together with the VPH Network of Excellence (NoE). To integrate these and new data sources into the data management platform, there is a need for on-demand data transformation.

Data exposed within VPH-Share will be employed in the context of the infostructure and will be exposed to VPH-Share stakeholders following security and privacy requirements. Datasets that have been identified for the provisioning via the data infrastructure include data sources from the European projects @neurIST and ViroLab, as well as the NHS IC database [7], and the STH Cardiac data set.

The @neurIST dataset holds information in the domain of cerebral aneurysm research, including images, comprehensive demographic, and physiological information obtained from six European member states. The ViroLab data set includes several thousand records associated with HIV/AIDS research including genomic sequences, genotypes, treatment history, clinical and demographic data. The dataset from the NHS IC contains a range of national health and social care datasets that describe the demographics, lifestyles, burden on the health and social care system and interaction with this system. A longitudinal data set including cardiac data is utilized at the Sheffield Teaching Hospital (STH) and can possibly be utilized during the project as well. A number of additional data sets have been identified and it has yet to be decided if they can be included in the data management platform based on the data holders requirements and legal restrictions.

3.2   Data Services

The VPH-Share project will provide a generic data management and integration framework that supports the provisioning and deployment of data services.

---

[7] NHS Information Centre, `http://www.ic.nhs.uk/`

The data service infrastructure will enable the virtualization of heterogeneous scientific databases and information sources as Web services which do allow transparent access to and integration of relational databases, XML databases and flat files. The development of data services is based on the Vienna Cloud Environment (VCE) [5],[6] and the @neurIST data service infrastructure [7] and utilizes advanced data mediation and distributed query processing techniques. Data services hide the details of distributed data sources, resolving heterogeneities with respect to access language, data model and schema. These services comprise data access services to expose data sources via a Web Service interface. Additionally, data mediation services are provided in order to transparently combine different data sources and data access services in a mediated fashion as high-level services. Data mediation services preserve the autonomy of underlying data sources and ensure always up-to-date data, both key requirements of the project. A customised set of these services forms the basis for an on-demand dataspace which can be utilized by the workflows and the end users.

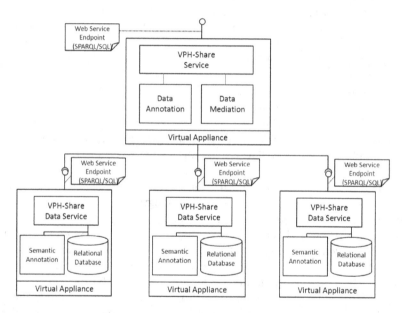

Fig. 2. VPH-Share Data Services: Data Services are hosted in virtual appliances and expose data sources as Web service endpoints

The data service infrastructure, as outlined in Fig. 2, is being built on top of state-of-the art Web service technologies. Data access services provide a uniform interface, utilizing WSDL and REST, to expose data sources. By utilizing mediation technology, data services will be able to integrate data exposed via different services. Hosting VPH-Share services follows the virtual appliance approch enabling the hosting of services in the Cloud. Client applications usually access data services by submitting an SQL query, or, in the case of semantically annotated data sources, a SPARQL query, and download the query results in respective formats (e.g. WebRowSet or RDF triples). The data service framework internally utilizes established data access and integration technologies capabilities including OGSA-DAI [8] and OGSA-DQP [9].

The hosting of data services relies on the concept of virtual appliances. A virtual appliance can be defined as a software package pre-installed on a virtual machine image to enable provisioning of the software in the Cloud. The VPH-Share Cloud infrastructure will enable on-demand hosting of data sources exposed as services and provided via virtual appliances in the Cloud.

4   VPH Semantics

The VPH-Share semantics layer aims at providing 'knowledge level' functionality to the stakeholder by establishing an abstraction over the lower-level compute and data services.

VPH-Share will provide facilities for assisting users in selecting suitable ontologies and annotating datasources with them. Informed by these annotations VPH-Share will provide means for exposing and integrating distributed datasets exploiting linked data principles [15]. In particular, supported by this technology the project shall support accessing the underlying information through different semantic views and combining these different view for carrying out global analysis. Similarly, VPH-Share will provide support for annotating computational services so as to exploit these annotations in order to better assist data analysts in the discovery of applicable analysis services, as well as to help composing and invoking them. In this respect, the project shall leverage linked services technologies notably their integration with linked data as a processing infrastructure [16].

Finally, supported by the ability to integrate and process distributed data, the project shall devise a number of data inference services. These services will leverage domain knowledge, data mining, and machine learning technologies to analyse the wealth of information captured in order infer and estimate additional information, thus allowing practitioners to reach previously unattainable insights which would presumably lead to further and better informed decisions.

5   Related Work

Building an infrastructure for modelling and managing biomedical information has been addressed by multiple projects. The @neurIST project dealt with supporting the research and treatment of cerebral aneurysms. An advanced service-oriented IT infrastructure for the management of all processes linked to research, diagnosis, and treatment development for complex and multi-factorial diseases has been developed.

Another project in the domain of VPH, called Health-e-Child, creates an information modelling methodology based around three complementary concepts: data, metadata, and semantics. The goal is to give clinicans a comprehensive view of a child's health by integrating biomedical data, information and knowledge. The utilized data spans from imaging to genetic to clinical and epidemiological.

The caCORE infrastructure [11], developed by the National Cancer Institute (NCI), United States provides tools for the development of interoperable information management systems for data sharing and is particularly focused on biological data in the cancer domain. Additional projects, relying on the model-driven software architecture of caCORE for managing biomedical research information haven been started (caGrid [12], CaBIG [13]).

The PhysiomeSpace [14] is a digital library service for biomedical data and has been developed in the LHDL project. PhysiomeSpace provides services for sharing biomedical data and models with a mixed free/pay-per-use business model that should ensure long term sustainability.

6 Conclusion

The VPH-Share project is part of the VPH initiative of the European Commission with the goal of providing a systematic framework for understanding physiological processes in the human body in terms of anatomical structure and biophysical mechanisms at multiple length and time scales. The project will provide a systematic framework for the understanding of physiological processes in the human body.

The VPH-Share project introduces the concept of a patient avatar which can be defined as a coherent digital representation of each patient including information relevant to different contexts. For managing data the project relies on the DIKW pyramid describing the path from data, information, and knowledge, to wisdom. A flexible, semantically enhanced, data management platform will be created supporting this approach and relying on the concept of data services to enable the vision of patient avatars.

The infrastructure will be developed based on the requirements of four flagship workflows (@neurIST, euHeart, VPHOP, and Virolab). These workflows serve as the empirical basis and benchmarks for the support structure to be developed.

The VPH-Share project will provide a Cloud infrastructure facilitating on-demand access to data and compute resources. On top of the Cloud infrastructure, VPH-Share services including data access, data mediation, semantic, and compute services, as well as workflows, will be hosted on demand.

References

1. ARGOS: Transatlantic Observatory for Meeting Global Health Policy Challenges through ICT-Enabled Solutions (2011), http://argos.eurorec.org/
2. Hunter, P., Coveney, P., de Bono, B., Diaz, V., Fenner, J., Frangi, A., Harris, P., Hose, R., Kohl, P., Lawford, P., McCormack, K., Mendes, M., Omholt, S., Quarteroni, A., Skår, J., Tegner, J., Thomas, S., Tollis, I., Tsamardinos, I., van Beek, J., Viceconti, M.: A vision and strategy for the virtual physiological human in 2010 and beyond. Phil. Trans. Royal Society A, 2595–2614 (2010)

3. Dunlop, R., Arbona, A., Rajasekaran, H., Iacono, L.L., Fingberg, J., Summers, P., Benkner, S., Engelbrecht, G., Chiarini, A., Friedrich, C.M., Moore, B., Bijlenga, P., Iavindrasana, J., Hose, R.D., Frangi, A.F.: @neurIST - Chronic Disease Management through Integration of Heterogeneous Data and Computer-interpretable Guideline Services. In: Proceedings of Healthgrid (2008)

4. Franklin, M., Halevy, A., Maier, D.: From Databases to Dataspaces: A new abstraction for information management. ACM SIGMOD (2005)

5. Benkner, S., Engelbrecht, G., Koehler, M., Woehrer, A.: Virtualizing scientific applications and data sources as grid services. In: Cao, J. (ed.) Cyberinfrastructure Technologies and Applications. Nova Science Publishers (2009)

6. Koehler, M., Benkner, S.: VCE - A Versatile Cloud Environment for Scientific Applications. In: The Seventh International Conference on Autonomic and Autonomous Systems, ICAS (2011)

7. Benkner, S., Arbona, A., Berti, G., Chiarini, A., Dunlop, R., Engelbrecht, G., Frangi, A.F., Friedrich, C.M., Hanser, S., Hasselmeyer, P., Hose, R.D., Iavindrasana, J., Koehler, M., Iacono, L.L., Lonsdale, G., Meyer, R., Moore, B., Rajasekaran, H., Summers, P.E., Woehrer, A., Wood, S.: @neurist: Infrastructure for advanced disease management through integration of heterogeneous data, computing, and complex processing services. IEEE Transactions on Information Technology in Biomedicine 14(6), 1365–1377 (2010)

8. Antonioletti, M., Atkinson, M., Baxter, R., Borley, A., Hong, C., Neil, P., Collins, B., Hardman, N., Hume, A.C., Knox, A., Jackson, M., Krause, A., Laws, S., Magowan, J., Paton, N.W., Pearson, D., Sugden, T., Watson, P., Westhead, M.: The design and implementation of grid database services in ogsa-dai: Research articles. Concurrency and Computation: Practice and Experience 17(2-4), 357–376 (2005)

9. Alpdemir, M.N., Mukherjee, A., Gounaris, A., Paton, N.W., Watson, P., Fernandes, A.A.A., Fitzgerald, D.J.: OGSA-DQP: A Service for Distributed Querying on the Grid. In: Bertino, E., Christodoulakis, S., Plexousakis, D., Christophides, V., Koubarakis, M., Böhm, K. (eds.) EDBT 2004. LNCS, vol. 2992, pp. 858–861. Springer, Heidelberg (2004)

10. Branson, A., Hauer, T., McClatchey, R., Rogulin, D., Shamdasani, J.: A Data Model for Integrating Heterogeneous Medical Data in the Health-e-Child Project. In: Proceedings of HealthGrid (2008)

11. Komatsoulis, G.A., Warze, D.B., Hartel, F.W.: caCORE version 3: Implementation of a model driven, service-oriented architecture for semantic interoperability. Journal of Biomedical Informatics 41(1), 106–123 (2008)

12. Oster, S., Langella, S., Hastings, S., Ervin, D.: caGrid 1.0: An Enterprise Grid Infrastructure for Biomedical Research. Journal of the American Medical Informatics Association 15(2), 138–149 (2008)

13. Buetow, K.H., Niederhuber, J.: Infrastructure For A Learning Health Care System: CaBIG. Health Affairs 28(3), 923–924 (2009)

14. Testi, D., Quadrani, P., Viceconti, M.: PhysiomeSpace: digital library service for biomedical data. Phil. Trans. R. Soc. 368(1921), 2853–2861 (2010)

15. Bizer, C., Heath, T., Berners-Lee, T.: Linked Data - The Story So Far. International Journal on Semantic Web and Information Systems (IJSWIS) (2009)

16. Pedrinaci, C., Domingue, J.: Toward the Next Wave of Services: Linked Services for the Web of Data. Journal of Universal Computer Science 16(13), 1694–1719 (2010)

SLM and SDM Challenges in Federated Infrastructures

Matti Heikkurinen[1,2] and Owen Appleton[1,2]

[1] Emergence Tech. Limited
[2] gSLM Project
{matti,owen}@emergence-tech.com
www.emergence-tech.com
www.gslm.eu

Abstract. Federation of computing resources imposes challenges in service management not seen in simple customer-supplier relationships. Federation is common in e-Infrastructure and growing in clouds through the growth of hybrid and multiclouds. Relationships in federated environments are complex at present, and must be simplified to allow structured service management to be improved. Input can be taken from commercial service management techniques such as ITIL and ISO/IEC20000 but special features of federated environments, such as complications in inducement and enforcement must be considered.

Keywords: Cloud, multicloud, e-Infrastructure, Grid, HPC, Service Level Management, Service Delivery Management, Service Level Agreement.

1 Setting the Scene

Online and distributed services are now essentially endemic in the IT sector, so much so that their nature is often ignored by end users of systems such as Gmail or various online storage services like Dropbox. Both the academic and industrial/commercial sectors are likewise awash with distributed services. In the commercial sector there is a long history of network based IT services, but recently Cloud computing has been the focus of attention. Clouds are online services based on large numbers of virtual machines that can be used to provide compute, storage and other services.

In the academic sector the umbrella term for distributed services in Europe is e-Infrastructure (cyberinfrastructure in the USA). This term includes a wide range of "facilities, resources and collaboration tools" that allow for "computing, connectivity, storage and instrumentation"[1]. This is a stack of services, from pan-European network services such as GÉANT at the bottom of the stack up through an infrastructure layer of high performance or high throughput computing systems up to service layers that are exposed to users. High throughput computing, also known as Grid computing, involves the coupling of geographically distributed heterogeneous, generally commodity resources into a system similar to a computing cluster. In comparison, high performance computing (HPC) involves tightly coupled and geographically local high specification machines, so-called supercomputers. HPC does also work in a distributed manner, through connections between supercomputers, but it is a different approach to distribution.

M. Alexander et al. (Eds.): Euro-Par 2011 Workshops, Part I, LNCS 7155, pp. 64–72, 2012.

In all these cases, there is an element of dynamic federation. These systems are designed for users with variable needs that for a range of reasons choose not to work with fixed local resources.

2   The Nature of Federated Infrastructures

2.1   The ICT Management Challenge

There is no way around the need for management of IT services. Provision of infrastructure services (i.e. large-scale, general purpose IT services) will always involve an important management component. Correct architectural design, fault-tolerant soft- and hardware and other technical solutions can improve the reliability of the infrastructure and convince users to migrate their applications.

However, management processes and organizational approaches are key in ensuring that Quality of Service (QoS) can be maintained in situations that automatic tools cannot cope with. Such situations are inevitable in complex systems reliant on variable networks and used by fallible users.

These challenges have been addressed by the commercial and public sector in the last few decades, and a large body of knowledge addressing this management challenge has been collected under the disciplines of Service Level Management (SLM) and Service Delivery Management (SDM). They collect, analyze and derive sets of processes that are used to define, agree, monitor and manage the provision of a huge range of services. These provide a structured approach to the service provision lifecycle, from offering service catalogues to negotiating enforceable legal agreements, coping with service failures and closing agreements. While SLM-SDM has legal elements and can specify technical metrics, it also pays attention to reaching common understandings and other human elements in the service domain. These themselves are necessary for legal reasons, as for instance in most systems contracts must represent a meeting of the minds to be legally enforceable.

In the commercial IT service sector, SLM-SDM is a mature area, a component of IT Service Management (ITSM). Several internationally accepted systems for SLM-SDM exist, notably ITIL, ISO/IEC 20000, eTOM and COBIT. However, these systems have not been used in the e-Infrastructure domain beyond small-scale pilots focusing on the activities within a single site. In fact, even when addressing complex, cross-organizational value networks, these SLM/SDM frameworks have always assumed a fairly static contractual model that can be broken down into bilateral "producer-consumer" agreements that have been negotiated well in advance. Dynamically federated e-Infrastructures, such as Grids, challenge this model and necessitate adaptation of many of the tools and procedures on the management level.

In clouds, SDM-SLM has been considered, as one would expect from commercial organizations already familiar with he concepts, but the implemented service level agreements (SLAs) for instance, are very weak by any normal IT service management standard. SDM-SLM also seems to ignore the need to federate, or so called Hybrid and Multi-cloud infrastructures. It appears that cloud providers assume (or hope) that any 'federation' you need can be accomplished within their service. However, such vendor lock-in will not suit all customers by any means.

In both clouds and academic e-Infrastructure, participants have tried to shortcut the management challenge through automation. For instance, in the Grid field automated SLA negotiation has long been the most commonly seen effort in the SLM-SDM area, but has ignored the more fundamental questions of agreement and negotiation. Rather one-size fits all SLAs have been attempted with only limited success.

Automation is an important step, but one might summarize the service management meta-process as understand, communicate, manage, monitor and then finally automate. Grids and some other e-Infrastructure have tried to jump to the end of this process, and hence found they have an automated system that lacks SLAs anyone will agree to.

2.2   Why Federation Is Necessary?

There are a number of drivers for federation of resources, through cloud, Grid, HPC or any other system. These include requirements for high capacity resources, mitigating risk through vendor independence, simplification of remote service accessibility or perhaps increased service redundancy. At heart most of these can be expressed in economic terms. High capacity resources might be needed transiently (peak demand) but might be unaffordable to provision permanently and locally. Equally vendor lock-in might present a dependence on an outside firm that presents a major financial risk.

Politics can also play a part. The original motivation for development and deployment of Grids came from the need for very large scale resources, that were either economically infeasible in one location, or if not, were politically impossible to select a single location for.

In the cloud domain, there are some basic questions on federation. Clouds are often presented as federating individual compute or storage units - conventionally virtual machines – into a consistent whole. But Clouds often aggregate the resources instead of federating them. While a cloud brings together many virtual machines their ability to act as a seamless distributed whole is limited. In comparison, Grids show lower reliability but more completely unify resources Grids, despite their issues can also scale redundantly as they are based on open standards and heterogeneous resources. Failure of a single site, or even the sites in a whole country is not terminal for a user. Partly due to their experimental and academic pedigree, Grids can cope better than Clouds with local failures and the diversity of software, equipment and groups involved provides security. For example, recent failures in the Amazon cloud services took down many major websites. Industry commentators have since noted that many firms rely on single cloud providers such as Amazon, despite never allowing it with local resources, where a backup system for key infrastructure was long a given [2].

The multi-cloud approach recognises and avoids these risks by spreading services across multiple providers. Hybrid clouds are similar, mixing internal and external cloud resources. Both emphasise provision of vendor-neutral interfaces to various Infrastructure/Platform as a Service (IaaS/PaaS) services.

Whatever their differences, the e-Infrastructure and cloud visions both contain – implicitly or explicitly – the ideas of easy, instant access to remote resources that for whatever reason, exceed the capacities and capabilities of a single organisation. At the same time, both Grid and Cloud domains have matured to the level where solving the interoperability issues between different solutions is seen as a key challenge: benefiting from the economies of scale is only possibly if the resources are – in one way or the other – put into a single pool.

2.3   Examples of Federated Infrastructures

For the moment, the largest federated e-Infrastructures are most likely the European HPC and Grid services. For example, EGI (the European Grid Initiative) acts as an umbrella organisation for an infrastructure consisting of almost 350 resource providers from 57 different countries with hundreds of thousands of CPU cores[3]. The federated supercomputing infrastructure PRACE consists of 21 European supercomputing centres that share resources to solve high-end HPC challenges[4].

In the cloud domain, the main providers are companies such as Amazon, Rackspace, Salesforce, Google and Microsoft's Azure. In the academic space, many installations are based on Eucalyptus (an open source private cloud solution compatible with Amazon's offerings) or make use of OpenNebula (a toolkit for heterogeneous cloud resources).

The multicloud space, however, remains smaller. RightScale provides a multicloud management and monitoring system supporting services including Amazon cloud services, Rackspace and the open source and Eucalyptus based clouds. Open source option Scalr offers most of the same functionality, and there are several other open source multicloud projects in the academic space, but they are not yet widely adopted. While currently a relatively small sector, it seems likely that as the hype on clouds dies down and the limitations of single vendor solutions become apparent, multiclouds will grow rapidly, and likely match if not surpass the size of current e-Infrastructure services.

2.4   The State of Federated SLM

We consider the current state of federated SLM rather weak. In the e-Infrastructure domain, the services' academic origins meant that systems were developed based on informal sharing, without financial customer-provider relationships. Imposing such models early on would have likely stifled innovation as academic and academic organisations are generally wary of engaging in financial relationships but very open to less formal collaborative ones. While at the network level, SLM is quite thorough, in the Grid layers, SLM is generally limited to very weak SLAs which are not easily enforceable.

The cloud does feature SLAs, but the service guarantees are rather trivial. The Amazon EC2 SLA [5] has a maximum penalty of 10% of a customer bill for periods where annual availability falls below 99.95%. Furthermore, the 10% is not a refund, but credit against future Amazon EC2 purchases. Rackspace LoadBalancer service offers 5% of fees paid for each hour the SLA is not met, up to a total of 100% of fees paid. However, again this is paid as credit toward future purchases.

Multiclouds seem to offer initially just collections of the SLAs of the individual services. This is essentially aggregation rather than federation. While it may be sufficient for simply replicating a single system, running a service with interdependent components means that a failure of one Cloud can take down the whole service but compensation is based on the value of the failed part.

For the multicloud or e-Infrastructures to be broadly successful, they will require SLM-SDM that inspires confidence in their client base. In the e-Infrastructure domain, the European Commission has funded the gSLM project [6] to bring approaches from the commercial SDM-SLM arena to the area.

2.5   The SLM Problem

We have described and demonstrated the need for an approach to SLM in federated environments, here we try and consider how a model can be formed. A first step is to consider that while experience, inspiration and expertise from commercial SDM-SLM can be extremely useful, one cannot simply drop SDM-SLM into a multicloud or e-Infrastructure. Dynamically federated systems have specific challenges that must be addressed to implement effective service management.

In e-Infrastructure, multiple organisations contribute to a single, large-scale service. These organisations are connected through relationships that began informally though they now start to seek formal connection. Jumping from no formal agreements to highly formal agreements would not be well accepted by the participants, who appear generally nervous about codifying service levels, even if they are at a level that is easily achievable. There are also complex issues about delegated responsibility. If a single party fails, causing a service provided by a large number of participants to fail, customers must be compensated, but neither penalizing one organisation for the total value of the service, not penalizing all organisations for the failure of one are fair or likely to be accepted. SLAs, the most common form of SLM attempted in the e-Infrastructure sphere, also tend to assume availabilities not seen in Grids and some other e-Infrastructure. Due to the complexity and heterogeneity of the system, availability or success rates around of 65% are not uncommon, which makes many commercial approaches hard to implement.

In the cloud, the product is standardised in a way e-Infrastructure generally isn't. They also have real SLAs that apply to all users, but while SLAs tend to promise good availability, they are weak on penalties for non-performance. They can also decouple user level value from the unit of sale. While the individual value of a single virtual machine may be low to the provider versus the whole pool, it might be high to the user. A complex service requiring many virtual machines running together might be rendered ineffective by a single failure, in a way that say, Grids would recognise and cloud providers would not. Such a failure might be within the bounds of acceptable failure on Cloud SLAs, and is one reason that clouds have not simple replaced e-Infrastructures. This would be a case for single clouds showing features of aggregation rather than federation, and currently multi clouds (apparently more federated) would show the same problem unless the multicloud providers provide their own SLA and accepts the risk themselves.

2.6   Modelling Federated SLM Relationships

In trying to bring a new model to the federated computing landscape, there are a number of steps that can be taken to start the process. The first of these is to map the relationships and risks in each service type.

Plain clouds show a simple relationship model (customer-provider), but for reasons previously discussed, single providers may not serve all needs. In the multicloud, we have several options for how relationships can be structured. Figure 1 shows the relationships in two types of potential multicloud situation.

Customer 1 pays directly two cloud providers and the multicloud provider to control and monitor their multiple cloud resources. While the aggregated multicloud provider may guarantee their service (as in their dashboard availability etc) they make no promises about the services they aggregate. Thus their service can be relatively low cost, as they assume no risk. From a customer point of view this multicloud scenario works best when using different cloud providers per purpose, e.g. storage from one and compute from another.

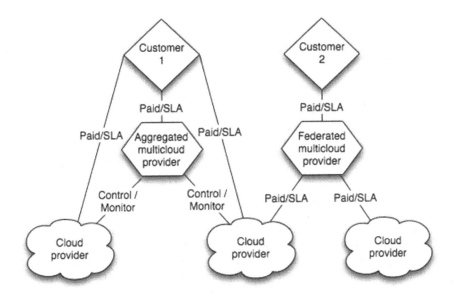

Fig. 1. Two kinds of multicloud relationship maps

Customer 2 deals only with the federated multicloud provider, who provides an abstraction layer that hides the various clouds used to provision their service. They then have SLAs with the cloud providers themselves. In this case the customer deals with a single interface that federates resources such that failure of the overall service will be managed by the multicloud providers (perhaps by redeploying from a failing cloud provider to a working one). Clearly taking on this risk will incur costs, but the costs will provide the user with security not present in the aggregated model.

In e-Infrastructures, particularly Grid infrastructures, reducing the number of relationships to the logical minimum is a challenge complicated by the number of actors. Figure 2 illustrates this relationships challenge.

An ideal situation would be a strictly hierarchical chain where users through various intermediaries accesses resources, this is however complicated by the existence of Grid Infrastructures (essentially federators) of different scales. Countries operate federating bodies for resources, but equally some subject areas or other groups may operate as federators. Both deal with resource owners at so-called sites. There are then secondary federators that collect primary ones into larger bodies. On the customer side, user groups come together as virtual organisations.

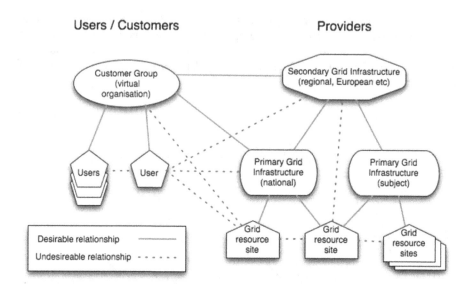

Fig. 2. Relationships in Grid type e-Infrastructure

At present almost every possible relationship occurs, whether desirable or not - including the unnecessary relationships of Figure 2. Reduction to a single chain would let the system be considered, in SLA terms, as an SLA between a user group and a federating Grid infrastructure, which would then have operational Level Agreements (OLAs) or Underpinning Contracts (UCs) with other federators and/or individual sites. The current situation is more complex in several regards. First, many relationships are captured only in Memoranda of Understanding (MoUs) or at best extremely weak SLAs. Second, many relationships that undermine a clear schema for responsibility exist, such as individual users having connections to resource owners, bypassing the federation of both users and resources. Third, the schema shown in Figure 2 ignores the underlying network layer, where each site (and potentially user) will have a relationship with a network infrastructure to support it, though network SDM-SLM is considerable more mature.

In both the cloud and Grid type e-Infrastructure cases we might say the ideal model is the one with the fewest relationships possible. These relationships should be those that can resemble to the greatest extent a conventional commercial customer-provider relationship, where the provider should assume responsibility for all downstream provision issues, even if this imposes risk that must be shared or represented in the contract with the user.

2.7   Enforcement, Inducement and Penalisation

Once a working schema for relationships is derived (and implemented) then agreements must be structured that are not only acceptable, but sufficiently enforceable. Currently cloud agreements appear technically enforceable, but sanctions may not be sufficient to justify major investments in reliability. On the other hand, e-Infrastructures codify very low levels of service and recognise the impact of failure, but offer no path for enforcement or penalisation on failure. The cloud domain may at the first glance seem to be in a better state, but the SLM-SDM as implemented refers almost exclusively to single providers. The Multi-cloud, with its hopefully federated resources currently offers no meaningful SDM-SLM at all.

On both sides a balance must be struck between guarantees strong enough to tempt a user to adopt a system but not so draconian as to discourage providers. In the cloud this should be simple, since at least all participants are legal entities and agreements between participants are formal. The issue will be to induce single cloud providers to recognise that they must provide SDM-SLM that is compatible with their services being federated. Users must then recognise that the federators assume a risk on their behalf, for which they must be compensated. A similar situation has been seen in software licensing, where all distributed computing systems require rethinking of license models. It is unreasonable for a user that uses 10 copies of an analysis package all month but then uses 10,000 copies on a cloud one day to pay for 10,000 licenses. Equally it is unreasonable for cloud providers to be able to ignore that users require their services to be aggregated in the SDM-SLM they offer.

For Grids the challenges stem from the lack of economic basis to many agreements. One simply cannot impose financial exchanges and penalties in an academic system that has operated on a model of sharing and informal agreement overnight. The multinational nature of Grids and other distributed e-Infrastructure also means that disputes are often between organisations that do not have formal bilateral agreements, and are often in different countries. For instance a site in one country failing may cause a service failure dealing with a federator in a second country, causing many sites federated by that body to lose business, time or custom. At present there is little recourse for those that suffer from failure without being responsible for it. The only sanctions available tend to be embarrassment and loss of professional reputation. Anything beyond this generally involves exclusion from the service, which is a 'nuclear option' that becomes immediately a political problem. This means that small failures are not punished, and there is little inducement to perform well beyond avoiding catastrophic, politically unpleasant failures.

One option, short of instituting financial relationships, is some sort of quanta of credit, whether it is for service delivery or for service quality. Even though such a 'currency' might be of no economic value, by quantifying it, small changes in service quality could be easily demonstrated. By engaging competition to perform against the yardstick of ones service credit balance, e-Infrastructure could engage organisations in improving their service in the same way social networks encourage participants to make ever more connections through metrics relating to social activity.

3   Conclusions and Future Work

This paper offers only the first steps in a model for federated SDM-SLM, by examining two kinds of system that show (or will show) federation. They clearly have some common issues though many individual ones. In both cases lessons can be learned from commercial SDM-SLM, though systems such as ITIL cannot be wholesale imported. New approaches in areas such as inducement and enforcement must be considered. These issues will be considered by the gSLM project [5] in the next year and will be presented at future events. The gSLM project also intends to produce a maturity model for SDM-SLM in Grid infrastructures. The concept being to show Grid providers and users a path for evolutionary improvement of service management, such that they can select appropriate SLM-SDM measures as infrastructures grow and develop. This will also form part of a strategic roadmap to be released in last 2012 on the larger issues of SLM-SDM in Grids.

The authors of this paper and colleagues from the gSLM project will also seek to collaborate with members of the cloud community on common issues of federated SDM-SLM. This has already begun through participation at the IEEE BDIM2011 workshop [7] on Business Driven IT Management where the issues were discussed with SDM-SLM experts from the commercial sector, including major IT service providers. It will continue through collaboration with projects such as mOSAIC, and results will be released through the gSLM web site.

Acknowledgements. This paper was produced in part through the gSLM project, which is co-funded by the European Commission under contract number 261547.

References

1. Definition of e-Infrastructure taken from the European Commission website,
   http://cordis.europa.eu/fp7/ict/e-infrastructure/
   (accessed 04.07 2011)
2. http://www.infoworld.com/d/cloud-computing/the-failure-behind-the-amazon-outage-isnt-just-amazons-107?page=0,1
   (accessed 03.07.2011)
3. http://www.egi.eu/infrastructure/Figures_and_utilisation/
   (accessed 01.07.2011)
4. http://www.prace-ri.eu/ (accessed 29.06.2011)
5. http://aws.amazon.com/ec2-sla/ (accessed 04.07.2011)
6. http://www.gslm.eu (accessed 30.06.2011)
7. BDIM 2011 formed part of the 12th IFIP/IEEE International Symposium on Integrated Network Management (IM 2011), http://www.ieee-im.org/,
   http://www.bdim2011.org/Workshop/Welcome.html (accessed 01.07.2011)

Rapid Prototyping of Architectures on the Cloud Using Semantic Resource Description

Houssam Haitof

Technische Universität München, Germany
haitof@in.tum.de

Abstract. We present in this paper a way for prototyping architectures based on the generation of service representations of resources. This generated "infrastructure" can be used to rapidly build on-demand settings for application/scenario requirements in a Cloud Computing context where such requirements can be as diverse as the applications running on the Cloud. The resources used to build the infrastructure are semantically described to capture their properties and capabilities. We have also developed a framework called the Managed Resource Framework (MRF) to automatically generate service descriptions with an added manageability interface from these semantic description. These services are then ready for deployment. Our work was materialize in the SEROM Software.

1   Introduction

One of the biggest advantages of Cloud Computing is that the back-end of the Cloud infrastructure is invisible to the user, especially for the Software as a Service (SaaS) and Platform as a Service (PaaS) types of Cloud. This advantage is less prominent when we deal with the Infrastructure as a Service (IaaS) type of Clouds where the user has more control, and hence, more visibility on the infrastructure. Another difficulty with the IaaS is that the Cloud is often pre-configured with some services suitable for an application or a certain scenario, and once the requirements change, that configuration needs to be adapted by adding or removing some services or some other infrastructure components.

Depending on the application settings, resources are instantiated to answer the requirements needed by the application. If, for instance, the requirements include some database servers and web servers, then these requirements and the relationship among them are described in a semantic document and a match-making routine searches for the appropriate resources using their semantic descriptions and, using the Managed Resource Framework, actual service representations of the resources are generated and deployed with minimum human intervention. This prototype architecture can be then reviewed and validated by an administrator if there is need for that.

For every service representation, a standard interface for managing the service is generated. This interface can then be used by other software agents for management purposes or for querying about the resource capabilities and properties. The resource that can be used in this setting have to be first semantically described following a basic model called an Abstract Managed Resource Model.

M. Alexander et al. (Eds.): Euro-Par 2011 Workshops, Part I, LNCS 7155, pp. 73–82, 2012.

Our architectural model is based on the Service Oriented Architecture and we use semantics with a formal language representation based on description logic for the knowledge level.

2 Description and Knowledge Levels

Our system needs a certain level of conformity and defined expectation, especially when dealing with system components. Confronting the Software components with unknown system representations where resources may take unknown forms, use unknown communication protocols or present unknown control interfaces is a real challenge that is out of the scope of this work. We believe that such system configuration is too complex to be dealt with and we think that it is extremely difficult to come up with a system capable of navigating through such a configuration. We assume that all the system component have a certain degree of conformity making it (i.e. the system) a homogeneous and integrated system. This conformity is expressed at the level of component description and at the possible ways to interact with those components. This level of predictability is necessary whenever we deal with an automated or semi-automated management model, where several management tasks are offloaded to software agents.

2.1 The Need for SOA

Having this conformity of resources at the description level coincide with the service encapsulation that the service orientation model follows. Where the service represents a single, contained and self-standing set of functionalities. In this model, everything is a service that shares similar communication protocols with all other services, allowing other software agents, services or not, to handle them in a predictable way. This important characteristic of service orientation is an appealing argument that motivated the use of that model as our conceptual model. The service orientation model is quite vague in its definitions leaving the room open for interpretation and assumptions related to many design principles. Although, it offers a lot of flexibility, this vagueness leads often to incompatible service oriented architectures defying the whole purpose off the model. This is why we wanted to stick, as much as possible, to an abstraction level that would, at the same time, adhere to the guiding principles for a service oriented system, while being extensible and compatible with the defacto standards used for creating service oriented systems and the design decision that lead to them. This, in fact, justifies some design decision such as the choice of WS*-[1] stack over REST even if the latter is easier and has a more perfo urmant implementation than the first, because the first is indeed the defacto standard used in implementing service oriented systems.

---

[1] WS-* is used to refer to the collection of specifications related to the Web Services.

2.2 The Need for Semantics

Even though modeling everything as a service would ease handling system components by software agents, these latter would still miss the semantic of the functionalities they are dealing with. In other terms, the software agents would have access to the "technical" description of the services and would be able to initiate and endure communication with the services, however, they will not be able to know what the service is actually doing, or to distinguish (or find, as a matter of redundancy support for instance) between different services supposedly doing the same thing. Another layer of information is needed to allow software agents to understand what they are dealing with in a manner close to what a human would do to apprehend the *usefulness* of a service. This layer is called the *knowledge layer*. But, why would the software agents need an access to the knowledge layer? In fact, it is not that difficult to automatize a system, in a majority of cases it comes down to writing a set of scripts. The real value is coming from enabling software agents to become more than automated agents and be adaptive and even more: to behave in an autonomic manner.

3   Semantic Resource Description and Resource Management

Describing the the resource characteristics, capabilities, interaction possibilities and management potential in a formal language is not enough for other software components to figure out the exact purpose of the resource and the meaning of its capabilities. Using such language provides only syntactic level description that necessitate the intervention of humans to appreciate the value or the purpose of the resource. Hence the resources need to be augmented by a semantic description that would capture the fore-mentioned meaning. A serious problem in today's IT management is the lack of information related to the managed resources [10]. This lack of information can be sensed at different levels which add to the complexity of the problem.

3.1   Lack of Information Effects

At the Level of IT System. There is a lack of information on what is installed and where it is installed. Often the purpose of the system it self is ambiguous if not unknown. Sometimes whole parts of the system that are unused are up and running and nobody can make a clear decision of the necessity of those components or if any other part of the system *may* depend on those components.

At the Level of the Resources Relationships. Often the information of the relationships of resources to one another is missing. Information about why and how a set of resources is generally not documented making failures analysis an extremely difficult task as well as problem source determination. Another problem that is also related to the first point is that with the lack of such information, predicting the impact of a change in a system is nearly impossible, with cascading effects and latent effects being the worse types of problems that may happen.

At the Level of the Resource Itself. There is a lack of information about the resource itself, its purpose, capabilities and requirements. If this information is ever stored, it is done separately of the resource in external repositories that can get inconsistent if there is no system capable of reflecting in it the status of the resources in real-time. If such information was available, maintenance would be done in an easier manner as data about the resource is available, allowing to offer it its needed ecosystem or changing it with an equivalent resource.

3.2 Semantically Augmented Resources

Describing resources semantically is crucial to understand what they are, what they do and how to interact with them. This semantic augmentation amounts to adding meta-data to resources as descriptive layer, thus publishing information about the resources in a standardized, machine-readable way. If we want management systems in our model to interact with the resources, we need more than the capacity to how to read information about the resource (syntax parsing), but also what does the information mean (semantics).

3.3 Managing Resources

One important principle behind the creation of web services was for application integration, including legacy applications that were written using heterogeneous technologies and platforms. This was also the case for management applications that not only had to deal with heterogeneous resources, were themselves not inter-operable. Using web services principles, it is possible for management applications to use common messaging protocols between themselves and the manageable resources, thus becoming vendor-neutral and platform-independent solutions [7]. In the WS-* landscape, there are two important and competing sets of specifications that describe management messaging protocols on top of the web service stack, namely WSDM [7,20,8,9] and WS-Man [15]. There is an ongoing effort to merge the two specifications [2] as conformity and standardization was a key objective in the design of both specifications. Both specifications have a resource centric view of management, where the common messaging protocol is used to communicate directly with the resource through a standardized interface. Contrast this with the traditional model where management applications were often contacting agents on behalf of the resources. This standard interface is the interface of the web service that represents the resources. In other words, resources can be accessed only through the End Point Reference of the web service.

3.4   Representing Resources as Services

There is nothing special about representing a resource using a web service, if that resource is already offering some API to access its capabilities and properties. It would be a matter of writing an interface to this API, accessible through a well-defined web service. However there are some issues related to the intrinsic nature of web services and resources. The most prominent difference is the fact that web services are stateless, meaning that they do not keep data (a state) between different invocations. This contradicts the view of the physical resource that keeps a state during its lifetime. This stateless characteristic of web services is not a limitation as it was a design choice aiming at the web services being light-weight software components. There is mechanisms that permits to emulates a statefull behavior for web services, with the most traditional being session cookies or using persistent storage of state like a database or using WS-Session.

WSRF [3] propose an elegant and integrated solution to the stateless issue of web services by using descriptive document called *ResourceProperties* and introducing the concept of *WS-Resource*. The WSRF provides a general solution using web services to an originally specific problem: describing and representing Grid resources that are statefull in nature. Another relevant feature of WSRF is that it brings a solution for management of a resource lifetime, faults and properties. Rendering resources as WS-Resource and decomposing software component into services is the first step toward a SOA enabled management architecture with all the advantages that it can bring such as ease of management, adaptability and automation.

4   Managed Resource Framework (MRF)

This section discuses the *Managed Resource Framework (MRF)*, a framework for automatically generating ready-to-deploy service representations of resources from their semantic representations. The objective is to have a computer aided process by which resources can be rapidly *instantiated,* deployed and managed in a relatively quick and transparent manner for the user.

The framework assumes the existence of a semantic representation of a resource written in OWL that extends an Abstract Managed Resource Model and outputs a deployable service representation called *Managed Resource Archive (MRA)*. The only "human" intervention during this process would be in the case there were custom capabilities defined in the semantic representation and that lack an implementation (see figure 1).

Using the Managed Resource Framework, it is possible to generate resource artifacts that would eventually constitute the Managed Resource Archive. MRF assumes a target-based mechanism by which, only one or several constituent of the MRA could be generated as needed instead of the monolithic MRA.

The Managed Resource Archive is a deployable service representation of the resource that is generated by the Managed Resource Framework. The MRA is a

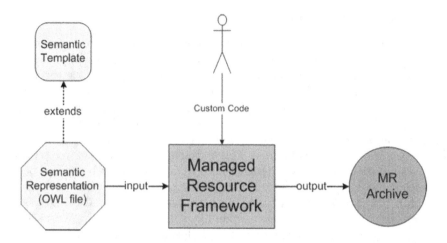

Fig. 1. Managed Resource Framework (MRF) input/output

Web application formed by a bundle of servlets, classes and other resources and intended to run on Managed Resource Containers or on Java Servlet Containers with, however, a loss of capabilities.

Once deployed, every MRA has a unique URI represented by its location in the container. An example would be `http://www.example.com/site1/res_A42`. Requests to the resource would have to start with that URL as a prefix. Every request is then forwarded to the `ServletContext` representing the resource. The `ServletContext` is an interface that defines a servlet's view of the Web application. It is up to the container provider to provide an implementation to the `ServletContext` and to ensure the one to one correspondence between every resource and a single `ServletContext`. A Web application may consist of servlets, utility Java Classes, static documents, client-side Java applets, beans, and classes and descriptive meta information.

5 Implementation

5.1 SEROM

We developed a full implementation of the Managed Resource Framework called SEROM to materialize some concepts presented in this work. The development environment was constituted of the Java programming language, eclipse and maven. We used Java for the richness of its libraries and APIs and its portability. We used eclipse as IDE and maven as project management tool.

MRF is being developed as a modular, plug-in based software to insure the future extendability of the framework. It comes in two versions a command line tool and an API to be programatically invoked. MRF is target-based, meaning that a target needs to be specified while invoking the framework and these targets can be: `model`, `wsdl`, `doc`, `source`, `proxy`, `build` or `all`. model can only be invoked programatically, all the other targets can also be invoked from the command line tool. The `model` target generates an internal model of the resource, this model is needed by all the developed modules. `wsdl` generates the WSDL document from the model, `doc` the online documentation, `source` the server stub and the proxy skeleton source code, `proxy` the proxy client library, while `build` builds the WAR archive and finally `all` generates all of the above and packages the archive into a deployable artifact. Every new module can provide new targets but it has to specify its required inputs from the existing targets. MRF uses a templating system to generate the different documents. Appropriate templates are loaded at run-time and processed using the in memory model of the resource. The WSDM implementation used by MRF is Apache muse.

5.2   Under the Hood

MRF implementation of the management mechanisms is done following the Web Services Distributed Management (WSDM) set of standards [20,8,9]. WSDM defines protocols to allow services to expose their manageability interface in a standard way such that any consumer that is WSDM-compliant is able to access the service manageability functions. WSDM specification relies on several WS-* standards for its operations, namely WS-MetadataExchange, WS-ResourceFramework [3], WS-ResourceProperties, WS-ResourceLifetime [18], WS-ServiceGroup and WS-Notification. The manageability of a service is exposed through a Web Service and is accessed through that service EPR, called a manageability endpoint. Any software application that accesses the manageability endpoint is called manageability consumer. The manageability consumer can interact with the manageability endpoint, and hence, the resource, in three distinct ways:

- The manageability consumer can retrieve management information from the managed resource through calls to its management capabilities.
- The manageability consumer can affect the state of the managed resource by changing its state through calls to its management capabilities.
- The manageability consumer can receive notifications from the managed resource if the consumer had subscribed to receive events from the managed resource.

The methods stated above show that the relationship between the managed resource and the manageability consumer can be a pull or a pushed based communication mechanism depending on the nature of the resource and the consumer and the rate by which the resource can produce events. Producing events by the resource is, however, optional. WSDM does not, in general, define the content of the messages exchanged between the managed resource and the consumer, but only the communication protocol and the format of the exchanged data. Using MRF, the user can also specify some WSDM-defined management capabilities to be added to the resource definition. The MRF takes then care of generating the proper configuration files and capabilities implementation. The following section describes the WSDM-defined capabilities as well as other capabilities inherited from the other supporting WS-* standards.

6 Related Works

There are numerous works done in the field of semantic web services, such as WSDL-S [1] that tries to extend WSDL by adding some semantic annotation to the file as XML tags that can reference entities in models outside the WSDL document. WSDL-S builds on the establishment of WSDL as a service description language for ease of migration. WSDL-S is intended to be a minimalist approach that tries to extend the pre-existing Web Services with semantic annotation, which is quite different from the other methods that tries to create a more complete, sometimes complex frameworks. Another effort is the Web Service Modeling Language (WSMO) that tries to describe all aspects of semantic web services with the goal of automating the discovery, selection, composition, execution and other tasks related to the integration of web services. WSMO is based on the Web Service Modeling Framework (WSMF) [13] and has three working groups: WSMO [11], Web Service Modeling Language (WSML) [12] that represents a family of languages used as representation format for WSMO and Web Service Execution Environment (WSMX) [16] that acts as a reference implementation of WSMO. WSMO is composed of four elements: ontologies that define the common representation of information, web services that represent the services, goals that describes aspects of the requests to web services and finally mediators that act like connector between the different layers of WSMO. The major drawbacks of WSMO are that it is a quite complex framework that uses proprietary technologies at almost every level. It does not use WSDL, but instead a new representation formalism, it ignores UDDI for its own solution, and uses a family of languages that are not XML conform and are meant to be replacement to the already established languages such as OWL and RDF. Another work is OWL-S [14], an effort to define an ontology for semantic markup of Web Services. OWL-S was meant to be a replacement to the WSDL, however this effort was not successful. Other works on semantic web services worth mentioning here are IRS-II [17], Meteor-S [19] and SWSF [4,5,6].

7 Conclusion

The work presented in this paper aimed to bring a simple solution for rapid prototyping of architectures on the Cloud. We brought simplicity by providing a mechanism to model resource in a standard and uniform way using an expressive language for the purpose of generating software components that would provide a standard management interface to access and manage the resources represented by these components. The simplicity is apparent in modeling the resources, in the process by which the service artifacts were generated and the end-result: simple manageable components. The use of semantics allowed to capture the characteristics of the resources with simple and minimum set of descriptive classes and relationships among them and yet powerful enough to allow the conversion to other representation formats such as the service representation generated by the MRF. The use of open standards and plug-in based architecture of MRF allow for future extension of the system and ease of adaptation to other requirements.

References

1. Akkiraju, R., Farrell, J., Miller, J., Nagarajan, M., Schmidt, M., Sheth, A., Verma, K.: Web service semantics - wsdl-s. Technical report, World Wide Web Consortium (November 2005)
2. Antony, J., et al.: Wsdm/ws-man reconciliation. Technical report, IBM (August 2006)
3. Banks, T.: Web services resource framework (wsrf) - primer v1.2. Technical report, OASIS (May 2006)
4. Battle, S., Bernstein, A., Boley, H., Grosof, B., Gruninger, M., Hull, R., Kifer, M., Martin, D., McIlraith, S., McGuinness, D., Su, J., Tabet, S.: Semantic web services framework (swsf) overview. Technical report, World Wide Web Consortium (September 2005)
5. Battle, S., Bernstein, A., Boley, H., Grosof, B., Gruninger, M., Hull, R., Kifer, M., Martin, D., McIlraith, S., McGuinness, D., Su, J., Tabet, S.: Semantic web services language (swsl). Technical report, World Wide Web Consortium (September 2005)
6. Battle, S., Bernstein, A., Boley, H., Grosof, B., Gruninger, M., Hull, R., Kifer, M., Martin, D., McIlraith, S., McGuinness, D., Su, J., Tabet, S.: Semantic web services ontology (swso). Technical report, World Wide Web Consortium (September 2005)
7. Bullard, V., Murray, B., Wilson, K.: An introduction to wsdm. Technical report, OASIS Official Committee Specification (February 2006)
8. Bullard, V., Vambenepe, W.: Web services distributed management: Management using web services (muws 1.1) part 1. Technical report, OASIS Web Services Distributed Management TC (August 2006)
9. Bullard, V., Vambenepe, W.: Web services distributed management: Management using web services (muws 1.1) part 2. Technical report, OASIS Web Services Distributed Management TC (August 2006)
10. Chess, D.M., Hanson, J.E., Pershing, J.A., White, S.R.: Prospects for simplifying itsm-based management through self-managing resources. IBM Systems Journal 46(3), 599–608 (2007)
11. de Bruijn, J., Bussler, C., Domingue, J., Fensel, D., Hepp, M., Kifer, M., Knig-Ries, B., Kopecky, J., Lara, R., Oren, E., Polleres, A., Scicluna, J., Stollberg, M.: Web service modeling ontology (wsmo). Technical report, WSMO (April 2005)
12. de Bruijn, J., Lausen, H., Krummenacher, R., Polleres, A., Predoiu, L., Kifer, M., Fensel, D.: The web service modeling language (wsml). Technical report, WSMO (October 2005)
13. Fensel, D., Bussler, C.: The web service modeling framework (wsmf). Technical report, Vrije Universiteit Amsterdam (2002)
14. Martin, D., Burstein, M., Hobbs, J., Lassila, O., McDermott, D., McIlraith, S., Narayanan, S., Paolucci, M., Parsia, B., Payne, T., Sirin, E., Srinivasan, N., Sycara, K.: Owl-s: Semantic markup for web services. Technical report, White Paper, DARPA Agent Markup Language (DAML) Program
15. McCollum, R., Murray, B., Reistad, B.: Web services for management (ws-management) specification. Technical report, DMTF (2008)
16. Moran, M., Zaremba, M.: Wsmx architecture. Technical report, WSMO (June 2004)
17. Motta, E., Domingue, J., Cabral, L., Gaspari, M.: Irs-ii: A framework and infrastructure for semantic web services. Technical report, Knowledge Media Institute at the Open University, Milton Keynes, UK

18. Srinivasan, L., Banks, T.: Web services resource lifetime 1.2 (ws-resourcelifetime). Technical report, OASIS (April 2006)
19. Verma, K., Gomadam, K., Sheth, A.P., Miller, J.A., Wu, Z.: The meteor-s approach for configuring and executing dynamic web processes. Technical report, LSDIS Lab, University of Georgia (June 2005)
20. Wilson, K., Sedukhin, I.: Web services distributed management: Management of web services (wsdm-mows) 1.1. Technical report, OASIS Web Services Distributed Management TC (August 2006)

Cloud Patterns for mOSAIC-Enabled Scientific Applications

Teodor-Florin Fortiş[1,2], Gorka Esnal Lopez[3], Imanol Padillo Cruz[3],
Gábor Ferschl[4], and Tamás Máhr[4]

[1] Institute e-Austria, Timişoara, Romania
[2] West University of Timişoara, Romania
fortis@info.uvt.ro
[3] Tecnalia (Industrial Systems Unit), San Sebastián, Spain
{gorka.esnal,imanol.padillo}@tecnalia.com
[4] AITIA International, Inc., Budapest, Hungary
{gferschl,tmahr}@aitia.ai

Abstract. Cloud computing has a huge potential to change the way data- and computing-intensive applications are performing computations. These specific categories of applications raise different concerns and issues that can be bypassed by identifying relevant reusable cloud computing patterns, on the top of specific cloud computing use cases. Development of new cloud patterns will help offering a better support for the development and deployment of scientific distributed application over a cloud infrastructure.

Keywords: Cloud computing, cloud use cases, cloud patterns.

1 Introduction

Cloud computing, with its different deployment and service models, has a huge potential to change the way we are performing computations, by moving it from a traditional model to a service-based model – utility computing –, as a next generation of commodity computing.

The National Institute of Standards and Technology (NIST) [13] offered a very clear and simple definition of cloud computing , as *"a model for enabling ubiquitous, convenient, on-demand network access to a shared pool of configurable computing resources [...] that can be rapidly provisioned and released with minimal management effort or service provider interaction."* A similar point of view was expressed in a white paper from the UC Berkeley RAD Labs [1] : *"cloud computing refers to both the applications delivered as services over the Internet and the hardware and systems software in the datacenters that provide those services."*

However, in Berkley RAD Lab's white paper a separation between utility computing and private clouds was identified. As a consequence, provided that cloud computing can be identified as *"the sum of SaaS and utility computing"* [1], the same kind of separation exists between cloud computing and private clouds.

M. Alexander et al. (Eds.): Euro-Par 2011 Workshops, Part I, LNCS 7155, pp. 83–93, 2012.

With a slightly different point of view, G. Perry [14] specified that "*cloud computing is a broader concept than utility computing and relates to the underlying architecture in which the services are designed*", that can be applied both to utility computing and internal corporate data centers.

With a growing interest in cloud computing, there are a series of research challenges, as identified in [19], that still require specific attention from the research communities. These challenges include *automated service provisioning, data security, software frameworks, storage technologies and data management*, or *novel cloud architectures*. In addition, having different approaches for the various setting of cloud computing, several important issues, like *open standards interfaces, opportunity of service level agreements* (SLA) for service delivery, *security in different service delivery models* [18], or *commonly accepted programming models* [12], still need to be addressed.

The mOSAIC project[1], developed in the framework of the FP7-ICT programme, is addressing a series of the issues and research challenges related with cloud computing, as specified above, to deliver an open-source platform that enables applications to negotiate cloud services as they are requested by their respective users, and to develop an open-source cloud API, by which applications will be able to specify and communicate their requirements to the platform.

Special attention is paid to the identification of a set o reusable patterns and use cases relevant to the selected set of mOSAIC-enabled applications [15], [11], that will be used both for validating the core of the mOSAIC platform [6], and the different mOSAIC specific components. The set of mOSAIC specific components include a semantic engine and a cloud agency [2], that will help applications to have a better response in relation with their requirements in terms of cloud resources, service level agreements (SLA) or quality of service.

2   Cloud Use Cases and Cloud Patterns

Different efforts were performed in order to identify cloud computing patterns. In [10] several sets of patterns were described, closely related with the capabilities offered by the Azure platform. Different categories of patterns were identified, including computing (on-demand application instance, worker patterns), storage (blob storage, structured storage patterns), communication (service interface, service-oriented integration, and messaging patterns), and administration (cloud deployment, design for operations, service instance management, managements alerts, and service level management patterns). A different approach was offered by a Sun presentation [17], where a set of software and infrastructure patterns were identified, in relation with cloud computing[2].

The different approaches for data- and computing-intensive applications (see [12], [16], [4], [9], [7]) identified different concerns and issues related with cloud computing. On the top of these issues and concerns, a common point of view

---

[1] Detailed information available on project's web site: http://www.mosaic-cloud.eu

[2] Also available on SUN wiki: http://wikis.sun.com/display/cloud/Patterns

can be developed by identifying and specifying a common set of reusable cloud computing patterns, and the set of complementary cloud computing use cases.

2.1 Cloud Computing Use Cases

The Cloud Computing Use Cases Group defined a set of use case scenarios for cloud computing [5], by using both the experience of cloud vendors, and cloud consumers. The document offers a consumer-oriented view of cloud usage, and highlights several concerns related with interoperability, standards and standardization, security and SLA. Seven core cloud usage scenarios were identified, and the specific interaction concerns related with these usage scenarios were exposed: *end user to cloud, enterprise to cloud to end user, enterprise to cloud, enterprise to cloud to enterprise, private cloud, changing cloud vendors,* and *hybrid cloud* [5, pp. 18-19]. Also, Cloud Computing Use Cases Group provided an uniform view of the relationships between cloud requirements and specific use cases, as well as a set of developer requirements for cloud-based applications.

NIST, with the Standards Acceleration to Jumpstart Adoption of Cloud Computing (SAJACC) initiative, developed a set of cloud use cases [3], by combining the experience from industry, government agencies and academia. The efforts of the SAJACC initiative were oriented to *"facilitate Standards Development Organizations in their efforts to develop high-quality standards"*, addressing the important needs identified, on the basis of a pool of use case scenarios that were developed to better support portability, interoperability and security.

With the document [7], the Distributed Management Task Force (DMTF), via its Open Cloud Standards Incubator, offered the basis for a reference architecture for managing clouds, and identified specific requirements oriented to management, security and resource models. Different interaction patterns were identified along with this reference architecture, covering four larger categories. Based on the set of interaction patterns, a distinct document was offered for a uniform view of cloud management use cases [8]. These use cases were aligned with NIST definitions for cloud computing [13], offering a distinctive view on cloud management, security and cloud government requirements and concerns.

3   Usage Scenario: A mOSAIC Perspective

Different data- and computing-intensive applications were considered for mOSAIC implementation, as proof-of-the-concept applications. Cloud usage patterns and cloud use cases were identified after a detailed analysis of these applications, starting from typical usage scenarios, as in [15]. Considered data-intensive applications, include applications used for process optimization and maintenance in different industrial sectors, storage and data distribution, fast data access for crisis situations, or running simulations on the cloud, with different configured simulation scenario. The area of usage cases covered by the minimal set of mOSAIC applications range from virtual storage, data distribution, peak in processing resource demand, fast data access for crisis situations,

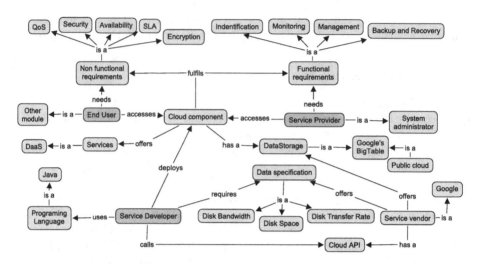

Fig. 1. Ontological view: data storage and data access (data intensive, [11])

data-intensive telemetry scenario, on-demand and distributed storage allocation, balanced computing, to computing-intensive scenario.

Data Intensive Applications. The Intelligent Maintenance System (IMS) allows the maintenance of devices from different industrial scenarios (wind turbines, airplanes, machine tools, etc) through early diagnosis of faults in critical components and real-time monitoring of key variables. It uses specific Artificial Intelligence techniques that permit modelling the experience of expert technical people and reason about it to support IMS in making decisions about maintenance actions and advance warning of critical situations.

IMS is associated with a SLA template customized to its needs. The system automatically acquires data from distributed sensors and stores them into a cloud-based datastore. Once data is acquired, a knowledge extraction process over raw data is executed, using a cloud-based infrastructure, in order to get enough information that will assist in the detection process of potentially critical situations. These diagnoses are also stored in a cloud-based datastore.

After the data has been stored properly in a cloud storage system, registered users have the ability to query these data. For this purpose, users must be properly registered in the system and they must have sufficient permissions. Users who meet these requirements can access stored data (as raw data storage and diagnoses) in an asynchronous way, i.e. while the system continues storing new data and generating new diagnoses.

For this specific application type several usage scenarios are possible, on the basis of which one can identify the set of specific requirements and relationships, as depicted in Figure 1, and described in [11].

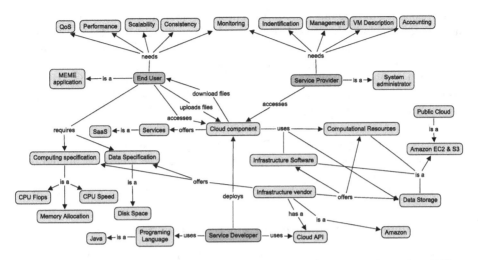

Fig. 2. Ontological view: distributed parameter sweep (computing intensive, [11])

Computing Intensive Applications. The Model Exploration Portal (MEP) is a service and website that enables researchers to run social simulation models in the cloud. Various user needs can be satisfied when renting computational resources for the users. They can run agent-based simulations in an 'as-fast-as-possible' mode by acquiring as many resources as needed. Alternatively, in a so called 'best-effort' mode, it is possible to use the spare resources in the system which become available when a simulation finishes without using its resources to the full time. Finally, users may set a deadline for the simulations, and the system will automatically determine the proper operational mode. Users can monitor the progress of their simulations and modify the SLA online. The development of agent-based models requires repeated experimentation with the model, which in turn means that a large amount of simulations have to be run.

One of the typical usage is to run *parameter-sweep* experiments, where the parameter space of the model is explored to get an overview of the general behavior. This particular usage scenario was fully described in [11], and the set of identifiable requirements and relationships was specified as in Figure 2.

4   Execution Scenarios for mOSAIC-Enabled Applications

Based on the initial analysis of the data- and computing-intensive applications (implementing simulation scenarios and intelligent maintenance), a series of requirements were identified for further implementation of SLA, and for implementing specific cloud policies and constraints. These requirements are reflecting both the functional and non-functional requirements that are coming from the analyzed applications, see [11], and express a wide range of cloud-specific concerns.

Functional requirements that were identified in [11], and depicted in Figure 1 and Figure 2, include the following: (1) consistency, (2) identifications, (3) monitoring, (3) backup and recovery, (4) replication, (5) management, (6) accounting, (7) virtual machine descriptions, (8) encryption. Non-functional properties include (1) availability, (2) QoS, (3) communication (non-functional part), (4) computing (non-functional part), (5) security, (6) scalability, (7) performance, (8) autonomous, (9) data (non-functional part), (10) reliability.

Starting from the set of functional and non-functional properties, and complemented by the discussion about SLA from Cloud Computing Use Cases Group's document [5, p. 54], a set of basic SLA requirements was identified, including, but not limited to: (1) compliance, (2) transparency, (3) security, (4) metric, (5) privacy, (6) auditability, (7) data encryption, (8) monitoring, (9) certification.

4.1   Intelligent Maintenance System Execution Scenarios

On the top of the identified use cases for an Intelligent Maintenance System (IMS), several execution scenario are possible for an IMS-enabled application. These execution scenarios respond to specific requirements from application point of view.

IMS Synchronous Execution Scenario. In this scenario data acquired from distributed sources (sensors) by the IMS system is automatically stored. A knowledge extraction process over these acquired raw data is executed, in order to get information that will help to detect possible critical situations. Storage of these diagnoses is subsequently performed. The entire process is carried out in synchronous mode, without any interaction required from expert or specialized user to the system.

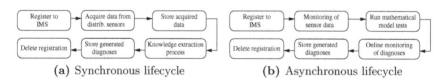

(a) Synchronous lifecycle   (b) Asynchronous lifecycle

Fig. 3. IMS execution scenarios

The implementation of this scenario is based on the existence of several use cases, as specified in Figure 3a, including *data acquisition from distributed sources*; *storing acquired data from distributed sources*; *running knowledge extraction processes*; *storing generated diagnoses*.

IMS Asynchronous Execution Scenario. This scenario is applicable to a situation where expert or specialized users access generated data (e.g. reports, statistics) by using a specialized web interface. Moreover, expert users have the ability to access independent applications through which they have the possibility to configure (change, or add) the rules on which the intelligent system is based. Additionally, the ability to deploy algorithms is ensured, such that the newly configured rules can be used. Different use cases, including *IMS regis-tration*; *online monitoring of data from sources*; *running mathematical model tests*; *online monitoring of diagnoses*; *storing generated diagnoses*; *registration deletion*, are used for this execution scenario, as identified in Figure 3b.

4.2   Model Exploration and Service Level Agreement Execution Scenarios

With the model exploration series of execution scenarios, different usages are described for this system, including a model exploration portal (MEP) as an administrative cloud application, the model exploration service (MES), which enables distributed simulations and collection of simulation results, the model exploration management in cloud (MEMiC), which is responsible with provision-ing of cloud resources, including negotiation of a service level agreement (SLA) with the cloud providers, resource acquisition and monitoring, and the model exploration module (MEME), a system used to run agent based simulations for building experiment's designs.

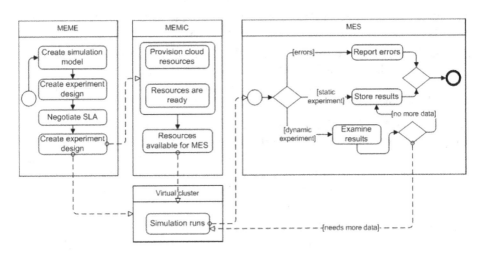

Fig. 4. Simulation execution scenario: activity workflow

Simulation Execution Scenario. The simulation execution scenario is used for conducting both static and dynamic simulation experiments. In both situa-tion a simulation model was identified, and an analysis of this model is to be performed by running it with various settings, in order to follow its behavior. For a dynamic experiment design, an initial set of parameter settings will be run, and based on results analysis new sets of parameter settings will be identified and run, until a stopping condition was met. On the other hand, in the case of static exper-iment design, there is only one set of parameter settings that will be run, then the simulation is ended. Different use cases, including *creating a simulation model*;

setting up model exploration; choosing an SLA template; contracting an SLA; provisioning cloud resources; running, monitoring and simulation maintenance, are used for this execution scenario.

SLA Execution Scenario. This complex scenario is in relation with the model exploration module (MEME) and the model exploration management in cloud (MEMiC). The SLA is being negotiated with MEME, and is based on interactions with MEMiC for establishing SLA options. The scenario offers the necessary support for SLA preparation, enabling SLA, as well as modifying the SLA. However, this execution scenario depends on the capability of the MES provider to define and modify SLA templates in MEMiC, and to offer the necessary support for negotiations.

4.3   Cloud Patterns for mOSAIC-Enabled Applications

On the top of identified use cases and typical execution scenario, a set of cloud patterns can be extracted in order to support the development of mOSAIC-enabled applications. The identified cloud patterns could be categorized, following category description, as in [7] and [10]. The common identified patterns, together with additional pattern categories and applicable security federation pattern categories, as specified in [5], are as follows.

Establish Identity (identify [7, p.18]**).** Establish the identity of accessing user of a scientific application. Different security policies, including *trust; identity management; single sign-on/sign-off* [5, pp.46-47]; can be used in the implementation of this pattern.

Establish SLA (identify). A complementary pattern for establishing identity. An SLA contract was established for the accessing entity and the cloud provider for accessed services. The 'Establish SLA' pattern is responsible with enforcing the established SLA. Security policies and federation patterns, like *trust; access management; audit and compliance* [5, pp.46-47]; as well as cryptography-related security controls, are applicable for this pattern.

Browse Available Offerings (administer [7, p.18]**).** A generic pattern, usable for browsing offerings, related with available (e.g. sensor) data collections; available data storage facilities; available components for monitoring. The *configuration management* security federation pattern [5, p.47] can be used in the implementation of this pattern.

Establish Parameters (administer). Parameters, as metadata of accessed scientific services, can be specified for different aspects (e.g. processes) of sample mOSAIC applications: parameters for simulations, parameters for knowledge extraction, parameters for data mining, monitoring parameters. Usable security federation patterns include *trust* and *access management* [5, pp.46-47].

Update SLA (administer). Updating a previously generated SLA to better respond to requirements of the accessing user. The mOSAIC SLA Generation Tool (MSGT), used for the generation of the SLA, could be used for this pattern, too.

Same security federation patterns as for the 'Establish SLA' pattern could be used in the implementation of this pattern.

Obtaining Metadata of Provisioned Services (administer). Different metadata of provisioned services, like parameters, SLA information, or diagnoses results are the subject of this pattern. The security federation pattern usable for implementing this pattern is *configuration management* [5, p.47].

Online Adjustment and Negotiation of Resources (deploy and update [7, p.19]**).** Adjustment and negotiation of resources are necessary when cloud resources initially allocated to the execution of the scientific processes (e.g. simulation) may not fulfill anymore the accessing entity's requirements (e.g. established SLA). An automatic monitoring of the scientific process (e.g. simulation) and online adjustments of cloud resource allocation are performed. *Access management*; *audit and compliance*; and *configuration management* [5, pp.46-47] are the security policies applicable for this situation.

Provision Scientific Process (deploy and update [7, p.19]**).** Scientific processes require access to large quantities of data: sensor data, simulation data, satellite images, as well as large quantities of resources. This pattern is responsible with uploading of selected data for the execution of scientific processes, as well as provisioning of resources that satisfies established SLAs. A set of security policies similar with those specified for the 'Update SLA' and 'Online adjustment and negotiation of resources' patterns, are usable for this case.

Data Storage and Aggregation (steady state). A generic cloud pattern, for storing data outputs from scientific application, like results of knowledge extraction process, of simulation results. Aggregated and raw data are the subject of this identified pattern. While *access management* is the basic security federation pattern, it can come into effect accompanied by several security controls, like *data/storage security* [5, pp.44-46].

Monitoring and Notification of Data Models (steady state). This pattern is related with execution of the knowledge extraction process; execution of simulations for adjusting provisioned resources, or job distribution. *Audit and compliance*; *configuration management*; *access management* [5, pp.46-47] are the security policies usable for the implementation of this pattern.

5   Conclusions

The cloud offers an ideal environment for developing and deploying of data- and computing-intensive scientific applications. These applications have to use complex mechanisms for assuring SLA, or QoS, like negotiation, brokering or provisioning, in order to maximize the utilization of a cloud infrastructure.

Typical usage of these mechanisms could be captured by the specification of a set of cloud patterns, oriented to scientific applications, in addition to previously described patterns, as in [10] and [17], and offer the basis for the development of powerful reusable building blocks for cloud-enabled applications.

Identification of the new cloud patterns was based on data- and computing-intensive applications, that are considered as proof-of-the-concept mOSAIC applications. Different execution scenarios were considered for the identification of specific cloud use cases, and specification of corresponding cloud patterns. By putting the newly identified patterns in relation with already specified pattern categories, and linking them with interaction patterns, security federation patterns, as well as with security controls, a high level of reusability for the set of considered cloud patterns is achieved.

Acknowledgments. This research was partially supported by the grant FP7-ICT-2009-5-256910 (mOSAIC).

References

1. Armbrust, M., Fox, A., Griffith, R., Joseph, A.D., Katz, R.H., Konwinski, A., Lee, G., Patterson, D.A., Rabkin, A., Stoica, I., Zaharia, M.: Above the clouds: A Berkeley view of cloud computing (February 2009),
   http://www.eecs.berkeley.edu/Pubs/TechRpts/2009/EECS-2009-28.html
2. Aversa, R., di Martino, B., Rak, M., Venticinque, S.: Cloud agency: A mobile agent based cloud system. In: Barolli, L., Xhafa, F., Vitabile, S., Hsu, H.H. (eds.) CISIS, pp. 132–137. IEEE Computer Society (2010)
3. Badger, L., Bohn, R., Chandramouli, R., Grance, T., Karygiannis, T., Patt-Corner, R., Voas, J.: Cloud computing use cases (October 2010),
   http://www.nist.gov/itl/cloud/use-cases.cfm
4. Beloglazov, A., Buyya, R., Lee, Y.C., Zomaya, A.: A taxonomy and survey of energy-efficient data centers and cloud computing systems. Advances in Computers 82, 47–111 (2011)
5. Cloud Computing Use Cases Group: Cloud computing use cases white paper (July 2010), http://opencloudmanifesto.org/Cloud_Computing_Use_
   Cases_Whitepaper-4_0.pdf
6. Di Martino, B., Petcu, D., Cossu, R., Goncalves, P., Máhr, T., Loichate, M.: Building a Mosaic of Clouds. In: Guarracino, M.R., Vivien, F., Träff, J.L., Cannataro, M., Danelutto, M., Hast, A., Perla, F., Knüpfer, A., Di Martino, B., Alexander, M. (eds.) Euro-Par-Workshop 2010. LNCS, vol. 6586, pp. 571–578. Springer, Heidelberg (2011)
7. DMTF: Architecture for managing clouds (June 2010),
   http://dmtf.org/sites/default/files/standards/documents/
   DSP-IS0102-1.0.0.pdf
8. DMTF: Use cases and interactions for managing clouds (June 2010),
   http://www.dmtf.org/sites/default/files/standards/documents/
   DSP-IS0103_1.0.0.pdf
9. Guo, W., Gong, J., Jiang, W., Liu, Y., She, B.: OpenRS-cloud: A remote sensing image processing platform based on cloud computing environment. SCIENCE CHINA Technological Sciences 53, 221–230 (2010)
10. Joseph, J.: Patterns for high availability, scalability, and computing power with Windows Azure. MSDN Magazine (May 2009)
11. Lazkanotegi, I., Esnal, G.: Cloud usage patterns (March 2011),
    http://www.mosaiccloud.eu/dissemination/deliverables/
    FP7-256910-D3.1-1.0.pdf

12. Malawski, M., Meizner, J., Bubak, M., Gepner, P.: Component approach to computational applications on clouds. Procedia Computer Science 4, 432–441 (2011)
13. Mell, P., Granc, T.: The NIST definition of cloud computing (January 2011),
    http://csrc.nist.gov/publications/drafts/800-145/
    Draft-SP-800-145_cloud-definition.pdf
14. Perry, G.: How cloud and utility computing are different (February 2008),
    http://gigaom.com/2008/02/28/how-cloud-utility-computing-
    are-different/
15. Petcu, D.: Identifying cloud computing usage patterns. In: Proceedings of Cluster 2010, pp. 1–4. IEEE Computer Society (September 2010)
16. Rafique, M.M., Butt, A.R., Nikolopoulos, D.S.: A capabilities-aware framework for using computational accelerators in data-intensive computing. Journal of Parallel and Distributed Computing 71(2), 185–197 (2011)
17. Stanford, J., Mattoon, S., Pepple, K.: Practical cloud computing patterns (2009),
    http://wikis.sun.com/download/attachments/116065636/
    Practical-Cloud-Patterns-S311528.pdf
18. Subashini, S., Kavitha, V.: A survey on security issues in service delivery models of cloud computing. Journal of Network and Computer Applications 34(1), 1–11 (2011)
19. Zhang, Q., Cheng, L., Boutaba, R.: Cloud computing: state-of-the-art and research challenges. Journal of Internet Services and Applications 1, 7–18 (2010)

Enhancing an Autonomic Cloud Architecture with Mobile Agents*

A. Cuomo[1], M. Rak[2], S. Venticinque[2], and U. Villano[1]

[1] Università del Sannio, Benevento, Italy
{antonio.cuomo,villano}@unisannio.it
[2] Seconda Università di Napoli, Aversa (CE), Italy
{massimiliano.rak,salvatore.venticinque}@unina2.it

Abstract. In cloud environments application scheduling, i.e., the matching of applications with the resources they need to be executed, is a hot research topic. Autonomic computing provides viable solutions to implement robust architectures that are enough flexible to tackle scheduling problems. CHASE is a framework based on an autonomic engine, designed to optimize resource management in clouds, grids or hybrid cloud-grid environments. Its optimizations are based on real-time knowledge of the status of managed resources. This requires continuous monitoring, which is difficult to be carried out in distributed and rapidly-changing environments as clouds. This paper presents a monitoring system to support autonomicity based on the mobile agents computing paradigm.

1 Introduction

Cloud computing [15] is evolving at a steady pace, putting itself forward as a convenient way for structuring and deploying applications and infrastructures both in the commercial and in the academic world. The crosscutting nature of the cloud paradigm ("everything as a service") has promoted its diffusion into many different areas of computer engineering, ranging from applications (Software-as-a-Service) to development platforms (Platform-as-a-Service) to the provisioning of basic computing resources as processing units, storage and networks (Infrastructure-as-a-Service). It could be argued that the very basic concept of "resource", whether it is a piece of software, a developing platform or a hardware component, has changed due to the use of resource *virtualization*, the driving technological force behind the cloud paradigm. Virtualization of resources brings new opportunities (e.g., the acquisition of virtually infinite computing elements) which are partly balanced by new issues and challenges (assessing the effect of virtualization on system performance, extracting information on the physical resources "hidden" behind a virtual interface, . . .).

---

* The work described in this paper has been partially supported by the MIUR-PRIN 2008 project "Cloud@Home: a New Enhanced Computing Paradigm" and by the FP7-ICT-2009-5-256910 (mOSAIC) EU project.

M. Alexander et al. (Eds.): Euro-Par 2011 Workshops, Part I, LNCS 7155, pp. 94–103, 2012.

In the HPC context the current trend is the integration of grids and clouds into unified architectures [9,11,2,17]. To this aim, we have recently proposed *cloudgrid*, a novel architecture for the integration of clouds and grids, and developed its implementation, PerfCloud [13,4]. Among other things, PerfCloud makes it possible to set up a cloud-based provision of computing resources taken from an existing grid. The leased virtual resources are usually organized in virtual clusters, which are automatically integrated in the underlying grid [4].

One of the main open issues in hybrid cloud-grid architectures is *application scheduling*, that is, the matching of applications to the resources they need to be executed. There exists a wide and consolidated body of literature dealing with the scheduling of applications in grids, which is a complex problem by itself. But, nowadays, schedulers should also address the highly dynamic nature of hybrid cloud-grid architectures.

We are currently working on a scheduler which leverages the principles of *autonomic computing* to add self-optimization capabilities to hybrid cloud/grid architectures [18]. Autonomic computing [10] has emerged as a paradigm able to cope with complex and rapidly-mutable environments. Currently, high research effort is directed to investigate how to design cloud and grid environments endowed with autonomic management capabilities [3,11,16]. CHASE, our prototype implementation of autonomic engine, has been designed to tackle the scheduling problem in PerfCloud. However, its design is not tied to the architecture of a *cloudgrid*, but it is sufficiently general to be integrated with any cloud, grid or hybrid cloud-grid environment.

This paper takes a further step towards the definition of an autonomic cloud architecture by showing how some common tasks which are required in this architecture, namely system configuration mining and monitoring may be easily achieved by employing *mobile agents*. Mobile agents are the last evolution of mobile code-based systems. They add mobility to the well-known and largely appreciated features of ordinary software agents systems, such as reactivity, proactivity, communication and social ability. In essence, a mobile agent is a program, which is able to migrate across the network bringing over its own code and execution state. To support our autonomic architecture, a set of specialized agents has been devised that can extract information about the system configuration and perform monitoring tasks.

The rest of the paper is organized as follows. First of all, a synthetic overview of the architecture of CHASE, originally presented in [18], is given, focusing on the requirements for extracting system information and monitoring. Then the mobile agent platform is presented, showing how it can satisfy these requirements. A concrete use case is dealt with in section 4. After a presentation of related work, the paper closes with our final considerations and a sketch of future work.

2   An Autonomic Engine for Managing Clouds

The CHASE architecture (Figure 1) has been described in [18]. At its core, it is a resource manager whose choices are driven by the predictive evaluation of the application performance for different possible resource assignment scenarios. Performance predictions are obtained by simulation of the application for a given resource assignment by means of a discrete-event simulator which acts on the basis of information both static (essentially, the system configuration) and dynamic (system load).

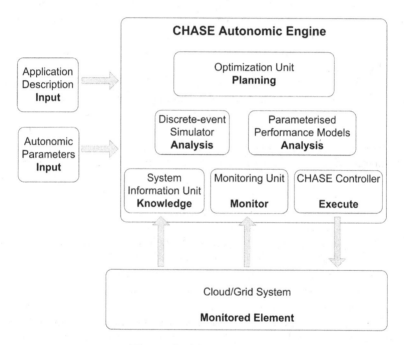

Fig. 1. CHASE architecture

The engine is designed as an autonomic manager capable of controlling different elements as clouds or grids. Figure 1 shows the logical mapping from the CHASE components to the corresponding autonomic building blocks described in [10]. The **Input** to the autonomic engine consists of an *Application Description*, which is a synthetic representation of the application behavior used for driving the simulations, and one or more *Autonomic Performance Parameters*, which can be application performance goals, or constraints on the selection of the resources. The input section is more thoroughly described in [18].

The architectural building blocks are:

– **Planning**, consisting of the Optimization Unit (OU). This is the "smart" component of the architecture. It selects a minimal set of possible resource assignments that have to be simulated in order to find the best one.

- **Analysis**, which is the component capable of performing system evaluation. For a given system configuration, the performance prediction is performed by the Discrete-event Simulator. This is a Java-based prototype that represents the evolution of our previous heterogeneous system simulator, HeSSE [14].
- **Knowledge**, the module responsible for obtaining information about the configuration of the controlled system. We will generally call such information *resource metadata*. The Knowledge module is implemented by the System Information Unit. Subsection 2.1 introduces the requirements for this module, whereas the next section introduces the proposed solution based on mobile agents.
- **Monitor**, which is implemented by a monitoring unit responsible for obtaining dynamic information about the system. The unit can possibly generate alerts when failures or degradations that may cause violations of performance contracts have occurred or are about to occur, thus making it possibly to apply countermeasures.
- **Execute.** The Execute module, implemented by the CHASE Controller, is the system actuator. It is interfaced with the underlying cloud/grid platform, and translates the devised resource assignment plan into actual cloud resource management commands (e.g., virtual machine creation/start/stop, application launch/termination).

2.1   Gathering Resource Metadata

To perform the predictions, the autonomic engine needs information about the the resources of the underlying cloud/grid system. These *resource metadata* can be classified in two macro areas: system configurations and system benchmarks figures. Table 1 reports the current organization of these metadata, as used by our autonomic system.

System configuration is the set of resource parameters that describe how a specific element (system, node, network) is configured. This comprises, for example, frequencies and microarchitecture for the computing elements or latencies and bandwidths for the networks.

System benchmark figures are selected measurements of the system. The outcome of the benchmarks are used to tune the simulator for accurate performance prediction.

The main requirements for resource metadata gathering are:

- *Flexible Structure.* It is not easy, neither desirable, to impose a rigid structure to the classes of information that must be gathered. As an example, new hardware may be introduced that has not been taken into account in the system configuration specification.
- *Mining Capabilities.* While some cloud/grid systems directly expose resource metadata, this is not generally true. Even when some metadata are present, they may be not detailed enough to serve as a basis for configuring the simulations. After all, the intrinsic goal of a cloud is to hide the complexity

of the underlying infrastructure. Thus, methods as general as possible must
be devised to extract these information directly from the system.
- *Support for Extending the Benchmarks.* Defining once and for all which
  benchmarks will be supported is not a viable solution. It is widely recognized that no single benchmark can represent how the system will behave
  with every possible application. Better benchmarks may be defined later in
  time, and the possibility of dynamically changing the measurements to be
  performed is of paramount importance.

Table 1. Resource metadata as gathered by the Knowledge Module

System Configuration		
Scope	**Name**	**Description**
System	No. of nodes	Number of nodes that are available to the system
System	Networks	Available networks (e.g. 10Gb Ethernet, Infiniband)
Node	Hypervisor	Virtual machine monitor of a node (e.g. Xen, KVM, VirtualBox, or none for physical nodes)
Node	No. of CPU	Number of CPUs, number of cores per CPU
Node	Amount of memory	Amount of main memory, amount and configuration of cache memories
Node	Network interface cards	Per-node interfaces to the system networks

System Benchmark Figures	
Benchmark Class	**Description**
CPU	Raw computational speed benchmarks (includes FLOPS and MIPS measurements)
Memory	Sequential/Random read/write access, cache access times
Network	Includes latency and bandwidth benchmarks
Disk	File creation/read/write benchmarks

2.2 Requirements for Monitoring

Static configuration of the resources is just a part of the whole picture: measurements are needed to gain knowledge about the current status of the resources. A
monitoring infrastructure is required to evaluate at least two parameters: system
load and system availability.

System load refers to all the metrics that can be gathered to measure the load
of the different resources (CPUs, networks). These data are fed to the simulator
to contextualize the performance prediction process to a specific system load
(current or future).

System availability comprises data about the liveness of the resources. Periodical checks must be performed to verify that an entire virtual machine or a
single application are still up and running.

3 Introducing Mobile Agents

3.1 The mAGDA Toolset

The mAGDA toolset runs on an agent-enabled cloud composed of one or more virtual machines, and accessible by a WSRF/REST interface that is available to all authenticated users. Service binding is statically defined, but service execution can take place on any nodes belonging to the cloud. An agent-enabled cloud consists of a mobile agents platform distributed on different virtual machines which are connected by a real or a virtual network. Figure 2 shows how a client can use a WSRF/REST stub to invoke agent based services. A software agent, to be installed on a front-end, acts as a proxy between the WSRF/REST and agents technology by translating incoming requests into ACL messages (ACL: Agent Communication Language). Specialized agents are distributed in the cloud to perform their specific role. An agent platform is composed of Jade containers. Jade is a FIPA[1] compliant agent technology developed in Java. A container is a peer-to-peer application that supports execution of agents. We will call agent-node a machine that hosts at least an agent container.

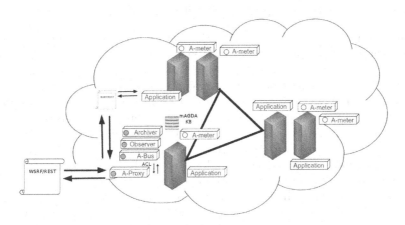

Fig. 2. mAGDA architecture

Any type of agent service can be built on top of this infrastructure: in the following, the set of agent based services that has been conceived to support monitoring and management of cloud resources at infrastructure level will be described. Agents will be in charge of configuring the system, performing measures, computing statistics, collecting and managing information, detecting critical situation and applying reactions according to the decisions notified by the CHASE autonomic engine.

---

[1] Foundation of Intelligent Physical Agents, www.fipa.org

3.2   Supporting the Knowledge Function with mAGDA

The expected output from mAGDA is a profile of the cloud that is composed of a static and a dynamic part. The static part corresponds to resource metadata, as described in section 2.1. It includes information about what are the available resources, how they are connected and their qualitative and quantitative technological parameters. An example could be a virtual machine with 2 dual core x64 CPUs, a given amount of memory and storage, a 100Mb/s network connection and a software installation. The knowledge of the available computing infrastructure is necessary to be aware of the expected application performance and how the resource can be managed optimally. When this information is not made available by the infrastructure, it can be collected by sending agents on the target resource, at start-up or in course of its operation. mAGDA mobile agents can also carry with them benchmark codes, which are executed on the target resource producing benchmark figures which are collected in the cloud profile. The profile also includes information about the configuration of the monitoring infrastructure, as the number of agents, the monitored resources, the active statistics and the controlled performance indexes.

3.3   Supporting the Monitoring Function with mAGDA

Besides the static configuration, mAGDA has to provide a dynamic knowledge about the actual usage of resources. The dynamic part of the cloud profile is updated during the monitoring activity, whose requirements have been described in section 2.2. The monitoring data is composed of statistics of performance parameters which are periodically measured by dedicated agents. To support autonomic behavior, the choice of performance parameters and statistics to be gathered is not fixed, but can be tailored with the configuration of the agent. The monitoring service of mAGDA has been designed as a multi-agent system that distributes tasks among specialized agents. It contemplates both static and mobile agents: the former are responsible for performing complex reasoning on the knowledge base, so they are statically executed where the data reside; the latter usually need to move to the target resources in order to perform local measurements or to get system information. The *Archiver* is a static agent that configures the monitoring infrastructure, collects and stores measurements, computes statistics. According to the parameters to be monitored, the kind of measurement and the provider technology, the archiver starts different *Meters*, which are implemented as mobile agents that the Archiver can dispatch where it needs. *Observers* periodically check a set of rules to detect critical situations. They query the Archiver to know about the statistics and eventually notify applications if some checks have failed. Applications can use a *Agent-bus* service to subscribe themselves for being alerted about each detected event. They can also invoke mAGDA services to start, stop or reconfigure the monitoring infrastructure. Finally, applications can access the complete knowledge base to retrieve information about cloud configuration, monitoring configuration, statistics and the history of past failed checks.

4   An Example Use Case: The Cloud@Home System

Cloud@Home [5] is a project, funded by the Italian Government, which aims at merging the cloud and *volunteer* computing paradigms. Cloud@Home collects infrastructure resources from many different resource providers and offers them through a uniform interface, with an *Infrastructure as a Service* (IaaS) model. The resource providers can range from commercial cloud providers to academic partners, or even to individually volunteered desktop machines. Cloud@Home gives great emphasis to the management of Service Level Agreements (SLAs) and Quality of Service (QoS), and provides dedicated components for these tasks. Through these components, Cloud@Home is capable of performing virtual machine creation on the resource it manages, possibly governed by a resource-oriented Service Level Agreement. CHASE and mAGDA have been designed to enrich the Cloud@Home system with application-oriented performance prediction capabilities and a monitoring infrastructure. A prototype implementation has been realized to verify the effectiveness of the approach. In the prototype scenario, a Cloud@Home installation has been deployed on two academic clusters, PoweRcost and Vega, respectively placed at University of Sannio and Second University of Naples. As a test case, CHASE had to provide an application scheduling for a well-known HPC code, the NAS/MPI 2.4 LU Benchmark, on the IaaS cloud provided by Cloud@Home. This cloud was composed of 8 virtual machines which had been previously obtained from the system. The scheduling goal was the minimization of execution time. The engine workflow went on as described in the following:

1. Input - The performance goal, together with an application description, is fed to the CHASE engine.
2. Knowledge - CHASE instructs mAGDA to launch mobile agents on the C@H virtual machines to recover system configuration. The agents recover information about the structure of the nodes and the network and launch benchmarks to obtain performance data. Most of this information does not vary between executions and is thus stored to allow immediate retrieval in future application requests.
3. Monitoring - CHASE instructs mAGDA to launch mobile monitoring agents on every virtual machines. The agents periodically report information about system load and availability.
4. Planning - CHASE begins selecting possible variations of resource assignments that have to be simulated. Techniques to reduce the number of configurations have been described in [18].
5. Analysis- Every chosen configuration, together with system load data, is fed to the simulator, which reports predicted execution time to the engine.
6. Planning - The planning unit compares the predictions and chooses the best configuration.
7. Execute - The engine schedules the launch of the application on the selected resources.

The correct minimized execution time was selected: results of these execution have been reported in [18].

5   Related Work

A wide body of literature deals with resource management in physical grids [12]. The resource provisioning problem in virtualized systems has been tackled in the Shirako system from Duke University [8] and in the Haizea architecture from University of Chicago/Argonne National Laboratory [19]. Both systems hinge on the concept of *leases*, contracts that define which resources are assigned to users and the duration of these assignments. Compared to these solutions, our engine presents an application centric perspective, where the user has not to provide direct resource requests, but can express his needs in terms of desired application performance. An approach more similar to the CHASE one is used in AppLeS [1], a methodology for adaptive application scheduling on physical Grids. In AppLeS, applications are associated with a customized scheduling agent that monitors and predicts available resource performance an dynamically generates a schedule for the application. Some previous work has been done on the application of mobile code to monitoring and management of resources, mainly in the grid context [20,7]. Few applications of mobile agents to cloud systems are starting to spread, most of which tackle issues different than the ones covered here, like intrusion detection [6] and cloud federation [21].

6   Conclusions

In this paper we have shown how some key parts of an autonomic system can be implemented through the use of mobile agents. These enhancements have been applied to CHASE, an autonomic engine for the development of self-optimizing applications in cloud environments. Two key functions in the CHASE architecture are system configuration mining and resource monitoring. These have been implemented through mAGDA, a mobile agent based platform. A prototypal use case has been developed on the Cloud@Home platform. Future work will focus on testing the engine on a larger set of real applications and cloud platforms.

References

1. Berman, F., Wolski, R., Casanova, H., Cirne, W., Dail, H., Faerman, M., Figueira, S., Hayes, J., Obertelli, G., Schopf, J., et al.: Adaptive computing on the grid using AppLeS. IEEE Transactions on Parallel and Distributed Systems 14(4), 369–382 (2003)
2. Blanco, C., Huedo, E., Montero, R., Llorente, I.: Dynamic provision of computing resources from grid infrastructures and cloud providers. In: Proceedings of the 2009 Workshops at the Grid and Pervasive Computing Conference, pp. 113–120. IEEE Computer Society (2009)
3. Brandic, I.: Towards self-manageable cloud services. In: 33rd Annual IEEE International Computer Software and Applications Conference, pp. 128–133 (2009)
4. Casola, V., Cuomo, A., Rak, M., Villano, U.: The *CloudGrid* approach: Security and performance analysis and evaluation. Future Generation Computer Systems (to be published, 2012), special section: Quality of Service in Grid and Cloud Computing

5. Cuomo, A., Di Modica, G., Distefano, S., Rak, M., Vecchio, A.: The Cloud@Home Architecture - Building a Cloud infrastructure from volunteered resources. In: CLOSER 2011, The First International Conference on Cloud Computing and Service Science, Noordwojkerhout, The Netherlands, May 7-9 (2011)
6. Dastjerdi, A.V., Bakar, K.A., Tabatabaei, S.: Distributed intrusion detection in clouds using mobile agents. In: 2009 Third International Conference on Advanced Engineering Computing and Applications in Sciences, pp. 175–180. IEEE (2009)
7. Di Martino, B., Rana, O.F.: Grid performance and resource management using mobile agents. In: Performance Analysis and Grid Computing, pp. 251–263. Kluwer Academic Publishers, Norwell (2004)
8. Grit, L., Irwin, D., Yumerefendi, A., Chase, J.: Virtual machine hosting for networked clusters: Building the foundations for autonomic orchestration. In: Proceedings of the 2nd International Workshop on Virtualization Technology in Distributed Computing, p. 7. IEEE Computer Society (2006)
9. Keahey, K., Foster, I.T., Freeman, T., Zhang, X.: Virtual workspaces: Achieving quality of service and quality of life in the grid. Scient. Progr. 13(4), 265–275 (2005)
10. Kephart, J.O., Chess, D.M.: The vision of autonomic computing. Computer 36(1), 41–50 (2003)
11. Kim, H., et al.: An autonomic approach to integrated hpc grid and cloud usage. In: 2009 Fifth IEEE International Conference on e-Science, pp. 366–373. IEEE (2009)
12. Krauter, K., Buyya, R., Maheswaran, M.: A taxonomy and survey of grid resource management systems for distributed computing. Software: Practice and Experience 32(2), 135–164 (2002)
13. Mancini, E.P., Rak, M., Villano, U.: Perfcloud: Grid services for performance-oriented development of cloud computing applications. In: WETICE, pp. 201–206 (2009)
14. Mazzocca, N., Rak, M., Villano, U.: The Transition from a PVM Program Simulator to a Heterogeneous System Simulator: The HeSSE Project. In: Dongarra, J., Kacsuk, P., Podhorszki, N. (eds.) PVM/MPI 2000. LNCS, vol. 1908, pp. 266–273. Springer, Heidelberg (2000)
15. Mell, P., Grance, T.: The nist definition of cloud computing (2009)
16. Murphy, M.A., Abraham, L., Fenn, M., Goasguen, S.: Autonomic clouds on the grid. Journal of Grid Computing 8(1), 1–18 (2010)
17. Ostermann, S., Prodan, R., Fahringer, T.: Resource Management for Hybrid Grid and Cloud Computing. Computer Communications, 179–194 (2010)
18. Rak, M., Cuomo, A., Villano, U.: CHASE: an Autonomic Service Engine for Cloud Environments. In: WETICE 2011 - 20th IEEE International Conference on Collaboration Technologies and Infrastructures. pp. 116–121. IEEE (2011)
19. Sotomayor, B., Keahey, K., Foster, I.: Combining batch execution and leasing using virtual machines. In: Proceedings of the 17th International Symposium on High Performance Distributed Computing. pp. 87–96. ACM (2008)
20. Tomarchio, O., Vita, L.: On the use of mobile code technology for monitoring grid system. In: CCGRID 2001: Proceedings of the 1st International Symposium on Cluster Computing and the Grid, p. 450. IEEE Computer Society, Washington, DC (2001)
21. Zhang, Z., Zhang, X.: Realization of open cloud computing federation based on mobile agent. In: IEEE International Conference on Intelligent Computing and Intelligent Systems, ICIS 2009, vol. 3, pp. 642–646. IEEE (2009)

Mapping Application Requirements
to Cloud Resources

Yih Leong Sun, Terence Harmer, Alan Stewart, and Peter Wright

The Queen's University of Belfast,
University Road, Belfast, BT7 1NN, Northern Ireland, UK
{ysun05,t.harmer,a.stewart,p.wright}@qub.ac.uk
http://www.qub.ac.uk

Abstract. Cloud Computing has created a paradigm shift in software
development. Many developers now use the Cloud as an affordable platform on which to deploy business solutions. One outstanding challenge is
the integration of different Cloud services (or resources), offered by different Cloud providers, when building a Cloud-oriented business solution.
Typically each provider has a different means of describing Cloud resources and uses a different application programming interface to acquire
Cloud resources. Developers need to make complex decisions involving
multiple Cloud products, different Cloud implementations, different deployment options, and different programming approaches. In this paper,
we propose a model for discovering Cloud resources in a multi-provider
environment. We study a financial use case scenario and suggest the use
of a provider-agnostic approach which hides the complex implementation
details for mapping the application requirements to Cloud resources.

Keywords: Cloud Computing, Cloud Programming Model, Resource
Discovery.

1 Introduction

The emergence of Cloud Computing is creating a paradigm shift in software
development. The International Data Corporation (IDC) published a research
report in 2010 forecasting that the estimated spending on Public Cloud services
will grow from $16.5 billion in 2009 to over $55 billion in 2014 [24]. The first
wave of Public Cloud services was dominated by Software-as-a-Service (SaaS)
applications, which contributed to 49% of Public Cloud spending in 2009. However, forecasts suggest that an increasing share of services will be provided by
Platform-as-a-Service (PaaS), 16%, and Infrastructure-as-a-Service (IaaS), 20%,
in 2014. A growing number of developers are using Cloud as the most affordable
platform on which to deploy business solutions [25].

Cloud Computing offers many benefits to businesses. The consumption of
Cloud services is usually on a pay-as-you-use pricing model. This can significantly reduce the upfront cost of purchasing software licenses or infrastructure
hardware. It provides great flexibility for businesses to scale resources according to demand. In addition to that, the advantages of Cloud Computing includes

M. Alexander et al. (Eds.): Euro-Par 2011 Workshops, Part I, LNCS 7155, pp. 104–112, 2012.
© Springer-Verlag Berlin Heidelberg 2012

dynamic resource provisioning, efficient multi-tenancy and server utilization which brings environmental benefits by reducing energy consumption and carbon emission [18].

There has been a significant growth in the number of Cloud service providers offering on-demand software services, application, storage and compute resources in the market. Providers may have different application programming interfaces to obtain and configure required Cloud services. From the application developer's point of view, there is a challenge to assemble Cloud services together, from various Cloud providers, in order to build a complete Cloud-oriented business solution. Application developers are not only interested in compute resources, such as CPU, memory, operating system type but are also interested in integrating other Cloud services, such as storage, database, messaging and communication services. When building a Cloud-oriented application, a developer must take into account requirements such as fault-tolerance, self-healing, self-management as well as the cost of Cloud services.

There is a need to develop an advanced high-level programming model for building Cloud-oriented business solutions in a multi-provider environment. The high-level model should enable cross-Cloud implementations and avoid a low-level technical restriction to a single Cloud provider. In this paper, we describe the concept of using a constraints-based model to map an application to a set of Cloud resources, which are to be used to execute the application, in a multi-provider environment. It should provide an abstract software layer that excludes implementation details from the issue of selecting Cloud resources.

1.1   Paper Organisation

The remainder of this paper is organised as follows. In section 2, we present a brief summary of our study on the management of Cloud resources. In section 3, a financial sector use case scenarios is presented. In section 4, we describe our proposed resource discovery model. In section 5, we present a prototype demonstrator. In section 6, we study some related work. Section 7 suggests future work.

2   Cloud Resource Management

There are numerous Cloud management toolkits which manage and control infrastructure resources across multiple Cloud provider or virtualisation environments. These toolkits provide functionality for managing compute resources on the Cloud. Eucalyptus [6] provides an EC2-compatible programming interface and one-stop management console to manage hybrid clouds and private clouds with mixed hypervisor environments (XEN, KVM, vSphere, ESX, ESXi). It supports features such as storage integration, monitoring and auditing. OpenNebula [15] provides a standard-based open source cloud computing toolkit for building private, public or hybrid clouds using an interface which enables dynamic deployment and reallocation of virtual machines. Haizea [7] is an open source resource leasing manager which can be used as a VM scheduler for OpenNebula to provide leasing capabilities, such as resource reservation. Nimbus [10] is an open source toolkit that turns a cluster into an IaaS cloud. The Nimbus cloud client allows provisioning of compute nodes with a leasing model based on Amazon EC2 interface.

Most of the resource management toolkits in the market offer useful management features, however, they do not provide a search capability for Cloud resources that satisfy application's requirements. A developer needs to have preexisting knowledge of the infrastructure capabilities and pricing structures offered by different providers before using these toolkits to allocate infrastructure resources. Moreover, most of these toolkits are focused at the infrastructure layer, i.e. compute resources or virtual machines. There are a small number of toolkits for managing applications, such as, Message Queue Service [1,16,4], Storage Service [12,3] and Database Service [2,5,11].

3   Financial Use Case Scenarios

In [30], an SLA (Service Level Agreement) focused financial services infrastrucutre framework is described. Two financial business scenarios are described. One of the financial business use cases requires the application developer to build a financial application to revalue a customer's stock or portfolio on a day to day basis in order to comply with internal market risk controls and national regulatory requirements. The execution of such application is very complex and requires computational intensive techniques. It requires high-end compute resources and large storage space. Extra compute power is needed, usually at short notice, if several large portfolios are to be valued at the same time. It needs an application platform to host a specific software bundle. It needs access to market data from a market feed services, such as Bloomberg market data feed. And one of the regulatory requirements is that data can not be held or transmitted outside the UK.

The other business use case presented in the paper is the building of a financial application that integrates different remote services and has the potential to run on multiple remote compute resources. It requires access to third-party financial services and compute resources on demand in order to run a financial market *back-test* simulation. It needs to pull historical data from different stock exchanges, such as London and New York. To ensure data quality and integrity, historical data needs to be verified and audited by a third-party data verification service. The verified data is fed into the financial application which runs on multiple remote compute resources. Large storage space is required to keep the historical data, verified data and the simulation result for further analysis. It must guarantee a low response time within a certain time range in the day. In addition, it has a maximum budget per month for running such application.

3.1   Application Requirement's Challenges

The financial sector is a challenging domain which requires high data volumes and rapid data processing with stringent security and confidentially requirements.

Financial applications depends heavily on process and data intensive computations. It is highly regulated with national and international regulatory requirements. From the business use case scenarios described above, we identify the following key challenges when implementing a financial application in the Cloud:

- *Performance Requirement.* In the financial services sector, high availability of resources is at primary important. To ensure infrastructure resilience, multiple identical mirror infrastructures must be provisioned. It needs a very fast automatic mechanism to discover and re-provision resources when failure is detected.
- *Compliance Requirement.* Legislation regulation requirements are essential to the finance sector. A financial application must ensure the data quality, integrity and confidentiality in order to comply with the national and international regulations.

4   Using Constraints to Discover Cloud Resources

It is highly desirable to develop a novel programming model adhering to the service-oriented nature of Cloud Computing, allowing Cloud-oriented application to be constructed rapidly. It is proposed that a Cloud programming model provides a means of reasoning about user requirements or constraints (Fig. 1). In this paper, we propose a method for mapping an application with an associated set of constraints to a set of resources, that could be used to support the application. Examples of constraints include (but not limited to) the followings:

- *Hardware constraints.* Does the application have any hardware requirements; if so, how can we select a Cloud resource that meet the requirements.
- *Software constraints.* Does the application utilise any software; if so, is the software offered in a Cloud or must it be pre-installed by the user on an application platform.
- *Storage constraints.* Does the application need a storage space to keep data such as files or raw logs; if so, are these files stored in the Cloud.
- *Data constraints.* Does the application utilise a database; if so, is the database in a Cloud.

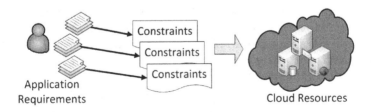

Fig. 1. Mapping Application Requirements to Cloud Resources

– *Security constraints.* Does the application have any security or trust concerns; if so, is this security feature available from any Cloud provider.
– *Performance constraints.* Does the application need to fulfil a Quality of Service (QoS) or Service Level Agreement (SLA) requirement; if so, can a set of Cloud resources be found to meet the QoS or SLA.
– *Cost constraints.* Does the application have a budget or cost restriction; if so, can a set of Cloud resources be acquired within this budget.
– *Compliance constraints.* Does the application need to abide by any regulator or compliance requirement; if so, can a set of Cloud resources be found to meet the legal requirement.

Constraints can be simple, such as bandwidth of 1 gigabit, storage resilience of at least 99.9999%, geographical location (resources must be in the UK), or business regulatory (must be in a TIA942 compliant datacentre).

As a simple example application consider a server which will host a large database. The resource must have at least 4 CPU cores, 8GB of RAM and 1TB of local disk space. A more interesting example would be the provision of a financial infrastructure. Two identical mirror infrastructures must be provisioned, ideally widely separated, in order to ensure high resilience and high availability. The infrastructure being provisioned must:

– enforce financial regulatory requirements that the data must not be held or transmitted outside the UK;
– enforce performance requirements for a demanding application which requires high availability (99.9999%) of compute power and data storage;
– balance the separation of the mirrored infrastructures against the performance need to keep the response time as low as possible (low latency).

The selection of resources must fulfil the regulatory requirements and balance the *functional requirements* required for the resources and the *non-functional requirements* required for high resilience.

Using a constraints-based model, the above example could be expressed as follow:

```
SoftwareConstraint os = new
                    OperatingSystemConstraint(UBUNTU_10_04)
HardwareConstraint cpu = new CPUCoreConstraint(4)
HardwareConstraint ram = new RAMConstraint(8, GIGABYTES)
StorageConstraint storage = new StorageConstraint(1,
                    TERABYTES, new StorageResilence(99.9999))
LocationConstraint location = new CountryConstraint(Country.UK)
CompliantConstraint compliant = new
                    DatacenterConstraint(Compliance.TIA942)

Resource[] resources = FindResourcesByConstraints(os, cpu, ram,
                    storage, location, compliant)
```

It is necessary to have a clear description of Cloud resources in order to map the constraints to resources. Cloud resources can be described using semantic web techniques [19,29]. Once the resources are defined, it is possible to translate the application requirements into constraints, which can be mapped to resource descriptions.

5   Demonstrator

We have implemented a simple prototype using the proposed constraints-based resource discovery model. In this prototype, Cloud resources are restricted to infrastructure compute resources (virtual machines) and storage resources (remote file storage) only. Amazon AWS and internal hardware infrastructures are used in this prototype to provision the resources. Following the approach of previous work [23], Cloud resources are described in terms of Resource Template with different attributes such as hardware specification, operating system type, storage capacity and datacenter location. Application requirements are translated into a set of constraints. In our experiment, we apply different hardware constraints (cpu, memory), software constraints (operating system), storage constraints (storage space) and regulatory constraints (geographical location) to *search* for viable resources. The performance of the demonstrator depends on the set of constraints being supplied. For example, searching resources in the EU region is much faster than searching for resources across all geographical regions. The experiment results show that the demonstrator can *search* and *provision* a set of Cloud resources that satisfy the application's requirements, using the proposed constraints-based model, in a multi-provider environment.

6   Related Works

The RESERVOIR project [28] presents an Open Federated Cloud Computing architecture that allows service providers to be grouped together so as to create a seemingly infinite pool of compute resources. The model separates the functional roles of service providers from infrastructures. Service providers need not necessarily own computational resources but may lease resources from infrastructure providers. This provides a clean separation of responsibilities and hides low level infrastructure details from the service providers. The RESERVOIR proposes a service definition manifest to specify the application configurations–using a service specification language [22] based on the DMTF's Open Virtualisation Format (OVF) standard [14]. The service manifest includes VM details, application settings and deployment settings. In contrast to the RESERVOIR approach, we prefer a high-level constraints model which provides an application-focused (user-centric) rather than a provider-focused view of resources.

Aneka [31] is a PaaS (Platform as a Service) type of middleware for deploying Cloud applications. It provides a platform and framework for developing distributed applications on the Cloud. Aneka is being developed on top of EMCA

Common Language Infrastructure [17]. It requires the application to be implemented on .NET Framework [8] or Mono [9] only. A Platform Abstraction Layer is introduced in Aneka to encapsulate all of the platform dependencies on the hosting platform behind a common interface. An Aneka Container, the basic deployment unit of Aneka Cloud, supports different programming models including Task, Distributed Thread and MapReduce[20].

Mosaic [21,26,27] project intends to develop an open-source Cloud application programming interface and a platform for developing applications in a multi-Cloud environment. It studies patterns from related architectures (service-oriented, parallel computing) and proposes a few Cloud Computing patterns such as Data storage and Multi-tenancy pattern. It proposes a resource negotiation solution based on software agents and semantic data processing. It presents a few functionalities that should be exposed by the Mosaic's API at the Storage, Communication, Monitoring and Provisioning level. It aims to provide a generic Cloud API by extending the OGF OCCI [13] proposal. It proposes an application model in terms of Cloud Building Block which can be a Cloud Resource under the Cloud provider control or a Cloud Component controlled by the application user. Mosaic is still under development. The first version of API will be made available in autumn 2011 and the full platform in another two years.

7 Conclusion and Future Works

Cloud application developers currently need to deal with a complex choice among multiple Cloud products, different Cloud implementations, different deployment options, and different programming approaches. Our proposed model is intentionally simple and attempts to reflect an ideal for the application user who wishes to specify services or resources without knowing the internal behaviour of the underlying provider - insulating the user from the different provider approaches and frequent changes in the underlying APIs. This approach means that the application can take a dynamic, commodity approach to service usage. A Cloud-oriented application can be deployed and scaled according to application and system constraints, stay within a strict budget and be portable between all available Cloud providers.

Most of the concepts described in this paper and the prototype demonstrator are still in preliminary stage. This research will serve as a base for future studies of a standard programming model for developing applications in the Cloud. We aim to develop a provider-agnostic mechanism in searching for Cloud resources in a multi-provider environment. The ability to map an application's requirements to a set of Cloud resources, based on a constraints-based model, can narrow the viable choices and allow automatic discovery of resources during application runtime.

References

1. Amazon Simple Queue Service (Amazon SQS), http://aws.amazon.com/sqs
2. Amazon SimpleDB, http://aws.amazon.com/simpledb/

3. AT&T Synaptic Storage as a Service, http://www.synaptic.att.com
4. CloudMQ Message Queuing as a Service, http://www.cloudmq.com/
5. Database.com, http://www.database.com/
6. Eucalyptus, The Open Source Cloud Platform, http://open.eucalyptus.com/
7. Haizea, An Open Source VM-based Lease Manager, http://haizea.cs.uchicago.edu/
8. Microsoft .NET Framework, http://www.microsoft.com/net/
9. MONO, Cross platform open source .NET development framework, http://www.mono-project.com/
10. Nimbus Project, http://www.nimbusproject.org/
11. NimbusDB, http://www.nimbusdb.com/
12. Nirvanix Storage Delivery Network, http://www.nirvanix.com/
13. OCCI - Open Cloud Computing Interface, http://occi-wg.org/
14. Open Virtualization Format (OVF) Specification. DSP0243 1.0.0. Distributed Management Task Force (February 2009), http://www.dmtf.org/standards/ovf
15. OpenNebula, The Open Source Toolkit for Cloud Computing, http://www.opennebula.org
16. RabbitMQ Messaging that just works, http://www.rabbitmq.com/
17. Standard ECMA-335 Common Language Infrastructure (CLI), http://www.ecma-international.org/publications/standards/Ecma-335.htm
18. Accenture, Microsoft, WSP: Cloud Computing and Sustainability: The Environmental Benefits of Moving to the Cloud (2011), http://www.zdnet.co.uk/white-papers/view/server-platforms-os/cloud-computing-and-sustainabilitythe-environmental-benefits-of-movingto-the-cloud-261937611/2/
19. Bernstein, D., Vij, D.: Using semantic web ontology for intercloud directories and exchanges. In: International Conference on Internet Computing, pp. 18–24 (2010)
20. Dean, J., Ghemawat, S.: MapReduce: Simplified Data Processing on Large Clusters. In: OSDI 2004, pp. 137–150 (2004)
21. Di Martino, B., Petcu, D., Cossu, R., Goncalves, P., Máhr, T., Loichate, M.: Building a Mosaic of Clouds. In: Guarracino, M.R., Vivien, F., Träff, J.L., Cannataro, M., Danelutto, M., Hast, A., Perla, F., Knüpfer, A., Di Martino, B., Alexander, M. (eds.) Euro-Par-Workshop 2010. LNCS, vol. 6586, pp. 571–578. Springer, Heidelberg (2011), http://dx.doi.org/10.1007/978-3-642-21878-1_70
22. Galán, F., Sampaio, A., Rodero-Merino, L., Loy, I., Gil, V., Vaquero, L.M.: Service specification in cloud environments based on extensions to open standards. In: Proceedings of the Fourth International ICST Conference on Communication System Software and Middleware, COMSWARE 2009, pp. 19:1–19:12. ACM, New York (2009), http://doi.acm.org/10.1145/1621890.1621915
23. Harmer, T., Wright, P., Cunningham, C., Perrott, R.: Provider-Independent Use of the Cloud. In: Sips, H., Epema, D., Lin, H.-X. (eds.) Euro-Par 2009. LNCS, vol. 5704, pp. 454–465. Springer, Heidelberg (2009), http://dx.doi.org/10.1007/978-3-642-03869-3_44
24. IDC: IDC's Public IT Cloud Services Forecast: New Numbers, Same Disruptive Story, http://blogs.idc.com/ie/?p=922
25. IDC: The Single Biggest Reason Public Clouds Will Dominate the Next Era of IT, http://blogs.idc.com/ie/?p=345
26. Petcu, D.: Identifying cloud computing usage patterns. In: 2010 IEEE International Conference on Cluster Computing Workshops and Posters (CLUSTER WORKSHOPS), pp. 1–8 (September 2010)

27. Petcu, D., Craciun, C., Rak, M.: Towards a cross-platform cloud api. components for cloud federation. In: 1st International Conference on Cloud Computing & Services Science, pp. 166–169 (2011)

28. Rochwerger, B., Breitgand, D., Levy, E., Galis, A., Nagin, K., Llorente, I.M., Montero, R., Wolfsthal, Y., Elmroth, E., Caceres, J., Ben-Yehuda, M., Emmerich, W., Galan, F.: The Reservoir model and architecture for open federated cloud computing. IBM Journal of Research and Development 53(4), 4:1 –4:11 (2009)

29. Sheu, P.Y., Wang, S., Wang, Q., Hao, K., Paul, R.: Semantic Computing, Cloud Computing, and Semantic Search Engine. In: IEEE International Conference on Semantic Computing, ICSC 2009, pp. 654–657 (2009)

30. Sun, Y.L., Perrott, R., Harmer, T., Cunningham, C., Wright, P.: An SLA Focused Financial Services Infrastructure. In: International Conference on Cloud Computing & Virtualization 2010, Singapore (2010)

31. Vecchiola, C., Chu, X., Buyya, R.: Aneka: A Software Platform for .NET-based Cloud Computing, pp. 267–295. IOS Press Inc. (2009)

CoreGRID/ERCIM Workshop on Grids, Clouds and P2P Computing – CGWS2011

Marco Danelutto[1], Frédéric Desprez[2], Vladimir Getov[3], and Wolfgang Ziegler[4]

[1] Univ. of Pisa (I)
[2] INRIA and ENS Lyon (F)
[3] Univ. of Westminster (UK)
[4] Fraunhofer SCAI (D)

CoreGRID is a European research Network of Excellence (NoE) that was initiated in 2004 as part of the EU FP6 research framework and run up to 2008. CoreGRID partners, from 44 different countries, developed theoretical foundations and software infrastructures for large-scale, distributed Grid and P2P applications. An ERCIM sponsored CoreGRID Working Group was established to ensure the continuity of the CoreGrid programme after the official end of NoE. The working group extended its interests to include the emerging field of (service based) cloud computing which is of great importance to the European software industry. Its main goals consist in i) sustaining the operation of the CoreGRID Network, ii) establishing a forum to encourage collaboration between the Grid and P2P Computing research communities, and (iii) encourage research on the role of cloud computing as a new paradigm for distributed computing in e-Science.

In particular, the ERCIM CoreGRID working group managed to organize an annual CoreGRID workshop, traditionally associated to the Euro-Par conference, thus continuing the tradition of the CoreGRID workshops regularly run once per year during the NoE activities. Past ERCIM CoreGRID workshops have been organized in Delft (2009) and Ischia-Naples (2010). In 2011 the workshop has been organized in Bordeaux. As usual the topics of interest included Service Level Agreements, Data & Knowledge Management, Scheduling, Virtual environments, Network monitoring, Volunteer Computing Systems, Trust & Security, Self-* and adaptive mechanisms, Advanced programming models, IaaS, PaaS and SaaS, Tools and Environments for Application Development and Execution.

The 2011 ERCIM CoreGRID workshop gathered around 40 researchers from the european community, on August 29, 2011. Nine papers were presented after one keynote talk.

The keynote talk was given by Franoise Baude (Univ. de Nice, CNRS, INRIA Sophia Antipolis) about an overview of the Grid Component Model (GCM) that allows large applications to be ported in a seamless way over Grids and now Clouds.

The first paper presented a study of the mapping of evolving applications over resource managers. Results showed that resource usage and application response time can be significantly improved with short scheduling times. The second paper discussed the use of model checking to support conflict resolution in multiple non-functional concern management. A trade-off must be found between the ability to develop independently management of the individual concerns and the detection and resolution of conflicts that may arise when combining the independently developed management code. The next paper showed how consistent reconfiguration protocols can be derived for stream-based ASSISTANT applications, and their costs was characterized in terms of proper performance models. The fourth paper described challenges around highly interactive virtual environments, also known as Real-Time Online Interactive Applications (ROIA). A dynamic resource management system RTF-RMS which implements a load-balancing strategy for ROIA on Clouds was presented. In the fifth paper, the architecture of Contrail federations of Clouds were presented and motivated. Beside supporting user authentication and applications deployment, Contrail federations aim at providing extended SLA management functionalities, by integrating the SLA management approach of SLA@SOI project in the federation architecture. The sixth paper presented a novel tool to synthesize ontologies for the Abstract Grid Workflow Language (AGWL). Experiments based on two separate application domains were shown that demonstrate the effectiveness of our approach by semi-automatically generating ontologies which are then used to automatically create workflow applications. The seventh paper presented the chemical machine, an interpreter for the Higher Order Chemical Language. The design follows that of logic/functional languages and bridges the gap between the highly abstract chemical model and the physical machine by an abstract interpreter engine. The next paper described OP2, an "active" library framework for the solution of unstructured mesh applications. The OP2 code generation and compiler framework which, given an application written using the OP2 API, generates efficient code for state-of-the-art hardware (e.g. GPUs and multi-core CPUs) were discussed. The last paper proposed a dynamic load balancing strategy to enhance the performance of parallel association rule mining algorithms in the context of a Grid computing environment.

We wish to thank all those that contributed to the success of the workshop: authors submitting papers, invited speakers, colleagues participating in the refereeing process / discussion sessions and Euro-Par 2011 organizers whose invaluable support greatly helped in the organisation of the Workshop.

October 2011   *M. Danelutto, F. Desprez, V. Getov, W. Ziegler*

A Perspective on the *CoreGRID* Grid Component Model

Françoise Baude

INRIA, I3S-CNRS, University of Nice Sophia-Antipolis,
2004 route des Lucioles, Sophia Antipolis, France
Francoise.Baude@inria.fr

The Grid Component Model is a software component model designed partly in the context of the *CoreGRID* European Network of Excellence, as an extension of the Fractal model, to target the programming of large-scale distributed infrastructures such as computing grids [3]. These distributed memory infrastructures, characterized by high latency, heterogeneity and sharing of resources, suggest the efficient use of several CPUs at once to obtain high performances. To address these characteristics, GCM features

- primitive components that can be deployed on different locations of the grid, through the notion of Virtual Nodes and their associated XML-based deployment descriptors,
- composite and distributed components exporting server and client interfaces of their inner components
- collective interfaces (multicast, gathercast, MxN)
- and, as in Fractal, an open control part giving GCM components full introspection and reconfiguration capabilities.

Moreover, the control part itself can be designed as a composition of distributed GCM components [4], allowing for full expressiveness and more importantly, full adaptability of the control part even at runtime. A GCM membrane (control part) can for instance implement an autonomic adaptation of the parallelism degree of the composite parallel component it controls (a.k.a. behavioral skeleton [1]) i.e. configure the number of inner components working in parallel to achieve a given task.

The GCM specification (API, Architecture Description Language for initially describing a GCM application, and GCMA/GCMD deployment descriptors) has been approved as an ETSI standard by the technical body in charge of grids and clouds.

A reference implementation of GCM relying upon the open source ProActive parallel suite (proactive.inria.fr) relies on Virtual Nodes concrete instantiation, and the use of Active Objects to implement distributed components. Server and client interfaces method invocations thus rely on asynchronous method invocations with futures. Moreover, futures are first-class which is key to propagate interface calls, in particular within composite components. Strategies to update future values have also been deeply experimented with, and the way components interact through requests has been formalized and proved correct (using the Isabelle theorem prover) [5]. Behavioural specifications of GCM interfaces enable hierarchical and thus scalable model cheking of whole GCM applications [2].

GCM has been successful in building applications acting as high-level middlewares. MPI-like applications can be executed on top of on any combination of heterogeneous computing resources from different administrative domains i.e. acquired from different

M. Alexander et al. (Eds.): Euro-Par 2011 Workshops, Part I, LNCS 7155, pp. 115–116, 2012.
© Springer-Verlag Berlin Heidelberg 2012

clusters, grids and even clouds, thanks to a GCM-based substrate [6]. Such substrate handles the efficient and seamless inter domain routing of application-level messages exchanged between processes of the non-embarrassinly parallel application. The obtained performances are competitive in regard to existing implementations of MPI on grids. Handling the routing of application-level messages across domains can be useful in other situations, as when building federations of Enterprise Service Busses [6].

GCM has been given an *SCA (Service Component Architecture)* personality, meaning one can design a GCM application as an SCA one, including the use of SCA intents. Moreover, GCM primitive components can be implemented as BPEL documents (according to the SCA-BPEL specification). The links to orchestration engines through specific GCM controllers allow partner links dynamic adaptation and opens the way for distributed orchestration. SCA/GCM components can be equiped with a GCM membrane specially designed as a MAPE-compliant framework for flexible SOA applications. This means the SOA application can flexibly be recomposed and redeployed if needed, according to some SLAs, in an autonomic way [7].

GCM is also being used to program peer-to-peer applications. More specifically, it is used to build up a cloud-based system for storing and brokering semantically described (RDF) events, relying upon a structured CAN-based overlay architecture. Peers and associated proxies of this system named *Event cloud* are programmed so to fulfill the Event Level Agreements dictated by the services that are publishing or subscribing to events.

As a conclusion, GCM is becoming a mature technology for programming large-scale distributed and parallel applications on grids, clouds and any combination of them.

References

1. Aldinucci, M., Campa, S., Danelutto, M., Vanneschi, M., Kilpatrick, P., Dazzi, P., Laforenza, D., Tonellotto, N.: Behavioral skeletons in GCM: automatic management of Grid components. In: 16th Euromicro Conference on Parallel, Distributed and Network-Based Processing (2008)
2. Barros, T., Boulifa, R., Cansado, A., Henrio, L., Madelaine, E.: Behavioural Models for Distributed Fractal Components. Annals of Telecommunications 64(1) (2009)
3. Baude, F., Caromel, D., Dalmasso, C., Danelutto, M., Getov, V., Henrio, L., Pérez, C.: GCM: A Grid Extension to Fractal for Autonomous Distributed Components. Annals of Telecommunications 64(1), 5–24 (2009)
4. Baude, F., Henrio, L., Naoumenko, P.: Structural reconfiguration: an autonomic strategy for GCM components. In: 5th International Conference on Autonomic and Autonomous Systems (ICAS 2009), pp. 123–128. IEEE Xplore (2009)
5. Henrio, L., Khan, M.: Asynchronous Components with Futures: Semantics and Proofs in Isabelle/HOL. In: FESCA 2010. ENTCS (2010)
6. Mathias, E., Baude, F.: A Component-Based Middleware for Hybrid Grid/Cloud Computing Platforms. In: Concurrency and Computation: Practice and Experience (to appear, 2012)
7. Ruz, C., Baude, F., Sauvan, B.: Flexible Adaptation Loop for Component-based SOA applications. In: 7th International Conference on Autonomic and Autonomous Systems (ICAS 2011). IEEE Explorer (2011) Best paper awarded

Towards Scheduling Evolving Applications*

Cristian Klein and Christian Pérez

INRIA/LIP, ENS de Lyon, France
{cristian.klein,christian.perez}@inria.fr

Abstract. Most high-performance computing resource managers only allow applications to request a static allocation of resources. However, evolving applications have resource requirements which change (evolve) during their execution. Currently, such applications are forced to make an allocation based on their peak resource requirements, which leads to an inefficient resource usage. This paper studies whether it makes sense for resource managers to support evolving applications. It focuses on scheduling fully-predictably evolving applications on homogeneous resources, for which it proposes several algorithms and evaluates them based on simulations. Results show that resource usage and application response time can be significantly improved with short scheduling times.

1 Introduction

High-Performance Computing (HPC) resources, such as clusters and super-computers, are managed by a Resource Management System (RMS) which is responsible for multiplexing computing nodes among multiple users. Commonly, users get an exclusive access to nodes by requesting a static allocation of resources (i.e., a *rigid job* [1]), characterized by a node-count and a duration. Scheduling is mostly done using First-Come-First-Serve (FCFS) combined with backfilling rules such as EASY [2] or CBF [3]. Once the allocation has started, it cannot be grown nor shrunken.

As applications are becoming more complex, they exhibit **evolving** resource requirements, i.e., their resource requirements change during execution. For example, Adaptive Mesh Refinement (AMR) [4] simulations change the working set size as the mesh is refined/coarsened. Applications which feature both temporal and spatial compositions [5,6] may have non-constant resource requirements as components are activated/deactivated during certain phases of the computation. Unfortunately, using only static allocations, evolving applications are forced to allocate resources based on their maximum requirements, which may lead to an inefficient resource utilisation.

We define three types of applications. **Fully-predictably evolving** applications know their complete evolution at submittal. **Marginally-predictable** can predict changes in their resource requirements only some time in advance. **Non-predictably evolving** applications cannot predict their evolution at all.

---

* This work was supported by the French ANR COOP project, n° ANR-09-COSI-001.

M. Alexander et al. (Eds.): Euro-Par 2011 Workshops, Part I, LNCS 7155, pp. 117–127, 2012.

This paper does an initial study to find out whether it is valuable for RMSs to support evolving applications. It focuses on fully-predictably evolving applications. While we agree that such an idealized case might be of limited practical use, it is still interesting to be studied for two reasons. First, it paves the way to supporting marginally-predictably evolving applications. If little gain can be made with fully-predictably evolving applications, where the system has complete information, it is clear that it makes little sense to support marginally-predictable ones. Second, the developed algorithms might be extensible to the marginally- and non-predictable case. Each time an application submits a change to the RMS, the scheduling algorithm for fully-predictable applications could be re-run with updated information.

The contribution of this paper is threefold. First, it presents a novel scheduling problem: dealing with evolving applications. Second, it proposes a solution based on a list scheduling algorithm. Third, it evaluates the algorithm and shows that significant gains can be made. Therefore, we argue that RMSs should be extended to take into account evolving resource requirements.

The remaining of this article is structured as follows. Section 2 presents related work. Section 3 gives a few definitions and notations used throughout the paper and formally introduces the problem. Section 4 proposes algorithms to solve the stated problem, which are evaluated using simulations in Section 5. Finally, Section 6 concludes this paper and opens up perspectives.

2   Related Work

Increased interest has been devoted to dynamically allocate resources to applications, as it has been shown to improve resource utilization [7]. If the RMS can change an allocation during run-time, the job is called **malleable**. How to write malleable applications [8,9] and how to add RMS support for them [10,11] has been extensively studied.

However, supporting evolving applications is different from malleability. In the latter case, it is the RMS that decides when an application has to grow/shrink, whereas in the former case, it is the application that requests more/fewer resources, due to some internal constraints.

The Moab Workload Manager supports so-called "dynamic" jobs [12]: the RMS regularly queries each application what its current load is, then decides how resources are allocated. This feature can be used to dynamically allocate resources to interactive workloads, but is not suitable for batch workloads. For example, let us assume that there are two evolving applications in the system, each using half of the platform. If, at one point, both of them require additional resources, a dead-lock occurs, as each application is waiting for the requested resources. Instead, the two applications should be launched one after the other.

In the context of Cloud computing, resources may be acquired on-the-fly. Unfortunately, this abstraction is insufficient for large-scale deployments, such as those required by HPC applications, because "out-of-capacity" errors may be encountered [13]. Thus, the applications' requirements cannot be guaranteed.

3 Problem Statement

To accurately define the problem studied in this paper, let us first introduce some mathematical definitions and notations.

3.1 Definitions and Notations

Let an **evolution profile (EP)** be a sequence of **steps**, each step being characterized by a *duration* and a *node-count*. Formally, $ep = \{(d_1, n_1), (d_2, n_2), \ldots, (d_N, n_N)\}$, where N is the number of steps, d_i is the duration and n_i is the node-count during Step i.

An evolution profile can be used to represent three distinct concepts. First, a **resource EP** represents the resource occupation of a system. For example, if 10 nodes are busy for 1200 s, afterwards 20 nodes are busy for 3600 s, then $ep_{res} = \{(1200, 10), (3600, 20)\}$.

Second, a **requested EP** represents application resource requests. For example, $ep_{req} = \{(500, 5), (3600, 10)\}$ models a two-step application with the first step having a duration of 500 s and requiring 5 nodes and the second step having a duration of 3600 s and requiring 10 nodes. Non-evolving, rigid applications can be represented by an EP with a single step.

Third, a **scheduled EP** represents the number of nodes actually allocated to an application. For example, an allocation of nodes to the previous two-step application might be $ep_s = \{(2000, 0), (515, 5), (3600, 10)\}$. The application would first have to wait 2000 s to start its first step, then it would have to wait another 15 s ($= 515\,\text{s} - 500\,\text{s}$) to start its second step.

We define the expanded and delayed EPs of $ep = \{(d_1, n_1), \ldots, (d_N, n_N)\}$ as follows: $ep' = \{(d'_1, n_1), \ldots, (d'_N, n_N)\}$ is an **expanded EP** of ep, if $\forall i \in \{1, \ldots, N\}, d'_i > d_i$; $ep'' = \{(d_0, 0), (d_1, n_1), \ldots, (d_N, n_N)\}$ is a **delayed EP** of ep, if $d_0 > 0$.

For manipulating EPs, we use the following helper functions:

- $ep(t)$ returns the number of nodes at time coordinate t,
  i.e., $ep(t) = n_1$ for $t \in [0, d_1)$, $ep(t) = n_2$ for $t \in [d_1, d_1 + d_2)$, etc.
- $\max(ep, t_0, t_1)$ returns the maximum number of nodes between t_0 and t_1,
  i.e., $\max(ep, t_0, t_1) = \max_{t \in [t_0, t_1)} ep(t)$, and 0 if $t_0 = t_1$.
- $\text{loc}(ep, t_0, t_1)$ returns the end-time of the last step containing the maximum, restricted to $[t_0, t_1]$,
  i.e., $\text{loc}(ep, t_0, t_1) = t \Rightarrow \max(ep, t_0, t) = \max(ep, t_0, t_1) > \max(ep, t, t_1)$.
- $\text{delay}(ep, t_0)$ returns an evolution profile that is delayed by t_0.
- $ep_1 + ep_2$ is the sum of the two EPs, i.e., $\forall t, (ep_1 + ep_2)(t) = ep_1(t) + ep_2(t)$.

3.2 An RMS for Fully-Predictably Evolving Applications

To give a better understanding on the core problem we are interested in, this section briefly describes how fully-predictably evolving applications could be scheduled in practice.

Let us consider that the platform consists of a homogeneous cluster of n_{nodes} computing nodes, managed by a centralized RMS. Fully-predictably evolving applications are submitted to the system. Each application i expresses its resource requirements by submitting a requested EP[1] $ep^{(i)}$ ($ep^{(i)}(t) \leq n_{nodes}, \forall t$). The RMS is responsible for deciding when and which nodes are allocated to applications, so that their evolving resource requirements are met.

During run-time, each application maintains a session with the RMS. If from one step to another the application increases its resource requirements, it keeps the currently allocated nodes and has to *wait* for the RMS to allocate additional nodes to it. Note that, the RMS can *delay* the allocation of additional nodes, i.e., it is allowed to expand a step of an application. However, we asssume that during the wait period the application cannot make any useful computations: the resources currently allocated to the application are **wasted**. Therefore, **the scheduled EP** (the EP representing the resources effectively allocated to the application) must be equal to the requested EP, optionally **expanded** and/or **delayed**.

If from one step to another the node-count decreases, the application has to release some nodes to the system (the application may choose which ones). The application is assumed fully-predictable, therefore, it is not allowed to contract nor expand any of its steps at its own initiative.

A practical solution to the above problem would have to deal with several related issues. An RMS-Application protocol would have to be developed. Protocol violations should be detected and handled, e.g., an application which does not release nodes when it is required to should be killed. However, these issues are outside the scope of this paper.

Instead, this paper does a preliminary study on whether it is meaningful to develop such a system. For simplicity, we are interested in an offline scheduling algorithm that operates on the queued applications and decides how nodes are allocated to them. It can easily be shown that such an algorithm does not need to operate on node IDs: if for each application, a scheduled EP is found, such that the sum of all scheduled EPs never exceeds available resources, a valid mapping can be computed at run-time. The next section formally defines the problem.

3.3   Formal Problem Statement

Based on the previous definitions and notations, the problem can be stated as follows. Let n_{nodes} be the number of nodes in a homogeneous cluster. n_{apps} applications having their requested EPs $ep^{(i)}$ ($i = 1 \ldots n_{apps}$) queued in the system ($\forall i, \forall t, ep^{(i)}(t) \leq n_{nodes}$). The problem is to compute for each application i a scheduled EP $eps_s^{(i)}$, such that the following conditions are simultaneously met:

C1 $eps_s^{(i)}$ is equal to $ep^{(i)}$ or a delayed/expanded version of $ep^{(i)}$ (see above why);
C2 resources are not overflown ($\forall t, \sum_{i=1}^{n_{apps}} eps_s^{(i)}(t) \leq n_{nodes}$).

Application completion time and resource usage should be optimized.

---

[1] Note that this is in contrast to traditional parallel job scheduling, where resource requests only consist of a node-count and a wall-time duration.

4   Scheduling Fully-Predictably Evolving Applications

This section aims at solving the above problem in two stages. First, a list-scheduling algorithm is presented, which transforms requested EPs into scheduled EPs. It requires a `fit` function which operates on two EPs at a time. Second, several algorithms for computing a `fit` function are described.

4.1   An Algorithm for Offline Scheduling of Evolving Applications

Algorithm 1 is an offline scheduling algorithm that solves the stated problem. It starts by initializing ep_r, the resource EP, representing how resource occupation evolves over time, to the empty EP. Then, it considers each requested EP, potentially expanding and delaying it using a helper `fit` function. The resulting scheduled EP $ep_s^{(i)}$ is added to ep_r, effectively updating the resource occupation.

The `fit` function takes as input the number of nodes in the system n_{nodes}, a requested EP ep_{req} and a resource EP ep_{res} and returns a time coordinate t_s and ep_x an expanded version of ep_{req}, such that $\forall t, ep_{res}(t) + \text{delay}(ep_x, t_s)(t) \leq n_{nodes}$. A very simple `fit` implementation consists in delaying ep_{req} such that it starts after ep_{res}.

Throughout the whole algorithm, the condition $\forall t, ep_r(t) \leq n_{nodes}$ is guaranteed by the post-conditions of the `fit` function. Since at the end of the algorithm $ep_r = \sum_{i=1}^{n_{apps}} ep_s^{(i)}$, resources will not be overflown.

4.2   The `fit` Function

The core of the scheduling algorithm is the `fit` function, which expands a requested EP over a resource EP. It returns a scheduled EP, so that the sum of the resource EP and scheduled EP does not exceed available resources.

Because it can expand an EP, the `fit` function is an element of the efficiency of a schedule. On one hand, a step can be expanded so as to interleave applications, potentially reducing their response time. On the other hand, when a step is expanded, the application cannot perform useful computations, thus resources are wasted. Hence, there is a trade-off between the resource usage, the application's start time and its completion time.

In order to evaluate the impact of expansion, the proposed `fit` algorithm takes as parameter the **expand limit**. This parameter expresses how many times the duration of a step may be increased. For example, if the expand limit is 2, a step may not be expanded to more than twice its original duration. Having an expand limit of 1 means applications will not be expanded, while an infinite expand limit does not impose any limit on expansion.

Base `fit` Algorithm. Algorithm 2 aims at efficiently computing the `fit` function, while allowing to choose different expand limits. It operates recursively for each step in ep_{req} as follows:

Algorithm 1. Offline scheduling algorithm for evolving applications

---

Input: $ep^{(i)}, i = 1 \ldots n_{apps}$, requested EP of the application i,
    n_{nodes}, number of nodes in the system,
    $\mathtt{fit}(ep_{src}, ep_{dst}, n_{nodes}) \to (t_s, ep_s)$, a $\mathtt{fit}$ function
Output: $ep_s^{(i)}$, scheduled EP of application i

1   $ep_r \leftarrow$ empty EP ;
2   **for** $i = 1$ **to** n_{apps} **do**
3      $t_s^{(i)}, ep_x^{(i)} \leftarrow \mathtt{fit}(ep^{(i)}, ep_r, n_{nodes})$;
4      $ep_s^{(i)} \leftarrow \mathrm{delay}(ep_x^{(i)}, t_s^{(i)})$;
5      $ep_r \leftarrow ep_r + ep_s^{(i)}$;

Algorithm 2. Base $\mathtt{fit}$ Algorithm

Input: $ep_{req} = \left\{ \left(d_{req}^{(1)}, n_{req}^{(1)} \right), \ldots, \left(d_{req}^{(N_{req})}, n_{req}^{(N_{req})} \right) \right\}$, EP to expand,
    $ep_{res} = \left\{ \left(d_{res}^{(1)}, n_{res}^{(1)} \right), \ldots, \left(d_{res}^{(N_{res})}, n_{res}^{(N_{res})} \right) \right\}$, destination EP,
    n_{nodes} : number of nodes in the system,
    l : maximum allowed expansion ($l \geq 1$),
    i : index of step from ep_{req} to start with (initially 1),
    t_0 : first moment of time where ep_{req} is allowed to start (initially 0)
Output: ep_x : expanded ep_{req},
    t_s : time when ep_x starts **or** time when expansion failed

1   **if** $i > N_{req}$ **then**
2      $t_s \leftarrow t_0$; $ep_x \leftarrow$ empty EP ; **return**

3   $d \leftarrow d_{req}^{(i)}$; $n \leftarrow n_{req}^{(i)}$;   /* duration and node-count of current step */
4   $t_s \leftarrow t_0$;
5   **while** *True* **do**
6   **if** $n_{nodes} - \max(ep_{res}, t_s, t_s + d) < n$ **then**
7          $t_s \leftarrow \mathrm{loc}(ep_{res}, t_s, t_s + d)$; **continue**
8   **if** $i > 1$ **then**
9          $t_{eas} \leftarrow t_s - l \cdot d_{req}^{(i-1)}$ /* earliest allowed start of previous step */
10   **if** $t_{eas} > t_0 - d_{req}^{(i-1)}$ **then**
11              $t_s \leftarrow t_{eas}$; $ep_x \leftarrow \varnothing$; **return**

12   **else if** $n_{nodes} - \max(ep_{res}, t_0, t_s) < n_{req}^{(i-1)}$ **then**
13              $t_s \leftarrow \mathrm{loc}(ep_{res}, t_0, t_s)$; $ep_x \leftarrow \varnothing$; **return**

14      $t_s^{tail}, ep_x \leftarrow \mathtt{fit}(ep_{req}, ep_{res}, n_{nodes}, i + 1, t_s + d)$;
15   **if** $ep_x = \varnothing$ **then**
16          $t_s \leftarrow t_s^{tail}$; **continue**

17   **if** $i > 0$ **then** prepend $(t_s^{tail} - t_s, n)$ to ep_x ;
18   **else**
19   prepend (d, n) to ep_x ;
20          $t_s \leftarrow t_s^{tail} - d$;

21   **return**

---

1. find t_s, the earliest time coordinate when the current step can be placed, so that n_{nodes} is not exceeded (lines 4 – 7);
2. test if this placement forces an expansion on the previous step, which exceeds the expand limit (lines 8 – 11) or exceeds n_{nodes} (lines 12 – 13);
3. recursively try to place the next step in ep_{req}, starting at the completion time of the current step (line 14);
4. prepend the expanded version of the current step in ep_x (line 17). The first step is delayed (i.e., t_s is increased) instead of being expanded (line 20).

The recursion ends when all steps have been successfully placed (lines 1–2).

Placement of a step is first attempted at time coordinate t_0, which is 0 for the first step, or the value computed on line 14 for the other steps. After every failed operation (placement or expansion) the time coordinate t_s is increased so that the same failure does not repeat:

– if placement failed, jump to the time after the encountered maximum (line 7);
– if expansion failed due to the expand limit, jump to the first time which avoids excessive expansion (computed on line 11, used on line 16).
– if expansion failed due to insufficient resources, jump to the time after the encountered maximum (computed on line 13, used on line 16);

Since each step, except the first, is individually placed at the earliest possible time coordinate and the first step is placed so that the other steps are not delayed, the algorithm guarantees that the application has the earliest possible completion time. However, resource usage is not guaranteed to be optimal.

Post-processing Optimization (Compacting). In order to reduce resource waste, while maintaining the guarantee that the application completes as early as possible, a **compacting** post-processing phase can be applied. After a first solution is found by the base `fit` algorithm, the expanded EP goes through a compacting phase: the last step of the applications is placed so that it ends at the completion time found by the base algorithm. Then, the other steps are placed from right (last) to left (first), similarly to the base algorithm. In the worst case, no compacting occurs and the same EP is returned after the compacting phase.

The base `fit` algorithm with compacting first optimizes completion time then start time (it is optimal from expansion point-of-view), but because it acts in a greedy way, it might expand steps with high node-count, so it is not always optimal for resource waste.

4.3   Discussions

This section has presented a solution to the problem stated in Section 3.3. The presented strategies attempt to minimize both completion time and resource waste. However, these strategies treat applications in a pre-determined order and do not attempt to do a global optimization. This allows the algorithm to be easier to adapt to an online context in future work for two reasons. First, list scheduling algorithms are known to be fast, which is required in a scalable RMS implementation. Second, since the algorithms treat application in-order, starvation cannot occur.

5 Evaluation

This section evaluates the benefits and drawbacks of taking into account evolving resource requirements of applications. It is based on a series of experiments done with a home made simulator developed in Python. The experiments are first described, then the results are analyzed.

5.1 Description of Experiments

The experiments compare two kinds of scheduling algorithms: `rigid`, which does not take into account evolution, and variations of Algorithm 1. Applications are seen by the `rigid` algorithm as non-evolving: the requested node-cound is the maximum node-count of all steps and the duration is the sum of the durations of all steps. Then, `rigid` schedules the resulting jobs in a CBF-like manner.

Five versions of Algorithm 1 are considered to evaluate the impact of its options: base fit with no expansion (`noX`), base fit with expand limit of 2 without compacting (`2X`) and with compacting (`2X+c`), base fit with infinite expansion without compacting (`infX`) and with compacting (`infX+c`).

Two kinds of metrics are measured: system-centric and user-centric. The five system-centric metrics considered are: (1) *resource waste*, the resource area (nodes×duration, expressed as percent of total resources), which has been allocated to applications, but has not been used to make computations (see Section 3.2); (2) *resource utilisation*, the resource area that has been allocated to applications; (3) *effective resource utilisation*, the resource area (expressed as percent of total resources) that has been effectively used for computations; (4) *makespan*, the maximum of the completion times; (5) *schedule time*, the computation time taken by a scheduling algorithm to schedule one test on a laptop with an Intel®Core™2 Duo processor running at 2.53 GHz.

The five user-centric metrics considered are: (1) per-test average application completion time (`Avg. ACT`); (2) per-test average application waiting time (`Avg. AWT`); (3) the number of expanded applications (`num. expanded`) as a percentage of the total number of applications in a test; (4) by how much was an application expanded (`App Expansion`) as a percentage of its initial total duration; (5) per-application `waste` as a percentage of resources allocated to the application.

As we are not aware of any public archive of evolving application workloads, we created synthetic test-cases. A test case is made of a uniform random choice of the number of applications, their number of steps, as well as the duration and requested node-count of each step. We tried various combinations that gave similar results. Table 1 and 2 respectively present the results for the system- and user-centric metrics of an experiment made of 1000 tests. The number of applications per test is within $[15, 20]$, the number of steps within $[1, 10]$, a step duration within $[500, 3600]$ and the node-count per step within $[1, 75]$.

Table 1. Comparison of Scheduling Algorithms (System-centric Metrics)

Name	Waste (%)			Utilisation (relative)			Eff. Util. (%)			Makespan (relative)			Sch. Time (ms)		
	min	avg	max	min	avg	max	min	avg	max	min	avg	max	min	avg	max
rigid	43	70	116	1	1	1	30	40	51	1	1	1	4.64	6.2	9.41
noX	0	0	0	.46	.58	.69	49	61	73	.49	.65	.82	11.4	24.7	55.8
2X	0	2	11	.47	.60	.71	50	63	75	.48	.64	.82	11.4	24.4	45.4
2X+c	0	ϵ	4	.46	.59	.70	53	63	75	.48	.63	.82	17.1	36.7	88.6
infX	0	7	22	.49	.63	.78	52	64	73	.49	.63	.78	11.4	23.4	49.2
infX+c	0	1	11	.46	.59	.71	55	64	74	.47	.62	.78	17.6	36	124

Table 2. Comparison of Scheduling Algorithms (User-centric Metrics)

Name	Avg. ACT (relative)			Avg. AWT (relative)			Num. expanded (%)			App expansion (%)			Per-app. waste (%)		
	min	avg	max	min	avg	max	min	avg	max	min	avg	max	min	avg	max
rigid	1	1	1	1	1	1	0	0	0	0	0	0	0	67	681
noX	.42	.61	.84	.36	.55	.81	0	0	0	0	0	0	0	0	0
2X	.45	.61	.84	.36	.54	.80	0	22	56	0	4	76	0	2	75
2X+c	.44	.60	.84	.37	.54	.81	0	7	40	0	ϵ	60	0	ϵ	41
infX	.43	.62	.81	.27	.53	.76	0	26	62	0	19	884	0	6	360
infX+c	.44	.60	.81	.35	.53	.76	0	13	47	0	5	1354	0	1	119

5.2 Analysis

Administrator's Perspective rigid is outperformed by all other strategies. They improve effective resource utilisation, reduce makespan and drastically reduce resource waste within reasonable scheduling time. Compared to rigid, all algorithms reduce resource utilization. We consider this to be a desired effect, as it means that, instead of allocating computing nodes to applications which do not effectively use them, these nodes are release to the system. The RMS could, for example, shut these nodes down to save energy.

There is a trade-off between resource waste and makespan (especially when looking at maximum values). However makespan differs less between algorithms than waste. If maintaining resources is expensive, an administrator may choose the noX algorithm, whereas to favour throughput, she would choose 2X+c.

User's Perspective. When compared to rigid, the proposed algorithms always improve both per-application resource waste and average completion time. When looking at maximum values, the trade-off between expansion / waste vs. completion time is again highlighted. Algorithms which favor stretching (infX, infX+c) reduce average waiting time, but not necessarily average completion time.

The results show that waste is not equally split among applications, instead, few applications are expanded a lot. Since most cluster / grid systems are subject to accounting (i.e., in a way, users pay for the resources that are allocated to them), using the infX and infX+c algorithm (which do not guarantee an upper bound on the waste) should be avoided. Regarding algorithms which limit expansion, the benefits of using 2X+c instead of noX are small, at the expense of significant per-application resource waste. Therefore, users might prefer not to expand their applications at all.

Global Perspective. From both perspectives, expanding applications has limited benefit. Therefore, the noX algorithm seems to be the best choice. Taking into account evolving requirements of applications enables improvement of all metrics compared to an algorithm that does not take evolvement into consideration.

6 Conclusions

Some applications, such as adaptive mesh refinement simulations, can exhibit evolving resource requirements. As it may be difficult to obtain accurate evolvement information, this paper studied whether this effort would be worthwhile in term of system and user perspectives. The paper has presented the problem of scheduling fully-predictable evolving applications, for which it has proposed an offline scheduling algorithm, with various options. Experiments show that taking into account resource requirement evolvement leads to improvements in all measured metrics, such as resource utilization and completion time. However, the considered expansion strategies do not appear valuable.

Future work can be divided into two directions. First, the algorithm has to be adapted to online scheduling. Second, as real applications are not fully-predictable, this assumption has to be changed and the resulting problem needs to be studied.

References

1. Feitelson, D.G., Rudolph, L., Schwiegelshohn, U.: Parallel Job Scheduling — A Status Report. In: Feitelson, D.G., Rudolph, L., Schwiegelshohn, U. (eds.) JSSPP 2004. LNCS, vol. 3277, pp. 1–16. Springer, Heidelberg (2005)
2. Lifka, D.: The ANL/IBM SP Scheduling System. In: Feitelson, D.G., Rudolph, L. (eds.) JSSPP 1995. LNCS, vol. 949, pp. 295–303. Springer, Heidelberg (1995)
3. Mu'alem, A.W., Feitelson, D.G.: Utilization, predictability, workloads, and user runtime estimates in scheduling the IBM SP2 with backfilling. TPDS 12(6) (2001)
4. Plewa, T., Linde, T., Weirs, V.G. (eds.): Adaptive Mesh Refinement – Theory and Applications. Springer (2003)
5. Bouziane, H.L., Pérez, C., Priol, T.: A Software Component Model with Spatial and Temporal Compositions for Grid Infrastructures. In: Luque, E., Margalef, T., Benítez, D. (eds.) Euro-Par 2008. LNCS, vol. 5168, pp. 698–708. Springer, Heidelberg (2008)
6. Ribes, A., Caremoli, C.: Salome platform component model for numerical simulation. COMPSAC 2, 553–564 (2007)

7. Hungershofer, J.: On the combined scheduling of malleable and rigid jobs. In: SBAC-PAD (2004)
8. Buisson, J., Sonmez, O., Mohamed, H., et al.: Scheduling malleable applications in multicluster systems. Technical Report TR-0092, CoreGRID (2007)
9. El Maghraoui, K., Desell, T.J., Szymanski, B.K., Varela, C.A.: Dynamic malleability in iterative MPI applications. In: CCGRID (2007)
10. Cera, M.C., Georgiou, Y., Richard, O., Maillard, N., Navaux, P.O.A.: Supporting MPI malleable applications upon the OAR resource manager. In: COLIBRI (2009)
11. Buisson, J., Sonmez, O., Mohamed, H., et al.: Scheduling malleable applications in multicluster systems. Technical Report TR-0092, CoreGRID (2007)
12. Adaptive Computing Enterprises, Inc.: Moab workload manager administrator guide, version 6.0.2, http://www.adaptivecomputing.com/resources/docs/mwm
13. Cycles, C.: Lessons learned building a 4096-core cloud HPC supercomputer, http://blog.cyclecomputing.com/2011/03/cyclecloud-4096-core-cluster.html

Model Checking Support for Conflict Resolution in Multiple Non-functional Concern Management

Marco Danelutto[1], P. Kilpatrick[2], C. Montangero[1], and L. Semini[1]

[1] Dept. Computer Science, University of Pisa
[2] Dept. Computer Science, Queen's University Belfast

Abstract. When implementing autonomic management of multiple non-functional concerns a trade-off must be found between the ability to develop independently management of the individual concerns (following the separation of concerns principle) and the detection and resolution of conflicts that may arise when combining the independently developed management code. Here we discuss strategies to establish this trade-off and introduce a model checking based methodology aimed at simplifying the discovery and handling of conflicts arising from deployment–within the same parallel application–of independently developed management policies. Preliminary results are shown demonstrating the feasibility of the approach.

Keywords: Autonomic managers, model checking, non-functional concerns, structured parallel computations.

1 Introduction

The past ten years have seen a major shift in the nature of distributed and parallel computing systems. While traditionally systems were relatively unchanged throughout their lifetime and existed in more or less stable environments, the pervasive nature of many modern systems and their composition from grid or cloud services mean that often they need the capability to adapt automatically to changes in their environment and/or changes to their constituent services. This has relatively little impact on the core functionality, which tends to lend itself to precise definition, but has significant implications for non-functional aspects such as performance, security, etc. These aspects may not be so clearly defined and often the code to handle them is interwoven with the core functionality. In previous work we have proposed a means of isolating such code by introducing, in the notion of behavioural skeleton, an amalgam of algorithmic skeleton (parallel pattern) – for example, farm, pipeline – together with one or more managers of non-functional concerns (such as performance, power usage, security). A manager monitors the performance of its associated skeleton with respect to a particular concern and has the capacity to initiate changes to the skeleton behaviour with respect to that concern. However, when bringing together managers of differing concerns, these managers may not sit comfortably together and indeed may be in conflict. For example,

M. Alexander et al. (Eds.): Euro-Par 2011 Workshops, Part I, LNCS 7155, pp. 128–138, 2012.

it is conceivable that a power manager may be prompting removal of a worker from a task farm (to reduce power consumption) while a performance manager is (more or less) simultaneously indicating that a worker be added to boost performance. In earlier work [2] we proposed a protocol for coordinating the activities of managers to deal with such conflicts and showed how this protocol might operate in practice [3]. There the conflicts were identified simply by human inspection. Here we extend that work by using a model checking approach to identify potential conflicts and generate a trace showing the origin of the conflict. This trace allows us to modify the design to avoid the possibility of conflict or to deal with such conflict dynamically.

2   Rule Based Management

In [1] we introduced the concept of a behavioural skeleton comprising an algorithmic skeleton (parallel pattern), e.g., farm, pipe, etc. *and* an autonomic manager taking care of non-functional aspects of the computation, such as performance, security, etc. The manager has the capacity to modify the behaviour of the associated skeleton by prompting a change to the structure or operation of the skeleton. It runs a classic MAPE loop: it *M*onitors the behaviour of the pattern with respect to a given non-functional concern (e.g., throughput for performance); *A*nalyses the monitored values to determine if the skeleton is operating satisfactorily; if adjustment is necessary it *P*lans for a modification; and finally *E*xecutes the modification. The MAPE loop then recurs. The MAPE cycle may in practice be implemented as a set of *pre-condition*→*action* rules [3].

From a separation of concerns viewpoint it is best if autonomic management can be developed as a set of separate managers, each handling a single concern. Each manager may thus be developed by an expert in the concern at hand. The challenge then lies in coordinating the activities of these managers so that cooperation rather than conflict within a given MAPE cycle is achieved. To identify conflicts it is necessary to have a means of cataloguing the structural or operational changes to a skeleton that may be initiated by a manager. For this it is useful to have the concept of an *application graph* [2] whose nodes represent parallel/distributed activities and whose arcs represent communications/synchronizations among these activities (Fig. 1). Each node and arc can be labelled with metadata specifying non-functional properties. To identify conflicts one must first identify actions on the application graph which are clearly in opposition (such as add-worker/remove-worker) and determine if there is a possible evolution of the system which would lead to two such actions being invoked in the same MAPE cycle. It is in this latter activity that model checking proves beneficial, as will be seen in section 4. First we discuss more generally strategies for managing non-functional concerns in distributed systems.

3   Multiple Non-functional Concern Management

When dealing with multiple non-functional concerns within a parallel application, conflicts may arise when two or more management policies demand changes

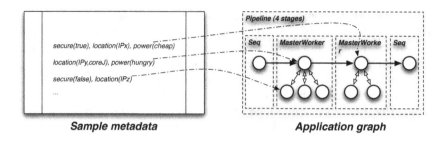

Fig. 1. Sample Application Graph

to the application graph which are incompatible, as discussed above. Here we will describe three approaches to resolution of such conflicts. These vary in the degree of coordination required and in the timing of this coordination. In principle, autonomic non-functional concern management of parallel or distributed computations should be designed by experts in parallel computing *and* in the single non-functional concern at hand to ensure the maximum impact of the management. The approaches presented differ in how they attempt to resolve the tension that exists between separation of concerns at the development stage and the need to bring these concerns together in a unified running system.

3.1 Fully Coordinated Co-design

In the *fully coordinated design* approach we sacrifice separation of concerns for ease of consolidation. A single expert (or a single team of experts) is in charge of developing management policies for all the non-functional concerns considered. As a result, the management policies may be coordinated from the beginning and conflict may be *prevented by design*.

Situations raising conflicts are detected by the single (team of) expert(s) and rules in the managers are (re)programmed so that their combined effect no longer raises conflicts. For example, consider the case where performance security and power consumption are the non-functional concerns to be managed. When programming rules to increase the program throughput by augmenting the parallelism degree, both recruitment of non power-hungry processing resources and the deployment of secure communication mechanisms will be considered. As a result of consideration of both concerns, a simple rule stating that if throughput is low[1] the parallelism degree should be increased:

R1   performance low $\rightarrow$ recruit resource; deploy code; link resource to par. computation;

will be replaced by the following pair of rules:

R1a   performance low **and** R is available and low power resource **and** secure(R) $\rightarrow$ recruit(R); deploy code; link R to parallel computation;
R1b   performance low **and** R is available and low power resource **and** unsecure(R) $\rightarrow$ recruit(R); deploy secure code; link R to parallel computation;

merging knowledge of performance, security and power management concerns.

---

[1] e.g. with respect to some user agreed SLA or *contract*.

3.2 Coordinated Decision Commitment

In the *coordinated decision commitment* approach, emphasis is placed on separation of concerns and an attempt is made to build into the rules for each separate concern the ability to identify and resolve conflicts *at runtime*. Here distinct (teams of) experts design the policies for the autonomic management of distinct non-functional concerns. However, the policies are designed in such a way that they can also work when policies for the management of other concerns are concurrently applied in the same context. In a sense, a coordinated commitment of independently taken decisions is implemented – hence the name.

To achieve this coordination a two-phase distributed agreement protocol such as that proposed in [2] may be adopted. In this case, when according to the policies managing concern C_i a decision d_j is to be taken, a *consensus* is sought from managers of all other concerns different from C_i. The consensus is sought on the new application graph resulting from the implementation of decision d_j. If all the other managers agree on the feasibility of the new graph, the decision is taken. If at least one of the other managers (e.g. the one managing concern C_k) indicates that the decision would eventually lead to an unfeasible application graph – according to the concern managed, C_k – then the decision is aborted and the priority of the rules firing the decision is lowered. The last, and more interesting, case is where all managers agree on the feasibility of the new application graph, but some request that an additional feature be taken into account when implementing the decision d_j. In this case the decision is committed by the manager managing concern C_i using an alternative implementation plan which ensures the additional requirements.

If we consider the rule R1 discussed in Sec. 3.1 leading to an increase of the current parallelism degree, in this case we will eventually arrive at the set of rules:

R1.1 performance low **and** R is available $\rightarrow$ ask consensus on recruitment of resource R to other managers

R1.2 all managers grant unconditional consensus $\rightarrow$ recruit resource R; deploy code; link resource to parallel computation

R1.3 one manager negates consensus $\rightarrow$ abort decision; lower priority for R1.1

R1.4 all managers grant consensus provided properties $P_1, \ldots, P_k$ are ensured $\rightarrow$ change original decision plan A' to A'' such that A'' ensures P_1 to P_k; commit decision through plan A''

In this case, the knowledge needed to implement a different decision plan comes in part from the knowledge of the concern of the manager using these rules and in part from the concerns managed by autonomic managers requiring properties P_i. If consensus is granted, provided that $P_0 = $ **security** is ensured, then the original plan:

recruit(R); deploy code; link R to parallel computation;

will be substituted by the new plan:

recruit(R); deploy secure code; link R to parallel computation;

With this approach the separation of concerns principle is compromised somewhat by the need for the individual rule systems to be designed so as to be able to accommodate future interactions with rule systems pertaining to other concerns. Insofar as the interactions are described in terms of modifications to the application graph, this can reasonably be achieved, although the fact that the graph contains metadata relating to various concerns (and not just structure) means that full separation is not possible.

3.3   *Ex Post* Independent Manager Coordination

Coordinated commitment may be regarded as an *interpretive* approach to coordination. When we deploy more than a single manager in the same application, we pre-configure a number of conflict situations that may eventually arise (managers ask consensus) and pre-configure modified decision commitment plans taking care of these conflicts.

The consensus building phase takes time, however. Even in the case of no conflicts, communications must be performed between the manager taking the decision and those checking the decision is safe w.r.t. their own policies. This means of implementing management is thus a *reactive* process, and the reaction time of the system critically impacts the efficiency of the whole management process. Thus any delay should be reduced as much as possible.

As is usual in computer science, moving from interpreters to compilers improves performance.

In the third approach, we retain the idea of coordinated decision making but implement it through the *compilation* of a modified set of management rules *before* the system is actually run. In particular, we perform the following steps:

- We analyze the independently developed sets of rules, looking for those rules which, if fireable at the same time, may lead to conflicting actions. The key point here is again to identify the conflicting actions in terms of the application graph.
- Then we derive a new set of rules possibly including some (modified version) of the initial set of rules from the different managers together with new rules managing the conflict situations.

Note that the knowledge required to determine this modified set of rules is roughly the same as that needed to implement the coordinated decision commitment approach.

For example, consider a performance manager having a rule that increases the parallelism degree when low throughput is experienced ($R_{pd-increase}$), and a power manager with a rule stating that "power hungry" resources must be dismissed when too much power is consumed by the computation ($R_{pw-decrease}$). In this case a conflict arises if the performance manager wants to increase the parallelism degree and the power manager wants to dismiss a resource. Adopting an "ex post coordination" approach, we can look at the condition of the rules used in the conflict situation and implement a new rule, with a higher priority w.r.t. to both $R_{pd-increase}$ and $R_{pw-decrease}$, stating that if performance is low and power consumption high we should increase parallelism degree by selecting low consumption resources or by releasing high consumption resources and replacing them with a larger number of low consumption resources.

4   Model Checking for Conflict Resolution

The ability to develop independent managers and modify them to accomplish coordinated management of multiple concerns looks attractive in that it enforces modular design and reuse as well as allowing better use of domain specific knowledge relative to different non-functional concerns.

However, combining a set of single-concern managers in both coordinated decision commitment and ex post independent manager coordination may be difficult to achieve unless the developer is an expert in *all* of the non-functional concerns to be coordinated. Even then, the sheer number of evolution paths of the combined managers may make it extremely difficult for the human to identify possible conflict.

Model checking tools may, however, provide useful support. When considering a complex set of management rules, such as those describing a number of different non-functional concern managers, an approach such as that proposed in [9] can be used. There, "conflicts" in rule based management systems can be *detected* using a model checker after identifying conflicting atomic actions.

Here we modify that methodology to support conflict detection in rules describing independently developed managers. As the "ex post" approach looks the more promising, we consider the use of a model checker to support compilation of a coordinated set of rules from a set of independently developed rules. We propose a methodology in which:

- Independent experts design policies for distinct non-functional concerns. We assume the rules are expressed using APPEL [10]. This allows better structuring of the manager rules. In particular, we use APPEL triggers to start rule evaluation. In previous work, we used JBoss rule syntax to express management rules. In that case rules were tested cyclically for fireability. The period of the cycle *de facto* determined the MAPE loop efficiency, as "too slow" loops react poorly and "too fast" loops may lead to overly rapid decisions. By using the concept of APPEL triggers to start rule evaluation, we avoid problems related to MAPE loop polling.
- A set of conflicting actions is defined, such that a pair of actions a_i, a_j are in the set *iff* action a_i "undoes" action a_j and vice versa. As actual atomic actions only affect the application graph, this step does not require any specific knowledge of non-functional concerns.
- A formal model of the system is derived, which is fed to a model checker. The model is generated following the approach outlined in [9]. APPEL policies are automatically mapped to a UMC specification, i.e. the textual description of a UML state machine, in the UMC input format. The mapping is based on the APPEL formal semantics, as given in [7].

- The model checker is used to check formulas stating that conflicting actions may coincide, that is occur in the same MAPE loop iteration. Traces of actions leading to conflicts are produced.
- Knowledge obtained from the traces is used to develop the additional rules to be included in the rule system to handle conflicts.[2]

5   Preliminary Results

To evaluate the feasibility of the proposed approach, we ran experiments using the model checker UMC [11, 8]. UMC is an on-the-fly analysis framework which allows the user to explore interactively the UML state machine, to visualize abstract behavioural slices of it and to perform local model checking of UCTL formulae. UCTL is an action- and state-based branching-time temporal logic [5]. Its syntax thus allows one to specify the properties that a state should satisfy and to combine these basic predicates with advanced temporal operators dealing with the actions performed.

Layouni et al. in [6] experimented with the use of the model checker Alloy [4] to support policy conflict resolution. In view of its current widespread use in industrial practice, we considered UML a better candidate: it has good tool support, and, besides supporting conflict detection, will also help in understanding and resolving them.

The results reported here were obtained using a prototype translator to automate the translation from the APPEL rules to an equivalent UMC specification, dubbed *Appel2UMC*, and written in OCaml. *Appel2UMC* is structured as a syntax definition module, a *Compiler*, and an *Unparser*. The *Compiler* translates APPEL to UMC, at the abstract syntax level, and the *Unparser* generates the textual version needed by the model checker. These core modules depend on a further one that defines the domain dependent features (triggers, conditions and actions), thus ensuring adaptability of the tool. At the moment, the syntax is about 100 lines, the core modules are slightly over 500 lines, and the domain dependent part less than 80 lines, and translation times are not an issue.

In our experiment we considered merging two independently developed managers taking care respectively of performance and power management concerns (part of these rules were introduced in [2]). The performance manager has a rule stating that in case of poor throughput the parallelism degree may be increased. The power manager has a rule stating that in case of too high power consumption the parallelism degree may be decreased. Both managers operate on the application graph executing actions from a set including "LinkWorker" and "UnLinkWorker", including or removing a worker node in/from the current computation, respectively. These link/unlink actions are marked as "atomic conflict" as they clearly negate one another.

---

[2] At the moment conflicts are identified by the model checker, but then the actions needed to resolve the situation (i.e. the modifications to the manager rules) are performed by humans. Ideally this part would also be executed automatically.

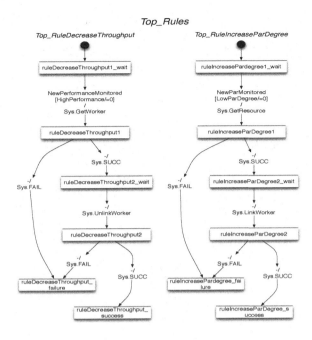

Fig. 2. Model checker output: UML parallel state machine

The result of the compilation of the parallel composition of the power and performance manager rules is the UML parallel state machine in Figure 2, whose graphical representation is produced by the UMC framework. In this simple example it is clear, by inspection, that the conflict will arise. To detect it automatically, however, we load the model into the model checker, together with the formalization in UCTL of the relevant question: may a conflict occur in one MAPE cycle? In terms of traces: is there no trace among those generated by the automaton, which includes both link and unlink? Formally:

(not EF EX{LinkWorker} EF{UnlinkWorker} true) & (not EF EX{UnlinkWorker} EF{LinkWorker} true)

The question has to be formulated in this way, since UMC translates the input model into a standard finite state machine, resolving parallelism with interleaving: "parallel" actions appear in sequence, in different orders, in several traces. The traces of the automaton are shown in Figure 3.

The answer given by the model checker is "false" and the explanation outlines the traces leading to the situation where the formula is demonstrated false. To solve the conflict, the user can then also reason on the UML state machine, which is more expressive than the graph of the traces, including the names of the states and complete labelling of the transitions.

According to the methodology outlined in Sec. 4 we are able to collect the knowledge necessary to produce a modified set of rules that avoid the conflict from the traces exposed by the model checker. From the traces in Fig. 3 we can evince that:

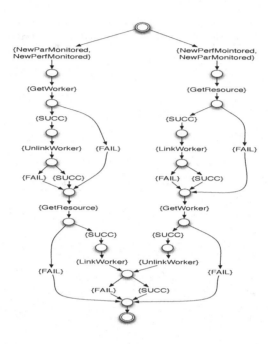

Fig. 3. Model checker output: Traces

- the situation leading to the conflicting actions is determined by the presence of both triggers firing the power manager "reduce power usage" and the performance "increase parallelism degree" rules. This is evidenced by the triggers at the beginning of the two traces.
- both paths leading to the conflict (relative to different interleavings of the same actions) include the actions in the "reduce power usage" and the "increase parallelism degree" rules.

Based on this knowledge, we can conclude that handling of the detected conflict may be achieved by a high priority rule (or a set of rules):

- that includes both triggers[3]; and
- whose action part consists in a plan whose effect is an increase of the parallelism degree with reduced power consumption.

Alternatively, we may solve the conflict by assigning a priority to one of the conflicting rules, in such a way that only the higher priority rule is executed.

This is a very simple case. We modelled just two rules and so we get a very compact model and useful "explanations" in terms of traces. In fact, the number of states generated in the UMC model is below one hundred and the response time of the model checker is of the order of a fraction of a second.

---

[3] possibly a new trigger logically corresponding to the conjunction of the two triggers, as APPEL does not support the conjunction of triggers but only trigger disjunction.

However, we also made more realistic experiments with a set of up to 6 rules with complex action parts.

Fig. 4 shows times needed to execute the model checker with different rules sets and queries (the AG(true) query gives the upper bound in execution times, as it requires the model checker to visit all possible paths in the model). This confirmed to us that the approach is feasible in more realistic situations. We do not show sample

Rules#	∃conflict	AG(true)
2	0.03	0.02
4	0.05	0.12
6	0.06	0.25

Fig. 4. Execution times (in seconds) with different sets of rules and queries

output from the model checker in this case, as the graphs are significantly larger and do not fit easily on a page.

6 Future Work and Conclusions

This paper builds on previous results in the field of multiple non-functional concern management. To the best of our knowledge, the classification of the possible approaches for autonomic management of multiple non-functional concerns presented in Sec. 3 is original. The proposal for using model checking to support merging of independently developed autonomic managers is also new.

In previous work [9] some of the authors presented a compositional, but manual, translation from APPEL to UML and then to UMC. In this paper we automate the translation and introduce a shortcut for those situations where starting from a UML graphical presentation of the rules is not a requirement. Moreover, if we wish to build a transformer from a UML state machine, as generated by a design environment, to a checkable UMC model, we can reuse at least the *Unparser*.

We are currently improving the methodology outlined in this paper. In particular, we are performing more experiments with the model checker to refine the technique (both in the design of the queries and in the interpretation of the analysis) and we are using more realistic rule sets to check that the approach remains feasible.

Acknowledgements. We thank Franco Mazzanti for his support with the model checker. This work is partially supported by Italian PRIN project "SOFT".

References

[1] Aldinucci, M., Campa, S., Danelutto, M., Dazzi, P., Kilpatrick, P., Laforenza, D., Tonelletto, N.: Behavioural skeletons for component autonomic management on grids. In: Making Grids Work, CoreGRID, Chapter Component Programming Models, pp. 3–16. Springer (August 2008)

[2] Aldinucci, M., Danelutto, M., Kilpatrick, P.: Autonomic managenemt of multiple non-functional concerns in behavioural skeletons. In: Grids, P2P and Services Computing (Proc. of the CoreGRID Symposium 2009), CoreGRID, pp. 89–103. Springer, Delft (2010)

[3] Aldinucci, M., Danelutto, M., Kilpatrick, P., Xhagjika, V.: LIBERO: A Framework for Autonomic Management of Multiple Non-functional Concerns. In: Guarracino, M.R., Vivien, F., Träff, J.L., Cannatoro, M., Danelutto, M., Hast, A., Perla, F., Knüpfer, A., Di Martino, B., Alexander, M. (eds.) Euro-Par-Workshop 2010. LNCS, vol. 6586, pp. 237–245. Springer, Heidelberg (2011)

[4] Alloy Community, http://alloy.mit.edu/community/

[5] ter Beek, M.H., Fantechi, A., Gnesi, S., Mazzanti, F.: An Action/State-Based Model-Checking Approach for the Analysis of Communication Protocols for Service-Oriented Applications. In: Leue, S., Merino, P. (eds.) FMICS 2007. LNCS, vol. 4916, pp. 133–148. Springer, Heidelberg (2008)

[6] Layouni, A., Logrippo, L., Turner, K.: Conflict Detection in Call Control using First-Order Logic Model Checking. In: Proceedings International Conference on Feature Interactions in Software and Communication Systems (ICFI 2007), pp. 66–82. IOS Press (2007)

[7] Montangero, C., Reiff-Marganiec, S., Semini, L.: Logic-based Conflict Detection for Distributed Policies. Fundamenta Informaticae 89(4), 511–538 (2008)

[8] ter Beek, M.H., Fantechi, A., Gnesi, S., Mazzanti, F.: A state/event-based model-checking approach for the analysis of abstract system properties. Science of Computer Programming 76, 119–135 (2011)

[9] ter Beek, M.H., Gnesi, S., Montangero, C., Semini, L.: Detecting policy conflicts by model checking uml state machines. In: ICFI 2009, pp. 59–74 (2009)

[10] Turner, K.J., Reiff-Marganiec, S., Blair, L., Campbell, G.A., Wang, F.: APPEL: An Adaptable and Programmable Policy Environment and Language. Technical Report CSM-161, Univ. of Stirling (2011), http://www.cs.stir.ac.uk/~kjt/techreps/pdf/TR161.pdf

[11] UMC v3.7, http://fmt.isti.cnr.it/umc

Consistent Rollback Protocols
for Autonomic ASSISTANT Applications

Carlo Bertolli[1], Gabriele Mencagli[2], and Marco Vanneschi[2]

[1] Department of Computing, Imperial College London 180 Queens Gate, London,
SW7 2AZ, UK
`c.bertolli@imperial.ac.uk`
[2] Department of Computer Science, University of Pisa Largo B. Pontecorvo 3,
I-56127, Pisa, Italy
`{mencagli,vannesch}@di.unipi.it`

Abstract. Nowadays, a central issue for applications executed on heterogeneous distributed platforms is represented by assuring that certain
performance and reliability parameters are respected throughout the system execution. A typical solution is based on supporting application components with adaptation strategies, able to select at run-time the better
component version to execute. It is worth noting that the efficacy of a reconfiguration may depend on the time spent in applying it: in fact, albeit
a reconfiguration may lead to a better steady-state behavior, its application could induce a transient violation of a QoS constraint. In this paper
we will show how consistent reconfiguration protocols can be derived for
stream-based ASSISTANT applications, and we will characterize their
costs in terms of proper performance models.

1 Introduction

Today distributed platforms include heterogeneous sets of parallel architectures,
such as clusters (e.g. Roadrunner), large shared-memory platforms (e.g. SGI
Altix) and smaller ones, as off-the-shelf multi-core components also integrated
into mobile devices. Examples of applications that enjoy such heterogeneity are
Emergency and Risk Management, Intelligent Transportation and Environmental Sustainability. Common features are the presence of computationally demanding components (e.g. emergency forecasting models), which are constrained
by the necessity of providing results under a certain *Quality of Service* (QoS).
To assure that the QoS is respected, applications must be *autonomic*, in the
sense that their components must apply proper adaptation and fault-tolerance
strategies.

A reconfiguration can dynamically modify some implementation aspects of a
component, such as its parallelism degree. In some cases, when components are
provided in multiple alternative versions, a reconfiguration can also dynamically
select the best version to be executed. Multiple versions can be provided in order
to exploit in the best way as possible different architectures on which the computation may be currently deployed and executed. For this reason programming

M. Alexander et al. (Eds.): Euro-Par 2011 Workshops, Part I, LNCS 7155, pp. 139–148, 2012.

models for autonomic applications include a *functional logic*, which is in charge of performing the computation, and a *control logic* (or manager), aimed at assuring the required QoS levels in the face of time-varying execution conditions. In this paper we do not focus on the policy under which a reconfiguration is taken. Rather we are interested in how reconfigurations are implemented, and their impact on the application performance.

The complexity of a reconfiguration protocol depends on the way in which the application semantics (*computation consistency*) is preserved during the reconfiguration itself. Several research works, especially in the Grid computing area, have studied consistent reconfiguration protocols for general parallel applications (e.g. MPI computations), by applying coarse-grained protocols [1] involving the whole set of functional logic processes, and for specific programming models (e.g. Divide-and-Conquer applications), in which reconfigurations are applied at task granularity [2] level. In many cases we may experience a strong reconfiguration overhead, that could avoid the component to respect the required QoS. In other words, even if a reconfiguration leads to a better situation from a performance standpoint, the cost of a reconfiguration protocol should be taken into account if we want to develop effective adaptation models.

In this paper we show how to derive consistent reconfiguration protocols, focusing on the specific case of dynamic version selection. Our approach is characterized by performance models that can be used to dynamically predict the reconfiguration cost and its impact on the provided QoS. We show our contribution for the **ASSISTANT** programming model [3], which is our research framework for studying autonomic high-performance applications.

The paper is organized as follows: Section 2 introduces the main points of the ASSISTANT programming model. In Section 3 we describe a high-level modeling framework for deriving consistent reconfiguration protocols and we provide a specific technique based on a rollback approach. In Section 4 we assess the correctness of the reconfiguration model through experiments.

2   The ASSISTANT Programming Model

ASSISTANT is our framework for autonomic applications and it is based on structured parallel programming [4] to express alternative parallel versions of a same component. ASSISTANT allows programmers to define parallel applications as graphs of parallel modules (i.e *ParMod*), interconnected by means of streams, i.e. possibly unlimited sequences of typed elements. The ParMod semantics is characterized by two interacting logics:

- *Functional Logic* or Operating Part: it encapsulates multiple versions of the parallel module, each one with a different behavior according to several parameters (e.g. memory utilization and expected performance). Only one version at time is allowed to be active;
- *Control Logic* or Control Part: it implements the adaptation strategy by analyzing the current platform and application behavior and by issuing reconfiguration commands to the Operating Part.

We introduce a new construct, called *operation*, implementing the functional part of a version and the corresponding adaptation strategy applied when that version is executed. A ParMod includes multiple operations which totally describe its functional and control logics. For lack of space in this paper we focus on the interactions between the control and the functional logic, which follows the abstract scheme depicted in Figure 1. The computation performed by the functional logic can be reconfigured at implicitly identified reconfiguration points (e.g. between the reception of two subsequent tasks).

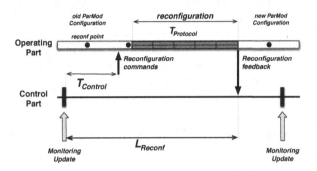

Fig. 1. Interaction scheme between functional and control logics

When a context update is received by the ParMod monitoring, the Control Part decides the set of reconfigurations by executing a control algorithm ($T_{Control}$). After that, a set of reconfiguration commands are sent to the Operating Part which applies them at the first reconfiguration point. For applying them, the Operating Part processes cooperatively execute a reconfiguration protocol, which induces a corresponding overhead (i.e. $T_{Protocol}$). We focus on two general structured parallelism models, namely task-farm and data-parallel. A *task-farm* computation is based on the replication of a given functionality F (e.g. a user-provided function) which is applied to a set of elements scheduled from an input stream. Each application of F to an input element gives place to a result, hence the set of results forms an output stream. From an implementation level an emitter process receives input elements and schedules them to workers; the collector receives results and delivers them to the output stream. A performance model can be formally derived: let us denote with T_E, T_W and T_C respectively the service time of the emitter, worker and collector. By considering them as successive stages of a pipeline system, we can calculate the inter-departure time of results from the collector as $T_{farm} = \max\{T_E, T_W/N, T_C\}$, where N is the parallelism degree (i.e. the number of workers).

A *data-parallel* computation in ASSISTANT is, like task-farm ones, stream-based, where each input task gives places to a composite state, which is scattered amongst a set of workers by a scatter process. The workers apply a same user-provided function (say G) sequentially on each element of their partition and for a fixed number of iterations (or steps) or until some convergence condition is satisfied. At each step workers may be required to communicate between themselves, in this case the data-parallel program is characterized by some form of stencil. At the end of the computation the resulting composite state is gathered on a gather process and delivered to the output stream. A simple performance model for data-parallel programs considers the scatter, workers and gather processes as successive stages of a pipeline graph. The results inter-departure time is $T_{dp} = \max\{T_S, T_W, T_G\}$, where T_S, T_W and T_G are the service times of the three functionalities. In particular T_W is the worker execution time: this value depends on the number of steps performed and it accounts for the calculation time and the communication time at each step of the data-parallel computation.

Finally, the ParMod implementation also includes a set of manager processes that implement the Control Logic. Managers may be replicated on different architectures on which the computation can be executed to assure their reliability in face of failures. A replicated set of managers along with the related processes implementing the functional part of a version, can be dynamically deployed and started during a reconfiguration phase.

3   Consistent Reconfiguration Protocols

We suppose a model which is quite general for a broad class of parallel applications: tasks are independent (no internal state of the ParMod survives between different task executions) and idempotent (a task can be repeatedly calculated without getting the ParMod into an inconsistent state).

If we take a computation snapshot, there are: (i) a set of tasks T_{IN} which are still to be received and which are stored in the input streams; a set of tasks T_P currently in execution on the ParMod; and a set of task results T_{OUT} previously produced by the ParMod on the output streams. *The goal of a consistent reconfiguration protocol is to properly manage the set T_P of tasks.* We can formalize the concept of consistency according to two notions:

Definition 1 (Weak Consistency). *All input tasks should be processed by the ParMod and their results delivered to the intended consumers.*

Note that this definition does not admit to loose any result but it permits their replication.

Definition 2 (Strong Consistency). *All elements produced on the input stream are processed by the ParMod and their results delivered to the intended consumers at most one time.*

We introduce a formalization methodology which is based on a proper modeling tool enabling us to define protocols in terms of tasks and results.

3.1   Formalization

Our methodology is inspired by the ***Incomplete Structure*** model (shortly I-Structure), introduced with other purposes in data-flow programming models [5] and previously used in [6] to model fault-tolerance protocols. An I-Structure is a possibly unlimited collection of typed elements, uniquely identified by sequence identifiers. There are two ways of accessing an I-Structure:

- we can read (**get**) the element stored at a given position. If it is empty, the operation blocks the caller until a value is produced on that position;
- we can write (**put**) a value to a given position. A write semantics assures the write-once property: i.e. it is not possible to perform a write more than once on the same position.

In Figure 2 is depicted how the I-Structure tool is used: each task input stream of a ParMod is mapped to a single I-Structure denoted with *IN*, and result output streams are mapped to a further I-Structure denoted with *OUT*.

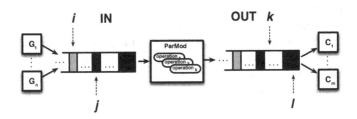

Fig. 2. I-Structure model applied to a ParMod

For a correct understanding of how I-Structures are used, note that there is not any notion of ordering between the IN and OUT elements: broadly, a task produced on an input stream has an index that may be different w.r.t the index of the corresponding result. For each I-Structure we can identify two indexes: one of the last consumed element (e.g. j and l in Figure 2) and the one of the last produced element (e.g. i and k). By using them we can precisely characterize the sets T_P, T_{IN} and T_{OUT}. For instance T_P is the set of elements with indexes on the IN I-structure from 0 to j to which we have to subtract all elements whose results have been produced to the output streams, i.e. results with indexes on the OUT I-Structure from 0 to k.

Although a formal description of proofs about reconfiguration protocols can be expressed through the I-Structure methodology, in this paper we are mainly interested in defining reconfiguration protocols at the level of implementation, by using the information derived from the abstract I-Structure model.

3.2   Implementation

At the implementation level interactions between ParMods are exploited by proper typed communication channels. In order to correctly implement the I-Structure model, we have to extend the basic ParMod implementation [3]: in fact the model requires that elements can be recovered at any time during the computation, simply passing their unique identifier. In a classical channel implementation, when a message is received (i.e. extracted) from the channel buffer, its content can be overwritten by successive messages. To this end we have two main implementation choices:

- the channel run-time support can be equipped with message logging techniques [7]: i.e. when a message is stored in the channel buffer, it is also copied into an external memorization support that can not be overwritten;
- message recovery can be faced directly at the application level: i.e. we can require that application components can re-generate elements on-demand.

Even if the first approach may induce an additional communication overhead, it is completely transparent from the application viewpoint. Nevertheless in this paper we suppose to adopt the second approach: i.e. every ParMod is able to re-generate past tasks/results. Anyway the presented protocols are independent on the way in which stream elements are recovered.

Therefore we can map the two I-Structures IN and OUT to different communication channels Ch_{IN} and Ch_{OUT}. For the purpose of re-generation, input tasks are labeled with their input sequence identifiers, whereas the results include a reference to the sequence identifier of the corresponding input task. In this way we assure that all ParMods have a common view of task and result identifiers.

Finally, we define the notion of **Vector Clock** (VC). A VC models a correspondence between output stream identifiers and input stream identifiers. It is a set of pairs of the form $(1, k_1), (2, k_2), \ldots, (N, k_N)$, where the first element of each pair is an result identifier, and the second one is the corresponding task identifier. Another important notion for our purpose is the *maximum contiguous sequence identifier* (shortly MC), which is the maximum task identifier on the input stream such that all its predecessors are included in the vector clock.

3.3   Description of Reconfiguration Protocols

In this section we describe consistent reconfiguration protocols focusing on version switching reconfigurations, in which we stop executing a *source* operation and we start executing a *target* one. Two techniques can be identified:

- we can wait for the source operation to perform all tasks in T_P and then make the target operation start from the first task which was not consumed by the source operation. We denote this technique as **rollforward protocols**;
- when the Control Part notifies an operation switching, the source operation can simply stop its execution. Then the control is passed immediately to the target operation that has to re-obtain the tasks in set T_P and re-start their execution. We denote this kind of approach as **rollback protocols**.

In this paper we focus on a generic rollback protocol, and we show how to optimize it for data-parallel programs. In the description we assume that the target operation has been previously deployed and it is ready to start its execution. For a comprehensive analysis of rollforward protocols, interested readers can read [8].

In a rollback protocol, the target operation needs to obtain all tasks in T_P from the related generators. To this end the Control Part should provide to the target operation some kind of information. Depending on the data passed we obtain different protocols:

- the information passed is the MC value: in this case the target operation will request the generators to re-generate elements whose identifier starts from $MC + 1$ to the sequence identifier of the message on the top of the Ch_{IN} buffer queue. Note that this techniques may induce a duplication of results: therefore it implements the weak consistency definition;
- the source operation can pass the whole Vector Clock to the target one, that drives the re-generation of T_P by issuing to generator components only the missing identifiers. Note that this protocol avoid the re-execution of previously performed tasks, hence it implements the strong consistency definition.

The choice of applying this kind of protocol depends on the amount of work which can be lost. We can quantify it depending on the parallelization scheme adopted by the source operation. If the source operation implements a task-farm computation, we have to re-execute at most $N + 4$ tasks (i.e. one task for each of the N workers; two tasks on the emitter and the collector; two tasks on the input and the output channels). In addition, in the first version of the protocol, we have also to sum up all tasks whose results have been delivered in an unordered way to the output stream. On the other hand, if the source operation implements a data-parallel program, we have to re-execute at most 5 tasks: one on the scatter process; one currently executed by workers; one corresponding to the result processed by the gather process; one on the input channel and a result on the output channel. In this scheme the input and the output streams are ordered between themselves, therefore, in both the versions of the protocol there are no further tasks that must be executed.

Optimizations Based on Checkpointing Techniques. Let us suppose a special case in which source and target operations are data-parallel programs with the same characteristics (e.g. in terms of the stencil definition). In this case we can think to transfer the partially transformed state from the source to the target operation in order to reduce the rollback overhead (time spent in re-executing tasks belonging to the set T_P). Of course this optimization is applicable only if it does not compromise the computation consistency, i.e. depending on the specific properties of the two data-parallel versions.

If this approach is viable, a straightforward solution is to take a snapshot of (all the workers) the computation of the source operation and transfers it to the target operation. The snapshot includes also all messages currently stored in the channel buffers, as well as in-transit messages. As it can be noted, this snapshot-based solution is valid only under the hypothesis that the source and target operations have the same parallelism degree. Moreover the whole computation state formed by the local state of each worker may be inconsistent, due to the fact that workers may be computing at different stencil steps. The reason behind this is that we consider data-parallel programs not based on a step-synchronous logic, but workers are allowed to proceed in their computation depending only on the availability of their input stencil information (i.e. their data dependencies).

Therefore, the main point consists in how a consistent state is reached by workers. A solution to this problem is based on *checkpointing*: workers can perform periodic checkpointing activities of their local partitions at the very same frequency (e.g. every d steps). Note that checkpointing activities can be performed independently by workers, with the consequence that the last checkpoint from a worker can be different to the ones of others (see [6]). Therefore, to assure that the transferred state is consistent, when workers are issued to perform an operation switching they have to first identify the last checkpointing step which all have passed (a.k.a a *recovery line*), and then transfer the corresponding checkpoints. The selection of the recovery line can be performed by running a two-phase leader-based protocol as described in [6].

4   Experiments

We have tested the behavior of the rollback protocol on a flood emergency management application, developed in the context of the Italian In.Sy.Eme. project (Integrated System for Emergency). This application includes three ParMods: a *Generator* of environmental data, providing input tasks describing the current state of each point of a discretized space of a river basin; a *Forecasting ParMod* implementing a flood forecasting model, that for each input point resolves a system of differential equations. The numerical resolution of the system gives place to four tri-diagonal linear systems, which are solved according to an optimized direct method (see [9] for further details). This ParMod includes two operations, respectively based on a task-farm and on a stencil data-parallel parallel program; the last ParMod implements a *Client* visualizing the results.

In these tests the task-farm is mapped to a cluster including 30 production workstations. The data-parallel operation is executable on two multi-core architectures: (1) a dual-processor Intel Xeon E5420 Quad-Core featuring 8 cores; (2) a dual-processor Intel Xeon E5520 Quad-Core featuring 8 cores. The operations have been implemented using the MPI library: on the cluster architecture we supported the task-farm with the LAM/MPI implementation, while on the multi-cores we have used the shared-memory version of MPICH.

The generic rollback protocol has been tested on the operation switching from the task-farm to data-parallel version. The optimized protocol is exploited for switching between two instances of the data-parallel operation mapped to the two multi-cores. Figures 3a and 3b show the behavior of the the reconfiguration overhead L_{reconf} (i.e. total time in seconds for applying the reconfiguration) by varying the parallelism degree of the source operation and the size of the solved systems. Consider the case of systems of size $32\,MB$ and parallelism degree equals to 8. In this case, the mean service time of each worker is $10.25\,sec.$ and by applying the performance models of parallelism schemes introduced in Section 2 and the reconfiguration cost model introduced in Section 3.3 we obtain that $L_{reconf} \leq (N + 4)\,T_W = 123.023\,sec.$. This value is a slight overestimation

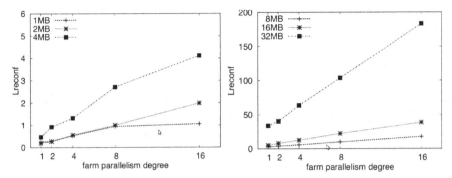

(a) L_{reconf} by varying the parallelism de-**(b)** L_{reconf} by varying the parallelism de-gree and the task size (1, 2 and 4 MB).   gree and the task size (8, 16 and 32 MB).

Fig. 3. Evaluation of rollback protocol for Task-Farm to Data-Parallel switching

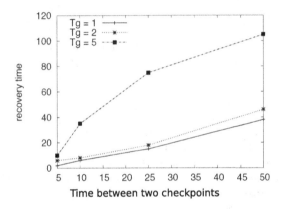

Fig. 4. Recovery time on the target operation by varying the checkpointing frequency and the G grain

than the real experienced one (i.e. 103.6233 *sec.*), due to the fact that in this experiment the number of rolled-back elements has been 11 instead of 12.

Figure 4 shows the time needed to perform the optimized recovery protocol on the target operation by varying the checkpointing frequency and the cost of applying the function G on the local partition of each worker. Clearly, this time also depends on the instant at which reconfiguration is issued, aside of the check-pointing frequency: for instance, if we perform checkpointing with low frequency but the reconfiguration must be applied immediately after a checkpoint, clearly the recovery cost is small. Nevertheless, the behavior of the recovery cost, in average, decreases with the checkpointing frequency. As we can see with these tests, with a grain of $T_G = 5$ *sec.*, the selected pattern for issuing reconfiguration commands makes the recovery time strongly increase when the checkpointing frequency decreases. From this, we can see that higher T_G times should be supported by more frequent checkpointing operations, if our target is to minimize the recovery time.

5   Conclusions

In this paper we have introduced two consistent reconfiguration protocols for ASSISTANT applications, supporting version switching activities. The first protocol supports the switching between any kind of parallel computations. The second protocol represents an optimization when the source and target operations are "similar" data-parallel programs. It is based on a periodic checkpointing protocol and on transferring the state of the last recovery line from the source to the target operation. For the protocols we have introduced performance models to predict their overhead, and we have assessed the expected results by real experiments.

References

1. Kennedy, K., et al.: Toward a framework for preparing and executing adaptive grid programs. In: Proceedings of the 16th International Parallel and Distributed Processing Symposium, IPDPS 2002, pp. 322–326. IEEE Computer Society, Washington, DC (2002)
2. Blumofe, R.D., Lisiecki, P.A.: Adaptive and reliable parallel computing on networks of workstations. In: Proceedings of the Annual Conference on USENIX Annual Technical Conference, p. 10. USENIX Association, Berkeley (1997)
3. Bertolli, C., Mencagli, G., Vanneschi, M.: A cost model for autonomic reconfigurations in high-performance pervasive applications. In: Proceedings of the 4th ACM International Workshop on Context-Awareness for Self-Managing Systems, CASEMANS 2010, pp. 3:20–3:29. ACM, New York (2010)
4. Cole, M.: Bringing skeletons out of the closet: a pragmatic manifesto for skeletal parallel programming. Parallel Comput. 30, 389–406 (2004)
5. Arvind, Nikhil, R.S., Pingali, K.K.: I-structures data structures for parallel computing. ACM Trans. Program. Lang. Syst. 11, 598–632 (1989)
6. Bertolli, C., Vanneschi, M.: Fault tolerance for data parallel programs. Concurrency and Computation: Practice and Experience 23(6), 595–632 (2011)
7. Elnozahy, E.N.M., Alvisi, L., Wang, Y.M., Johnson, D.B.: A survey of rollback-recovery protocols in message-passing systems. ACM Comput. Surv. 34, 375–408 (2002)
8. Bertolli, C., Mencagli, G., Vanneschi, M.: Consistent reconfiguration protocols for adaptive high-performance applications. In: The 7th International Wireless Communications and Mobile Computing Conference. Workshop on Emergency Management: Communication and Computing Platforms (2011) (to appear)
9. Bertolli, C., Buono, D., Mencagli, G., Vanneschi, M.: Expressing Adaptivity and Context Awareness in the ASSISTANT Programming Model. In: Vasilakos, A.V., Beraldi, R., Friedman, R., Mamei, M., et al. (eds.) Autonomics 2009. LNICST, vol. 23, pp. 32–47. Springer, Heidelberg (2010), doi:10.1007/978-3-642-11482-3_3

A Dynamic Resource Management System for Real-Time Online Applications on Clouds

Dominik Meiländer, Alexander Ploss, Frank Glinka, and Sergei Gorlatch

University of Muenster, Germany
{d.meil,a.ploss,glinkaf,gorlatch}@uni-muenster.de

Abstract. We consider a challenging class of highly interactive virtual environments, also known as Real-Time Online Interactive Applications (ROIA). Popular examples of ROIA include multi-player online computer games, e-learning and training applications based on real-time simulations, etc. ROIA combine high demands on the scalability and real-time user interactivity with the problem of efficient and economic utilization of resources, which is difficult to achieve due to the changing number of users. We address these challenges by developing the dynamic resource management system RTF-RMS which implements load balancing for ROIA on Clouds. We illustrate how RTF-RMS chooses between three different load-balancing actions and implements Cloud resource allocation. We report experimental results on the load balancing of a multi-player online game in a Cloud environment using RTF-RMS.

1 Introduction and Related Work

This paper is motivated by the challenges of the emerging class of *Real-Time Online Interactive Applications (ROIA)*. Popular and market-relevant representatives of these applications are multi-player online computer games, as well as real-time training and e-learning based on high-performance simulation. ROIA are characterized by: short response times to user actions (about 0.1-1.5 s); frequent state computation (up to 50 Hz); large and frequently changing number of users in a single application instance (up to 10^4 simultaneously).

The high demands on ROIA performance usually cannot be satisfied by a single server. Therefore, distributed, multi-server application processing with suitable scalability concepts is required. A major problem in this context is the efficient utilization of multiple server resources for application provision, which is difficult to achieve for ROIA due to a variable number of users who are continuously connecting to the application and disconnecting from it.

In this paper, we study how Cloud Computing with its *Infrastructure-as-a-Service (IaaS)* approach can be utilized for ROIA applications. We are developing a novel resource management system for ROIA, called *RTF-RMS*, that is implemented on top of the *Real-Time Framework (RTF)* [1]. RTF is our middleware platform for a high-level development of scalable ROIA that provides a rich set of distribution and monitoring mechanisms. RTF-RMS utilizes a

M. Alexander et al. (Eds.): Euro-Par 2011 Workshops, Part I, LNCS 7155, pp. 149–158, 2012.

Cloud infrastructure to lease virtualized hardware resources on demand and provides dynamic load balancing for ROIA, taking into account the monitoring data provided by RTF.

A number of research projects studied the potential of Cloud Computing for cost-efficient provision of particular application classes, e.g., batch execution systems [2], scientific astronomy workflows [3], and market-oriented resource management systems [4]. However, none of these approaches targets applications with requirements similar to ROIA. Rather than general challenges for efficient Cloud resource management, e.g., different performance characteristics of identical resource types [5] or data inconsistency in Cloud storage solutions [6], this work addresses the particular challenges of cost-effectively leasing Cloud resources and reducing their startup times for ROIA.

We showed the impact of virtualized Cloud resources on concrete ROIA implementations in our previous work [7] which proved that the performance requirements of ROIA can be fulfilled on commercial Cloud systems like the Amazon EC2 [8]. In [9], the influence of Cloud resources allocation on the hosting process of multi-player online games was analyzed, showing that load balancing is a critical challenge for ROIA provision on Clouds, as targeted in this paper.

Cloud platforms offer services that provide monitoring and load balancing for their Cloud resources, e.g., Amazon Cloud Watch or Amazon Elastic Load Balancing [8]. However, these services only provide generic system information about resource utilization (CPU, memory, bandwidth, etc.). This information is not sufficient for up- and down-scaling of ROIA sessions since ROIA have a specific runtime behaviour: e.g., regardless of the current number of users, an online game may run with a constant CPU load of 100 % in order to deliver the highest state update rate possible. In this paper, we aim at a dynamic load-balancing strategy based on application-specific monitoring information (e.g., update rate) that is more suitable for ROIA.

The paper is organized as follows. Section 2 describes our target class of Real-Time Online Interactive Applications (ROIA) and the Real-Time Framework (RTF) for their development and execution. Section 3 presents our new dynamic resource management system RTF-RMS and illustrates its strategy for load balancing and Cloud resource allocation. Section 4 presents our experimental results in a Cloud environment, and Section 5 concludes the paper.

2   Scalable ROIA Development with RTF

Typically, there are multiple users in a Real-Time Online Interactive Application (ROIA) who access a common application state and interact with each other concurrently within one virtual environment. The users connect to the application from different client machines and control their avatars that interact with other users' avatars or computer-controlled characters (*entities*). Since ROIA usually have very high performance requirements, the application state processing should be performed on multiple servers. Hence, ROIA are highly distributed applications with new challenges for application development and provision, such as: short response times to user actions, high concurrency, frequent state computation, ad-hoc user connections, and variable numbers of users.

We use the *real-time loop* model [10] for describing ROIA execution on both physical and Cloud resources. One iteration of the real-time loop is called a *tick*. The time required for one iteration of the real-time loop (*tick duration*) is directly related to the application's response time to user actions, and, hence, is a suitable criterion for dynamic up- and down-scaling of ROIA sessions. A loop iteration consists of three major steps (on the left-hand side of Fig. 1):

1. Servers receive user actions from the clients connected to them.
2. Servers compute a new application state according to the application logic.
3. Servers send the new state to their clients and to other servers.

Steps 1 and 3 involve communication to transmit the user inputs and state updates between processes. The computation of a new application state (step 2) involves quite compute-intensive calculations which apply the application logic to the current state, taking into account the newly received users' actions.

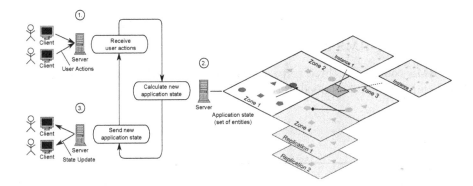

Fig. 1. One iteration of the real-time loop (left); RTF distribution methods (right)

The *Real-Time Framework (RTF)* [11] is our high-level development platform for ROIA which supports the application developer in three essential tasks:

1. *Application State Distribution:* RTF supports three major methods of partitioning the virtual environment among servers (on the right-hand side of Fig. 1): zoning, replication and instancing, and combinations of them. Zoning assigns the processing of the entities in disjoint areas (*zones*) to distinct servers. Instancing creates separate independent copies of a particular zone; each copy is processed by a different server. In the replication approach, each server keeps a complete copy of the application state, but each server is responsible for computing a disjoint subset of entities. A more detailed description of the distribution methods in RTF can be found in [11].

2. *Communication Handling:* RTF provides automatic serialization for entities to be transferred, implements marshalling and unmarshalling of data types, and optimizes the bandwidth consumption of communication.
3. *Monitoring and Distribution Handling:* RTF offers a high-level Hoster Management Interface (HMI) which allows developers to send controlling commands directly into a running RTF-based server application (*ROIA process*), as well as to receive monitoring values from RTF inside a ROIA process. Controlling commands include, e.g., adding physical resources, changing the game world in an online game during runtime, etc.

3   Resource Management for ROIA on Clouds

A major problem for an efficient ROIA execution is the economical utilization of server resources, which is difficult to achieve due to a continuously changing number of users. Cloud Computing promises the potential to distribute application processing on an arbitrary number of resources and to add/remove resources on demand. We develop a Resource Management System (RTF-RMS) as a software component on top of RTF for dynamic up- and down-scaling of ROIA sessions on Cloud resources during runtime.

3.1   The RTF-RMS Architecture

RTF-RMS consists of three software components which are shown in Fig. 2 (left-hand side) and described in the following.

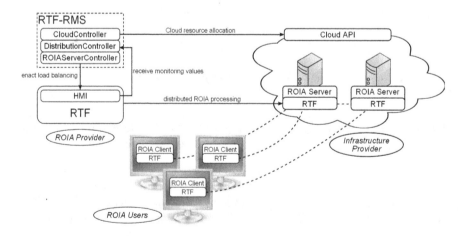

Fig. 2. Composition of RTF-RMS and RTF

The `CloudController` implements the communication with the interface (API) of the Cloud system. RTF-RMS currently implements Cloud resource allocation for the Amazon Compute Cloud (EC2). A particular challenge in the implementation of the `CloudController` is the compensation of a comparatively long startup time of Cloud resources that can be up to several minutes. Furthermore, cost optimization is an important issue since Cloud resources are typically leased for a certain usage period. We address these challenges in Section 3.3.

The `DistributionController` implements our new load-balancing strategy that dynamically changes the workload distribution between application servers. For this purpose, it receives monitoring values from HMI which are used to determine the load of application servers. If the `DistributionController` identifies an overloaded server, it chooses between three different load-balancing actions, as described in Section 3.2.

The `ROIAServerController` enacts load-balancing actions on request from the `DistributionController`, e.g., adding a new resource to the application processing. The `ROIAServerController` uses HMI's distribution handling functionalities (Section 2) to integrate new servers in the application session.

3.2   A Load-Balancing Strategy for ROIA on Clouds

In order to identify the demand for load-balancing actions, a suitable workload analysis is required. RTF-RMS is configured for the workload analysis of a particular application by specifying an *application profile* that defines the monitoring values of interest, e.g., tick duration in ms, update rate in Hz, etc., see Listing 1 for an example. RTF-RMS allows the application developer to specify upper and lower thresholds for each monitoring value in the profile. If a monitoring value exceeds the upper threshold, a new resource is added to the application processing; if monitoring values drop below the lower threshold then the dispensable resources are removed. The application profile also allows application developers to define the maximum number of active replicas for each zone, in order to limit the overhead for inter-server communication caused by the replication. The developer can find suitable thresholds for all parameters in the application profile by considering the runtime behaviour of the application on physical resources and calculating the virtualization overhead, or by conducting benchmark experiments in the Cloud environment.

Listing 1. Example application profile for a fast-paced action game

```
<appProfileData>
  <maxNumReplications>2</maxNumReplications>
  <metric>
    <name>TickDuration</name>
    <monitoringInterval>1</monitoringInterval>
    <upperThreshold>40</upperThreshold>
    <lowerThreshold>10</lowerThreshold>
  </metric>
</appProfileData>
```

RTF-RMS implements workload analysis as follows. The `Distribution-Controller` creates for each application session a `TimerTask` object, responsible for collecting the monitoring values specified in the profile and received from RTF. Each `TimerTask` registers an event listener at RTF which updates the monitoring values with the frequency specified in the application profile.

In RTF-RMS, we implement a load-balancing strategy for Cloud resources that chooses between the following three load-balancing actions:

1. *User Migration*: users are migrated from an overloaded server to an underutilized server which is replicating the same zone. For this purpose, RTF-RMS uses HMI's `migrate` method that switches user connections from one server to another. The `migrate` method expects a so-called `MigrationPolicy` which specifies the amount of migrated users; RTF-RMS provides by default a `MigrationPolicy` that distributes an equal amount of users onto each application server for a particular zone.
   User migration is the preferred action if the load of an overloaded server can be compensated by running resources.

2. *Replication Enactment*: new game servers are added in order to provide more computation power to the highly frequented zone. For this purpose, RTF-RMS uses HMI's `activateReplication` method that assigns a new server to the processing of a new replica; a number of users are migrated to the new replica in order to balance the load. Replication implies an additional inter-server communication and thus, its scalability is limited.
   If the number of active replicas for a particular zone is below the maximum number of replicas specified by the profile, then replication is used; otherwise the resource substitution action (described next) is preferred.

3. *Resource Substitution*: an existing resource in the application processing is substituted by a more powerful resource in order to increase the computation power for highly frequented zones. RTF-RMS replicates the targeted zone on the new resource (using `activateReplication`) and migrates all clients to the new server (using `migrate`). The substituted server is shut down.

In order to choose the optimal load-balancing action, the `Distribution-Controller` creates *reports* for each application server (Fig. 3). A report describes the load of a particular server, e.g., current tick duration in ms. A *zone report* is created for each zone by collecting all reports from servers involved in the zone processing and calculating the average load of these servers. The zone report is the basis for choosing the load-balancing action as described above.

Fig. 3 illustrates an example of how zone reports are used to choose a load-balancing action. We assigned Server A to the processing of Zone 1, and Server B and C were assigned to Zone 2. The zone report of Zone 1 identifies an average tick duration of 45 ms. Given an upper threshold of 40 ms, RTF-RMS decides to enact a new replication for Zone 1. The zone report of Zone 2 identifies an average tick duration of 30 ms which is below the threshold, but Server B has a tick duration of 45 ms. Hence, RTF-RMS migrates users from Server B to Server C in order to distribute the workload equally on both servers.

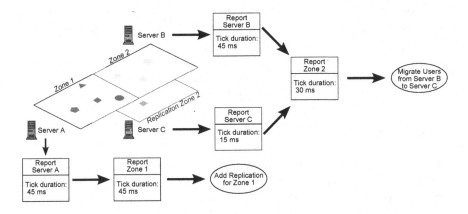

Fig. 3. Finding a suitable load-balancing action using zone reports

3.3   Cloud Resource Allocation

An important factor that may limit the performance of applications on Clouds is the long startup time of Cloud resources which may take up to several minutes. Since ROIA are highly responsive applications, finding a compensation of long startup times is an important task.

To start multiple resources as quickly as possible, the `CloudController` of RTF-RMS sends multiple requests in parallel to the Cloud API. Moreover, the `DistributionController` introduces a *resource buffer* to which a predefined number of Cloud resources are moved in advance, i.e. before they are demanded by the application. The `CloudController` tags resources that are currently running the application as *running* in contrast to *buffered* resources that are currently not used. If any resource changes its state from buffered to running, the `DistributionController` checks whether new Cloud resources must be started in order to keep a certain number of resources in the resource buffer. The number of buffered resources is configured in the application profile.

By leasing and buffering Cloud resources in advance, additional overhead is generated. Therefore, the size s of the resource buffer should be chosen carefully. Given n clients and m servers for a particular zone, the time $t_{\mathrm{integr}}(r, n, m)$ for integrating a single resource r from the resource buffer R is split up into time $t_{\mathrm{intro}}(r, m)$ for the introduction of r to m other servers and time $t_{\mathrm{migr}}(r, n)$ for migrating users to the new server, i.e., $t_{\mathrm{integr}}(r, n, m) = t_{\mathrm{intro}}(r, m) + t_{\mathrm{migr}}(r, n)$. The overall time required for integrating all resources $r_1, ..., r_s$ from the resource buffer R in the application processing should be less than the time $t_{\mathrm{leas}}(p)$ required for leasing a new single Cloud resource from the infrastructure provider p. Therefore, the following condition describes a reasonable limit for the size s of the resource buffer: $1 \leq s \leq \max\{i \in \mathbb{N} \mid \sum_{j=1}^{i} t_{\mathrm{integr}}(r_j, n, m) < t_{\mathrm{leas}}(p)\}$.

Another important issue for the cost-efficient ROIA provision on Clouds is the consideration of leasing periods. In commercial Cloud systems, resources are typically leased and paid per hour or some longer leasing period. Since ROIA have dynamically changing user numbers, the time after which Cloud resources become dispensable is very variable. However, resources will not be used cost-efficiently if they are shut down before the end of their leasing period. Hence, RTF-RMS removes the resources that have become dispensable from the application processing and moves them to the resource buffer. Cloud resources in the buffer are shut down at the end of their leasing period or they are integrated in the application processing again if required.

4   Experiments

While the scalability of the proposed load-balancing actions was already demonstrated in [7], we evaluate the suitability of the proposed load-balancing actions to overcome performance bottlenecks in an example multi-player action game. This game, RTFDemo, is developed using RTF and is a representative of the first-person shooter online game category. In RTFDemo, zoning and replication are used for the distribution of the game state. We use the tick duration as the monitoring value for up- and down-scaling of the RTFDemo session. In order to provide a seamless gaming experience, users should not receive less than 25 updates per second over a longer time period. Hence, we configured RTF-RMS by specifying the upper threshold of 40 ms for the tick duration.

In our experiments, we use a private Cloud environment with the Eucalyptus framework (version 2.0.2) [12]; servers are Intel Core Duo PCs with 2.66 GHz and 2 GB of RAM running CentOS 5.3. Since Eucalyptus and Amazon EC2 use the same API, no adaptation of the `CloudController` was required.

For our first experiment, we have started two servers, with all clients initially connected to server 1, which implies an imbalanced load on application servers. We apply load balancing by user migration without leasing new Cloud resources. Fig. 4 shows that the tick duration of server 1 initially grows with the number of connected clients. When the tick duration reaches the threshold of 40 ms, RTF-RMS migrates half of the users (i.e., 120 users) from server 1 to server 2. This action reduces the tick duration of server 1 from 40 ms to 10-15 ms.

Our second experiment demonstrates load balancing by replication enactment. We start a single RTFDemo server and connect multiple clients to it. Fig. 5 shows that as soon as the tick duration of server 1 exceeds the threshold, RTF-RMS requests a new Cloud resource from the resource buffer (for this experiment, the size of the buffer was 1). Although the requested resource is already started up (since it is in the buffer), we observe that a certain time period is still required to add the new server to the application processing and start user migration. This delay of approximately 10 sec is caused by the initialization and inter-server communication required to integrate the new server in the application processing. After the migration is accomplished, the tick duration of server 1 is significantly reduced. Note that if the resource were not in the buffer and would have been started up from scratch, the delay would be much longer, in the order of 130 sec.

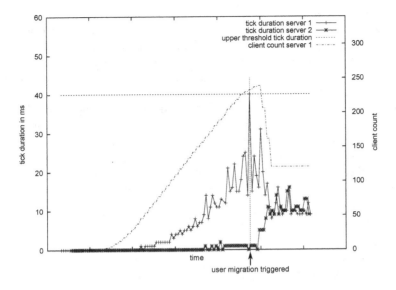

Fig. 4. Load balancing by user migration

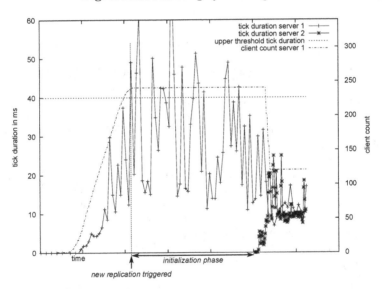

Fig. 5. Load balancing by replication enactment

5   Conclusion

This paper presents our new resource management system RTF-RMS for executing Real-Time Online Interactive Applications (ROIA) on Cloud systems. We have described our load-balancing strategy for ROIA on Clouds which chooses between three possible load-balancing actions: user migration, replication enactment, and resource substitution. The strategy is based on the application-specific monitoring values provided by the Real-Time Framework (RTF), and goes beyond the state-of-the-art load balancing on Clouds which is based on generic system information. RTF-RMS allows for a cost-effective leasing of Cloud resources on demand by buffering unused resources; thereby the startup times of Cloud resources are reduced. Our experiments demonstrate the use of RTF-RMS load balancing by user migration and replication enactment for improving the performance of a multi-player, real-time online game on a Cloud.

Acknowledgment. Our research has received funding from the European Community's Seventh Framework Programme FP7/2007-2013 under grant agreement 215483 (S-Cube).

References

1. Real-Time Framework, RTF (2011), http://www.real-time-framework.com
2. Freeman, T., Keahey, K.: Flying Low: Simple Leases with Workspace Pilot. In: Luque, E., Margalef, T., Benítez, D. (eds.) Euro-Par 2008. LNCS, vol. 5168, pp. 499–509. Springer, Heidelberg (2008)
3. Deelman, E., Singh, G., Livny, M., Berriman, B., Good, J.: The Cost of Doing Science on the Cloud: The Montage Example. In: Supercomputing Conference, pp. 1–12 (2008)
4. Buyya, R., Yeo, C.S., Venugopal, S.: Market-Oriented Cloud Computing: Vision, Hype, and Reality for Delivering IT Services as Computing Utilities. In: Int. Conf. on High Performance Computing and Communications, pp. 5–13 (2008)
5. Dejun, J., Pierre, G., Chi, C.-H.: Resource provisioning of Web applications in heterogeneous clouds. In: Proceedings of the 2nd USENIX Conference on Web Application Development (2011)
6. Wei, Z., Pierre, G., Chi, C.-H.: CloudTPS: Scalable transactions for Web applications in the cloud. IEEE Transactions on Services Computing (2011) (to appear)
7. Ploss, A., Meiländer, D., Glinka, F., Gorlatch, S.: Towards the Scalability of Real-Time Online Interactive Applications on Multiple Servers and Clouds. Advances in Parallel Computing, vol. 20, pp. 267–287. IOS Press (2011)
8. Amazon Web Services, AWS (2011), http://aws.amazon.com
9. Nae, V., Iosup, A., Prodan, R., Fahringer, T.: The Impact of Virtualization on the Performance of Massively Multiplayer Online Games. In: 8th Annual Workshop on Network and Systems Support for Games (NetGames), pp. 1–6 (2009)
10. Valente, L., Conci, A., Feijó, B.: Real Time Game Loop Models for Single-Player Computer Games. In: SBGames 2005 – IV Brazilian Symposium on Computer Games and Digital Entertertainment (2005)
11. Glinka, F., Ploss, A., Gorlatch, S., Müller-Iden, J.: High-Level Development of Multiserver Online Games. International Journal of Computer Games Technology 2008, 1–16 (2008)
12. Nurmi, D., Wolski, R., Grzegorczyk, C., et al.: The Eucalyptus Open-Source Cloud-Computing System. In: 9th IEEE/ACM International Symposium on Cluster Computing and the Grid, pp. 124–131. IEEE Computer Society (2009)

Cloud Federations in Contrail

Emanuele Carlini[1,2], Massimo Coppola[1], Patrizio Dazzi[1],
Laura Ricci[3], and Giacomo Righetti[1,3]

[1] ISTI-CNR, Pisa, Italy
[2] IMT Lucca, Lucca, Italy
[3] Dept. Computer Science, Univ. of Pisa, Italy

Abstract. Cloud computing infrastructures support dynamical and
flexible access to computational, network and storage resources. To date,
several disjoint industrial and academic technologies provide infrastructure level access to Clouds. Especially for industrial platforms, the evolution of de-facto standards goes together with worries about user lock-in to
a platform. The Contrail project [6] proposes a federated and integrated
approach to Clouds. In this work we present and motivate the architecture of Contrail federations. Contrail's goal is to minimize the burden on
the user and increase the efficiency in using Cloud platforms by performing both a vertical and a horizontal integration. To this end, Contrail
federations play a key role, allowing users to exploit resources belonging
to different cloud providers, regardless of the kind of technology of the
providers and with a homogeneous, secure interface. Vertical integration
is achieved by developing both the Infrastructure- and the Platform-as-
a-Service levels within the project. A third key point is the adoption of
a fully open-source approach toward technology and standards. Beside
supporting user authentication and applications deployment, Contrail
federations aim at providing extended SLA management functionalities,
by integrating the SLA management approach of SLA@SOI project in
the federation architecture.

1 Introduction

Cloud computing is a computing model aimed at providing resources as services
according to a pay-per-use paradigm. The provided resources differ in type and
level of abstraction. While the basic candidates are computational power and
storage, resources can be provided to users from the infrastructure level (IaaS,
e.g. virtual machines, virtual storage), the platform level (PaaS, e.g. programming libraries, application templates and components) and the software level
(SaaS, e.g. complete applications like Google Documents). Almost all current
IT behemoths offer their own cloud computing solution: Amazon [1], Google [7],
Microsoft [2] and many others. Unfortunately, this leads to some issues. Each
cloud provider forces its users to operate according to specific models, e.g. communication protocols and virtualization formats. This is known as *vendor-lock
in* and from users perspective it leads to a major disadvantage. Namely, even

M. Alexander et al. (Eds.): Euro-Par 2011 Workshops, Part I, LNCS 7155, pp. 159–168, 2012.

if users running their applications in a certain cloud find better providers to exploit, the burden of cloud switching may lead to cut this solution off.

As the resources offered by each provider belong to different levels of abstraction, standardization decreases. Typically providers offer somewhat interchangeable services only at a low level of abstraction, while higher level services provide a low or no degree of personalization. Any user willing to exploit resources belonging to different levels while keeping the option open to move across provider boundaries, needs to cope with the burden of adapting the applications. In order to address these issues, in recent times several standards like Open Cloud Computing Interface [8] and Open Virtualization Format [9] have been proposed to provide cooperation among different cloud solutions. Each of these standards covers, however, only specific aspects and portions of the Cloud management stack, and no standard is universally adopted by cloud providers, so far.

The Contrail approach to cloud federation tackles the issue of integration among heterogeneous clouds. Important factors are the open-source choice and the collaborations with other projects involved in Cloud research. On top of this, as a main line of research, Contrail aims at a two-way integration: (i) a *vertical* integration, which provides a unified platform for the different kind of resources and (ii) a *horizontal* integration that abstracts the interaction models of different cloud providers. In this work we describe the general architecture of Contrail cloud federations, thereby focusing on horizontal integration and on the federation services which are essential in allowing vertical integration.

Section 2 explores the motivations and commitments of a cloud federations, with a particular stress on users ID managements, Service Level Agreement (SLA) integration and application execution. Section 3 gives an overview of the Contrail federation architecture and how appliances are deployed. Section 4 presents a selection of current research work on cloud federations. Finally Section 5 concludes the paper.

2   Contrail Federations: Motivations and Commitments

From a practical point of view, a federation can be considered as a bridge linking cloud users and cloud providers. As the role of the federation goes beyond mere interface adaptation, federation services act as mediators between users and providers. From a user's perspective, the components and the services supporting the federation (we will refer to them as *federation-support* in the rest of the paper) act as a broker for the resources owned by providers participating to the federation. As each provider has its own, potentially specific, mechanisms and policies for managing resources, the goal of the federation-support is to provide translation and mapping mechanisms for matching user needs and exploiting federated cloud providers.

The pay-per-use concept relies on the existence of a formally agreed SLA between the user and the provider(s), and the ability to monitor, enforce and account service use and QoS. Besides the resource selection functionalities across multiple providers and the consistent management of resources, a Contrail federation coordinates the SLA support of cloud providers. Indeed, as cloud providers have their own SLA management mechanisms which is useful to exploit, the role of the federation is to setup, coordinate and enforce a global SLA, eventually negotiating SLAs with providers on behalf of the users. This leads to the possibility of a *vertical SLA management*, allowing to define PaaS services which are provider-invariant and also supporting interactions between public and private cloud providers. The federation-support has to monitor the application in order to verify that SLA is fulfilled by providers, and to react to SLA violations.

Federation-Level User ID Management. A federation has to provide users with mechanisms to specify their preferences about cloud providers and resources. Federation-support manages the user identities for accessing to cloud providers, and users have also to be informed about their actual and historical usage of resources (accounting, billing).

The task of protecting personal user-related information, like user identities, is only the first stone when building security into a federated cloud approach. One of the problems related with federations is to save the users from the burden of authenticating with resources belonging to different cloud providers, especially as many of the actions on the resources have to be automated and performed 24/7. The federation should exploit proper mechanisms and credentials, in accordance with both user preferences and the authentication support of the providers.

Appliance Deployment. An application is composed by: (i) a set of appliances and (ii) a SLA description that provides the user requirements on a per appliance basis. With the term appliance we identify a set of VM images strictly cooperating to realize an application fundamental block (e.g. a pool of web servers, or a firewall and back-end database combination). The federation has to map those appliances in the federation resources according to both user requirements and preferences, as specified in the application SLA and possibly as constrained by user identity and related resource policies.

In order to effectively set up and enact the application-resources mapping the federation needs static (geographic location, cost-models, installed software) and dynamic information regarding cloud providers and their resources. It is also relevant to record past history of providers with respect to SLA violations, in order to evaluate their reliability.

SLA Coordination. SLAs negotiated by the federation-support and users define a set of functional and non-functional requirements that have to be addressed and enforced in order to properly execute user's appliances. In the Contrail project we assume that every cloud provider belonging to the federation has proper mechanisms able to deal with the SLA descriptions regarding the appliances it has to execute.

Most of those mechanisms and the underlying formalism are inherited from the SLA@SOI [12] [13] project. In particular, the SLA management yielded by Contrail cloud providers is based on three main entities: (i) SLA, (ii) SLA Template and (iii) SLA Manager. The SLA is a structured description of user and appliance requirements, which is derived by a SLA Template. A SLA template provides a customizable base that can be exploited in order to derive specific SLAs. A SLA@SOI SLA Manager monitors a running appliance and reacts in case the appliance misbehaves with respect to its associated SLA. The actions enacted by a SLA Manager include intra-cloud appliance migration, appliance reconfiguration and network set-up. The federation-support should intervene to coordinate the involved SLA Managers, in case one or more SLA Managers were unable to enforce the SLA of one or more appliances.

Non-functional Requirements. In addition to the functional commitments, the federation-support has also to address specific non-functional requirements. They are mainly related with platform scalability, flexibility and security. Scalability and flexibility are key performance aspects for a federation, dealing with a relevant amount of resources and users, and can be regarded as a non-functional requirement of the federation design. These considerations influence the design of the federation-support, presented in Section 3.

Other classical non-functional goals of application execution, once the application gets deployed on a Cloud in accordance with an SLA, become functional requirements for the federation-support. Besides performance, one of the major concerns of the federation-support is security. Security plays an important role in the federation as well as in the whole Contrail project, since it directly affects the acceptance with respect to possible customers. The federation-support must offer a secure environment in which users execute applications, and store their data and personal information. In this context protection is two-fold: first, both the users data and their applications should be protected from unauthorized accesses and modifications. For instance, the federation should protect users from affecting each other, from snooping on each other one's jobs, or data. Second, the federation shall protect itself from malicious or erratic applications.

3   Federation Architecture

The federation acts as a bridge between users and cloud providers. The *federation-support* offers to users, in an uniform fashion, resources belonging to different cloud providers. A Contrail federation can exploit two kind providers, those based on the Contrail cloud infrastructure and the ones based on other public and commercial infrastructures. As shown in Figure 1 the federation architecture is composed of three layers. Every layer is in turn composed by modules, where each module addresses a well defined commitment.

The top-most layer, called *interface*, gives a view on the federation and provides proper ways to interact with the federation. The interface gathers requests from users as well as from other Contrail components that rely on the federation functionality and facilities. The interface layer includes a CLI and HTTP interface, from which is possible to access to REST services. The mid layer, called *core*, contains modules that fulfill the functional (e.g. application life-cycle management) and non-functional (e.g. security) requirements of the federation. The bottom layer, called *adapters*, contains the modules that retrieve information

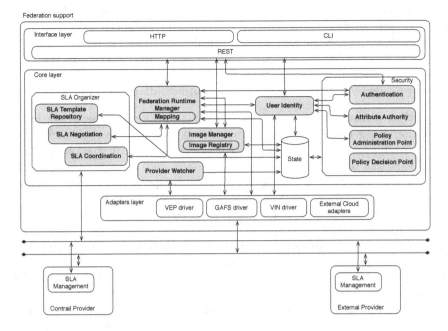

Fig. 1. Federation-support architecture

and operate on different cloud providers. This layer provides also a unified interface that possibly copes with heterogeneity of providers. A detailed description of mechanisms provided by the interface layer are beyond the scope of this paper, therefore they are not presented. In the next sections we present a detailed description of the modules belonging to the core and adapters layer.

3.1 Core Layer

The core layer contains the modules that implement the business logic of the federation. These modules solve the three main commitments demanded to the federation-support, namely identity management, application deployment and SLA coordination. These modules are in turn supported in their activities by additional auxiliary modules. In the following of this chapter we present in detail the modules that implement the business logic of the federation as well as the state module, which is in charge of the federation state management. We refer to the auxiliary modules whenever it is necessary.

User Identity. The federation-support provides to each user a federation-level account. By using this account the user can have access to all the resources owned by the federated cloud providers. In order to interact with different providers, the federation-level user account is bound with different local providers identities. The *user identity* module is in charge of realizing the aforementioned bind. The actual connection between the module and the providers is done through the Adapter layer (discussed later).

The access to resources is managed in a seamless way, i.e., once authenticated to a Contrail federation, users should not be prompted again to access federated Cloud providers (e.g. single sign-on). The local cloud identities are stored in the state module. In order to guarantee isolation and data integrity, of the user-related data, the federation-support takes advantages of the mechanisms and policies provided by the authentication and authorization modules.

Federation Runtime Manager. One of the core task of the federation is application deployment. This is not a trivial task, since the user will expect the federation-support to find proper mappings between submitted appliances and clouds belonging to the federation.

In order to devise a good mapping onto the compute, storage and network services of the federation, the *federation runtime manager* (FRM) uses a set of heuristics that consider different aspects, such as to minimize economical cost and to maximize performance levels. This actual task and the heuristics are implemented by the *mapping* component, while the FRM is in charge of the orchestration between the mapping component, the SLA management system and the drivers layer. In particular, the FRM is responsible of the application life cycle management. The FRM gathers information to cover these aspects from the State module. The information is both static and dynamic. *Static* information is mainly related with general properties about cloud providers; it includes, for instance, their geographic location, their resource- and cost-models as well as the installed software. *Dynamic* information is related to the status of cloud provider resources, as well as to cloud providers as autonomous entities forming the federation. It is the kind of information obtained by monitoring resource availability either on a per cloud-provider basis or by recording and analysing the past history of each provider with respect to violated SLA. This information can be exploited to evaluate their reliability.

Image Manager. From the user's perspective the images can be managed in two ways: they can be packed inside an OVF archive or referenced within the OVF files by using URI. The task of deciding what is the best storage solution is carried out by the *Image Manager*. It associates metadata to the images and decides when is necessary to copy an image or when indirection can be exploited. The actual metadata are kept inside the State module; however an *Image Registry* is introduced to decouple federation code from being modified whenever State module is modified moving from the centralized scenario to the distributed one.

Provider Watcher. This component is responsible for the State update, upon receiving monitoring information from the Adapter layer. It decouples the State from doing this task leading to a more cohesive architectural design.

SLA Organizer. The *SLA Organizer* is a collection of modules related to SLA management at the Federation level, which is achieved by leveraging and coordinating SLA agreements stipulated with the federated resource providers. These modules are:

- **SLA Coordination.** The *SLA Coordination* module checks that running appliances comply with the user provided and agreed SLA, and plans corrective actions as needed. Upon being notified a violation, the SLA Coordination module logs the event, evaluates the current status of all related appliances and providers, and tries to define a reconfiguration plan for the application which compensates the violation. The SLA coordination module undertakes actions that may involve either a single cloud provider, or, in more complex scenarios, multiple providers and the federation-support.
- **SLA Negotiation.** The *SLA Negotiation* is responsible of the negotiation protocols with providers. Its main purpose is to decouple the protocols for SLA (re)negotiation from the core Business logic of the Federation Runtime manager.
- **SLA Template Repository.** This module gathers and stores SLA templates published by the providers. The Federation SLA Template Repository acts primarily as a cache of the Provider's SLA Template Registries, supporting scalable SLA-based queries and user interface template selection within the federation. The repository can as well holds federation-specific SLA templates not bound to any provider.

The State Module. The *state* module collects, aggregates and provides information exploited by the federation-support. Information is subject to diverse constraints in terms of frequency, atomicity and consistency of updates, thus different architectural solutions may be needed to fulfil scalability and reliability.

The involved issues become relevant when deploying the federation in a highly distributed scenario, with many federation access points. The specific purpose of the State module is to keep the core business logic of the federation unaware of the distribution aspects, only exposing the choice among different classes of data services. Each kind of information and the related constraints can be addressed by specific design patterns, whose use we will investigate further during the project. The federation modules require the state to manage different kinds of information.

- The User Identity module, security modules and the Federation Runtime Manager need read or write capability to access/manage user identity information and system-wide preferences;
- The Provider Watcher needs write capability to keep an up-to-date view of available resources belonging to federated and external cloud providers;
- The Provider Watcher module and the SLA Organizer gather a characterization of cloud providers, such as their geographic location, SLA templates, cost models and peculiar features;
- The Federation Runtime Manager accesses meta-data about providers (reputation, availability) and running appliances (including associated SLA).

Clearly, such an approach requires a proper distributed communication mechanism to support the flow of information among the state modules. To this end, we plan to integrate different distributed communication patterns. The decoupling of distributed communication within the State module is allowed since most tasks requiring atomicity are performed at the provider level (e.g. resource pre-reservation and commitment), thus simplifying the implementation of the federation state.

3.2 Adapters Layer

This layer contains the modules that enable the access to infrastructural services for both Contrail cloud and External clouds. They are referred respectively as *internal* and *external* adapters. These components enrich the typical cloud infrastructural services with additional features targeting federations.

Internal Adapters. The components of the internal adapters module are: (i) the Virtual Infrastructure Network (VIN) which provides network, (ii) the Global Autonomous File System (GAFS) which provides storage and (iii) the Virtual Execution Platform (VEP) which provides computing power.

The VIN provides APIs to define a virtual network among multiple virtual machines, both intra- and inter-provider. Also the VIN provides API to know the QoS level of an inter-provider link, and if it is possible, the proper mechanisms to enforce a given QoS. The GAFS provides shared data space, with the possibility for an application spanning in multiple providers to access a virtual volume. Finally, the VEP provides the proper OCCI interfaces to enable access to provider resources. Its APIs include mechanisms for reservation and configuration of resources, and starting and monitoring of machines.

External Adapters. In order to extend Contrail's functionality onto external clouds and at the same time to maintain modularity, the federation has been designed in a provider-agnostic fashion. This means that each module of the federation-support do not have any knowledge if it is issuing command to a Contrail cloud or to an external cloud. Commands toward external cloud are issued via a type-specific adapter, which translates requests from the federation support into requests that are understood by the provider. This task is assigned to the *External Provider* module of the federation Model. This module does not contain any driver supporting the VIN, GAFS, or VEP. Instead, an External-Provider exploits the interface exposed by the public cloud.

4   Related Work

In this section we briefly describe state-of-the-art solutions dealing with federations of clouds. InterCloud [3] is a federated cloud computing environment that addresses the issue of provisioning application services in a scalable computing environment, achieving QoS under variable workload, resource and network conditions. InterCloud performs application scheduling, resource allocation and migration of workloads. The authors implemented it on top of CloudSim [4], a framework to model and simulate cloud computing infrastructures and services. Their solution is built on three concepts: Cloud coordinators, Cloud Brokers and

Cloud Exchange. A *Cloud Coordinator* (CC) exports the services provided by a cloud to the federation by implementing basic functionalities for resource management such as scheduling, allocation, workload and performance models. This actor also supports virtualization, dynamic sensing/monitoring, discovery, and application composition. CCs periodically update the *Cloud Exchange* (CEx) with their availability, pricing, and SLAs policies. This information repository aggregates information supplied by CCs in order to support the Cloud Brokers activity. The *Cloud Broker* identifies suitable cloud service providers published on the CEx, negotiating with CCs for an allocation of resources that meets QoS needs of users. Since Contrail's brokers interact with each others, instead of having single-user context brokering, our federation-support can exploit information of what other users are requesting. This means a more reactive scenario in which better reservation strategies can be adopted. In addition, to the best of our knowledge, Contrail adopts a more cloud independent approach. Indeed, in our solution the federation plays a more central role, incorporating most of the functionalities described into InterCloud's CC.

The authors of [11] describe the architecture of an open federated cloud computing platform in the context of the Reservoir [10] project. In the Reservoir model, each resource provider is an autonomous entity with its own business goals. A provider can choose the providers with which to federate. There is a clear separation between the functional roles of *service providers* and *resource providers*. Service providers are the entities that matches the user needs by finding resources that their application need. However, service providers do not own the resources. They lease such resources from resource providers. Reservoir succeeds in defining a reference architecture capable of dealing with common IaaS requirements and even new ones, such as service-orientation and separation between infrastructure and services. Nevertheless, Contrail tries to built upon its results, adding vertical integration of IaaS and PaaS service models.

In [5] the authors propose *Dynamic Cloud Collaboration* (DCC), an approach for setting up highly dynamic cloud federations. The cloud provider (CP) that wants to setup a federation assumes the role of the *primary cloud provider* (pCP), whereas the federated cloud providers are called *collaborating CPs*. To federate new collaborating CPs, adding their resource/services to a DCC platform, an approval of other providers based on their own policies is needed. Users request services published on the service catalogue of the pCP. Then the pCP finds suitable partners based on the business objectives, and stipulate a contract with specific SLAs requirements for each partner involved. If after a distributed negotiation an agreement among all partners is reached a new dynamic cloud became operational.

5   Conclusions

This position paper presents the cloud federations of the Contrail project. A Contrail cloud federation supports the horizontal integration of different cloud providers by easing the task of distributing applications among different cloud providers as well as managing them in order to fulfil negotiated SLAs. In order to achieve this goal, a Contrail federation manages users identities, coordinates application deployment and the SLA management conducted by single cloud providers. In this paper we presented these commitments in detail. Then, we described the architecture of the cloud federation-support by showing the main software modules it is composed of, and describing the relationships among those modules. This description is an outline for the future work that has to be conducted in order to realize Contrail cloud federations.

Acknowledgment. The authors acknowledge the support of Project FP7-257438, Contrail: Open Computing Infrastructures for Elastic Services (2010-2013).

References

1. Amazon Elastic Compute Cloud, http://aws.amazon.com/ec2/
2. Windows Azure, http://www.microsoft.com/windowsazure/
3. Buyya, R., Ranjan, R., Calheiros, R.N.: InterCloud: Utility-Oriented Federation of Cloud Computing Environments for Scaling of Application Services. In: Hsu, C.-H., Yang, L.T., Park, J.H., Yeo, S.-S. (eds.) ICA3PP 2010. LNCS, vol. 6081, pp. 13–31. Springer, Heidelberg (2010)
4. Calheiros, R.N., Ranjan, R., Beloglazov, A., De Rose, C.A.F., Buyya, R.: Cloudsim: a toolkit for modeling and simulation of cloud computing environments and evaluation of resource provisioning algorithms. Software: Practice and Experience 41(1), 23–50 (2011)
5. Celesti, A., Tusa, F., Villari, M., Puliafito, A.: How to enhance cloud architectures to enable cross-federation. In: 3rd International Conference on Cloud Computing, pp. 337–345. IEEE (2010)
6. Contrail project, http://www.contrail-project.eu
7. Google App Engine, http://code.google.com/appengine/
8. Open Cloud Computing Interface, http://occi-wg.org/
9. The Open OVF project, http://www.dmtf.org/standards/ovf
10. Reservoir project, http://www.reservoir-fp7.eu
11. Rochwerger, B., Breitgand, D., Levy, E., Galis, A., Nagin, K., Llorente, I.M., Montero, R., Wolfsthal, Y., Elmroth, E., Caceres, J.: The reservoir model and architecture for open federated cloud computing. IBM Journal of Research and Development 53(4), 4 (2010)
12. The SLA@SOI project, http://sla-at-soi.eu/
13. Theilmann, W., Yahyapour, R., Butler, J.: Multi-level sla management for service-oriented infrastructures. In: Towards a Service-Based Internet, pp. 324–335 (2008)

Semi-automatic Composition
of Ontologies for ASKALON Grid Workflows*

Muhammad Junaid Malik, Thomas Fahringer, and Radu Prodan

Institute of Computer Science, University of Innsbruck,
Technikerstraße 21a, A-6020 Innsbruck, Austria
{malik,tf,radu}@dps.uibk.ac.at

Abstract. Automatic workflow composition with the help of ontologies has been addressed by numerous researchers in the past. While ontologies are very useful for automatic and semiautomatic workflow composition, ontology creation itself remains a very important and complex task.

In this paper we present a novel tool to synthesize ontologies for the Abstract Grid Workflow Language (AGWL) which has been used for years to successfully create Grid workflow applications at a high level of abstraction. In order to semi-automatically generate ontologies we use an AGWL Ontology (AGWO - an ontological description of the AGWL language), structural information of one or several input workflows of a given application domain, and semantic enrichment of the structural information with the help of the user. Experiments based on two separate application domains (movie rendering and meteorology) will be shown that demonstrate the effectiveness of our approach by semi-automatically generating ontologies which are then used to automatically create workflow applications.

1 Introduction

The Grid [7] has eliminated the need for dedicated computational facilities and enables the scientists to leverage the computational power of resources located at geographically remote distances.

The Grid workflow programming model [19] has been highly successful in the last decade in facilitating the composition of medium to large-scale applications from existing basic activities defining a sequence of tasks to manage computational science processes. A Grid workflow application represents a collection of computational tasks (activities) interconnected in a directed graph through control and data flow dependencies that are suitable for execution on the Grid.

Domain scientists create Grid workflows with the help of Grid workflow composition tools and execute them with runtime environments [6], [5], [20], and [3]. These tools have greatly simplified the effort of a workflow designer through features such as auto-completion and design suggestions [11], [3] for workflows.

* This research is partially funded by the "Tiroler Zukunftsstiftung", Project name: "Parallel Computing with Java for Manycore Computers" and by the European Union under grant agreement number 261585/SHIWA project.

M. Alexander et al. (Eds.): Euro-Par 2011 Workshops, Part I, LNCS 7155, pp. 169–180, 2012.

Nevertheless manual workflow creation is still a very demanding task. It not only requires comprehensive application domain knowledge but also sufficient skills of the incorporated workflow composition tool.

Numerous research projects tried to automatically generate workflows [6], [3], and [17]. Most of these approaches are based on the analysis of the input data and functional description of the workflow activities with the help of domain ontologies [16]. Successful approaches rely on the completeness of domain ontologies (a formal representation of knowledge as a set of classes within a given application domain) which commonly must be manually created.

A major problem faced by scientists when they try to manually create domain ontologies is that manual ontology creation not only requires extensive domain knowledge and excellent ontology development skills but is also very time consuming.

Semi-automated ontology synthesis expedites the process of ontology creation and automatic updates of ontologies. To address the above mentioned problem, this paper proposes a new method for semi-automatic ontology synthesis for Grid workflows specified with AGWL.

Our approach for ontology creation is performed in three phases. In the first phase one or several AGWL activities or workflows of the same application domain are parsed and analyzed for the information available in the input AGWL data. We extract information about activities and their input and output ports which we refer to as classes. The next phase associates these classes (for instance, all data ports are associated with an AGWL *Data* class) with the AGWL ontology, which results in an intermediate ontology. Thereafter, in the final phase the user has to provide semantic information for these classes which is used to derive the final ontology associated with the domain of the input AGWL data. The final ontology can then be used to automatically create workflows of the given domain.

The paper is organized as follows; Section 2 provides the prerequisites and terminology for the proposed method. In Section 3 we introduce our novel method for semi-automatically creating ontologies. Section 4 presents experimental results, followed by Section 5 that discusses related work. Finally, Section 6 provides the concluding remarks and potential future research.

2   Prerequisite

An account of the terminology used in this paper is presented in this section. A real-world movie rendering algorithm workflow (Fig.1) known as *POVray* [8] is used as an example workflow. The *POVray* workflow is composed of three independent activities.

The first activity takes scene data as input and initializes the process by creating multiple *initialization* files for parallel execution of the Render activity. The Render activity takes this input from the *initialize* activity and generates images for individual frames of the movie. It then packs the frames into a *tarball*, which is consumed by the third activity *Convert* that combines these individual

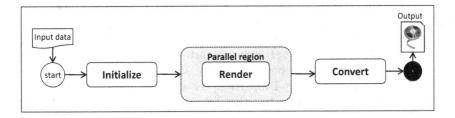

Fig. 1. *POVray* movie rendering workflow

frames and creates a movie. A Grid workflow is a collection of computational tasks (activities) orchestrated in a predefined order to achieve the required execution goals on the Grid. Each activity is described using a number of attributes such *name*, *type*, and *function*.

We use the Askalon Grid application development environment [6] for creating and executing Grid workflows. Askalon simplifies the development and execution of Grid applications, in particular workflows. It is based on a set of high level services which realize the automatic enactment and execution of Grid workflows in a transparent and efficient manner. With the help of its high level middleware services (scheduling, resource management, performance prediction, and enactment) Askalon hides the underlying details of the Grid from the user.

Askalon uses AGWL to describe Grid workflows. AGWL is an XML-based language designed in such a way that the user can concentrate on creating scientific applications without dealing with either the complexity of the Grid or any specific implementation technology such as Web/Grid services. it provides a rich set of constructs to simplify the specification of Grid workflow applications. AGWL has been used for creating workflows from diverse scientific domains, like material sciences, meteorology, astrology, mathematics, and computer graphics. The activity representation in AGWL is called ActivityType *(AT)*. An *AT* is comprised of function description, data *inPorts* and data *outPorts*.

In order to specify ontologies for the semantic description of workflows OWL [9] is used. AGWL ontology (AGWO) is the ontological representation of the AGWL constructs in the form of an OWL document. These constructs encoded as OWL classes are inherited from the *OWL Thing* class (the base class for all OWL ontologies). These classes are used as parent class for the domain specific classes when creating a new ontology. AGWO contains two base classes *Function* and *Data*; that provide foundations for the extended domain classes. Each of these classes may have one or more associated properties, or subclasses. These properties are used to specify additional features or attributes of these classes. An AGWL activity comprises a description of the computational task and its input/output, these components of the activity are represented using the base classes *Function* and *Data* respectively in the AGWO. Further semantic information for these classes is added by specifying *rdfs:onProperty*, and by declaring them as subclasses of existing classes in the ontology using *rdfs:subClassOf* construct. The object-Properties defined for the *Function* class include *hasInput* and *hasOutput*. Whereas the class *Data* has object-Properties *hasRepresentation, isInputTo, isOutputOf, isPartOf,* and *hasPart* etc. The two base classes *Function* and *Data* of AGWO, are extended for each new domain ontology by creating subclasses *[Domain]Function* and *[Domain]Data*. For instance, activities from the *POVray* domain will be inherited from the class *POVrayFunction*, which is in turn inherited from *Function*. The *Function* and *Data* base classes are also related to each other using *hasInput* and *hasOuput* object-Properties. For example, a *POVray* movie rendering function is a *POVrayFunction* that takes as input some *POVrayData* and will produce some *POVrayData* as output. Fig.2 shows the definition of these ontological classes for AGWO.

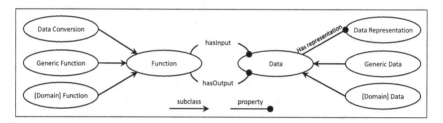

Fig. 2. AGWL ontology (AGWO) *Function* and *Data* classes

To synthesize ontologies, the proposed system extracts and processes extensive information which is stored in the Lexicon database *LDB* and in the Ontology database *ODB*. The *LDB* contains the lexicon of classes with semantic information (e.g. an image in a specific format is provided through an *inPort*), whereas the *ODB* contains the AGWL data and intermediate ontology structure etc., created during the ontology synthesis process.

3   Methodology

The proposed ontology synthesis system is built as part of the ASKALON [6] grid workflow development environment. The three phases of the ontology synthesis process are explained in the following subsections. A block-diagram of the overall system is shown in Fig.3.

3.1   Parsing and Canonicalization

The first component of the system the AGWL parser takes one or a set of AGWL activity constructs belonging to a certain scientific domain as user input. Fig.4 shows an input AGWL activity representation.

The parsing process extracts datasets (e.g. activity datasets such as *{activity, name, type, function}* and data *inPort* datasets such as *{data port, name, type, category, source}*) from the input AGWL data. As all the AGWL activity elements are not structurally identical, and also the attributes of similar workflow elements may vary in number, these datasets need to be normalized before they

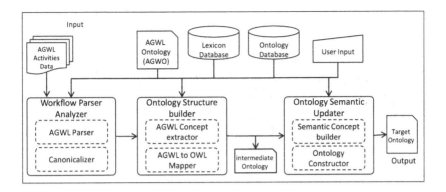

Fig. 3. Block diagram of the ontology synthesis system

can be canonicalized and stored in the database. For instance, some activities may not have a function attribute because they were not meant to be used for semantic analysis. Normalization is the process of adding missing attributes to these AGWL activities thus all the elements have the same set of attributes. After normalization, these datasets are transformed into the canonicalized form, which can be analyzed and processed using standard SQL commands.

```
<activity function="" name="Convert" type="Povray:Convert">
  <dataIns>
    <dataIn category="" name="movieyuv" source="gsiftp://..." type="agwl:file">
      <dataRepresentation>
        <storageType>FileSystem</storageType>
        <contentType>File</contentType>
        <archiveType>none</archiveType>
        <cardinality>multiple</cardinality>
      </dataRepresentation>
    </dataIn>
  </dataIns>
  <dataOuts>
    <dataOut category="" name="movie.avi" saveto="gsiftp://..." type="agwl:file">
      <dataRepresentation>
        <storageType>FileSystem</storageType>
        <contentType>File</contentType>
        <archiveType>none</archiveType>
        <cardinality>single</cardinality>
      </dataRepresentation>
    </dataOut>
  </dataOuts>
</activity>
```

Fig. 4. AGWL representation of the activity *Convert* from *POVray* workflow

In the canonicalization process, all the attributes of the extracted AGWL structures are analyzed. When an attribute without a value is found, the missing information is added to it, this information is collected from existing data contained in the *LDB* or otherwise through user input. The canonicalized form (database relations) of a sample AGWL activity appearing in Fig.4 is shown in Fig.5, which illustrates the three database relations, *activity*, *activity_port* and *data_representation*. The canonicalization process filled the missing attribute values for *function* in *activity*, and *category* in *activity_port* relation.

ACTIVITY				
Id	wf-id	name	type	function
1	1	Convert	Povray:Convert	MovieConv

ACTIVITY_PORT							
id	parent	element	name	category	type	source	saveto
1	1	DataIn	movieyuv	Movie	agwl:file	gsiftp://	NULL
2	1	DataOut	movieavi	Movie	agwl:file	NULL	gsiftp://

DATA_REPRESENTATION					
Id	parent	storage	content	archive	cardinality
1	1	FileSystem	File	None	multiple
2	2	FileSystem	File	tgz	single

Fig. 5. Canonical form (in relational format) of the activity shown in Fig.4

The process is repeated for all the datasets. and the canonicalized information is stored in the ontology database *ODB*. The *ODB* has five relations. The workflow and activity related data is stored in the relations *workflow* and the *activity* respectively. The remaining three relations *act_port* and *wf_port* and *data_representation* are used to store information about activity dataports, workflow dataports, and their corresponding data representations respectively.

3.2   Creation of an Intermediate Ontology

In this phase the intermediate structure of the ontology is created. This is done by retrieving the canonical information for each AGWL element from the Ontology database *ODB* and transforming this information into a unique OWL class representation. Each newly created class is inherited from a *Data* or *Function* class (input/output port or activity) in the AGWO. This process results in an intermediate ontology. Continuing our *POVray* example, the structure of the ontology created for the *convert* activity (Fig.4) is shown in Fig.6. Only one *POVray* activity *Convert* is being used to create the intermediate ontology. The declaration of class *#Convert* is show in Fig.6 which is a placeholder for the *Function* class named *Convert* taken from the AGWL data of the activity.

```
1   <?xml version="1.0"?>
2   <!--ENTITY DECLARATIONS -->
3   <!--NAMESPACE DECLARATIONS -->
4     <owl:Ontology rdf:about=""> <owl:imports rdf:resource="http://www.askalon.org/ontologies/agwl"/></owl:Ontology>
5     <owl:Class rdf:about="#POVRAYFunction"><rdfs:subClassOf rdf:resource="&agwl;Function"/> </owl:Class>
6     <owl:Class rdf:about="#POVRAYData"><rdfs:subClassOf rdf:resource="&agwl;Data"/> </owl:Class>
7     <owl:Class rdf:about="#Movieyuv"/> <rdfs:subClassOf rdf:resource="#POVRAYData"/> </owl:Class>
8     <owl:Class rdf:about="#Movieavi"/> <rdfs:subClassOf rdf:resource="#POVRAYData"/> </owl:Class>
9     <owl:Class rdf:about="#Convert">
10    <rdfs:subClassOf rdf:resource="#POVRAYFunction"/>
11     <rdfs:onProperty rdf:resource="&AGWL;hasInput"/>
12       <rdf:Description rdf:about="#Movieyuv"/>
13     <rdfs:onProperty rdf:resource="&AGWL;hasOutput"/>
14       <rdf:Description rdf:about="#Movieavi"/>
15    </owl:Class>
16   </rdf:RDF>
```

Fig. 6. Structure of intermediate ontology before semantic enrichment

3.3   Semantic Association and Meaning Specification

The last phase deals with the semantic enrichment of the intermediate ontology. As discussed earlier there are two base classes, i.e. *Data* and *Functions*. Similarly an AGWL element can be either AGWL data (input/output port) or an AGWL activity. Every class from the intermediate ontology representing AGWL data or AGWL activity is presented to the user who then has to provide the semantic information for each of these classes. The user can also choose the semantic information for these classes from the *LDB*. Which means specifying a meaningful name for the class and its association with the appropriate parent class in the AGWO.

In case of an input/output port, a name is given to the port which specifies the contents of the port (e.g. an image in a specific data format). The port is declared as a new class inherited from the *[domain]Data* class, which, in turn, is a subclass of the *Data* AGWO class.

The user can also create a new class to specify a certain type of a *Data* class. For example, if the data port represents a *png* or *jpeg* image format, the user might create a class *image* as a subclass of *[Domain]Data* and then declare this data port as a subclass of the *image* class. Similarly in case of activities, the meaningful name provided by the user describes the function performed by each activity, and is declared as a subclass of *[domain]Function* class which, in turn, is a subclass of *Function* AGWO class. Again the user can create new class definitions to categorize the activities by function they perform as done for the data ports. During this interactive process all the information given by the user is stored in the *LDB*. The final ontology created for the activity *Convert* from the *POVray* workflow is illustrated in Fig.7. For the sake of simplicity, the definitions for the OWL entities and XML namespaces have been omitted. In the intermediate ontology the classes *Movieyuv* and *Movieavi* (line 7,8 Fig.6) are extended from the *POVrayData* class. The function *Convert* is by default declared as the subclass of *POVrayFunction* class. In the final ontology (Fig.7) which is enriched with the semantic information there are more class definitions.

On (line 7,8) the definition of *MovieData* and *MovieConv* appears as sub-classes of *POVRAYData* and *POVRAYFunction* respectively. The classes *Movieyuv* and *Movieavi* are now extended from the *MovieData* class (line 9,10), and the *Convert* class is extended from *MovieConv* class. Also as a result of the semantic enrichment the function definition (lines 13-34) of the *Convert* class has complete description of the input port of the function. This final ontology is used by Askalon automatic workflow composition tools to generate Grid workflows.

4   Experiments

Two types of experiments are performed; first to evaluate (validity checking) the ontologies and secondly to measure the performance of our ontology synthesis approach.

```
1   <?xml version="1.0"?>
2   <!--ENTITY DECLARATIONS -->
3   <!--NAMESPACE DECLARATIONS -->
4   <owl:Ontology rdf:about=""><owl:imports rdf:resource="http://www.askalon.org/ontologies/agwl"/></owl:Ontology>
5   <owl:Class rdf:about="#POVRAYFunction"><rdfs:subClassOf rdf:resource="&agwl;Function"/></owl:Class>
6   <owl:Class rdf:about="#POVRAYData"><rdfs:subClassOf rdf:resource="&agwl;Data"/></owl:Class>
7   <owl:Class rdf:about="#MovieData"> <rdfs:subClassOf rdf:resource="#POVRAYData"/></owl:Class>
8   <owl:Class rdf:about="#MovieConv"><rdfs:subClassOf rdf:resource="#POVRAYFunction"/></owl:Class>
9   <owl:Class rdf:about="#Movieyuv"/> <rdfs:subClassOf rdf:resource="#MovieData"/></owl:Class>
10  <owl:Class rdf:about="#Movieavi"/>    <rdfs:subClassOf rdf:resource="#MovieData"/></owl:Class>
11  <owl:Class rdf:about="#Convert">
12  <rdfs:subClassOf rdf:resource="#MovieConv"/>
13   <rdfs:onProperty rdf:resource="&AGWL;hasInput"/>
14      <owl11:onClass>
15          <owl:Class>
16              <owl:intersectionOf rdf:parseType="Collection">
17                  <rdf:Description rdf:about="#Movieyuv"/>
18                  <owl:Restriction>
19                  <owl:onProperty rdf:resource="http://www.askalon.org/ontologies/agwl#hasRepresentation"/>
20                      <owl:intersectionOf rdf:parseType="Collection">
21                          <rdf:Description rdf:about="http://www.askalon.org/ontologies/agwl#DataRepresentation"/>
22                          <owl:Restriction>
23                          <owl:onProperty rdf:resource="http://www.askalon.org/ontologies/agwl#hasStorageType"/>
24                              <owl:hasValue rdf:resource="http://www.askalon.org/ontologies/agwl#FileSystem"/>
25                              <owl:onProperty rdf:resource="http://www.askalon.org/ontologies/agwl#hasContentType"/>
26                              <owl:someValuesFrom rdf:resource="#File"/>
27                              <owl:cardinality rdf:datatype="http://www.w3.org/2001/XMLSchema#nonNegativeInteger">
28                              1
29                              </owl:cardinality>
30                          </owl:Restriction>
31                      </owl:Restriction>
32                  </owl:intersectionOf>
33              </owl:Class>
34          </owl11:onClass>
35      <rdfs:onProperty rdf:resource="&AGWL;hasOutput"/>
36      <!--DETAILS OMITTED -->
37      </owl:Class>
38  </rdf:RDF>
```

Fig. 7. Structure of the final ontology

4.1   Ontology Evaluation

For the evaluation of domain ontologies the gold standard approach [13] is most
widely used. This approach is based on comparison of the newly synthesized
ontologies to existing ontologies in the same domain. These reference ontologies
in the domain which are known to be valid and are known as "gold standard".
Other approaches include real life testing of the ontologies [15], verification of ontologies manually; involving human effort [12], and by comparing the ontology to
the source data [2] that is used to generate the ontology. For our experiment, we
combine the "gold standard" approach with a real life application of ontologies
to evaluate the domain ontologies synthesized by using the described method of
this paper.

For the gold standard evaluation an existing manually created ontology from
the meteorology domain is used as the "gold standard" ontology [16]. We used
existing AGWL activities of the meteorology domain to semi-automatically synthesize a meteorology ontology based on the described approach of this paper.
The resulting ontology has then been used to automatically generate a meteorology workflow with the Askalon workflow synthesis tool [16]. The so generated
workflow represents the same functionality as given by the workflow created by
hand or when using the gold standard meteorology ontology with the main difference that our approach takes much less time (see Table.1). Apart from the

major objective of synthesizing valid ontologies, the secondary goal of the ontology synthesis approach was to improve user experience and reduce the effort required to synthesize ontologies. Table.1 shows the time needed to generate the workflow manually versus semi-automatically based on our approach. It took almost two weeks to manually create the gold standard meteorology ontology (used as reference ontology in our experiments) after after acquiring complete domain knowledge. Whereas our approach required substantially less time which was in the order of several hours.

4.2 Performance Measurements for Ontology Synthesis Process

To evaluate the performance behavior of the ontology synthesis tool, We used the AGWL data from the movie rendering workflow *POVray* [8]. The movie rendering application used for the experiments takes four parameters: a set of input frames, initialization file, configuration file, and number of frames to be processed per activity. The original *POVray* workflow contains only three activities as shown in Fig.1. We introduce intermediate artificial activities in the workflow to evaluate the performance behavior of the tool with higher number of activities. These additional activities are just data conversion activities and do not change the actual functionality of the workflow.

Table.1 tabulates the time required to synthesize the ontologies for the above mentioned variations of the *POVray* workflow. The manual input is taking most of the time in the synthesis process. Yet it is clear from the time measurements that by using our ontology synthesis approach, the time required to create ontologies for AGWL data is substantially shorter than a pure manual approach.

Table 1. The Ontology synthesis system performance measurements

Method	Activities	I/O ports	Database seek	Processing	Manual input	Total
				Time in seconds.		
Movie Rendering Domain (Workflow:: *POVray*)						
Semi-Automatic	3	12	0.104	1.56	620	621.664
Semi-Automatic	6	18	0.379	8.338	1200	1208.717
Semi-Automatic	8	24	0.711	17.775	1800	1818.486
Semi-Automatic	10	30	1.273	36.917	2800	2838.19
Meteorology Domain (Workflow:: *MeteoAG*)						
Semi-Automatic	15	79	3.53	11.47	17567	17582
Manual	15	71	≈ 120 work hours			

5 Related Work

The use of ontologies in the context of automatic workflow composition has driven the scientists towards the development of automatic ontology synthesis techniques.

Two approaches are particularly similar to our method, which use three phases for ontology creation. The OBO-Edit tool [22] involves the extraction of terms or keywords for ontologies from the source text. This leads to definitions of the terms (classes) by using online information. Relationships between the terms are explored which lead to ontology classes. The OBO-framework loads classes from existing ontologies. Only these classes can act as potential parents for the newly discovered classes. In our approach, besides the use of a lexicon database for searching existing classes, we extend this functionality by providing the user an opportunity to create new classes on-the-fly, if no suitable parent class is found automatically. Moreover, our system automatically establishes relations based on the occurrences of such classes in AGWO. This reduces the chance of having incorrect relations between two classes because AGWO is proven to be correctly defined for AGWL [16].

Another attempt on automatic ontology synthesis [14], synthesizes ontologies based on existing ontologies for similar input information. This approach introduces two additional phases, namely validation and evolution. It tries to match and align the newly found classes with existing classes in the reference ontologies. This method very much depends on the availability and richness of existing ontologies, whereas in our approach ontologies can be generated from scratch without any need of existing domain ontologies. Numerous other attempts explored ontology synthesis [18], [4], [21] and [10], all of them largely focused on very specific aspects of a full ontology synthesis scenario. For example, a comprehensive study of the classification of classes and matching and alignment techniques is presented in [4]. In [10] a detailed analysis of ontology alignment techniques is presented.

In [1] the idea of mapping XSD file entities to OWL classes is described. A limitation of their approach is the absence of relations between different types of classes.

6   Conclusion

A crucial aspect towards automatic generation of Grid workflow applications is the availability of effective ontologies. This paper introduces a novel tool for semi-automatic synthesis of domain ontologies as a basis for the automatic generation of Grid workflows (written in the language AGWL). For this purpose we use an AGWL Ontology, structural information as AGWL data of a given domain, and semantic enrichment of the structural information with the help of the user. Experiments have been shown based on two separate application domains (movie rendering and meteorology) that demonstrate the quality of our approach. Semi-automatically generated ontologies are used by ASKALON to automatically generate workflows. Furthermore, performance experiments shown in the Table 1 reflect that the time it takes to synthesize ontologies even for large number of input activities is very reasonable.

References

1. Bohring, H., Auer, S.: Mapping xml to owl ontologies. In: Jantke, K.P., Fhnrich, K.-P., Wittig, W.S. (eds.) Leipziger Informatik-Tage. LNI, vol. 72, pp. 147–156. GI (2005)
2. Brewster, C., Alani, H., Dasmahapatra, S., Wilks, Y.: Data driven ontology evaluation. In: Proceedings of the International Conference on Language Resources and Evaluation (LREC), Lisbon, Portugal (2004)
3. Callahan, S.P., Freire, J., Santos, E., Scheidegger, C.E., Silva, C.T., Vo, H.T.: Vistrails: visualization meets data management. In: Proceedings of the 2006 ACM SIGMOD International Conference on Management of Data, SIGMOD 2006, pp. 745–747. ACM, New York (2006)
4. Castano, S., Ferrar, A., Montanelli, S., Hess, G.N., Bruno, S.: State of the art on ontology coorination and matching. deliverable 4.4 version 1.0 final (2007)
5. Deelman, E., Singh, G., Su, M.H., Blythe, J., Gil, A., Kesselman, C., Mehta, G., Vahi, K., Berriman, G.B., Good, J., Laity, A., Jacob, J.C., Katz, D.S.: Pegasus: a framework for mapping complex scientific workflows onto distributed systems. Scientific Programming Journal 13, 219–237 (2005)
6. Fahringer, T., Jugravu, A., Pllana, S., Prodan, R., Seragiotto, C., Truong, H.L.: ASKALON: a tool set for cluster and Grid computing. Concurrency - Practice and Experience 17(2-4), 143–169 (2005)
7. Foster, I., Kesselman, C. (eds.): The grid: blueprint for a new computing infrastructure. Morgan Kaufmann Publishers Inc., San Francisco (1999)
8. Povray, http://www.povray.org/
9. Web ontology language, http://www.w3.org/2004/OWL/
10. Euzenat, J., Le Bach, T., Barrasa, J., Bouquet, P., De Bo, J., Dieng, R., Ehrig, M., Hauswirth, M., Jarrar, M., Lara, R., Maynard, D., Napoli, A., Stamou, G., Stuckenschmidt, H., Shvaiko, P., Tessaris, S., Van Acker, S., Zaihrayeu, I.: State of the art on ontology alignment. knowledge web deliverable d2.2.3 (2004)
11. Junaid, M., Berger, M., Vitvar, T., Plankensteiner, K., Fahringer, T.: Workflow composition through design suggestions using design-time provenance information. In: 5th IEEE International Conference on E-Science Workshops, pp. 110–117 (December 2009)
12. Lozano-Tello, A., Gómez-Pérez, A.: Ontometric: A method to choose the appropriate ontology. Journal of Database Management 15(2) (April-June 2004)
13. Maedche, A., Staab, S.: Measuring Similarity between Ontologies. In: Gómez-Pérez, A., Benjamins, V.R. (eds.) EKAW 2002. LNCS (LNAI), vol. 2473, pp. 251–263. Springer, Heidelberg (2002)
14. Automatic Ontology Generation: State of the Art. University of Versailles Technical report. Ivan bedini and benjamin nguyen (2007)
15. Porzel, R., Malaka, R.: A Task-based Approach for ontology Evaluation. In: Workshop on Ontology Learning and Population, ECAI 2004 (2004)
16. Qin, J., Fahringer, T.: A novel domain oriented approach for scientific grid workflow composition. In: Proceedings of the 2008 ACM/IEEE Conference on Supercomputing, SC 2008, pp. 21:1–21:12. IEEE Press, Piscataway (2008)
17. Slota, R., Zieba, J., Kryza, B., Kitowski, J.: Knowledge evolution supporting automatic workflow composition. In: e-Science, p. 37. IEEE Computer Society (2006)
18. Sure, Y., Studer, R., Fensel, C.D., Lebensversicherungsund, S., Reimer, C.U.: On-to-knowledge methodology - final version (2002)

19. Taylor, I., Deelman, E., Gannon, D., Shields, M.: Workflows for e-science. XXII, 530 p. 181 illus., Hardcover (2007)
20. Taylor, I., Wang, I., Shields, M., Majithia, S.: Distributed computing with triana on the grid: Research articles. Concurr. Comput.: Pract. Exper. 17, 1197–1214 (2005)
21. Vrandecic, D., Pinto, H.S., Sure, Y., Tempich, C.: The diligent knowledge processes. Journal of Knowledge Management 9(5), 85–96 (2005)
22. Wächter, T., Schroeder, M.: Semi-automated ontology generation within obo-edit. Bioinformatics 26, i88–i96 (2010)

The Chemical Machine: An Interpreter for the Higher Order Chemical Language

Vilmos Rajcsányi and Zsolt Németh

MTA SZTAKI Computer and Automation Research Institute,
P.O. Box 63, H-1518 - Hungary
zsnemeth@sztaki.hu

Abstract. The notion of chemical computing has evolved for more than two decades. From the seminal idea several models, calculi and languages have been developed and there are various proposals for applying chemical models in distributed problem solving where some sort of autonomy, self-evolving nature and adaptation is sought. While there are some experimental chemical implementations, most of these proposals remained at the paper-and-pencil stage. This paper presents a general purpose interpreter for the Higher Order Chemical Language. The design follows that of logic/functional languages and bridges the gap between the highly abstract chemical model and the physical machine by an abstract interpreter engine. As a novel approach the engine is based on a modified hierarchical production system and turns away from imperative languages.

1 Introduction

The advent of large scale distributed systems (such as grids, service oriented architectures) introduced a group of problems that are hard to solve by humans or by any machinery in an exact way due to the very large number of entities, their heterogeneous nature, partial lack of information of their state, unpredictable, error prone behavior and many other factors. Approximately the same time appeared the notion of autonomic computing [17] where entities are supposed to monitor and control themselves according to some strategies: self-configuration, self-optimization, self-healing and self-protection. Since then a large number of reflective, self-* properties of computing entities have been proposed and realized. This new notion of computing naturally attracted non-conventional approaches; in fact the seminal paper [17] also took inspiration from the nervous system [13]. There is a large group of models that mimic various biological, chemical, physical, ethological processes and phenomenons or simply take them as metaphors.

In the chemical programming paradigm, instead of computing steps (instructions) and their strict order, a program is conceived as a chemical solution where data and procedures are molecules floating around and computation is a series of reactions between these molecules. Note, that in this case chemistry is just an inspiration or an abstract metaphor as opposed to chemical models (artificial chemistries) where computation closely simulates some chemical processes [12]. This vision of chemical computing is formalized in the γ-calculus [3] as (without the chemical guise) a declarative functional computational model where terms are commutative and associative.

M. Alexander et al. (Eds.): Euro-Par 2011 Workshops, Part I, LNCS 7155, pp. 181–190, 2012.

The chemical model and the γ-family (the calculus and the related languages) has already been investigated in various distributed scenarios, like self-organizing systems [8] where a self-healing, self-optimizing and self-protecting mail system is studied. Grids are obviously a good target for applying the chemical model in some well-known problems like coordinating a ray-tracing example on desktop grids [7], enacting workflows on-the-fly with strong emphasis on dynamicity both in the environment and in the workflow structure [11] and modeling self-developing secure virtual organisations [2]. Recently service oriented techniques and clouds also attracted great attention and proposals like chemical based service orchestration [6], dynamic service composition [5], dynamic service composition with partial instantiations and re-using instantiations [18] and others. Note, that the chemical model in all these cases is not applied for problem solving (in terms of solving any computational tasks) but *coordinates* the execution so that it may exhibit some of the features of the chemical metaphor like timely response to events, adaptation, self-evolution, intrinsic concurrency, independency, maximum parallelism and many others.

Albeit application of the chemical metaphor in grids and service oriented systems is well studied and various concepts are elaborated, appropriate interpreter and development tools for executing programs expressed in the chemical metaphor are largely missing. Most of these models require framework that is (i) able to execute the code expressed in a chemical language and (ii) provides interfaces to the embedding system so that some processes can be controlled by the chemical program meanwhile monitored data can be gathered. The work introduced in this paper is focused on (i) and aimed at creating an *interpreter* that supports the entire Higher Order Chemical Language (HOCL), a language that is based on and extends the γ-calculus. While the chemical model is quite different from any other widespread computing models and languages, careful study revealed similarities in other paradigms and the combination of techniques related to declarative languages and those of production systems allowed a realization of the interpreter in a short development cycle. At deciding the implementation means attention was paid to (ii) so that the interpreter can be interfaced with various tools and environments in the future. The work is focusing on the *design* and *realization* of the interpreter. Establishing autonomic or adaptive behaviour in the chemical framework is on one hand presented in papers [7][11] [5][8][18], etc., on the other hand related to the *application* of the interpreter and not presented here.

2 The Chemical Computational Model

Most algorithms are expressed sequentially even if they describe inherently parallel activities. Gamma (General Abstract Model for Multiset Manipulation) [4] aimed at relaxing the artificial sequentializing of algorithms. It is a multiset rewriting system where the program is represented by a set of declarative rules that are atomic, fire independently and potentially simultaneously, according to *local* and *actual* conditions. There is no concept of any centralized control, ordering, serialization rather, the computation is carried out in a non-deterministic, self-evolving way. It has been shown in [4] that some fundamental problems of computer science (sorting, prime testing, string processing, graph algorithms, etc.) can be expressed in Gamma in a concise and elegant way.

The γ-calculus is a formal definition of the chemical paradigm. The fundamental data structure is the multiset M. γ-terms (molecules) are: variables x, γ-abstractions $\gamma\langle x\rangle.M$, multisets (M_1, M_2) and solutions $\langle M\rangle$. Juxtaposition of γ-terms is commutative ($M_1, M_2 \equiv M_2, M_1$) and associative ($M_1, (M_2, M_3) \equiv (M_1, M_2), M_3$). Commutativity and associativity are the properties that realize the 'Brownian-motion', i.e., the free distribution and unspecified reaction order among molecules . The γ-abstractions are the reactive molecules that can take other molecules or solutions and replace them. Due to the commutative and associative rules, the order of parameters is indifferent; molecules, solutions participating in the reaction are extracted by pattern matching – *any* of the matching ones may react. The semantics of a γ-reduction is $(\gamma\langle x\rangle.M), \langle N\rangle \rightarrow_\gamma M[x := N]$ i.e., the two reacting terms on the left hand side are replaced by the body of the γ-abstraction where each free occurrence of variable x is replaced by parameter N if N is inert . Reactions may depend on certain conditions expressed as C in $\gamma\langle x\rangle\lfloor C\rfloor.M$ that can be reduced only if C evaluates to true before the reaction . Reactions can capture multiple molecules in a single atomic step. The universal symbol ω matches any pattern. Reactions are governed by: (i) law of locality , i.e. if a reaction can occur, it will occur in the same way irrespectively to the environment; and (ii) membrane law , i.e. reactions can occur in nested solutions or in other words, solutions may contain sub-solutions separated by a membrane. The γ-calculus is a *higher order* model, where abstractions – just like any other molecules – can be passed as parameters or yielded as a result of a reduction [8][3].

The Higher Order Chemical Language (HOCL) [3] is a language based on the Gamma principles more precisely, the γ-calculus extended with expressions, types, pairs, empty solutions and names. HOCL uses the self-explanatory **replace... by... if...** construct to express rules. **replace** P **by** M **if** C formally corresponds to $\gamma(P)\lfloor C\rfloor.M$ with a major difference: while γ-abstractions are destroyed by the reactions, HOCL rules are n-shot and remain in the solution nevertheless, single-shot γ-style rules can also be added. **replace... by... if...** is followed by **in** $\langle...\rangle$ that specifies the solution the active molecule floats in. Notable features (extensions) of HOCL are: types,= that can be added to patterns for matching; pairs in form of $A_1 : A_2$ where A_1 and A_2 are atoms; and naming that allows to identify and hence, match rules, e.g. **let** $inc =$ **replace** x **by** $x + 1$ **in** $\langle 1, 2, 3, inc\rangle$ specifies an active molecule called inc which captures an integer and replaces it with its successor, floating in a solution together with integers 1, 2, 3. Some possible reduction steps can be (note, the model is non-deterministic, there are different possible execution paths):

$$\langle 1, 2, 3, inc\rangle \rightarrow \langle 2, 2, 3, inc\rangle \rightarrow \langle 3, 2, 3, inc\rangle \rightarrow \langle 3, 2, 4, inc\rangle \rightarrow \langle 3, 3, 4, inc\rangle$$

3   The Concept of the Chemical Interpreter

In case of declarative languages, the semantics of the execution model and that of the underlying physical architecture is quite different therefore, they are usually executed via an abstract, hypothetic engine placed inbetween. The program is first transformed (compiled) into the language of the abstract engine that successively interprets the input and executes it. From the programmer's point of view the abstract engine is a machine that is able to execute the high-level language natively, it hides all the details of the real physical machine whereas, the abstract engine and its language is closer to the physical machine and can be executed in a simpler way (the semantic gap is narrower.) The most known such engine is the Warren's Abstract Machine (WAM) for executing Prolog [1] or SECD and Lispkit [15] for executing functional languages but there are many such examples like some implementations of (early) Pascal [19] or less known and more specific languages like Palingol [10].

The design of our chemical engine is also based on this principle. Thus, in our approach HOCL is first transformed into the code of the abstract engine and then this intermadiate code is interpreted. It is easy to see that HOCL execution resembles that of (i) functional languages with the exception of commutative and associative properties and (ii) production systems with the exception of hierarchical knowledge base and concurrent execution; yet not equivalent to any of these. To shorten the development cycle we carefully examined the similarities and differences in the computational models and opted to realize the HOCL abstract engine based on the notion of a production system. A production system consists of facts (knowledge) and rules (behaviour) applied to facts. If the facts fulfill conditions assigned to a certain rule, the rule is activated. From many activated rules one is selected by conflict resolution and fired. Firing a rule means executing its action part that updates the facts and leads to firing further rules. This so called production cycle is repeated over again.

Some of the key requirements of an efficient and simple realization of interpreting HOCL. (i) Efficient pattern matching. Production systems often apply the RETE-algorithm [14] in such a way, a highly efficient pattern matching, the most important cornerstone of the realization is available ready-made. This is the main inspiration of realizing the HOCL interpreter on the foundation of a production system. (ii) Nested solutions (hierarchical knowledge base). Most production systems assume a global knowledge base and do not allow the structured or hierarchical facts. This aspect needs a careful elaboration in the HOCL abstract engine as it is different in production systems. (iii) Concurrency. The concept of locality (molecules react with their "neighbor" molecules) is simulated by a random choice of potential molecules. Yet, the dynamics of the chemical system is quite different from that of a production system and the random conflict resolution needs further refinement. (iv) Level of parallelism. The γ-model is inherently concurrent and this behavior should be modeled with multiple concurrent execution threads yet, their level (granularity) can be different. To keep the granularity at a reasonable level yet, to enable concurrent behavior, we assigned an execution thread to each solution thus, solutions can evolve independently whereas concurrency within a solution (race condition among molecules) is represented by random choice of reacting molecules.

The conceptual representation of various elements of a HOCL program will be introduced by Dijkstra's Dutch flag [4], as an example. The aim of the Dutch flag problem is to order three colors, white, red and blue in a randomized array so that they are arranged according to the stripes of the Dutch national flag: red, white and blue.

let red = **replace** $\langle i, red \rangle, \langle j, white \rangle$ **by** $\langle i, white \rangle, \langle j, red \rangle$ **if** $i > j$ **in**
let $white$ = **replace** $\langle i, white \rangle, \langle j, blue \rangle$ **by** $\langle i, blue \rangle, \langle j, white \rangle$ **if** $i > j$ **in**
let $blue$ = **replace** $\langle i, red \rangle, \langle j, blue \rangle$ **by** $\langle i, blue \rangle, \langle j, red \rangle$ **if** $i > j$ **in**
$\langle \langle 1, blue \rangle, \langle 2, white \rangle, \langle 3, white \rangle, \langle 4, red \rangle, \langle 5, blue \rangle, \langle 6, white \rangle, red, white, blue \rangle$

We introduce a simplified, easy-to-read pseudo code for representing and explaining the code of the production system. While they show all the necessary information many irrelevant details are eliminated. A production system represents its knowledge in facts like (1) or (1 2 3). Some facts can have named slots like ((x 1) (y 2) (z 3)). A rule has a left hand side (LHS) pattern that must be matched to enable the rule followed by $\Rightarrow$ and a right hand side (RHS) action that is triggered if the rule fires.

Molecules. As one may expect, a *passive molecule* is simply transformed into a fact like $1 \rightarrow$ (molecule (value 1)) or $red \rightarrow$ (molecule (color red)). A straightforward (and naive) approach would be to represent *active molecules* as production rules. This way however, makes it very hard to realize the higher order property of the HOCL model where active molecules can be captured transformed, canceled or added just like any other molecule. Therefore, active molecules are represented by a rule *and* a fact. Thus, molecule red is transformed into a fact (rule red) and a rule with pattern shown as (some parts to be refined later):

```
(defrule red
        (rule red)
        ;match <i, red> and <j, white> if i>j
   ⇒
        ;swap <i, red> and <j, white>
```

This rule can fire if fact (rule red) is present in the same solution. All modifications to the active molecules (added, withdrawn, transferred) are performed on this fact that enables the rule. For instance, moving the active red molecule from one solution to another is simply moving the (rule red) fact.

Solutions are two faced entities: they are data if inert and are separate running processes (and thus, unable to be matched) if active. Solutions can hold passive molecules, active molecules, other solutions or pairs and can be nested in arbitrary depth. Unfortunately, production systems usually do not allow nesting the facts hence, there is no straightforward representation. We opted for a Prolog-like representation of compound terms [1] where not actual terms but references to terms that are stored. Therefore, molecules are augmented with identifiers so that references can be put to them. For instance, $\langle 1, blue \rangle$ is represented as two facts (molecule (value 1) (in id_k)) and (molecule (color blue) (in id_k)) and then the solution itself is a fact (solution id_k) (just the idea is shown here, there is more information related to solutions and molecules). This representation seemingly calls for a complicated recursive pattern-matching but it can be solved very efficiently in a flat manner as (following the above example):

```
(defrule red
         (rule red)
         (solution x)
         (molecule (value i)(in x))
         (molecule (color red)(in x))
         (solution y)
         (molecule (value j)(in y))
         (molecule (color white)(in y))
         (test i > j)
     ⇒
         ;swap <i, red> and <j, white>
```

where the matching variables represent the constraint so that molecules belonging to the given solution are selected. Similarly, multiply nested solutions are represented in the same way. Pairs are a special case of solutions: they have exactly two molecules inside and their order *is* relevant. With minor differences, all the principles introduced for solutions are used for pairs, too.

Transfer between Solutions. Molecules can be moved between solutions for instance, in **replace** $\langle i, red \rangle, \langle j, white \rangle$ **by** $\langle i, white \rangle, \langle j, red \rangle$ the two color molecules are exchanged between the two solutions. This is a very simple example but there are cases where multiple molecules are moved, or every molecule (ω) moved except some. Furthermore, deleting a molecule can be traced back to the same situation where it is taken from a solution but put nowhere. In order to handle all these cases efficiently and uniformly, we categorized the following cases as types

- **replace** $a : \langle \omega_a \rangle, b : \langle \omega_b \rangle$ **by** $a : \langle \rangle, b : \langle \omega_a, \omega_b \rangle$ – moving *all* molecules, e.g. from solution tagged a to solution b
- **replace** $a : \langle a, b, c, \omega_a \rangle, b : \langle \omega_b \rangle$ **by** $a : \langle \omega_a \rangle, b : \langle a, b, c, \omega_b \rangle$ – moving certain molecules, e.g. a, b, c form solution a to solution b
- **replace** $a : \langle a, b, c, \omega_a \rangle, b : \langle \omega_b \rangle$ **by** $a : \langle a, b, c \rangle, b : \langle \omega_a, \omega_b \rangle$ – moving all but certain molecules, e.g. all molecules from solution a to b except a, b, c

They can be further classified if the source and target solutions are top-level or nested ones or nil. Altogether 15 types of operations belong to this category. In fact, in reactions most of the actions are putting molecules around therefore, this operation must be very simple in the language (and efficient in the implementation). The intermediate language therefore is extended with (relocate toMove, notToMove, from, to), a special custom function. Thus, we can finalize the example as

```
(defrule red
 (rule red)
 (solution x)
 (molecule (value i)(in x))
 (molecule (color red)(in x))
 (solution y)
 (molecule (value j)(in y))
 (molecule (color white)(in y))
 (test i > j)
⇒
```

```
(relocate (molecule (value i)(in x)) nil (solution x)(solution y))
(relocate (molecule (value j)(in y)) nil (solution y)(solution x))
```

Hence, the active molecule *red* has been rewritten into `rule red` of the intermediate language. It is important to mention that – just like the HOCL reaction – firing a rule is an atomic step. That is, in the above example molecules are transferred in a single step and there are no intermediate inconsistent states.

4   Implementation

The principles of an HOCL interpreter based on a production system drafted above have been implemented in jess [16], a Java based production system. Here some additional, implementation related details are explained only.

The Intermediate Language. HOCL programs are transformed (compiled) into an intermediate language that is based on the jess script language with (i) some restrictions and (ii) an added function. Restriction means a fixed template of molecules and a strict pattern in the head of rules. These principles were shown in Section 3 but in reality molecules contain more information (technical details) than presented before; there is an inherent need to keep them consistent. Therefore, there is a `molecule` template that defines all the necessary slots and all other passive molecules are derived from that. Restrictions are also present in the head of rules: capturing a molecule has a certain pattern sequence that must be strictly followed. The added function is the `relocate` introduced earlier. It is important to notice that this is the only one function that is not part of the jess script language and a large area of possible cases are realized by this single instruction. Due to the minimal changes introduced, the intermediate language is very close to the jess script. One familiar with jess or other production systems can easily read, understand and modify the intermediate language. Minimal changes also ensure that the intermediate language is executed as efficiently as the native jess script.

The Interpreter. We kept the same principle: introduce as little changes as possible thus, the HOCL interpreter is just a slightly modified jess engine. Furthermore, in case of the interpreter all these changes are transparent to the user. Albeit invisible, some important modifications and extensions must have been added to the basic execution mechanism of jess mainly due to the required support of hierarchical knowledge base. These include activities related to spawning a new RETE-engine (initiate a new solution) or opposedly, stop a RETE-engine. In such cases transferring data to a new process and vice versa by maintaining consistency, correctness and avoid synchronization problem is a complex task. To achieve these goals efficiently, Java procedures operate on the internal data structures of jess. Similarly, the realization of *relocate* is encoded in the interpreter as a custom Java function. Furthermore, the random conflict resolution must have been modified, see the explanation in Section 5. Measurements showed that these additional functionalities in the jess engine do not add significant overhead or cause performance degradation.

User Interface, Program Control and External Interfaces. There is a simple user interface developed that facilitates the execution, tracing and debugging of HOCL programs (Figure 1). The main fields show the current reactions, the possible reactions in each solution and the solution structure. The latter is augmented with some graphical aids to see where reactions are possible and what are the inert solutions. Solutions and molecules are clickable: new molecules can be added to solutions at run-time whereas breakpoints can be added or withdrawn on active molecules. Tracing and debugging is supported by various run modes: step-by-step, continuous run with variable speed and breakpoint. For specific applications custom-made user interfaces can be made for instance, an experimental tic-tac-toe game table was implemented (see Section 5). This latter also demonstrates how easily the interpreter can be interfaced with other programs that is a fundamental requirement for coordinating tasks the chemical paradigm is aimed at. In this case the game board is a separate process and steps made by the user are external events imported into the chemical engine whereas steps made by the computer are events that are exported and displayed graphically. In the same way, other sources of events and control can be realized in different scenarios.

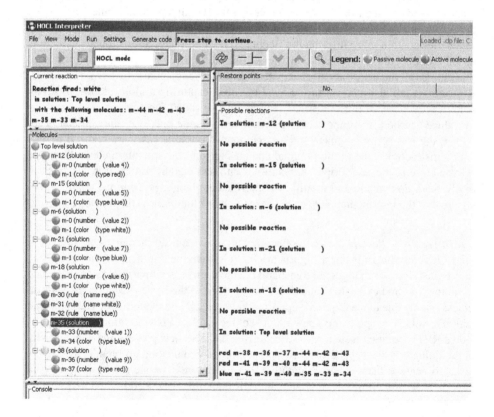

Fig. 1. Graphical interface for the HOCL interpreter

5   Experiences Learned

The interpreter was tested by a large set of toy examples to verify the correctness of elementary constructs in the language. Also, it was tested by some nontrivial problems listed in [4][8]. Here we present two experiences we learned beyond the simple correctness tests.

An implementation of the foxes and rabbits problem (Lotka-Volterra equations [9]) revealed that dynamicity in the chemical model is a crucial issue. This type of applications should oscillate (the number of foxes and rabbits change periodically) but our initial attempts diverged. The problem was caused by the random conflict resolution of the production system that did not really simulate the random mixture of molecules and must have been replaced by a custom made one. While this sensitivity seemingly affects a very little portion of computational problems, the chemical approach is associated with realizing self-* autonomic systems where evolution and dynamicity of certain populations is of fundamental importance and such aspects must be carefully researched and elaborated.

A player vs. machine tic-tac-toe game revealed the importance of the appropriate transformation of HOCL into the intermediate language. A very simple implementation of this game was encoded in HOCL in a concise way and was executed by the interpreter. Yet, as the size of the field grew, performance problems started to appear and around the table size of 30*30 the game became unplayable due to large response times. The root of the problem was in expressing the HOCL program in the intermediate language. While HOCL allows a very expressive and elegant problem statement, pattern matching works more efficiently on numerous but simple rules. Therefore, a complex HOCL statement must be transformed into the intermediate language so that it is broken into simpler, more specific rules that facilitate pattern matching; tic-tac-toe was successfully hand coded so that it became scalable. While the transformation of HOCL into the intermediate language (compiler construction) can be described easily, taking into consideration such performance issues requires more research work.

6   Conclusions

In this paper we presented the design and implementation principles of an HOCL interpreter for executing programs written in a higher order chemical language. The chemical computing model is an upcoming candidate for realizing autonomic properties in various distributed settings (such as grid and service based environments, see [5] [11] [18]).

The proposed execution of HOCL programs is an interpreter realized as an abstract engine. The engine is based on a production system that lends its state-of-the-art pattern matching mechanism but modified to support the hierarchical notion of knowledge base of the chemical semantics and fulfill other technical challenges. The interpreter supports the entire HOCL language and has a graphical user interface and a basic support for tracing and debugging. The realization of the interpreter also makes possible to interface it to other systems for observation and control.

Test experiments proved the correctness of the interpreter. They also revealed the importance of efficient representation of the HOCL program at the intermediate level and that of the dynamic behavior. Both are strongly related to self-evolving properties of autonomic systems and therefore, will play crucial role in real-life applications. These aspects are targets of further research.

Acknowledgements. The research leading to these results has received funding from the European Community's Seventh Framework Programme FP7/2007-2013 under grant agreement 215483 (S-Cube).

References

1. Aït-Kaci, H.: Warren's Abstract Machine: A Tutorial Reconstruction. MIT Press (1991)
2. Arenas, A.E., Banâtre, J.-P., Priol, T.: Developing Autonomic and Secure Virtual Organisations with Chemical Programming. In: Guerraoui, R., Petit, F. (eds.) SSS 2009. LNCS, vol. 5873, pp. 75–89. Springer, Heidelberg (2009)
3. Banâtre, J.-P., Fradet, P., Radenac, Y.: Generalised multisets for chemical programming. Math. Struct. in Comp. Science 16, 557–580 (2006)
4. Banâtre, J.-P., Le Métayer, D.: Programming by multiset transformation. Commun. ACM 36(1), 98–111 (1993)
5. Banâtre, J.-P., Priol, T.: Chemical programming of future service-oriented architectures. JSW 4(7), 738–746 (2009)
6. Banâtre, J.-P., Priol, T., Radenac, Y.: Service Orchestration Using the Chemical Metaphor. In: Brinkschulte, U., Givargis, T., Russo, S. (eds.) SEUS 2008. LNCS, vol. 5287, pp. 79–89. Springer, Heidelberg (2008)
7. Banâtre, J.-P., Le Scouarnec, N., Priol, T., Radenac, Y.: Towards "chemical" desktop grids. In: eScience, pp. 135–142 (2007)
8. Banâtre, J.-P., Fradet, P., Radenac, Y.: Programming self-organizing systems with the higher-order chemical language. International Journal of Unconventional Computing 3(3), 161–177 (2007)
9. Berryman, A.A.: The origins and evolution of predator-prey theory. Ecology (73) (1992)
10. Billoud, B., Kontic, M., Viari, A.: Palingol: a declarative programming language to describe nucleic acids secondary structures and to scan sequence database. Nucleic Acids Res. (24), 1395–1403 (1996)
11. Caeiro, M., Németh, Z., Priol, T.: A chemical model for dynamic workflow coordination. In: PDP, pp. 215–222 (2011)
12. Dittrich, P., Ziegler, J., Banzhaf, W.: Artificial chemistries-a review. Artificial Life 7(3), 225–275 (2001)
13. Dobson, S., Sterritt, R., Nixon, P., Hinchey, M.: Fulfilling the vision of autonomic computing. IEEE Computer 43(1), 35–41 (2010)
14. Forgy, C.: Rete: A fast algorithm for the many patterns/many objects match problem. Artif. Intell. 19(1), 17–37 (1982)
15. Henderson, P.: Functional programming - application and implementation. Prentice Hall International Series in Computer Science, pp. 1–355. Prentice Hall (1980)
16. Hill, E.F.: Jess in Action: Java Rule-Based Systems. Manning Publications Co., Greenwich (2003)
17. Kephart, J.O., Chess, D.M.: The vision of autonomic computing. IEEE Computer 36(1), 41–50 (2003)
18. Di Napoli, C., Giordano, M., Pazat, J.-L., Wang, C.: A Chemical Based Middleware for Workflow Instantiation and Execution. In: Di Nitto, E., Yahyapour, R. (eds.) ServiceWave 2010. LNCS, vol. 6481, pp. 100–111. Springer, Heidelberg (2010)
19. Nori, K.V., Ammann, U., Jensen, K., Nageli, H.H., Jacobi, C.: Pascal-p implementation notes. In: Pascal - The Language and its Implementation, pp. 125–170 (1981)

Design and Performance of the OP2 Library for Unstructured Mesh Applications[*]

Carlo Bertolli[1], Adam Betts[1], Gihan Mudalige[2], Mike Giles[2], and Paul Kelly[1]

[1] Department of Computing, Imperial College, London
[2] Oxford e-Research Centre, University of Oxford

Abstract. OP2 is an "active" library framework for the solution of unstructured mesh applications. It aims to decouple the scientific specification of an application from its parallel implementation to achieve code longevity and near-optimal performance by re-targeting the back-end to different multi-core/many-core hardware. This paper presents the design of the OP2 code generation and compiler framework which, given an application written using the OP2 API, generates efficient code for state-of-the-art hardware (e.g. GPUs and multi-core CPUs). Through a representative unstructured mesh application we demonstrate the capabilities of the compiler framework to utilize the same OP2 hardware specific run-time support functionalities. Performance results show that the impact due to this sharing of basic functionalities is negligible.

1 Introduction

OP2 is an "active" library framework for the solution of unstructured mesh applications. It utilizes code generation to exploit parallelism on heterogeneous multi-core/many-core architectures. The "active" library approach uses program transformation tools, so that a single application code written using the OP2 API is transformed into the appropriate form that can be linked against a target parallel implementation (e.g. OpenMP, CUDA, OpenCL, AVX, MPI, etc.) enabling execution on different back-end hardware platforms.

Such an abstraction enables application developers to focus on solving problems at a higher level and not worry about architecture specific optimisations. This splits the problem space into (1) a higher application level where scientists and engineers concentrate on solving domain specific problems and write code that remains unchanged for different underlying hardware and (2) a lower implementation level, that focuses on how a computation can be executed most efficiently on a given platform by carefully analysing the data access patterns. This paves the way for easily integrating support for any future novel hardware architecture.

---

[*] This research is partly funded by EPSRC (grant reference numbers EP/I00677X/1, EP/I006079/1), the UK Technology Strategy Board, and Rolls- Royce plc through the SILOET programme.

M. Alexander et al. (Eds.): Euro-Par 2011 Workshops, Part I, LNCS 7155, pp. 191–200, 2012.
© Springer-Verlag Berlin Heidelberg 2012

To facilitate the development of unstructured mesh applications at a higher hardware agnostic level, OP2 provides both a C/C++ and a Fortran API. Currently an application written using this API can be transformed into code that can be executed on a single multi-core and/or multi-threaded CPU node (using OpenMP) or a single GPU (using NVIDIA CUDA). In this paper we introduce the design of the code transformation/compiler framework, which supports OP2's multi-language/multi-platform development capability. We show how, hardware specific optimisations can be utilised independently of the application development language and present key issues we encountered and their performance effects during the execution of a representative CFD application written using the OP2 API.

More specifically we make the following contributions:

1. We present the design of the OP2 compiler framework, which translates an application written using the OP2 API in to back-end hardware implementations. Key design features of this framework are illustrated with a stepwise analysis of this process and the resulting optimisation opportunities, during code transformation.
2. A representative CFD application written using the OP2 C/C++ API is re-developed using the OP2 Fortran API and the contrasting performance of these two applications are explored on two modern GPU platforms (NVIDIA GTX460 and Fermi M2050).
3. Both C/C++ and the Fortran based applications uses the same hardware specific back-end irrespective of the application language; we show that the impact due to this sharing of basic functionalities is negligible.

The paper is organised as following: Section 2 describes relevant related work. Section 3 gives an overview of the OP2 functions. Section 4 describes the compiler architecture, and its implementation. In Section 5 we provide results of experiments on C/C++ and Fortran programs for CUDA. Finally, Section 6 concludes with plans for future research.

2   Related Work

OP2 is the second iteration of OPlus (Oxford Parallel Library for Unstructured Solvers) [3]. OPlus provided an abstraction framework for performing unstructured mesh based computations across a distributed-memory cluster. It is currently used as the underlying parallelisation library for Hydra a production-grade CFD application used in turbomachinery design at Rolls-Royce plc. OP2 builds upon the features provided by its predecessor but develops an "active" library approach with code generation to exploit parallelism on heterogeneous multi-core/many-core architectures.

Although OPlus pre-dates it, OPlus and OP2 can be viewed as an instantiation of the AEcute (access-execute descriptor) [9] programming model that separates the specification of a computational kernel with its parallel iteration space, from a declarative specification of how each iteration accesses its data. The decoupled Access/Execute specification in turn creates the opportunity to apply powerful optimisations targeting the underlying hardware. A number of related research projects have implemented similar programming frameworks. The most comparable of these is LISZT [4,5] from Stanford University.

LISZT is a domain specific language specifically targeted to support unstructured mesh application development. The aim, as with OP2, is to exploit information about the structure of data and the nature of the algorithms in the code and to apply aggressive and platform specific optimisations. Preliminary performance figures from the LISZT framework have been presented in [5]. The authors report the performance of Joe, a fluid flow unstructured mesh application using a mesh of 750K cells, on a Tesla C2050 (implemented using CUDA) against an Intel Core 2 Quad, 2.66GHz processor. Results show a speed-up of about 30× in single precision arithmetic and 28× in double precision relative to a single CPU thread.

3   OP2

Unstructured meshes are used over a wide range of computational science applications. They are applied in the solution of partial differential equations (PDEs) in computational fluid dynamics (CFD), computational electro-magnetics (CEM), structural mechanics and general finite element methods. Usually, in three dimensions, millions of elements are often required for the desired solution accuracy, leading to significant computational costs.

Unlike structured meshes, they use connectivity information to specify the mesh topology. In OP2 an unstructured mesh problem specification involves breaking down the algorithm into four distinct parts: (1) sets, (2) data on sets, (3) connectivity (or mapping) between the sets and (4) operations over sets. These lead to an API through which any mesh or graph can be completely and abstractly defined. Depending on the application, a set can consist of nodes, edges, triangular faces, quadrilateral faces, or other elements. Associated with these sets are data (e.g. node coordinates, edge weights) and mappings between sets which define how elements of one set connect with the elements of another set.

Fig. 1 illustrates a simple quadrilateral mesh that we will use as an example to describe the OP2 API. The mesh can be defined by two sets, nodes (vertices) and cells (quadrilaterals). There are 16 nodes and 9 cells, which can be defined using the OP2 API as shown in Fig. 2. In our previous work [8] we detailed the OP2 API for code development in C/C++. Here we introduce the Fortran API.

The connectivity is declared through the mappings between the sets. The integer array `cell_map` can be used to represent the four nodes that make up each cell, as shown in Fig. 2.

Each element of set `cells` is mapped to four different elements in set `nodes`. The `op_map` declaration defines this mapping where `mcell` has a dimension of 4 and thus its index 0,1,2,3 maps to nodes 0,1,5,4, and so on. When declaring

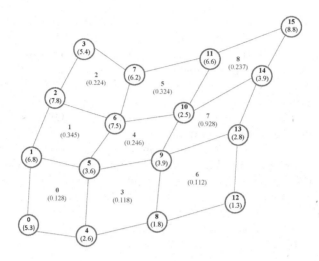

Fig. 1. A mesh example used through the paper

```
integer(4)  ::  numNodes = 16
integer(4)  ::  numCells = 9

type(op_set)  ::  nodes,  cells

integer(4),  dimension(36)  ::  cell_map = (/  0,1,5,4,  1,2,6,5,  2,3,7,6,  &
    & 4,5,9,8,5,6,10,9,6,7,11,10,  &
    & 8,9,13,12,9,10,14,13,10,11,15,14  /)

type(op_map)  ::  cellsToNodes

call  op_decl_set  ( numNodes, nodes )
call  op_decl_set  ( numCells, cells )

call  op_decl_map  ( cells, nodes, 4, cell_map, cellsToNodes )
```

Fig. 2. Example of declaration of op_set and op_map variables

a mapping we pass the source and destination sets (**cells** and **nodes**), the dimension of each map entry, which for **mcell** it is 4, and the mapping data array (**cell_map**).

Once the sets are defined, data can be associated to them. In Fig. 3 we show some data arrays that contain double precision data associated with the cells and the nodes respectively. Note that here a single double precision value per set element is declared. A vector of a number of values per set element could also be declared (e.g. a vector with three doubles per node to store the X,Y,Z coordinates).

All numerically intensive computations in the application can be described as operations over sets. This corresponds to loops over a given set, accessing data through the mappings (i.e. one level of indirection), performing some calculations, then writing back (possibly through the mappings) to the data arrays. If the loop involves indirection we refer to it as an indirect loop; if not, it is called a direct loop.

```
real(8), dimension(9) :: cell_data = (/ 0.128, 0.345, 0.224, 0.118, &
& 0.246, 0.324, 0.112, 0.928, 0.237 /)

real(8), dimension(16) :: nodes_data = (/ 5.3, 6.8, 7.8, 5.4, &
& 2.6, 3.6, 7.5, 6.2, 1.8, 3.9, 2.5, 6.6, 1.3, 2.8, 3.9, 8.8 /)

type(op_dat) :: dataCells, dataCellsUpdated, dataNodes

call op_decl_dat ( cells, 1, cell_data, dataCells )
call op_decl_dat ( nodes, 1, nodes_data, dataNodes )
```

Fig. 3. Example of data array declaration and OP2 variables

The OP2 API provides a parallel loop function which allows the user to declare the computation over sets. Consider the sequential loop in Fig. 4, operating over each mesh cell. Each cell updates its data value using the data values held on the four nodes connected to that cell. An application developer declares this loop using, together with the "elemental" kernel function, as shown in Fig. 5. OP2 handles the architecture specific code generation. The elemental kernel function takes six arguments in this case and the parallel loop declaration requires the access method of each to be declared (OP_WRITE, OP_READ, etc). OP_ID indicates that the data is to be accessed without any indirection (i.e. directly). dnodes on the other hand is accessed through the mcell mapping using the given index.

OP2's general decomposition of unstructured mesh algorithms imposes no restrictions on the actual algorithms, it just separates the components of a code. However, OP2 makes an important restriction that the order in which elements are processed must not affect the final result, to within the limits of finite precision floating-point arithmetic. This constraint allows the program to choose its own order to obtain maximum parallelism. Moreover the sets and mappings between sets must be static and only one level of indirection is allowed.

The OP2 API targets explicit relaxation methods such as Jacobi iteration; pseudo-time-stepping methods; multi-grid methods which use explicit smoothers; Krylov subspace methods with explicit preconditioning. However, algorithms based on order dependent relaxation methods, such as Gauss-Seidel or ILU (incomplete LU decomposition), lie beyond the capabilities of the API.

```
subroutine seqLoop ( numCells, cell_map, cellDataUpdated, cellData, &
                & nodeData )
    integer(4) :: numCells
    integer(4), dimension(:) :: cell_map
    real(8), dimension(:) :: cellDataUpdated, cellData, nodeData

    integer(4) :: i
    do i = 1, numCells
        cellDataUpdated(i) = cellData(i) + nodeData( cell_map(4*i) ) + &
        nodeData( cell_map(4*i +1) ) + nodeData( cell_map(4*i +2) ) + &
        nodeData( cell_map(4*i +3) )   )
    end do
end subroutine seqLoop
```

Fig. 4. Example of sequential loops

```
subroutine kernel ( cellUpdated , cell , node1 , node2 , node3 , node4 )
   real (8) , dimension(1) :: cellUpdated , cell , node1 , node2 , node3 , node4

   cellUpdated(1) = cell (1) + node1 (1) + node2 (1) + node3 (1) + node4 (1)
end subroutine kernel

call op_par_loop ( kernel , cells , &
                 & dataCellsUpdated , −1, OP_ID , OP_WRITE,
                 & dataCells , −1, OP_ID , OP_READ,
                 & dataNodes , 1, cellsToNodes , OP_READ,
                 & dataNodes , 2, cellsToNodes , OP_READ,
                 & dataNodes , 3, cellsToNodes , OP_READ,
                 & dataNodes , 4, cellsToNodes , OP_READ )
```

Fig. 5. Example of op_par_loop corresponding to the sequential loops showed above

4   OP2 Code Generation and Compiler Framework

The OP2 compiler is based on the ROSE framework [10], which is a framework for building source-to-source translators. ROSE supports front ends for C/C++ and Fortran 77-2003; it generates an Abstract Syntax Tree (AST) of the input program, which we use to analyse, optimise and transform the input OP2 programs. Our compiler infrastructure, illustrated in Figure6, performs the following set of tasks:

1. Type and consistency checks. For instance, the compiler checks that the basic type of an *op_dat* is the same as a corresponding formal parameter in a user kernel declaration.
2. Host subroutine generation. This subroutine partitions the iteration set and colours the partitions and their elements to avoid race conditions over indirectly accessed data. Then, for all partitions with the same colour, it applies a back-end specific subroutine (next item)
3. Backend-specific subroutine generation. In CUDA, this subroutine is a kernel, while in OpenMP it is a vanilla subroutine invoked in parallel by the threads. Its main task is to call the user kernel to perform the required computations over a single partition. As partitions are internally coloured, to avoid race conditions and hence the need for locks, this subroutine iterates over such colours, serially invoking the user kernel on all elements with same colours.
4. Transformation of the user kernel. In the case of CUDA some additional labels are needed to inform the back-end compiler which subroutines intend to run on the device. Also, Fortran CUDA [1] requires that all device subroutines be included in the same Fortran module.

Currently, the compiler produces a CUDA implementation of C/C++ and Fortran OP2 programs, while we are developing OpenCL and AVX/SSE back-ends. Further back-ends will include optimised code generation for new heterogeneous architectures, like AMD's APU [2].

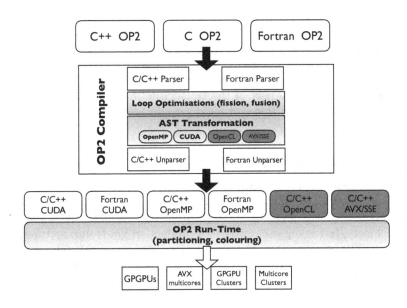

Fig. 6. Architecture of the OP2 ROSE-based compiler. Shaded grey blocks represent the main OP2 functionalities, where darker squared blocks are features currently under development.

Optimisations are the cardinal points of this development: as shown in Fig. 6, a set of program transformations, like loop fusion and fission, will be independent of the input language. This independence is easily obtained because ROSE maps input programs of different input languages to an orthogonal AST representation, called Sage III. The ASTs for C and Fortran programs are mainly based on the same AST node types, except for some minor differences which we treat as special cases. However, the need of defining optimisations at this level might require a further abstraction over the AST, to easily manipulate the program without dealing with low-level compiler details.

Other transformations and configurations are instead dependent on the target architecture, and they define the design choices that our compiler targets. For instance, the compiler can select optimal thread numbers in a different way for NVIDIA and AMD GPUs.

In the same figure we also show a further cardinal point in the design of OP2. If we consider different generated back-end programs, originated from different input languages and targeting different architectures, we can see that some of them share a same C-based run-time support. The run-time includes basic OP2 declaration routines (e.g. *op_decl_set*), as well as the colouring and partitioning logics. In other words, a same colouring and partitioning algorithm is used by different back-ends. For instance, both Fortran and C++ generated programs targeting CUDA and OpenMP make use of the same implementation of colouring and partitioning algorithms.

This choice comes at a performance cost for Fortran generated programs. In fact, they need to interoperate with C run-time support functions, and to transform the resulting variables from Fortran to C notation. The compiler generates code to minimise the number of variables which have to be transformed, but in some cases, either due to algorithmic reasons, or to lower level compiler bugs, we are forced to re-execute part of the transformation at each invocation of a op_par_loop . The extent of this cost is targeted in Section 5.

5   Performance

The example application used in this paper, Airfoil, is a non-linear 2D inviscid Airfoil code that uses an unstructured grid [7]. It is a much simpler application than the Hydra [6] CFD application used at Rolls-Royce plc. for the simulation of turbomachinery, but is representative of a production grade unstructured mesh application. The mesh used in our experiments is of size 1200×600, consisting in over 720K nodes, 720K cells and about 1.5 million edges. The code consists of five parallel loops: save_soln, adt_calc, res_calc, bres_calc, update. The most compute intensive loop res_calc has about 100 floating-point operations performed per mesh edge and is called 2000 times during total execution of the application. save_soln and update are direct loops while the other three are indirect loops.

In this section we show the performance measurements on two GPUs of the Airfoil application, implemented in Fortran and C++, based on double precision floating point numbers. The used GPUs are: a popular consumer graphics card (Nvidia GeForce GTX460) and a high performance computing card (NVIDIA Fermi M2050). For space reasons, we only show results related to the execution on GPUs, while we will target in future work specific optimisations and performance measurements for multicore processors.

Target of these performance measurements is to understand which is the cost of the use of a common run-time support, implemented in C, for both Fortran and C/C++ OP2 generated programs. From the Fortran side this involves: (i) to define a proper interface between C functions and Fortran code, to allow interoperability of function calls; (ii) to translate variables generated in the C functions to Fortran variables. Both points are implemented by using the Fortran 2003 standard binding support, supported by the ISO_C_BINDING Fortran module. At run-time, we employ the c_f_pointer function to convert variables from C to Fortran.

Another main difference between C/C++ and Fortran lies in the different implementation of the CUDA kernels, which are language dependent. Practically, while the C implementation makes extensive use of pointers to the GPU shared memory to address specific sub-portion of op_dat variables, the Fortran implementation lacks of a support for such kinds of pointers, and it is forced to re-compute the offset for shared memory variables.

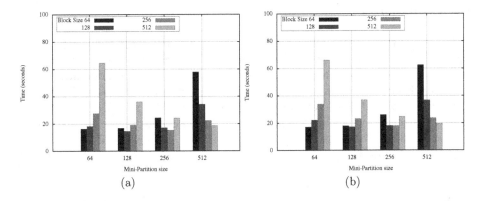

Fig. 7. Performance of C++ (left) and Fortran (right) Airfoil on a M2050

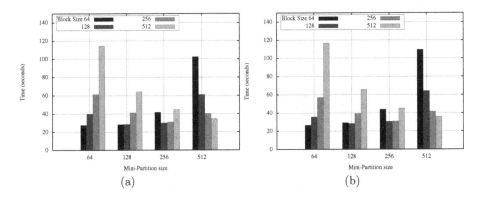

Fig. 8. Performance of C++ (left) and Fortran (right) Airfoil on a GTX460

Unlike the previous interoperability issue, this latter one represents the critical point in the difference between the Fortran and C implementation of OP2 on GPUs. For this reason, our performance measurements specifically target the execution time in the kernel code.

Fig. 7 shows the performance measurements on the M2050 GPU, by varying the number of set elements in each block (*partition size*), and the number of threads in a CUDA block (*block size*). If the partition size is equal to the block size, then each thread is assigned a single set element to which it applies the kernel. If the partition size is a multiple of the block size, then each thread applies the kernel on multiple set elements. Finally, if the block size is a multiple of the partition size, then a section of the threads in a block is not used, leaving executing threads more resources.

Similar results, even if with a lower performance, are shown in Fig. 8 for the execution of the C++ and Fortran program on the GTX 460 GPU.

6 Conclusion

In this paper we have described the source-to-source compiler framework for OP2 applications, targeting unstructured mesh CFD applications. The compiler currently supports different input languages (namely C/C++ and Fortran), and it generates back-end architecture implementation for multicores, using OpenMP, and GPUs, using CUDA. We have shown the specific design choices in the compiler architecture, which are the basis over which we will provide language and back-end independent optimisations, as well as back-end dependent optimal configurations. In addition, the generated code for Fortran and C/C++ makes use of the same set of core run-time OP2 functions, implementing main application logics, like mesh colouring and partitioning.

We have presented performance results of the execution of a CFD application on two GPUs, showing a almost identical performance for Fortran and C/C++ CUDA implementations.

References

1. Pgi cuda fortran (2011), http://www.pgroup.com/resources/cudafortran.htm/
2. The amd fusion family of apus (2011),
   http://sites.amd.com/us/fusion/apu/Pages/fusion.aspx
3. Burgess, D.A., Crumpton, P.I., Giles, M.B.: A parallel framework for unstructured grid solvers. In: Proc. of the 2nd European Computational Fluid Dynamics Conf., pp. 391–396. John Wiley and Sons, Germany (1994)
4. Chafi, H., DeVito, Z., Moors, A., Rompf, T., Sujeeth, A.K., Hanrahan, P., Odersky, M., Olukotun, K.: Language virtualization for heterogeneous parallel computing. In: Proc. of the OOPSLA 2010 Applications, pp. 835–847. ACM, USA (2010)
5. DeVito, Z., Joubert, N., Medina, M., Barrientos, M., Oakley, S., Alonso, J., Darve, E., Ham, F., Hanrahan, P.: Liszt: Programming mesh based pdes on heterogeneous parallel platforms (October 2010), http://psaap.stanford.edu
6. Giles, M.B.: Hydra (1998-2002),
   http://people.maths.ox.ac.uk/gilesm/hydra.html
7. Giles, M.B., Ghate, D., Duta, M.C.: Using automatic differentiation for adjoint CFD code development. Computational Fluid Dynamics J. 16(4), 434–443 (2008)
8. Giles, M.B., Mudalige, G.R., Sharif, Z., Markall, G., Kelly, P.H.J.: Performance analysis of the op2 framework on many-core architectures. SIGMETRICS Perform. Eval. Rev. 38, 9–15 (2011)
9. Howes, L.W., Lokhmotov, A., Donaldson, A.F., Kelly, P.H.J.: Deriving Efficient Data Movement from Decoupled Access/Execute Specifications. In: Seznec, A., Emer, J., O'Boyle, M., Martonosi, M., Ungerer, T. (eds.) HiPEAC 2009. LNCS, vol. 5409, pp. 168–182. Springer, Heidelberg (2009)
10. Schordan, M., Quinlan, D.: A Source-To-Source Architecture for User-Defined Optimizations. In: Böszörményi, L., Schojer, P. (eds.) JMLC 2003. LNCS, vol. 2789, pp. 214–223. Springer, Heidelberg (2003)

Mining Association Rules on Grid Platforms

Raja Tlili and Yahya Slimani

Department of Computer Science, Faculty of Sciences of Tunisia,
Campus Universitaire, 1060 Tunis, Tunisia
raja_tlili@yahoo.fr, yahya.slimani@fst.rnu.tn

Abstract. In this paper we propose a dynamic load balancing strategy to enhance the performance of parallel association rule mining algorithms in the context of a Grid computing environment. This strategy is built upon a distributed model which necessitates small overheads in the communication costs for load updates and for both data and work transfers. It also supports the heterogeneity of the system and it is fault tolerant.

Keywords: Association rules, Performance problem, Distributed algorithms, Grid computing, Dynamic load balancing.

1 Introduction

The fast development of data acquisition and storage technologies led to an exponential growth in worldwide data. In order to decrease the gap between data and useful information, a group of architectures and utilities, some of them are new and others exist since a long time, are grouped under the term data mining. Association rule mining is one of the most important data mining techniques [8, 3]. The most important challenge for this technique is quickly and correctly finding interesting correlation relationships between items in large databases. The algorithms of this technique are computationally and input/output intensive, due to the fact that they have to mine voluminous databases. High performance parallel and distributed computing can relieve current association rule mining algorithms from the sequential bottleneck, providing scalability to massive data sets and improving response time.

Grid computing [9] is recently regarded as one of the most promising platform for data and computation-intensive applications like data mining. In such computing environments, heterogeneity is inevitable due to their distributed nature.

Almost all current parallel association rule mining algorithms assume the homogeneity and use static load balancing strategies. Thus applying them to Grid systems will degrade their performance. The load imbalance that occurs during execution time is caused by the dynamic nature of these algorithms and also by the heterogeneity of such distributed systems. Because of that we have to develop new methodologies to handle this problem, which is the focus of our research.

In this paper, we develop and evaluate a run time load balancing strategy for mining association rule algorithms under a grid computing environment.

M. Alexander et al. (Eds.): Euro-Par 2011 Workshops, Part I, LNCS 7155, pp. 201–210, 2012.

The rest of the paper is organized as follows: Section 2 introduces association rule mining technique and related work. Section 3 describes the load balancing problem. Section 4 presents the system model of a Grid. In section 5, we propose the dynamic load balancing strategy. Experimental results obtained from implementing this strategy are shown in section 6. Finally, the paper concludes with section 7.

2   Related Work

Association rules mining (ARM) finds interesting correlation relationships among a large set of data items. A typical example of this technique is market basket analysis. This process analyses customer buying habits by finding associations between different items that customers place in their "shopping baskets". Such information may be used to plan marketing or advertising strategies, as well as catalog design [8]. Each basket represents a different transaction in the transactional database, associated to this transaction the items bought by a customer. Given a transactional database D, an association rule has the form $A => B$, where A and B are two itemsets, and $A \cap B = \emptyset$. The rule's support is the joint probability of a transaction containing both A and B at the same time, and is given as $\sigma(A \cup B)$. The confidence of the rule is the conditional probability that a transaction contains B given that it contains A and is given as $\sigma(A \cup B)/\sigma(A)$. A rule is frequent if its support is greater than or equal to a pre-determined minimum support and strong if the confidence is more than or equal to a user specified minimum confidence.

Many sequential algorithms for solving the frequent set counting problem have been proposed in the literature. We can define two main methods for determining frequent itemsets supports: with candidate itemsets generation [3, 11] and without candidate itemsets generation [14].The Apriori algorithm [3] was the first effective algorithm proposed in the literature. This algorithm uses a generate-and-test approach which depends on generating candidate itemsets and testing if they are frequent. It uses an iterative approach known as a level-wise search, where $k-$itemsets are used to explore $(k+1)-$itemsets. During the initial pass over the database the support of all $1-$itemsets is counted. Frequent $1-$itemsets are used to generate all possible candidate $2-$itemsets. Then the database is scanned again to obtain the number of occurrences of these candidates, and the frequent 2-itemsets are selected for the next iteration.The DCI algorithm proposed by Orlando and others [11] is also based on candidate itemsets generation. It adopts a hybrid approach to compute itemsets supports, by exploiting a counting-based method (with a horizontal database layout) during its first iterations and an intersection-based technique (with a vertical database layout) when the pruned dataset can fit into the main memory.The FP-growth algorithm [14] allows frequent itemsets discovery without candidate itemsets generation. First it builds from the transactional database a compact data structure called the FP-tree then extracts frequent itemsets directly from the FP-tree. Sequential algorithms suffer from a high computational complexity which derives from the size of its search space and the high demands of data access. Parallelism is expected to relieve these algorithms from the sequential bottleneck, providing the ability to scale the massive datasets, and improving the response time. However, parallelizing these algorithms is not trivial and is facing many challenges including the workload balancing problem. Many parallel algorithms for solving the frequent set counting problem have been proposed. Most of them use Apriori algorithm [3] as fundamental algorithm, because of its success on the sequential setting. The reader could refer to the survey of Zaki on association rules mining algorithms and relative parallelization schemas [18]. Agrawal et al. proposed a broad taxonomy of parallelization strategies that can be adopted for Apriori in [2].

There also exist many grid data mining projects, like Discovery Net, GridMiner, DMGA [12] which provide mechanisms for integration and deployment of classical algorithms on grid. Also the DisDaMin project that deals with data mining issues (as association rules, clustering, etc.) using distributed computing [7].

3   Load Balancing: Problem Definition

Work load balancing is the assignment of work to processors in a way that maximizes application performance [6]. The process of load balancing can be generalized into four basic steps: (1) Monitoring processor load and state; (2) Exchanging workload and state information between processors; (3) Decision making; and (4) Data migration. The decision phase is triggered when the load imbalance is detected to calculate optimal data redistribution. In the fourth and last phase, data migrates from overloaded processors to underloaded ones. According to different policies used in the previously mentioned phases, Casavant and kuhl [5] classify work-load balancing schemes into three major classes: (1) Static versus dynamic load balancing; (2) Centralized versus distributed load balancing ; (3) Application-level versus system-level load balancing.

Static load balancing can be used in applications with constant workloads, as a pre-processor to the computation. Other applications require dynamic load balancers that adjust the decomposition as the computation proceeds [6, 15]. This is due to their nature which is characterized by workloads that are unpredictable and change during execution. Data mining is one of these applications.

Parallel association rule mining algorithms have a dynamic nature because of their dependency on the degree of correlation between itemsets in the transactional database which cannot be predictable before execution.

Although intensive works have been done in load balancing, the different nature of a Grid computing environment from the traditional distributed system, prevent existing static load balancing schemes from benefiting large-scale applications. An excellent survey from Y. Li et al. [10], displays the existing solutions and the new efforts in dynamic load balancing that aim to address the new challenges in Grid. The work done so far to cope with one or more challenges brought by Grid: heterogeneity, resource sharing, high latency and dynamic system state, can be identified by three categories as mentioned in [16]: (1) Repartition methods focus on calculating data distribution in a heterogeneous way, but don't pay much attention to the data movement in Grid; (2) Divisible load theory based schemes well model both the computation and communication, but loose validity in case of adaptive application; (3) Prediction based schemes need further investigation in case of long-term applications. C. Yang et al. Proposed a heuristic data distribution scheme for data mining applications on grid environments [16]. They induced load balancing through a heuristic data partition technique that aims to reduce the total execution time of the program. K. Yu et al. proposed a weighted distributed parallel Apriori algorithm [17] in which the transaction identifier of itemsets is stored in a table to compute their occurrence. The algorithm takes the factor of itemset counts into consideration in order to balance workloads among processors and reduce processor idle time.

4   The Grid Model

In our study we model a Grid as a collection of T sites with different computational facilities and storage subsystem. Let $G = (S_1, S_2, ..., S_T)$ denotes a set of sites, where each site S_i is defined as a vector with three parameters $S_i = (M_i, Coord(S_i), L_i)$, where M_i is the total number of clusters in S_i, $Coord(S_i)$ is the workload manager, named the coordinator of S_i, which is responsible of detecting the workload imbalance and the transfer of the appropriate amount of work from an overloaded cluster to another lightly loaded cluster within the same site (intra-site) or if it is necessary to another remote site (inter-sites). This transfer takes into account the transmission speed between clusters which is denoted $\zeta_{ijj'}$ (if the transmission is from cluster cl_{ij} to cluster $cl_{ij'}$). And L_i is the computational load of S_i. Each cluster is characterized by a vector of four parameters $cl_{ij} = (N_{ij}, Coord(cl_{ij}), L_{ij}, \omega_{ij})$, where N_{ij} is the total number of nodes in cl_{ij} , $Coord(cl_{ij})$ is the coordinator node of cl_{ij} which ensures a dynamic smart distribution of candidates to its own nodes, L_{ij} is the computational load of cluster cl_{ij} and ω_{ij} is its processing time which is the mean of processing times of cluster's nodes. Figure 1 shows the Grid system model. To avoid keeping global state information in a large-scale system (where this information would be very huge), the proposed load balancing model is distributed in both intra-site and inter-sites. Each site in the Grid has a workload manager, called the coordinator, which accommodates submitted transactional database partitions and the list of candidates of the previous iteration of the association rules mining algorithm. Each coordinator aims at tracking the global workload status by periodically exchanging a "state vector" with other coordinators in the system. Depending on the workload state of each node, the frequency of candidate itemsets may be calculated in its local node or will be transferred to another lightly loaded node within the same site. If the coordinator cannot fix the workload imbalance locally, it selects part of transactions to be sent to a remote site through the network. The destination of migrated work is chosen according to the following hierarchy : First The coordinator of the cluster $Coord(cl_{ij})$ selects the available node within the same cluster; If the workload imbalance still persists then $Coord(cl_{ij})$ searches for an available node in

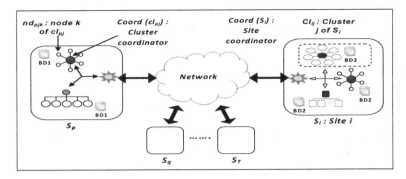

Fig. 1. The system model of a Grid

another cluster but within the same site; Finally, in extreme cases, work will be send to a remote site. The coordinator of the site $Coord(S_i)$ will look for the nearest site available to receive this workload (i.e. least communication cost). If the coordinator node does not give response within a fixed period of time, an election policy is invoked to choose another coordinator node.

5   The Dynamic Load Balancing Strategy

Our proposed load balancing strategy depends on three issues: (i) Database architecture (partitioned or not); (ii) Candidates set (duplicated or partitioned); (iii) network communication parameter (bandwidth).

Our strategy could be adopted by algorithms which depend on candidate itmesets generation to solve the frequent set counting problem. It combines between static and dynamic load balancing and this by interfering before execution (i.e. static) and during execution (i.e. dynamic).

To respond to the heterogeneity of the computing system we are using (Grid) the database is not just partitioned into equal partitions in a random manner. Rather than that, the transactional database is partitioned according to the characteristics of different sites, where the size of each partition is determined according to the site processing capacity (i.e., different architecture, operating system, CPU speed, etc.). It's the responsibility of the coordinator of the site $Coord(S_i)$ to allocate to its site the appropriate database portion according to the site processing capacity parameters stored in its information system.

Our load balancing strategy acts on three levels: (1) level one is the migration of work between nodes of the same cluster. If the skew in workload still persists the coordinator of the cluster $Coord(cl_{ij})$ moves to the next level; (2) level two depends on the migration of work between clusters within the same site; (3) and finally if work migration of the previous two levels is not sufficient then the coordinator of the overloaded cluster $Coord(cl_{ij})$ asks from the coordinator of the site $Coord(S_i)$ to move to the third level which searches for the possibility of migrating work between sites. Communication between the coordinators of different sites is done in a unidirectional ring topology via a token passing mechanism. This choice was made based on the study conducted by H. Renard [13] which states that the ring topology is the most effective for iterative algorithms under distributed environments.

The following workload balancing process is invoked when needed. It is the responsibility of distributed coordinators to detect that need dynamically according to the charge status of their relative nodes (i.e. equilibrated or overloaded). Where the charge status of a node is determined by the number of candidates waiting for treatment:

1. From the intra-site level, coordinators of each cluster update their global workload vector by acquiring workload information from their local nodes. From the Grid level, coordinators of different sites periodically calculate their average workload in order to detect their workload state (overloaded or under-loaded). If an imbalance is detected, coordinators proceed to the following steps.
2. The coordinator of the overloaded cluster makes a plan for candidates migration intra-site (between nodes of the same site). If the imbalance still persists, it creates another plan for transactions migration inter-sites (between clusters of the Grid).
3. The concerned coordinator (the coordinator of the overloaded cluster or the coordinator of the overloaded site) sends migration plan to all processing nodes and instructs them to reallocate the work load.

5.1 The Dynamic Load Balancing Algorithms

Computing node (nd_{ijk})

Loop :

-- Receives a group of candidates from the coordinator of the cluster
-- Calculates their supports
-- Sends local supports to cluster's coordinator which performs the global supports reduction

---

Cluster coordinator (coord(cl_{ij}))

Loop :

-- Distributes candidate itemsets between nodes according to their capacities. Candidates are distributed by their (k-1) commun prefix
-- Performs the global reduction of supports to obtain global frequencies
-- Constructs frequent itemsets (L_k step)
-- Constructs candidates itemsets of the following iteration $C_{(k+1)}$ step
-- Every n steps :
   o Save the local state : ch_{ij},
   o Update if necessary $C_{(k+1)}$ step

Site coordinator (Coord(S_i))
Loop :
-- Updates the global state vector of the site Average(chi))
-- Finds the Max overloaded cluster and the max underloaded cluster
    ○ $Cl_{ijmax} \Rightarrow {}_{j}^{max} (ch_{ij}) > Avg(ch_i)$
    ○ $Cl_{ijmin} \Rightarrow {}_{j}^{min} (ch_{ij}) < Avg(ch_i)$
-- Finds the Max x_c (with the same prefix) on Cl_{ijmax}
    1. $Ch_{ijmin} + x_c.\omega_{ijmin} \le Avg(ch_i)$
      // To find the best number of candidates to migrate in order
      to not overload the destination cluster
  AND
    2. $x_c.\omega_{ijmax} - (x_c.\omega_{ijmin} + len(x_c).\zeta_{ijmaxjmin}) > Seuil_{mc}$
      // $Seuil_{mc}$: le seuil qui va dclencher la migration
-- If x_c exists Then informs the overloaded cl_{ijmax} and the
  underloaded cl_{ijmin} and updates (ch_i)
-- Asks from the overloaded cluster to send the family of candidates
  having the same prefix

Where T is the total number of sites; M_i is the total number of clusters of the site S_i ; N_{ij} is the total number of nodes of the cluster cl_{ij} ; $Coord(cl_{ij})$ is the coordinator node of cl_{ij} ; $coord(S_i)$ is the coordinator of S_i ; $\zeta_{ijj'}$ is the transmission speed between clusters cl_{ij} and $cl_{ij'}$; ω_{ijk} is the cycle time of nd_{ijk} ; ch_i is the charge of S_i ; ch_{ij} is the charge of cl_{ij} ; ω_{ij} is the average (ω_{ijk}); $seuil_{mc}$ is the significant time limit to trigger candidate itemsets migration between clusters; $seuil_{mt}$ is the significant time limit to trigger task migration between sites and x_c is the number of candidates to migrate from one cluster to another.

6 Performance Evaluation

In order to evaluate the performance of our workload balancing strategy we parallelized the sequential Apriori which is the fundamental algorithm for frequent set counting algorithms with candidate itemsets generation. It is important to mention that our load balancing could be applied to the entire class of association rule mining algorithms that depends on candidate itemsets generation.

The performance evaluations presented in this section were conducted on Grid'5000 [4], a dedicated reconfigurable and controllable experimental platform featuring 13 clusters, each with 58 to 342 PCs, interconnected through Renater (the French Educational and Research wide area Network). It gathers roughly 5000 CPU cores featuring four architectures (Itanium, Xeon, G5 and Opteron) distributed into 13 clusters over 9 cities in France. We used heterogeneous clusters in order to generate the maximum workload imbalance. We conducted several experiments, by varying the number of sites, clusters and computational nodes. Due to space limitation, we will present in what follows only the results obtained by using two sites, each site containing two clusters and with 20 computational nodes distributed as follows: 4 nodes/cluster1, 3 nodes/cluster2, 6 nodes/cluster3 and 7 nodes/cluster4. We allocated clusters with different sizes to show the effectiveness of our approach in dealing with the heterogeneity of the system. The datasets used in tests are synthetic, and are generated using the IBM-generator [1]. Table 1 shows the datasets characteristics.

Table 1. Transactional databases characteristics

Database	Characteristics			
	Items Number	Avg. Trans. Length	Transactions Number	Database Size
DB100T13M	4000	25	1300000	100 Mb
DB300T39M	6000	30	3900000	300 Mb
DB600T78M	8000	35	7800000	600 Mb

The first iteration of association rule mining algorithm is a phase of initiation for workload balancing (i.e. creating state vectors and processing time estimates, etc). For the first dataset (DB100T13M) the algorithm performed 11 iterations in order to generate all possible frequent itemsets. Candidate itemsets migration (intra-site) is initiated two times during the second iteration, and once during the third and fourth iterations. Figure 2 illustrates the speedup obtained as a function of the number of processors used in execution. We can clearly see that for the different datasets we achieved better speed up with the load balancing approach. The drop in speedup for relatively higher support values is due to the fact that when the support threshold increases the number of candidate itemsets generated decreases (i.e. less computation to be performed). In this case it would be better to decrease the number of nodes incorporated in execution so that the communication cost will not be higher than the computation cost. In fact, there is not a fixed optimal number of processors that could be used for execution. The number of processors used should be proportional to the size of data sets to be mined. The easiest way to determine that optimal number is via experiments.

Performance's Comparisons: Table 2 illustrates the differences between: Our Dynamic Load Balancing Approach (DLBA), the Weighted Distributed Parallel Apriori algorithm (WDPA) proposed in [17] and Heuristic Data Distribution Scheme (HDDS) introduced in [16]. Both WDPA and HDDS are based on a centralized (master/slave) load balancing approach where there is one master responsible of data distribution and n computing slaves. This would cause a scalability problem. Our approach is totally distributed in order to respond to the high level of distribution in grid systems. For input size 1000 transactions and by using 9 processors, the speed up obtained by the WDPA algorithm is

Table 2. Approaches comparison

Approach Name	Approach used to Balance Load	Characteristics	Speed Up (using 9 procs)
WDPA	One Master/P Slaves	Centralized	7.5
HDDS	One Master/P Slaves	Centralized	5.5
DLBA	Hierarchy of coordinators	Distributed	8.95

equal to 7.5, the speed up obtained by executing the HDDS algorithm is equal to 5.5, while the speed up of our dynamic load balancing approach (DLBA) is equal to 8.95.

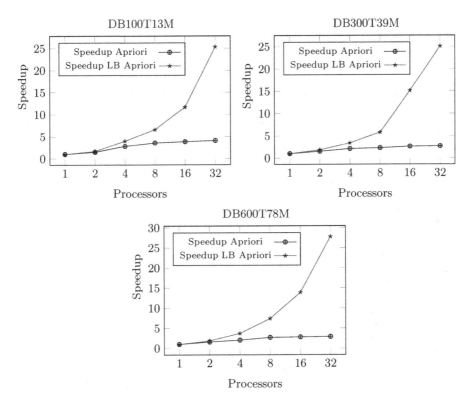

Fig. 2. Comparing the speedup of parallel Apriori with and without load balancing

7   Conclusion

Data mining algorithms have a dynamic nature during execution time which causes load-imbalance between the different processing nodes. Such algorithms require dynamic load balancers that adjust the decomposition as the computation proceeds. Numerous static load balancing strategies have been developed where dynamic load balancing still an open and challenging research area. In this article we developed a dynamic load balancing strategy for association rule mining algorithms, with candidate itemsets generation, under a Grid computing environment. Experimentations showed that our strategy succeeded in achieving better use of the Grid architecture assuming load balancing and this for large sized datasets. In the future, we plan to study the effect of the database type (dense and sparse) on our strategy. We also aim to adopt our strategy to association rule mining algorithms without candidate itemsets generation.

References

[1] Generator of databases site, http://www.almaden.ibm.com/cs/quest
[2] Agrawal, R., Shafer, J.C.: Parallel mining of association rules (December 1996)
[3] Agrawal, R., Srikant, R.: Fast algorithms for mining associations rules in large databases (September 1994)
[4] Cappello, F., Caron, E., Dayde, M., Desprez, F., Jegou, Y., Primet, P.V.B., Jeannot, E., Lanteri, S., Leduc, J., Melab, N., Mornet, G., Quetier, B., Richard, O.: Grid'5000: a large scale and highly reconfigurable grid experimental testbed (November 2005)
[5] Casavant, T.L., Kuhl, J.G.: Taxonomy of scheduling in general purpose distributed computing systems (February 1988)
[6] Devine, K., Boman, E., Heaphy, R., Hendrickson, B.: New challenges in dynamic load balancing (2005)
[7] Fiolet, V., Toursel, B.: Distributed data mining. in scalable computing: Practice and expériences (scpe) (March 2005)
[8] Han, J., Kamber, M.: Data mining: concepts and techniques (2000)
[9] Foster, I., Kesselman, C.: The Grid2: Blue print for a New Computing Infrastructure (2003)
[10] Li, Y., Lan, Z.: A survey of load balancing in grid computing (2004)
[11] Orlando, S., Palmerini, P., Perego, R.: A scalable multi-strategy algorithm for counting frequent sets (2002)
[12] Perez, M., Sanchez, A., Robles, V., Herrero, P., Pena, J.: Design and implementation of a data mining grid-aware architecture (2007)
[13] Renard, H.: Equilibrage de Charge et Redistribution de donnes sur Plates-formes htrognes (December 2005)
[14] Wang, K., Tang, L., Han, J., Liu, J.: Top down fp-growth for association rule mining in pakdd 2002 (May 2002)
[15] Willebeek-LeMair, M.H., Reeves, A.P.: Strategies for dynamic load balancing on highly parallel computers (September 1993)
[16] Yang, C.T., Shih, W.C., Tseng, S.S.: A heuristic data distribution scheme for data mining applications on grid environments (June 2008)
[17] Yu, K.M., Zhou, J.L.: A weighted load-balancing parallel apriori algorithm for association rule mining (2008)
[18] Zaki, M.: Parallel and distributed association mining: A survey (December 1999)

5th Workshop on System-Level Virtualization for High Performance Computing (HPCVirt 2011)

Stephen L. Scott[1,2], Geoffroy Vallée[1], and Thomas Naughton[1]

[1] Oak Ridge National Laboratory
[2] Tennessee Tech. University

The emergence of virtualization enabled hardware, such as the latest generation AMD and Intel processors, has raised significant interest in High Performance Computing (HPC) community. In particular, system-level virtualization provides an opportunity to advance the design and development of operating systems, programming environments, administration practices, and resource management tools. This leads to some potential research topics for HPC, such as failure tolerance, system management, and solution for application porting to new HPC platforms.

The workshop on System-level Virtualization for HPC (HPCVirt 2011) is intended to be a forum for the exchange of ideas and experiences on the use of virtualization technologies for HPC, the challenges and opportunities offered by the development of system-level virtualization solutions themselves, as well as case studies in the application of system-level virtualization in HPC.

Performance Evaluation
of HPC Benchmarks on VMware's ESXi Server

Qasim Ali, Vladimir Kiriansky, Josh Simons, and Puneet Zaroo

VMware
{qali,vkiriansky,simons,puneetz}@vmware.com

Abstract. A major obstacle to virtualizing HPC workloads is a concern about the performance loss due to virtualization. We will demonstrate that new features significantly enhance the performance and scalability of virtualized HPC workloads on VMware's virtualization platform. Specifically, we will discuss VMware's ESXi Server performance for virtual machines with up to 64 virtual CPUs as well as support for exposing virtual NUMA topology to guest operating systems, enabling the operating system and applications to make intelligent NUMA aware decisions about memory allocation and process/thread placement. NUMA support is especially important for large VMs which necessarily span host NUMA nodes on all modern hardware. We will show how the virtual NUMA topology is chosen to closely match physical host topology, while preserving the now expected virtualization benefits of portability and load balancing. We show that the benefit of exposing the virtual NUMA topology can lead to performance gains of up to 167%. Overall, we will show close to native performance on applications from SPEC MPI V2.0 and SPEC OMP V3.2 benchmarks virtualized on our prototype VMware's ESXi Server.

Keywords: Non Uniform Memory Architecture (NUMA), ESXi, High Performance Computing (HPC), virtual NUMA (vNUMA), virtualization.

1   Introduction

Interest in system virtualization technologies for HPC applications is increasing [12, 14, 5–7, 4, 9]. While much of this interest stems from a desire to exploit cloud computing approaches, virtualization offers additional values for HPC [11, 6, 10]. These include both proactive and reactive application resiliency; dynamic resource management for scheduling efficiency and power management; multi-tenant security; and operational flexibilities.

Despite these potential values, adoption of virtualization for HPC will be determined in large part by the performance achievable on relevant workloads in virtualized environments. And that performance will be determined primarily by two factors: the hardware support for virtualization and the capabilities of the virtual infrastructure that provides the virtual machine (VM) abstraction to the guest operating system instance and its applications.

M. Alexander et al. (Eds.): Euro-Par 2011 Workshops, Part I, LNCS 7155, pp. 213–222, 2012.

While there are many aspects of the VM abstraction that contribute to the delivered performance of an application, this paper focuses on two such capabilities of particular importance to HPC. The first is support for VMs with many virtual CPUs which is required to allow thread-parallel OpenMP and other similar codes including hybrid MPI/OpenMP applications to take full advantage of the underlying cores in modern multi-core systems. The second is support for exposing the NUMA topology of the underlying hardware to the guest operating system so that it, along with any NUMA-aware runtime libraries, can optimally co-locate compute and data where possible.

The paper presents a brief overview of ESXi server, VMware's commercial hypervisor, with an emphasis on its scalability properties. We then describe how ESXi exposes a virtual NUMA topology to guest operating systems, and finally present experimental results using SPEC OMP and SPEC MPI as representative workloads.

2   ESXi Server Architecture

VMware ESXi Server is VMware's bare-metal hypervisor which runs directly on physical hardware. It multiplexes physical hardware among multiple VMs and works in conjunction with the virtual machine monitor (VMM), an instance of which runs per VM. By managing hardware resources directly, ESXi Server achieves high performance by reducing virtualization overhead [13].

In about a decade of existence, VMware's server virtualization platform has undergone many advancements to increase its scalability and performance. The scalability improvements have led to support for larger physical and virtual processor counts and memory sizes, as well as higher VM consolidation rates. These scalability increases have been enabled by advancements in both the virtual machine monitor and ESXi hypervisor. Some key features which have enabled these advances are architectural changes to support large virtual processor counts (large SMP VMs), support for 64 bit x86 architecture and efficient use of hardware virtualization support [2], along with advanced physical CPU, memory and IO management [13]. Supporting large SMP VMs required careful data structure design, coscheduling improvements [3], fine-grained locking, and best software engineering practices to enable support for 64 virtual CPUs in a VM with minimal virtualization overhead. In the next section, we discuss the presentation of a virtual NUMA topology to guest operating systems running inside VMs, which proved crucial to the performance of virtualized HPC workloads.

3   Virtual NUMA Support

Current generation operating systems, runtime libraries and applications are expected to be NUMA-aware for improved performance, e.g. they would allocate memory and schedule execution threads to take advantage of the NUMA topology. To support this within a virtual environment, we introduce the concept of a *virtual NUMA topology* which can be exposed to a guest operating system.

This abstraction is then mapped by the ESXi NUMA scheduler to an intermediate level of abstraction *physical NUMA node*, which is in turn dynamically bound to specific *machine NUMA node* resources on the host system. This hierarchy of (virtual, physical, machine) is analogous to that used to implement virtual memory in a virtualized environment. It should be noted that there is not necessarily a one-to-one correspondence between virtual and physical NUMA nodes since multiple physical NUMA nodes may be required to provision the required CPUs and interleaved memory for a virtual NUMA node. Similarly, multiple physical NUMA nodes may be scheduled on the same machine NUMA node, and even over-commit available CPU and memory resources.

The number of virtual NUMA nodes, the number of virtual CPUs (vCPUs) and the amount of memory associated with the virtual nodes normally remain fixed for the lifetime of a VM. We also support hot-plug add of CPU and memory resources, though not all OSes support hot-plug remove or dynamic changes to NUMA topology. Our virtual BIOS exposes the ACPI Static Resource Affinity Table (SRAT) [1] and ACPI PXM methods to guest OSes to reveal which memory regions and vCPUs belong to which virtual NUMA node. Minimally NUMA aware OSes only distinguish between local vs remote allocation; most modern ones take into account the minimal inter node latencies (or number of hops); yet more advanced OSes need to track maximum link bandwidths, and ultimately total system bandwidth for optimal scheduling. There are no standard facilities for exposing the actual link topology connecting NUMA nodes, e.g. Intel QPI or AMD HyperTransport frequency, number of lanes, lane widths, and for partially connected systems the routes and congestion policies that determine the maximum total interconnect bandwidth. We don't expose ACPI System Locality Information Table (SLIT) [1] information which would only provide fixed latency information. Most modern guest OSes measure during initialization the unidirectional access costs for a vCPU from one virtual NUMA node accessing memory on another virtual NUMA node.

There are several scenarios in which the NUMA topology deduced by the guest OS may become inaccurate over the lifetime of the virtual machine and the remote memory access latency and bandwidth may change. First, the VM might get powered on, suspended and resumed, or live migrated to hosts with different machine NUMA topology than the original system. If different number of physical nodes may be needed, e.g. if originally 4 nodes were used and now 8 nodes are needed, memory interleaving across pairs of physical nodes will be necessary. The physical NUMA node abstraction accommodates even a VM started with 8 vCPUs per NUMA node after it is migrated to a node with 6 PCPUs per NUMA node with best efforts to minimize the performance impact. Second, even if the same number of physical nodes are needed they may use a different NUMA topology. For example, when no subset of 4 machine nodes on an 8-socket host is fully connected, a 4-node VM would need more hops for some remote accesses, instead of symmetric accesses on a fully connected 4-socket host.

It is also possible for the ESXi NUMA scheduler to choose different actual NUMA nodes for placement based on the system workload. Physical NUMA nodes belonging to the same VM which are smaller than the machine NUMA node may be either consolidated or spread over multiple machine nodes. For example, a single VM workload may benefit from spreading over four NUMA nodes to gain higher memory bandwidth and cache capacity, but two such VMs should each be using two non-overlapping NUMA nodes and links.

Trading off maximum single VM performance versus optimal total system performance and overall fairness across VMs can add additional constraints. While the optimal choices are specific to the VM workload, the best physical NUMA topology and placement on machine nodes depends on the overall load on the system and each NUMA node load. Other VMs' CPU utilization, cache capacity, and memory bandwidth consumption may impact the scheduler choices as well. We expose manually configurable policies that affect both the fixed virtual NUMA topology, initial physical NUMA topology placement, and load balancing.

If the memory bandwidth demands of the VM are very high, then using multiple memory controllers will be more beneficial and thus spreading over multiple machine NUMA nodes would be favored. If there are high levels of inter-thread communication, sharing the same last level cache will be preferred and thus consolidation over fewer machine nodes will be favored. Finally, a VM may be configured to favor using SMT hyperthreads instead of full cores - appropriate when the lower latency of local memory may outweigh the disadvantage of not using the full resources of a core. This benefits workloads with higher level of inter-thread communication or external I/O, where cores will otherwise be underutilized. So, for example, a VM with 16 vCPUs, on a host with four 8-core (16 SMT) sockets will perform best with either one, two, or four NUMA nodes, depending on the workload.

The above complexities and potential divergence over time of guest OS determined topology are most pronounced for heterogeneous workloads consolidated on hosts in heterogeneous clusters. Maximum performance of a single VM running on hosts with identical machine NUMA topology is an equally important scenario. In our experimental evaluation we discuss performance of VMs with maximum vCPU count with matching virtual, physical and machine topology. We expect these to be typical configurations for virtualized HPC environments which generally will not over-subscribe hardware resources and which employ homogeneous clusters.

4   Experimental Evaluation

We evaluated our prototype ESXi Server using four applications from the SPEC MPI V2.0 suite and seven applications from SPEC OMP V3.2 suite. SPEC MPI workloads are meant to be evaluated on distributed memory machines but can be useful for performance evaluation on shared memory machines as well. SPEC OMP is designed for use on shared-memory machines and is well-suited to evaluate the performance of large SMP virtual machines for HPC. All the experimental results reported here were gathered on 2.27 GHz Intel(R)

Xeon(R) CPU X7560 processors based on the Nehalem-EX architecture. All the benchmarks were compiled using gcc-4.3 and gfortran. We present three types of results in this paper:

- Gains obtained due to vNUMA
- Native to virtual runtime ratio showing virtual performance
- Native and virtual scaling

Our virtual NUMA(vNUMA) results start at 16 vCPUs since this represents the two-socket case on our test system. Native to virtual ratio is obtained by dividing the completion time of an application in the native case by the completion time of the virtual run. A ratio greater than 1 indicates that a VM runs faster than the native. Scaling results are reported starting at four vCPUs / processes / threads because some MPI tests failed to run using fewer than four processes. All of the SPEC benchmark applications were run for two iterations, which is not SPEC-compliant. Run-to-run variation was within 1-2%. The numbers reported here are the average of the two runs.

4.1 SPEC MPI Results

The SPEC MPI applications were evaluated on a Dell PowerEdge R910, which has four sockets and a total of 256 GB memory. RHEL 5.4 was used as a native and guest OS with kernel version 2.6.18-164. All VMs were configured with 128 GB of virtual RAM. We used Open MPI v1.4 [8] and the SPEC MPI medium dataset for our tests.

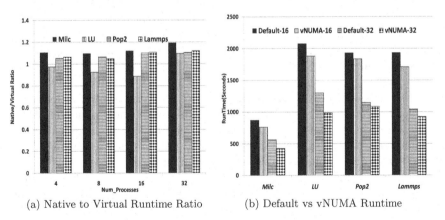

(a) Native to Virtual Runtime Ratio   (b) Default vs vNUMA Runtime

Fig. 1. SPEC MPI Virtualization performance, and Interleaving vs vNUMA with vCPU count = Number Of Physical Cores = 32

We conducted two sets of experiments. In the first set, the number of vCPUs is equal to the number of physical cores in the system (32 in this case) and the number of processes spawned is the same as in the case of native. This config-uration is similar to the native setup in the sense that the guest OS scheduler would schedule as it would on a native system with the minor difference that in the native case it would schedule on 64 logical threads, while in the virtual case, it would schedule on 32 vCPUs and the 32 vCPUs would then be scheduled by the ESXi scheduler on the 64 logical threads. We do not expose hyper-threading information to the guest and for this workload we need full cores for each vCPU. While this configuration has the best performance, we discuss alternative VM size configurations later in our evaluation. In the second set of experiments, the number of vCPUs configured for a VM is set equal to the number of processes spawned in each SPEC MPI run – we size the VM equal to the size of the MPI job.

Figure 1(a) shows the native to virtual runtime ratio for four applications from the SPEC MPI V2.0 suite. The ratio for most of the applications is close to one which indicates that virtualization is adding little or no overhead in this case. In certain cases we see up to 20% better virtual performance than native as in the case of the milc application run with 32 processes. We observed that native Linux scheduler gives better performance if HT is OFF versus when it is ON (32-process SPEC MPI applications on the 64 logical threads). We also observed that many SPEC MPI applications on a native system with 64 processes on a 64 logical core system like the Nehalem-EX system were not gaining much over the performance of the 32-process run. Hence we sized the VM with 32 vCPUs (because there were 32 physical cores in the system). Also typically in HPC applications, processes/threads are spawned based on number of physical cores rather than logical cores.

Figure 1(b) shows the performance gain obtained due to exposing to the guest OS a virtual NUMA topology matching the machine topology. In this figure, Default-16 means that vNUMA is disabled (memory is interleaved over the physical NUMA nodes) and the suffix 16 means that sixteen MPI processes were spawned within the MPI application, whereas vNUMA-16 means that vNUMA is enabled (virtual NUMA nodes match physical NUMA nodes). The gain due to vNUMA for milc were 12.3% and 25% for the 16 and 32 vCPU cases, respectively. Similarly for LU, the gains are 9.3% and 24% for 16 and 32vCPU VMs. Noticeable gains were also observed for the pop2 and lammps applications.

In order to better understand the trade-offs in performance, we modified the virtual experiments so that the number of vCPUs configured for a VM is equal to the number of processes spawned in SPEC MPI applications. Figure 2(a) shows the results with the number of vCPUs equal to number of processes.

In Figure 2(a), milc and LU actually lose performance for 4, 8 and 16 rank runs when compared to results in Figure 1(a). This is because the scheduling decisions in native and virtual environments were different. For example, in the native four-process case the Linux scheduler spreads the workload across multiple sockets, which increases the effective cache size and delivers better performance for applications that benefit from larger cache sizes. ESXi instead will schedule the four virtual processors on a single socket for better consolidation and to increase cache sharing effects. That is the reason why LU's native to VM ratio is in between 0.7 and 0.9 for 4, 8 and 16vCPU runs. In the light of these results,

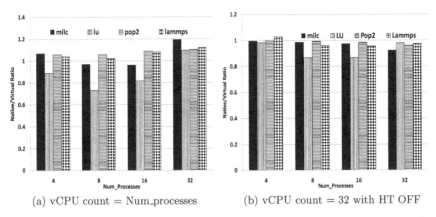

(a) vCPU count = Num_processes   (b) vCPU count = 32 with HT OFF

Fig. 2. SPEC MPI Virtualization Performance with vCPUs = processes, and with hyper-threading off

the best practice would be to size your VMs depending on your application's cache footprint.

Both Figure 1(a) and Figure 2(a) show that native suffers performance degradation with HT. To test whether HT is responsible for this degradation, we disabled HT from the system BIOS. Figure 2(b) shows the native to virtual ratio with HT OFF in both the VM and the native case with vCPU count equal to 32. The ratio is less than one for almost all cases (expect lammps which is slightly higher). Given the fact that both native and virtual configurations represented in Figure 2(b) have same amount of cache, we conclude that the ESXi scheduler is more optimal than the native scheduler in this case.

Figure 3(a) shows native and virtual scaling of the four applications from the SPEC MPI V2.0 suite. The suffix "-N" means native run and "-V" means virtual run. In this figure, HT is ON, which explains why virtual numbers are sometimes better than native, e.g., the 32-process data point.

In the light of the above results, for the virtual runs, HT ON and number of vCPUs being equal to the physical cores in the system is the best configuration. We used this configuration for SPEC OMP V3.2 benchmarks in the next section.

4.2   SPEC OMP Results

SPEC OMP applications were evaluated on an HP ProLiant DL980 G7, with eight sockets and 512 GB RAM. RHEL 6.0 was used as a native and guest OS with kernel version 2.6.32-71.el6. All VMs were configured with 128 GB of virtual RAM. The large data sets were used for all SPEC OMP experiments. Figure 4(a) shows the virtualization performance for SPEC OMP V3.2 benchmarks. The native to virtual runtime ratio was close to one for all applications expect for equake (four process and 64 process run) and fma3d (4 process run) where the ratio was greater than one. As was explained earlier, this is because native scheduling with HT ON is sub-optimal.

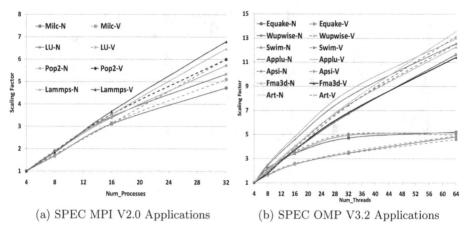

(a) SPEC MPI V2.0 Applications   (b) SPEC OMP V3.2 Applications

Fig. 3. Native and Virtual Scaling with vCPUs = No. Of Physical Cores

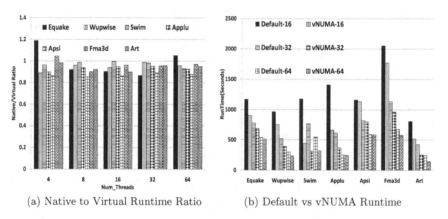

(a) Native to Virtual Runtime Ratio   (b) Default vs vNUMA Runtime

Fig. 4. SPEC OMP Virtualization performance, and Interleaving vs vNUMA with vCPU count = Number Of Physical Cores = 64

Figure 4(b) shows performance gains due to vNUMA for seven different applications from the SPEC OMP V3.2 suite.

Strikingly, swim with 16 threads and virtual NUMA performs better than 32 or even 64 threads without virtual NUMA topology! This shows the memory bandwidth demands of this benchmark are much more critical than the thread count. With 16 threads the gains on swim from vNUMA are 167%, but with 64 threads the benefit is down to 72%, probably because of saturated memory bandwidth.

Art starts with 56% vNUMA gains at 16 threads, and the benefits increase to 71% at 64 threads. Most likely memory bandwidth becomes a bigger bottleneck at higher thread counts and bandwidth is still available.

Fma3d and Wupwise have a relatively constant gain from vNUMA at different thread counts respectively 17% and 30% where both peak at 32 threads. Given that the increased memory bandwidth demand of higher number of threads doesn't affect performance, these applications are probably latency-sensitive but not bandwidth-sensitive. Our hypothesis is that instead of 12.5% locality when using 8 sockets, the lower latency for accessing up to 100% local memory is the main reason for these gains.

Applu and Equake gain significantly at 16-threads respectively 114% and 30%, but at 64-threads the vNUMA gains drop to 2% and 5%. This implies that initially memory bandwidth was the biggest bottleneck but new bottlenecks emerge at higher thread counts. Little gain in Apsi was observed probably because of a smaller memory bandwidth demand.

Overall at 64 threads two applications get more than 70% gains from vNUMA, and the geometric mean of the performance gains over all applications is 25%. All applications achieve their best performance at 64 threads but don't scale equally well.

Figure 3(b) shows native and virtual scaling for the seven applications. All applications show similar trends for virtual and native scaling. Some virtual and scaling data points were not close due to the difference in HT scheduling. One important point to note here is that Apsi, Swim and Equake are not scaling as nicely as other applications beyond 16 threads. Evaluating a multi-VM scenario on a single host as well on a cluster of hosts will be covered in future work.

5   Conclusion

We demonstrated that HPC workloads on VMware's virtualization platform achieve close to native performance (in some cases even 20% better than native) with applications from SPEC MPI and SPEC OMP benchmarks. We evaluated the new features in VMware's ESXi Server that significantly enhance the performance and scalability of HPC workloads.

Exposing a virtual NUMA topology that closely matches the physical host topology is a major feature, bridging the gap between native and virtual performance for VMs with large memory and high vCPUs counts. Gains of up to 2.67x were observed.

Virtual machines with up to 64 virtual CPUs now achieve their best performance when a virtual NUMA topology is exposed to guest operating systems. This allows operating systems and applications to make intelligent decisions about memory allocation and process/thread placement. We discussed the features required for a production system that exposes virtual NUMA topology. We preserve the now-expected virtualization benefits of portability and load balancing both within a host and a cluster, yet with with minimal overhead for a single VM.

Acknowledgments. We'd like to thank our colleagues Jeffrey Buell, Ishaan Joshi, and Seongbeom Kim for helpful experiments and suggestions, and our monitor and VMkernel group colleagues for making this work possible.

References

1. Advanced Configuration and Power Interface specification, rev 4.0a (2009),
   `http://www.acpi.info/spec40.htm`
2. Agesen, O., Garthwaite, A., Sheldon, J., Subrahmanyam, P.: The evolution of an x86 virtual machine monitor. Operating Systems Review 44(4) (2010)
3. Scalable Infrastructure with the CPU scheduler in VMware ESX 4.1,
   `http://www.vmware.com/files/pdf/techpaper/VMW_vSphere41_cpu_schedule_ESX.pdf`
4. Gavrilovska, A., Kumar, S., et al.: High-Performance Hypervisor Architectures: Virtualization in HPC Systems. In: HPCVirt 2007: 1st Workshop on System-level Virtualization for High Performance Computing (2007)
5. Huang, W., Gao, Q., Liu, J., Panda, D.K.: High performance virtual machine migration with RDMA over modern interconnects. In: Proceedings of the 2007 IEEE International Conference on Cluster Computing, CLUSTER 2007, pp. 11–20. IEEE Computer Society, Washington, DC (2007)
6. Mergen, M.F., Uhlig, V., Krieger, O., Xenidis, J.: Virtualization for high-performance computing. SIGOPS Oper. Syst. Rev. 40, 8–11 (2006)
7. Nagarajan, A.B., Mueller, F.: Proactive fault tolerance for HPC with Xen Virtualization. In: Proceedings of the 21st Annual International Conference on Supercomputing (ICS 2007), pp. 23–32. ACM Press (2007)
8. Open MPI: Open Source High Performance Computing (2011),
   `http://www.open-mpi.org`
9. Ranadive, A., Kesavan, M., Gavrilovska, A., Schwan, K.: Performance implications of virtualizing multicore cluster machines. In: Proceedings of the 2nd Workshop on System-Level Virtualization for High Performance Computing, HPCVirt 2008, pp. 1–8. ACM, New York (2008)
10. Rao, D., Schwan, K.: vNUMA-mgr: Managing VM memory on NUMA platforms. In: 2010 International Conference on High Performance Computing (HiPC), pp. 1–10 (December 2010)
11. Simons, J.E., Buell, J.: Virtualizing high performance computing. SIGOPS Oper. Syst. Rev. 44, 136–145 (2010)
12. Valle, G., Engelmann, C., Scott, S.L., Naughton, T., Ong, H.: System-Level Virtualization for High Performance Computing, February 13-15 (2008)
13. Waldspurger, C.A.: Memory resource management in VMware ESX server. In: OSDI 2002: Proceedings of the 5th Symposium on Operating Systems Design and Implementation, pp. 181–194. ACM Press, New York (2002)
14. Youseff, L., Seymour, K., You, H., Dongarra, J., Wolski, R.: The impact of paravirtualized memory hierarchy on linear algebra computational kernels and software. In: Proceedings of the 17th International Symposium on High Performance Distributed Computing, HPDC 2008, pp. 141–152. ACM, New York (2008)

Virtualizing Performance Counters

Benjamin Serebrin and Daniel Hecht

VMware
{serebrin,dhecht}@vmware.com

Abstract. Virtual machines are becoming commonplace as a stable and flexible platform to run many workloads. As developers continue to move more workloads into virtual environments, they need ways to analyze the performance characteristics of those workloads. However, performance efforts can be hindered because the standard profiling tools like VTune and the Linux Performance Counter Subsystem do not work in most modern hypervisors. These tools rely on CPUs' hardware performance counters, which are not currently exposed to the guests by most hypervisors. This work discusses the challenges of performance counters due to the trap and emulate method of virtualization and the time sharing of physical CPUs among multiple virtual CPUs. We propose an approach to address these issues to provide useful and intuitive information about guest performance and the relative costs of virtualization overheads.

1 Introduction

Virtualization is a method to decouple physical hardware from an operating system by running the guest OS in a virtual machine, or VM. Virtualization has found uses in both development, to isolate systems-under-test, and in data centers, to provide server consolidation, migration, and manageability functions. Workloads are increasingly likely to be virtualized. Many companies are using remote desktop viewing products to replace developers' and users' dedicated desktop machines. With these trends, developers face an increasing need to use native performance tools like VTune[13], CodeAnalyst[3], and the Linux Performance Counter Subsystem[6] inside VCPUs.

VMware is investigating the virtualization of hardware performance counters for its future products. This paper discusses the typical use cases for the counters and the ways to properly represent a useful view of performance events. The typical uses of virtualization present several challenges not present on non-virtualized (native) systems. For example, a virtual CPU (VCPU) does not occupy a physical CPU (PCPU) 100% of the time, which breaks many assumptions a profiler may make about the passage of time. Sharing the PCPU with multiple VMs requires that the hypervisor not only context switch the hardware counter resources, but also adjust some of the results to match what the profiler is expecting.

These event count adjustments are also required to expose the resource and time consumption of emulated instructions, and to match the semantics of a

M. Alexander et al. (Eds.): Euro-Par 2011 Workshops, Part I, LNCS 7155, pp. 223–233, 2012.

small set of counters that relate to instruction retirement. For example, a hypervisor often completes a trapped privileged instruction on behalf of the guest. Without additional hypervisor bookkeeping, this emulation would not appear as having consumed execution resources or retired any instructions if the counters are paused while the hypervisor is running. Conversely, if counters are allowed to freely run in both contexts, confusing results may arise when hypervisor events are counted. Our work seeks to find the best mix of performance counter emulations to represent performance events in a way that supports existing profiling tools.

The hypervisor strives to provide a virtual CPU as similar as possible to physical hardware; it should present virtualized performance counters that enable a guest to profile itself as well as it could on a native system. This work treats the hypervisor itself as an opaque extension of the CPU with respect to the in-guest profiling system; this enables the hypervisor to agnostically support all profilers that use the standard CPU interface to performance counters.

Enabling performance counter use in guests allows profilers to use hardware performance counters to measure metrics including cache misses, translation lookaside buffer (TLB) pressure, and instructions per cycle (IPC). These profiling tools produce per-process and system metrics based on sampled hardware counts to indicate where performance improvement opportunities exist. High performance computing developers frequently use such performance tools to find bottlenecks and inefficiencies. Virtualization is under discussion in HPC contexts to provide abstraction, migration, and reliability, and hypervisor vendors must support the same performance monitoring capabilities that developers use to tune native systems.

2   x86 Performance Counter Hardware

Intel[8] and AMD[1] provide similar interfaces to their performance counting hardware. Each CPU has its own set of performance counters and performance event select registers. The event select register is used to specify which microarchitectural event is to be counted, and contains bits to enable, filter the count results, and raise interrupts if the counter overflows from negative to positive. Typical modern hardware has between 2 and 8 general purpose counters and up to 3 fixed counters, each dedicated to a single event.

The encodings of events are generation-specific, though Intel has defined a small set of events that are encoded consistently across generations, and similar events on AMD appear consistent as well. Events common across many architectures include cycle counts (relative to core cycles and to constant-rate cycles), TLB accesses and misses, last-level cache accesses and misses, and instruction and branch retired counts. In addition to these common events, each CPU generation has its own assortment of architecture-specific events including store-to-load forwarding failure counts and functional unit stall events. AMD and Intel each have mechanisms to enable and disable individual counters during the state transition between the hypervisor's own code and running the guest.

A typical usage of the performance counters could include configuring Event Select 0 to count Last-Level Cache misses in all privilege levels with the overflow interrupt disabled and configuring Event Select 1 to count Last-Level Cache accesses with identical privilege and interrupt settings. A profiler then samples the Event Counts 0 and 1 and calculates per-sample period differences to track the ratio of cache misses to accesses. In addition, the interrupt facility of the hardware counters can be enabled to cause interrupts after a set number of events. In this example, setting the Event Select's interrupt-enable bit and setting the corresponding counter to -10,000 would cause the hardware to raise an interrupt after the 10,000th cache miss.

Extensions such as PEBS (Precise Event-Based Sampling) and LWP (Lightweight Profiling) are not discussed in detail in this paper, but may be virtualized with similar methods. However, each of these has memory-access characteristics that present more virtualization challenges than the simple Model-Specific Register (MSR) interface of the core event counters. Uncore or Northbridge counters are shared among multiple PCPUs and thus are less amenable to time-multiplexing.

3   Profilers

Profilers commonly use a sampling mode where one or more events are allowed to raise interrupts after a specified number of counts. The user or profiler sets the overflow limit to achieve a desired approximate frequency of events, based on an estimated expected rate of events. For example, if 1000 TLB misses occur per second on average, and a 10Hz sampling rate is desired, the event counter is initialized to -100.

The profilers are given knowledge of a binary's code layout and symbols and are often integrated with an IDE programming environment like Visual Studio or Eclipse. They run one or multiple passes of a program and record the instruction pointer and possibly the call stack information in place at the time of a performance counter interrupt. The profilers present a visualization of the average cost of a given function or even an individual instruction based on this information.

A programmer commonly writes a program and runs it under the profiler, providing a typical input set. The programmer can iteratively apply optimizations based on profiler results.

4   Time-Sharing Physical CPUs

Many datacenters perform CPU overcommittment using hypervisors, running multiple VMs on a single computer where the total VCPU count exceeds the total number of PCPUs. The hypervisor must share PCPUs among all the VCPUs, giving each VCPU a fraction of the total runtime of the system. The sharing of hardware resources requires the hypervisor to apply heuristics to enable guest operating systems to accurately keep track of absolute time, often called wall-clock time.[14]

The guest operating system wall-clock should track absolute time over the long term. To achieve this, while the VM is descheduled, VMware's virtual timer devices that are used by the guest operating system for timekeeping are allowed to fall behind real time and later catch up faster than real time when the VM is rescheduled. This way, over the longer term, these devices track absolute real time. Profilers, on the other hand, are more concerned with relative time differences over the short term, and want to count only the time that the VCPU is scheduled on a PCPU.

This tension over the desired semantics of a timer device requires the hypervisor to carefully trade off keeping a guest's notion of wall-clock time correct and giving a notion of time appropriate for profilers' use. Both Intel and AMD CPUs provide an event called core cycles not halted, which tracks the CPU cycle count independently of wall-clock time. CPU frequency can increase or decrease due to power saving modes, and CPU cycles can stop entirely if the OS has executed the HLT instruction. The notion of core cycles not halted is thus a convenient hardware interface that can be extended for profiling in a virtual environment. The hypervisor can define core cycles not halted to count only core clock cycles when the VCPU is in context on a PCPU, including time spent in the hypervisor on that VCPU's behalf. Fortunately, the use of core cycles not halted appears to be common practice in profilers, and our extension of its meaning is consistent with common calculations of events per unhalted cycle ratios.

The RDTSC instruction is a common source of total elapsed time. However, an instructions per cycle calculation that uses RDTSC results for elapsed time as its denominator might under-count the IPC. In this case, the hypervisor is actively managing the RDTSC instruction to track absolute real time. The more correct method would be to measure instructions retired in one performance counter while measuring core-cycles not halted in another. Fortunately, there is incentive on native systems for that practice, as most modern processors support some form of hardware-mediated cycle speed boosting that the OS does not control. Boosting provides a similar distortion as hypervisor time manipulation when RDTSC is used as a cycle count.

Sharing hardware leads to other, less direct effects. Just as multiple processes may compete for cache and other resources, multiple VCPUs and other unrelated hypervisor threads that share a physical core can pollute each other's caches, branch predictors, TLBs, and other microarchitectural state. This work intentionally avoids attempting to condition these types of counters, both due to the difficulty of properly recalculating the non-sharing values of such dynamic counts, and due to a desire to appropriately show the effects of sharing resources. While a program may not be causing cache misses itself, it may still experience them in a time-shared machine, and the programmer could benefit from such knowledge.

The hypervisor context switches all relevant CPU state when each VCPU is scheduled and descheduled. To virtualize performance counters as we describe, the hypervisor must context switch the active performance counter state, in addition to the context switching of general purpose registers and control state. This serves to time-multiplex the CPU and performance counter hardware resources and guarantee that virtual counters do not advance while that VCPU is out of context. The context switching of the counter state satisfies our extended definition of unhalted core-cycles.

5   Trapping and Emulation

When a non-privileged guest instruction is executed by the physical CPU, the guest is said to be in *direct execution* mode. Modern hypervisors trap and emulate[12] to handle privileged guest instructions and events. In well-tuned systems, the rate of traps is low and guests spend most of their time in direct execution. However, a guest may execute a trapped instruction, such as the CPUID instruction, which is then intercepted by the hypervisor. The hypervisor decodes and emulates the instruction, and resumes with direct execution beginning at the next guest instruction. Other mandatory traps include IN and OUT instructions, page faults that are induced by lazy context evaluation in shadow or nested paging modes, and accesses to virtual devices.

If a hypervisor were to naïvely pause the virtual counters when exiting direct execution, an emulated instruction would never cause any counters to increment. Conversely, if the hypervisor were to allow all counters to continue running while emulating the instruction, the instructions retired count would match the number of hypervisor instructions executed. For example, if the following code snippet were in an inner loop, a non-virtualized profiler would discover that many cycles were spent executing the CPUID instruction (which is fairly expensive at approximately 100 cycles on modern CPUs) and that IPC is very low. However, a hypervisor that paused virtual counters would fail to increment cycles or even instruction retired counts for the CPUID instruction, and the profiler would interpret the event counts as saying the CPUID instruction had zero cost. Alternatively, if all counters increment freely during emulation of the CPUID instruction, IPC may appear to be high since most of the hypervisor instructions used to emulate CPUID will be normal high-throughput instructions. This design choice would also hide the cost of executing CPUID in a VM. Our work aims to categorize ways to appropriately and efficiently emulate performance events in such cases.

```
int popcnt(int i) {
   if (cpuid(1).ecx & POPCNT_MASK != 0) {
      return __builtin_popcnt(i);
   } else {
      return SoftwarePopcnt(i);
   }
}
```

6   Speculative and Non-speculative Events

Many performance events are subject to run-to-run variation due to processor speculation, varying cache and branch predictor temperature, variable cache miss costs, and other non-deterministic effects. These *speculative* [1] events include cache, branch predictor, and TLB statistics as well as microarchitecture-specific events. A cache miss counter, for instance, could experience run-to-run variation due to execution of mispredicted code, OS context switch costs, cache misses due to thread migration to different cores, and memory bandwidth competition due to other cores.

Other events can be considered deterministic and *non-speculative*: for a given program execution, the counts of retired instructions and branches can be expected to be repeatable and determined from an in-order execution of the program. For example, after a 3-instruction code loop that executes 1000 times, the retired branch instruction event should report 1000 branches and the retired instruction event should report 3000 instructions.

7   Combining Native and Emulated Performance Counters

As discussed above, one approach is to allow the counters to run during execution of the inner portions of the emulation code, and to pause the counters only on context switches away from the current VCPU. Another approach pauses all counters at the boundary between hypervisor and hardware execution of guest code.[4] Finally, a third approach emulates the hardware counters to attempt to represent the microarchitecture's counts for a small subset of events.[5]

This paper proposes a hybrid approach: for non-speculative events, the emulation code will ensure correctness, while speculative counters will present a view of the hypervisor's effect on hardware even for emulated guest instructions and events.

When the hypervisor is emulating one or more guest instructions, it has full knowledge of the counts of non-speculative guest events and can increment the counters. However, it is impractical to provide a CPU simulator in order to properly represent cache miss rates, TLB hits, cycle counts, and other speculative events. Instead, this work allows speculative events to count both in the guest context and during hypervisor emulation of the instruction. As discussed above, if the hypervisor switches context to another VCPU, the virtual counters are paused. When the current VCPU context is restored, the virtual counters resume.

Our approach gives the guest a glimpse into the costs of the hypervisor's implementation, but does not propose to expose hypervisor addresses or symbols. Instead, hypervisor effort for emulation is attributed to the instruction that required the emulation by allowing the non-speculative events to continue counting in the hypervisor. In the code example above, our approach causes CPUID to appear to consume the number of cycles that were required to emulate the instruction, and to increment the retired instruction count by one.

This design leads to some interesting surprises. For example, a natively-executed CPUID instruction never causes TLB misses or cache misses. However, the emulation code does require memory accesses and is likely to induce both TLB and cache events. We deliberately pass such counts through to the guest. This kind of induced event incrementing is visible only to a spot inspection of a particular instruction. A typical profiler must tolerate imprecision including the variable number of cycles a performance counter interrupt can require to arrive. Therefore, such surprising events like unexpected cache misses on non-memory instructions, which do not occur on native hardware, are unlikely to confuse the profiler's results.

Our design results in approximate correctness: expensive events do appear expensive when viewed in the profiler, whether the instruction causing that event was trapped-and-emulated or executed by hardware.

7.1   Hybrid Performance Counter Example

Figure 1 demonstrates how the various classes of performance events can behave under our design. Instructions retired is a non-speculative event, so does not increment while the VCPU is descheduled. However, at the point indicated by the arrow, the hypervisor has emulated one or more instructions and has incremented the counter accordingly. The hypervisor (VMM) runs between the VMexit and VMentry times. TLB accesses is a speculative event and is allowed to run during that time. Cycles not halted, while not related to speculative execution, is treated in the same manner. All VCPU counters are stopped when the VCPU is descheduled.

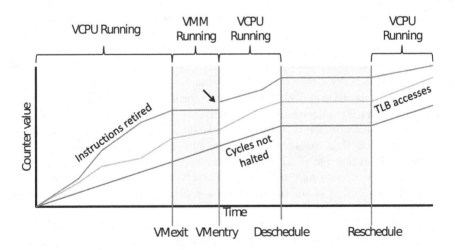

Fig. 1. Example graph of speculative and nonspeculative counters

8 Performance Counter Hardware Virtualization Methods

VMware hypervisors have historically largely avoided paravirtualized interfaces to basic hardware features in an effort to focus performance optimization at supporting a wide range of virtualization-unaware guests. In general, guest accesses to privileged state are trapped and emulated by the hypervisor. The hypervisor's handling of guest performance counter resource accesses follows this pattern: each guest performance counter MSR access is trapped and proxied, largely unaltered, to the underlying hardware.[1] A guest performance counter that is configured to raise an interrupt will cause the hypervisor to enable the interrupt on the corresponding hardware resource. The hypervisor will trap the resulting performance monitor interrupt and forward it synchronously to the guest.

The hypervisor configures the hardware performance counters with a few small differences to enable the hypervisor to share performance counters with other hypervisor software services, and to enable the guest-only filtering capabilities of the hardware when appropriate for the event type.

9 Discussion

An open item of discussion for this workshop is to explore whether these design choices are correct and adequate.

One question is how the hypervisor should properly filter events that a profiler might use in a ratio. If the profiler mixes speculative and non-speculative events in the same ratio, the speculative events will have been allowed to increment during hypervisor emulation code, while the non-speculative events will count only guest events. Example ratios include TLB misses or accesses per retired instruction. A hypervisor cannot predict whether the profiler or user wants to include only events incurred while running guest code, but a modification to our design could assume the use of retired instruction events implies such a ratio and thus conditionally pause speculative event counts during emulation.

Generally, it is expected that unmodified profiling tools will function correctly under this virtualization scheme. Directed tests running natively and in VMs observe performance counter results that match within close tolerances, and it is expected that variances due to the timesharing and virtualization will cause similarly minor disruptions to profiling tools' results. The user bears some responsibility for understanding profiler results in the native case, and some additional understanding about the nature of virtualized workloads will be vital to effective performance tuning.

Certain phases of a workload should be minimally impacted by virtualization, while others may experience a range of performance effects. For example, a computation-heavy workload phase that does not pressure the TLB significantly

---

[1] Optimizations to allow the guest to write some MSRs directly are not the focus of this paper. The hypervisor can usually allow the guest to write the count MSRs directly, but often must mediate access to configuration and interrupt control registers.

should provide the same profile results when run in a VM or natively. The profiler would be expected to show significant profile differences if, for example, the VM's memory is misconfigured and resides on an inappropriate memory controller. The shape of the profile for other workloads can be expected to change under virtualization. For example, using hardware page table virtualization (Intel EPT or AMD Nested Paging) can increase the cost of a TLB miss.[2] A garbage-collected workload with a large working set could experience greater performance degradations while virtualized, and the costs will be visible in the profile.

The profilers discussed here are often considered vertical profilers[7], in that they have sampling and symbol visibility to multiple layers of the system, including hardware, operating system, various middle layers, language virtual machine, and application. While software counters can be used for the upper layers of the system, the hardware's own performance counters are typically used for measuring the hardware layer. This work can be considered to support vertical profiling by extending the definition of hardware to include the CPU emulation efforts of the hypervisor. This definition serves to abstract away specific knowledge of the hypervisor from the guest profiler while exposing the related costs, in a manner analogous to the level of visibility into the CPU's hardware itself.

10   Future Work

This work focuses on enabling existing unmodified performance tools. By inferring the appropriate way to emulate speculative and non-speculative counters, we assume knowledge of the profiler's intentions. A virtualization-aware profiler could express its interest in how a hypervisor should emulate its counters.

Analogous to the commonality of many of the basic microarchitectural events, hypervisors could expose synthesized events that are common to most hypervisor implementations, especially events that pertain to implementation of CPU emulations. For example, a shadow-paging hypervisor could expose the number of hidden page faults that required hypervisor intervention for events like accessed and dirty bit setting. A hypervisor in any paging mode, including hardware-supported nested paging, can expose an event containing the number of hidden page faults due to lazy population of guest memory or copy-on-write collisions.

Timeslicing a machine is a fertile area of exploration for adding performance metrics. A guest may be interested in estimating the number of cycles stolen due to resource sharing (for example, to understand video frame rates or other time-sensitive measurements). Disk events, hypervisor lock statistics, and NUMA migration counts are other potential events that could provide insight into the system.

11   Related Work

Generally, existing profiling tools that can be used with virtual machine environments are modified and either run on the host or have some cooperation from and communication with the hypervisor. [9] discusses a system-wide profiling framework, Xenoprof, implemented in Xen. It includes a hypervisor component and a domain level component that coordinate to provide a system-wide profiler. OProfile has been ported to the Xenoprof interface. [16] allows a Linux host running the KVM VMM to collect guest OS statistics using the Linux perf utility. [15] can count hardware performance events on an ESX hypervisor.

[4], [5] and [11] discuss recent performance counter extensions to KVM and Xen, respectively. [4] and [5] discuss *guest-wide profiling*, which is similar in intent to our approach. [4] and [5] also discuss two choices for multiplexing the performance counter hardware: *CPU switch* and *domain switch*. [11] describes an infrastructure for Xen, perfctr-xen, that allows access to the hardware performance counters in a virtual environment. The infrastructure relies on a hypervisor component along with modifications to the guest OS kernel.

[4] mentions the requirement of synchronous interrupt delivery, which should be straightforward for all hypervisors: each performance counter interrupt is generated locally on the PCPU where the VCPU currently resides, and the hypervisor must have a fault injection mechanism that can be leveraged for interrupt injection. [10] describes whole-system profiling with the help of agents at each level of the virtualization hierarchy.

12   Conclusion

This paper presented a proposed solution for virtualizing and time-sharing performance counters while providing reasonable and intuitive counter results. The proposed implementation distinguishes between speculative events, which are allowed to count while a hypervisor is emulating guest code, and non-speculative events, which are faithfully emulated to match in-order program flow. In this way, unmodified profiling tools can be used inside a VM to gather useful performance profiles that do not conceal overheads caused by virtualization.

Acknowledgements. The authors would like to thank Hussam Mousa of Intel for collaboration and investigation of performance counter implementation and usage across processor generations and profiler versions.

References

1. AMD Bios and Kernel Developer Guide,
   http://support.amd.com/us/Processor_TechDocs/31116.pdf
2. Bhargava, R., Serebrin, B., Spadini, F., Manne, S.: Accelerating two-dimensional page walks for virtualized systems. ASPLOS XIII, Seattle, WA
3. CodeAnalyst, http://developer.amd.com/tools/codeanalyst/pages/default.aspx
4. Du, J., Sehrawat, N., Zwaenepoel, W.: Performance Profiling in a Virtualized Environment. In: Hotcloud 2010, Boston, MA (2010)
5. Du, J., Sehrawat, N., Zwaenepoel, W.: Performance Profiling of Virtual Machines. In: Virtual Execution Environments 2011, Newport Beach, CA (2011)
6. Gleixner, T.: Linux Performance Counter announcement,
   http://lkml.org/lkml/2008/12/4/401

7. Hauswirth, M., Sweeney, P., Diwan, A., Hind, M.: Vertical Profiling: Understanding the Behavior of Object-Oriented Applications. In: OOPSLA 2004, Vancouver, British Columbia, Canada (2004)

8. Intel Software Developer Manual, vol. 3, http://www.intel.com/Assets/PDF/manual/325384.pdf

9. Menon, A., Santos, J.R., Turner, Y., Janakiraman, G., Zwaenepoel, W.: Diagnosing Performance Overheads in the Xen Virtual Machine Environment. In: Virtual Execution Environments, Chicago, IL (2005)

10. Mousa, H., Doshi, K., Sherwood, T., Ould-Ahmed-Vall, E.: VrtProf: Vertical Profiling for System Virtualization. Hawaii International Conference on System Sciences, Koloa, HI

11. Nikolaev, R., Back, G.: Perfctr-Xen: A Framework for Performance Counter Virtualization. Virtual Execution Environments, Newport Beach, CA (2011)

12. Popek, G., Goldberg, R.: Formal Requirements For Virtualizable Third Generation Architectures. Commun. ACM 17(7), 412–421 (1974)

13. VTune, http://software.intel.com/en-us/articles/intel-vtune-amplifier-xe/

14. VMware: Timekeeping In Virtual Machines, http://www.vmware.com/files/pdf/Timekeeping-In-VirtualMachines.pdf

15. VMware: VMkperf for VMware ESX 5.0 (2011)

16. Zhang, Y.: Enhanced perf to collect KVM guest os statistics from host side, http://lwn.net/Articles/378778/

A Case for Virtual Machine Based Fault Injection in a High-Performance Computing Environment*

Thomas Naughton, Geoffroy Vallée, Christian Engelmann, and Stephen L. Scott

Oak Ridge National Laboratory,
Computer Science and Mathematics Division,
Oak Ridge, TN 37831, USA

Abstract. Large-scale computing platforms provide tremendous capabilities for scientific discovery. As applications and system software scale up to multi-petaflops and beyond to exascale platforms, the occurrence of failure will be much more common. This has given rise to a push in fault-tolerance and resilience research for high-performance computing (HPC) systems. This includes work on log analysis to identify types of failures, enhancements to the Message Passing Interface (MPI) to incorporate fault awareness, and a variety of fault tolerance mechanisms that span redundant computation, algorithm based fault tolerance, and advanced checkpoint/restart techniques.

While there is much work to be done on the FT/Resilience mechanisms for such large-scale systems, there is also a profound gap in the tools for experimentation. This gap is compounded by the fact that HPC environments have stringent performance requirements and are often highly customized. The tool chain for these systems are often tailored for the platform and the operating environments typically contain many site/machine specific enhancements. Therefore, it is desirable to maintain a consistent execution environment to minimize end-user (scientist) interruption.

The work on system-level virtualization for HPC system offers a unique opportunity to maintain a consistent execution environment via a virtual machine (VM). Recent work on virtualization for HPC has shown that low-overhead, high performance systems can be realized [7,15]. Virtualization also provides a clean abstraction for building experimental tools for investigation into the effects of failures in HPC and the related research on FT/Resilience mechanisms and policies. In this paper we discuss the motivation for tools to perform fault injection in an HPC context. We also present the design of a new fault injection framework that can leverage virtualization.

1 Introduction

Large-scale computing platforms provide tremendous capabilities for scientific discovery. These systems have hundreds of thousands of compute cores, hundreds of terabytes of memory, and enormous high-performance interconnection networks. As these platforms increase in size to accommodate the performance demands of the computational

---

* ORNL's work was supported by the U.S. Department of Energy, under Contract DE-AC05-00OR22725.

M. Alexander et al. (Eds.): Euro-Par 2011 Workshops, Part I, LNCS 7155, pp. 234–243, 2012.

science community, their component counts and overall system complexity increase. These massive node/component counts also yield increased occurrence of failure. As such, fault tolerance/resilience (FT/R) are key factors for effective utilization of high-performance computing (HPC) systems.

Going forward, failures will become something that developers and scientific users of these HPC platforms will be forced to manage in their applications as they move toward multi-petaflop and exascale systems. There is already active work on this topic, to include log analysis for identification of failure types/modes, enhancements to the Message Passing Interface (MPI) to incorporate fault awareness, and a variety of fault tolerance mechanisms that span redundant computation, algorithm based fault tolerance, and advanced checkpoint/restart techniques.

However, there are few tools to aid in the evaluation and experimentation of HPC failures. The methodical investigation of failure in these systems is hampered by their scale, and a lack of tools for controlled experiments. The area of system-level virtualization offers a promising basis to support such experimentation. Virtualization has received much attention in recent years, which was primarily driven by commercial efforts (e.g., server consolidation), such that vendors are including hardware support for virtual machines. This trend and wide-scale industry adoption is likely to lead to virtualization as a standard capability of modern hardware/operating systems.

As the importance of fault tolerance increases, methods for experimentation into new mechanisms and policies is critical. The widespread availability of virtualization, combined with its strong isolation and user-customizable/adaptable execution environments, makes it an interesting platform for fault-tolerance testbeds. The virtual machine allows various operating systems, middleware, and applications to run unmodified in a controlled environment, where dependability can be evaluated at a very generic level, e.g., via virtual machine based fault injection.

Motivated by work in FT/R for HPC and current efforts in virtualization, we argue that tools for FT/R experimentation are needed and that system-level virtualization provides an interesting basis to develop such tools. We highlight prior work into the use of fault-injection for FT/R evaluation. We also discuss some of the unique requirements that emerge when working in an HPC environment.

The remainder of the document is organized as follows: Section 2 presents existing solutions for fault injection that are representative of the current state of the art, as well as a classification of these different solutions; Section 3 motivates the work presented in this document and Section 4 presents the specifics of the HPC context. Section 5 proposes a new framework architecture for fault injection in the context of HPC, and Section 6 concludes.

2 Background

Fault injection is the purposeful introduction of faults (or errors) into a target [5]. It has been used extensively for testing and experimentation of fault-tolerance mechanisms. These injections may be via specialized hardware or through software implemented fault injection (SWIFI). The software based approach offers more flexibility in terms of how to implement and detect the faults, but are limited in scope to areas accessible via software [5]. For example, radiation induced memory "soft errors" can be injected via hardware/environmental approaches but can only be emulated through software by techniques like bit-wise operations to force memory bit-flip(s).

The past work has included testing for distributed environments (NFTAPE) [12], which involved some experiments with MPI applications. In their MPI tests, they made minor modifications to the target application to accommodate the cluster based launch mechanism. In more recent work, FAult Injection Language (FAIL), provides a user the ability to express fault injection scenarios in a high-level language for distributed systems [4]. The language includes a compiler and execution context for performing the distributed fault-injection campaigns. The initial FAIL framework used the FCI (FAIL Cluster Implementation) to perform remote startup. In later work [3], they extended the tool to support dependability benchmarking of a fault-tolerant implementation of MPI.

Earlier studies have looked at the effects of faults on parallel applications running on a 4 node Parsytec PowerXplorer Transputer based machine [11]. This work leveraged hardware capabilities, e.g., performance counters and debug registers, to create low-overhead fault injection mechanisms (Xception) [6]. This provided a method to inject faults into any process, to include system software.

In systems that support dynamic loading of shared libraries, a common approach is to use the LD_PRELOAD mechanism to interpose on library calls and introduce faults, e.g., library level fault injection (LFI) [9]. This is a generic approach that does not require source code modifications of the target, and allows for runtime additions via the shared library wrapper routines.

Virtual machines have been used to aid in application robustness testing. In "FastFI with VMs" [13], they used virtual machines to aid in fault injection, specifically to reduce the complexity in capturing state associated with an application under test. They inject faults within the VM (e.g., API robustness for system calls from application), and export the post-fault analysis results and experimental state to the host before a VM rollback. Their focus is on using this efficient shapshot/rollback to reduce the overall runtime for extensive fault-injection campaigns. They mention the challenges with capturing state for fast rollback when working without VMs (their prior work employed fork()) and how some experiments would result in residual effects from the FI post-rollback, which was avoided with the isolation/encapsulation of the VM. They mention that distributed applications can be tested by using VM's, and virtualizing the network by running all on a single host. However, it appears they restrict their use of VM's and FI to a single physical machine, even in the case of testing distributed applications. Additionally, their work was focused on software error handling using fault injection at the API level.

The FAUmachine [10] project has produced a hardware simulation platform that provides fine grained fault injection capabilities. They use VHDL to model the hardware and leverage this detail to create more realistic SWIFI scenarios. They report that running unmodified operating systems and applications on the virtual CPU of FAUmachine, with its just-in-time compiler, results in a 5-20% reduction in performance in comparison to native execution. Their system supports a variety of faults, to include [10]: CPU, IDE controller, network adapter, serial terminal, monitor, power, and keyboard/mouse (input) errors.

A stated goal of the FAUmachine project is to maintain the fidelity of the hardware, as opposed to other virtualization efforts which seek increased performance in spite of true execution behavior. Restated, FAUmachine attempts to keep the hardware details consistent with real actions, whereas other virtual machine based system seek to improve performance and may adjust execution to achieve this goal.

In [8] the advantages and challenges associated with using virtualization for SWIFI are discussed. They cite the ability to isolate the system under test and avoid cumbersome situations when injecting into system running directly on the physical machine (e.g., self-crashes, log corruption). The challenge when working with VMs are to maintain sufficient fidelity with standard (bare machine) execution when performing injections, i.e., inject into proper context and avoid indirect virtualization related side effects. They use their tool, *Gigan*, to perform fault injection from within the VM (guest kernel) and from the VMM, for both para-virtualized and fully virtualized VMs. They tested a non-virtualized instance (where guest would normally run on physical machine) and virtualized case (to test resilience of VM and VMM platform itself).

Table 1. The projects discussed in this background section fall into three groups: (i) tools for distributed systems, (ii) mechanisms that leverage hardware/software features, and (iii) FI systems that employ virtualization

Distributed Systems	Leverage HW/SW Features	Virtualization
FAIL-FCI/-MPI	LFI	FAUmachine
NFTAPE	Xception	FastFI-VM
		Gigan

3   Motivation

Testing and experimentation are fundamental components of computer research and development. As systems increase in size this process becomes increasing difficult due to factors like distributed resources and concurrent execution. Additionally, it is becoming increasingly apparent that large-scale computing platforms must cope with an increased occurrence of failures. While this aspect has been embraced in purely distributed environments, it has been less common in high-performance computing (HPC) due to a more optimistic view on failures for these tightly coupled platforms. This leads to a growing recognition that failures are an unavoidable reality in large-scale high-performance computing (HPC) systems. Therefore, the system software that underpins these HPC systems must evolve to provide better fault tolerance (FT). Additionally, the applications themselves must also cope with failures and make effective use of any/all available FT mechanisms. An apparent indication of this merger of FT and HPC is the recent message passing interface (MPI) v3 working group on fault tolerance, MPI3-FT. Another indication that current and future large-scale systems must find new methods to cope with these interruptions is high-lighted in the recent DoE Exascale workshops and associated proposal calls. The objective being to design and implement the next generation software stack for future exascale computing platforms.

As fault-tolerance continues to push the research and development in HPC system software, the tools and techniques to properly test proposed solutions becomes more critical. Therefore, a systematic method for experimentation into fault-tolerance is necessary to help in the development of future HPC systems. The focus of our work is to provide such tools and create experimental environments for continued research and development. To that end, we discuss requirements and challenges associated with buildings failure testbeds supported by system-level virtualization. The use of virtualization provides two key benefits: (i) leverages modern hypervisor technology to reduce the overhead of running a guest testing domain, and (ii) provides a consistent execution environment for the target software stack, which is isolated from the native/physical platform. This enables the fault-tolerance efforts to develop as needed, while maintaining a consistent base testing/experimentation platform.

4 HPC Environments

There are several constraints associated with tools for HPC systems. In this section we highlight some significant aspects involved in building tools for those environments, with the purpose being to indicate properties that may affect fault injection tools for HPC environments. Also, in Table 2 we provide a brief contrasting of the prior work mentioned in Section 2 with the HPC oriented properties discussed in this section.

4.1 Batch Allocation Systems

These large systems are generally run using some form of job management system where applications (jobs) are submitted to a batch scheduling system, e.g., PBS/Torque, SLURM. In batch scheduled environments the job is allocated a dedicated set of resources for a given period of time. However, access to those resources may be highly restricted. For example, process startup may be limited to a remote invocation interface with no direct (interactive) access granted to the compute resources. That is to say the user may only be able to startup a task, but may not actually have a local shell to each processing element (node). This requires the tool chain to support these remote execution interfaces. This may also have ramifications on how the actual fault-injection experiments are carried out or detection is performed on the remote processes.

4.2 Executable Linkage

The compute node execution environments on HPC systems may be highly specialized. There may not be a local hard drive on the node, and there may be a minimalistic runtime environment. This often constraints how the executable binary is compiled. In many instances, there are no shared libraries on the compute nodes or dynamic shared library loading support is disabled entirely. This may limit the applicability of existing fault injection frameworks for practical use in an HPC environment. For example, the compiled binaries may require static linkage for execution on the compute nodes. This precludes the direct use of many fault-injection techniques that leverage shared libraries to interpose on application execution, e.g., LD_PRELOAD.

4.3 Performance Sensitive

The tool chain must be as low-overhead as possible. This has noticeable effects on infrastructure that must scale to support large numbers of processes. The tools may be forces to avoid centralized approaches due to added load on the network communication links, which could affect the performance of the application. In the context of fault-injection, this may manifest as constraints on monitoring frequency and volume of reporting information. Additionally, the concept of "performability" may be relevant, where performance and availability are criteria in the evaluation of the given application. Since fault-tolerance and performance often share many parallels, these aspects are likely to be relevant in the fault-injection infrastructure driving FT/R experiments.

4.4 Exotic Hardware

The hardware for these systems may be rather "exotic", and therefore require additional insights for its use. This may be in the form of additional software interfaces or device drivers. This is often the case in the interconnection network of HPC systems, which may influence the communication API provided to the tools. The software infrastructure may also have to accommodate idiosyncrasies in the hardware.

Note, the difference in HPC hardware may also influence the ways faults occur, i.e., "fault types". This is very important when defining fault-injection experiments. The mapping of applications to the system resources will also influence how the system behaves in the presence of faults. For example, the HPC interconnection network has greater bandwidth along one axis. Then failures in this direction could generate congestion, which could result in clients failing in their writes to the parallel file system. The point being that these errors were influenced by characteristics of the hardware and expectations on system balance, which can lead to complex failure scenarios that are unique to these platforms.

Table 2. Summary of HPC oriented properties supported by FI projects from Section 2

a The distributed MPI test cases with NFTAPE required modification to the source to cope with cluster launch

HPC Oriented Properties	FAIL-FCI	NFTAPE	LFI	Xception	FAUmachine	FastFI-VM	Gigan
Target Source Modifications	N	Y_a	N	N	N	N	N
Distributed Environment	Y	Y	N	Y	N	N	N
Full Execution Environment	N	N	N	Y	Y	Y	Y
HPC System Interfaces	Y	N	N	N	N	N	N
Require Dynamic Linkage	N	N	Y	N	N	N	N

5 Design

Our approach is to leverage existing work in HPC system software to build a framework for testing the effects of failure. By leveraging existing HPC infrastructure we can better manage some of the issues outlined earlier in Section 4. The major components of the system can be broken down into the following areas: (i) front-end and distributed control, (ii) experiment setup/management, (iii) monitoring and event logging, and (iv) fault injection mechanisms. The user interacts with the framework via the front-end to drive an experiment to test the effects of failure on a target application. The basic structure of the system is shown in Figure 1. The remainder of this section describes the aspects of these areas, to include what parts of the existing system software will be leveraged and/or extended.

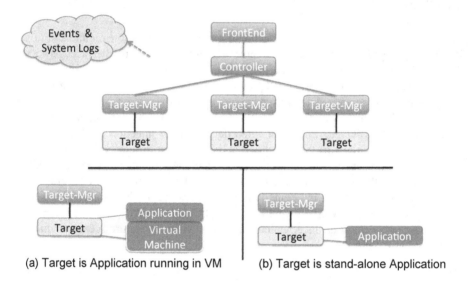

(a) Target is Application running in VM   (b) Target is stand-alone Application

Fig. 1. Basic structure for the tool

5.1 Front-End and Distributed Control

The interface provided to users of HPC systems is generally in the form of a launcher that the user invokes, which in turn invokes platform interfaces for remote task startup and control. This runtime environment (RTE) provides a basic communication and distributed control layer that applications may use to interact. The message passing interface (MPI) programming model is a common example that will be familiar to most users of HPC systems. The RTE provides MPI applications a way to bootstrap tasks and their communication handles. This is the same kind of functionality that is needed to startup and manage our fault injection experiments. Therefore, we leverage the RTE code base of the Scalable Tools and Communication Infrastructure (STCI) project [1]. This is a component-based RTE platform being developed at Oak Ridge National Laboratory.

In Figure 1 the STCI related parts are delimited by the blue boxes. This includes a Frontend and Controller that provide the interface between the user and system respectively. A customized agent is created called a "Target Manager". This provides the interface between the control runtime and the actual experiment "Target". The Frontend, Controller and Target Manager share a common communication space provided by STCI. The Target Manager is responsible for the bootstrap and control of the "Target", which will be discussed in more detail below.

5.2 Experiment Setup/Management

A fault injection experiment includes a configuration that defines what events (faults) should be introduced and how the experiment should be carried out. The steps to carry out this experiment are managed by the testing framework. The system under test (SUT), or "Target", is the entity upon which the experiment is focused. The *Target* is paired with a *Target Manager*. This allows for a clean separation of the SUT from the infrastructure used to manage the experiment. In the context of our framework, the Target could be an application binary or a virtual machine with the application running inside the VM. This has an effect on what injectors and faults may be employed for the experiment, but these details should be hidden from the end-user as much as possible.

In the case where the Target involves virtualization, the Target Manager is responsible for VM bootstrapping and management. This VM interface leverages prior work for Virtual System Environments [14], specifically the *LibV3M* abstraction layer. This library provides a VM management interface that the Target Manager uses to start, stop and monitor the VM based experiment.

5.3 Monitoring and Event Logging

While experiments are taking place, the system should be monitored using existing tools like Ganglia, syslog analyzers, etc. Additionally, a specific event notification channel is established so faults may be published as they are injected and used to correlate with actual failures detected throughout the system. The STCI runtime provides basic monitoring and failure detectors that could be useful for experiment monitoring. The publish/subscribe services in STCI and CiFTS Fault Tolerant Backplane (FTB) [2] are also good candidates for implementing these event notification channels.

5.4 Fault Injection Mechanisms

The controlled injection of synthetic faults, i.e., fault-injection (FI), requires that the system under test be sufficiently isolated. The strong isolation capabilities of virtual machines provide a sound platform for this requirement. It is beneficial to keep as much, if not all, of the FI infrastructure outside of the VM in order to maintain these isolation properties. Therefore extending the VM interface to support FI capabilities allows for access from the host operating system, and avoids complications when performing the injections in the same execution environment as the FI infrastructure.

There are a number of approaches to implement fault injection mechanisms. Two key characteristics of the mechanisms are: (a) how they are invoked, and (b) where the fault should be introduced.

The invocation may be based on a timer or some other external trigger (i.e., user input). It could also be based upon access to some resource, i.e., read from a given memory address. This leads to the second facet, fault location. In the case of VM-based injectors, the VMM/VM have full access to the resources and have full control to interpose on their access. However, to make the experiments more meaningful, often details about the application running in the VM must be exported to improve context for fault placement. This is a significant part of the experiment procedure, and something that will require careful consideration during experiment design. The current work in the V3VEE project has added initial support to Palacios for generating exceptions (faults) for specific memory locations at the VM-level, which are then serviced by the guest operating system. The FI framework would provide a way to configure tests that could leverage this to perform injections over a set of machines.

6   Conclusion

As HPC systems increase in size, concerns about failures and application resilience also increase. There is a growing effort to explore techniques to provide improved fault-tolerance/resilience (FT/R) for HPC platforms. This includes research and development at both the system and applications levels of the software stack. However, there is a significant gap in the set of tools available to assist in experimentation for FT/R mechanisms and policies. In this paper we have provided motivation for tools to address this gap and comments as to why existing tools for fault-injection experiments may face challenges for reuse in an HPC context. We also described an initial architecture for a new fault injection framework, which is based on existing HPC system software and tools, to help overcome this gap. We also argue that current work in system-level virtualization provides a good basis for developing fault-injection tools for HPC due to its strong isolation capabilities and complete access to resources used by the application (via virtual machine abstraction).

References

1. Buntinas, D., Bosilica, G., Graham, R.L., Vallée, G., Watson, G.R.: A Scalable Tools Communication Infrastructure. In: Proceedings of the 22nd International High Performance Computing Symposium (HPCS 2008), June 9-11, session track: 6th Annual Symposium on OSCAR and HPC Cluster Systems (OSCAR 2008). IEEE Computer Society (2008), http://www.csm.ornl.gov/oscar08/
2. Gupta, R., Beckman, P., Park, B.H., Lusk, E., Hargrove, P., Geist, A., Lumsdaine, A., Dongarra, J.: Cifts: A coordinated infrastructure for fault-tolerant systems. In: International Conference on Parallel Processing, ICPP (2009)
3. Hoarau, W., Lemarinier, P., Herault, T., Rodriguez, E., Tixeuil, S., Cappello, F.: Fail-mpi: How fault-tolerant is fault-tolerant mpi? In: IEEE International Conference on Cluster Computing, pp. 1–10 (September 2006)

4. Hoarau, W., Tixeuil, S., Vauchelles, F.: Fail-fci: Versatile fault injection. Future Generation Computer Systems 23(7), 913–919 (2007), http://www.sciencedirect.com/science/article/pii/S0167739X07000209

5. Hsueh, M.C., Tsai, T.K., Iyer, R.K.: Fault injection techniques and tools. Computer 30(4), 75–82 (1997)

6. Carreira, J., Madeira, H., Silva, J.G.: Xception: A Technique for the Experimental Evaluation of Dependability in Modern Computers. IEEE Transactions on Software Engineering 24(2) (February 1998), http://www.xception.org/files/IEEETSE98.pdf

7. Lange, J., Pedretti, K., Hudson, T., Dinda, P., Cui, Z., Xia, L., Bridges, P., Jaconette, S., Levenhagen, M., Brightwell, R., Widener, P.: Palacios and Kitten: High Performance Operating Systems For Scalable Virtualized and Native Supercomputing. Tech. Rep. NWU-EECS-09-14, Northwestern University, July 20 (2009), http://v3vee.org/papers/NWU-EECS-09-14.pdf

8. Le, M., Gallagher, A., Tamir, Y.: Challenges and Opportunities with Fault Injection in Virtualized Systems. In: First International Workshop on Virtualization Performance: Analysis, Characterization, and Tools, Austin, Texas, USA (April 2008), http://www.cs.ucla.edu/~tamir/papers/vpact08.pdf

9. Marinescu, P.D., Candea, G.: LFI: A Practical and General Library-Level Fault Injector. In: Proceedings of the 39th Annual IEEE/IFIP International Conference on Dependable Systems and Networks (DSN 2009), June 29 - July 2. IEEE (2009), http://dslab.epfl.ch/pubs/lfi/index.html

10. Potyra, S., Sieh, V., Cin, M.D.: Evaluating fault-tolerant system designs using FAUmachine. In: Proceedings of the 2007 Workshop on Engineering Fault Tolerant Systems (EFTS 2007), p. 9. ACM, New York (2007)

11. Silva, J.G., Carreira, J., Madeira, H., Costa, D., Moreira, F.: Experimental assessment of parallel systems. In: Proceedings of the 26th Annual International Symposium on Fault-Tolerant Computing (FTCS 1996), June 25-27, pp. 415–424 (1996)

12. Stott, D.T., Floering, B., Burke, D., Kalbarczyk, Z., Iyer, R.K.: NFTAPE: A framework for assessing dependability in distributed systems with lightweight fault inectors. In: Proceedings of the 4th IEEE International Computer Performance and Dependability Symposium (IPDS), pp. 91–100. IEEE (March 2000)

13. Süßkraut, M., Creutz, S., Fetzer, C.: Fast fault injection with virtual machines (fast abstract). In: Supplement of the 37th Annual IEEE/IFIP International Conference on Dependable Systems and Networks (DSN2007) (June 2007), http://wwwse.inf.tu-dresden.de/papers/preprint-suesskraut2007DSNb.pdf

14. Vallée, G., Naughton, T., Scott, S.L.: System Management Software for Virtual Environments. In: Proceedings of the ACM International Conference on Computing Frontiers (CF 2007), Ischia, Italy, May 7-9 (2007)

15. Youseff, L., Seymour, K., You, H., Dongarra, J., Wolski, R.: The impact of paravirtualized memory hierarchy on linear algebra computational kernels and software. In: Proceedings of the 17th International Symposium on High Performance Distributed Computing (HPDC 2008), pp. 141–152. ACM, New York (2008)

HPPC 2010:
5th Workshop on
Highly Parallel Processing on a Chip

Martti Forsell[1] and Jesper Larsson Träff[2]

[1] VTT, Technical Research Centre of Finland,
Oulu, Finland
`Martti.Forsell@vtt.fi`
[2] Faculty of Computer Science, Department of Scientific Computing,
University of Vienna, Vienna, Austria
`traff@par.univie.ac.at`

1   Introduction

Despite the processor industry having more or less successfully invested already 10 years to develop better and increasingly parallel multicore architectures, both software community and educational institutions appear still to rely on the sequential computing paradigm as the primary mechanism for expressing the (very often originally inherently parallel) functionality, especially in the arena of general purpose computing. In that respect, parallel programming has remained a hobby of highly educated specialists and is still too often being considered as too difficult for the average programmer. Excuses are various: lack of education, lack of suitable easy-to-use tools, too architecture-dependent mechanisms, huge existing base of sequential legacy code, steep learning curves, and inefficient architectures. It is important for the scientific community to analyze the situation and understand whether the problem is with hardware architectures, software development tools and practices, or both. Although we would be tempted to answer this question (and actually try to do so elsewhere), there is strong need for wider academic discussion on these topics and presentation of research results in scientific workshops and conferences.

The workshop on Highly Parallel Processing on a Chip (HPPC), now in its 5th incarnation, is dedicated to the interface between single-chip/node multi- and manycore architectures and programming paradigms, models, and languages towards supporting parallel algorithms and applications development in an efficient and manageable way. HPPC is intended as a forum for bold, new ideas on architectural organization (general- and special-purpose processors, heterogeneous designs, memory organization, on-chip communication networks, etc.), parallel programming models, languages, and libraries, manycore parallel algorithms, and application studies on both existing and envisaged architectures. In response to the call-for-papers that was issued (late) on April 6, 2011, HPPC 2011 received only a relatively low number of 7 submissions, that were, however, all of relevance to the general workshop themes. Based on relevance and quality of the submissions as judged by the program committee (which did most of the reviewing with few external reviewers) four papers were selected for presentation by the program chairs. This made for an acceptance rate of 57%. The workshop organizers and program chairs thank sincerely all contributing authors, and hope that they will also find it worthwhile to submit contributions next year (assuming the HPPC workshop series will be continued). All contributions received five reviews, and were thus given an all in all fair consideration. The members of the program committee are likewise all thanked for the time and expertise they put into the reviewing work, and for getting it done within the rather strict time limit.

The Euro-Par 2011 workshop day featured a number of workshops, and was very lively, well-attended and generally well-organized. The HPPC workshop was conducted in an informal atmosphere and gave, hopefully, enough room for interaction and discussion between presenters and audience. HPPC 2011 had a relatively high, cumulative attendance of more than 50. In addition to the four contributed talks, the workshop featured a longer, invited talk by Rick Hetherington on "Extreme Thread-Level-Parallelism on Sparc Processors", which turned out to be very good summary of techniques and architectural issues related to the Ultra SPARC T3 and T4 CMT processors and was well-received by the audience. The workshop organizers thank all attendees, who contributed much to the workshop with questions, comments and discussion, and hope they found something of interest in the workshop, too. We also thank the Euro-Par organization for creating the opportunity to arrange the HPPC workshop in conjunction with the Euro-Par conference, and of course all Euro-Par 2011 organizers for their help and support both before and during the workshop. HPPC sponsors VTT, University of Vienna, and Euro-Par 2011 are warmly thanked for the financial support that made it possible to invite Rick Hetherington, who we sincerely thank for accepting our invitation to speak and for his excellent talk. One of the workshop organizers unfortunately could not make it to the workshop.

These post-workshop proceedings include the final versions of the presented HPPC 2011 papers (accepted papers not presented at the workshop will not be included in the proceedings, but HPPC 2011 had all authors present and presenting), taking the feedback from reviewers and workshop audience into account. In addition to the reviews by the program committee prior to selection, an extra, post-workshop (blind) "reading" of each presented paper by one of the other presenters has been introduced with the aim of getting fresh, uninhibited high-level feedback for the authors to use at their discretion in preparing their final version (no papers would have been rejected at this stage bar major flaws). This idea was introduced with HPPC 2008, and will be continued also for HPPC 2012. The contributed papers are printed in the order they were presented at the workshop. Thematically, the contributed papers cover aspects of high-throughput computing CMPs ("Thermal Management of a Many-Core Processor under Fine-Grained Parallelism" by Keceli, Moreshet and Vishkin) and programming and optimization of CMPs ("Mainstream Parallel Array Programming on Cell" by Keir, Cockshott and Richards, "Generating GPU Code from a High-level Representation for Image Processing Kernels" by Membarth, Lokhmotov and Teich, "A Greedy Heuristic Approximation Scheduling Algorithm for 3D Multicore Processors" by Xu, Liljeberg and Tenhunen).

This year the number of submissions, only 7, was too low, and unless this can be significantly raised there is no reason to continue the workshop. The organizers are analyzing the reasons, and hope to find reasons and a way to organize HPPC again in conjunction with Euro-Par 2012.

October 2011

Martti Forsell, VTT, Finland
Jesper Larsson Träff, University of Vienna, Austria

Thermal Management of a Many-Core Processor under Fine-Grained Parallelism

Fuat Keceli[1], Tali Moreshet[2], and Uzi Vishkin[1]

[1] University of Maryland, College Park, MD, USA
[2] Swarthmore College, Swarthmore, PA, USA

Abstract. In this paper, we present the work in progress that studies the run-time impact of various DTM techniques on a proposed 1024-core XMT chip. XMT aims to improve single task performance using fine-grained parallelism. Via simulations, we show that relative to a general global scheme, speedups of up to 46% with a dedicated interconnection controller and 22% with distributed control of computing clusters are possible. Our findings lead to several high level insights that can impact the design of a broader family of shared memory many-core systems.

1 Introduction

Thermal feasibility has become a first-class architectural design constraint reflected in specifications of modern processors. It is typical to incorporate dynamic thermal management (DTM) in order to improve the power envelope without having to adopt more expensive cooling solutions. Going forward, it is important to advance the understanding of DTM techniques for efficiently supporting the architecture trend of increase in core count.

We base our work on the eXplicit Multi-Threading (XMT) architecture. XMT is a general-purpose many-core platform for fine-grained parallel programs, with significant evidence on ease-of-programming (e.g., [24]) and competitive performance (e.g., [3]). The reasons for choosing XMT as our platform are: *(a)* As noted in [25], ease-of-programming is crucial for the success of parallel computers and XMT constitutes a competitive and realistic direction in this respect, *(b)* The XMT simulator allows for evaluation of DTM techniques and such an infrastructure is not publicly available for other current many-core platforms.

In this paper, we evaluate the potential benefits of several DTM techniques on XMT. We focus on a system which executes one parallel task at a time. The relevance and the novelty of our work can be better understood by answering the following two questions.

Why Is Single Task Fine-Grained Parallelism Important? On a general-purpose many-core system the number of concurrent tasks is unlikely to often reach the number of cores (i.e., thousands). Parallelizing the most time consuming tasks is a sensible way for both improved performance and taking advantage

M. Alexander et al. (Eds.): Euro-Par 2011 Workshops, Part I, LNCS 7155, pp. 249–259, 2012.
© Springer-Verlag Berlin Heidelberg 2012

of the plurality of cores. The main obstacle then is the difficulty of programming for single-task parallelism. Scalable fine-grained parallelism is natural for easy-to-program approaches such as XMT.

What Is New in Many-Core DTM? DTM on current multi-cores mainly capitalizes on the fact that cores show different activity levels under multi-tasked workloads [5]. In a single-tasked many-core, the source of imbalance is likely to lie in the structures that did not exist in the former architectures such as the large scale on-chip interconnection network (ICN) and distributed shared caches.

Contribution. This paper introduces XMTSim+dtm, a new, DTM-enabled cycle-accurate simulator based on XMTSim [16]. Using XMTSim+dtm we measure the performance improvements introduced by several DTM techniques for a 1024-core XMT chip. We compare techniques that are tailored for a many-core architecture against a global DTM (GDVFS), which is not specific to many-cores. Following are the highlights of the insights we provide: (a) Workloads with scattered irregular memory accesses benefit more from a dedicated ICN controller (up to 46% runtime improvement over GDVFS). (b) In XMT, cores are arranged in clusters. Distributed DTM decisions at the clusters provide up to 22% improvement over GDVFS for high-computation parallel programs, yet overall performance may not justify the implementation overhead.

Our work is relevant for architectures that consider similar design choices as XMT (for example the Plural system [7]) which promote the ability to handle both regular and irregular parallel general-purpose applications competitively (see Section 3.1 for a definition of regular and irregular). These design choices include an integrated serial processor, no caches that are local to parallel cores, and a parallel core design that provides for a true SPMD implementation. We aim to establish high-level guidelines for designers of such systems.

A comprehensive body of previous work is dedicated to dynamic power and thermal management techniques for multi-core processors [13]. However, in most cases (e.g., [6, 12, 21]), authors assume a pool of uncorrelated serial benchmarks as their workload, and capitalize on the variance in the execution profiles of these benchmarks. The study by Ma, et al. [22] is notable, as they simulate a set of parallel benchmarks, however, it focuses on power rather than thermal management and considers up to only 128 cores. To our knowledge, our work is among the first to evaluate DTM techniques on a many-core processor for single task parallelism.

2   Experimental Platform

2.1   The XMT Architecture

The primary goal of the eXplicit Multi-Threading (XMT) general-purpose computer architecture [28] has been improving single-task performance through parallelism. XMT was designed from the ground up to capitalize on the huge on-chip resources becoming available in order to support the formidable body of knowledge, known as Parallel Random Access Model (PRAM) algorithmics [18], and the latent, though not widespread, familiarity with it. Driven by the repeated programming difficulties of parallel machines, ease-of-programming was a leading design objective of XMT. Indeed, considerable amount of evidence was developed on *ease of teaching* and improved *development time* with XMT (e.g., [24])[1].

The XMT architecture includes an array of lightweight cores, Thread Control Units (TCUs), and a serial core with its own cache (Master TCU). The architecture includes several clusters of TCUs connected to mutually-exclusive shared cache modules by a high-throughput interconnection network [1]. XMT does not feature writable private caches. Moreover, since the cache modules are mutually exclusive, no cache coherence is required. TCUs include lightweight ALUs, but the more heavy-weight units are shared by all TCUs in a cluster. XMT is programmed in XMTC, a simple extension of the C language which contains succession of serial and parallel code sections. The code of a parallel section is expressed in the SPMD (single program, multiple data) style, specifying an arbitrary number of virtual threads sharing the same code. Further details on the XMT architecture can be found in [28].

2.2   Simulation Environment

The simulation environment used in this work is XMTSim+dtm, an extension of publicly available XMTSim [16]. XMTSim is the cycle-accurate simulator of the XMT computer architecture, built to model the on-chip components that constitute the ASIC and FPGA prototypes of XMT. XMTSim has been validated against the FPGA prototype and cycle counts are shown to be accurate within a margin of 15% [17]. The parameters of the power model used in XMTSim is based on other validated tools: McPat [20] and Cacti [29]. The details of this estimation are the subject of a companion paper [15]. More details on the simulator than presented hereafter can be found in [14, 16, 17].

The high level specifications of the 1024-TCU XMT chip that we simulated in our experiments are given in Table 1a. The values in the table were compiled to match the chip area of an advanced GPU, NVIDIA GTX280. Details of this analysis are given in [3].

Power Estimation. XMTSim estimates power based on the activity that a benchmark induces on the clusters, ICN and the shared caches. Effect of die temperatures is included in calculation of the leakage power. The power model used in XMTSim is similar to the model proposed in [11] and explained in detail in [14, 17]. The model reflects the assumptions that a components implement clock gating and voltage gating. Table 1a lists the maximum powers of the components in the simulated XMT chip.

The Temperature Model. XMTSim uses HotSpot [27] to estimate the temperatures of the clusters and the maximum temperature of the area dedicated to the ICN routing. We set the thermal limit at 65C, whenever required, and

---

[1] A complete list of references can be found at
http://www.umiacs.umd.edu/users/vishkin/XMT/index.shtml#publications

Table 1. (a) The specifications of the 1024-TCU XMT. Given in parentheses are the maximum cumulative power for each group of components. (b) Checkerboard floorplan for a 1024 TCU XMT. Vertical strips with light gray color are reserved for interconnection network routing and the black colored rectangle is the Master TCU.

Processing Clusters (240.7W)
·1024 In-order 5–stage TCUs with ALUs, 2-bit br. prediction, 16 prefetch buffers ·64 Mult./Div. and 64 Float. Point units ·2K read-only cache per cluster
Interconnection Network (45.3W)
·64-to-128 Mesh-of-Trees [1]
Shared Parallel Cache (80.4W)
·128 modules x 32K. 4MB total ·2-way associative
Other Specifications
·Max. clock freq.: Clusters – 1.3 GHz, ICN – 2.6 GHz ·Max. DRAM bwidth.: 141.7 GB/sec

(a)   (b)

simulated our benchmarks with a heatsink convection resistance of 0.05W/K, observed in advanced cooling solutions [10]. Fig. 1b denotes the simulated XMT floorplan. It is motivated by previous work that shows it is thermally more efficient to place the clusters and shared caches in a checkerboard pattern rather than keeping them separately [10].

Simulating DTM. XMTSim samples the power and computes temperature at regular intervals. At each interval, DTM algorithm calculates a new set of frequencies for the clusters and the ICN. In order to avoid very long simulation times, we use steady-state temperature computations. Steady-state is an approximation to transient solutions for very long intervals with steady inputs. We observed that the behaviors of the kernels we simulated do not change significantly with larger data sets, except that the phases of consistent activity stretch in time. Therefore, we interpret the steady-state results obtained from simulating relatively short kernels with narrow sampling intervals as indicators of potential results from longer kernels. The sampling intervals, ranging from 5K to 200K clock cycles, are determined empirically to filter the noise in the activity patterns.

3   Performance under Thermal Constraints

In this section, we discuss the performance of the XMT chip under thermal constraints and evaluate a set of dynamic thermal management techniques that can potentially improve the performance. Our main objective is obtaining the

Table 2. Benchmark properties. Results are clock cycles, average power and temperature, consecutively

Name	Results	Description	Characteristic and Dataset
BFS-I	1.825M, 161W, 60C	Breadth-first search on graphs.	Hi-P. 1M nodes, 6M edges. Low cluster and moderate ICN activity. Irregular.
BFS-II	135.2M, 118W, 56C		Low-P. 200K nodes, 1.2M edges. Very low activity. Irregular.
Bprop	3.990M, 118W, 56C	Back Propagation machine learning alg.	Hi-P. 64K nodes. Low activity. Irregular.
Conv	0.885M, 215W, 66C	Image convolution with separable filter.	Hi-P. 1024x512. Highest activity. Regular.
FFT	4.905M, 194W, 63C	1-D fixed point Fast-Fourier transform.	Hi-P. 1M points. Moderate activity. Regular.
Mmult	10.6M, 180W, 63C	Multiplication of two integer matrices.	Low-P. 512x512 elts. Moderate cluster and high ICN activity. Regular.
Msort	3.625M, 161W, 60C	Merge-sort algorithm.	Hi-P. 1M keys. Variable moderate to low activity. Irregular.
NW	1.725M, 166W, 61C	Needleman-Wunsch sequence alignment.	Low-P. 2x2048 seqs. Variable moderate to low activity. Irregular.
Reduct	0.67M, 185W, 63C	Parallel reduction (sum).	Hi-P. 16M elts. Moderate cluster and high ICN activity. Regular.
Spmv	0.31M, 205W, 64C	Sparse matrix - vector multiplication.	Hi-P. 36Kx36K, 4M non-zero. Moderate cluster and high ICN activity. Irregular.

shortest execution time for a benchmark without exceeding a predetermined temperature limit. Note that energy efficiency is not within the scope of this objective.

3.1   Benchmarks

We consider it essential for a general-purpose architecture to perform well on a range of applications. Therefore we include both regular benchmarks, such as graphics processing, and irregular benchmarks, such as graph algorithms. In a typical regular benchmark, memory access addresses are predictable and there is no variability in control flow. In an irregular benchmark, memory access addresses and the control flow (if it is data dependent) are less predictable. Since it is our purpose to make the results relevant to other many-core platforms, we select benchmarks that commonly appear in the public domain [2, 4, 8, 23, 26]. Where applicable, benchmarks use single precision floating point format, except FFT, which uses fixed point arithmetics (i.e., utilizing the integer functional units instead of the FP units).

Table 2 provides a summary of the benchmarks that we use in our experiments. Execution times (in clock cycles), average power and temperature values are obtained from simulating benchmarks with no thermal constraint. Power and temperature estimations assume a global clock frequency of 1.3 GHz and $R_c = 0.05W/K$. Each benchmark is characterized in terms of its degree of parallelism, regularity and activity. More detail on these will follow next.

The degree of parallelism for a benchmark is defined to be low (*low-P*) if the number of TCUs executing threads is significantly smaller than the total number of TCUs when averaged over the execution time of the benchmark. Otherwise the benchmark is categorized as highly parallel (*hi-P*). According to Table 2, three of our benchmarks, *BFS-II*, *Mmult* and *NW*, are identified as low-P. In *Mmult*, the size of the multiplied matrices is 512×512 and each thread handles one row, therefore only half of the 1024 TCUs are utilized. *BFS-II* shows a random distribution of threads between 1 and 11 in each one of its 300K parallel sections. *NW* shows varying amount of parallelism between the iterations of a large number of synchronization steps (i.e., parallel sections in XMTC).

As mentioned above, regularity of a benchmark is affected by the predictability of memory access patterns and the control flow. For instance, *BFS*, *Msort* and *Spmv* are irregular due to their memory access patterns, whereas *BFS* also shows data dependent control flow. *FFT* is another benchmark with irregular memory access patterns, however it is classified as regular since the uniform distribution of work among TCUs was the dominant factor in this case. Some of the other factors that play a role in the regularity of a benchmark are the amount and variability of parallelism (e.g., *NW*), and memory bottlenecks (e.g., *Bprop*). *Bprop* is a complex irregular program with heavy memory queuing.

The activity profile of a benchmark plays an important role in the behavior of the system under thermal constraints, as we demonstrate in Section 3.3. It can be observed in Table 2 that there is a direct correlation between the regularity and activity/power value of a benchmark. For example, *Conv*, *Reduct* and *Mmult* are typical regular benchmarks with steady and high activity and power values.

In addition to regularity, cluster and ICN activities are determined by a number of additional factors, such as the computation to memory operation ratio of the threads and amount of parallelism (even if it is constant). An example is fixed-point *FFT*, which has lower activity than the other regular benchmarks, partly because it performs integer operations rather than floating point, spending less time in computation. Another example, *Mmult*, despite being very regular, is not as active as *Conv* due to the fact that it is a low-P benchmark.

3.2 Dynamic Thermal Management

Dynamic thermal management is the general term for various algorithms used to increase, or more efficiently utilize, the power envelope without exceeding a limit temperature at any location on the chip, as observed by thermal sensors. DTM alters the operation of the system during runtime via tools such as dynamic voltage and frequency scaling (DVFS), clock gating and voltage gating. These tools are commonly implemented in current processors [9, 13, 19].

In our experiments, we evaluated the following DTM techniques that are motivated by previous work on single and multi-cores [13]. We adapted these techniques to our many-core platform. The DTM decisions for each technique are determined during runtime and based on proportional-integral (PI) controllers which take temperatures as input and output the clock frequency and voltage level [27]. The clusters and ICN are assumed to feature one or more temperature sensors that report their maximum temperatures. The exact sensor configuration is beyond the scope of this work. In the distributed DVFS algorithms, a controller assigned to a certain component in the chip (for example, the ICN or a cluster) responds to the temperature of that component. Further details can be found in [14].

Global DVFS (GDVFS): All clusters, caches and the ICN are connected to one central controller which converges to the maximum frequency/voltage values possible without exceeding limit temperature. Global DVFS is the simplest DTM technique in terms of physical implementation, therefore, any other technique should perform better in order to justify its added design complexity.

Coarse-Grain Distributed DVFS (CG-DDVFS): The ICN is assigned a separate controller while the rest of the chip remains connected to the global controller as in GDVFS. Some many-cores, such as GTX280, already have separate clock domains for the computation elements and the interconnection network, leading us to conclude that the implementation cost of this technique is acceptable.

Fine-Grain Distributed DVFS (FG-DDVFS): Each cluster is connected to an isolated voltage/frequency domain and assigned a separate controller. The shared caches are connected to a common domain and their frequency is set to the average frequency of the clusters. The ICN is assigned a dedicated controller as in CG-DDVFS. The implementation of distributed DVFS may be prohibitively expensive on large systems due to the high number of voltage/frequency domains.

3.3   Analysis of DTM Results

A chip with no dynamic thermal management is designed to work at the highest possible clock frequency with which it can tolerate the thermal stress of the worst case (i.e., the most active, most power intensive) benchmark. Consequently, applications that are not as thermally demanding are penalized, since they are subject to the same clock frequency. DTM techniques provide the highest improvement on the execution time of such benchmarks compared to the *no-DTM* case. Consistent with this statement, throughout this analysis it can be observed that benchmarks identified as low activity in Section 3.1 show the highest speedups with DTM techniques.

In evaluating the DTM techniques introduced in Section 3.2, we set an XMT chip with *no-DTM* as the baseline and express the performance of a DTM technique in terms of speedups over the baseline. We assume that the *no-DTM* system is optimized to run at the fastest clock frequency that is thermally feasible for *Conv*, which is the most thermally active benchmark according to Section 3.1. We determined the baseline clock frequency as 900MHz. The thermal limit was set at 65C, as indicated in Section 2.2.

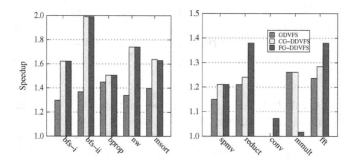

Fig. 1. Benchmark speedups for the DTM algorithms. The benchmarks are grouped into low (left) and high (right) cluster activity. Note that the two groups have different y-axis ranges.

In Fig. 1, we present the benchmark speedups when simulated with the examined DTM techniques. If thermal management is present, the clock frequencies of the clusters and caches can be dynamically scaled up to 1.3GHz. We also assume that ICN frequency can be raised to a maximum of 2.6GHz. A higher interconnect speed is possible due to the simplicity of the pipeline stages in the Mesh-of-Trees ICN (as in [9]). The speedup of a benchmark is calculated using the following formula: $S = Exec_{base}/Exec_{dtm}$, where $Exec_{base}$ and $Exec_{dtm}$ are the execution times on the baseline, *no-DTM* system and with thermal management, respectively.

As a general trend, the benchmarks that benefit the most from the DTM techniques are benchmarks with low cluster activity factors, namely *BFS-I*, *BFS-II*, *Bprop*, *NW* and *Msort* (note the scale difference between the y axes of the two rows of Fig. 1). The highest speedups are observed for *BFS-II* since it has very low overall activity and runs at the maximum clock speed without even nearing the limit temperature. Moreover, CG-DDVFS and FG-DDVFS performs up to 46% better than GDVFS for *BFS-II*, which is mainly bound by memory latency, hence benefits greatly from the independently increased ICN frequency. On the other extreme, *Conv* has the highest cluster activity and was used as the worst case in determining the feasible baseline clock frequency, and therefore shows the least improvement in most experiments.

In the remainder of this section we elaborate on the performance of CG-DVFS and FG-DVFS separately.

CG-DDVFS. Our experiments show that the CG-DDVFS algorithm presents a very reasonable trade-off between hardware complexity and performance. However, performance of certain benchmarks can suffer from the CG-DDVFS algorithm without the modification explained next.

We observed that the performance of the originally proposed CG-DDVFS algorithm is adversely affected by the fact that the ICN and cluster temperatures are correlated. The conduction of the heat generated by the ICN activity adds to the temperature of the clusters, requiring a slowdown in the cluster clock frequency. Moreover, when the ICN frequency is increased, the cores spend less time idling on memory operations and the cluster power escalates. As a consequence, CG-DDVS is most effective on benchmarks with low cluster activity, and may hurt the performance of a computation bound benchmark by causing the cluster frequency to drop excessively while trying to increase the ICN frequency for an insignificant gain. Therefore, we modified the algorithm to fall back to GDVFS when the ICN activity is lower than the cluster activity (this criterion was determined empirically). Fig. 1 reflects the results of this modification.

The CG-DDVFS technique provides better performance than GDVFS on *BFS-I* (25% faster), *BFS-II* (46% faster), *NW* (30% faster) and *Msort* (17% faster), which have irregular memory accesses and low computation to memory operation ratios. For these benchmarks, the performance bottleneck is the amount of time that TCUs wait on memory operations. CG-DDVFS shortens the wait time by increasing the ICN clock frequency. Irregularity of memory accesses implies that the ICN is not saturated, and it is not fully utilizing its power envelope. Therefore, ICN has sufficient thermal slack that can be picked up by increasing its clock frequency. *Bprop* does not benefit from CG-DDVFS significantly, due to the high degree of queuing on the shared memory modules with this benchmark. We also observed that CG-DDVFS can cause a performance degradation of up to 12% with respect to GDVFS for the remainder of the benchmarks if the GDVFS fall-back is not implemented.

Insight: For a system with a central ICN component such as XMT, workloads that are characterized by scattered irregular memory accesses usually benefit more from dedicated ICN thermal monitoring and control. Conversely, CG-DDVFS can hurt the performance and should be disabled for regular parallel programs which usually have higher computation to memory operation ratios. Performance of CG-DDVFS improves for more advanced cooling solutions.

FG-DDVFS. For the single-tasked system such as the one we examine in this work, the activity does not vary significantly among the clusters when averaged over a sufficiently long time window. The said time window is shorter than the duration required for a significant change in temperature to occur. Therefore, the only benefit that FG-DDVFS can provide is due to the temperature gradient between the middle of the die, where it is harder to remove the heat, and the edges. FG-DDVFS tries to pick up the thermal slack at the edge clusters by increasing their clock frequency. However, the performance of FG-DDVFS suffers from the interaction between the temperatures of the center and edge clusters: as the temperature of the edge clusters rises, so does the temperature of the center clusters, and the controllers in the middle will respond by converging at lower clock frequencies, diminishing the performance gain.

FG-DDVFS exhibits speedups similar to CG-DDVFS on the low activity benchmarks. This is due to the dedicated ICN clock controller introduced in CG-DDVFS. The added value of the dedicated cluster controllers of FG-DDVFS is observed on *Spmv*, *Reduct*, *Conv* and *FFT*, which are the high activity benchmarks. For these benchmarks, runtimes with FG-DDVFS are faster than GDVFS by 14%, 7% and 11%, respectively. *Mmult* is the only benchmark that shows a slowdown over GDVFS due to its low-P characteristic.

Insight: Individual temperature monitoring and control for computing clusters may be worthwhile even in a single-tasking system with fairly uniform workload distribution. The gains are noteworthy for regular parallel programs with high amounts of computation. Conversely, the overall performance of FG-DDVFS on the low activity benchmarks may not justify its added cost for some systems. It should also be noted that FG-DDVFS has advantage over CG-DDVFS only for cases where the overall speedups are lower than average.

4   Conclusion

In this paper, we outline ongoing work in which we tailor various DTM techniques that exist in uniprocessors and multi-cores to a many-core architecture. We evaluate these techniques on the easy-to-program XMT many-core architecture according to their implementation/design complexity and improvement in single task execution time. We observed that in a many-core processor with fine-grained parallel workloads, the dominant source of thermal imbalance is often between the cores and the interconnection network. According to preliminary results, a DTM technique that exploits this imbalance by individually managing the interconnect can perform up to 46% better than the global DTM for irregular parallel benchmarks. This paper provides several other high-level insights on the effect of individually managing the interconnect and the computing clusters. Our analysis is a step forward from the previous work on multi-core DTM which exclusively focused on systems with a small number of relatively complex serial processors and uneven distribution of the load among these cores. Future work will extend the results presented here to a multi-tasked environment, where the XMT chip will be able to simultaneously execute multiple fine-grained parallel tasks. This extension poses an interesting optimization problem where the management algorithm will also determine the number of threads to be run from each task and how they map on the TCUs.

Acknowledgment. Partial support by NSF grants 0325393, CCF-0811504, 0834373 and 0926237 is gratefully acknowledged.

References

1. Balkan, A.O., Horak, M.N., Qu, G., Vishkin, U.: Layout-accurate design and implementation of a high-throughput interconnection network for single-chip parallel processing. In: Proc. Hot Interconnects (2007)
2. Bell, N., Garland, M.: Implementing sparse matrix-vector multiplication on throughput-oriented processors. In: Proc. SC (2009)
3. Caragea, G., Keceli, F., Tzannes, A., Vishkin, U.: General-purpose vs. GPU: Comparison of many-cores on irregular workloads. In: Proc. HotPar (2010)
4. Che, S., Boyer, M., Meng, J., Tarjan, D., Sheaffer, J.W., Lee, S.H., Skadron, K.: Rodinia: A benchmark suite for heterogeneous computing. In: Proc. IISWC (2009)
5. Donald, J., Martonosi, M.: Techniques for multicore thermal management: Classification and new exploration. In: Proc. ISCA (2006)

6. Ge, Y., Malani, P., Qiu, Q.: Distributed task migration for thermal management in many-core systems. In: Proc. DAC (2010)
7. Ginosar, R.: The plural architecture (2011), www.plurality.com, also see course on Parallel Computing, Electrical Engineering, Technion, http://webee.technion.ac.il/courses/048874
8. Hoberock, J., Bell, N.: Thrust: A parallel template library version 1.1 (2009), http://www.meganewtons.com/
9. Howard, J., Dighe, S., et al.: A 48-core IA-32 message-passing processor with DVFS in 45nm CMOS. In: Proc. ISSCC (2010)
10. Huang, W., Stan, M.R., Sankaranarayanan, K., Ribando, R.J., Skadron, K.: Many-core design from a thermal perspective. In: Proc. DAC (2008)
11. Isci, C., Martonosi, M.: Runtime power monitoring in high-end processors: Methodology and empirical data. In: Proc. MICRO (2003)
12. Kadin, M., Reda, S., Uht, A.: Central vs. distributed dynamic thermal management for multi-core processors: which one is better? In: Proceedings of the Great Lakes Symposium on VLSI (2009)
13. Kaxiras, S., Martonosi, M.: Computer Architecture Techniques for Power Efficiency. Morgan and Claypool Publishers (2008)
14. Keceli, F.: Power and Performance Studies of the Explicit Multi-Threading (XMT) Architecture. Ph.D. thesis, University of Maryland (2011)
15. Keceli, F., Moreshet, T., Vishkin, U.: Power-performance comparison of single-task driven many-cores, submitted for publication
16. Keceli, F., Tzannes, A., Caragea, G., Vishkin, U., Barua, R.: Toolchain for programming, simulating and studying the XMT many-core architecture. In: Proc. HIPS (2011), in conj. with IPDPS
17. Keceli, F., Vishkin, U.: XMTSim: Cycle-accurate Simulator of the XMT Many-Core Architecture. Tech. Rep. UMIACS-TR-2011-02, Univ. of Maryland (2011)
18. Keller, J., Kessler, C., Traeff, J.L.: Practical PRAM Programming. John Wiley & Sons, Inc., New York (2001)
19. Kumar, R., Hinton, G.: A family of 45nm IA processors. In: Proc. ISSCC (2009)
20. Li, S., Ahn, J.H., Strong, R.D., Brockman, J.B., Tullsen, D.M., Jouppi, N.P.: McPAT: an integrated power, area, and timing modeling framework for multicore and manycore architectures. In: Proc. MICRO (2009)
21. Liu, S., Zhang, J., Wu, Q., Qiu, Q.: Thermal-aware job allocation and scheduling for three dimensional chip multiprocessor. In: Proceedings of the International Symposium on Quality Electronic Design (2010)
22. Ma, K., Li, X., Chen, M., Wang, X.: Scalable power control for many-core architectures running multi-threaded applications. In: Proc. ISCA (2011)
23. NVIDIA: CUDA SDK 2.3 (2009), www.nvidia.com/cuda
24. Padua, D., Vishkin, U.: Joint UIUC/UMD parallel algorithms/ programming course. In: Proc. EduPar (2011), in conj. with IPDPS
25. Patterson, D.: The trouble with multicore: Chipmakers are busy designing microprocessors that most programmers can't handle. IEEE Spectrum (July 2010)
26. Satish, N., Harris, M., Garland, M.: Designing efficient sorting algorithms for many-core GPUs. In: Proc. IPDPS (2009)
27. Skadron, K., Stan, M.R., Huang, W., Velusamy, S., Sankaranarayanan, K., Tarjan, D.: Temperature-aware microarchitecture. In: Proc. ISCA (2003)
28. Wen, X., Vishkin, U.: FPGA-based prototype of a PRAM on-chip processor. In: Proc. Comp. Front. (2008)
29. Wilton, S., Jouppi, N.: CACTI: an enhanced cache access and cycle time model. IEEE J. Solid-State Circuits 31(5), 677–688 (1996)

Mainstream Parallel Array Programming on Cell

Paul Keir[1], Paul W. Cockshott[1], and Andrew Richards[2]

[1] School of Computing Science, University of Glasgow, UK
[2] Codeplay Software Ltd., Edinburgh, UK

Abstract. We present the E♯ compiler and runtime library for the 'F' subset of the Fortran 95 programming language. 'F' provides first-class support for arrays, allowing E♯ to implicitly evaluate array expressions in parallel using the SPU co-processors of the Cell Broadband Engine. We present performance results from four benchmarks that all demonstrate absolute speedups over equivalent 'C' or Fortran versions running on the PPU host processor. A significant benefit of this straightforward approach is that a serial implementation of any code is always available, providing code longevity, and a familiar development paradigm.

1 Introduction

Collection-oriented programming languages [1] are characterised by the provision of a built-in selection of operations to manipulate aggregate data structures in a holistic manner. Idiomatic code in these languages will commonly eshew the use of loop constructs. The potential to extract parallelism from this style of programming is consequently, and firstly, due to the *divisibility* of these aggregate data types; and secondly to the lack of side-effects in the expressions or constructs which stand in place of the imperative loops. Collection-oriented programming has often been applied to distributed parallel architectures, however it is just as relevant in the setting of heterogeneous multicore.

A perennial concern of performance-critical code structured around imperative loops appears within the context of implicit, or automatic, parallelism. An auto-parallelising compiler faced with a side-effecting loop which exhibits a sequential execution semantics, may overcome the challenge by a code transformation which introduces parallelism, along with locks or semaphores. The user of such a compiler is soon compelled to understand a new layer of diagnostic messages, which gradually cajole them towards an alternative, highly structured, coding style. The resulting code will often be data-parallel, and specify behaviour equivalent to that common to collection languages, though considerably more verbose.

In this paper we present a mainstream solution for scientific computing in the auto-parallelising array compiler, E♯, which targets the heterogeneous architecture of the Cell Broadband Engine. We also discuss the design decisions behind our implementation of four classic benchmarks[1], before presenting an analysis of performance experiments.

---

[1] Available at
http://www.dcs.gla.ac.uk/people/personal/pkeir/hppc11code.7z

M. Alexander et al. (Eds.): Euro-Par 2011 Workshops, Part I, LNCS 7155, pp. 260–269, 2012.
© Springer-Verlag Berlin Heidelberg 2012

1.1 Related Work

The seminal array language, originating in the 1960s, is Kenneth Iverson's APL. Subsequent decades brought a number of *parallel* array languages, for *distributed architectures*: HPF, NESL, and ZPL being notable examples. Recent trends towards multicore systems have brought about a renaissance in the design of parallel array languages.

Single Assignment C (SAC) is a pioneering functional array research language based on the syntax and semantics of 'C'. SAC is distinguished by its first-class arrays, absent pointers and side-effects, and an advanced typing system capable of shape-polymorphic array function definitions. SAC has also recently targeted the heterogeneous GPU architecture via a CUDA backend [2]. The absence of a stack in CUDA however necessitates that no function calls are present within the SAC WITH-loops which provide the sites for parallelisation.

Cray's Chapel language, and IBM's X10, were the two finalists from the ten year DARPA High Productivity Computing Systems (HPCS) [3] programme. Both use a partitioned global address space (PGAS) model, and allow high-level, holistic, and parallelisable manipulation of arrays. The two standard implementations of these languages target distributed parallel architectures.

Microsoft's Accelerator project [4] targets homogeneous x86, and heterogeneous GPU architectures, using a data-parallel .NET array library which, by delaying the evaluation of array expressions, can minimise the creation of intermediate structures.

By virtue of the highly expressive Haskell typing system, the Repa [5] parallel array *library*, is refreshingly akin to an embedded array *language*. Absolute parallel performance comparable to serial 'C' derives from optimisations such as array fusion; and mandatory unboxed, strictly evaluated array elements. For the end user, performance can still depend on careful application of the force function; which replaces a *delayed* with a *manifest* array. Repa builds on the long-running Data-Parallel Haskell research strand, and for now targets only homogeneous multicore systems.

2 Implicit Parallelism Using the 'F' Programming Language

Fortran was originally developed by John Backus and others at IBM in the 1950s. Like 'C', Fortran is a statically typed, imperative language. Fortran has historically differentiated itself from 'C' by its absent pointer arithmetic; longstanding support for complex numbers; argument passing by reference; and with *Fortran 90*, first-class array types. The Fortran language is ISO standardised, and *Fortran 2008* has been approved. Of the mainstream programming languages, Fortran has distinguished itself within the field of computational science, due to its relatively high level, and good performance.

The 'F' programming language is a subset of *Fortran 95* designed with the intention of providing a lightweight version of Fortran, free of the requirement to support 40 years of language artifacts. The primary motivation of the language design was to create a Fortran-based language for education, however 'F' is a perfectly adequate general-purpose language. Furthermore, any Fortran compiler will compile a program conforming to the 'F' language standard.

Having the requisite support for arrays, the 'F' programming language is therefore a suitable language to explore the use of array expressions as a mechanism to drive implicit parallelism for scientific computing on a heterogeneous architecture such as the Cell Broadband Engine (Cell B.E.).

2.1 A Language Primer

The following code excerpt demonstrates an entire 'F' program, equivalent to a 'C' *main* function. The assignment on line 3 will *pointwise* multiply the elements of the two arrays bound by b and c, before adding the result to a third array induced by the literal 3. Once all operations on the right hand side of the assignment are completed, the result is copied to the array bound to a.

```
1   program p
2     real, dimension(2,3) :: a, b = 1, c = 2
3     a = b * c + 3
4     a = muladd(b,c,3)
5   end program p
```

Fig. 1. Assignments involving intrinsic and user defined elemental functions

The dimension attribute specification on line 2 of Figure 1 declares three arrays, each with an explicit *shape* vector of 2;3. The length of an array's shape vector provides another useful metric: its *rank*, and is therefore 2 in this case. The terms in an array expression must all have equal shape, and in doing so, the shapes are said to *conform*. Scalar values, such as the numeric literals 1, 2 and 3, are promoted, or lifted, to an array type of conforming shape, when their context within an expression requires it. The induced array is then populated by elements of the same value as the inducing scalar. In Figure 1, the expression b * c + 3 is therefore an array expression with a rank of 2, and shape of 2;3. This is in fact true of all the expressions in Figure 1.

For the E♯ compiler, an array expression involving one or more functions, or operators, will be evaluated in parallel. The array expression b * c + 3 from Figure 1 will therefore qualify, and so trigger the appropriate compiler transformations to ensure a parallel execution.

Scalar functions free of side-effects may also be applied to array arguments with conforming shapes. Such functions in Fortran are classified as *elemental*. The call to muladd on line 4 of Figure 1 represents a user defined elemental function producing the same result as the elemental arithmetic expression on line 3.

Unlike many auto-parallelising compilers, the E♯ user has the certainty that *all* array expressions will execute in parallel. Consequently, other iterative constructs of the 'F' language, such as do or while loops remain useful. Such constructs should be used where there is insufficient work to justify the small cost of thread adminstration and direct memory access (DMA) operations.

3 The E♯ Compiler

E♯ is a source to source compiler, translating from the 'F' subset of Fortran 95 to Offload C++ [6]: a C++ language extension utilising pointer locality. The compiler targets heterogeneous multicore architectures, and in particular the Cell B.E. The 'F' language has a large standard library, and this is made available to both the PPU and the SPU using the GNU Fortran runtime libraries. A C++ template class has also been developed which both abstracts over the multifarious internal array representations of essentially all Fortran compilers; and is also compatible with the dual memory address hierarchy exposed by Offload C++. The E♯ compiler is written in the pure functional programming language Haskell. Haskell's Parsec parsing library allowed the structure of the published 'F' grammar to be followed exactly, while the Scrap Your Boilerplate package was used to perform the crucial transformations of the abstract syntax trees.

```
1  offloadThread_t tid = offload {
2    int outer *po = &g;
3    int i = *po;
4    int inner *pi = &i;
5    *pi = *pi+1;
6    *po = i;
7  };
8
9  offloadThreadJoin(tid);
```

Fig. 2. A simple asynchronous offload block expression

3.1 Targeting Offload C++

E♯ translates from 'F' to Offload C++, a C++ language extension and runtime library [6] targeting heterogeneous architectures. The most prominent language feature of Offload C++ is the *offload block* which provides a traditional 'C' compound statement, prefixed with the keyword offload, to be executed asynchronously to the main thread. Running on the Cell B.E, each new thread will be executed by the next available SPU. An offload block returns an integer thread identifier and, like Pthreads, performance parallelism is achieved through the launch of multiple threads; subsequently joined with a call to offloadThreadJoin. A related benefit of this approach, is *automatic call-graph duplication*: with little or no annotation, a function, or variable reference, defined once, may be used both outside and inside an offload block.

The C++ type system is also extended to allow statically assigned pointer locality. In Offload C++ a pointer is, either implicitly or explicitly, identified either with an *inner* or *outer* locality. Pointer arithmetic and assignment between those of differing localities is statically prohibited by the compiler. More proactively, the dereferencing of an *outer* pointer from within an offload block corresponds to a DMA transfer from main memory to SPU scratch memory; while assignment to an *outer* pointer results in a DMA transfer in the opposite direction. Figure 2 demonstrates the concept: assuming the variable g is defined at global scope, the resulting effect of the offload block is for

```
1  template <typename T, int Od>
2  struct PtrWrapper {
3    T inout(Od) *m_p;
4  };
```

Fig. 3. Offload C++ template struct with pointer member

g to be incremented by one. Note that the `inner` and `outer` pointer qualifiers on lines 2 and 4 in Figure 2 are optional and would be automatically inferred.

Flexibility in the locality of class or struct pointer members may be obtained using the static `inout` qualifier and an integer template parameter, as shown in Figure 3.

3.2   A C++ Template Interface to Fortran Runtime Libraries

Neither the 'F' nor Fortran language standards specify an application binary interface (ABI) for arrays. With over a dozen Fortran compilers it would be unfortunate to restrict the E♯ compiler to only one of the associated runtime libraries. The Chasm project [7] helps to address this issue by providing a low-level 'C' API targeting the internal "dope vectors" used by each Fortran compiler. For E♯, two new C++ array template classes have been designed and implemented: `ArrayT`; and the statically sized `ArrayTN`. Each provides high-level support for Fortran array features such as sectioning; serialisation; de-serialisation; and fast indexing with optional non-1 lower bound.

3.3   Parallel Operational Semantics

The E♯ compiler attempts a human-readable, one-to-one correspondence between 'F' input and C++ output language constructs. An exception occurs at a parallelised array expression. In this instance, the array expression is transformed into a nested `for` loop[2], with depth equal to an expression's rank. A team of threads is then launched, each assigned a statically allocated and contiguous chunk of the outermost iteration space. The precise number of threads is set on program startup using an environment variable, `ESHARP_NUM_THREADS`, and may range from 1 to 128. Each individual thread is given the full resources of an SPU, and sits in a notional FIFO queue until one is available. While it can be assumed that launching one thread for each SPU will incur the lowest thread administration costs, and maximise resource usage, a program with a large working set may need to be split into more than six pieces. For example, an array expression with a 6000KiB working set, will exceed the 256KiB local store of an SPU if partitioned across six threads. With 32 or more threads, the program should run.

4   The Benchmark Programs

The first two benchmark programs we will examine, BlackScholes and Swaptions, are financial simulations from Princeton Univerity's PARSEC benchmark suite, converted by hand to 'F' from original C and C++. Our Mandelbrot program allows us to look at DMA transfer bottlenecks. while exploring differing approaches to parallel decomposition. Finally, a simulation of the n-body problem is examined.

---

[2] The operation is also recursively applied to array subexpressions.

4.1 Blackscholes

Blackscholes is a financial simulation which prices a portfolio of options using a partial differential equation now known as the *Black-Scholes equation*. Scalability in performance is obtained using a chunked, fine-grained decomposition, and calculating multiple options in parallel. The original implementation of Blackscholes uses Threading Building Blocks (TBB) and Pthreads to facilitate parallelism, with both using an *array of structs* configuration. Beneath the requisite file IO and threading boilerplate, there are two functions within the call graph of the parallel region: `BlkSchlsEqEuroNoDiv`, and a "callee" function `CNDF`. The kernel is given 100 runs, each of which is launched by an application of the TBB `parallel_for` template. This invokes multiple calls to a user-defined worker class's overloaded function operator. The 'F' version requires only that we mark the function as `elemental`, and the kernel launch is then

`prices = BlkSchlsEqEuroNoDiv(dat)`

4.2 Swaptions

The Swaptions program prices a portfolio of interest-rate swap options using Monte-Carlo simulation. The original program consists of around fifteen C++ source files, then converted to 'F'.

Parallel decomposition on both TBB and Pthread implementations was, like Blackscholes, static and course-grained, though distinguished by a significantly larger working set. An *array of structs* configuration was again present in the C++ code, and the kernel was dominated by a single 16-parameter function, `HJM_Swaption_Blocking`, applied in parallel to chunks from an one-dimensional iteration space.

The `HJM_Swaption_Blocking` function was ultimately a suitable target for `elemental` status, however the element type of two of its arguments are pointers to 1D and 2D arrays. An 'F' `elemental` function cannot accept arrays as a "scalar" element type, so necessitating the definition of two array wrapper types. With the 1D *pdYield* array, this amounts to the type shown in Figure 4.

```
1  type, public :: yieldT
2    real(kind=ki), dimension(m_iN) :: y
3  end type yieldT
```

Fig. 4. A scalar 'F' datatype wrapping an array

The C++0x code generated by E♯ from Figure 4 is shown in Figure 5. Notice that the `struct` has a template parameter, used to specify the *locality* of the data accessed via the `ArrayTN` member at line 18. That this is an `ArrayTN`, rather than an `ArrayT`, is an automatic optimisation due to the `m_iN` from line 2 of Figure 4 being a compile-time constant; the integer template argument `11` specifies the statically-allocated data size.

4.3 Mandelbrot

Estimation of the Mandelbrot set requires iteration of the complex function $z_{n+1} = z_n^2 + c$. Of the two Mandelbrot benchmarks we have developed, the first is more straightforward. An array of the same size as the 8-bit output image is initialised with positive

```
1   template <int Od>
2   struct yieldT {
3     inline yieldT () {};
4     inline yieldT (const ArrayTN<__compiler,float,1,11,Od> &&y)
5       : y(y) {};
6     inline friend ostream & operator << (ostream &o,
7                                          const yieldT<Od> &t) {
8       o << t.y; return o;
9     };
10    inline friend istream & operator >> (istream &i,
11                                         yieldT<Od> &t) {
12      i >> t.y; return i;
13    };
14    template <int Od2>
15    inline yieldT &operator= (const yieldT<Od2> &rhs) {
16      y = rhs.y; return *this;
17    };
18    ArrayTN<__compiler,float,1,11,Od> y;
19  };
```

Fig. 5. The C++ struct generated from Figure 4 by E♯

integer coordinate pairs within the appropriate range, leaving the `elemental` function to create the complex value upon which it iterates. A second, blocked, version of the program partitions the coordinate array into squares. A user defined type is used for the squares, and is the scalar type upon which the requisite `elemental` function is defined.

4.4   The n-Body Problem

From earlier work [8] we were aware that an $O(n^2)$ "all-pairs" n-body simulation on Cell B.E. can exhibit good scaling at the expense of wall clock time, and so a tiled decomposition of the problem, inspired by research at Nvidia [9], was developed.

The kernel of our n-body algorithm performs the $O(n^2)$ force calculation in parallel while the remaining leapfrog-Verlet integration [9] updates the positions and velocities, and is run in serial by the host processor. This choice seems reasonable as having only linear complexity, the percentage of runtime expended on the remaining integration stage becomes insignificant with larger body counts. A square shaped tile of the pairwise body interactions, maximises the number of calculations that can be performed per body. That is to say, a DMA transfer of $2p$ body positions and masses, will provide p^2 components of force for the integrator.

The E♯ compiler parallelises only the outermost of the generated loops. To fully exploit the two-dimensional decomposition already outlined, a "flattened", *one-dimensional*, array is used to feed the requisite driving `elemental` function. User-defined scalar types, are once again required for the input and output elements. For input and output respectively the two types `pchunk2d` and `accel_chunk` are shown in Figure 6.

```
1  type, public :: pchunk2d
2    type(vec4), pointer, dimension(:) :: ivec4, jvec4
3  end type pchunk2d
4
5  type, public :: accel_chunk
6    type(vec3), dimension(CHUNK_SIZE) :: avec3
7  end type accel_chunk
```

Fig. 6. The n-body kernel input (pchunk2d) and output (accel_chunk) wrapper types

5 Experimental Evaluation

The following benchmark results were measured and averaged across five runs on a PlayStation 3 running Fedora Core 7. Single-precision was used throughout, due to the SPU's slow double-precision execution. In addition to the 4.1.1 versions of the GNU C, C++, and Fortran compilers provided with the installed IBM Cell SDK v3.0, version 4.6 of GCC is also installed. Where a speedup metric is presented, the fastest available PPU serial version is used, with selection based on source language; compiler; and the often powerful GCC switch: -mcpu=cell. The Offload C++ compiler version is 2.0.2, patched to use SPU GCC 4.6. All compilers use the -O3 switch throughout.

BlackScholes. This benchmark exceeds the memory limitations of the SPU at low thread counts. However, with 18 threads the E♯ version outperforms GCC after 4K options. With 64 threads, 256K options become possible, and provide a final speedup of over 11; shown in Figure 7. The surprisingly horizontal E♯ curves indicate that the problem is dominated by thread administration. The serial results also demonstrate that the 'F' version performs competitively with the independently constructed 'C' version.

Swaptions. Though speedup values also increased, slightly, with input data size, Figure 8 shows only a maximum speedup of almost 1.8x over GCC 4.6 with the "Large" data set. Lower thread counts for Swaptions are possible, and the graph demonstrates good scaling to 6 threads. While greater thread counts, up to 128, are shown as redundant in this configuration, it is encouraging to see that increasing thread administration overheads have no noticeable effect, as no fall in speedup is observed.

Mandelbrot. As anticipated, the blocked version of Mandelbrot, using 64x64 squares, outperformed the naïve version, presumably due to reduced DMA traffic. The blocked version was also able to create a 2048x2048 image, and so achieve a speedup of almost 12x. Mandelbrot reaches a similar maximum speedup as Blackscholes; though a distinctive fall-off is also observed. See Figure 9.

The n-Body Problem. Using 16x16 square tiles speedups increase gradually with data sizes, reaching a 3.4x speedup against the fastest 'C' configuration on PPU; which uses the older GCC 4.1.1 and the -mcpu=cell switch. In comparison to times obtained from the PPU only, using GFortran 4.1.1 -mcpu=cell, and the same 'F' code, a speedup of 4.9x is obtained with 16384 bodies; shown in Figure 10.

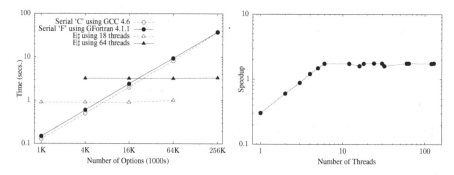

Fig. 7. Wallclock Blackscholes Kernel Timings for 100 iterations

Fig. 8. E♯ Speedup with Swaptions and "Large" data set

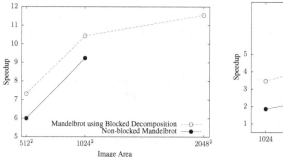

Fig. 9. Relative Mandelbrot Speedups against Image Area

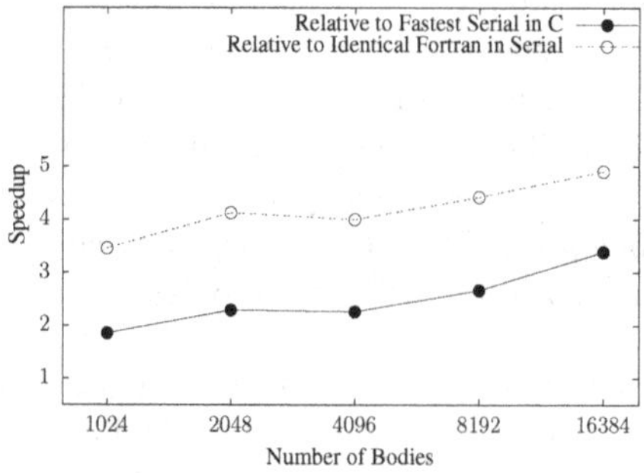

Fig. 10. Relative n-Body Speedups against Input Data Size

6   Conclusion

We have demonstrated the auto-parallelising array compiler, E♯, targeting the heterogeneous architecture of the Cell Broadband Engine. Encouraging performance results from four benchmarks are presented, and show speedups ranging from 2-11x over serial versions running on PPU only. The language employed, 'F', is a simple, useable, and standard dialect of modern Fortran, and is therefore well positioned for expected users from the scientific programming community. In addition, 'F' codes developed for use by E♯ are also valid Fortran; and shown to perform competitively in serial.

E♯ would benefit from the inclusion of streaming, rather than the current static partitioning of the iteration-space. This should allow access to a larger range of problem sizes, and hopefully more routine access to high performance. Also, as array expressions are free of side-effects, we can expose a finer level of granularity than currently offered by E♯, which presently partitions only the outermost rank. This should help load balancing on problems with small outer rank extents.

The techniques described here for the Cell B.E. could also be applied to new multi-core processors such as Intel's Single-Chip Cloud Computer (SCC), or Knight's Corner. In the case of the SCC it would be possible to produce an E♯ compiler provided that a version of the Offload system were ported to the SCC. This is likely to result in some-what lower performance than the Cell because of 3 factors: a) processors on the SCC can not initiate reads from host memory, b) inter-process communication on the SCC relies on a software library, RCCE, rather than the Cell B.E.'s DMA hardware; c) the performance of the individual SCC processors is slower than the host Xeon, whereas the Cell SPUs are capable of higher throughput than the host PPC. For shared memory ma-chines like Knight's Corner, we anticipate implementing E♯ by compiling to C++ with OpenMP pragmas. Some prototype work has already been done using this approach.

References

1. Sipelstein, J., Blelloch, G.E.: Collection-Oriented Languages. Proceedings of the IEEE 79, 504–523 (1991)
2. Guo, J., Thiyagalingam, J., Scholz, S.-B.: Breaking the GPU programming barrier with the auto-parallelising SAC compiler. In: Proceedings of the Sixth Workshop on Declarative As-pects of Multicore Programming, pp. 15–24. ACM Press (2011)
3. Weiland, M.: Chapel, Fortress and X10: novel languages for HPC. EPCC, The University of Edinburgh, Tech. Rep. HPCxTR0706 (October 2007)
4. Tarditi, D., Puri, S., Oglesby, J.: Accelerator: Using Data Parallelism to Program GPUs for General-Purpose Uses. In: Proceedings of the 12th International Conference on Architectural Support for Programming Languages and Operating Systems. ACM Press (2006)
5. Keller, G., Chakravarty, M.M., Leshchinskiy, R., Peyton Jones, S., Lippmeier, B.: Regular, shape-polymorphic, parallel arrays in Haskell. In: Proceedings of the 15th ACM SIGPLAN International Conference on Functional Programming, pp. 261–272. ACM Press (2010)
6. Cooper, P., Dolinsky, U., Donaldson, A.F., Richards, A., Riley, C., Russell, G.: Offload – Automating Code Migration to Heterogeneous Multicore Systems. In: Patt, Y.N., Foglia, P., Duesterwald, E., Faraboschi, P., Martorell, X. (eds.) HiPEAC 2010. LNCS, vol. 5952, pp. 337–352. Springer, Heidelberg (2010)
7. Rasmussen, C.E., Sottile, M.J., Shende, S.S., Malony, A.D.: Bridging the language gap in scientific computing: the Chasm approach. Concurrency and Computation: Practice and Ex-perience 18, 151–162 (2006)
8. Donaldson, A.F., Keir, P., Lokhmotov, A.: Compile-Time and Run-Time Issues in an Auto-Parallelisation System for the Cell BE Processor. In: César, E., et al. (eds.) Euro-Par 2008 Workshops. LNCS, vol. 5415, pp. 163–173. Springer, Heidelberg (2008)
9. Lars Nyland, M.H., Prins, J.: Fast N-Body Simulation with CUDA. In: Nguyen, H. (ed.) GPU Gems 3, pp. 677–694. Addison-Wesley Professional (2007)

Generating GPU Code from a High-Level Representation for Image Processing Kernels

Richard Membarth[1,*], Anton Lokhmotov[2], and Jürgen Teich[1]

[1] Hardware/Software Co-Design, Department of Computer Science,
University of Erlangen-Nuremberg, Germany
{richard.membarth,teich}@cs.fau.de
[2] Media Processing Division, ARM,
Cambridge, United Kingdom
anton.lokhmotov@arm.com

Abstract. We present a framework for representing image processing kernels based on decoupled access/execute metadata, which allow the programmer to specify both execution constraints and memory access pattern of a kernel. The framework performs source-to-source translation of kernels expressed in high-level framework-specific C++ classes into low-level CUDA or OpenCL code with effective device-dependent optimizations such as global memory padding for memory coalescing and optimal memory bandwidth utilization. We evaluate the framework on several image filters, comparing generated code against highly-optimized CPU and GPU versions in the popular OpenCV library.

1 Introduction

Computer systems are increasingly heterogeneous, as many important computational tasks, such as multimedia processing, can be *accelerated* by special-purpose processors that outperform general-purpose processors by 1–2 orders of magnitude, importantly, in terms of energy efficiency as well as in terms of execution speed.

Until recently, every accelerator vendor provided their own application programming interface (API), typically based on the C language. For example, NVIDIA's API called CUDA C [6] targets systems accelerated with Graphics Processing Units (GPUs). In CUDA, the programmer dispatches compute-intensive data-parallel functions (*kernels*) to the GPU, and manages the interaction between the CPU and the GPU via API calls. Ryoo et al. [7] highlight the complexity of CUDA programming, in particular, the need for exploring thoroughly the space of possible implementations and configuration options. OpenCL [8], a new industry-backed standard API that inherits many traits from CUDA, aims to provide software portability across heterogeneous systems: correct OpenCL programs will run on any standard-compliant implementation. OpenCL per se, however, does not address the problem of *performance portability*; that is, OpenCL code optimized for one accelerator device may perform dismally on another, since performance may significantly depend on low-level details, such as data layout and iteration space mapping [4].

---

* This work was partly done during the author's internship at ARM, which was sponsored by the European Network of Excellence on High Performance and Embedded Architectures and Compilation (HiPEAC).

M. Alexander et al. (Eds.): Euro-Par 2011 Workshops, Part I, LNCS 7155, pp. 270–280, 2012.
© Springer-Verlag Berlin Heidelberg 2012

Low-level programming increases the cost of software development and maintenance: whilst low-level languages can be robustly compiled into efficient machine code, they effectively lack support for creating portable and composable software.

High-level languages with domain-specific features are more attractive to domain experts, who do not necessarily wish to become target system experts. To compete with low-level languages for programming accelerated systems, however, domain-specific languages should have an acceptable performance penalty.

We present a framework for image processing that allows programmers to concentrate on developing algorithms and applications, rather than on mapping them to the target hardware. While previous work shows that running the same kernels (e. g., written in OpenCL) on different hardware (from AMD and NVIDIA) can have significant impact on the performance [3], this framework serves to protect investments in software in the face of the ever changing landscape of computer systems.

The framework is implemented as a library of C++ classes (§2.1) and a Clang-based compiler producing host and device code in CUDA C and OpenCL (§2.2). Our framework is most similar in spirit to Cornwall *et al.*'s work on indexed metadata for visual effects [2] but introduces additional device-specific optimizations such as global memory padding for memory coalescing and optimal bandwidth utilization. We evaluate the framework by comparing generated code against highly-optimized CPU and GPU versions in the popular OpenCV library (§3).

2 Image Processing Framework

Our framework provides a library of C++ classes for representing image processing kernels (§2.1) and a source-to-source compiler for translating library constructs into host and device code in CUDA or OpenCL (§2.2). The library is based on the concept of decoupled access/execute metadata, which capture both execution constraints and memory access patterns of a kernel [4]. The compiler is built using Clang [1], an open source frontend for C-family languages.

2.1 Library

The library consists of built-in C++ classes that describe the following three basic components required to express image processing on an abstract level:

- *Image*: Describes data storage for the image pixels. Each pixel can be stored as an integer number, a floating point number, or in another format such as RGB, depending on instantiation of this templated class. The data layout is handled internally using multi-dimensional arrays.
- *Iteration Space*: Describes a rectangular region of interest in the output image, for example the complete image. Each pixel in this region is a point in the iteration space.
- *Kernel*: Describes an algorithm to be applied to each pixel in the region of interest.

These components are an instance of decoupled access/execute metadata [4]: the *Iteration Space* specification provides ordering and partitioning constraints (execute metadata); the *Kernel* specification provides a pattern of accesses to uniform memory (access metadata). Currently, the access/execute metadata is mostly implicit: we assume that the iteration space is parallel in all dimensions and has a 1:1 mapping to work-items (threads), and that the memory access pattern is obvious from the kernel code.

Example. We illustrate our image processing framework using a grayscale vertical mean image filter, for which the output pixel with coordinates (x,y) is the average of D input column pixels:

$$\mathbf{O}_{x,y} = \frac{1}{D} \sum_{k=0}^{D-1} \mathbf{I}_{x,y+k}, \text{ where } 0 \leq x < W, 0 \leq y < H - D. \tag{1}$$

- **I** is an input image of $W \times H$ pixels;
- **O** is an output image of $W \times H$ pixels;
- D is the *diameter* of the filter, that is, the number of input pixels over which the mean is computed (typically, $D \ll H$).

To express this filter, the framework user derives a class from the built-in *Kernel* class and implements the virtual *kernel* function, as shown in Listing 1. The *kernel* function (line 10) takes an *ElementIterator* argument that represents the output pixel for which the algorithm is run. To access the pixels of an image, the parenthesis operator ( ) is used, taking the *ElementIterator* argument as a mandatory parameter, and the column (dx) and row (dy) offsets as optional parameters. The user instantiates the class with input and output images, an iteration space, and other parameters that are member variables of the class.

```
1  class VerticalMeanFilter : public Kernel {
2    private:
3      Image<float> &Input, &Output;
4      int d;
5
6    public:
7      VerticalMeanFilter(IterationSpace &IS, Image<float> &
             Input, Image<float> &Output, int d) :
8        Kernel(IS), Input(Input), Output(Output), d(d) {}
9
10     void kernel(IterationSpace::ElementIterator EI) {
11       float sum = 0.0f;
12
13       for (int k=0; k<d; ++k) {
14         sum += Input(EI, 0, k);
15       }
16
17       Output(EI) = sum/(float)d;
18     }
19 };
```

Listing 1. The vertical mean filter expressed in our framework

In Listing 2, the input and output *Image* objects IN and OUT are defined as two-dimensional $W \times H$ grayscale images, having pixels represented as floating-point numbers (lines 8–9). The *Image* object IN is initialized with the host_in pointer to a plain C array with raw image data, which invokes the = operator of the *Image* class (line 12). The region of interest VIS contains all image columns but excludes the last d rows to simplify border handling in this example (line 15). The kernel is initialized with the iteration space object, image objects and kernel diameter *d* (line 18), and executed by a call to the *execute()* method (line 21). To retrieve the output image, the host_out pointer to a plain C data array is assigned the *Image* object OUT, which invokes the getData() operator (line 24).

```
1   const int width = 5120, height = 3200, d = 40;
2
3   // pointers to raw image data
4   float *host_in = ...;
5   float *host_out = ...;
6
7   // input and output images
8   Image<float> IN(width, height);
9   Image<float> OUT(width, height);
10
11  // initialize input image
12  IN = host_in; // operator=
13
14  // define region of interest
15  IterationSpace VIS(width, height-d);
16
17  // define kernel
18  VerticalMeanFilter VMF(VIS, IN, OUT, d);
19
20  // execute kernel
21  VMF.execute();
22
23  // retrieve output image
24  host_out = OUT.getData();
```

Listing 2. Example code that initializes and executes vertical mean filtering

2.2   Compiler

This section describes the design of our source-to-source compiler and the single steps taken to create CUDA C and OpenCL code from a high-level description of image objects, iteration space objects and kernel objects.

Our source-to-source compiler is based on the latest Clang/LLVM compiler framework. The Clang frontend for C/C++ is used to parse the input files and to generate an AST representation of the source code. Our backend uses this AST representation to generate host and device code in CUDA or OpenCL.

Kernel Code. The compiler creates the kernel code AST in multiple steps.

First, the kernel declaration is created. The kernel parameters are identified from the *Kernel* class constructor. Each variable, reference, or pointer has to be initialized in the constructor of the *Kernel* class and a corresponding kernel parameter is added to the declaration. In doing so, references to image objects are replaced by global memory

pointers to the pixel type. The existing kernel method argument—the *ElementIterator*—
is removed. Some additional parameters such as the image width and height are added
for index calculations and for future uses like border handling.

Second, the kernel body is created from the *kernel* method of the class. To get an AST
for the kernel body, the original AST is copied with certain AST nodes replaced. References to *Image* objects are replaced with references to corresponding arrays. Instead of
using the *ElementIterator* to calculate the image index, the compiler adds statements at
the beginning of the kernel that calculate the pixel location from the thread index and
block index in CUDA C or the global indices in OpenCL. Similarly, each class member
expression – access to a member variable of the kernel class – is translated to a reference to the corresponding kernel function parameter. After the translation, we get an
AST that can be used for further transformations.

After transformations, the AST is pretty printed and stored to a file. During pretty
printing, CUDA C and OpenCL C specific function and variable qualifiers are emitted.
For example, the __global__ qualifier in CUDA C and the __kernel qualifier in
OpenCL are emitted for entry functions.

Host Code. Unlike for device code, we create no AST for host code. Rather, we use
Clang's *Rewriter* functionality to change the textual representation of AST nodes, whilst
leaving the nodes intact.

To invoke previously generated device kernels, the framework code gets translated
into corresponding CUDA or OpenCL API calls as follows:

- *Image declarations* (line 8 and 9): Get translated into device memory allocation
  using cudaMalloc or clCreateBuffer.
- *Memory assignments* (line 12): Get translated into memory transfers using cuda-
  Memcpy or clEnqueueWriteBuffer.
- *IterationSpace declaration* (line 15): Defines the kernel execution configuration.
- *Kernel declaration* (line 18): Gets translated into loading the kernel source. For
  CUDA C, this step is not required. For OpenCL, the kernel source is loaded from
  a file, an OpenCL program for the loaded source is created, and the kernel is com-
  piled.
- *Kernel execution* (line 21): Gets translated into launching the kernel, using the ex-
  ecution configuration obtained from from the corresponding IterationSpace
  declaration.
- *Memory assignments* (line 24): Get translated into memory transfers using cuda-
  Memcpy or clEnqueueReadBuffer.

In addition to the above changes, further changes are required to get proper CUDA C
or OpenCL code. First of all, include directives for the CUDA C or OpenCL headers
are added. In addition, the CUDA C kernel sources are included at the beginning of the
file. To initialize the runtime, we add the corresponding functionality at the beginning
of the main function. In particular, for OpenCL this initialization is an important part
since it sets up the platform and device to be used for execution. After these changes,
the generated host and device files can be compiled.

Padding Support. To avoid conflicts in accessing image pixels in global memory, our
compiler adds padding to allocated host and device memory. For host code, special
memory allocation functions are required to allocate memory so that each image row

is padded to get the desired data alignment. For device code, array index calculations are changed to take padding into account. The compiler handles padding automatically, given the desired alignment amount for the target device.

3   Results

3.1   Vertical Mean Filtering

A naïve parallel algorithm can run $N = W \times (H - D)$ threads, each producing a single output element, which requires $\Theta(ND)$ reads and arithmetic operations. A good parallel algorithm, however, must be efficient and scalable [5]. Therefore, we use an algorithm that *strips* the computation, where up to T outputs in the same strip are computed serially in two *phases* [4]: The first phase computes $\mathbf{O}_{x,y0}$ according to (1), while the second phase computes $\mathbf{O}_{x,y}$ for $y \geq y0 + 1$ as $\mathbf{O}_{x,y-1} + \left(\mathbf{I}_{x,y+D-1} - \mathbf{I}_{x,y-1}\right)/D$.

This algorithm performs $\Theta(N + ND/T)$ reads and arithmetic operations, considerably reducing memory bandwidth and compute requirements for $T \gg D$, whilst allowing up to $\lceil N/T \rceil$ threads to run in parallel. Thus, this algorithm trades off work efficiency against parallelism.

Listing 3 shows the implementation of this algorithm in our framework. Since our framework supports currently only a 1:1 mapping of output pixels to threads, we use the offset specification to calculate the pixel location for a 1:N mapping. We will provide special syntax for a 1:N mapping in the future.

```
1  class VerticalMeanFilterRollingSum : public Kernel {
2    ...
3    void kernel(IterationSpace::ElementIterator EI) {
4      float sum = 0.0f;
5      int t0 = EI.getY();
6
7      // first phase: convolution
8      for (int k=0; k<d; ++k) {
9        sum += Input(EI, 0, k + (t0*NT-t0));
10     }
11     Output(EI, 0, (t0*NT-t0)) = sum/(float)d;
12
13     // second phase: rolling sum
14     for (int dt=1; dt<min(NT, height-d-(t0*NT)); ++dt) {
15       int t = (t0*NT-t0) + dt;
16       sum -= Input(EI, 0, t-1);
17       sum += Input(EI, 0, t-1+d);
18       Output(EI, 0, t) = sum/(float)d;
19     }
20   }
21 };
```

Listing 3. Kernel description of the vertical mean filter using a rolling sum

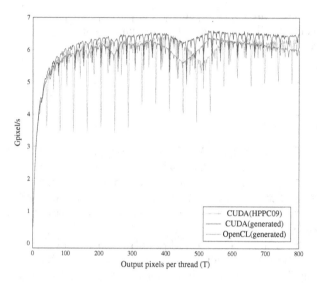

Fig. 1. Throughput of the generated CUDA C/OpenCL sources in Gpixel/s for the vertical mean filter on an image of 5120×3200 pixels in comparison to the hand-written CUDA code from [4]

We compare the performance of code generated by our framework against that of hand-written code reported in [4].[1] We run the vertical mean filter with different values for T, that is, changing the number of pixels calculated by one thread. Figure 1 shows the execution times of the vertical mean filter applied to an image of 5120×3200 pixels. Processing more than one pixel increases the throughput from 0.53 Gpixel/s for $T = 1$, up to the peak throughput of 6.6 Gpixel/s at several points (e. g., for $T = 528$).

The results show that the generated CUDA code achieves the same performance as the optimized hand-written CUDA code.[2] However, our high-level implementation is concise and has only a fraction of the complexity of the low-level implementation of [4]. For instance, in terms of lines of code, the low-level implementation consists of about 500 lines of host and device code, whilst the high-level implementation consists of fewer than 50 lines of code.

In the previous example, the image width of 5120 is a multiple of the SIMD width of the underlying hardware (which is 32). This results in optimal memory transfers utilizing memory bandwidth best. However, if the image width is not a multiple of the SIMD width and not properly aligned, bandwidth throughput drops. For instance, increasing image width by one pixel using an image of 5121×3200 pixels, gives us a peak throughput of 3.9 Gpixel/s which is roughly half of the throughput we got before. Using our framework allows to pad images and changes the kernel source to take padding into account. The amount of padding required for best performance depends on the underlying hardware. For the used graphics hardware, best memory throughput

---

[1] We use the same configuration: thread block dimensions 128×1, kernel diameter $D = 40$. However, we use Quadro FX 5800, rather than GTX 280.

[2] The generated OpenCL code is slightly slower than the generated CUDA code, which we attribute to the relative immaturity of the OpenCL implementation.

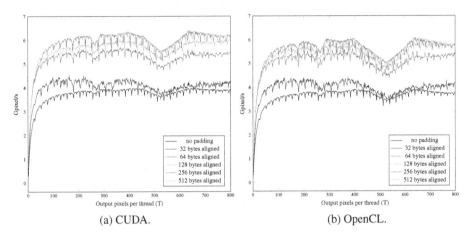

(a) CUDA.   (b) OpenCL.

Fig. 2. Throughput of the generated CUDA C sources in Gpixel/s for the vertical mean filter on an image of 5121×3200 pixels with padding. The generated CUDA C and OpenCL source pads the image width to a multiple of 32-, 64-, 128-, 256-, or 512-bytes.

can be achieved when the image is padded to a multiple of the memory transaction size that can be handled by the GPU in one transaction. This size can be 32-, 64-, and 128-byte segments of aligned memory. Doing so improves the peak throughput as shown in Fig. 2 for an image of 5121×3200 pixels with image lines padded to the different memory transaction sizes. The peak throughput of 6.4 Gpixel/s is achieved for aligning to 256-bytes, which is double the maximum transaction size.

3.2 OpenCV Library

One widely used library for image processing is the *Open Source Computer Vision* (OpenCV) library [9]. Image processing algorithms are optimized in OpenCV to make use of the SIMD units and multiple cores of modern processors. Beginning with version 2.2, selected algorithms (mostly convolution kernels) can also be executed on the GPU. Instead of implementing these kernels from scratch, OpenCV relies on the NVIDIA Performance Primitives (NPP) library. To compare the performance of code generated by our framework to such state-of-the-art approaches, we used the framework to implement all six convolution kernels from OpenCV that utilize NVIDIA GPUs. These kernels mostly support the 8-bit *unsigned char* type and the 3×3 and 5×5 window dimensions, which we use for evaluation. (Note, there is no 5×5 GPU implementation of the laplace convolution filter.) However, we can also generate code for other configurations with only minor modifications to the high-level description as for the 5×5 laplace convolution filter.

Figure 3 shows the execution times of the OpenCV implementations on a CPU (Core 2 Quad @3.00 GHz) and three GPUs: NVIDIA's Quadro FX 5800 and Tesla C2050 and AMD's Radeon HD 5870. For the NVIDIA cards, the OpenCV implementation and CUDA/OpenCL code generated by our framework are compared, while on the AMD card only generated OpenCL code is available. Generated code is as fast as OpenCV code (actually, faster in most cases). With larger filter window size also

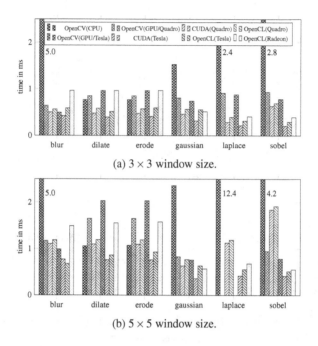

(a) 3×3 window size.

(b) 5×5 window size.

Fig. 3. Comparison of the execution time of convolution kernels from OpenCV and our framework for an image of 1024×1024 pixels on a Quadro FX 5800, Tesla C2050, and Radeon HD 5870. The results for a window size of 3×3 is shown in (a) and for a window size of 5×5 in (b).

execution time increases. Again, the generated CUDA code is slightly faster than the OpenCL code. The GPU implementation of OpenCV relies on NPP, resulting in longer execution times. While our DSL approach generates GPU code from a high-level representation of the desired convolution kernel, the OpenCV library and NPP[3] provide more general implementations that are not optimized for the selected convolution kernel properties like the kernel size. The performance of the vectorized OpenCV code varies considerably. For some convolution kernels, their CPU implementation is almost as fast as our generated GPU code (e. g., for dilate and erode); for most kernels, however, their CPU implementation is an order of magnitude slower than generated GPU code (e. g., for blur, laplace, and gaussian). One big advantage of our framework is that we can generate code for any pixel data type, while the OpenCV implementations are mostly restricted to *unsigned char*.

4   Future Work

The framework presented in this paper allows abstract description of algorithms for image processing which is translated and transformed into device-dependent,

---

[3] The NPP source code is not available for detailed analysis.

optimized source codes. While this works for simple kernels and convolution kernels, we are planning to extend our current framework to provide better support for a broader range of image processing specific features and applications.

The current version of our framework does not support border handling for image processing. The user has to specify border handling in the high-level algorithm description. Instead, our compiler can generate border handling support for images, like clamping to the last valid value, repeating the values beyond the border, mirroring the values at the border, or using a constant value.

Currently, the access/execute metadata is mostly implicit: we assume that the iteration space is parallel in all dimensions and has a 1:1 mapping to work-items (threads), and that the memory access pattern is obvious from the kernel code. In the vertical mean filter example, we use the offset specification to realize a 1:N mapping. More elegant, native support for such mappings allow not only more concise code, but also optimizations on the generated code.

The configuration for a kernel can be specified by a user or determined by the framework. Currently, our framework falls back to a default configuration of 128×1, which is generally suboptimal. However, the compiler can detect a suitable configuration for a kernel and use this setting.

Often, to reduce overheads for dispatching kernels and communicating intermediate data between them, the programmers *manually* bundle several kernels (related by data flow, not necessarily by the application logic!) into a single kernel. Since we have AST information for kernel functions, we can perform kernel fusion and other optimizations automatically if they are allowed by iteration space specifications and data dependences.

5   Conclusion

In this paper, we introduced a performance-portable framework for image processing. Our framework provides C++ classes that allow to describe image processing kernels based on decoupled access/execute metadata, which allows programmers to concentrate on developing algorithms and applications, rather than on mapping them to the target hardware.

The framework performs source-to-source translation of kernels expressed in high-level framework-specific C++ classes into low-level CUDA C and OpenCL code with effective device-dependent optimizations such as global memory padding for memory coalescing and optimal memory bandwidth utilization. Our source-to-source compiler is based on Clang and creates AST for kernel functions, which leaves room for future intra- and inter-kernel optimizations.

Our experiments show that code generated from our abstract description is as fast as hand-optimized and hand-tuned CUDA code for vertical mean filtering. While the performance for images that lead to misaligned memory layouts decreases almost by 50 %, our compiler pads the memory layout so that almost no performance penalty can be observed. In terms of lines of code, our concise high-level description requires only one tenth of the hand-written CUDA implementation. Supporting different backends, our source-to-source compiler produces CUDA C and OpenCL code that is faster than the OpenCV/NPP implementation for the available OpenCV convolution kernels that run on the GPU.

References

1. Clang: Clang: A C Language Family Frontend for LLVM (2007–2011),
   http://clang.llvm.org
2. Cornwall, J., Howes, L., Kelly, P., Parsonage, P., Nicoletti, B.: High-Performance SIMT Code
   Generation in an Active Visual Effects Library. In: Proceedings of the 6th ACM Conference
   on Computing Frontiers, pp. 175–184. ACM (2009)
3. Du, P., Weber, R., Luszczek, P., Tomov, S., Peterson, G., Dongarra, J.: From CUDA to
   OpenCL: Towards a Performance-portable Solution for Multi-platform GPU Programming.
   Tech. rep. (2010)
4. Howes, L., Lokhmotov, A., Donaldson, A.F., Kelly, P.H.J.: Towards Metaprogramming for
   Parallel Systems on a Chip. In: Lin, H.-X., Alexander, M., Forsell, M., Knüpfer, A., Prodan, R.,
   Sousa, L., Streit, A. (eds.) Euro-Par 2009. LNCS, vol. 6043, pp. 36–45. Springer, Heidelberg
   (2010)
5. Lin, C., Snyder, L.: Principles of Parallel Programming. Addison-Wesley Publishing Company, USA (2008)
6. NVIDIA: CUDA (2006–2011), http://www.nvidia.com/cuda
7. Ryoo, S., Rodrigues, C., Stone, S., Stratton, J., Ueng, S., Baghsorkhi, S., Hwu, W.: Program Optimization Carving for GPU Computing. Journal of Parallel and Distributed Computing 68(10), 1389–1401 (2008)
8. The Khronos Group: OpenCL (2008–2011), http://www.khronos.org/opencl
9. Willow Garage: Open Source Computer Vision (OpenCV) (1999–2011),
   http://opencv.willowgarage.com/wiki

A Greedy Heuristic Approximation Scheduling Algorithm for 3D Multicore Processors[*]

Thomas Canhao Xu, Pasi Liljeberg, and Hannu Tenhunen

Turku Center for Computer Science, Joukahaisenkatu 3-5 B, 20520, Turku, Finland
Department of Information Technology, University of Turku, 20014, Turku, Finland
{canxu,pasi.liljeberg,hannu.tenhunen}@utu.fi

Abstract. In this paper, we propose a greedy heuristic approximation scheduling algorithm for future multicore processors. It is expected that hundreds of cores will be integrated on a single chip, known as a Chip Multiprocessor (CMP). To reduce on-chip communication delay, 3D integration with Through Silicon Vias (TSVs) is introduced to replace the 2D counterpart. Multiple functional layers can be stacked in a 3D CMP. However, operating system process scheduling, one of the most important design issues for CMP systems, has not been well addressed for such a system. We define a model for future 3D CMPs, based on which a scheduling algorithm is proposed to reduce cache access latencies and the delay of inter process communications (IPC). We explore different scheduling possibilities and discuss the advantages and disadvantages of our algorithm. We present benchmark results using a cycle accurate full system simulator based on realistic workloads. Experiments show that under two workloads, the execution times of our scheduling in two configurations (2 and 4 threads) are reduced by 15.58% and 8.13% respectively, compared with the other schedulings. Our study provides a guideline for designing scheduling algorithms for 3D multicore processors.

1 Introduction

The number of circuits integrated on a chip have been increasing continuously which leads to an exponential rise in the complexity of their interaction. Traditional digital system design methods, e.g. bus-based System-on-Chip (SoC) will encounter communication bottlenecks. To address these problems, Network-on-Chip (NoC) was proposed as a promising communication platform solution for future multicore systems [1]. Network communication methodologies are brought into on-chip communication. Figure 1 shows a NoC with 4×4 mesh (16 nodes). The underlying network is comprised of network links and routers (R), each of which is connected to a processing element (PE) via a network interface (NI). The basic architectural unit of a NoC is a tile/node (N) which consists of a router, its attached NI and PE, and the corresponding links. Communication among PEs is achieved via network packets. Intel[1] has demonstrated an 80 tile,

---

[*] This work is supported by Academy of Finland and Nokia Foundation.
[1] Intel is a trademark or registered trademark of Intel or its subsidiaries. Other names and brands may be claimed as the property of others.

M. Alexander et al. (Eds.): Euro-Par 2011 Workshops, Part I, LNCS 7155, pp. 281–291, 2012.

100M transistor, 275mm^2 2D NoC under 65nm technology [2]. Recently, an experimental microprocessor containing 48 cores (x86) on a chip has been created, using 4×6 2D mesh topology with 2 cores per tile [2].

Traditional 2D chip interconnection will result long global wire lengths, causing a high delay, high power consumption and low performance [3]. Besides 2D chips have larger die size in multiprocessor implementations. The 3D integration has the potential to increase device density, providing shorter wire lengths and faster on-chip communication compared with the 2D integration. Traditional stacking technologies such as System-in-Package (SiP) and Package-on-Package (PoP) have been integrated into manufacturing technology. Recent researches have focused on TSV [4]. TSV is a viable solution in building 3D chips by stacking IC layers together using vertical interconnects. These interconnects are formed through the silicon die to enable communication among layers. Layers with different functionalities can be implemented in a 3D chip. The manufacturing process of the TSV is complex and expensive [4], therefore finding an optimal number and placement of TSVs is critical. It is presented that, the balance between performance and manufacturing cost is essential in designing a 3D chip [5].

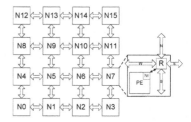

Fig. 1. An example of 4×4 NoC using mesh topology

With limited resources between layers, it is obvious that better or even optimal efficiency can be achieved through appropriate scheduling of multi-threaded tasks in large scale 3D multicore processors. The design of operating system schedulers is one of the most important issues for CMPs. Several multiprocessor scheduling policies such as round robin, co-scheduling and dynamic partitioning have been studied and compared in [6]. However, these policies are designed mainly for the conventional shared bus based communication architecture. Many heuristic-based scheduling methods have been proposed [7,8]. These methods are based on different assumptions, e.g. the prior knowledge of the tasks and execution time of each task in a program, presented as a directed acyclic graph. Hypercube scheduling has been proposed for off-chip systems [9]. Hypercube systems, usually based on Non-Uniform Memory Access (NUMA) or cache coherent NUMA architectures [10], are different from CMPs. Task scheduling for 2D NoC platforms is studied in [11] and [12]. The impact of limited resources between layers is not considered in these papers.

In our paper, we propose and discuss a novel greedy heuristic approximation scheduler for TSV constrained 3D multicore processors which aims to reduce the average network latency between caches and processing cores. With the decrease of the latencies, lower power consumption and higher performance can be achieved. To confirm our theory, we model and analyze a 64-core, 2-layer NoC with 8×8 meshes, present the performance of an application with different allocation strategies using a full system simulator.

2   3D NoC with through Silicon via Constraints

A modern multi-core processor is composed of several parts, e.g. processor core, shared last level cache, I/O and memory controller. Processor core and shared cache consume over 80% of the die area [13]. The total area of Sun SPARC chip is 396mm^2 with 65nm fabrication technology. Each core has an area of 14mm^2, thus with 16 cores the total area of cores is 224mm^2 (56.6%). Shared caches and other components occupy 172mm^2 (43.4%). As explained above, nearly half of the die area is devoted to cores and the other half is devoted to shared caches and other circuits. A natural way of applying 3D integration is to partition all the processors to one layer and other components to the other layer.

2.1   Processors and Caches

There is a significant concern for thermal hot-spots brought by packing layers vertically. It is expectable that since the processors consume overwhelming majority of power in a chip, stacking multiple processor layers would be unwise for heat dissipation. According to [5], heat dissipation is a major problem by stacking multiple processor layers even if processors are interlaced vertically. Therefore, in consideration of heat dissipation of current CMP, the processor layer should be on top of the chip.

In our paper, based on the above analysis, we use a 3D multicore processor model of two layers. The top layer is an 8×8 mesh of 64 Sun SPARC cores. Each core, scaled to 32nm technology, has an area of 3.4mm^2. We simulate the characteristics of a 64MB, 64 banks, 64-bit line size, 4-way associative, 32nm cache by CACTI [14]. Results show that the total area of cache banks is 204.33mm^2. Each cache bank, including data and tag, occupies 3.2mm^2. The cache layer has an 8×8 mesh of cache banks. Routers are quite small compared with processors and caches, e.g. we calculate a 7-port 3D router to be only 0.096mm^2

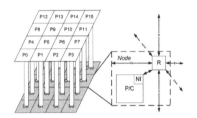

Fig. 2. A 3D NoC with one processor layer (upper) and one cache layer (lower), layers are fully connected by TSVs

under 32nm. The total area of the processor is supposed to be below 300mm^2. Figure 2 shows a model with two layers and 16 processors only.

2.2   Constraints of the through Silicon via

TSV is the most promising solution for building 3D chips. There are several types of TSVs, e.g. data signal transmission, control signal transmission, power distribution and thermal dissipation. In our paper, a pillar is defined as a bunch of TSVs, including TSVs for data, control and power distribution. On the assumption that the power supply voltage is 1V, a practical aspect ratio for TSVs is between 10:1 to 5:1, in which signal TSVs are dominant ones [15]. As it is shown in Figure 1, routers in the 2D NoC have five ports to connect to five directions, namely, North, East, West, South and Local PE. For the vertical communication between different layers, routers in a generic 3D NoC model have two more ports and the corresponding virtual channels, buffers and crossbars to connect to the Up and Down pillars (Figure 2). It is noteworthy that routers in our 3D NoC require less than seven ports, e.g. router of P12 in Figure 2 has only four ports (East, South, Local PE and Down).

It is obvious that the maximum performance can be achieved by full layer-layer connection, e.g. all routers are connected with up/down routers by pillars. However, as the number of tiles grow, it might not be practical to assume that each tile will be connected with corresponding TSVs because of the manufacturing cost and chip area. Assuming that a flit in a NoC is 128 bits, full layer-layer connection for an 8×8 NoC would require $128 \times 8 \times 8 = 8,192$ TSVs for parallel data signals. Other TSVs are required for power, thermal and control. Several researches have shown that [4,16], TSV processing cost is the dominating cost for a 3D wafer. It is cheaper to manufacture a 3D chip with a fewer pillars between layers, in this case, multiple

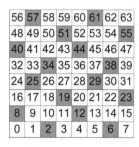

Fig. 3. Each gray nodes is attached to a pillar. Numbers denote the sequence of nodes.

nodes have to share a pillar, high congestion could be created on a pillar, leading to communication bottlenecks. In [5], the placement of pillars is studied, an optimal placement of TSVs for an 8×8 mesh with 16 pillars is presented to minimize traffic contention between layers (Figure 3). The overall performance and total number of TSVs are 92% and 20% compared with full layer-layer connection respectively, achieving a good balance between performance and manufacturing cost.

Assuming XYZ deterministic routing, Equation 1 shows the access time (latency) required for a core-cache communication. The latency involves in-tile links (Between NI and PE, L_{Link_delay1}), router (L_{Router_delay}), tile-tile links (L_{Link_delay2}), the number of hops required to reach the destination (n_{hop}) and the delay caused by TSV (L_{TSV_delay}). Since the delays of link, router and TSV are fixed, hop count is the most important metric in determining latency. Figure 4 shows the average hop counts required for a core to access the shared cache nodes (AHPC). Obviously, without proper schedule, the communication overhead can be an obstacle. For example, nodes at corners of the NoC have much higher AHPC than nodes in the center. However, nodes directly connected with a pillar usually

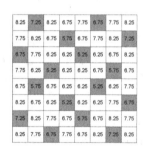

Fig. 4. Gray nodes are attached with a pillar, number means average hop counts to all cache nodes

have lower AHPC, sometimes even lower than inner nodes, e.g. the AHPC for the node 38 is 5.75, lower than 6.75 of the node 37. Scheduling a task to the node 38 is therefore preferable than 37, since the average delay to the shared caches is lower.

$$L_{CoreCache} = 2 \times L_{Link\_delay1} + (n_{hop} + 1) \times L_{Router\_delay} +$$
$$n_{hop} \times L_{Link\_delay2} + L_{TSV\_delay} \qquad (1)$$

3   The Scheduling Algorithm

Our proposed scheduling algorithm takes into consideration of on-chip topology and TSV placement, scheduling decisions are made based on these information. The aim of the algorithm is to minimize average network latency of the system, which is an important factor of system performance. We use a 3D NoC model as described below.

Definition 1. *A 3D NoC $N(P(X,Y), C(X,Y))$ consists of a layer of PE mesh $P(X,Y)$ (width X, length Y); and a layer of cache mesh $C(X,Y)$. Layers are connected by TSVs, only a quarter of nodes are connected (Figure 3).*

Definition 2. *Each node is denoted by a coordinate (x,y), where $0 \leq x \leq X - 1$ and $0 \leq y \leq Y - 1$.*

Definition 3. *The Manhattan Distance between two PEs $n_i(x_i, y_i)$ and $n_j(x_j, y_j)$ is $MD(n_i, n_j)$, $MD(n_i, n_j) = |x_i - x_j| + |y_i - y_j|$. Two nodes in the same layer $n_1(x_1, y_1)$ and $n_2(x_2, y_2)$ are interconnected by a router and related link only if they are adjacent, e.g. $MD(n_1, n_2) = 1$.*

Definition 4. *A task $T(n)$ with n threads requests the allocation of n cores.*

Definition 5. *n_{Free} is a sorted list of all unallocated nodes in P, such that: $AHPC_{nFree1} \leq AHPC_{nFree2} \leq AHPC_{nFree3} \leq \ldots AHPC_{nFreek}$.*

Definition 6. *$R(T(n))$ is a unallocated region in P with n cores for $T(n)$.*

To schedule a task efficiently, several metrics have to be considered, e.g. MD, AHPC and so on. Scheduling a task with only 1 thread is relatively easy. In this case, nodes 19, 29, 34 and 44 are considered in the first place, if they are not utilized by other applications. The reason is that, these four nodes have the lowest AHPC (5.25). However, as the requested number of threads grows, other metrics have to be included. For example, a 2-thread task can be scheduled to nodes 19 and 29. In this case, the Inter Process Communication (IPC) between threads will suffer higher delay, since the messages have to go through nodes 20 and 21 according to XY routing. Another problem is fragmentation. Non-contiguous allocation of cores in a dynamic system can cause degradation of overall system performance. The 2-thread task can be scheduled to nodes 19 and 20 as well. Despite the fact that the AHPC is increased by 1 for node 20 compared with node 29, the adjacent allocation will alleviate IPC bottleneck, and reduce fragmentation. We introduce Average Core-access Time (ACT), which is defined as the number of nodes a message has to go through from a PE to other PEs, $\forall i, j \in P$.

$$ACT = \frac{\sum MD(n_i, n_j)}{n} \tag{2}$$

Such that: $\forall i \neq j \in P$ and $n_i \neq n_j$

According to the equation, the ACT is 3 and 1 for nodes 19/29 and 19/20, respectively. The delay for a core-core communication is shown in Equation 3. Obviously, allocation 19/29 will incur much higher router delay and delay of tile-tile links, comparing with allocation 19/20. It is noteworthy that a core-core communication is a intra-layer communication, while a core-cache communication is a inter-layer communication.

$$L_{CoreCore} = 2 \times L_{Link\_delay1} + (n_{hop} + 1) \times L_{Router\_delay} + n_{hop} \times L_{Link\_delay2} \tag{3}$$

For a rectangular core allocation with $A \times B$ nodes, according to [17], ACT can be calculated in an easier way (Equation 4). For example, 4×4 and 2×8 are possible rectangular core allocations for a task with 16 threads. However, the value of ACT in 4×4 is smaller than in 2×8 (2.5 and 3.125). In consideration of ACT, an allocation shape have a lower ACT number if it is closer to a square. Figure 5a and 5b show two core allocation schemes for a task with 15 threads. In Figure 5b, the number of ACT is lower than in Figure 5a (2.4177 and 2.4888 respectively).

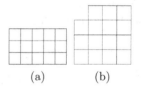

(a)   (b)

Fig. 5. Comparison of two core allocation schemes for 15 threads

$$ACT = \frac{A + B}{3} \times (1 - \frac{1}{A \times B}) \tag{4}$$

A scheduling algorithm should have a low computation complexity and should deliver an optimal or near-optimal results. This is due to the scheduling has to be solved online, and the time for solving the scheduling is a part of the overall system response time. It is clear that we should not try to solve the scheduling problem optimally, in case the computation complexity is too high. Given a task with n executing threads, we define the problem as determining the near-optimal core allocation for the task by selecting a region containing of n cores. The pseudo code of the algorithm is shown in Algorithm 1.

Algorithm 1. The Greedy Heuristic Approximation Scheduling Algorithm

---

Input: A mesh based NoC N with TSV constrains, a task with n threads
Output: An allocated region R, containing n processors

1 Pop the first node as an initial node u_0 from n_{Free}, and push u_0 to R

2 $n_{MD} := n_{Free}$ sorted as $\text{MD}(u_0, n_{Free})$

3 while n_{MD} *is not empty* **do**
4   Pick a node $u_n(x_i, y_i)$ from n_{MD} with smaller AHPC
        if *several nodes with same AHPC* **then**
5   pick a node $u_n(x_i, y_i)$ with smaller ACT in the result region
6   **end**
7   **if** *several nodes with same ACT* **then**
8   pick a node $u_n(x_i, y_i)$ which $x_i \to \frac{X}{2}$ and $y_i \to \frac{Y}{2}$
9   **end**
10   Pop $u_n(x_i, y_i)$ from n_{MD}, and push u_n to R
11 end

Line 1 sets the starting node of the algorithm, which is the one with the lowest AHPC. A list n_{MD} contains nodes sorted based on MD from the starting node. The adjacent nodes are always considered first, in terms of AHPC. ACT will be calculated, in case several nodes are with the same AHPC. If ACTs for the allocation strategies are still the same, a node closer to the center of the network will be selected (considering the statistical variance of the coordinates of two nodes, Equation 5). This is due to the fact that, nodes in the center usually have lower AHPC than nodes in the border, following steps may have better results from this heuristic.

$$Var(n) = \frac{1}{2} \times [(x_i - \frac{X}{2})^2 + (x_j - \frac{Y}{2})^2] \qquad (5)$$

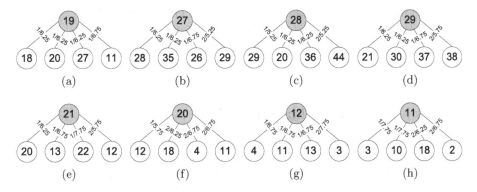

Fig. 6. The node selection steps for the algorithm

We analyze an example of the algorithm. Figures 6a to 6h shows the steps for node selection, starting from node 19. The number between two nodes n_i and n_j means $MD(n_i,n_j)$ and $AHPC(n_j)$. Note that we only show 4 child nodes in these figures. The actual list n_{MD} and n_{Free} may contain more nodes. As illustrated in Figure 6a, node 19 has 4 adjacent nodes and 3 of them are with the same AHPC and ACT. However, in terms of distance to the center, node 27 is selected ($Var(27) < Var(20) < Var(18)$). The selection of the next node follows the similar rule: same AHPC, same ACT, same variance. In this case we choose node 28, having a smaller node number than node 35. Figure 6c demonstrates that, node 29 is selected due to its lowest MD and AHPC. The next step involves different ACTs: both node 21 and node 30 have the lowest AHPC, however the ACTs for the two nodes are different (2 for node 30, and 1.8 for node 21). Node 20 and 12 are selected as the sixth and seventh node, respectively, due to their lowest AHPC. The next node (11) is picked out, on account of its lower ACT than the others. It is noteworthy that the aforementioned greedy heuristic approximation algorithm generates near-optimal scheduling solution in most cases. However, in our algorithm we put adjacent nodes as the first priority, the AHPC and ACT are considered next. This strategy may generate non-optimal scheduling for certain applications.

Take a 4-thread application for example. As shown in Figure 7, the algorithm will choose nodes 19, 27, 28 and 29 for allocation.

An IPC-intensive application may suffer from the long distance communication of node 19 and 29. In this case, node 20 is a better choice than 29 since the ACT is lower. Despite our goal is to find a near-optimal scheduling using MD, AHPC and ACT, the weight of these metrics should be considered as well. Different applications have their own profile: some have higher demand of caches, some have higher volume of IPC. It is difficult to determine the behavior of an application automatically beforehand, since there are millions of them and the number is still increasing. One feasible way is to add an interface between the application and the OS, the application will tell the OS its behavior. Another way is to add a low overhead profiling module inside the OS. Program access patterns are traced dynamically, and possibly migrated for better allocations.

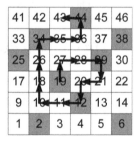

Fig. 7. The execution of our algorithm, starting from node 19 and selected 16 nodes

4   Experimental Evaluation

4.1   Experiment Setup and Application

The simulation platform is based on a cycle-accurate NoC simulator which is able to produce detailed evaluation results. The platform models the routers and links accurately. The router includes a routing computation unit, a virtual channel allocator, a switch allocator, a crossbar switch and 4 input buffers. Deterministic XYZ routing algorithm has been selected to avoid deadlocks. We use a 64-core multiprocessor which models a single-chip CMP for our experiments. The 3D architecture in this paper has two layers; the first layer contains PEs (each running at 2GHz with a private L1 cache, split I+D, each 16KB, 4-way associative, 64-bit line, 3-cycle), the second layer consists of shared L2 caches (unified 64 banks, each 1MB, 64-bit line, 6-cycle). The simulations are run on Solaris 9 based on UltraSPARCIII+ instruction set in-order issue structure. The simulated memory/cache architecture mimics Static Non-Uniform Cache Architecture. A two-level directory cache coherence protocol called MOESI, based on MESI, has been implemented in our memory hierarchy in which each L2 bank has its own directory. We use Simics [18] as our full system simulation platform.

We select FFT [19] and Radix [20] as experiment applications. The FFT algorithm is a one-dimensional, radix-n, six-step algorithm optimized to minimize IPC. The communication between processors only take place at the last stage of the execution. However the network traffic and cache miss rate are very high. The Radix sort algorithm assigns each processor a part of the sorting keys. For every iteration in the algorithm, a permutation for the keys is required to create a new array for the next iteration. This will incur all-to-all communication among processes. Hence Radix represents an application with high IPC.

4.2   Result Analysis

We evaluate performance in terms of Average Network Latency (ANL), Execution Time (ET) and Cache Hit Latencies (CHL). ANL represents the average number of cycles required for the transmission of all messages. The number of required cycles for each message is calculated from the injection of the message header into the network at the source node, to the reception of the tail flit at the destination node. Under the same configuration and workload, lower values are favorable. We analyze two core allocations for a 2-thread task: *T2-1* is from our algorithm, which contains nodes 19 and 27. It has lowest ACT values, however the AHPC is not optimal. *T2-2* is an alternative allocation, which contains nodes 19 and 29. In this case, the AHPC is minimized. The *T4-1*, *T4-2* and *T4-3* are three core allocations for a 4-thread task: *T4-2* contains nodes 19, 20, 27 and 28, represents lowest ACT; *T4-3* contains nodes 19, 29, 34 and 44, represents lowest AHPC. Our algorithm selects *T4-1*, it has neither lowest ACT nor AHPC numbers. However we believe it could be a good balance for the two metrics.

The results are illustrated in Figure 8. The core allocation of our scheduling algorithm for 2 threads outperforms the other in terms of ANL. The improvement is more notable in 2-thread FFT and Radix, with 9.26% and 11.77% reduced latency, respectively, compared with the *T2-2* allocation. This is primarily due to the reduced communication overhead between two PEs. We note that the reduced AHPC in *T2-2* failed to compensate the increasing ACT, in terms of ANL. The CHL in *T2-2* directly reflects the reduced AHPC. However, the average runtime of two applications show that, our algorithm spends 15.58% shorter time than *T2-2*. Considering a 4-thread task, we note that both ACT and AHPC

play important roles in overall performance. For example, despite the fact that
T4-2 has lowest ACT, the
ANL for two applications is
3.76% higher than in our algorithm. This leads to a higher
ET as well. Allocation *T4-3* performs better than our
scheduling in the 4-thread
FFT. This is because of, in
FFT, the communication between threads only happens
at the last stage of the exe-

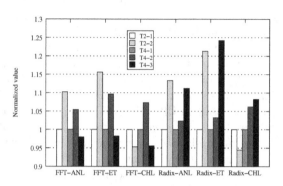

Fig. 8. Performance for FFT and Radix

cution. In this case, we observe that the trade-off for ACT is worthy. However,
applications that heavily rely on IPC, e.g. Radix, will suffer from the *T4-3*. The
ET of *T4-3* is 24.24% longer than in *T4-1*.

5   Conclusion and Future Work

In this paper, we studied the problem of process scheduling for future 3D multicore processors. A model for NoC-based 3D CMP was defined. We analyzed
process scheduling in terms of average hop counts for core-cache accesses (AHPC)
and average core access time (ACT) in 3D CMPs with constraints of inter-layer
connections. A greedy heuristic approximation algorithm was proposed to reduce
overall on-chip communication latencies and improve performance. Results have
shown that, with proper scheduling, performance improved significantly in most
cases. The impact of ACT and AHPC was discussed. The results of this paper
give a guideline in designing schedulers for future 3D CMPs. Our next step is to
evaluate more applications with different access profiles and number of threads.
The weight of AHPC and ACT will be analyzed and compared, and the trade-off
for finding the best allocation strategy will be studied.

References

1. Dally, W.J., Towles, B.: Route packets, not wires: on-chip inteconnection networks. In: Proceedings of the 38th Conference on Design Automation, pp. 684–689
   (June 2001)
2. Intel: Intel research areas on microarchitecture (May 2011),
   http://techresearch.intel.com/projecthome.aspx?ResearchAreaId=11
3. Sylvester, D., Keutzer, K.: Getting to the bottom of deep submicron. In: ICCAD
   1998, pp. 203–211 (November 1998)
4. Velenis, D., Stucchi, M., Marinissen, E., Swinnen, B., Beyne, E.: Impact of 3d design
   choices on manufacturing cost. In: IEEE 3DIC 2009, pp. 1–5 (September 2009)
5. Xu, T.C., Liljeberg, P., Tenhunen, H.: Optimal number and placement of through
   silicon vias in 3d network-on-chip. In: Proc. of the 14th DDECS. IEEE (2011)

6. Leutenegger, S.T., Vernon, M.K.: The performance of multiprogrammed multiprocessor scheduling algorithms. In: Proc. of the SIGMETRICS, pp. 226–236 (April 1990)
7. Chen, C., Lee, C., Hou, E.: Efficient scheduling algorithms for robot inverse dynamics computation on a multiprocessor system. IEEE Transactions on Systems, Man and Cybernetics 18(5), 729–743 (1988)
8. Hakem, M., Butelle, F.: Dynamic critical path scheduling parallel programs onto multiprocessors. In: Proceedings of 19th IEEE IPDPS, p. 203b (April 2005)
9. Sharma, D.D., Pradhan, D.K.: Processor allocation in hypercube multicomputers: Fast and efficient strategies for cubic and noncubic allocation. IEEE Transactions on Parallel and Distributed Systems 6(10), 1108–1123 (1995)
10. Laudon, J., Lenoski, D.: The sgi origin: a ccnuma highly scalable server. In: Proc. of the 24th International Symposium on Computer Architecture, pp. 241–251 (June 1997)
11. Chen, Y.J., Yang, C.L., Chang, Y.S.: An architectural co-synthesis algorithm for energy-aware network-on-chip design. J. Syst. Archit. 55(5-6), 299–309 (2009)
12. Hu, J., Marculescu, R.: Energy-aware communication and task scheduling for network-on-chip architectures under real-time constraints. In: DATE 2004, p. 10234. IEEE Computer Society, Washington, DC (2004)
13. IBM: Ibm power 7 processor. In: Hot Chips 2009 (August 2009)
14. Shyamkumar, T., Naveen, M., Ho, A.J., Jouppi Norman, P.: Cacti 5.1. Technical Report HPL-2008-20, HP Labs (2008)
15. Semiconductor Industry Association: The international technology roadmap for semiconductors (itrs) (2007),
   http://www.itrs.net/Links/2007ITRS/Home2007.htm
16. Lau, J.H.: Tsv manufacturing yield and hidden costs for 3d ic integration. In: Proc. of the 60th ECTC, pp. 1031 –1042 (June 2010)
17. Lei, T., Kumar, S.: A two-step genetic algorithm for mapping task graphs to a network on chip architecture. In: DSD, pp. 180–187 (September 2003)
18. Magnusson, P., Christensson, M., Eskilson, J., Forsgren, D., Hallberg, G., Hogberg, J., Larsson, F., Moestedt, A., Werner, B.: Simics: A full system simulation platform. Computer 35(2), 50–58 (2002)
19. Bailey, D.H.: Ffts in external or hierarchical memory. The Journal of Supercomputing 4, 23–35 (1990), doi:10.1007/BF00162341
20. Blelloch, G.E., Leiserson, C.E., Maggs, B.M., Plaxton, C.G., Smith, S.J., Zagha, M.: A comparison of sorting algorithms for the connection machine cm-2. In: Proceedings of the 3rd SPAA, pp. 3–16. ACM, New York (1991)

Algorithms and Programming Tools for Next-Generation High-Performance Scientific Software HPSS 2011

Stefania Corsaro[1,2], Pasqua D'Ambra[2], and Francesca Perla[1,2]

[1] University of Naples "Parthenope"
[2] Institute for High-Performance Computing and Networking (ICAR), CNR

The workshop *Algorithms and Programming Tools for Next-Generation High-Performance Scientific Software* (HPSS) focuses on recent advances in algorithms and programming tools development for next-generation high-performance scientific software as enabling technologies for new insights into Computational Science.

Scientific Software is a key component in developing effective instruments for Computational Science. Prototyping and developing scientific codes in terms of reliable, efficient and portable building blocks allow users to reduce the time-to-solution of a computational problem and to simplify the inclusion and comparison of new physical/mathematical models and solvers. The history of open-source high-performance scientific libraries and frameworks, such as ScaLapack, FFTW, PETSc, Trilinos, ATLAS, only to cite some of the most widely used, is a history of success. Some of the mentioned packages represent both "de facto" standard platforms for scientific code development and benchmarks for new proposals of hardware/software architectures devoted to high-performance computing. On the other hand, we are currently living a discontinuity in software design procedures due to the need of efficient use of near future highly parallel machines, where multiple levels of parallelism and heterogeneous components will be integrated. Relevant changes are happening from programming models to base software, thus scientific software community is thinking and working on new challenges of tomorrow's scientific software infrastructure for Computational Science. Designing and implementing high-quality, reusable, extensible and portable scientific software require inputs and skills from different areas of Mathematics and Computer Science. Many issues have to be considered, such as targeting theoretical efficiency when designing new algorithms, being at the same time aware of architectural limitations; analyzing performance of such algorithms on emerging computers by realistic performance models as well as by practical implementation; using advanced programming tools for simplicity of usage and portability of the resulting software.

HPSS is intended to bring together applied mathematicians, computer scientists and computational scientists from different areas, in order to discuss recent challenges and results in modern technology issues for high-performance computing as well as in developing open-source high-quality software for Computational Science.

The contributions of the authors certainly work togheter to reach this aim and are representative of outstanding research in the context of design and development of algorithms and software for high-performance scientific computing. We want to thank all the authors for having submitted papers to HPSS 2011.

Our gratitude also goes to Iain Duff and Laura Grigori for accepting our invitation to give a lecture.

In this book are collected 11 contributed papers selected among 21 submissions by a peer review process. Moreover, we are very grateful to Iain Duff for allowing us to include his paper in the book. The paper focuses on the European Exascale Software Initiative, a recent project funded by European Community, which had the final aim to build a european vision and roadmap to address the challenges of the new generation of parallel systems providing exaflop performance in the near future.

We wish to thank all the members of the Program Committe of HPSS 2011 and the reviewers for their contribution in the definition of the workshop program. We thank the Euro-Par 2011 organizers for providing us the opportunity to make HPSS 2011 in conjunction with the conference. Finally, we are grateful to the University of Naples "Parthenope" and the Institute for High-Performance Computing and Networking for financial support.

October 2011   Stefania Corsaro
                                                     Pasqua D'Ambra
                                                     Francesca Perla

European Exascale Software Initiative: Numerical Libraries, Solvers and Algorithms

Iain S. Duff[1,2]

[1] RAL, Oxfordshire, UK
[2] CERFACS, Toulouse, France

Abstract. Computers with sustained Petascale performance are now available and it is expected that hardware will be developed with a peak capability in the Exascale range by around 2018. However, the complexity, hierarchical nature, and probable heterogeneity of these machines pose great challenges for the development of software to exploit these architectures.

This was recognized some years ago by the IESP (International Exascale Software Project) initiative and the European response to this has been a collaborative project called EESI (European Exascale Software Initiative). This initiative began in 2010 and has submitted its final report to the European Commission with a final conference in Barcelona in October 2011. The main goals of EESI are to build a European vision and roadmap to address the international outstanding challenge of performing scientific computing on the new generation of computers.

The main activity of the EESI is in eight working groups, four on applications and four on supporting technologies. We first briefly review these eight chapters before discussing in more detail the work of Working Group 4.3 on Numerical Libraries, Solvers and Algorithms. Here we will look at the principal areas, the challenges of Exascale and possible ways to address these, and the resources that will be needed.

1 Introduction

Computers with sustained Petascale performance are now available and it is expected that hardware will be developed with a peak capability in the Exascale range by around 2018. However, the complexity, hierarchical nature, and probable heterogeneity of these machines pose great challenges for the development of software to exploit these architectures.

It is widely recognized that the major bottleneck in the exploitation of Exaflop computing lies more in the software than the hardware and also that insufficient attention has been paid in the past to supporting efforts in software development. The hardware costs for this forthcoming generation of high performance computers are estimated to be in the order of $200 million with probably at least $20 million a year in electricity costs to run them. It is against this background that we present relatively modest costs for the software effort that will be necessary if we are to capitalize on the thousand-fold increase in computing power over today's fastest machines.

M. Alexander et al. (Eds.): Euro-Par 2011 Workshops, Part I, LNCS 7155, pp. 295–304, 2012.

Of course, we are working on the assumption that we need to exploit future generation machines and recognize that Exaflop computing is on the horizon. Clearly such power (10^{18} floating-point operations per second) is needed for more accurate and complicated simulations. Applications include: multiphysics, multiscale, inverse problems, and optimization.

This was recognized some years ago by the IESP (International Exascale Software Project) initiative and the European response to this has been a collaborative project called EESI (European Exascale Software Initiative). This initiative began in 2010 and submitted its final report to the European Commission with a final conference in Barcelona in October 2011.

We first give a brief review of the main structure of the EESI project in Section 2 before discussing in more detail the work of Working Group 4.3 on Numerical Libraries, Solvers and Algorithms in Section 3. After outlining the topics covered by the Working Group, we then in separate subsections highlight some major issues raised by our investigation. We conclude this short report in Section 4 by highlighting the areas that we need to address to ensure European competitiveness and by summarizing briefly the resources that will be needed.

This note is based on a talk given at the HPSS 2011 Workshop at EuroPar 2011 in Bordeaux. It is particularly noticeable for its lack of references. This reflects somewhat the deliverable of the Working Group although the main report includes references to several web sites. This main report will shortly be available as deliverable D4.5, referenced through our EU contract number EESI 261513.

2   EESI: European Exascale Software Initiative

The European Exascale Software Initiative (EESI) is supported by the EU under the Infrastructure thematic of Support and Collaborative Action (CSA). The 18 months project began on 1 June 2010. The final conference to present our findings was in Barcelona from 11-12 October 2011.

The organizations that are involved in EESI can be grouped into three categories, viz.

- The *contractual partners* are: ARTTIC, BSC, CINECA, EDF, EPSRC, GENCI, JSC, and NCF.
- The *associated partners* are: CEA, CECAM, CERFACS, CMCC, CNRS, CSC, EMBL-EBI, ENES, EPCC, INGV, INRIA, NAG, STFC, Ter@tec, TOTAL, STRATOS, and Univ Edinburgh.
- There is also an active group of *contributing partners*: Univ Tennessee, Tokyo Inst Tech, SNECMA, Airbus, ESF, IACAT, DEISA, LRZ, OeRC, and PROSPECT.

The main goals of EESI are:

To build a European vision and roadmap to address the international outstanding challenge of performing scientific computing on the new generation of computers (multi-Petaflop now and Exaflop in 2020).

The more specific aims are to:

- Investigate how Europe is located, its strengths and weaknesses, in the overall international HPC landscape and competition.
- Identify priority actions.
- Identify the sources of competitiveness for Europe induced by the development of Peta/Exascale solutions and usages.
- Investigate and propose programmes in education and training for the next generation of computational scientists.
- Identify and stimulate opportunities of worldwide collaboration.

We are working closely with the IESP (International Exascale Software Project) led by Pete Beckman (Argonne and Chicago) and Jack Dongarra (Tennessee and Manchester). The main funding for IESP is from the DOE Office of Science and the NSF Office of Cyberinfrastructure. The IESP involves researchers from the US, Europe (including Russia), China, and Japan and has held several workshops beginning with one in Santa Fe in April 2009. The workshops have also been attended by researchers from Australia, Saudi Arabia, South Korea, and Taiwan.

The goal of IESP is to "Improve the world's simulation and modeling capability by improving the coordination and development of the HPC software environment". The aim of the many workshops held internationally by the project is to *"Build an international plan for coordinating research for the next generation open source software for scientific high-performance computing"*.

The EESI project is split into five workpackages. WP 1 on administration, WP 2 on international networking, and WP 5 on dissemination. The main part of the project is based around eight working groups in workpackages 3 and 4; four based on applications and four based on underlying technologies. We list the Working Groups in Table 1.

Table 1. EESI Working Groups

	Chair	Vice-chair
WP3: Application Grand Challenges WP Chair: Stéphane Requena (GENCI)		
WG 3.1 Industrial and Engineering Applications	Philippe Ricoux (TOTAL)	Jean-Claude André (CERFACS)
WG 3.2 Weather, Climatology and Earth Sciences	Giovanni Aloisio (ENES-CMCC)	Massimo Cocco (INGV)
WG 3.3 Fundamental Sciences (Chemistry, Physics)	Godehard Sutmann (CECAM)	Jean-Philippe Nominé (CEA)
WG 3.4 Life Science and Health	Modesto Orozco (BSC)	Janet Thornton (EBI)
WP4: Enabling Technologies for Exaflop Computing WP Chair: Bernd Mohr (Jülich)		
WG 4.1 Hardware Roadmaps, Links with Vendors	Herbert Huber (STRATOS-LRZ)	Sanzio Bassini (CINECA)
WG 4.2 Software Eco-system	Franck Cappello (INRIA-UIUC)	Bernd Mohr (Jülich)
WG 4.3 Numerical Libraries, Software and Algorithms	Iain Duff (STFC-RAL and CERFACS)	Andreas Grothey (Edinburgh University)
WG 4.4 Scientific Software Engineering	Mike Ashworth (STFC-DL)	Andrew Jones (NAG)

Each Working Group consists of a Chair, a Vice-Chair, and from ten to fifteen experts, chosen for both topical and geographical coverage. In the case of the Working Group on Numerical Libraries, Software and Algorithms, the composition of the Team is shown in Table 2. The input from all these experts should be acknowledged both in the production of the Working Group report but also in providing the base material for my talk in Bordeaux and this subsequent short report.

Table 2. Composition of Working Group 4.3

Iain Duff	STFC/CERFACS	UK	Sparse Linear Algebra
Andreas Grothey	University of Edinburgh	UK	Cont & Stoch Optimization
Patrick Amestoy	ENSEEIHT-IRIT, Toulouse	FR	Sparse Direct Methods, Solvers
Peter Arbenz	ETH Zürich	CH	Eigenvalues, HPC
Jack Dongarra	Tennessee/Manchester	UK/US	HPC, Numerical LA
Salvatore Filippone	Università di Roma	IT	Numerical Software
Mike Giles	University of Oxford	UK	GPU, CFD/Finance
Luc Giraud	INRIA Bordeaux	FR	Iterative & Hybrid Methods
Thorsten Koch	Zuse-Institut Berlin	DE	Combinatorial Optimization
Bo Kågström	Umeå University	SE	HPC, Dense Linear Algebra
Karl Meerbergen	K.U. Leuven	BE	Preconditioners, ExaScience Lab
Volker Mehrmann	TU Berlin	DE	Linear Algebra, HP Applications
Gerard Meurant	ex-CEA	FR	HPC, PDE solution
François Pellegrini	Université de Bordeaux & INRIA	FR	Partitioning
Julius Žilinskas	Vilnius University	LT	Global Opt, Meta-heuristics

3   Numerical Libraries, Solvers and Algorithms

The area addressed by Working Group 4.3 is very much an enabling technology and so inherits the impact and societal benefits of the enabled applications. Indeed we are very much motivated by the needs of applications and our work is critical to the success of these applications even more so in the forthcoming computing regime than at present.

3.1   Main Areas Covered in the WG 4.3 Report

We started our discussions on which topics to include by basing these on the original Colella's dwarves[1] and extensions of these. The original seven dwarves were: structured grids, unstructured grids, fast Fourier Transform, dense linear algebra, sparse linear algebra, particles, and Monte Carlo, but it was soon apparent that these only cover a limited range of the main areas that we felt we should include. After some discussion, we chose the list:

- Dense linear algebra
- Graph and hypergraph partitioning
- Sparse direct methods
- Iterative methods for sparse matrices
- Eigenvalue problems, model reduction
- Optimization
- Control of complex systems
- Structured and unstructured grids

The above list has been ordered according to a software stack where entries further down the stack use those above them in the stack. This hierarchical structure is important when considering the mapping of our algorithms and libraries to the hierarchically structured computers of the new emerging architectures. For example in the stack:

---

[1] D. Patterson (2005) Colella, Phillip. Defining software requirements for scientific computing.
http://www.lanl.gov/orgs/hpc/salishan/salishan2005/david patterson.pdf

- BLAS
- Dense linear algebra
- Sparse solver
- Hybrid solver
- Optimization/Eigenvalues/Control

the BLAS are at the most basic level and are used extensively by dense linear algebra codes that in turn can be used to factorize submatrices in sparse direct solvers. In turn, the solution of the linear system might be effected by using the sparse direct solver within a hybrid solver, for example to solve subproblems in a domain decomposition approach. Finally the linear system may be solved within the inner loop of optimization, eigensystem, or control software. Note that we need not be preoccupied with achieving Exascale performance at every level. It can often be sufficient, particularly lower in the stack to obtain Peta or even Terascale performance. For example, if the BLAS executes on a multicore node at a Terascale level, the execution of the software at the highest level could well be at Exascale.

3.2   Algorithmic Issues

There were several algorithmic issues that were identified in more than one subtopic and we discuss these in this subsection. We should point out that there are a huge number of algorithms in our portfolio, and the most suitable one will depend not only on the functionality and the target architecture. Clearly, the problem will define the general approach but the structure and size of the problem is also of crucial importance, for example is the problem sparse or in some way structured and can we exploit this structure?

We already mentioned the software stack that gave rise to a hierarchy of library calls with consequent multiple possibilities for exploiting parallelism at many levels. However, even with seemingly tightly defined algorithms or kernels there is often scope for a hierarchically structured algorithm that might match well to emerging computer architectures. An example is in my own field of the direct solution of sparse equations. Here there might be an initial dependency on graph partitioning algorithms and then the construction and use of a computational tree where the units of computation are akin to a dense matrix factorization which in turn uses possibly highly-tuned BLAS algorithms. Further levels of parallelism can be obtained from the context of the sparse direct solver. For example, it could be in the inner loop of an eigensystem solver or at each step of an optimization algorithm. This algorithmic modularity also supports the exploitation of heterogeneous systems.

There are several barriers to the efficient exploitation of parallel architectures. One is synchronization where there can be significant inefficiencies if one thread is held waiting for others to finish. This is epitomized by the fork-join construct and much recent work has sought to remove this bottleneck and express algorithms in terms of a task graph (normally a directed acyclic graph or dag). Several powerful algorithms for both dense and sparse linear algebra use dags as their basis for assigning work to processors and scheduling the computation.

Of course, as has long been recognized, even on older generations of machines, the main bottleneck is not the floating-point execution time but rather the cost of moving data to the arithmetic units that can be increasingly costly on modern very non-NUMA architectures with many levels of memory and cache hierarchy.

One of the main algorithmic tricks to reduce this bottleneck is to block the computation so that the ratio of data fetching to arithmetic is reduced. A simple example of this is the Level 3 BLAS. We note that there can be extra costs in doing this, for example data might have to be reordered or restructured or repartitioned with concomitant costs.

This type of blocking or data rearrangement is often at the heart of so-called communication avoiding algorithms which often rely on blocking to reduce the amount of communication. An allied issue is that of communication hiding where strong attempts are made to ensure that any data movement is masked by simultaneous arithmetic processing on other data. Care has to be taken both to ensure algorithms remain stable and to avoid extra synchronization costs. We note that, if data movement and communication can be reduced then less energy may be needed to effect the computation, a potentially major issue when dealing with such high performance computers. The concept of energy aware algorithms has indeed become a big issue in high performance computation.

3.3   Software Issues

In the previous section, we discussed generic algorithmic issues which should be addressed if we are to obtain good performance on Peta and Exascale machines. We now discuss some software issues, most of which have existed for some time but many have been brought into sharper focus by the development of high performance computing.

Interoperability is always an important feature of software libraries and this is even more true in the current regime. The Exascale setting intensifies the need to draw on multiple areas of expertise and to have various toolkits interacting with each other.

The Exascale target is a moving one so that any software needs to have a good support structure so that it can continually be adapted to meet the demands of new architectural features. Also, partly in order to attract users for the software (and this is by no means guaranteed), it really is important to have and be seen to have long term support over a period of several years or even decades.

Any code supported by the European Union should certainly be open source to promote its widest dissemination within the research and educational communities. This will also contribute strongly to the future development and support of the code and enhancement of it from third parties. The issue of licensing is more fraught and has not really been grasped by the EU. A licence like LGPL allows open dissemination but could hamper its use in applications although it does open the possibility of commercializing the code (sometimes encouraged in EU projects).

Above all, the interface and documentation of the codes are of prime importance partly because the environment in which they will be used is getting increasingly complex, not just from the hardware point of view but also in a software context where codes may be used in effecting stochastic approaches or in the solution of inverse problems.

3.4   Fault Tolerance

Fault tolerance is a major issue in Exascale computation as, even with a high chip yield, a billion core machine will quite likely experience the failure of a core at an intervals that potentially will cause problems in application and numerical library codes. There are various estimates of the severity of this but it is universally agreed to be a significant problem. One thing to note is the difference between MTBF (mean time between failures) that could be in the order of hours or less and MTTI (mean time to interrupt) which is when the code might have to take significant action. The order of this depends on hardware support for handling the chip failures but could be in the order of a day and thus will be less likely to require dramatic remedial action. Certainly our hope is that the vendors will be able to give support for automatically recovering from some faults although the detection of these can be as hard as the subsequent corrective action.

At the level of MPI, there has been some discussion of handling fault tolerance and we encourage further work on FT-MPI.

A standard way of guarding against such a failure is to use checkpointing so that the computation can be restarted if a problem is detected. This is, however, expensive and can be difficult to schedule without introducing extra synchronization points. A faster means of checkpointing data, say to FLASH memories, may help. On some computations, for example sparse direct factorization, checkpointing can be a problem but for sparse iterative methods it might be more easily accommodated.

In addition to checkpointing or when checkpointing is not feasible, there are other algorithmic tricks that can be done. Examples are to do a backward computation from the point of failure (possible for the more simple algorithms) or to perform additional computations that can also be very useful in detecting when there is a problem. This is reminiscent of check sum computations when using hand held computers and indeed some suggested approaches are very close to these earlier methods.

3.5   Uncertainty Quantification

As we move to ever more complicated computation sometimes with inexact data, the issue of uncertainty quantification looms high in the desires of application scientists for support from algorithm and code designers. It is, however, very important to recognize that such issues span very many levels. For example there can be problems or uncertainties with: input data, modelling of physical phenomena, uncertainty in observed data, approximation of continuous by discrete model, solution of resulting equations, and the effect of finite-precision arithmetic.

Many of these are more in the domain of the application scientist although we can and should provide tools for assisting them in this important quest. For example: stochastic optimization and stochastic partial differential equations, the use of mixed-precision arithmetic and refinement, and software for assessing accuracy.

3.6   Programmability

While the core of our numerical algorithms might continue to be in standard languages like C or Fortran probably using MPI for parallel constructs, it is recognized that there are and perhaps need to be further developments to both make the programming more efficient and robust and also to be able to exploit more complicated parallel architectures. Certainly stronger support for multi-level parallelism is needed, perhaps better combinations of MPI or OpenMP and further developments of MPI to include improved collectives, including sparse and non-blocking collectives and stronger support for fault tolerance.

Other developments of programming languages based on a partitioned global address space (PGAS) parallel programming model are also available and may become more widely used. Prime examples of these are UPC and co-array Fortran.

3.7   Floating-Point Issues

It is all very well to develop algorithms that perform well on high performance computers but there is little point in getting an answer quickly if it is wrong! It is thus particularly important to ensure that any new algorithm is stable. This can be an issue in block algorithms of the kind we mentioned in Section 3.2.

In that section, we also emphasized the problem of data movement and clearly a lower precision floating-point number will require less storage than one at higher precision. Thus if we can compute in lower precision but still get acceptable results then the amount of data handled and potentially moved could be less. This has led to the rediscovery and development of algorithms that perform much of the computation in single precision but have some kind of corrective action, perhaps in higher precision, to ensure that the final accuracy is not compromised. An example of this is the use of iterative refinement when computing the solution of linear equations, where only the residual need be computed in the higher precision. This results in mixed-precision arithmetic. On the other end of the scale, some applications require very high accuracy in some parts of the computation so the mixed arithmetic could also involve some computations in extended precision.

A further issue in floating-point arithmetic is the problem of reproducibility, particularly acute when computing in parallel. This problem is mainly caused by the lack of associativity in floating-point arithmetic so that the sequence of performing the arithmetic operations can influence the result. This sequence could be changed in a parallel environment because of influences outside the program itself and this indeterminacy mitigates against reproducibility. Getting different results for different runs of the same computation can be disconcerting for users even if, in a sense, both results are correct. Giving an estimate of the backward or forward error in the computation may help but it can be useful if the vendor could have a mode of running which would be far less efficient but could give a better possibility of getting a reproducible result. This would also be very useful for debugging purposes.

3.8 Training

Training is crucial in many ways both in order to develop and maintain the skills necessary to develop the underlying mathematics and numerical algorithms and software but also to train potential application scientists to recognize and use the tools so developed. In addition to the mathematics, the former group will need training in using programming models and basic tools, for example in partitioning or the use of basic algebra kernels.

The report also noted the relationship to already existing European initiatives involving training including DEISA, PRACE, and HPC-Europa.

4 Conclusions

The main conclusion of our Working Group was that the work of European scientists is recognized at a high global level and there is much interaction between individuals and teams in Europe and groups from outside Europe, particularly with the USA. This is true in all the domains addressed by our study. However, there are four main reasons why we cannot be complacent with the current situation and why more resources are required if Europe is to maintain its competitive edge.

The *first* concerns the complexity of moving to the Exascale domain. Although we do not know the detail of the hardware that will be available, we can be certain that the level of parallelism will increase significantly, that machines will be more complex and heterogeneous, and that the hierarchical structure of many current Petascale systems will be even more pronounced. Thus, in common with our colleagues in the US and Japan, we recognize that considerably more effort and manpower will be required to even begin to address this complexity and so additional resources will be necessary just to stay still as it were.

The *second* concern is that most of the high level research in Europe is done by small groups some of which are only just of critical mass. Thus support is needed to strengthen such groups to keep them at or above critical mass, both for today's challenges and those in the future.

The *third* concern that is also primarily a problem in Europe is that the networking of the groups is not at a level to sustain European competence at this next stage. Indeed many groups have closer contact with America than with their peers in other European countries. Thus there is a great need for support with networking.

The *fourth* concern is the lack of long-term funding to support the maintenance of software libraries, including their porting to new hardware platforms. This is extremely important because application developers will not commit to using software libraries if they are not positive that they will remain supported. In the US, the Department of Energy labs have played a major role in parallel software development, and one of the keys to their success has been the fact that they have the continuity of funding and users trust them to continue supporting the software packages they develop. In the European setting, this could be addressed through a co-design centre that would also involve hardware vendors. Their involvement would be particularly important in the development of kernels optimized to the new architectures. This centre would also house experts with extensive expertise in software engineering and parallel computing who could assume the task of maintaining the software base. Thus the centre could address the two main European weaknesses of fragmentation of research effort and long-term support for software.

In our report, estimates of the number of person years for each topic are presented, broken into subareas. From these, we have calculated that a total of around 2000 person years of effort needs to be funded to keep existing groups at a critical mass and to address the aforementioned Exascale challenges. Our request is thus for general support for all the topics mentioned at a level of a little over 10 million euros per year for the 2012-2030 timeframe. We would envisage support through normal research mechanisms: targeted calls, support for students, postdocs, and engineers, for networking and training. We are also proposing a co-design centre at a cost of roughly 4 million euros a year for the centre including an extensive visitor programme.

To put the request for funding into context note that the amount suggested is **small** relative to the costs of Exascale hardware; perhaps $200 million with around $20 million per year in electricity costs!

Acknowledgements. The talk at EuroPar and Sections 3 and 4 of this report were largely prepared from the report of Working Group 4.3. Thus the involvement of all the people listed in Table 2 is gratefully acknowledged.

On Reducing I/O Overheads
in Large-Scale Invariant Subspace Projections

Hasan Metin Aktulga[1], Chao Yang[1], Ümit V. Çatalyürek[2], Pieter Maris[3],
James P. Vary[3], and Esmond G. Ng[1]

[1] Lawrence Berkeley National Laboratory, Berkeley CA 94720, USA
[2] The Ohio State University, Columbus OH 43210, USA
[3] Iowa State University, Ames IA 50011, USA

Abstract. Obtaining highly accurate predictions on properties of light
atomic nuclei using the Configuration Interaction (CI) method requires
computing the lowest eigenvalues and associated eigenvectors of a large
many-body nuclear Hamiltonian, H. One particular approach, the J-
scheme, requires the projection of the H matrix into an invariant subspace. Since the matrices can be very large, enormous computing power
is needed while significant stresses are put on the memory and I/O sub-
systems. By exploiting the inherent localities in the problem and making
use of the MPI one-sided communication routines backed by RDMA operations available in the new parallel architectures, we show that it is
possible to reduce the I/O overheads drastically for large problems. This
is demonstrated in the subspace projection phase of J-scheme calculations on ^{6}Li nucleus, where our new implementation based on one-sided
MPI communications outperforms the previous I/O based implementation by almost a factor of 10.

1   Introduction

The direct solution of the quantum many-body problem transcends several areas
of physics and chemistry. Nuclear physics faces the multiple hurdles of a very
strong interaction, three-nucleon interactions, and complicated collective motion
dynamics. The configuration interaction (CI) method requires computing the
many-body wavefunctions associated with the discrete energy levels of nuclei by
partially diagonalizing the nuclear many-body Hamiltonian, H, in a many-body
basis space constructed from harmonic oscillator single-particle wavefunctions
[1]. Typically, one is only interested in a limited number of low energy states
[2,3], but for certain applications, computing a relatively large number of states
(and their wavefunctions) with a prescribed total angular momentum J is crucial.
We will refer to this type of calculation as a *total-J calculation* throughout this
paper. Investigating nuclear level densities as a function of J and excitation
energy, and evaluating scattering amplitudes for different values of J [4,5] are
among the target applications for total-J calculations.

In the total-J approach, eigenvalues and eigenvectors associated with a given
J value are computed through a diagonalization of the total angular momentum

M. Alexander et al. (Eds.): Euro-Par 2011 Workshops, Part I, LNCS 7155, pp. 305–314, 2012.
© Springer-Verlag Berlin Heidelberg 2012

square operator $\hat{J}^2$ [6], followed by a diagonalization of the projection of H onto a desired (and common) invariant subspace of H and $\hat{J}^2$. There are three major stages in this approach:

1. Computing the invariant subspace of $\hat{J}^2$ for a given eigenvalue $\lambda = J(J+1)$,
2. Projecting the H matrix into this subspace,
3. Finally, extracting the desired spectral information from the resulting lower dimensional Hamiltonian.

In [6], we present a multi-level method based on a greedy load-balancing algorithm to compute the invariant subspace Z of $\hat{J}^2$ efficiently on a large-scale distributed memory machine. Here we tackle the second stage of the total-J calculation, namely the projection of the H matrix into the subspace spanned by the columns of Z, i.e., $H' = Z^T H Z$.

Subspace projection calculation consists of two successive matrix multiplications, where the many-body Hamiltonian H is a square sparse symmetric matrix and Z has a block diagonal structure. These special properties of the matrices involved allow the subspace projection task to be divided into many independent subproblems of smaller sizes (see Sect. 2). However, due to the large dimensions of H and Z, such calculations demand significant amounts of computational resources, especially in terms of storage spaces. For example, in the problems that we study in Sect. 4, the dimensions of the H matrix becomes as large as 1.7×10^8 and the number of columns of Z is approximately 2.7×10^7.

In this paper, we describe an efficient scheme for performing large-scale invariant subspace projections on distributed memory machines. To exploit parallelism, we decompose the projection calculation into a number of smaller computational tasks, each of which can be completed by a single processing unit, as described in Sect. 3. A major decision that we must make is where to store the Z matrix, whose size can be on the order of terabytes, and how to access its diagonal blocks efficiently. We discuss and compare two strategies for storing Z. In the first scheme, which we describe in Sect. 4, Z is stored on the disk. Each processing unit reads in the required blocks of Z whenever they are needed. We will refer to this scheme as the out-of-core (OOC) implementation. Clearly, the OOC implementation is prone to severe I/O overheads (see Sect. 4). Our alternative scheme described in Sect. 5 is based on distributing the diagonal blocks of Z among all processors and fetching data from potentially remote memory by efficient one-sided MPI calls. However, our incore implementation suffers from another kind of overhead: communication latency, which can easily be overcome by buffering. Our experiments and observations are summarized in Sect. 5.

2   The Strutures of H and Z Matrices

Figure 1 illustrates the structures of matrices H and Z. Each row (and column) of H corresponds to, what is known in nuclear configuration interaction calculation as, a many-body basis state, which is a Slater determinant of single-particle states (anti-symmetrized product of single-particle states). The total number of many-body states, D, is determined by the number of particles in the nucleus, n_{part}, and a truncation parameter, N_{max}. A higher N_{max} value yields a more accurate finite dimensional approximation to the nuclear many-body Hamiltonian at the expense of an exponential growth in its dimension. As shown in Fig. 1, H is sparse. Its sparsity pattern is determined by the type of interaction used: a 3-body potential leads to a less sparse matrix than a 2-body potential. We use a 2-body interaction potential for the simulations presented in this paper, which means an entry H_{ij} of the Hamiltonian is non-zero only when the number of different single-particle states corresponding to row i and column j of H is at most 2.

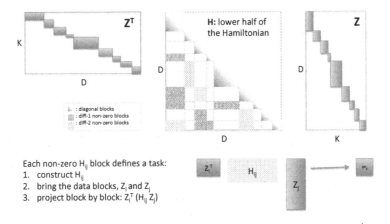

Fig. 1. Overview of the invariant subspace projection problem

The block structure of H seen in Fig. 1 results from a particular grouping of the many-body basis states based on their single particle quantum numbers (see [6] for details). Each non-zero block in H is itself sparse, and thus can be stored in a sparse matrix format. What is worth noting here is that each group of many-body basis state is invariant under the $\hat{J}^2$ operator. Consequently, such a grouping scheme produces a block diagonal representation of the $\hat{J}^2$ operator.

3   Task Decomposition for Parallel Processing

The special structures of H and Z matrices allow us to decompose the projection calculation into smaller tasks. Let i and j denote the block indices, then each non-zero H_{ij} block defines a subtask for the invariant subspace projection problem: $H'_{ij} = Z_i{}^T H_{ij} Z_j$, a sparse matrix multiplied with two dense blocks, resulting in a dense block of smaller dimensions (see Fig. 1). Accomplishing each small task involves construction of the H_{ij} block based on the interaction between the ith and jth many-body state groups and bringing the Z_i and Z_j blocks into local memory.

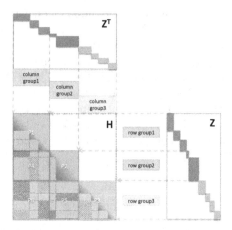

Fig. 2. Decomposition of the invariant subspace projection problem

Because H is symmetric, we configure processors into an $n_r \times n_r$ lower triangular grid T as shown in Fig. 2, so that the lower triangular part of the matrix can be distributed among $n_r(n_r + 1)/2$ processors. The partitioning of H is based on a cyclic distribution of the many-body basis groups over the diagonal processors of T. This partitioning also yields a logical partitioning of the Z blocks among the diagonal processors. Row and column processor groups are created within T to facilitate data communication. The partitioned Z blocks are to be shared (logically) among all processors within the same row and column groups. Such a distribution scheme maximizes the data locality during the subspace projection calculations.

Directly associated with the partitioning of the H matrix is the distribution of the subspace projection subtasks, $Z_i^T H_{ij} Z_j$. Each processor is responsible for computing the projection of non-zero H_{ij} blocks within its partition. In order to accomplish these subtasks, each off-diagonal processor needs only two sets of diagonal blocks of Z (one mapped to its row group, the other one mapped to its column group), while a diagonal processor needs only a single set of Z blocks. We will refer to the blocks of Z mapped to a processor's row group as that processor's row data blocks, similarly to the blocks of Z mapped to a processor's column group as its column data blocks.

4   An Out-of-Core Approach

A $Z_i^T H_{ij} Z_j$ subtask has three steps: (i) construction of the non-zero H_{ij} based on the interaction between the many-body groups i and j, (ii) bringing the associated row data block Z_i and column data block Z_j into local memory, (iii) and finally computing $Z_i^T H_{ij} Z_j$. Ideally, we would like to store all blocks of Z

that will be needed by a processor to perform all its projection subtasks in its local memory. However, for large problems, this is generally not possible due to the limited amount of memory on each processor. Therefore, it is important to carefully consider where to store the diagonal blocks of Z and how to bring them to local memory.

One approach we examined is to store the diagonal blocks of Z on the disk and let each processor read them from there whenever necessary. Algorithm 1 gives the pseudo-code for our out-of-core approach, which we will refer to as the OOC implementation. In order to reduce read contention on a single file, n_r files (one file per diagonal processor) are created to store the diagonal blocks of the Z matrix. To reduce I/O overheads in OOC, once a column data block Z_j is read from the disk, all subtasks associated with that data block are processed, *i.e.*, we follow a column-major order for processing non-zero blocks of H.

---

input : Processor column and row group indices: $mycol$ and $myrow$
output: Projection of the part of H assigned to the processor

Open $colfile$ that contains Z_j's mapped to the $mycol$th diagonal processor;
Open $rowfile$ that contains Z_i's mapped to the $myrow$th diagonal processor;

foreach $Z_j \in colfile$ **do**
    Read Z_j from $colfile$;
    foreach $Z_i \in rowfile$ **do**
        if $H_{ij} \neq 0$ **then**
            Read Z_i from $rowfile$;
            Construct H_{ij};
            $H'_{ij} = Z_i^T H_{ij} Z_j$;
        end
    end
end

Algorithm 1. An OOC algorithm for computing $H'_{ij} = Z_i^T H_{ij} Z_j$

We tested the performance of the OOC implementation on the Hopper system at the National Energy Research Scientific Computing Center (NERSC) [2]. Table 1 summarizes the performance of the OOC implementation on some of the real problems that we typically solve using the total-J code. OOC performs well when the size of the Z matrix is relatively small. We suspect that this is due to the availability of I/O buffers managed by the OS kernel, where the entire column and (more importantly) row files that contain the needed blocks of Z can be buffered effectively, when these files are small in size. However, as the Z matrix becomes larger, the efficiency of the OOC implementation drops sharply – the useful work done, which corresponds to the time spent when processors are not idle, for the $N_{max}=14$, J=3 case is only about 1%.

---

[2] See http://www.nersc.gov/users/computational-systems/hopper/

Table 1. Performance of the OOC implementation on total-J calculations of ^{6}Li with various parameters. $|Z|$ denotes the size of the Z matrix, n_{dblks} is the number of Z (data) blocks, n_{tasks} is the number of non-zero blocks in H. For each calculation, the total execution time (in seconds) and the percentage of overhead (*i.e.*, I/O time) is given.

calculation	$|Z|$ (GB)	n_{dblks}	n_{tasks}	n_{p}	overhead (%)	total (s)
$N_{\mathrm{max}}{=}12$, J=0	2.7	2.5×10^5	1.12×10^8	946	45%	159
$N_{\mathrm{max}}{=}12$, J=1	7.5	2.5×10^5	1.36×10^8	946	47%	204
$N_{\mathrm{max}}{=}12$, J=2	10.6	2.5×10^5	1.52×10^8	946	63%	319
$N_{\mathrm{max}}{=}12$, J=3	11.3	2.5×10^5	1.60×10^8	946	69%	358
$N_{\mathrm{max}}{=}12$, J=4	10.0	2.5×10^5	1.60×10^8	946	83%	551
$N_{\mathrm{max}}{=}14$, J=3	67.1	7.4×10^5	7.04×10^8	10,011	99%	9200

5   Distributed In-Core Approach

An alternative to the OOC implementation is to distribute and store a single copy of the blocks of Z in the local memory available to the processors. In a sense, we utilize the global address space available to the compute nodes as "disk". Our goal is to be able to tackle problems much bigger than the ones presented in Tab. 1 (*e.g.*, ^{6}Li, $N_{\mathrm{max}}{=}16$, J=5 where we expect $|Z| \approx 1$ TB excluding any auxiliary data structures) and to develop an implementation that can withstand the current trend of decreasing memory space per processor ratio. However, such an approach would require each processor to fetch data from remote memory belonging to a different processor during the projection calculation. The communication overhead may increase the turn-around time significantly, if regular MPI send/receives are used for fetching data. This overhead can be reduced by making use of one-sided MPI communication routines. On Hopper, each node is equipped with an RDMA engine which can handle remote memory access requests without interrupting the computation performed on processors residing on that node. So we take advantage of the one-sided **MPI_Get** operations available with Cray's xt-mpich2 MPI library on Hopper.

Our incore implementation balances the memory load among processors by distributing the blocks of Z logically mapped to the ith diagonal processor cyclically among processors that belong to the ith row and column communication groups. Before starting the projection calculations based on this distribution, each processor reads its share of Z blocks from its row and column data files into the memory. Contrary to our expectations, the incore version did not produce any improvements in terms of performance for the test cases listed in Tab. 1. A relatively small calculation for ^{6}Li, $N_{\mathrm{max}}{=}12$, J=0 took over 400 seconds on 946 processors. This performance compares unfavorably to the 159 seconds required in the OOC implementation. A detailed performance analysis reveals that reading the blocks of Z takes only about 20 seconds. The wall clock time spent in waiting for the completion of **MPI_Get** calls is about 250 seconds on average (more than 60% of the total completion time).

We believe that this unexpectedly large communication overhead is largely due to network latency, rather than the inadequacy of network bandwidth. Because in the ^{6}Li, $N_{max}=12$, J=0 case, individual Z blocks are not large in size, but there are over 100 million small tasks, each of which typically requires two different blocks of the Z matrix. Column major processing of tasks helps keeping the number of **MPI_Get** calls roughly equal to the number of tasks, which is still prohibitively high. MPI-2 specification [7] requires even read-only accesses to remote memory locations, which is the exclusive usage of MPI one-sided calls in our incore algorithm, to happen inside an epoch. The only way to start and end an epoch in MPI-2 without synchronization is to enclose remote memory accesses within a pair of **MPI_Win_lock** and **MPI_Win_unlock** calls. This locking–unlocking protocol incurs an overhead of 4α, where α denotes the network latency, for each **MPI_Get** call. As discussed by Gropp et. al. [8], it is possible to detect this special access pattern and reduce the latency overhead to 0 by combining the locking–unlocking phase with the **MPI_Get** call itself. But to the best of our knowledge, this optimization has not been included in Cray's xt-mpich2 implementation.

Algorithm 2 illustrates the final version of the incore implementation. To reduce the latency overheads associated with starting and ending epochs, all **MPI_Get** calls destined to the same remote memory address space are consolidated within a single epoch. Consequently, instead of looping over the column and row files as in the OOC algorithm, the incore algorithm loops over processor sub-groups which now store the needed Z blocks. Each processor maintains a list of destinations for the Z blocks it needs and issues **MPI_Get** calls to easily fetch them. Note that the **MPI_Getv** call in Alg. 2 is not actually an MPI-library call, it is a wrapper which initiates an epoch, issues a sequence of **MPI_Get** calls destined to a target processor, and terminates the epoch. So between the initial version of the incore algorithm described above and its final version given here, the number of **MPI_Get** calls stays the same. However, the number of epochs created by a processor is reduced from being roughly equal to the number of tasks assigned to it down to n_r^2. The effect of this reduction can be seen immediately in ^{6}Li, $N_{max}=12$, J=0 calculations on 946 processors where the running time of the final incore algorithm is 250 seconds (down from 400 seconds) and the communication overhead is reduced to 40% (down from over 60%).

In Fig. 3, we compare the performance of the OOC and the final distributed incore implementations for different J values in ^{6}Li, $N_{max}=12$ calculations on 946 processors. While the OOC version initially outperforms the incore implementation due to the small size of the Z matrix, the incore implementation delivers up to 2.8x speed-up over the OOC version for larger values of J where the size of the Z matrix is considerably larger (see Tab. 1). But the real advantage of the incore implementation becomes evident during the much larger ^{6}Li, $N_{max}=14$, J=3 calculations, where we obtain almost 10x speed-up over the OOC implementation, see Fig. 4.

```
input  : column & row group ids: mycol, myrow
input  : column & row group communicators: row_comm, col_comm
input  : manybody_groups (non-empty only on diagonal processors)
output: Projection of the part of H assigned to the processor

if diagonal processor then
 |  ids ← pids ∈ row_comm ∪ pids ∈ col_comm;
 |  host ← distribute manybody_groups cyclically over ids;
end
host ← Bcast(host, ids);
my_mb_groups ← Scatter(manybody_groups, ids);

cpids ← Bcast(ids, col_comm);      // processor subgroup to look for Zᵢs
rpids ← Bcast(ids, row_comm);      // processor subgroup to look for Zⱼs
my_dblks ← Load from column data file based on my_mb_groups;
my_dblks ← Load from row data file based on my_mb_groups;

foreach c ∈ cpids do
 |  cdlist ← {Zᵢ|need(Zᵢ) ∧ host(Zᵢ) = c};
 |  MPI_Getv(c, cdlist, cdblks);
 |  foreach r ∈ rpids do
 |   |  rdlist ← {Zⱼ|need(Zⱼ) ∧ host(Zⱼ) = r};
 |   |  MPI_Getv(r, rdlist, rdblks);
 |   |  foreach Zᵢ ∈ cdblks, Zⱼ ∈ rdblks do
 |   |   |  Construct Hᵢⱼ;
 |   |   |  H'ᵢⱼ = ZᵢᵀHᵢⱼZⱼ;
 |   |  end
 |  end
end
```

Algorithm 2. Pseudo-code for the incore implementation

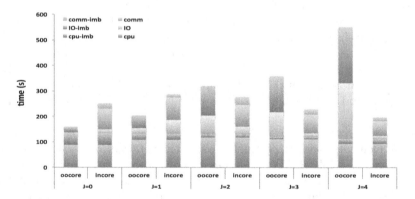

Fig. 3. Comparison of the performances of the incore and the OOC implementations. Total computation time (as denoted by the height of each bar) is examined in 6 parts: average CPU time (cpu), cpu load imbalance (cpu-imb), IO time (IO), IO time imbalance (IO-imb), communication time (comm), communication time imbalance (comm-imb). Note that, the OOC implementation does not do any communication. In the incore implementation, no IO-imb is measured.

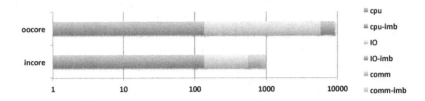

Fig. 4. Comparison of the performances of incore and OOC implementations for the ^{6}Li, $N_{\max}=14$, $J=3$ calculations on 10,011 processors, showing a 10x speed-up

6   Future Challenges

A detailed examination of the performance of incore algorithm reveals that the incore implementation is still prone to severe overheads. For example, for the $N_{\max}=14$, $J=3$ calculations on 10,011 processors, the percentage of useful computation (as measured by the ratio of average CPU time per processors to total wallclock time) is merely 10%. Out of the total 970 s, on average about 400 s is spent for reading the diagonal blocks of Z to memory and about 300 s is spent on communication. Another source of the inefficiency in the incore algorithm is the potential load imbalances among processors. Load imbalance caused by the basic round-robin distribution of tasks is not severe for ^{6}Li calculations where variations among task sizes are not drastic. But for heavier nuclei, we observe that there is a large variation among task sizes which could potentially cause severe load imbalances.

Some communication overheads may be reduced through further optimizations on Alg. 2. For example, one can pack multiple **MPI_Get** calls that are made to retrieve data from consecutive memory locations into one. Other one-sided communication libraries (such as ARMCI [10]) remains to be explored as they offer optimizations not present in the current MPI-2 implementations.

However, in order to alleviate the problems described above and further reduce overheads that were encountered in the subspace projection phase of total-J calculations, smarter heuristics, such as the technique presented in [9], which try to balance the task and memory load while minimizing communication overheads are necessary.

7   Conclusions

In this paper, we explore different approaches to tackle the challenging problem of large-scale invariant subspace projection problem arising in the context of total-J calculations and analyze their performances on real problems of interest to the nuclear physics community. We show that, by exploiting the inherent localities in the problem and making use of the MPI one-sided communication routines, it is possible to reduce the I/O and communication overheads drastically for large-scale data dependent problems. Despite the significant speed-ups achieved with the final version of the total-J code, our analysis shows that the useful work to total execution time ratio is still low (as low as 10%). We identify the sources of inefficiencies through a careful examination of the performance profiles of individual processors and lay out future research directions that may reduce overhead and provide better scalability to this important problem.

We realize that eigenvalue calculations are central to several problems in the area of computational science and engineering. Also high performance data-intensive computing is a field with growing interest. Therefore we believe that the results of this work and insights we have gained can be of much broader interest.

Acknowledgment. The computational results were obtained at the National Energy Research Scientific Computing Center (NERSC), which is supported under contract number DE-AC02-05CH11232. Research was supported in part by the DOE grants DE-FC02-09ER41582 (SciDAC-UNEDF), DE-FG02-87ER40371 and DE-FC02-06ER2775; by the NSF grants CNS-0643969, OCI-0904809, OCI-0904802 and NSF-0904782.

References

1. Vary, J.P., Maris, P., Ng, E., Yang, C., Sosonkina, M.: Ab initio nuclear structure: The Large sparse matrix eigenvalue problem. J. Phys. Conf. Ser. 180, 012083 (2009)
2. Maris, P., Shirokov, A.M., Vary, J.P.: Ab initio nuclear structure simulations: The Speculative F-14 nucleus. Phys. Rev. C 81, 021301 (2010)
3. Maris, P., Vary, J.P., Navratil, P., Ormand, W.E., Nam, H., Dean, D.J.: Origin of the anomalous long lifetime of 14C. Phys. Rev. Lett. 106, 202502 (2011)
4. Shirokov, A.M., Mazur, A.I., Zaytsev, S.A., Vary, J.P., Weber, T.A.: Nucleon nucleon interaction in the J matrix inverse scattering approach and few nucleon systems. Phys. Rev. C 70, 044005 (2004)
5. Shirokov, A.M., Mazur, A.I., Vary, J.P., Mazur, E.A.: Inverse scattering J-matrix approach to nucleon-nucleus scattering and the shell model. Phys. Rev. C 79, 014610 (2009)
6. Aktulga, H.M., Yang, C., Ng, E., Maris, P., Vary, J.P.: Large-scale Parallel null space calculation for nuclear configuration interaction. In: Proc. of HPCS 2011, Istanbul, Turkey, July 4 - 8 (2011)
7. Gropp, W., Huss-Lederman, S., Lumsdaine, A., Lusk, E., Nitzberg, B., Saphir, W., Snir, M.: MPI – The Complete Reference. The MPI-2 Extensions, vol. 2. MIT Press, Cambridge (1998)
8. Gropp, W., Thakur, R.: An Evaluation of Implementation Options for MPI One-Sided Communication. In: Di Martino, B., Kranzlmüller, D., Dongarra, J. (eds.) EuroPVM/MPI 2005. LNCS, vol. 3666, pp. 415–424. Springer, Heidelberg (2005)
9. Çatalyürek, Ü.V., Kaya, K., Uçar, B.: Integrated Data Placement and Task Assignment for Scientific Workflows in Clouds. In: Proc. of HPDC, The Fourth International Workshop on Data Intensive Distributed Computing (DIDC) (June 2011)
10. Nieplocha, J., Tipparaju, V., Krishnan, M., Panda, D.: High performance remote memory access comunications: The ARMCI approach. International Journal of High Performance Computing and Applications 20(2), 233–253 (2006)

Enabling Next-Generation Parallel Circuit Simulation with Trilinos

Chris Baker[1], Erik Boman[2], Mike Heroux[2], Eric Keiter[2], Siva Rajamanickam[2], Rich Schiek[2], and Heidi Thornquist[2]

[1] Oak Ridge National Laboratory, Oak Ridge, TN 37831, USA
[2] Sandia National Laboratories, Albuquerque, NM 87185, USA*

Abstract. The Xyce Parallel Circuit Simulator, which has demonstrated scalable circuit simulation on hundreds of processors, heavily leverages the high-performance scientific libraries provided by Trilinos. With the move towards multi-core CPUs and GPU technology, retaining this scalability on future parallel architectures will be a challenge. This paper will discuss how Trilinos is an enabling technology that will optimize the trade-off between effort and impact for application codes, like Xyce, in their transition to becoming next-generation simulation tools.

Keywords: circuit simulation, parallel computing, hybrid computing, preconditioned iterative methods, load balancing.

1 Motivation

Traditional analog circuit simulation, originally made popular by the Berkeley SPICE program [1], does not scale well beyond tens of thousands of devices, due to the use of sparse direct matrix solvers [2]. Given the importance of this simulation tool for circuit design verification, many attempts have been made to allow for faster, larger-scale circuit simulation. Fast-SPICE tools use event-driven simulation techniques and lookup tables for precomputed device evaluations, while hierarchical simulators use circuit-level partitioning algorithms [4,5] and more efficient data structures to enable the simulation of much larger problems. Unfortunately, the approximations inherent to these simulation approaches can break down under some circumstances, rendering such tools unreliable.

The availability of inexpensive clusters, multi-core CPUs, and GPUs, has resulted in significant interest for efficient parallel circuit simulation. Several approaches have been investigated for enabling parallel SPICE-accurate simulation. These generally involve a higher-level partitioning of the devices [6] or lower-level partitioning of the linear system of equations [7] to facilitate the creation of a more efficient parallel matrix solver. Recently, GPUs have been used

---

* Sandia National Laboratories is a multi-program laboratory managed and operated by Sandia Corporation, a wholly owned subsidiary of Lockheed Martin Corporation, for the U.S. Department of Energy's National Nuclear Security Administration under contract DE-AC04-94AL85000.

M. Alexander et al. (Eds.): Euro-Par 2011 Workshops, Part I, LNCS 7155, pp. 315–323, 2012.
© Springer-Verlag Berlin Heidelberg 2012

to accelerate transistor model evaluation [8], which can dominate time-domain circuit simulation. While these are examples of targeted improvements to parallel performance, efficient circuit simulation on next-generation architectures will require exploiting both coarse and fine-grained parallelism throughout the entire simulation flow.

Xyce [9], is a simulator designed "from-the-ground-up" to be distributed memory-parallel, and is intended for a spectrum of parallel platforms, from high-end supercomputers to multi-core desktops. It relies primarily upon a message-passing implementation (MPI) [10], but employs software abstractions that allow the simulator to adapt to other parallel paradigms. Xyce already leverages many of the high-performance scientific libraries provided by Trilinos [11] for its MPI-based implementation. This paper will present the enabling technologies provided by Trilinos that will allow Xyce to retain scalable performance on next-generation architectures.

2   Background

Circuit simulation adheres to a general flow, as shown in Fig. 1. The circuit, described by a netlist file, is transformed via modified nodal analysis (MNA) into a set of nonlinear differential algebraic equations (DAEs)

$$\frac{dq(x(t))}{dt} + f(x(t)) = b(t), \tag{1}$$

where $x(t) \in \mathbb{R}^N$ is the vector of circuit unknowns, q and f are functions representing the dynamic and static circuit elements (respectively), and $b(t) \in \mathbb{R}^M$ is the input vector. For any analysis type, the initial starting point is this set of DAEs. The numerical approach employed to compute solutions to equation (1) is predicated by the analysis type.

Transient and DC analysis are two commonly used simulation modes, in which the set of equations (1), more generally expressed as $F(x, x') = 0$, is solved by numerical integration methods corresponding to the nested solver loop in Fig. 1. Both analysis types require the solution to a sequence of nonlinear equations, $F(x) = 0$. Typically, Newton's method is used to solve these nonlinear equations, resulting in a sequence of linear systems

$$Ax = b$$

that involve the conductance, $G(t) = \frac{df}{dx}(x(t))$, and capacitance, $C(t) = \frac{dq}{dx}(x(t))$, matrices. For DC analysis, the q terms are not present in equation (1), so the linear system only involves the conductance matrix.

The computational expense in circuit simulation is dominated by repeatedly solving linear systems of equations, which are at the center of the nested solver loop (Fig. 1). Solving these linear systems requires their assembly, which depends upon device evaluations for the whole circuit. This means the computational expense includes both the device evaluations and the numerical method used to solve the linear systems. The linear systems solved during transient and DC

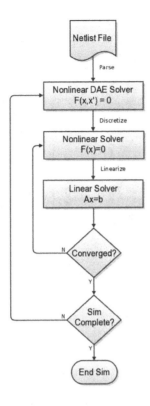

Fig. 1. General circuit simulation flow

analysis are typically sparse, have heterogeneous non-symmetric structure, and are often ill-conditioned. Direct sparse solvers [2,3] are the industry standard approach because of their reliability and ease of use. However, direct solvers scale poorly with problem size and become impractical when the linear system has hundreds of thousands of unknowns or more.

3   Xyce-Trilinos Interface

Xyce is written in ANSI C++ and exploits modern software paradigms to enable the development of a production simulator as well as a testbed for parallel algorithm research. Xyce uses abstract interfaces and runtime polymorphism throughout the code, which facilitates code reuse and algorithmic flexibility. Many of the higher-level abstractions, relating to the analysis type or time integration methods, have implementations that are contained in Xyce. However, the lower-level numerical abstractions, related to the nested solver loop in Fig. 1, have interfaces to the high-performance scientific libraries provided by Trilinos. The current Trilinos software stack that is employed by Xyce is illustrated in Fig. 2.

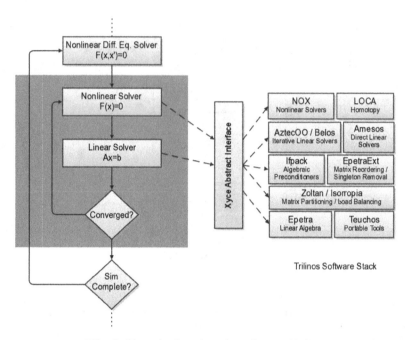

Fig. 2. Nested solver loop interface to Trilinos

Xyce employs these software abstractions to enable adaptation to future parallel paradigms and arithmetic precision strategies with minimal effort. Xyce currently uses MPI with double precision arithmetic through essential Petra (Epetra). However, future computational platforms may require the use of other parallel paradigms, such as hybrid techniques that combine MPI with threads, to achieve optimal performance. Furthermore, to address ill-conditioned matrices, it may prove useful to use higher precision arithmetic in the linear solvers. These next-generation computational strategies are the motivation for the newer Trilinos linear algebra packages: templated Petra (Tpetra) and Kokkos. Tpetra provides a templated interface to parallel linear algebra and Kokkos contains the underlying computational kernels enabling platform-dependent optimizations. Several pre-existing Trilinos packages can use Tpetra, like NOX, LOCA, Belos, and Teuchos, and many other packages are under development to provide direct solvers and preconditioners using Tpetra.

4   Next-Generation Circuit Simulation

Parallelism can be integrated into every step of the nested solver loop shown in Fig. 1. Furthermore, parallelism can be achieved through both coarse-scale (multi-processor) and fine-scale (multi-threaded) approaches. A composition of these two approaches will provide circuit simulation with the best performance impact on the widest variety of next-generation architectures. As discussed before, the majority of the computational time is spent in device evaluations and linear solvers, so this paper will present some of Trilinos' capabilities that will improve the parallelism pertaining to those specific tasks. In particular, the focus is on four packages that will enable more efficient circuit simulation in the migration to next-generation architectures: Epetra, ShyLU, and Zoltan. Numerical results will be presented for Epetra and ShyLU.

4.1   Computational Setup

Results presented in this section are generated by using Xyce (post release 5.2.1) and Trilinos release 10.8. The simulations are performed on a single node of a small cluster, where each node has a dual-socket/quad-core Intel Xeon® E5520 2.67 GHz processor and 36 GB of memory. Xyce and Trilinos are compiled using Intel 11.1 compilers, and the MPI library is supplied by OpenMPI version 1.3.3. Table 1 partially describes the circuits used in the numerical experiments. Two of the circuits, ckt2 and ckt3, are from the freely available and well known test suite CircuitSim90 [12], and respectively correspond to the chip2 and ram2k test cases. The other three circuits are proprietary integrated circuits.

Table 1. Circuits: matrix size(N), capacitors(C), MOSFETs(M), resistors(R), voltage sources(V), diodes (D)

Circuit	N	C	M	R	V	D
ckt1	63761	208236	11732	51947	56	0
ckt2	46850	21548	18816	0	21	0
ckt3	32632	156	13880	0	23	0
ckt4	25187	0	71097	0	264	0
ckt5	15622	7507	10173	11057	29	0

4.2   Epetra

Xyce currently uses Epetra underneath its abstract interface to provide serial and distributed parallel linear algebra objects (Fig. 2). As of Trilinos release 10.4, several of the linear algebra objects that Xyce interfaces to provide multi-threading capabilities via OpenMP to speed up basic computations. The classes that have been decorated with "parallel for" pragmas are **Epetra_Vector**, **Epetra_MultiVector**, **Epetra_CrsMatrix**, and **Epetra_CrsGraph**. Given that Xyce uses Epetra by default, it requires no code modifications to evaluate these hybrid (MPI with OpenMP) linear algebra computations. However, for Xyce, iterative linear solvers exercise these computations the most, which makes them necessary for illustrating the potential performance improvements.

For these numerical experiments, a preconditioned iterative solution strategy is employed that consists of several steps including the removal of dense rows or columns (singleton filtering), block triangular form (BTF) reordering, and hypergraph partitioning [13] to generate a block Jacobi preconditioner. This preconditioner, combined with AztecOO's Generalized Minimal Residual (GMRES) method, has been shown to speed up the simulation time for ckt2, ckt3,

Table 2. Comparison of Xyce simulation times using a non-threaded build of Epetra (MPI only; 2 MPI processes) versus a hybrid build of Epetra (MPI w/ OpenMP; 2 MPI processes, 2 threads per process)

Circuit	Linear Solver (sec.)			Total Simulation (sec.)		
	MPI only	MPI w/OpenMP	x Speedup	MPI only	MPI w/OpenMP	x Speedup
ckt2	92.8	66.1	1.40	165.9	143.3	1.15
ckt3	246.7	101.2	2.43	351.0	198.4	1.76
ckt4	36.2	23.4	1.54	186.5	157.3	1.18
ckt5	92.9	46.3	2.00	239.5	181.3	1.32

ckt4 and ckt5 [14]. For ckt1, this technique results in a large irreducible block, making this preconditioner inefficient, so ckt1 will not be considered for this test.

The results from performing a full transient simulation of these four circuits using Xyce compiled against a non-threaded (MPI only) and a hybrid (MPI w/ OpenMP) build of Trilinos is presented in Table 2. The simulations are performed with 2 MPI processes and, additionally, 2 threads per process for the hybrid build of Trilinos. The timings are averaged from three simulations of each scenario. Table 2 shows the speedup that was achieved using the hybrid build of Trilinos for both the linear solver, as well as for the whole simulation.

As previously mentioned, the potential performance improvements are concentrated in the linear solver, so the dramatic speedups achieved in that portion of the simulation are tempered by the rest of the simulation cost. Performance of the preconditioned iterative methods used in circuit simulation can degrade with an increasing number of MPI processes, as the preconditioner becomes less effective. Using hybrid techniques enable a performance improvement by leveraging shared memory techniques for fine-grained processes, like linear algebra, while maintaining the robustness of the preconditioner by reducing the number of distributed memory processes. The results presented in Table 2 indicate a total simulation speedup between 1.15 and 1.76 by making this minor change.

4.3   ShyLU

ShyLU provides a "hybrid-hybrid" sparse linear solver framework, based on Schur complements, that incorporates both direct and iterative methods, as well as coarse-scale (multi-processor) and fine-scale (multi-threaded) parallelism. It can serve as both a standalone black-box solver for medium-sized problems, and a subdomain solver or preconditioner within a larger distributed-memory framework. ShyLU is targeted towards next-generation architectures with many CPU-like cores within a single compute node, is based on Trilinos, and is also intended to become a Trilinos package.

The Schur complement approach solves the linear system $Ax = b$, by partitioning it into

$$A = \begin{bmatrix} D & C \\ R & G \end{bmatrix}, x = \begin{bmatrix} x_1 \\ x_2 \end{bmatrix}, b = \begin{bmatrix} b_1 \\ b_2 \end{bmatrix}, \tag{2}$$

Table 3. Comparison of average number of outer GMRES iterations using ShyLU as a preconditioner with the BTF-based and block Jacobi preconditioner. A dash indicates simulation failure.

Circuit	ShyLU	BTF	Block Jacobi
ckt1	2	-	151
ckt2	1	4	1
ckt3	1	7	60
ckt4	1	6	6
ckt5	2	9	131

where D and G are square, D is non-singular, and x and b are conformally partitioned to A. The Schur complement, after elimination of the top row, is $S = G - R * D^{-1}C$. Solving $Ax = b$ then consists of the three steps:

1. Solve $Dz = b_1$.
2. Solve $Sx_2 = b_2 - Rz$.
3. Solve $Dx_1 = b_1 - Cx_2$.

Iterative methods, based on Schur complement techniques, have proven effective and robust enough for circuit simulation [15,16]. In general, these approaches partition A so that the first and third steps can be performed quickly using direct methods, and the second step is performed inexactly by either approximating S or using an iterative method to solve $Sx_2 = b_2 - Rz$.

For these numerical experiments, ShyLU is used to generate a preconditioner for AztecOO's GMRES method. The Schur complement is dense for these circuits, so an approximation $\tilde{S} \approx S$ is constructed using value-based dropping with a threshold relative to the diagonal entries (10^{-2}). The approximation $\tilde{S}$ is used as a preconditioner to iteratively solve the Schur complement system, with a relative residual tolerance of 10^{-10} in at most 30 iterations. The initial partitioning of A is performed using the ParMETIS [18] graph partitioner through Zoltan. The simulations are performed with 2 MPI processes without any threads, since KLU [17] is used as the direct solver for the diagonal blocks of D.

The results from performing a full transient simulation of these five circuits using Xyce with different preconditioners is presented in Table 3. The average number of GMRES iterations needed to achieve convergence is reported for each of the three preconditioners: ShyLU (as described above), BTF-based preconditioning (described in Section 4.2), and block Jacobi preconditioning (KLU used to factor the diagonal blocks). While the BTF preconditioner is effective on four of the five circuits, ShyLU performs more consistently and robustly on all five circuits. Alternatively, the block Jacobi preconditioner is sporadically effective in solving these five circuits, performing well on ckt2 and ckt4, but poorly on ckt1, ckt3, and ckt5.

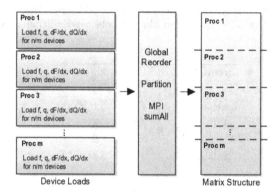

Fig. 3. Parallel load balance for device evaluation and matrix structure

4.4 Zoltan

In general, circuits of interest tend to be heterogeneous in structure, so the optimal parallel load balance for device evaluation (including matrix and residual vector assembly) will likely be different than for solving the linear system. For this reason, Xyce employs a different load balance for both these phases of the simulation, as illustrated in Fig. 3. Zoltan [19] is the parallel partitioning and load balancing library that Xyce currently uses to compute an efficient distributed-memory matrix partition. However, Zoltan can also be employed to develop a device evaluation phase that more intelligently balances the fine-grained computations performed by individual devices.

Xyce currently uses a naive partitioning of devices across MPI processes (Fig. 3), which has proven to be relatively well load balanced and reasonably scalable on current architectures. During the device evaluation phase, on each processor, devices are evaluated sequentially according to type. For example, given a transmission line (RLC circuit), all the resistors will be evaluated and loaded into the matrix and residual vector, then the capacitors, and finally the inductors. These fine-scale sequential computations can be accelerated through multi-threading techniques. However, to avoid race conditions, the static circuit connectivity (graph) can be leveraged to determine in what order the devices should be evaluated. Using the partitioning algorithms in Zoltan, a device ordering can be computed for each node that optimizes the thread-parallelism, and minimizes thread conflicts, during the matrix and residual vector load.

5   Conclusion

Scientific libraries that enable scalable performance of application codes on a wide variety of next-generation architectures are essential. Trilinos is one such project that is attempting to mitigate the challenge of this transition for application codes, like Xyce. This paper presents some enabling technologies delivered through the Epetra, ShyLU, and Zoltan packages that will facilitate this transition for circuit simulation.

References

1. Nagel, L.W.: SPICE 2, a Computer Program to Simulate Semiconductor Circuits, Memorandum ERL-M250, University of California, Berkeley (1975)
2. T. A. Davis: Direct Methods for Sparse Linear Systems. SIAM (2006)
3. Kundert, K.S.: Sparse Matrix Techniques, Circuit Analysis, Simulation and Design (1987)
4. Newton, A.R., Sangiovanni-Vincentelli, A.L.: Relaxation based electrical simulation. IEEE Trans. Comput.-Aided Design Integr. Circuits Syst. 4, 308–330 (1984)
5. White, J.K., Sangiovanni-Vincentelli, A.: Relaxation techniques for the simulation of VLSI circuits. Kluwer Academic Publishers (1987)
6. Fröhlich, N., Riess, B.M., Wever, U., Zheng, Q.: A New Approach for Parallel Simulation of VLSI-Circuits on a Transistor Level. IEEE Transactions on Circuits and Systems Part I 45(6), 601–613 (1998)
7. Peng, H., Cheng, C.K.: Parallel transistor level circuit simulation using domain decomposition methods. In: Proceedings of ASP-DAC 2009, pp. 397–402 (2009)
8. Gulati, K., Croix, J.F., Khatr, S.P., Shastry, R.: Fast circuit simulation on graphics processing units. In: Proceedings of ASP-DAC 2009, pp. 403–408 (2009)
9. Keiter, E.R., Thornquist, H.K., Hoekstra, R.J., Russo, T.V., Schiek, R.L., Rankin, E.L.: Parallel Transistor-Level Circuit Simulation. In: Advanced Simulation and Verification of Electronic and Biological Systems (2011)
10. Gropp, W., Lusk, E., Doss, N., Skjellum, A.: A high-performance, portable implementation of the MPI message passing interface standard. Parallel Computing 22(6), 789–828 (1996)
11. Heroux, M.A., et al.: An Overview of the Trilinos Project. ACM TOMS 31, 397–423 (2005)
12. Barby, J.A., Guindi, R.: CircuitSim93: A circuit simulator benchmarking methodology case study. In: Proc. of Sixth Annual IEEE International ASIC Conference and Exhibit (1993)
13. Devine, K.D., Boman, E.G., Heaphy, R.T., Bisseling, R.H., Catalyurek, U.V.: Parallel Hypergraph Partitioning for Scientific Computing. In: Proc. of 20th International Parallel and Distributed Processing Symposium (2006)
14. Thornquist, H.K., et al.: A Parallel Preconditioning Strategy for Efficient Transistor-Level Circuit Simulation. In: IEEE/ACM International Conference on Computer-Aided Design (ICCAD), pp. 410-417 (2009)
15. Basermann, A., Jaekel, U., Nordhausen, M.: Parallel iterative solvers for sparse linear systems in circuit simulation. Fut. Gen. Comput. Sys. 21(8), 1275–1284 (2005)
16. Bomhof, C.,, H.: vanderVorst: A parallel linear system solver for circuit simulation problems. Num. Lin. Alg. Appl. 7, 649–665 (2000)
17. Stanley, K., Davis, T.: KLU: a Clark Kent' sparse LU factorization algorithm for circuit matrices. In: SIAM Conference on Parallel Processing for Scientfic Computing (2004)
18. Karypis, G., Kumar, V.: ParMETIS: Parallel Graph Partitioning and Sparse Matrix Ordering Library, CS Dept., Univ. Minn (1997),
   http://glaros.dtc.umn.edu/gkhome/views/metis
19. Boman, E., Devine, K., Heaphy, R., Hendrickson, B., Mitchell, W.F., John, M.S., Vaughan, C.: Zoltan: Data-Management Services for Parallel Applications: User's Guide, Sandia National Laboratories (2004),
   http://www.cs.sandia.gov/Zoltan/Zoltan.html

DAG-Based Software Frameworks for PDEs

Martin Berzins[1], Qingyu Meng[1], John Schmidt[1], and James C. Sutherland[2]

[1] Scientific Computing and Imaging Institute,
[2] Institute for Clean and Secure Energy,
University of Utah, Salt Lake City, UT 84112, USA

Abstract. The task-based approach to software and parallelism is well-known and has been proposed as a potential candidate, named the silver model, for exascale software. This approach is not yet widely used in the large-scale multi-core parallel computing of complex systems of partial differential equations. After surveying task-based approaches we investigate how well the Uintah software and an extension named Wasatch fit in the task-based paradigm and how well they perform on large scale parallel computers. The conclusion is that these approaches show great promise for petascale but that considerable algorithmic challenges remain.

Keywords: Directed Acyclic Graph Task-Based Parallelism Scalability.

1 Introduction

The task-based approach to parallel computing is both well-known and widely-discussed as a potentially useful approach, but is not so often employed at large scales on parallel architectures as of yet. The central idea is to use a Directed Acyclic Graph (DAG) based approach to express the structure of the underlying software, see [8, 11, 24]. While the leading edge of present large-scale computing is focused on petascale computations, the anticipated move to exascale computing, [30], over the next decade has led to a discussion of task-based approaches as potential candidates for exascale software over the next decade. For example, the Silver model, [1], aims to:

1. provide an abstraction of parallel computation that exposes and exploits a high degree of algorithm concurrency, particularly from dynamic directed graph structure-based applications,
2. enable intrinsic latency hiding through automatic overlap of computation and communication through message-driven work-queue multi-threaded execution,
3. minimize impact of synchronization and other overheads for efficient scalable execution through lightweight object-oriented semantics,
4. support dynamic global address space scheduling for adaptive resource management, and
5. unify heterogeneous structure computing for diversity of processing modalities and exploitation of accelerator micro-architectures.

With this in mind, the aim of this paper is to explore the usefulness of DAG based approaches, such as the Silver Model, for computational frameworks which solve large

M. Alexander et al. (Eds.): Euro-Par 2011 Workshops, Part I, LNCS 7155, pp. 324–333, 2012.

systems of partial differential equations (PDEs) on existing large scale computers. This exploration will make use of the DAG-based parallel Uintah software framework for partial differential equations (PDEs) [21, 23] and its recent developments, [5, 14, 16, 19], to assess how well the Silver Model type approach works on present-day large-scale architectures for complex multi-physics multiscale applications. In order to assess how well the same approach also works when applied at multi-core level for complex physical applications, an approach, named Wasatch, proposed by one of the authors (Sutherland) and related to [20] will be considered. As a result of these investigations, a preliminary and tentative evaluation of the silver model type approach for PDE software infrastructures will be given.

2 A Brief Survey of Direct Acyclic Graph Approaches

The idea of the dataflow graph as an organizing structure for execution is well known and has been widely used in many different contexts. Only a non-exhaustive survey of a few salient approaches is given here. An appropriate starting point is Sarkar, [24], and the references within, while an example of a more recent discussion is [26]. One important distinction is the level of granularity at which the task-graph approach is applied. For example, the SISAL language compilers [25] used DAG concepts at a fine level of granularity to structure code generation and execution. More recently the PLASMA project uses these ideas at a sub-core level in a task-based linear algebra approach [13], to achieve speed-up over a conventional bulk-synchronous approach. The same ideas have also been extended to several thousand cores, [8]. An interesting language development explicitly designed for task-based paradigms is that of CnC [31]. A CnC approach has been shown to yield very good results in an automated way for linear algebra problems on multi-cores, [6]. While almost all of these approaches use data parallelism to achieve multi-core performance, that of [20] uses a functional decomposition of the complex system of PDEs being solved and will be discussed further below.

The use of a coarser granularity than the above examples makes it possible to apply the DAG approaches at a higher level. The SMARTS [28] dataflow engine used in the POOMA [2] toolkit shares a similar approach with Uintah, as described below, in that each caters to a particular higher-level presentation. SMARTS caters to POOMA's C++ implementation and its template-based approach. The Uintah software supports task graphs of C++ based mixed particle/grid algorithms on a structured adaptive mesh. Similar techniques are used by the well-known and successful Charm++ [11] framework which has a DAG-based dynamic runtime system and which has been successfully used on large scale parallel computers for a number of different applications.

3 Overview of Uintah Software

The Uintah Software was written in the University of Utah Center for the Simulation of Accidental Fires and Explosions (C-SAFE), a Department of Energy ASC center, which focused on providing science-based tools for the numerical simulation of accidental fires and explosions. Uintah is designed to solve complex multiscale multiphysics problems, by making use of a component design that enforces separation between large entities of software that can be swapped in and out, allowing them to be independently developed and tested within the entire framework. This has led to a very flexible simulation package that has been able to simulate a wide variety of problems including a small cylindrical steel container filled with a plastic bonded explosive subjected to convective and radiative heat fluxes from a fire, [9], shape charges, stage-separation in rockets, the biomechanics of microvessels, the properties of foam under large deformation, and the evolution of large pool fires caused by transportation accidents. The application of Uintah to a petascale problem arising from "sympathetic" explosions in which the collective interactions of a large ensemble of explosives results in dramatically increased explosion violence, was described in [5].

Uintah currently contains four main simulation algorithms:

(i) ICE is a "multi-material" CFD algorithm that was originally developed by Kashiwa and others at LANL [12] for incompressible and compressible flow regimes. This method conserves mass, momentum, energy, and the exchange of these quantities between materials and is used here on adaptive structured hexahedral mesh patches.

(ii) The Material Point Method (MPM) is a particle method that is used to evolve the equations of motion for the solid materials applications involving complex geometries, large deformations, and fracture. Originally described by Sulsky, et al., [27], MPM is an extension to solid mechanics of the well-known particle-in-cell (PIC) method for fluid flow simulation, that uses the ICE adaptive mesh as a computational scratchpad.

(iii) MPMICE is fluid-structure solver that combines MPM and ICE [9, 22].

(iv) The fixed-mesh Arches component solves turbulent reacting flows with participating media radiation. It is a three-dimensional, Large Eddy Simulation (LES) code that uses a low-Mach number, variable density formulation to simulate heat, mass, and momentum transport in reacting flows, [10]. Where implicit solvers are needed Uintah components such as Arches or ICE use MPI-based solver libraries, PETSc [3] and Hypre [7]. Uintah was originally capable of running on 4K cores and has now also been released as software[1] and now runs on up to 196K cores on DOE's Jaguar at Oak Ridge Laboratory.

4   Uintah as Viewed through the Silver Model

The heart of Uintah is a sophisticated computational framework that can integrate multiple simulation components, analyze the dependencies and communication patterns between them, and execute the resulting multi-physics simulation, [22]. Uintah may be seen as a precursor of a Silver Model type code and so we now describe how the two approaches are related.

Parallel Computing Abstraction: Uintah utilizes an abstract task-graph representation of parallel computation and communication to express data dependencies between multiple physics components. The task-graph is a directed acyclic graph of tasks. Each task consumes some input and produces some output (which is in turn the input of some future task). These inputs and outputs are specified for each patch in a structured AMR grid. Associated with each task is a C++ method which is used to perform the actual computation. Each component specifies a list of tasks to be performed and the data dependencies between them, [21, 23] The task-graph allows the Uintah runtime system to

---

[1] See http://www.uintah.utah.edu

analyze the structure of the computation to automatically enable load-balancing, data communication, parallel I/O, and checkpoint/restart. The task-graph approach of Uintah also shares many features with the migratable object philosophy of Charm++ [11].

Overlap of Computation and Communication: The philosophy used in Uintah is that tasks should execute in an asynchronous manner as possible to provide as much overlap as is possible between computation and communication. A scheduler component in Uintah sets up MPI communication for data dependencies and then executes the tasks that have been assigned to it. When a task completes, its outputs are sent to other tasks that require them. This procedure is completely asynchronous and has allowed parallelism to be integrated between multiple components while maintaining overall scalability, providing that there is enough work to keep each processor busy.

Table 1. AMR ICE Times as a function of mesh patch granularity

Patch Size	Scheduling Time	Regrid and Copydata	Task Wait MPI Time	Total Execution time
8	0.616	3.647	2.445	12.06
12	0.135	0.660	2.988	9.15
16	0.049	0.213	3.696	9.67
20	0.018	0.062	4.911	11.10

Minimize Impact of Synchronization and Other Overheads: Originally Uintah used a fixed execution pattern. After long MPI wait times were observed on large numbers of cores the internal task scheduler was rewritten so as to use both dynamic scheduling and out-of-order execution [19]. In particular the dynamic task scheduling mechanism in Uintah now allows tasks to run out of the sequential order that they are specified in the algorithm, if information obtained at runtime shows that this is permissible. Since Uintah is a general computational framework, it supports various tasks which may have asynchronous communications to different neighbors, write global variables, or even call third party libraries such as PETSc. The dynamic scheduler must be robust enough to guarantee that all these kinds of tasks are processed in such a way as to provide the correct result. This was accomplished by putting fine-grained computational tasks in a directed acyclic graph (DAG) and isolating the task memory. To achieve high scalability, a decentralized scheduling scheme was used; that is, each node schedules its tasks privately and communicates with other nodes regarding data dependencies only when necessary. Furthermore, Uintah's scheduler respects task priorities and supports scheduling global synchronization tasks. In order to create as many independent tasks as possible, we allow multiple versions of memory by adding a variable version table. This can help the system remove certain task dependencies and generate more independent tasks. Experiments in [19] varied mesh patch size on 24K cores and looked at trade-off between fewer larger patches, with fewer longer messages, less overhead and fewer parallel tasks and smaller patches with more tasks and more overhead and more shorter messages. Table 1 shows that a balance between sufficient parallel slackness and the associated overhead from scheduling regridding and wait time, was reached with patches of size 12x12x12 minimizing run time. This example illustrates some of the performance variations possible in a dynamically scheduled task-based execution environment.

Adaptive Resource Management: A low-cost load balancing method is an important part of adaptive resource management in Uintah. Uintah's load balancer utilizes space-filling curves in order to cluster patches together [14, 16]. This algorithm was driven by using a simple model of computational cost on each patch. For more complex situations such as adaptive mesh refinement, and combinations of complex physics involving rapidly moving particles and adaptive meshes, it becomes increasingly difficult to have a reliable cost model that reflects potential changes at every timestep. In order to address this imbalance, a new measurement and feedback-based approach technique has been developed which uses forecasting methods to predict the cost of each patch based on observations made at runtime. During task execution, the time to complete each task is recorded and used to update a simple forecasting model which is then used to predict the time to execute on each patch in the future. This provides a mechanism to accurately predict the cost of each patch while requiring little information from the user or component developer. This forecasting method is a simple exponential smoothing method [14], that has been used in a wide variety of applications because of its accuracy and simplicity. Although measurement based approaches have been used before, part of the reliability and robustness of this approach comes from the feedback loop.

Support for Heterogeneous Computing: The standard message passing paradigm that Uintah initially operated under was that any data that needed to be shared to a neighboring core must be passed via MPI. For multi-core architectures, the process of passing data that is local to a node is both wasteful in terms of latency from MPI sends and receives and in the duplication of identical data that is shared between cores. For these reasons we have moved to an architecture in which only one copy of global data is stored per node in Uintah's data warehouse. The task scheduler now spins off tasks to be executed on, say, nc cores using a threaded model, [18] which results in the memory used in a single shared data warehouse being a fraction of only nc^{-1} of what is required for multiple MPI tasks, one per each of the nc cores. Figure 1 shows dramatic memory saving and even more dramatic memory decrease when the MPICH buffer sizes are constrained. The memory saving from eliminating the duplication of data within a node allows us to to expand the scope and range of problems that we have been unable to explore up until now. This architecture also offers the possibility of being extended to spin off tasks to be executed on other types of processors, such as GPUs, in the near future.

5   The Silver Model and Applications

Regardless of the support provided by task-based infrastructures such as Uintah, in order for the underlying problem to scale in both a weak and strong sense, sufficient parallel slackness, [29], and linear complexity are both required [17]. An important feature of Uintah is its adaptive meshing capability and so, as a result, Uintah has had to rethink algorithms for mesh refinement from the well-known Berger-Rigoutsos [4] algorithm to the tiled algorithm proposed by [15] in which regular hexahedral patches or tiles are uniformly refined, [5, 14]. As each tile is searched, in parallel, for refinement

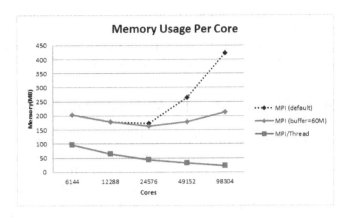

Fig. 1. Memory Reduction from Use of a Hybrid scheduler

flags without the need for communication and then refined if it contains refinement flags. This regridder is advantageous at large scales because cores only communicate once at the end of regridding when the patch sets are combined. Figure 3 (top) shows a simple example of Berger-Rigoutsos type patches and Figure 3 (bottom) shows the tiled approach applied to cylindrical refinement flags. Paradoxically the smaller number of patches resulting from the Berger-Rigoutsos algorithm makes it harder to distribute those patches evenly to large numbers of cores and the global communication required (or lack thereof) in each case is also significant, [15]. Figure 2 shows the performance results for an extended version of the time-dependent adaptive mesh refinement problem discussed in [5, 14]. The largest strong scaling case, as defined by the right most solid

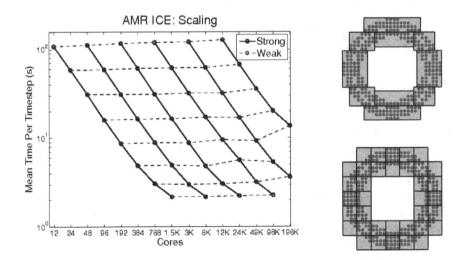

Fig. 2. Uintah Adaptive Mesh Scalability

Fig. 3. BR and Tiled Patch Example

line, shows scaling to 196K cores. It was not previously possible to run this problem due to a shortage of memory per core on Jaguar. While these results are preliminary they are very promising. Similar scalability results to 196K cores have also been obtained for the combustion problem relating to sympathetic explosions in [5].

6 Using the DAG Approach at the Multi-core Level with Wasatch

The complexity of the problems to which simulation is applied naturally increases with available computing power. For example turbulent combustion simulation of typical fuels involves $\mathcal{O}(10) - \mathcal{O}(100)$ species and $\mathcal{O}(10) - \mathcal{O}(10^3)$ reactions. This requires solution of very large sets of highly coupled, nonlinear PDEs that span many orders of magnitude in both space and time. In such highly dynamic, multi-physics systems, one may not be able to determine *a priori* the most appropriate models. Therefore, programming models which allow significant flexibility in the complex couplings that may occur for different model sets in multi-physics applications are required.

In the "expression" approach proposed by Sutherland, [20], the programmer writes pieces of code that calculate various mathematical expressions, explicitly identifying what data the code requires and produces/calculates. To create an algorithm, the programmer selects one or more expressions to be evaluated and the dependencies are recursively "discovered" resulting in a dependency graph. The dependency graph may be inverted to obtain the execution graph, which may be traversed in parallel if desired.

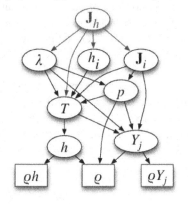

Fig. 4. Expression Tree for Heat Flux

As a simple example, consider a situation where we are solving PDEs for density (ρ), species mass (ρY_i), and enthalpy (ρh). One term in these equations is the energy diffusive flux, given by

$$\mathbf{J}_h = -\lambda \nabla T - \sum_{i=1}^{n_s} h_i \mathbf{J}_i, \qquad (1)$$

where λ is the thermal conductivity, h_i is the enthalpy of species i, and $\mathbf{J}_i$ is the mass diffusive flux of species i, given by another constitutive relationship. Defining the expression that calculates $\mathbf{J}_h$ as the root of the tree, we discover that we require expressions for λ, T, h_i and $\mathbf{J}_i$. We recursively obtain the graph shown in Figure 4. Each node in the graph represents a calculation performed over a subset of the mesh and can represent non-trivial operations. In Figure 4 boxes represent solution variables while ovals represent expressions and it is assumed that diffusivities are obtained from full kinetic theory and are functions of T, p, and Y_i. In the case of constant diffusion coefficients λ and D_{ij} do not depend on other values and the graph is simpler in structure. Moreover for any such changes in dependencies, the expressions for λ and $\mathbf{J}_i$ are simply modified and the tree recompiled, with no logic changes in the application software. Similarly, the constitutive relationship for J_i can be easily modified without any direct implications on the expression for J_h. While this is a very simple example, it illustrates the concept that complex relationships can be represented and abstracted well through the proposed expression approach.

In addition to the DAG expressions which expose the dependency and flow of the calculation, we employ an operator approach over strongly typed fields to form a domain specific language to achieve abstraction of field operations, including application of discrete operators such as interpolants, gradients, etc. This abstraction allows the programmer to work with fields in a MATLAB (vectorized) style while maintaining full compile-time type safety, ensuring that only valid field-field and operator-field operations can be performed. Furthermore, this level of abstraction also allows vectorized field operations to be automatically dispatched in parallel transparently to the programmer. Combined with the DAG strategy outlined above and the graph decomposition provided by Uintah, this provides three independent levels of parallelism that are easily exposed and exploited. Finally, when software is written using templated types, it is relatively simple to implement automatic differentiation techniques for C++ code.

Figure 5 shows strong scaling up to 512 processes, using the DAG expression approach. There are several curves, representing an increasing number of threads. For example, the 8 thread curve at 512 processes implies 64 MPI processes running on 64 nodes with 8 cores per node and 8 threads per node. Similarly, 1 thread at 512 processes implies 512 MPI processes running on 64 nodes with 8 cores per node. The threads are doing the task graph decomposition using the expression approach. These results are for a set of 16 PDEs that have all-to-all coupling in their source terms and also have spatial operations going on. The key point is that overall this approach is very competitive against a straight domain decomposition approach.

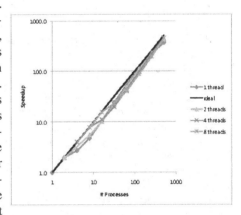

Fig. 5. Scalability of Wasatch Code

7 Summary

The Uintah results show that the DAG approach has promise for complex adaptive mesh calculations and is worth pursuing. The recent work on Wasatch shows that the same idea also has great promise in simplifying the solution of very complex PDE problems and in automating several parts of the parallel computation pipeline in a multi-core environment. In particular, the conclusion is that algorithm-decomposition parallelism, enabled by the expression approach, has the potential to be used in conjunction with MPI-based domain decomposition, as used in Uintah, to enable efficient scaling on modern multi-core architectures.

Acknowledgments. This work was supported by the National Science Foundation under subcontracts No. OCI0721659 and the NSF OCI PetaApps program, through award OCI 0905068, by DOE INCITE award CMB015 for time on Jaguar and by DOE NETL under NET DE-EE0004449.

References

1. Amarasinghe, S., Campbell, D., Carlson, W., Chien, A., Dally, W., Elnohazy, E., Hall, M., Harrison, R., Harrod, W., Hill, K., Hiller, J., Karp, S., Koelbel, C., Koester, D., Kogge, P., Levesque, J., Reed, D., Sarkar, V., Schreiber, R., Richards, M., Scarpelli, A., Shalf, J., Snavely, A., Sterling, T.: Exascale computing study: Software challenges in achieving exascale systems. Technical Report ECSS Report 101909, Georgia Institute of Technology (2009)
2. Atlas, S., Banerjee, S., Cummings, J.C., Hinker, P.J., Srikant, M., Reynders, J.V.W., Tholburn, M.: POOMA: A high-performance distributed simulation environment for scientific applications. In: Supercomputing 1995 Proceedings (December 1995)
3. Balay, S., Gropp, W.D., McInnes, L.C., Smith, B.F.: Efficient management of parallelism in object oriented numerical software libraries. In: Arge, E., Bruaset, A.M., Langtangen, H.P. (eds.) Modern Soft.Tools in Scien. Comput., pp. 163–202. Birkhäuser (1997)
4. Berger, M., Rigoutsos, I.: An algorithm for point clustering and grid generation. IEEE Trans. Systems Man Cybernet. 21(5), 1278–1286 (1991)
5. Berzins, M., Luitjens, J., Meng, Q., Harman, T., Wight, C.A., Peterson, J.R.: Uintah - a scalable framework for hazard analysis. In: TG 2010: Proceedings of the 2010 TeraGrid Conference. ACM, New York (2010)
6. Chandramowlishwaran, A., Knobe, K., Vuduc, R.: Performance evaluation of Concurrent Collections on high-performance multicore computing systems. In: Proc. IEEE Int'l. Parallel and Distributed Processing Symp (IPDPS), Atlanta, GA, USA (April 2010)
7. Falgout, R.D., Jones, J.E., Yangi, U.M.: The design and implementation of hypre, a library of parallel high performance preconditioners. In: Numerical Solution of Partial Differential Equations on Parallel Computers, pp. 267–294. Springer, Heidelberg (2006)
8. Bosilca, G., Bouteiller, A., Danalis, A., Faverge, M., Haidar, H., Herault, T., Kurzak, J., Langou, J., Lemariner, P., Ltaief, H., Luszczek, P., YarKhan, A., Dongarra, J.: Distibuted dense numerical linear algebra algorithms on massively parallel architectures: Dplasma. Technical report, Innovative Computing Laboratory, University of Tennessee (2010)
9. Guilkey, J.E., Harman, T.B., Banerjee, B.: An eulerian-lagrangian approach for simulating explosions of energetic devices. Computers and Structures 85, 660–674 (2007)
10. Spinti, J., Thornock, J., Eddings, E., Smith, P.J., Sarofim, A.: Heat transfer to objects in pool fires, in transport phenomena in fires. In: Transport Phenomena in Fires, Southampton, U.K. WIT Press (2008)
11. Kale, L.V., Bohm, E., Mendes, C.L., Wilmarth, T., Zheng, G.: Programming petascale applications with Charm++ and AMPI. Petascale Computing: Algorithms and Applications 1, 421–441 (2007)
12. Kashiwa, B.A.: A multifield model and method for fluid-structure interaction dynamics. Technical Report LA-UR-01-1136, Los Alamos National Laboratory, Los Alamos (2001)
13. Kurzak, J., Ltaief, H., Dongarra, J., Badia, R.: Scheduling dense linear algebra operations on multicore processors. Concurrency and Computation: Practice and Experience 22(1), 15–44 (2010)
14. Luitjens, J., Berzins, M.: Improving the performance of Uintah: A large-scale adaptive meshing computational framework. In: Proceedings of the 24th IEEE International Parallel and Distributed Processing Symposium, IPDPS 2010 (2010)

15. Luitjens, J., Berzins, M.: Scalable parallel regridding algorithms for block-structured adaptive mesh renement. In: Concurrency And Computation: Practice And Experience (2011)
16. Luitjens, J., Berzins, M., Henderson, T.: Parallel space-filling curve generation through sorting: Research articles. Concurr. Comput.: Pract. Exper. 19(10), 1387–1402 (2007)
17. Martin, I., Tirado, F.: Relationships between efficiency and execution time of full multigrid methods on parallel computers. IEEE Transactions on Parallel and Distributed Systems 8(6), 562–573 (1997)
18. Meng, Q., Berzins, M., Schmidt, J.: Using hybrid parallelism to improve memory use in the Uintah framework. In: TG 2011: Proceedings of the 2011 TeraGrid Conference. ACM, New York (2011)
19. Meng, Q., Luitjens, J., Berzins, M.: Dynamic task scheduling for the Uintah framework. In: Proceedings of the 3rd IEEE Workshop on Many-Task Computing on Grids and Supercomputers, MTAGS 2010 (2010)
20. Notz, P.K., Pawlowski, R.P., Sutherland, J.C.: Graph-based software design for managing complexity and enabling concurrency in multiphysics pde software. ACM Transactions on Mathematical Software (submitted)
21. Parker, S.G.: A component-based architecture for parallel multi-physics pde simulation. Future Gener. Comput. Syst. 22(1), 204–216 (2006)
22. Parker, S.G., Guilkey, J., Harman, T.: A component-based parallel infrastructure for the simulation of fluid-structure interaction. Engineering with Computers 22, 277–292 (2006)
23. Parker, S.G., Guilkey, J.E., Harman, T.: A component-based parallel infrastructure for the simulation of fluid structure interaction. Eng. with Comput. 22(3), 277–292 (2006)
24. Sarkar, V.: Partitioning and Scheduling Parallel Programs for Multiprocessors. MIT Press, Cambridge (1989)
25. Sarkar, V., Skedzielewski, S., Miller, P.: An automatically partitioning compiler for sisal. In: Proceedings of the Conference on CONPAR 1988, pp. 376–383. Cambridge University Press, New York (1989)
26. Sinnen, O., Sousa, L.A., Frode, E.S.: Toward a realistic task scheduling model. IEEE Trans. Parallel Distrib. Syst. 17, 263–275 (2006)
27. Sulsky, D., Zhou, S., Schreyer, H.L.: Application of a particle-in-cell method to solid mechanics. Computer Physics Communications 87, 236–252 (1995)
28. Vajracharya, S., Karmesin, S., Beckman, P., Crotinger, J., Malony, A., Shende, S., Oldehoeft, R., Smith, S.: Smarts: Exploiting temporal locality and parallelism through vertical execution (1999)
29. Valiant, L.G.: Optimally universal parallel computers, pp. 17–20. Prentice Hall Press, Upper Saddle River (1989)
30. Sarkar, V., Harrod, W., Snavely, A.E.: Scidac review: Software challenges in extreme scale systems. Journal of Physics: Conference Series 180 012045 (2009)
31. Budimlic, Z., Burke, M., Cavé, V., Knobe, K., Lowney, G., Newton, R., Palsberg, J., Peixotto, D.M., Sarkar, V., Schlimbach, F., Tasirlar, S.: Concurrent collections. Scientific Programming 18(3-4), 203–217 (2010)

On Partitioning Problems
with Complex Objectives

Kamer Kaya[1], François-Henry Rouet[2], and Bora Uçar[3]

[1] CERFACS, Toulouse, France
Kamer.Kaya@cerfacs.fr
[2] Université de Toulouse, INPT (ENSEEIHT)-IRIT, France
frouet@enseeiht.fr
[3] CNRS and ENS Lyon, France
bora.ucar@ens-lyon.fr

Abstract. Hypergraph and graph partitioning tools are used to partition work for efficient parallelization of many sparse matrix computations. Most of the time, the objective function that is reduced by these tools relates to reducing the communication requirements, and the balancing constraints satisfied by these tools relate to balancing the work or memory requirements. Sometimes, the objective sought for having balance is a complex function of a partition. We mention some important class of parallel sparse matrix computations that have such balance objectives. For these cases, the current state of the art partitioning tools fall short of being adequate. To the best of our knowledge, there is only a single algorithmic framework in the literature to address such balance objectives. We propose another algorithmic framework to tackle complex objectives and experimentally investigate the proposed framework.

Keywords: Hypergraph partitioning, graph partitioning, sparse matrix partitioning, parallel sparse matrix computations.

1 Introduction

Hypergraph and graph partitioning tools are used to partition work for efficient parallelization of many sparse matrix computations. Roughly speaking, the vertices represent the data and the computations, and the (hyper)edges represent dependencies of the computations on the data. For a parallel system of K processors, partitioning the vertices into K disjoint parts can be used to partition the data and the total work among the processors by associating each part with a unique processor. Therefore, a successful application of such partitioning tools should assign almost equal work/data to processors and should reduce the communication costs. The first of these goals is attained by associating weights to vertices and then by guaranteeing that the K resulting parts have almost equal weights, defined as a function of individual vertex weights. The second goal is achieved by reducing a function related to the (hyper)edges that straddle two or more parts. There are a number of widely used tools, including MeTiS [9], Mondriaan [19], PaToH [6], Scotch [14], and Zoltan [5], to achieve these goals.

M. Alexander et al. (Eds.): Euro-Par 2011 Workshops, Part I, LNCS 7155, pp. 334–344, 2012.

Sometimes the objective sought for having balance is simple. By this, we mean that one can assign weights to the vertices before partitioning, and then measure the weight of a part by simply adding up the weights of vertices in that part. For example, if a vertex represents a row of a sparse matrix, then the number of nonzeros in that row can be used as the weight of the corresponding vertex. In a given partition, the weight of a part corresponds to the total number of nonzeros assigned to that part, and hence balance can be obtained among processors easily by using the standard partitioning tools listed above. This standard approach, however, is not sufficient for many important classes of sparse matrix computations. We (in the accompanying technical report [11]) and Pınar and Hendrickson [15] discuss several class of computations (including the FETI class of domain decomposition-based solvers, iterative methods with incomplete LU or Cholesky preconditioners, overlapped Schwarz solvers, and direct methods based on multifrontal solvers) for which the standard approach falls short of achieving balance on the computational load of the processors. In these computations, the objective sought for balancing is a complex function of a partition and cannot be computed by looking at a set of a priori given vertex weights without taking a partition into account—resembling to the chicken-egg problem [15]. We give a toy example for this phenomena. Suppose that we want to partition a square matrix rowwise for efficient parallel computation of $y \leftarrow Ax$ where the input vector x and the output vector y are assigned to the processors conformally with the rows of A, i.e., a processor holding row i of A holds the vector entries y_i and x_i as well. Suppose also that we want to obtain balance on the number of nonzero entries with which the scalar multiply-add operations with the x-vector entries can be computed without communication. The objective is complex, because we cannot know which entries in a row will need an x-vector entry residing in another processor.

We discuss three special forms of sparse matrices in the next subsection. These forms embody most of the data partitioning approaches for efficient parallelization of sparse matrix computations with complex balance requirements. In Section 1.2, we survey the related work on similar problems and highlight our contributions. Section 2 includes the background material. In Section 3, we propose a general framework for the problem of partitioning for complex objectives and adjust it for two of the three matrix forms. For the third form, we just give a short summary and refer the reader to the technical report [11] for more details. A brief experimental evaluation is given in Section 4. We conclude the paper in Section 5 with a summary.

1.1 Problem Definition

Consider the following three forms of an $m \times n$ sparse matrix A for a given integer $K > 1$:

$$A_{SB}=\begin{bmatrix} A_{11} & & A_{1S} \\ & \ddots & \vdots \\ & & A_{KK}A_{KS} \end{bmatrix} \quad (1) \quad A_{BL}=\begin{bmatrix} A_{11}\cdots A_{1K} \\ \vdots \ddots \vdots \\ A_{K1}\cdots A_{KK} \end{bmatrix} \quad (2) \quad A_{DB}=\begin{bmatrix} A_{11} & & A_{1S} \\ & \ddots & \vdots \\ & & A_{KK}A_{KS} \\ A_{S1}\cdots A_{SK} A_{SS} \end{bmatrix} \quad (3).$$

The first form A_{SB} (1) is called the singly bordered block-diagonal form (by convention, we assume a columnwise border throughout the paper). The second one A_{BL} (2) is called the block form. The third one A_{DB} (3) is called the doubly bordered block diagonal form. These three forms have different uses in parallel sparse matrix computations. We assume that they are going to be used to partition the matrices among K processors. The following cases are common (see for example [3,8]). In the forms A_{SB} and A_{BL}, each processor holds a row stripe, i.e., processor k holds, respectively, $[A_{kk} \ A_{kS}]$ and $[A_{k1} \cdots A_{kk} \cdots A_{kK}]$. In A_{DB}, a processor holds the arrow-head formed by the blocks A_{kk}, A_{kS} and A_{Sk}, and perhaps parts of or all of A_{SS}.

The accompanying report [11] presents some applications which require a matrix to be put in one of the above three forms with the following complex partitioning requirements. In the A_{SB} form, the size of the border should be small, and the diagonal blocks should have an almost equal number of nonzeros. In the A_{BL} form, the total communication volume (the total number of nonzero off-diagonal column segments) should be small, the diagonal blocks should have an almost equal number of nonzeros, and each row stripe should have an almost equal number of nonzeros. The requirements for the A_{BL} form coincide with those of the toy example mentioned earlier. In the A_{DB} form, the size of the border should be small, the border blocks should have a balanced number of nonzeros, and the diagonal blocks should also have a balanced number of nonzeros.

1.2   Related Work and Contributions

The problem of partitioning for complex objectives was studied before for specific problems [4,13,18] and in a general setting [15] with some specific applications. The algorithmic framework in these studies is very similar and is called the predictor-corrector approach [13]. In the predictor-corrector approach, a partition is obtained by using the standard tools, with the standard (simple) objectives in the predictor step. Then, the partition is evaluated for the complex objectives and refinements to the current partition are performed in the corrector step. Certain methods [4,18] do not go back and forth between different objectives, rather they fix one of them and try to improve the others. The specific approach of [13] and the general framework of [15] apply move based improvement heuristics to improve the partition for all objectives.

There are a few difficulties and challenges that arise in the corrector step. Firstly, in order to efficiently compute and evaluate the complex functions, large two-dimensional data structures are required where one of the dimensions is K (also true for the simple objectives [2,16]). Secondly, efficient mechanisms that avoid cycles in the move based improvement approaches are hard to design. Furthermore, ties among the gains of moves arise almost always, and effective and efficient tie-breaking mechanisms are hard to design for the K-way refinement scheme (see [1] for those for the recursive bisection based approaches). Therefore, vertices are usually visited in a random order and best moves are performed (see [2,13]). This heuristic, although it can be helpful, can also be very shortsighted.

Direct K-way partitioning methods can handle complex partitioning objectives. This can be accomplished by replacing the standard refinement heuristics with those for the complex objectives. However, this method is akin to the predictor-corrector approach and suffers from the same difficulties.

We propose another approach for partitioning problems with complex objectives. The main idea is to use the recursive bisection based partitioning scheme and to evaluate the complex functions with respect to the existing coarser partition obtained as a result of the preceding bisections. Once the functions are evaluated, some weights can be assigned to the vertices, as the complex functions with respect to the coarser partition are now simple. This allows us to use available tools at each bisection step. The advantages of this framework is that one does not need to write a refinement routine, and the framework is easily applicable to graph and hypergraph models with differing objective functions. We will apply the framework with the standard hypergraph partitioning tools to address the complex partitioning problems for the A_{SB} and A_{BL} forms, and give a summary for that of the A_{DB} form.

2 Background

2.1 Hypergraph Partitioning

A hypergraph $\mathcal{H} = (\mathcal{V}, \mathcal{N})$ is defined as a set of vertices $\mathcal{V}$ and a set of nets (hyperedges) $\mathcal{N}$. Every net $n_j \in \mathcal{N}$ is a subset of vertices. Weights can be associated with the vertices. We use $w(v_i)$ to denote the weight of the vertex v_i. Given a hypergraph $\mathcal{H} = (\mathcal{V}, \mathcal{N})$, $\Pi = \{\mathcal{V}_1, \ldots, \mathcal{V}_K\}$ is called a K-way partition of the vertex set $\mathcal{V}$ if each part $\mathcal{V}_k$ is nonempty, parts are pairwise disjoint, and the union of parts gives $\mathcal{V}$. A K-way vertex partition of $\mathcal{H}$ is said to be balanced if $\frac{W_{max}}{W_{avg}} \leq (1 + \varepsilon)$, where $W_{max} = \max_k\{W(\mathcal{V}_k)\}$, $W(\mathcal{V}_k)$ is the weight of the part $\mathcal{V}_k$ defined as the sum of the weights of the vertices in $\mathcal{V}_k$, W_{avg} is the average part weight, and ε represents the allowed imbalance ratio.

In a partition Π of $\mathcal{H}$, a net that has at least one vertex in a part is said to *connect* that part. *Connectivity* λ_j of a net n_j denotes the number of parts connected by n_j. A net n_j is said to be *cut* (*external*) if $\lambda_j > 1$, and *uncut* (*internal*) otherwise. The set of external nets of a partition Π is denoted as $\mathcal{N}_E$. The partitioning objective is to minimize the cutsize defined over the cut nets. There are various cutsize definitions. Two relevant definitions are:

$$cutsize(\Pi) = \sum_{n_j \in \mathcal{N}_E} 1 \quad (4) \qquad cutsize(\Pi) = \sum_{n_j \in \mathcal{N}_E} (\lambda_j - 1) \quad (5) \, .$$

The NP-complete hypergraph partitioning problem [12] is defined as the task of dividing the vertices of a hypergraph into K parts such that the cutsize is minimized, while the balance criterion given above is met.

A recent variant of the above problem is the multi-constraint formulation [2,7,10,17] in which a set of T weights is associated with each vertex v, i.e., $w(v, 1), \ldots, w(v, T)$. Let $W(\mathcal{V}_k, t) = \sum_{v \in \mathcal{V}_k} w(v, t)$ denote the weight of part $\mathcal{V}_k$ for constraint t. Then, a partition Π is said to be balanced if $\forall t \in \{1, \ldots, T\}$ we have $\frac{W_{max}(t)}{W_{avg}(t)} \leq (1 + \varepsilon(t))$, where $W_{max}(t) = \max_k \{W(\mathcal{V}_k, t)\}$, $W_{avg}(t) = \sum_{v_i \in \mathcal{V}} w(v_i, t)/K$, and $\varepsilon(t)$ is the allowed imbalance ratio for the constraint t.

Different interpretations and applications of hypergraph partitioning can be used to permute a matrix into the A_{BL}, A_{SB} and A_{DB} forms (see Section 3).

2.2   Recursive Bisection Based Hypergraph Partitioning

We recall some important concepts in the recursive bisection based K-way hypergraph partitioning methods (see also [6]). The number of parts K is assumed to be a power of 2 for the ease of presentation, otherwise this is not a requirement. In this partitioning method, the vertices of a given hypergraph are partitioned into two balanced parts recursively until K parts are obtained. The recursive calls form a tree (called the *bisection tree*) with K leaves. The first bisection, or the root of the bisection tree, corresponds to partitioning the vertices of the original hypergraph into two. The leaf nodes correspond to the parts, and the two parts having the same parent are said to be of the same bisection.

While optimizing the cutsize metric (4), after a bisection step, one discards the cut nets and forms the two hypergraphs with two parts of vertices and the internal nets. This is referred to as *discarding the cut nets* during bisections. On the other hand, while optimizing for the other cutsize metric (5), one *splits the cut nets*. Let $\mathcal{V}_1$ and $\mathcal{V}_2$ be the two vertex partitions obtained at a bisection. Then for any net $n_j \cap \mathcal{V}_1 \neq \emptyset$, one puts a net containing the vertices $n_j \cap \mathcal{V}_1$ in the hypergraph containing vertices $\mathcal{V}_1$, and for any net $n_j \cap \mathcal{V}_2 \neq \emptyset$, one puts a net containing the vertices $n_j \cap \mathcal{V}_2$ in the hypergraph containing vertices $\mathcal{V}_2$.

3   A Framework for Complex Partitioning Objectives

We propose a framework within which standard tools of the hypergraph partitioning problem can be used effectively to address complex partitioning objectives. In this framework, we follow the recursive bisection paradigm. The first bisection is performed as it would be done for a simple objective case. Then, the subsequent recursive bisection steps use the partial (or coarse) partition information to set secondary constraints and use multi-constraint bisection routines. At each bisection step, the two parts will satisfy a balance constraint approximately, as the real balance can only be determined after the bisection. The abstract framework is given in Alg. 1, where concrete instantiations for the complex partitioning problems described in Section 1.1 are elaborated on in the next subsections. The initial call has the arguments $R = [1, \ldots, m]$, $C = [1, \ldots, n]$, $K = 2^\ell$ for some integer ℓ, $low = 1$, and $up = K$ for an $m \times n$ matrix A.

The advantage of this approach over the predictor-corrector approach is that it enables multi-level refinement (by harnessing such heuristics available in the standard tools) whereas the predictor-corrector approach does not. Writing down a multi-level refinement heuristic for the predictor-corrector approach will indeed be troublesome for the reasons outlined in Section 1.2. On the other hand, when the secondary constraints are not as important as the first one or when different and very loose imbalance ratios are used, predictions might well turn out to be acceptable, and one would not need to reduce the solution space by using multiple constraints.

3.1   The Singly Bordered Form

The off-the-shelf method to permute a matrix into the singly bordered form as shown in (1) is to use the column-net hypergraph model. In this model, an $m \times n$ matrix A is represented with a hypergraph $\mathcal{H} = (\mathcal{R}, \mathcal{C})$, where for each row i of A there is a vertex v_i in $\mathcal{R}$, for each column j of A there is a net n_j in $\mathcal{C}$, and $v_i \in n_j$ iff $a_{ij} \neq 0$. Each vertex v_i is assigned a weight of $|\{j : a_{ij} \neq 0\}|$, i.e., the number of nonzeros in the corresponding row. Then, partitioning this hypergraph into K parts under the objective function (4) can be used to permute the matrix A into the singly bordered form [3, Section 5]. The rows corresponding to the vertices in part k are permuted before the rows corresponding to the vertices in part ℓ for $1 \leq k < \ell \leq K$. This defines a row permutation where the permutation of the rows in a common block is arbitrary. The column permutation is found as follows. The columns corresponding to the nets that are internal to the part k are permuted before those corresponding to the nets internal to the part ℓ for $1 \leq k < \ell \leq K$. Then the coupling columns are permuted to the end. With this approach, one thus reduces the number of coupling columns and obtains balance on the number of nonzeros in the row stripes $[A_{kk} \ A_{kS}]$. This does not however imply balance on the diagonal blocks A_{kk}. In [3, Section 5], unit weighted vertices in an unconventional partitioning formulation in which one enforces balance on internal nets is used (the tool is not publicly available). This results in a singly bordered form where the diagonal blocks have a balanced number of rows as well as balanced a number of columns (but balance on the diagonal blocks is not addressed).

Our alternative is to use the outlined recursive bisection based framework to minimize the number of coupling columns while trying to obtain balance on the number of nonzeros in the diagonal blocks as well as in the row stripes. For this purpose, for each row vertex v_i, we associate two weights (after the first bisection) in the third line of Alg. 1:

$$w(v_i, 1) = |\{j : a_{ij} \neq 0\}|\,,$$
$$w(v_i, 2) = |\{j : a_{ij} \neq 0 \text{ and column } j \text{ is not cut yet}\}|\,.$$

Here $w(v_i, 1)$ is the number of nonzeros in row i and kept the same throughout the bisections to have balance in the row stripes $[A_{kk} \ A_{kS}]$. On the other hand

---

Algorithm 1. $RB(A, R, C, K, low, up)$

Input: A: a sparse matrix. R: row indices. C: column indices. K: number of parts.
    low, up: id of the lowest and highest numbered parts
Output: *partition*: partition information for the rows
 1: form the column-net model of the matrix $A(R, C)$
 2: **if** this is not the first bisection step **then**
 3:     use previous bisection information to set up the secondary constraints
 4: partition into two $\langle R_1, R_2 \rangle \leftarrow \text{BISECTROWS}(A(R, C))$ ▶ with standard tools
 5: set $partition(R_1) \leftarrow low$ and set $partition(R_2) \leftarrow up$
 6: create the two column sets, using net splitting or net discarding, giving C_1 and C_2
 7: $RB(A, R_1, C_1, K/2, low, (low + up - 1)/2)$ ▶ recursive bisection
 8: $RB(A, R_2, C_2, K/2, (low + up - 1)/2 + 1, up)$ ▶ recursive bisection

---

$w(v_i, 2)$ relates to the diagonal block weight, and by changing $w(\cdot, 2)$ at every bisection we make these weights become closer to the exact weight that will be seen at the end. Although each bisection step obtains two parts with a balanced $W(\cdot, 2)$, two parts from two different bisections are related only indirectly. The coupling columns are discarded at the sixth line of the framework, as we are interested in the cut-net metric (4).

3.2   The Block Form

The off-the-shelf method for this problem is to use the column-net hypergraph model with the objective function (5). The row permutation is done as in the previous section. The column permutation is determined in a post-process [4,18]. A straightforward post-process would be to first permute the internal columns as is done in the previous section and then to permute a coupling column j to the block which has the minimum number of nonzeros in the diagonal (so far) among those blocks that the coupling column j touches.

The proposed recursive bisection based framework can be used as follows. As the objective function is (5), we use the net splitting methodology. While doing so, we keep the copy with the higher number of nonzeros as the main copy (uncut nets are already main copies) with an intent to assign the associated columns to one of the parts that will be resulting from the recursive calls on the part of the main copy. That is, the net splitting operation marks either the copy in C_1 or the copy in C_2 of a cut net as the main one (assuming the cut net was a main copy). Consider a split net n_j whose main copy is put in C_1. Then in the following bisection $RB(A, R_1, C_1, \ldots)$, the vertex $i \in R_1$ for which $a_{ij} \neq 0$ will bear a weight of one for the split net n_j (that nonzero entry is in the diagonal block), whereas no vertex in R_2 will bear a weight for the same net. Formally, we propose assigning the following weights to the vertices:

$$w(v_i, 1) = |\{j : a_{ij} \neq 0\}|,$$
$$w(v_i, 2) = |\{j : a_{ij} \neq 0 \text{ and column } j \text{ is a main copy}\}|.$$

As before, keeping $w(\cdot, 1)$ always equal to the number of nonzeros in the corresponding row results in balance in the row stripes $[A_{k1}, \ldots, A_{kK}]$, whereas $w(\cdot, 2)$ will approximate the number of nonzeros in the diagonal blocks. Therefore, the last level bisections will be almost accurate. Again the weights of two distant parts will be loosely related.

3.3   The Doubly Bordered Form

We have instantiated the framework for the problem of permuting a sparse symmetric matrix into A_{DB} form with the complex objectives stated in Section 1.1. The details are in the accompanying technical report [11]. We give a short summary of what is achieved by the framework. The standard tools (based on graph partitioning methods) are demonstrated to be susceptible to drastic imbalances (up to 9, on diagonal blocks, and 32, on the border blocks, fold imbalance were reported in a 128-way partitioning of a matrix). On the other hand, the framework with some proper definition of vertex weights was able to improve the balance on the diagonal blocks always (the maximum was about 183%) and the balance on the border blocks by about (the maximum was about 137%). This comes however with an increase of about 35% in the border size on average.

In a recent study [20], the framework is adapted to attain some other complex partitioning objectives for the A_{DB} form (in which the border size should be small and linear system solves with the diagonal blocks and border blocks should be balanced). In that study, it has been demonstrated in practical experiments that the improved load balance can result in reduced execution time in spite of the increased border size.

4   Experiments

We have used three rectangular, nine square and pattern unsymmetric, and 23 pattern symmetric matrices from University of Florida sparse matrix collection (www.cise.ufl.edu/research/sparse/matrices/). The names and the properties of these matrices can be seen in [11]. We have partitioned the matrices into $K = \{32, 64, 128\}$ parts using the hypergraph partitioning tool PaToH [6]. As PaToH includes randomized algorithms, we run each experiment 10 times and report the average result. Below, we give a summary of results and refer the reader to [11] for detailed results, including those for the A_{DB} form.

4.1   The Singly Bordered Form

We compare the framework with the standard method (SM) of partitioning the column-net hypergraph model on all matrices in the data set. Both of the approaches obtained good balance on the number of nonzeros per row stripe (both are less than 0.04 on average). In 60 instances (among $35 \times 3 = 105$ partitioning instances), both of the methods obtained balance on the number of nonzeros in the diagonal blocks within 10% of the perfect balance—those instances are discarded. We normalized the cutsize and the imbalance obtained by the framework to those obtained by SM on the remaining instances. Some statistical indicators, the minimum, the median, the maximum, the average and the geometric mean (gmean), of these results are given in Table 1.

Table 1. Statistical indicators of the ratio of the results of the framework to the results of SM. "Cutsize" refers to the number of coupling columns and "Imbal(A_{kk})" refers to the imbalance on the number of nonzeros on the diagonal blocks.

	min	median	max	avg	gmean
Cutsize	0.78	1.08	1.74	1.11	1.10
Imbal(A_{kk})	0.36	0.64	1.57	0.70	0.67

As seen in Table 1, the framework obtains 30% better balance on the number of nonzeros in the diagonal blocks, on average. This comes with an increase of about 11% on the number of coupling columns. This degradation in the cutsize is expected as the standard method has only one constraint. Previously, the average increase in the cutsize with the metric (4) is reported to be around 34% (compare tables 2 and 5 in [2]) in the two-constraint case. We think therefore that the increase of 11% in the cutsize is well spent to reduce the imbalance of the diagonal blocks by 30%.

4.2   The Block Form

We compare the framework with the standard method (SM) of partitioning the column-net hypergraph model with the objective of minimizing the cutsize given in (5) on all square matrices of the data set. In all of these experiments, both of the approaches obtained balance on the number of nonzeros per row stripes quite satisfactorily (both are less than 0.06 on average). In 85 partitioning instances, both of the methods obtained balance on the number of nonzeros in the diagonal blocks within 10% of the perfect balance—those instances are discarded. We normalized the cutsize and the imbalance obtained by the framework to those obtained by SM on the remaining instances. Some statistical indicators, the minimum, the median, the maximum, the average and the geometric mean (gmean), of these results are given in Table 2.

Table 2. Statistical indicators of the ratio of the results of the framework to the results of SM. "Cutsize" refers to the total volume of communication and "Imbal(A_{kk})" refers to the imbalance on the number of nonzeros on the diagonal blocks.

	min	median	max	avg	gmean
Cutsize	1.00	1.10	1.53	1.15	1.16
Imbal(A_{kk})	0.35	0.78	2.00	0.84	0.75

As in the singly bordered case, we were expecting an increase in the cutsize. Compared to again previously reported results [2], 15% increase in the cutsize is acceptable. This resulted in 16% improvement in the balance on the number of nonzeros on the diagonal blocks. The small geometric mean indicates a few outliers with a large value. We have looked at the results closely and spotted only a few such cases (on one matrix the standard method and the framework obtained, respectively 0.08 and 0.10 imbalance, implying 25% better balance in favor of the standard method). Upon discarding those, the framework resulted in about 20% better balance, on average.

5 Conclusion

We have discussed three sparse matrix forms (the block form, the singly bordered block diagonal form, and the doubly bordered block diagonal form). These forms exemplify a broad range of sparse matrix computations whose efficient parallelization need some complex partitioning objectives to be attained. We have presented a framework to address such kinds of complex partitioning objectives, and evaluated the framework within hypergraph partitioning methods. We presented results for the singly bordered and block forms and reported results from [11] and another current study [20] in which the framework of the current paper was adapted to meet some objectives in the doubly bordered block diagonal form. In all cases, the framework is demonstrated to be able to trade an increase in the objective function with better load balance, and it improved running times in practical experiments with the doubly bordered form.

In general, the proposed framework is more effective with the increasing number of parts. The case $K = 2$, in particular, is not addressed at all.

References

1. Alpert, C.J., Kahng, A.B.: Recent directions in netlist partitioning: A survey. Integration, the VLSI Journal 19, 1–81 (1995)
2. Aykanat, C., Cambazoglu, B.B., Uçar, B.: Multi-level direct k-way hypergraph partitioning with multiple constraints and fixed vertices. J. Parallel Distr. Com 68, 609–625 (2008)
3. Aykanat, C., Pınar, A., Çatalyürek, Ü.V.: Permuting sparse rectangular matrices into block-diagonal form. SIAM J. Sci. Comput. 25, 1860–1879 (2004)
4. Bisseling, R.H., Meesen, W.: Communication balancing in parallel sparse matrix-vector multiplication. ETNA 21, 47–65 (2005)
5. Boman, E., Devine, K., Fisk, L.A., Heaphy, R., Hendrickson, B., Vaughan, C., Catalyurek, U., Bozdag, D., Mitchell, W., Teresco, J.: Zoltan 3.0: Parallel Partitioning, Load-balancing, and Data Management Services; User's Guide. Sandia National Laboratories, Albuquerque, NM (2007)
6. Çatalyürek, Ü.V., Aykanat, C.: PaToH: A multilevel hypergraph partitioning tool, ver. 3.0. Tech. Rep. BU-CE-9915, Bilkent Univ., Dept. Computer Eng. (1999)
7. Çatalyürek, Ü.V., Aykanat, C., Uçar, B.: On two-dimensional sparse matrix partitioning: Models, methods, and a recipe. SIAM J. Sci. Comput. 32, 656–683 (2010)

8. Hendrickson, B., Kolda, T.G.: Partitioning rectangular and structurally unsymmetric sparse matrices for parallel processing. SIAM J. Sci. Comput. 21, 2048–2072 (2000)
9. Karypis, G., Kumar, V.: MeTiS: A software package for partitioning unstructured graphs, partitioning meshes, and computing fill-reducing orderings of sparse matrices, version 4.0. Univ. Minnesota, Dept. Comp. Sci. Eng. (1998)
10. Karypis, G., Kumar, V.: Multilevel algorithms for multi-constraint graph partitioning. Tech. Rep. 98-019, Univ. Minnesota, Dept. Comp. Sci. Eng. (1998)
11. Kaya, K., Rouet, F.H., Uçar, B.: On partitioning problems with complex objectives. Tech. Rep. RR-7546, INRIA, France (2011)
12. Lengauer, T.: Combinatorial Algorithms for Integrated Circuit Layout. Wiley–Teubner, Chichester (1990)
13. Moulitsas, I., Karypis, G.: Partitioning algorithms for simultaneously balancing iterative and direct methods. Tech. Rep. 04-014, Univ. Minnesota, Dept. Comp. Sci. Eng. (2004)
14. Pellegrini, F.: SCOTCH 5.1 User's Guide. Laboratoire Bordelais de Recherche en Informatique (LaBRI) (2008)
15. Pınar, A., Hendrickson, B.: Partitioning for complex objectives. In: IPDPS 2001, CDROM, p. 121. IEEE Computer Society, Washington, DC (2001)
16. Sanchis, L.A.: Multiple-way network partitioning with different cost functions. IEEE T. Comput. 42, 1500–1504 (1993)
17. Schloegel, K., Karypis, G., Kumar, V.: Parallel Multilevel Algorithms for Multi-constraint Graph Partitioning. In: Bode, A., Ludwig, T., Karl, W.C., Wismüller, R. (eds.) Euro-Par 2000. LNCS, vol. 1900, pp. 296–310. Springer, Heidelberg (2000)
18. Uçar, B., Aykanat, C.: Encapsulating multiple communication-cost metrics in partitioning sparse rectangular matrices for parallel matrix-vector multiplies. SIAM J. Sci. Comput. 25, 1827–1859 (2004)
19. Vastenhouw, B., Bisseling, R.H.: A two-dimensional data distribution method for parallel sparse matrix-vector multiplication. SIAM Rev. 47, 67–95 (2005)
20. Yamazaki, I., Li, X.S., Rouet, F.H., Uçar, B.: Combinatorial problems in a parallel hybrid linear solver. In: Becker, M., Lotz, J., Mosenkis, V., Naumann, U. (eds.) Abstracts of 5th SIAM Workshop on Combinatorial Scientific Computing. pp. 87–89. RWTH Aachen University (2011)

A Communication-Avoiding Thick-Restart Lanczos Method on a Distributed-Memory System

Ichitaro Yamazaki* and Kesheng Wu

Lawrence Berkeley National Laboratory, Berkeley, CA, USA
ic.yamazaki@gmail.com

Abstract. The Thick-Restart Lanczos (TRLan) method is an effective method for solving large-scale Hermitian eigenvalue problems. On a modern computer, communication can dominate the solution time of TRLan. To enhance the performance of TRLan, we develop CA-TRLan that integrates communication-avoiding techniques into TRLan. To study the numerical stability and solution time of CA-TRLan, we conduct numerical experiments using both synthetic diagonal matrices and matrices from the University of Florida sparse matrix collection. Our experimental results on up to $1,024$ processors of a distributed-memory system demonstrate that CA-TRLan can achieve speedups of up to three over TRLan while maintaining numerical stability.

Keywords: thick-restart Lanczos, communication-avoiding.

1 Introduction

TRLan implements a thick-restart Lanczos method [12] on a distributed-memory system. It is effective for computing a few exterior eigenvalues λ and their corresponding eigenvectors v of a Hermitian matrix A:

$$Av = \lambda v.$$

On a modern computer, the time spent on communication (i.e., data access through memory hierarchy and data transfer between processors) can dominate the solution time of TRLan. To improve the performance of TRLan, in this paper, we study techniques to avoid communication. Several techniques to avoid communication of Krylov subspace methods have been proposed [5], but their performance on a distributed-memory system, especially for solving eigenvalue problems, has not yet been studied.

The rest of the paper is organized as follows: We first review TRLan in Section 2. Then, in Section 3, we develop a communication-avoiding version of TRLan (CA-TRLan). The experimental results of CA-TRLan are presented in Section 4. Finally, we conclude with final remarks in Section 5.

---

* Corresponding author.

M. Alexander et al. (Eds.): Euro-Par 2011 Workshops, Part I, LNCS 7155, pp. 345–354, 2012.

2   Thick-Restart Lanczos Method

Given a starting vector q, the i-th iteration of the Lanczos method [6] computes a new orthonormal basis vector q_{i+1} of a Krylov subspace,

$$\mathcal{K}_{i+1}(q, A) \equiv \mathrm{span}\{q, Aq, A^2q, \ldots, A^iq\} \equiv \mathrm{span}\{q_1, q_2, \ldots, q_{i+1}\}.$$

These basis vectors satisfy the relation

$$AQ_i = Q_iT_i + \beta_iq_{i+1}e_i^H, \tag{1}$$

where $Q_i = [q_1, q_2, \ldots, q_i]$, $\beta_i = q_{i+1}^H Aq_i$, e_i is the i-th column of the i-dimensional identity matrix I_i, $T_i = Q_i^H AQ_i$ is an $i \times i$ Rayleigh-Ritz projection of A onto $\mathcal{K}_i(A, q)$, and the superscript ^{H} indicates the conjugate transpose. Then, an approximate eigenpair $(\theta, x = Q_iy)$ of A is computed from an eigenpair (θ, y) of T_i, where θ and x are referred to as a Ritz value and Ritz vector, respectively. It is well known that Ritz values converge to exterior eigenvalues of A with a subspace dimension i that is much smaller than the dimension n of A [7,8].

A key feature that distinguishes the Lanczos method from other subspace projection methods is that T_i of (1) is symmetric tridiagonal:

$$T_i = \begin{pmatrix} \alpha_1 & \beta_1 & & & \\ \beta_1 & \alpha_2 & \beta_2 & & \\ & \beta_2 & \ddots & \ddots & \\ & & \ddots & \alpha_{i-1} & \beta_{i-1} \\ & & & \beta_{i-1} & \alpha_i \end{pmatrix}.$$

This leads to the following simple three-term recurrence:

$$\beta_iq_{i+1} = Aq_i - \alpha_iq_i - \beta_{i-1}q_{i-1}. \tag{2}$$

Subsequently, in theory, the new basis vector q_{i+1} can be computed by orthonormalizing the vector Aq_i against two preceding basis vectors, q_{i-1} and q_i. However, in finite precision arithmetic, the orthogonality among the basis vectors is lost even after a small number of iterations. To maintain orthogonality, TRLan reorthogonalizes the new basis vector q_{i+1} against all the previous vectors Q_i using a Classical Gram-Schmidt (CGS) procedure. As the basis size $i+1$ grows, this procedure becomes expensive in terms of both computation and storage.

To reduce the costs of computing a large subspace, TRLan restarts the iteration after a fixed number $m+1$ of the basis vectors is computed. At the $(j-1)$-th restart, TRLan sets k_j computed Ritz vectors and the last basis vector q_{m+1} as the first $k_j + 1$ basis vectors of the next projection subspace. To compute the (k_j+2)-th basis vector, TRLan computes $A\widehat{q}_{k_j+1}$ and orthonormalizes it against the previous basis vectors,[1]

$$\widehat{\beta}_{k_j+1}\widehat{q}_{k_j+2} = A\widehat{q}_{k_j+1} - \widehat{Q}_{k_j}(\widehat{Q}_{k_j}^H A\widehat{q}_{k_j+1}) - \widehat{q}_{k_j+1}(\widehat{q}_{k_j+1}^H A\widehat{q}_{k_j+1}), \tag{3}$$

---

[1] A hat distinguishes the i-th basis vector $\widehat{q}_i$ computed after the restart from the i-th basis vector q_i computed before the restart.

where $\widehat{Q}_{k_j}^H A \widehat{q}_{k_j+1} = \beta_m h$, $h = Y_{k_j}^H e_m$, and Y_{k_j} are the eigenvectors of T_m corresponding to the kept Ritz values.

In general, at the i-th iteration of the j-th restart-loop, the basis vectors satisfy the relation:

$$A\widehat{Q}_{k_j+i} = \widehat{Q}_{k_j+i}\widehat{T}_{k_j+i} + \widehat{\beta}_{k_j+i}\widehat{q}_{k_j+i+1}e_{k_j+i}^H,$$

where $\widehat{T}_{k_j+i} = \widehat{Q}_{k_j+i}^H A\widehat{Q}_{k_j+i}$ is of the form

$$\widehat{T}_{k_j+i} = \begin{pmatrix} D_{k_j} & \beta_m h \\ \beta_m h^H & \widehat{\alpha}_{k_j+1} & \widehat{\beta}_{k_j+1} \\ & \widehat{\beta}_{k_j+1} & \widehat{\alpha}_{k_j+2} & \widehat{\beta}_{k_j+2} \\ & & \widehat{\beta}_{k_j+2} & \ddots & \ddots \\ & & & \ddots & \widehat{\alpha}_{k_j+i-1} & \widehat{\beta}_{k_j+i-1} \\ & & & & \widehat{\beta}_{k_j+i-1} & \widehat{\alpha}_{k_j+i} \end{pmatrix}, \tag{4}$$

and D_{k_j} is a diagonal matrix whose diagonal elements are the kept Ritz values. In theory, the three-term recurrence is invalid only for computing q_{k_j+2} and is resumed afterward. However, to maintain orthogonality in finite precision arithmetic, TRLan reorthogonalizes each basis vector q_{k_j+i+1} against all the previous vectors. As a result, this full-reorthogonalization procedure and the matrix-vector multiplication often dominate the iteration time of TRLan. A detailed description of TRLan can be found in [11]. Effective auto-tuning schemes have been proposed to dynamically select the next subspace dimension m and the Ritz vectors to keep at each restart [12].

3 Communication-Avoiding TRLan

To compute q_{k_j+i+1} at the i-th iteration after the $(j-1)$-th restart, TRLan requires the *intra-processor* communication of the local portion of A and Q_{k_j+i} through the memory hierarchy, and also requires the *inter-processor* communication of all the required non-local data between the processors. This communication can dominate the iteration time of TRLan. To enhance the performance of TRLan, we develop CA-TRLan, which integrates techniques to avoid communication of Krylov subspace methods [5] into TRLan. The main idea is to compute a set of s basis vectors at each iteration. Below, we describe the t-th iteration of CA-TRLan to generate the next s basis vectors for the j-th restart-loop, where the basis vectors Q_{m_t+1} have been computed (i.e., $m_t = k_j + 1 + (t-1)s$).[2]

3.1 Krylov Subspace Generation

Given a starting vector q_{m_t+1}, the t-th iteration of CA-TRLan first generates basis vectors of the Krylov subspace $\mathcal{K}_{s+1}(q_{m_t+1}, A)$.[3] One option is to

---

[2] The last iteration generates $m - m_{t-1}$ basis vectors.

[3] The first starting vector q_{m_1+1} is q_{k_j+2} computed by the full-orthogonalization (3).

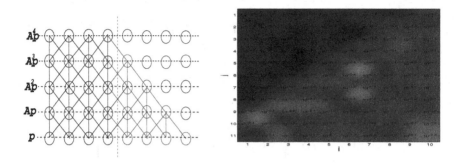

Fig. 1. Matrix-power kernel on a tridiagonal A (left) and orthogonality levels (right)

generate the monomial basis vectors $q_{m_t+1}, Aq_{m_t+1}, A^2q_{m_t+1}, \ldots, A^s q_{m_t+1}$, but the vector $A^s q_{m_t+1}$ converges to the principal eigenvector of A, leading to numerical instability in finite precision arithmetic. To avoid this instability, as suggested in [1,5], CA-TRLan generates the Newton basis vectors $P_+^{(t)} = [p_1^{(t)}, p_2^{(t)}, \ldots, p_{s+1}^{(t)}]$, where $p_i^{(t)} = \prod_{\ell=1}^{i-1}(A - \theta_\ell I)q_{m_t+1}$, and θ_ℓ are the Ritz values computed at the $(j-1)$-th restart in the Leja ordering. Notice that

$$AP^{(t)} = P_+^{(t)} B_+^{(t)}, \tag{5}$$

where $P^{(t)} = [p_1^{(t)}, p_2^{(t)}, \ldots, p_s^{(t)}]$ and $B^{(t)}$ is an $(s+1) \times s$ matrix whose diagonal entries are $\theta_1, \theta_2, \ldots, \theta_s$ and subdiagonal entries are ones. In order to obtain the shifts θ_ℓ, TRLan (without avoiding communication) is used for the first restart-loop of CA-TRLan.

The left figure in Fig. 1 illustrates our implementation of the matrix-power kernel to generate a set of s basis vectors $P_+^{(t)}$ for a tridiagonal matrix A (i.e., $s = 4$). In the figure, blue elements are the local portion of $P_+^{(t)}$, which must be computed by a processor, and edges between elements represent the data dependency. Our implementation first uses a k-way edge partitioning algorithm of METIS[4] to partition and distribute A into a block row format. The basis vectors $P^{(t)}$ are distributed in the conforming format. Now, at each t-th iteration to compute $P_+^{(t)}$, each processor first gathers all the required elements of q_{m_t+1} from the neighboring processors (the red elements of p in Fig. 1), and then it computes the local portion of $P_+^{(t)}$ without further communication. This requires the computation and storage of additional elements (the red elements in Fig. 1), but needs only one synchronization to compute the s vectors. The rows of A corresponding to the red elements of p in Fig. 1 are duplicated by the neighboring processors. A detailed discussion of the matrix-power kernel can be found in [4].

---

[4] http://glaros.dtc.umn.edu/gkhome/metis/metis.

3.2   Orthogonalization

Once the Newton basis vectors $P_+^{(t)}$ are computed as described in Section 3.1, CA-TRLan orthogonalizes $P_+^{(t)}$ and generates the orthonormal basis vectors $Q_+^{(t)} = [q_1^{(t)}, q_2^{(t)}, \ldots, q_{s+1}^{(t)}] = [q_{m_t+1}, q_{m_t+2}, \ldots, q_{m_t+s+1}]$. This is done by first orthogonalizing $P_+^{(t)}$ against the previous basis vectors Q_{m_t} and then orthogonalizing among the vectors in $P_+^{(t)}$. Note that the first vector $p_1^{(t)}$ is the last basis vector $q_{s+1}^{(t-1)}$ from the previous iteration, and it is already orthogonal to Q_{m_t}. Furthermore, because of the three-term recurrence (2), we have

$$p_{i+1}^{(t)} \in \text{span}\{q_{m_t-i+1}, q_{m_t-i+2}, \ldots, q_{m_t+i+1}\} \tag{6}$$

for $i = 1, 2, \ldots, s$. Hence, in theory, we can obtain the next basis vector q_{m_t+i+1} by orthonormalizing $p_{i+1}^{(t)}$ against the previous $2 \cdot i$ basis vectors. To illustrate this, the right figure of Fig. 1 shows the orthogonality level $r_{j,i+1}^{(t)}$ of $p_{i+1}^{(t)}$ against $q_j^{(t-1)}$ (i.e., $r_{j,i+1}^{(t)} = |q_j^{(t-1)H} p_{i+1}^{(t)}| / \|p_{i+1}^{(t)}\|_2$) at the second iteration of the second restart-loop for computing the 100 smallest eigenvalues of $\text{diag}(1^2, 2^2, \ldots, 10000^2)$ with $s = 10$.[5] We clearly see that $r_{j,i+1}^{(t)}$ diminishes for $j \leq s - i$. Only exception is at the first iteration (i.e., $t = 1$), where the full-orthogonalization is needed because $p_1^{(1)}$ is computed by (3), and $p_{i+1}^{(1)}$ does not satisfy (6).

Based on the above observations, the first step of our orthogonalization procedure uses CGS to orthogonalizes $P_+^{(t)}$ against the previous vectors Q_{m_t}. For this, xGEMM of level-3 BLAS is used once to compute $\bar{R}_-^{(t)} := Q_+^{(t-1)H} P_-^{(t)}$ and one more time to compute $\bar{P}_-^{(t)} := P_-^{(t)} - Q_+^{(t-1)} \bar{R}_-^{(t)}$.[6] The vector $p_{i+1}^{(t)}$ is orthogonalized against all the vectors in $Q_+^{(t-1)}$ even though it must be orthogonalized against only $i + 1$ vectors. This improves the data locality while increasing the operation count. TRLan also uses CGS for reorthogonalization, but it orthogonalizes one vector at a time using xGEMV of level-2 BLAS.

The second step of the orthogonalization procedure computes the QR factorization of $\bar{P}_-^{(t)}$ (i.e., $Q_-^{(t)} R_-^{(t)} = \bar{P}_-^{(t)}$). For this, we have implemented the following four approaches, where $\bar{P}_-^{(t)}$ and $Q_-^{(t)}$ are distributed among all the available p processors in a row block layout, while $R_-^{(t)}$ is duplicated on each processor:

- **CGS-Approach:** Similarly to TRLan, each vector of $\bar{P}_-^{(t)}$ is orthogonalized against the previous vectors based on CGS using xGEMV of level-2 BLAS. Communication is needed for orthogonalizing and normalizing each vector.
- **CholeskyQR-Approach:** xGEMM is first used to compute $\bar{P}_-^{(t)H} \bar{P}_-^{(t)}$ and then xPORTRF of LAPACK is used to compute its Cholesky factor $R_-^{(t)}$; i.e., $R_-^{(t)H} R_-^{(t)} = \bar{P}_-^{(t)H} \bar{P}_-^{(t)}$. Finally, xTRSM of LAPACK is used to compute $Q_-^{(t)}$

---

[5] A detailed description of the numerical experiment can be found in Section 4.
[6] For the full-orthogonalization at $t = 1$, we compute $\bar{R}_-^{(t)} := Q_{m_t}^H P^{(t)}$.

by solving the triangular system $R_-^{(t)H} Q_-^{(t)H} = \bar{P}_-^{(t)H}$. This approach requires about the same number of arithmetic operations as the CGS-approach. However, when the window size is much smaller than the local matrix size, i.e., $s \ll n/p$, most of the computation is performed using level-3 BLAS. Moreover, this approach achieves the lower-bound of the communication volume and message count for the QR factorization. Even though this approach was successful in our numerical experiments, it may be numerically unstable when A is ill-conditioned. More discussion of the numerical stability, and the computation and communication bounds can be found in [3,9].

- **ScaLAPACK-Approach:** The ScaLAPACK subroutines PxGEQRF and PxORGQR, which implement a numerically stable Householder QR factorization, were used. Even though ScaLAPACK expects $\bar{P}_-^{(t)}$ in a 2D block cyclic format, we used the row block layout to call ScaLAPACK in our numerical experiments. We also converted the matrix into a 1D block cyclic format, but the overhead of conversion can be significant, while the expected performance gain is small.
- **TSQR-Approach:** A communication-avoiding QR algorithm for tall-skinny matrices [3] is used. This algorithm obtains the lower-bound of communication and is as numerically stable as ScaLAPACK.

The resulting basis vectors satisfy the following relation:

$$P_{m_{t+1}+1} = Q_{m_{t+1}+1} R_{m_{t+1}+1}, \tag{7}$$

where $P_{m_{t+1}+1} = [Q_{k_j+1}, P_-^{(1)}, P_-^{(2)}, \dots, P_-^{(t)}]$, $R_{m_{t+1}+1} = \begin{pmatrix} R_{m_t+1} & \widehat{R}_-^{(t)} \\ & R_-^{(t)} \end{pmatrix}$,

$R_{m_1+1} = I_{k_j+2}$, and $\widehat{R}_-^{(t)} = Q_{m_t+1}^H P_-^{(t)}$. In theory, we have $\widehat{R}_-^{(t)} = \begin{pmatrix} 0_{m_t \times s} \\ \bar{R}_-^{(t)} \end{pmatrix}$ for

$t \geq 2$, where $0_{m_t \times s}$ is an $m_t \times s$ zero matrix, and $\bar{R}_-^{(t)}$ has the nonzero structure indicated by Fig. 1. To maintain orthogonality, however, CA-TRLan performs the full-reorthogonalization of $Q_-^{(t)}$ using the two-step procedure described in this section. As we will show in Section 3.3, only the bidiagonal elements of $R_-^{(t)}$ are needed in the remaining steps of CA-TRLan. Hence, after the reorthogonalization, only these required elements of $R_-^{(t)}$ are updated.

3.3 Tridiagonal Matrix Computation

Finally, to expand the tridiagonal matrix $\widehat{T}_{m_{t+1}}$ of (4), we compute the projected matrix $T_+^{(t)} = Q_+^{(t)H} A Q^{(t)}$, where $Q^{(t)} = [q_1^{(t)}, q_2^{(t)}, \dots, q_s^{(t)}]$. By (5) and (7), we have $T_+^{(t)} = R_+^{(t)} B^{(t)} (R^{(t)})^{-1}$, where $R_+^{(t)}$ and $R^{(t)}$ are the $(s+1) \times (s+1)$ and $s \times s$ lower-right submatrices of $R_{m_{t+1}+1}$ and $R_{m_{t+1}}$ of (7), respectively [5, Section 4.2.2]. Hence, the elements of $T_+^{(t)}$ are computed by the following simple recursion: for $i = 1, 2, \dots, s$,

$$\begin{cases} \alpha_i^{(t)} = (\theta_i r_{i,i}^{(t)} + r_{i,i+1}^{(t)} - \beta_{i-1}^{(t)} r_{i-1,i}^{(t)})/r_{i,i}^{(t)}, \\ \beta_i^{(t)} = r_{i+1,i+1}^{(t)}/r_{i,i}^{(t)}, \end{cases}$$

where $\alpha_i^{(t)} := \alpha_{m_t+i}$, $\beta_i^{(t)} := \beta_{m_t+i}$, $\beta_0^{(t)} = 0$, and $r_{i,j}^{(t)}$ is the (i,j)-th element of $R_+^{(t)}$. Notice that only the bidiagonal elements of $R_+^{(t)}$ are needed.

4 Numerical Experiments

We first study the effects of the window size s on the performance of CA-TRLan. Table 1 shows the results of computing the 100 smallest eigenvalues of the diagonal matrix $A_k(n) = \mathrm{diag}(1^k, 2^k, \ldots, n^k)$ of dimension $n = 10,000$ with $k = 1, 2$, or 3 on a single core of a Cray-XT4 machine at NERSC. The dimension of the projection subspace is fixed at $m = 200$ for $k = 1$ and 2, and at $m = 400$ for $k = 3$. A Ritz pair (θ, x) is considered to be converged when $\|Ax - \theta x\|_2 \leq 10^{-16}\|A\|_2$ and $\|A\|_2$ is approximated by the largest modulus of the computed Ritz values. In the table, "rest." is the number of restarts; "ops" is the number of matrix-operations; "res. norm" is the relative residual norm of the 100-th smallest computed eigenvalue; "time" shows the times required for the matrix-operations, orthogonalization, and restarts, and the total solution time in seconds. Under "time," we also show the time spent on the QR factorization of $\bar{P}_-^{(t)}$ in parentheses.

In the table, we see that the solution accuracy of CA-TRLan with s up to 20 was similar to that of TRLan in most cases. The only exceptions were when the CGS- or CholeskyQR-approach was used with $s = 15$ on A_3. In these cases, CA-TRLan failed to converge due to numerical instability. On the other hand, the ScaLAPACK- and TSQR-approaches were numerically stable with s up to 20. We also see that the orthogonalization time of CA-TRLan was much less than that of TRLan due to the reduced intra-processor communication on the single core. Furthermore, the first step of the orthogonalization procedure dominated the orthogonalization time. A larger value of s improved the data locality and reduced the time spent in this first step, but it increased the time required for the second step, which must orthogonalize the vectors in a larger window. Even though the TSQR-approach was faster than the ScaLAPACK-approach, these two approaches were significantly slower than the CGS- and CholeskyQR-approaches, especially with a larger value of s.

We next examine the parallel scalability of CA-TRLan. The left plot of Fig. 2 shows the solution times of CA-TRLan and TRLan computing the smallest 100 eigenvalues of $A_3(10,000)$. We used the CholeskyQR-based orthogonalization and the fixed parameters $m = 400$ and $s = 10$. The number above each bar is the speedup gained by CA-TRLan over TRLan using the same number of processors. A significant speedup was obtained by CA-TRLan on one processor due to the optimized intra-processor communication of level-3 BLAS. However, as the processor count increased (e.g., 4 to 64 processors), the local matrix size decreased, and so did the improvement gained using level-3 BLAS. Since the solution time was dominated by computation and intra-processor communication on a small number of processors, the speedups gained by CA-TRLan decreased. However, as the processor count increased further, inter-processor communication started to dominate the solution time (labeled by "MPI" in Fig. 2). CA-TRLan avoided

Table 1. Numerical results of CA-TRLan on synthetic diagonal matrices

s	rest.	ops	res. norm	time ops	orth	rest.	total	s	rest.	ops	res. norm	time ops	orth	rest.	total
— results with $A_1(10,000)$ —								— results with $A_2(10,000)$ —							
TRLan								TRLan							
	34	2.4K	9.3×10^{-12}	0	10 (0)	2	13		377	21.0K	1.0×10^{-8}	1	94 (0)	29	125
CA-TRLan with CGS-approach								CA-TRLan with CGS-approach							
5	34	2.5K	$9.9 \cdot 10^{-12}$	0	6 (0)	2	9	5	374	21.7K	$8.9 \cdot 10^{-8}$	1	59 (3)	29	92
10	34	2.5K	$9.7 \cdot 10^{-12}$	0	5 (1)	2	8	10	361	22.3K	$9.0 \cdot 10^{-8}$	1	46 (5)	28	78
15	34	2.6K	$1.4 \cdot 10^{-11}$	0	5 (1)	2	8	15	376	23.7K	$9.6 \cdot 10^{-8}$	1	50 (9)	29	83
20	34	2.7K	$1.7 \cdot 10^{-11}$	0	5 (1)	2	8	20	375	25.8K	$1.0 \cdot 10^{-7}$	1	53 (12)	29	86
CA-TRLan with CholeskyQR-approach								CA-TRLan with CholeskyQR-approach							
5	34	2.5K	$9.0 \cdot 10^{-12}$	0	6 (0)	3	9	5	370	21.7K	$9.0 \cdot 10^{-8}$	1	59 (3)	29	91
10	34	2.5K	$1.0 \cdot 10^{-11}$	0	5 (0)	3	8	10	362	22.5K	$1.0 \cdot 10^{-7}$	1	45 (4)	28	77
15	34	2.6K	$1.4 \cdot 10^{-11}$	0	5 (1)	3	8	15	367	23.7K	$9.1 \cdot 10^{-8}$	1	46 (5)	29	78
20	34	2.7K	$2.5 \cdot 10^{-11}$	0	5 (1)	3	8	20	364	25.2K	$9.6 \cdot 10^{-8}$	1	46 (6)	29	78
CA-TRLan with ScaLAPACK-approach								CA-TRLan with ScaLAPACK-approach							
5	34	2.5K	$1.6 \cdot 10^{-11}$	0	7 (1)	2	10	5	370	21.8K	$1.8 \cdot 10^{-7}$	1	65 (9)	29	97
10	34	2.5K	$1.8 \cdot 10^{-11}$	0	6 (1)	2	9	10	360	22.2K	$2.1 \cdot 10^{-7}$	1	55 (14)	28	87
15	34	2.6K	$4.2 \cdot 10^{-11}$	0	7 (2)	2	9	15	359	23.3K	$2.2 \cdot 10^{-7}$	1	61 (21)	28	93
20	34	2.7K	$4.0 \cdot 10^{-11}$	0	7 (3)	2	10	20	374	25.6K	$2.1 \cdot 10^{-7}$	1	70 (30)	29	103

s	rest.	ops	res. norm	time ops	orth	rest.	total	s	rest.	ops	res. norm	time ops	orth	rest.	total
— results with $A_3(10,000)$ —															
TRLan								CA-TRLan with ScaLAPACK-approach							
	2.4K	192K	$8.7 \cdot 10^{-4}$	6	1722 (0)	254	2002	5	2.7K	213K	$1.7 \cdot 10^{-3}$	12	1208 (85)	266	1541
CA-TRLan with CGS-approach								10	2.2K	199K	$2.4 \cdot 10^{-3}$	10	836 (129)	249	1141
5	2.6K	210K	$8.4 \cdot 10^{-4}$	12	1115 (27)	265	1445	15	2.4K	206K	$5.4 \cdot 10^{-3}$	11	869 (189)	253	1182
10	2.3K	200K	$8.6 \cdot 10^{-4}$	10	763 (49)	249	1070	20	2.6K	235K	$2.5 \cdot 10^{-2}$	12	984 (277)	262	1313
15	--	--	--	--	--	--	--	CA-TRLan with TSQR-approach							
CA-TRLan with CholeskyQR-approach								5	2.7K	212K	$8.7 \cdot 10^{-4}$	12	1163 (67)	266	1497
5	2.6K	210K	$8.5 \cdot 10^{-4}$	12	1109 (27)	265	1439	10	2.8K	227K	$9.2 \cdot 10^{-4}$	12	923 (98)	271	1262
10	2.5K	212K	$8.8 \cdot 10^{-4}$	11	799 (36)	262	1145	15	2.6K	213K	$1.6 \cdot 10^{-3}$	11	813 (108)	258	1134
15	--	--	--	--	--	--	--	20	2.6K	234K	$5.6 \cdot 10^{-3}$	12	841 (140)	258	1169

some of the inter-processor communication, and the improvement gained by CA-TRLan started to increase. The right plot of Fig. 2 shows the timing results of CA-TRLan and TRLan computing the smallest 30 eigenvalues of $A_2(10,000)$ with $m = 80$ and $s = 15$. In comparison to the left plot, the right plot shows more significant performance advantage of CA-TRLan because communication started to dominate the solution time of TRLan much sooner.

Finally, Table 2 shows the results of CA-TRLan computing the 30 smallest eigenvalues of four matrices (#1 Andrews, #2 torsion1, #3 cfd1, and #4 finan512) from the University of Florida sparse Matrix Collection (UFMC). For each ℓ-th matrix, we show #$\ell(n, nnz, \text{cond})$, where "$n$" is the matrix dimension in thousands, "nnz" is the number of nonzeros in thousands, and "cond" is the 1-norm condition number estimate computed using the MATLAB subroutine **condest**. Furthermore, "ln" and "lnz" show the minimum and maximum local dimensions and numbers of nonzeros in thousands. The experiments were conducted on 32 processors with the CholeskyQR-based orthogonalization and $(m, s) = (80, 10)$. In the table, "surf/vol" is the overhead of the matrix-power kernel discussed in Section 3.1. Specifically, under "A," we show the maximum ratio of the number of duplicated nonzeros of A over the number of local

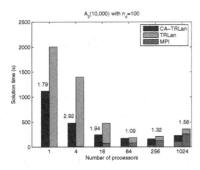
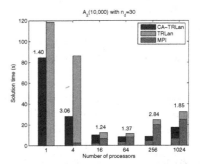

Fig. 2. Performance of CA-TRLan computing n_d eigenpairs of diagonal matrices

Table 2. Numerical results of CA-TRLan with matrices from UFMC collection

	surf/vol					time			surf/vol					time	
s	A^s	A	rest.	ops	res. norm	op	ort	tot	s	A^s	A	rest.	ops	res. norm	op	ort	tot
#1(60,760, 2.5×10^{17}), $ln(1.8, 2.0)$ $lnz(2.3, 2.5)$									#2(40, 198, 31), $ln = (1.2, 1.3)$ $lnz(5.6, 6.3)$						
TRLan									TRLan						
	0.0	0.0	24	865	$3.3 \cdot 10^{-14}$	2	1	4		0.0	0.0	118	3046	$1.1 \cdot 10^{-14}$	4	3	9
CA-TRLan									CA-TRLan						
1	0.0	0.0	24	865	$3.1 \cdot 10^{-14}$	2	2	4	1	0.0	0.0	116	3018	$1.1 \cdot 10^{-14}$	4	5	9
5	17.1	25.2	24	917	$3.1 \cdot 10^{-14}$	2	1	3	5	0.5	0.5	111	3234	$1.0 \cdot 10^{-14}$	1	1	3
10	--	32.0	24	972	$3.3 \cdot 10^{-14}$	5	1	6	10	1.2	1.3	116	3686	$1.2 \cdot 10^{-14}$	1	1	3
#3(71, 1.8, 1.3×10^{6}), $ln(2.1, 2.3)$ $lnz(53, 59)$									#4(75, 597, 98), $ln = (2.2, 2.2)$ $lnz(18, 19)$						
TRLan									TRLan						
	0.0	0.0	509	10318	$7.9 \cdot 10^{-15}$	17	15	36		0.0	0.0	78	1921	$1.2 \cdot 10^{-14}$	3	3	7
CA-TRLan									CA-TRLan						
1	0.0	0.0	644	12245	$9.4 \cdot 10^{-15}$	22	24	49	1	0.0	0.0	77	1910	$1.1 \cdot 10^{-14}$	3	4	8
5	4.3	3.9	510	11198	$8.3 \cdot 10^{-15}$	10	10	23	5	0.5	0.4	79	2112	$1.1 \cdot 10^{-14}$	1	1	3
10	11.6	12.2	587	14415	$1.5 \cdot 10^{-15}$	19	17	38	10	2.6	2.3	78	2306	$3.8 \cdot 10^{-14}$	1	1	3

nonzeros of A (corresponding to the red and blue elements, respectively, in Fig. 1)
on one processor. Under "A^s," we show the same ratio obtained computing the
k-way edge partition of explicitly computed A^s.[7] We see that the these two ratios are similar for the same value of s indicating that the partition of A was
as good as that obtained on A^s for these matrices. The numerical and timing
results are those with the partition of A. CA-TRLan obtained solution accuracy
similar to that of TRLan while achieving speedups of up to 3.54.

5   Conclusion

We have studied techniques to avoid communication of TRLan on a distributed-
memory system. The experimental results demonstrated that these techniques
can significantly reduce the solution time of TRLan while maintaining numerical
stability. Our matrix-power kernel has not yet been optimized for intra-processor
communication, and for this, we are planning to integrate the optimized sparse

---

[7] In the table "--" indicates insufficient memory to compute A^s.

kernel interface (OSKI) [10] into CA-TRLan. Furthermore, partitioning algorithms to enhance matrix-power kernels (e.g., [2]) is an important computational kernel of CA-TRLan, and we would like to study the effectiveness of such an algorithm for computing eigenpairs of general matrices with CA-TRLan.

Acknowledgements. We gratefully thank Mark Hoemmen, Magnus Gustafsson, James Demmel, and Julien Langou for helpful discussions. This research was supported in part by the Director, Office of Science, Office of Advanced Scientific Computing Research of the U.S. Department of Energy under Contract No. D-AC02-05CH11231, and the NSF PLASMA grant (#CCF-0811642) and the Microsoft PLASMA grant (MSRER RPD v3.1).

References

1. Bai, Z., Hu, D., Reichel, L.: A Newton basis GMRES implementation. IMA Journal of Numerical Analysis 14, 563–581 (1994)
2. Carson, E., Knight, N., Demmel, J.: Hypergraph partitioning for computing matrix powers. In: The Proceedings of SIAM Workshop on Combinatorial Scientific Computing (2011)
3. Demmel, J., Grigori, L., Hoemmen, M., Langou, J.: Communication-optimal parallel and sequential QR and LU factorizations. Technical Report UCB/EECS-2008-89, EECS Department, University of California, Berkeley (2008)
4. Demmel, J., Hoemmen, M., Mohiyuddin, M., Yelick, K.: Avoiding communication in sparse matrix computations. In: The Proceedings of IEEE International Symposium on Parallel and Distributed Processing (IPDPS), pp. 1–12 (2008)
5. Hoemmen, M.: Communication-avoiding Krylov subspace methods. PhD thesis, University of California, Berkeley (2010)
6. Lanczos, C.: An iteration method for the solution of the eigenvalue problem of linear differential and integral operators. J. Res. Nat. Bur. Stand. 45, 255–281 (1950)
7. Parlett, B.: The symmetric eigenvalue problem. Classics in Applied Mathematics. SIAM, Philadelphia (1998)
8. Saad, Y.: Numerical Methods for Large Eigenvalue Problems, 2nd edn. Classics in Applied Mathematics. SIAM, Philadelphia (2003)
9. Stathopoulos, A., Wu, K.: A block orthogonalization procedure with constant synchronization requirements. SIAM J. Sci. Comput. 23, 2165–2182 (2002)
10. Vuduc, R., Demmel, J., Yelick, K.: OSKI: A library of automatically tuned sparse matrix kernels. In: Proc. SciDAC, J. Physics: Conf. Ser., vol. 16, pp. 521–530 (2005), http://bebop.cs.berkeley.edu/oski/
11. Wu, K., Simon, H.: Thick-restart Lanczos method for large symmetric eigenvalue problems. SIAM J. Mat. Anal. Appl. 22, 602–616 (2000)
12. Yamazaki, I., Bai, Z., Simon, H., Wand, L.-W., Wu, K.: Adaptive projection subspace dimension for the thick-restart Lanczos method. ACM Trans. Math. Softw. 37 (2010), https://codeforge.lbl.gov/projects/trlan/

Spherical Harmonic Transform with GPUs

Ioan Ovidiu Hupca[1,3], Joel Falcou[1,3], Laura Grigori[1,3], and Radek Stompor[2]

[1] LRI - INRIA Saclay-Ile de France
{ioanovidiu.hupca,laura.grigori}@inria.fr, joel.falcou@lri.fr
[2] Astroparticule et Cosmologie, CNRS, Université Paris Diderot, Paris, France
radek@apc.univ-paris7.fr
[3] Université Paris-Sud 11, Orsay, France

Abstract. We describe an algorithm for computing an inverse spherical harmonic transform suitable for graphic processing units (GPU). We use CUDA and base our implementation on a FORTRAN90 routine included in a publicly available parallel package, s²HAT. We focus our attention on two major sequential steps involved in the transforms computation retaining the efficient parallel framework of the original code. We detail optimization techniques used to enhance the performance of the CUDA-based code and contrast them with those implemented in the FORTRAN90 version. We present performance comparisons of a single CPU plus GPU unit with the s²HAT code running on either a single or 4 processors. In particular, we find that the latest generation of GPUs, such as NVIDIA GF100 (Fermi), can accelerate the spherical harmonic transforms by as much as 18 times with respect to s²HAT executed on one core, and by as much as 5.5 with respect to s²HAT on 4 cores, with the overall performance being limited by the Fast Fourier transforms. The work presented here has been performed in the context of the Cosmic Microwave Background simulations and analysis. However, we expect that the developed software will be of more general interest and applicability.

Keywords: Spherical Harmonic Transform, NVIDIA CUDA, GPU, Cosmic Microwave Background.

1 Introduction

Spherical harmonic transforms are ubiquitous in diverse areas of science and practical applications, which need to deal with data distributed on a sphere. In particular, they are heavily used in various areas of cosmology, such as studies of the cosmic microwave background (CMB) radiation and its anisotropies, which have been our main motivations for this work. CMB is an electromagnetic radiation left over after the hot and very dense stage of early evolution of our Universe. Its measurements play a vital role in the present-day cosmology and have been a driving force behind turning it into a high precision, data-driven science it is today. A recent stunning increase in CMB data sets sizes, driven by the quick improvement of the detector technologies, has posed a formidable challenge for the CMB data analysis, which can only be met if efficient numerical algorithms and the latest computer hardware are employed to provide a sufficient,

M. Alexander et al. (Eds.): Euro-Par 2011 Workshops, Part I, LNCS 7155, pp. 355–366, 2012.

concurrent increase in our processing capability. Spherical harmonic transforms are some of the most fundamental tools used in the CMB data processing. This is because the CMB signal is naturally a function of the observational direction and thus can be adequately described as a field defined on a sphere. The spherical harmonic functions are a suitable basis to represent and manipulate such fields. The spherical harmonic transforms involve a decomposition of the signals defined on the sphere into a set of harmonic coefficients (i.e., a *direct* spherical harmonic transform) as well as synthesis of the sky signal given a set of harmonic expansion coefficients (i.e, an *inverse* transform). The latter is for instance a key step in massive Monte Carlo simulations used in the CMB data processing. As they usually require a very high resolution and precision, synthesis operations are particularly time and resources consuming. They are therefore the focus of this work, which discuss their implementation on the NVIDIA GPU architecture within the CUDA framework. We note that these transforms are commonly used beyond cosmology, for example, in geophysics, oceanography, or planetology and for all of which the implementation described here should be directly relevant.

There are several packages available implementing the spherical harmonic transforms with HEALPIX (http://healpix.jpl.nasa.gov/), CCSHT (http://crd.lbl.gov/~cmc/ccSHTlib/doc/), S^2HAT (http://www.apc.univ-paris7.fr/~radek/s2hat.html), GLESP (http://www.glesp.nbi.dk/), particularly popular in the CMB research. Here, we have used S^2HAT (Scalable Spherical Harmonic Transform) as the starting point for this research and a reference for performance comparisons. While all these packages implement similar numerical algorithms, only S^2HAT is not tied to any specific sky pixelization or discretization schemes. It is fully parallelized using MPI, and shows memory scalability, good speedup and load-balance over a wide range of considered problems.

Our primary final target are however heterogeneous, multi-processor systems made of multiple CPUs, each accompanied by a respective GPU. As the first step towards achieving this goal we focus on porting the two main, serial steps in the calculation of the transforms onto GPUs and retain the data distribution layout and communication structure of the original MPI code. Consequently, when run on a multi-processor/multi-GPU platform our code employs MPI calls to distribute the data and workload over all the CPUs, which then send them to their respective GPUs, where the bulk of the computation is performed. The performance tests presented in this paper focus specifically on the benefits due to GPUs and thus on single CPU/GPU. Cases with the multi-GPU/multi-CPU configurations are studied elsewhere [1].

2   Spherical Harmonic Transforms

2.1   Algebraic Background

Any real, band-limited, scalar field, s, defined on the $\mathcal{S}^2$-sphere can be represented as,

$$s\left(\theta_p, \phi_p\right) = \sum_{\ell=0}^{\ell_{max}} \sum_{m=-\ell}^{\ell} a_{\ell m} Y_{\ell m}\left(\theta_p, \phi_p\right) \tag{1}$$

Here the coefficients $a_{\ell m}$ define a harmonic representation of the field s, $Y_{\ell m}$ stands for a spherical harmonic. We assume, as it is usually the case in practical applications that the field, s is to be computed only on a discrete set of points, hereafter typically identified with a centers of sky pixels described by standard spherical coordinates, (θ_p, ϕ_p). The upper limit, ℓ_{max} in Eq. 1 defines the band-limit of the field s and is considered to be finite. In the CMB application it is usually determined by an experiment resolution and its typical values are $\ell_{max} = \mathcal{O}\left(10^3 - 10^4\right)$. The transform's objective is to reconstruct, or synthesize, the field, s, from its harmonic coefficients $a_{\ell m}$ on a grid of points p, and we will refer to it as the `alm2map` transform.

The spherical harmonics are defined as (hereafter, we will drop the index p for shortness)

$$Y_{\ell m}\left(\theta, \phi\right) \equiv \mathcal{P}_{\ell m}\left(\cos\theta\right) e^{im\phi} \tag{2}$$

where *renormalized* associated Legendre functions, $\mathcal{P}_{\ell m}\left(\cos\theta\right)$ are solutions of the Hemholtz equations, e.g., [2], normalized to ensure that $Y_{\ell m}$ constitute an orthonormal basis on the sphere. They can be computed via a 2-point recurrence, e.g., [2], with respect to the multipole number, ℓ, i.e.,

$$\mathcal{P}_{\ell+2,m}\left(x\right) = \beta_{\ell+2,m} \left[x\,\mathcal{P}_{\ell+1,m}\left(x\right) + \frac{1}{\beta_{\ell+1,m}}\mathcal{P}_{\ell m}\left(x\right)\right] \tag{3}$$

where $\beta_{\ell m} = \sqrt{(4\,\ell^2 - 1)/(\ell^2 - m^2)}$. The recurrence is initialized by the starting values,

$$\mathcal{P}_{mm}\left(x\right) = \mu_m \left(1 - x^2\right)^m, \quad \mu_m \equiv \frac{1}{2^m\,m!}\sqrt{\frac{(2m+1)!}{4\pi}} \tag{4}$$

$$\mathcal{P}_{m+1,m}\left(x\right) = \beta_{\ell+1,m}\,x\,\mathcal{P}_{mm}\left(x\right), \tag{5}$$

and is numerically stable but requires double precision and care has to be taken to ensure it does not under- or overflows. We describe a relevant algorithm in the next Section. On introducing,

$$\Delta_m\left(\theta\right) \equiv \begin{cases} \displaystyle\sum_{\ell=m}^{\ell_{max}} a_{\ell m}\,\mathcal{P}_{\ell m}\left(\cos\theta\right), & m \geq 0; \\[2ex] \displaystyle\sum_{\ell=|m|}^{\ell_{max}} a_{\ell|m|}^{\dagger}\,\mathcal{P}_{\ell|m|}\left(\cos\theta\right), & m < 0; \end{cases} \tag{6}$$

we can rewrite Eq. (1) as,

$$s\left(\theta, \phi\right) = \sum_{m=-\ell_{max}}^{\ell_{max}} e^{im\phi} \boldsymbol{\Delta}_m\left(\theta\right). \tag{7}$$

Eqs. 6 and 7 provide a basis for the numerical implementation of the spherical harmonic transforms.

2.2 Current Approach

A detailed description of the efficient serial implementation of the transforms can be found elsewhere [3,4]. Here we briefly outline the most important features, emphasizing the parallel aspects.

Numerical Complexity. From the sphere sampling considerations [5], we know that to properly sample a band-limited function with the band-limit set to ℓ_{max}, we need roughly $n_{pix} \sim \ell_{max}^2$ points on the sphere. Therefore to perform the operations required to calculate $\Delta\left(\theta\right)$, and as detailed in Eqs. 6, we need as many as $\mathcal{O}\left(n_{pix}^2\right)$ floating point operations (FLOPs). This is because for each of n_{pix} pixels we have to do the $\mathcal{P}_{\ell m}$ recurrence for all ℓ and m numbers, and there are $\mathcal{O}\left(\ell_{max}^2\right) \sim \mathcal{O}\left(n_{pix}\right)$ of (ℓ, m) pairs for a properly sample field. This is clearly a prohibitive scaling. It can however become more favorable if the problem is restricted to some specific sky pixelization/discretization schemes [5]. In particular, in the following we will always assume that all pixels/sky samples are arranged in a number of so-called iso-latitudinal rings, each of which have the same value of the polar angle, θ. Typically there will be $n_{rings} \sim \ell_{max}$ rings with each ring uniformly sampled $n_\phi \sim \ell_{max}$ times. Moreover, we will assume that the sky is pixelized symmetrically with respect to the equator. Such schemes indeed have been proposed and demonstrated to work well in practice [5,6,3,7] in a number of applications. With these constraints imposed on the pixelization the scaling for Eq. 6 is now $\mathcal{O}(n_{pix}^{3/2})$, given that the full $\mathcal{P}_{\ell m}$ recurrence needs to be now done only ones for each of the rings. The numerical cost of the final summation, Eq. 7, is then sub-dominant as it can be implemented using Fast Fourier transform (FFT) techniques, at the total cost of $\mathcal{O}\left(n_{pix} \ln n_\phi\right)$ FLOPs. We note here in passing that for this class of pixelizations even faster algorithms have been proposed with the complexity either on order of $\mathcal{O}[n_{pix}(\ln n_{pix})^2]$ [5] or $\mathcal{O}\left(n_{pix} \ln n_{pix}\right)$ [8]. However, they have a significant prefactor, involve complex algorithmic solutions, and have not been demonstrated to be numerically viable for $\ell_{max} \gg 100$.

Algorithm. The implementation of Eqs. 6 and 7 is rather straightforward. The pseudo code is outlined as Algorithm 1. Two steps which require somewhat more attention are the recurrence and the FFT. The two point recurrence as the one in Eq. 3 spans a huge dynamic range of values. This range depends on the values of ℓ, which need to be considered, but already for values as low as $\mathcal{O}\left(10^2\right)$ it exceeds

---

Algorithm 1. BASIC `alm2map` ALGORITHM

STEP 1 - $\boldsymbol{\Delta}_m$ CALCULATION

COMMENT: *Algorithm 2 has to be embedded below.*

for *every ring r* **do**

  for *every $m = 0, ..., m_{max}$* **do**

    for *every $\ell = m, ..., \ell_{max}$* **do**

      – *compute $\mathcal{P}_{\ell m}$ via the 2-point recurrence, Eq. 3;*

      – *update $\boldsymbol{\Delta}_m(r)$, given input $a_{\ell m}$ and computed $\mathcal{P}_{\ell m}$, Eq. 6;*

    end for *(ℓ)*

  end for *(m)*

STEP 2 - $\boldsymbol{s}$ CALCULATION

– *calculate $\boldsymbol{s}$ via FFT, given $\boldsymbol{\Delta}_m(r)$ pre-calculated for all m;*

end for *(r)*

Algorithm 2. 2-POINT ASSOCIATED LEGENDRE RECURRENCE

– *initialize the rescaling table;*

– *precompute $\boldsymbol{\mu}$ coefficients, Eq. 4;*

for *every ring r* **do**

  for *every $m = 0, ..., m_{max}$* **do**

    – *initialize the recurrence: $\mathcal{P}_{mm}$, $\mathcal{P}_{m+1,m}$, Eqs. 4 & 5, using precomputed μ_m;*

    – *precompute recurrence coefficients, $\beta_{\ell m}$ (fixed m, $\ell \in [m, \ell_{max}]$), Eq. 3;*

    for *every $\ell = m + 2, ..., \ell_{max}$* **do**

      – *compute $\mathcal{P}_{\ell,m}$ given $\mathcal{P}_{\ell-1,m}$ and $\mathcal{P}_{\ell-2m}$, given precomputed $\beta_{\ell m}$, Eq. 3;*

      – *test the value of $\mathcal{P}_{\ell+2m}$ against the rescaling table;*

      – *rescale $\mathcal{P}_{\ell+2,m}$ and $\mathcal{P}_{\ell+1,m}$ if needed, keep the info about the rescaling coefficient;*

      COMMENT: *$\mathcal{P}_{\ell m}$ needs to be scaled back before being used in the calculations of $\boldsymbol{\Delta}_m$;*

    end for *(ℓ)*

  end for *(m)*

end for *(r)*

---

that accorded to a double precision number on a typical processor. To solve this problem, real-time rescaling is employed. The newly computed values are tested if they approach over- or underflow limits and are rescaled if needed. The rescaling coefficients (e.g., in form of their logarithms) are kept tracked of and used to scale back the computed values of $\mathcal{P}_{\ell m}$ at the end. The scaling vector, referred to hereafter as a rescale table, uses a precomputed vector of values, sampling the dynamic range of the representable double precision numbers and thus avoids any explicit computation of numerically-expensive logarithms and exponentials.

The respective pseudo-code for the Legendre function recurrence is presented as Algorithm 2. The associated Legendre function recurrence is normally performed on-the-fly and Algorithm 2 is thus merged with the algorithm for the `alm2map` transform, Algorithm 1.

3   ALM2MAP with CUDA

Programming philosophy for CUDA dictates using fine grained parallelism and launching a very large number of threads in order to use all the available cores and hide memory latency. The loop computing the two-point recurrence is serial in nature and instead we consider two remaining choices for parallelization: the m-loop and the loop over the rings.

Algorithm 3. S^{2}HAT `alm2map` ALGORITHM - CUDA IMPLEMENTATION

STEP 1 - Δ_m CALCULATION
– STEP 1.1 - *assign rings for each* <u>*thread*</u>
for *every* $r \in \mathcal{R}_j$ **do**
   for *every* $m \in \mathcal{M}_i$ **do**
      – STEP 1.2 - *thread 0 in block computes a segment of* μ_m;
      for *every* $\ell = m + 2, ..., \ell_{max}$ **do**
         – STEP 1.3 - *use precomputed or, if needed, precompute in parallel a segment of* $\beta_{\ell m}$, *Eq. 3*;
         – STEP 1.4 - *use fetched or, if needed, fetch in parallel a segment of* $a_{\ell m}$ *map data*;
         – STEP 1.5 - *compute* $\mathcal{P}_{\ell m}$ *via the 2-point recurrence, Eq. 3*;
         – STEP 1.6 - *handle overflow/underflow using rescaling table*;
         – STEP 1.7 - *update* $\Delta_m(r)$, *given prefetched* $a_{\ell m}$ *and computed* $\mathcal{P}_{\ell m}$, *Eq. 6*;
      end for (ℓ)
   end for (m)
end for (r)
GLOBAL COMMUNICATION
– *redistribute* $\{\Delta_m(r),\ m \in \mathcal{M}_i,\ \text{all } r\} \overset{\texttt{MPI\_Alltoallv}}{\Longrightarrow} \{\Delta_m(r),\ r \in \mathcal{R}_i,\ \text{all } m\}$
STEP 2
– *using FFT calculate* $s(\theta, \phi)$ *for all samples for every,* $r \in \mathcal{R}_i$, *given* $\Delta_m(\theta)$ *stored for* $r \in \mathcal{R}_i$ & <u>*all*</u> m.

The CPU approach involved parallelizing only the m-loop, by having each process compute all the ring values for a subset of m values. This method of parallelization makes it easy to write code for MPI, as each process works on a subset of m values. This approach is not appropriate for the GPU due to shared memory limitations. The size of vector $\beta_{\ell m}$, Eq. 3, depends on ℓ_{max} and therefore cannot be stored in shared memory. Its values need to be recomputed for each m and are accessed sequentially in the ℓ-loop. However, these expensive, repeating calculations would seriously limit performance.

Parallelizing the ring loop (step 1.1 in algorithm 3) avoids this problem and has additional advantages. Each thread is assigned a number of rings for which it computes the 2-point recurrence for all m-values. The consequence is that each thread processes $a_{\ell m}$ values at the same m and ℓ coordinates, in parallel. This makes it easy to plan the computation of $\beta_{\ell m}$ and μ_m, Eq. 4, in segments, as well as caching the $a_{\ell m}$ values. An important added benefit is reusing these two vectors, by sharing them inside a thread block. Algorithm 3 shows the outline of the GPU computing kernel. It can be observed that the three new steps (1.2, 1.3, and 1.4) are designed to work around the high latency device memory and take advantage of the fast, but small, shared memory. Steps 1.2 and 1.3 calculate the values of the $\boldsymbol{\mu}_m$ and $\boldsymbol{\beta}_{\ell m}$ vectors in segments, as they do not fit in shared memory and it would be slow and wasteful to store them in global memory. Step 1.4 tries to keep a supply of $\boldsymbol{a}_{\ell m}$ values for the 2-point recurrence, therefore allowing a more continuous operation of the floating point units by decreasing memory wait time. Step 1.1 is where the threads select the rings on which to work upon. Since the m-loop and ring-loops are interchangeable, unlike the CPU version, the ring loop is first, allowing the sharing of the $\boldsymbol{\mu}_m$ and $\boldsymbol{\beta}_{\ell m}$ vectors.

4   Optimizations for GPU

GPU code optimization follows different rules than regular, CPU based code optimization. In fact, in some cases [9] even the most direct algorithm can outperform the CPU optimized one. On GPUs the relationship between the cost of memory access and amount of computations per kernel is exacerbated and it can be far more beneficial to recompute large segments of constant values instead of fetching them from main memory [10]. Performance loss can also stem from thread divergence due to asymmetrical branching in control flow. Such divergence though detectable by profilers, can be hard to avoid. Based on guidelines for CUDA kernel optimization [11,12,13] and our previous experiences, we focused here on limiting the effect of the slow global memory by buffering, precalculating or reusing data, removing branching in performance-critical sections and canceling warp serialization.

Array Segmentation. Due to shared memory small size, it is required to compute the $\boldsymbol{\beta}_{\ell m}$ vector in segments, on the fly (step 1.3). Pre-calculating it entirely in device memory (akin to the original CPU implementation) would be very slow, as completing one $P_{\ell m}$ value requires reading the entire vector. $\boldsymbol{\beta}_{\ell m}$ segments are computed inside the ℓ-loop. Since $\boldsymbol{\beta}_{\ell m}$ is accessed sequentially, a portion of the vector is computed then used in the following steps of the recurrence. When existing values are exhausted, the next portion is computed. The size of the segment influences code performance, as it can be seen in the performance section. The same philosophy is applied for the $\boldsymbol{\mu}_m$ vector. Only difference is that the segments are computed inside the m-loop (step 1.2). The advantage of having the code process the same $\boldsymbol{a}_{\ell m}$ data is that the two vectors are computed only once (in a parallel and serial fashion, respectively) and then reused by all threads in a thread block. As expected, the runtime decreases with increase in the number of threads.

A similar approach to segmentation is employed for offsetting memory latency for reading the $\boldsymbol{a}_{\ell m}$ coefficients and transferring them only once before being used by all threads in a block (step 1.4). The values $\boldsymbol{a}_{\ell m}$ are transferred in segments during the $P_{\ell m}$ computation in step 1.5. Optimal segment size for all three vectors is input size and platform dependent and has been found here by manual testing, a process, which could be however automated.

The nature of $\beta_{\ell m}$ and $a_{\ell m}$ allows their values to be obtained in parallel, by computing or fetching (steps 1.3 and 1.4, respectively). The number of threads which perform this operation is directly linked to segment size. In particular, the segment size must be a multiple of the number of threads. This avoids additional code for handling outlier indexes in performance-critical sections. Keeping in line with the CUDA guidelines on shared memory access for avoiding bank conflicts, the threads in a block calculate values sequentially, with a stride of block size. Due to its serial nature, μ_m is computed by a single thread, while others wait for its completion (step 1.2).

Branch Collapsing. Code branching can severely impair the performance of GPU code, as divergent code is executed sequentially, effectively canceling parallelism. This problem is solved by collapsing the branch into code that has the same outcome but can be executed in parallel by all threads. The computational overhead is smaller than that incurred by process-and-wait execution. Conditional assignments like if (c) v=tv else v=fv are converted to v=c | tv & !c | fv. The use of binary operators makes this expression very fast to compute. On the GPU however binary operators are not applicable to floating point operands. An equivalent version, based on multiplications and subtraction (v = tv*c + fv*(1-c)) severely increases overhead and is applicable only in some cases. For s^2HAT code, this version was employed in both full and short form (if-then) resulting in decreased branching but with limited influence on execution time.

Other approaches have been tried for using the resources of the GPU as much as possible. While none of them provides increased performance, they do offer some insight into the behavior of this new platform and serve as lessons for the future. We describe them briefly in the following.

Warp Serialization. Warp serialization for arrays of double precision floating point stored in shared memory is a problem for GT200 chips. Since a memory bank holds only 32 bit values, a 64 bit value is stored in two different banks. When the number of threads grows beyond half the number of banks, some values are accessed from the same bank. Bank access is not concurrent, so the threads are serialized. We tried splitting a 64 bit value into 2 32-bit ones stored in two different vectors, which are rejoined as needed [11, p. 156] but on the GT200 architecture, the computational cost outweighed that of warp serialization. The newer GT400 chips do not display such a problem.

Dedicated Scaling Table. The scaling table is subject to a different kind of warp serialization. When threads in a block enter the rescaling phase, they access the data inside the array in a random fashion. Given its small size (21 64-bit values), the simplest approach for canceling serialization is to replicate the table for each thread. However, experiments showed that though no serialization occurs, the time gain is insignificant even for small inputs. Also, for a large number of threads, the amount of shared memory used becomes a limiting factor (for just 64 threads, 10.5 KB are needed).

$\beta_{\ell m}$ **Precalculation.** Based on the ability to execute a very large number of mathematical operations and the drawback of high device memory latency, a method for obtaining a good throughput is computing values on-the-fly instead of precalculating them. This trades computing cycles for memory cycles and some algorithms gained significant performance in this manner. $\beta_{\ell m}$ calculation inside the ℓ-loop turned out to greatly increase computation time over both precalculation-based version and segment-based version. This is due to the high number of expensive operations involved in computing a single value of $\beta_{\ell m}$, making reuse essential. Computing the scaling factors on a need-basis showed a similar problem.

5 Experimental Results

Two platforms have been used for testing the code: GTX 260 for NVIDIA GT200 architecture and GTX 480 for the new NVIDIA GF100 (Fermi). Their host systems are: AMD Phenom 9850 (4 cores) with 8 GB of PC3200 DDR2 memory running on a MSI MS-7376 motherboard and Intel Core i7-960 CPU (4 cores, 8 processes with Hyperthreading) with 8 GB of PC3200 DDR2 memory running on a Gigabyte EX58-UD5, respectively. The number of theoretical double precision FLOPS is 2.2 and 3.2 times larger for the two GPU platforms respectively, when compared to the 51.2 GFLOPS double precision performance of Intel i7-960. The GPU FLOPS counts a FMADD operation as two separate ones, for an easier comparison with the CPU. It is also taken into account the fact that the Fermi chip can process a FMADD and ADD operation in parallel.

The s^2HAT Fortran algorithm was employed as reference for the CPU version. It was compiled with gfortran 4.3, using the default flags active at optimization level 3 (-O3). Manual tuning was applied to improve memory and cache performance. Accelerating spherical harmonics with SSE, could yield a 1.6-1.8x speedup, as suggested by [4] and our limited attempts on the code base, however more research is needed. Additional gains could also be obtained through proprietary compilers, like the Intel Fortran package, which is known to boost runtime by 5-20% over gfortran. Algorithm efficiency was computed using the FLOP count returned by the PAPI package.

For the GPU, the execution time is calculated using the `gettimeofday()` library call between kernel launch and result retrieval. Because the consumer-grade cards used have limited memory, the largest dataset used is 4096x4096 and 5120x5120, respectively. To assess performance for larger datasets, the output arrays were no longer allocated, leaving the entire card memory for the input. Results were written in a very small buffer (one value per thread), in order to maintain memory access and not distort the results. In this manner, the dataset limit was extended up to 9216x9216.

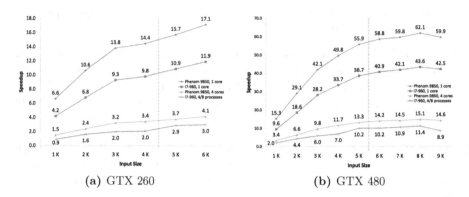

(a) GTX 260   (b) GTX 480

Fig. 1. Improvement factor obtained for Δ_m calculation of `alm2map` with CUDA with respect to the MPI version ran on the AMD Phenom and Intel i7 CPUs

5.1 Performance of Δ_m Computation

In this section we discuss the performance of the code on the two GPU platforms (from the latest two generations), with respect to the CPU implementation running on two different processors. The entire range of input sizes is tested with all variations of segment lengths. The best times are then selected and used for calculating the runtime improvement relative to the CPU implementation.

The improvement factor of the GPU version is calculated against the reference Fortran MPI code running on the CPU. For AMD, the time duration obtained by running the program with 1 and 4 processes is used. The Intel i7-960 is equipped with Hyperthreading and thus can run 8 threads on just 4 physical cores. However, we found that, in some cases, the 4 threads (MPI processes) version is faster. Therefore, one process and the best out of 4 or 8 processes is used as reference. The final runtime improvement factor for each input size is obtained by dividing the best time for each CPU by the best time of the GPU. When single-core is used as reference, the time measured while running the algorithm with just one process is divided by the best time of the GPU.

Figures 1a and 1b show the runtime improvement for the two platforms used for testing (the latest generation GTX 480 and the older GTX 260) while using the entire range of inputs. We observe how larger inputs result in a higher improvement factor. Values rise sharply before starting to level at 4K (GTX 260) or 5K (GTX 480). The graphs plot the values for input sizes that normally fit the cards used for testing as well as those that require output disabling. They are separated by a vertical line (normal inputs on the left).

The AMD Phenom is slower than the Intel i7, therefore the improvement factor could be expected to be higher. When comparing the GTX 480 runtimes to those of single core CPU code, the performance ratio levels out at 60x for the Phenom and at 42x for the i7. For the older GTX 260, the factor is 3-3.5 times lower, at 17x and 12x, respectively. However, the relevant values are those obtained when using the CPUs to their full potential, with all their cores.

The algorithm scales almost perfectly with the number of physical cores, the improvement values being generally one fourth of single core, with 14x and 10x for GTX 480 and 4x and 3x for GTX 260. Intel Hyperthreading does not appear to help by pushing scaling beyond the number of physical cores.

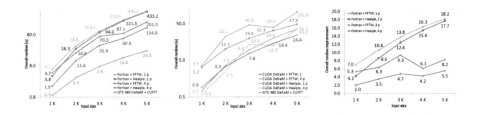

Fig. 2. alm2map overall runtime, Intel i7-960 (left) and NVIDIA GTX 480 (middle) and overall performance gain (right)

5.2   Overall Performance

The performance of the alm2map algorithm is greatly improved by offloading the Δ_m computation onto a GPU. In the original CPU-only code, the FFTs, performed as the second step, constitute 5-10% of the total runtime. Accelerating Δ_m calculation by a factor of 10 (Intel I7-960, 4 processes), results in the FFTs becoming dominant. We have tested two CPU FFT routines (FFT function implemented in HEALPIX [3] and FFTW[1] [14]) and one FFT routine for the NVIDIA GPUs (CUFFT [15]). We have not introduced any specific GPU optimizations in this part of the algorithm.

Left and middle panels of Fig. 2 show the overall (Δ_m + FFT) runtimes for all combinations of Δ_m computing code (Fortran on Intel i7-960 or CUDA on NVIDIA GTX 480), CPU FFT packages (Healpix or FFTW) and process count (1 or 4). Also, the runtime for a full GPU computation is plotted. Only the Intel i7-960 with NVIDIA GTX 480 results are shown. We notice that, relative to the FFTW routine, the HEALPIX FFT performs better for both 1 and 4 processes. We also observe that the best runtimes belong to the code running on the GPU.

Right panel of Fig. 2 plots the overall runtime improvement over the CPU code versions with respect to the best performing GPU code (labeled "GTX480 Δ_m + CUFFT" – middle panel). We observe that, in the best case, the improvement is just half of that obtained when considering only the Δ_m computation (Fig. 1b), but also significant, reaching factors from 5 to 18.

6   Conclusions

We have described an algorithm for computing the inverse spherical harmonic transform on GPUs and compared it with the inverse spherical harmonic transform provided in the s^2HAT library, and based on Fortran and MPI. The GPU

---

[1] FFTW: http://www.fftw.org/

algorithm leads to an improvement of up to a factor of 18 with respect to s^2HAT on a single core and up to a factor of 5.5 with respect to s^2HAT on 4 cores of an Intel i7-960 machine. The improvement is limited by the performance of Fast Fourier transforms.

Acknowledgment. This work has been supported in part by French National Research Agency (ANR) through COSINUS program (project MIDAS no. ANR-09-COSI-009) and used HPC resources from GENCI-CCRT/IDRIS (Grant 2011-066647).

References

1. Szydlarski, M., Esterie, P., Falcou, J., Grigori, L., Stompor, R.: Spherical harmonic transform on heterogeneous architectures using hybrid programming, INRIA, Rapport de recherche RR-7635 (April 2011),
   http://hal.inria.fr/inria-00597576/en/
2. Arfken, G.B., Weber, H.J.: Mathematical methods for physicists, 6th edn. Academic Press (2005)
3. Górski, K.M., et al.: HEALPix: A Framework for High-Resolution Discretization and Fast Analysis of Data Distributed on the Sphere. Astrophysical Journal 622, 759–771 (2005)
4. Reinecke, M.: Libpsht - algorithms for efficient spherical harmonic transforms. Astronomy and Astrophysics 526, A108+ (2011)
5. Driscoll, J.R., Healy, D.M.: Computing fourier transforms and convolutions on the 2-sphere. Advances in Applied Mathematics 15(2), 202–250 (1994)
6. Muciaccia, P.F., Natoli, P., Vittorio, N.: Fast Spherical Harmonic Analysis: A Quick Algorithm for Generating and/or Inverting Full-Sky, High-Resolution Cosmic Microwave Background Maps. Astrophysical Journal Letters 488, L63(1997)
7. Doroshkevich, A.G., et al.: First Release of Gauss-Legendre Sky Pixelization (GLESP) software package for CMB analysis. ArXiv Astrophysics e-prints (January 2005)
8. Tygert, M.: Fast algorithms for spherical harmonic expansions, ii. Journal of Computational Physics 227(8), 4260–4279 (2008)
9. Nukada, A., Matsuoka, S.: Auto-tuning 3-D FFT library for CUDA GPUs. In: SC 2009: Proceedings of the Conference on High Performance Computing Networking, Storage and Analysis, pp. 1–10 (2009)
10. Volkov, V., Demmel, J.W.: Benchmarking GPUs to tune dense linear algebra. In: ACM/IEEE Conference on Supercomputing, SC 2008 (2008)
11. Nvidia, NVIDIA CUDA Programming Guide (2010)
12. Nvidia, NVIDIA CUDA Best Practices Guide (2010)
13. Nvidia, Tuning CUDA Applications for Fermi (2010)
14. Frigo, M., Johnson, S.: The design and implementation of FFTW3. Proceedings of the IEEE 93(2), 216–231 (2005)
15. Nvidia, CUDA CUFFT Library (2010)

Design Patterns for Scientific Computations on Sparse Matrices

Davide Barbieri[1], Valeria Cardellini[1],
Salvatore Filippone[1], and Damian Rouson[2]

[1] University of Rome "Tor Vergata", Italy
salvatore.filippone@uniroma2.it, cardellini@ing.uniroma2.it
[2] Sandia National Laboratories
rouson@sandia.gov

Abstract. We discuss object-oriented software design patterns in the context of scientific computations on sparse matrices. Design patterns arise when multiple independent development efforts produce very similar designs, yielding an evolutionary convergence onto a good solution: a flexible, maintainable, high-performance design. We demonstrate how to engender these traits by implementing an interface for sparse matrix computations on NVIDIA GPUs starting from an existing sparse matrix library. We also present initial performance results.

1 Introduction

Computational scientists concern themselves chiefly with producing science, even when a significant percentage of their time goes to engineering software. The majority of professional software engineers, by contrast, concern themselves with non-scientific software. In this paper, we demonstrate the fruitful results of bringing these two fields together by applying a branch of modern software engineering design to the development of scientific programs.

Our meeting ground is the field of sparse matrices and related computations, one of the centerpieces of scientific computing. This paper covers how to handle certain kinds of design requirements, and illustrates what can be done by consciously applying certain design techniques. Specifically, we discuss the benefits accrued by the application of the widely used software engineering concept of *design patterns* in the context of scientific computation on sparse matrices. We choose as a case study the implementation of an interface for sparse matrix computations on NVIDIA GPUs starting from an existing sparse library.

A number of related projects provide libraries for constructing and using sparse (and dense) matrices and vectors, as well as provide solver libraries for linear, nonlinear, time-dependent, and eigenvalue problems. These projects include Trilinos [11], PETSc [1], and PSBLAS [8,7].

Trilinos focuses on the development of algorithms and enabling technologies within an object-oriented software framework for the solution of large-scale, complex multi-physics engineering and scientific problems. PETSc is the Portable,

M. Alexander et al. (Eds.): Euro-Par 2011 Workshops, Part I, LNCS 7155, pp. 367–376, 2012.

Extensible Toolkit for Scientific Computation. Many of the algorithms in PETSc and Trilinos can be interchanged via abstract interfaces without impacting application code. Both projects employ MPI to exploit distributed-memory, parallel computers and provide sparse matrix solvers for linear, nonlinear, and eigenvalue problems. They differ in implementation language: PETSc is written in C whereas Trilinos is written in C++. Language differences ultimately influence the programming paradigm and architectural style, with C supporting procedural programming and C++ explicitly enabling an object-oriented programming (OOP) style that facilitates the adoption of the architectural design patterns that comprise the focus of the current paper.

Parallel Sparse BLAS (PSBLAS) is a library of Basic Linear Algebra Subroutines for parallel sparse applications that facilitates the porting of complex computations on multicomputers. PSBLAS includes routines for multiplying sparse matrices by dense matrices, solving sparse triangular systems, and preprocessing sparse matrices; the library is mostly implemented in Fortran 95, with some additions of Fortran 77 and C. A Fortran 2003 version is currently under development, and forms the basis for the examples in this paper, because of the language support that we are going to describe.

Sparse matrices are widely used in scientific computations; most physical problems modeled by partial differential equations (PDEs) are solved via discretizations that transform the original equations into a linear system and/or an eigenvalue problem with a sparse coefficient matrix. A matrix is sparse when most of its elements are zero; this fact is exploited in devising a representation that does not store explicitly the null coefficients. This means abandoning the language's native array type along with the underlying assumption that one can infer the indices (i, j) associated with an element a_{ij} from the element's position in memory and vice versa. Any viable replacement for these assumptions must involve storing the indices explicitly. Despite the resulting overhead, in the vast majority of applications the scheme pays off nicely due to the small number of nonzero elements per row.

Variations on this concept abound in the COOrdinate, Compressed Sparse Rows, Compressed Sparse Columns, ELLpack, JAgged Diagonals, and other formats. Each storage format offers different efficiencies with respect to the mathematical operator or data transformation to be implemented (both typically map into an object "method"), and the underlying platform (including the hardware architecture and the compiler).

Sect. 2 of the current paper presents three design patterns: State, Builder, and Prototype, leveraging the newly available OOP constructs of Fortran 2003 in scientific applications. Sect. 3 presents interfaces for sparse matrix computations on GPUs starting from PSBLAS. Sect. 4 concludes.

2   Design Patterns

Many professionals will confirm that, when confronted with design patterns, their colleagues will often have a "recognition" moment in which they declare they have been doing things "the right way" all along, without knowing their fancy names.

Applying design patterns in a conscious way can be highly beneficial. Evidence from the literature suggests that these benefits have been reaped in the context of scientific applications only recently [10,14], the timing being due in part to the arrival of compilers that support the OOP constructs in Fortran 2003, the only language for which the international standards body has scientific programmers as its target audience. With this paper, we discuss implementations of design patterns not previously demonstrated in Fortran 2003.

2.1 "STATE" Is Your Friend

The State pattern allows the encapsulation of object state behind an interface that allows the object type to vary at runtime. Figure 1 shows a Unified Modeling Language (UML) class diagram of the State pattern, including the class relationships and the public methods. The diagram hides the private attributes.

Let us consider the problem of switching among different storage formats for a given object. An old-fashioned but feasible solution would be to have a data structure containing integer values driving the interpretation and dispatching of the various operations; however, this route is not very maintainable and scalable. Using an object-oriented design and language per se is not a solution either; indeed, while it seems that all variations in storage formats could be derived from a base class, switching at runtime would require the same object to change its class dynamically. This is generally not supported by object-oriented languages (with very rare exceptions [9]); the solution is to add a layer of indirection, encapsulating the "dynamic" object inside a normal one. The application to the sparse matrix case is shown here:

```
type :: psb_d_base_sparse_mat
contains
  procedure, pass(a) :: foo
end type psb_d_base_sparse_mat

type :: psb_dspmat_type
  class(psb_d_base_sparse_mat), allocatable :: a
contains
  procedure, pass(a) :: mat_foo
end type psb_dspmat_type

subroutine mat_foo(a)
    call a%a%foo()
end subroutine mat_foo
```

The methods of the outer class are always thrown onto the inner class, which is the actual workhorse. To enable a runtime class switch it is necessary to devise a conversion strategy; a viable choice we employed is to have one reference storage class, and to have all other classes provide methods to convert to/from it.

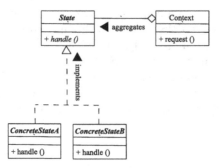

Fig. 1. UML class diagram for the State pattern: classes (boxes) and relationships (connecting lines), including abstract classes (bold italics) and relationship adornments (line labels) with arrows indicating the relationship direction. Line endings indicate relationship type: inheritance (open triangle) and aggregation (open diamond). Class boxes include: name (top), attributes (middle), and methods (bottom). Leading signs indicate visibility: public (+) or private (−). Italics denote an abstract method.

2.2 "PROTOTYPE" and "BUILDER" Are Good Ideas

This section is concerned with maintaining and extending a body of software, and how certain patterns can help. Suppose you are designing a library for sparse matrix computations; you spend a long time in thinking about the capabilities you have to implement, and how to combine them in a way that is both efficient and flexible. You have also spent a significant amount of effort in properly segregating the specifics of any given storage format to its class, and in optimizing the implementation of its methods. This is a success, everything works properly, and publication ensues; so far, so good.

However, at this point two issues arise: (1) your software has to be used on the latest BNE Tour-de-France processor; (2) Professor Hook in the University of Neverland absolutely wants to fit her favourite storage method into your framework, since she thinks it is so good (both her method and the framework). If your software is really successful, these requests might be coming in with an alarming frequency. Each time you have to derive a new class for the inner storage object (remember, we are systematically using the STATE pattern), and this is the (relatively) easy part, but you also have to adapt the library to handle its existence. You have to add constructors, converters, and what not; potentially, you have to touch multiple places, and break multiple things. How do you get out of this? The strategy that was devised in PSBLAS can be interpreted in terms of two design patterns: Builder and Prototype.

BUILDER. The Builder pattern in OO design allows for an abstract specification of the steps required to construct an object. Figure 2 shows a UML class diagram of the Builder pattern, including the class relationships and the public methods of the abstract parent. Child classes must provide concrete implementations of these methods (not shown). The diagram hides the private attributes.

The strategy to build a sparse matrix is: (1) initialize to some default; (2) add sets of coefficients by calling buildup methods in a loop; (3) assemble the results and bring the object to the desired final storage status. Most sparse matrix libraries (including Trilinos, PETSc, PSBLAS) are organized around these concepts; this is an example of "convergent evolution" towards a reasonable solution that is more or less forced by the constraints of the application domain.

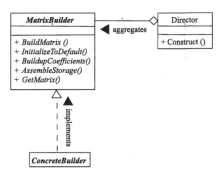

Fig. 2. UML class diagram for the Builder pattern

It should be clear that the only place where the desired output storage format has to be enforced explicitly is at the assembly step; in PSBLAS software, this is handled at the inner level, by allocating a new object of the desired class and converting to it from the existing inner object. It may appear that it is necessary to have an exact knowledge of the derived class of the new object at the time the assembly code is written; however this is not quite true. All that is needed is to know that it is derived from a given base class, and that it is capable of converting to/from a reference storage format. With this scheme, a conversion between arbitrary derived classes can always be implemented by at most one intermediate object of the reference class, even if the outer code invoking the conversion methods does not know the exact dynamic type involved. This scheme works fine, provided that the library code can allocate a new object with the correct dynamic type, which is only known at runtime: to this end we call the next design pattern to our rescue.

PROTOTYPE. This design pattern might also be defined as "copy by example": when a method needs to instantiate an object, it does it by referring to another object which is a "source" or a "mold". The class for copied object will include a cloning or molding method by which the desired copy can be obtained; the two variations refer to whether a full copy of the source object is created, or just an empty copy with the correct dynamic type.

Returning to our example of assembling a sparse matrix, you (or rather, your library code) gets a reference object for the inner storage; you do not need to know the details of its contents, as long as it is an extension of the base storage class, and it implements the necessary conversion methods to/from the reference format.

This idea is so good that in Fortran 2003/2008 it has become part of the language itself. To call into existence a polymorphic object the language provides a specification of dynamic type in the `ALLOCATE` statement; the most common way is shown in the following example:

```
class(base_sparse_mat), allocatable : mat_object
allocate(my_storage_format : mat_object)
```

where `my_storage_format` is the name of the desired dynamic type. However it is also possible to use the following alternatives:

```
class(base_sparse_mat) :: sourcemat;
allocate(mat_object, source=sourcemat)
```

or alternatively

```
allocate(mat_object, mold=sourcemat)
```

depending on whether the original contents of `sourcemat` have to be copied or not. The `MOLD=` variant is extensively used in PSBLAS to implement the PRO-TOTYPE pattern. In this way, a new storage format can be added by (1) defining a derived class from the base class, providing the necessary implementations of the methods; (2) using the new class in the main application, declaring a variable of the desired new class; (3) passing the "mold" variable to the assembly routine. This is it; no changes are necessary to the library code, not even a re-compilation, and the existing computational methods will happily use the new storage format.

3   An Example: Adding Support for NVIDIA GPUs

Graphics Processing Units (GPUs) have entered as an attractive choice the world of scientific computing, building the core of the most advanced supercomputers and even being offered as an infrastructure service in Cloud computing (e.g., Amazon EC2). We discuss here how our desing techniques help in interfacing sparse matrix computations kernels for the GPU into the existing sparse library PSBLAS.

The NVIDIA GPU architectural model is based on a scalable array of multi-threaded streaming multi-processors, each composed by a fixed number of scalar processors, one dual-issue instruction fetch unit, one on-chip fast memory with a configurable partitioning of shared memory, and L1 cache plus additional special-function hardware. CUDA is the programming model provided by NVIDIA for its GPUs; a CUDA program consists of a host program that runs on the CPU host, and a kernel program that executes on the GPU device. The host program typically sets up the data and transfers it to and from the GPU, while the kernel program processes that data. The CUDA programming environment specifies a set of facilities to create, identify, and synchronize the various threads involved in the computation. A key component of CUDA is the GPU memory hierarchy.

Memory on the GPU includes a global memory area in a shared address space accessible by the CPU and by all threads, a low-latency memory called the shared memory, which is local to each multiprocessor, and a per-thread private local memory, not directly available to the programmer.

3.1 Sparse Matrix Computation on GPU

The considerable interest in GPUs for General Purpose computation (GPGPU) is due to the significant performance benefits possible with its usage; for example, the works in [2,3,16] demonstrated how to achieve significant percentages of peak single-precision and double-precision throughput in dense linear algebra kernels. It is thus natural that GPUs (and their SIMD architecture) are considered for implementing sparse matrix computations; sparse matrix-vector multiplication has been the subject of intense research on every generation of high performance computing architectures.

Sparse matrix computations on the GPU introduce additional challenges with respect to their dense counterparts, because operations on them are typically much less regular in their data access patterns; recent efforts on sparse GPU codes include [4,5,6], and NVIDIA's CUSPARSE library [13].

Let us consider the matrix-vector multiplication $y \leftarrow \alpha Ax + \beta y$ where A is large and sparse and x and y are column vectors; we will need to devise a specific storage format for the matrix A to implement the sparse matrix computations of interest. Our starting point is a GPU-friendly format we developed; we will concentrate on how the design patterns discussed in Sect. 2 can be used to plug in the new formats and the GPU support code in the PSBLAS library.

Our storage format is a variation of the standard ELLpack (or ELL)format; an M-by-N sparse matrix with at most K nonzeros per row is stored as a dense M-by-K array `data` of nonzeros and array `indices` of column indices; all rows are zero-padded to length K; this format is efficient when the maximum number of nonzeros per row is close to the average. ELL fits a sparse matrix in a regular data structure; thus it is a good candidate to implement sparse matrix operations on SIMT architectures. The usage of ELL format and its variants on GPUs have been previously analyzed in [15,16].

Our storage format ELL-G takes into account the memory access patterns of the NVIDIA Tesla architecture [12], as well as other *many-threads* performance optimization patterns of the CUDA programming model.

A critical issue in interfacing with existing codes is the need to take care of the data movements from the main memory to the GPU RAM and vice versa; unfortunately data movement is very slow compared to the high bandwidth internal to the GPU, and this is one of the major problems in GPU programming. To add support for NVIDIA GPUs in the PSBLAS library we had to derive from ELL a new GPU class requiring the following modifications:

- At assembly time, copy the matrix to the GPU memory;
- At matrix-vector time, invoke the code on the GPU side;
- At deallocation time, release memory on both the host and device sides.

On the library side of things, a set of wrappers handles the communication with the application and sorts out the needed inter-language call details; attached to this layer there is the CUDA layer which performs the actual work. Thus, given the preparatory work discussed above, we can have the code

```
call psb_spmm(-done,a,x,dzero,y,desc_a,info,'n')
```

which performs the matrix-vector product; according to the dynamic type and state of the inner component(s) of a, x and y the code will run on the CPU or on the GPU, possibly including copying the vector data to the GPU side.

3.2   Performance Results

First of all, since this paper is dedicated to the design technique, let us state that after writing the CUDA kernel code, embedding the new format in the existing library required a development effort of just about a couple of days, including debugging. Our computational experiments were run on an NVIDIA GeForce GTX 285 graphics card, which has a maximum throughput of 94.8 Gflop/s in double precision. The computation rates are reported in Gflop/s; the number of arithmetic operations per matrix-vector is assumed to be $2NZ$ where NZ is the number of nonzeros in the matrix, and the rate is averaged over multiple runs. For the experiments we used a collection of sparse matrices arising from

Table 1. Sparse matrices used in the performance experiments

matrix name	N	NZ
pde05	125	725
pde10	1000	6400
pde20	8000	53600
pde30	27000	183600
pde40	64000	438400

matrix name	N	NZ
pde50	125000	860000
pde60	216000	1490400
pde80	512000	3545600
pde90	729000	5054400
pde100	1000000	6940000

a test three-dimensional partial differential equation (PDE) problem; the PDE is discretized with finite differences on a cubic domain. Table 1 summarizes the matrix characteristics, where N is the matrix size and NZ is the number of nonzeros. For the matrix-vector multiplication, in the experiments we set $\beta = 0$, i.e., we consider $y \leftarrow Ax$, and report results only for double precision computations.

In our experiments we compare the throughput of the sparse matrix-vector multiplication in PSBLAS exploiting the GPU and using our ELL-G storage format with that obtained by the standard PSBLAS library on CPU. For the experiments on CPU we used an AMD Athlon 64 processor running at 2.7 GHz; this is a dual-core processor, but we only run in serial mode for the purposes of this comparison. Figure 3(a) shows the performance improvement that we obtain implementing the PSBLAS interface for sparse matrix computations on GPUs even when we include the overhead of transferring the vector data from main memory; in this case the GTX 285 vs AMD matrix-vector multiplication gives a speedup between 2 and 3 depending on the sparse matrix.

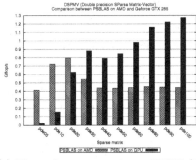

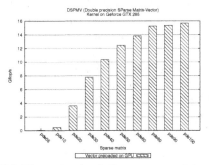

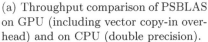

(a) Throughput comparison of PSBLAS on GPU (including vector copy-in overhead) and on CPU (double precision).

(b) Throughput of the sparse matrix-vector multiplication kernel on GPU (without vector copy-in overhead).

Fig. 3.

With the measurements shown in Figure 3(b) we report the same operations on the same data, but with the vectors prearranged in the GPU memory; this is more representative of usage of the kernels in a sparse iterative solver. Comparing these results with those in Figure 3(a), we see that data transfer overhead is very significant; having the vectors on the GPU enables a performance level that is essentially identical to that of the inner kernels. Arranging the vectors to be loaded on the GPU device memory is possible because the vectors undergo the same build cycle as the matrices; therefore by employing the State pattern for vectors we can have the data loaded on the device side "on demand". The high-level solver code looks exactly the same for GPU and CPU execution, but during the solution process only scalars are transferred between the CPU and the GPU; the solution vector itself is recovered upon exit from the iterative process.

4   Conclusions

In this paper, we have discussed how the well-known software engineering concept of Design Patterns can be applied with benefits in the context of sparse matrix computation. We have demonstrated how these patterns can be used to implement an interface for sparse matrix computations on GPUs starting from the existing PSBLAS library. Our experience shows that this solution provides good flexibility and maintainability and allows to exploit the GPU computation with its related performance benefits. While the ideas discussed have been tested in the PSBLAS framework, future work will include extension to multilevel preconditioners as well as interfacing with ForTrilinos. The techniques described in this paper can also be employed to encapsulate and use other storage formats, including the format used in the CUSPARSE library; a detailed performance analysis and comparison is the subject of currently ongoing work.

Acknowledgments. This research has been partially supported by the Italian Ministry of Instruction, University, and Research within the project FIRB 2007 "Studio, progettazione e sviluppo e sperimentazione di una nuova generazione competitiva di motori innovativi a basso consumo ed a basso impatto ambientale nellarco dellintero ciclo di vita."

Sandia National Laboratories is a multi-program laboratory managed and operated by Sandia Corporation, a wholly owned subsidiary of Lockheed Martin Corporation, for the U.S. Department of Energy's National Nuclear Security Administration under contract DE-AC04-94AL85000.

References

1. Balay, S., Gropp, W., McInnes, L.C., Smith, B.: PETSc 2.0 user manual. Tech. Rep. ANL-95/11 - Revision 2.0.22, Argonne National Laboratory (1995)
2. Barbieri, D., Cardellini, V., Filippone, S.: Generalized GEMM applications on GPGPUs: Experiments and applications. In: ParCo 2009. IOS Press (2009)
3. Barrachina, S., Castillo, M., Igual, F.D., Mayo, R., Quintana-Ortí, E.S., Quintana-Ortí, G.: Exploiting the capabilities of modern gpus for dense matrix computations. Concurr. Comput.: Pract. Exper. 21, 2457–2477 (2009)
4. Baskaran, M.M., Bordawekar, R.: Optimizing sparse matrix-vector multiplication on GPUs. Tech. Rep. RC24704, IBM Research (April 2009)
5. Bell, N., Garland, M.: Implementing sparse matrix-vector multiplication on throughput-oriented processors. In: Supercomputing 2009. ACM (2009)
6. Choi, J.W., Singh, A., Vuduc, R.W.: Model-driven autotuning of sparse matrix-vector multiply on GPUs. SIGPLAN Not. 45, 115–126 (2010)
7. D'Ambra, P., di Serafino, D., Filippone, S.: MLD2P4: a package of parallel algebraic multilevel domain decomposition preconditioners in Fortran 95. ACM Trans. Math. Softw. 37(3) (2010)
8. Filippone, S., Colajanni, M.: PSBLAS: a library for parallel linear algebra computations on sparse matrices. ACM Trans. on Math Software 26, 527–550 (2000)
9. Gamma, E., Helm, R., Johnson, R., Vlissides, J.: Design Patterns: Elements of Reusable Object-Oriented Software. Addison-Wesley (1995)
10. Gardner, H., Manduchi, G.: Design Patterns for e-Science. Springer (2007)
11. Heroux, M.A., Bartlett, R.A., Howle, V.E., Hoekstra, R.J., Hu, J.J., Kolda, T.G., Lehoucq, R.B., Long, K.R., Pawlowski, R.P., Phipps, E.T., Salinger, A.G., Thornquist, H.K., Tuminaro, R.S., Willenbring, J.M., Williams, A., Stanley, K.S.: An overview of the Trilinos project. ACM Trans. Math. Softw. 31(3), 397–423 (2005)
12. Lindholm, E., Nickolls, J., Oberman, S., Montrym, J.: NVIDIA Tesla: a unified graphics and computing architecture. IEEE Micro. 28, 39–55 (2008)
13. NVIDIA Corp.: CUDA CUSPARSE library version 4.0 (2011)
14. Rouson, D.W.I., Xia, J., Xu, X.: Scientific Software Design: The Object-Oriented Way. Cambridge University Press (2011)
15. Vazquez, F., Ortega, G., Fernández, J.J., Garzon, E.M.: Improving the performance of the sparse matrix vector product with GPUs. In: CIT 2010, pp. 1146–1151 (2010)
16. Volkov, V., Demmel, J.W.: Benchmarking GPUs to tune dense linear algebra. In: Supercomputing 2008 (2008)

High-Performance Matrix-Vector Multiplication on the GPU

Hans Henrik Brandenborg Sørensen

Informatics and Mathematical Modelling,
Technical University of Denmark, Bldg. 321, DK-2800 Lyngby, Denmark
hhs@imm.dtu.dk
http://www.gpulab.imm.dtu.dk

Abstract. In this paper, we develop a high-performance GPU kernel for one of the most popular dense linear algebra operations, the matrix-vector multiplication. The target hardware is the most recent Nvidia Tesla 20-series (Fermi architecture), which is designed from the ground up for scientific computing. We show that it is essentially a matter of fully utilizing the fine-grained parallelism of the many-core GPU in order to achieve high-performance for dense matrix-vector multiplication. We show that auto-tuning can be successfully employed to the GPU kernel so that it performs well for all matrix shapes and sizes.

Keywords: GPU, Matrix-Vector Multiplication, Dense linear algebra.

1 Introduction

The single-instruction-multiple-data (SIMD) parallel capabilities of Nvidia GPUs have been made accessible to scientists and developers through the CUDA programming model [1]. The most recent Fermi GPU architecture features up to 16 streaming multiprocessors (SM) having 32 single-precision cores each. Execution on this potent parallel hardware is controlled through CUDA keywords; a block is a 3D structure of up to 1024 threads and a grid is a 2D structure of blocks.

For many programmers, the key to good performance of numerical scientific applications is still linked to the availability of high-performance libraries for the most common dense linear algebra operations. Several such libraries have recently become available for GPUs, e.g., Nvidia's CUBLAS [2] and the open source MAGMA library [3]. In the case of matrix-vector multiplication, however, these libraries are currently not satisfactory and suffer from low utilization of the GPU hardware in particular for rectangular shaped problems [4].

In this paper, we seek to remedy this lack of performance for matrix-vector multiplication for all problem shapes and sizes. We will contribute to the present state of the art of GPU matrix-vector multiplication kernels by developing an auto-tunable rigorously parallel and versatile kernel, where threads can work together, not only within a block, but also between blocks. This provides the kernel with an additional layer of parallelism - at the grid level - which is essential in order to achieve high-performance for rectangular matrix-vector multiplication.

M. Alexander et al. (Eds.): Euro-Par 2011 Workshops, Part I, LNCS 7155, pp. 377–386, 2012.

The motivation from a parallel computing point of view is to maintain a good load balancing across the GPUs resources in all situations.

2   Related Work

Several previous works on matrix-vector multiplication kernels for GPUs exists of which we will mention some of the most recent. In 2008, Fujimoto [5] described a matrix-vector kernel written in CUDA that was specifically tuned for the Nvidia's GeForce 8800GTX graphics card. The performance he achieved was significantly better than the CUBLAS v1.1 library available at that time, reaching a maximum performance of 36 Gflops in single precision for a GPU with a theoretical memory bandwidth of 86 GB/s. The main design motivation for his kernel was an attempt to maximize data reuse of the x vector in combination with tiling of the matrix **A**. This led to important optimizations of the naive matrix-vector implementation such as a two-dimensional block structure and simultaneous reduction operations, which are also adopted in this work.

Later in 2009, Tomov and Dongarra et al. developed a fast matrix-vector kernel to be one of the key ingredients in their MAGMA library [6], which is a dense linear algebra package for heterogeneous CPU-GPU systems with the same functionality as the legacy LAPACK library [7]. Several generic optimization techniques were introduced to improve on the matrix-vector kernel performance, including pointer redirection [8] and auto-tuning [9]. For square matrices of sizes that are divisible by 32, they report a performance of up to 66 Gflops in single precision on a graphics card that has a theoretical memory bandwidth of 141 GB/s [6]. This result is a significant improvement over the CUBLAS 2.3 that was available in 2009. They also presented a kernel for transposed matrix-vector multiplication, which like Fujimoto's kernel, allows groups of threads within a block to work together followed by a required reduction operation. The maximum performance for the transposed version was 43 Gflops, which was more than twice of what CUBLAS 2.3 could deliver.

3   Matrix-Vector Multiplication Kernels

In this section, we describe the matrix-vector multiplication kernels we have developed for the C2050 card. To achieve high-performance for all shapes of matrix **A** we implement four different kernels to fit the four cases; very tall, tall and skinny, close to square, and wide and fat. The cases and the names of the kernels are illustrated in Fig. 1. We also combine the four kernels into a versatile generic kernel. We consider only the case of column major memory layout. In the next section we introduce auto-tuning of the versatile kernel in order to automatically select the best performing of the four kernels at runtime.

3.1   One Thread per Row

The typical implementation of a matrix-vector multiplication kernel, as illustrated in Fig. 2 (a), is where each thread performs a dot product between one

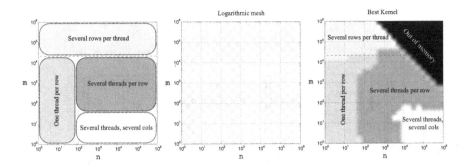

Fig. 1. Left; Four matrix-vector multiplication kernels designed to perform well at different shapes $m \times n$ of **A**. Middle; Tuning mesh. Right; Best kernel in practice. The dashed line indicates the minimum 21504 rows needed in **A** for full occupancy of the Nvidia Tesla C2050 card in a one-thread-per-row kernel. Note the logarithmic axes.

row of **A** and **x** to produce one element of the result **y**. The threads are then grouped in 1D blocks along the columns of **A**. For a given size of **A**, the only parameter required is the number of threads per block, which we will denote by BLOCKSIZE. The size of the grid specified when launching the kernel in CUDA is determined by the BLOCKSIZE parameter. Dividing the m rows of **A** into slices of size BLOCKSIZE, with the last slice possibly containing less than BLOCKSIZE rows, we have a one dimensional grid of size

$$\text{GRIDSIZE\_m} = (m + \text{BLOCKSIZE} - 1)/\text{BLOCKSIZE}.$$

Using a grid of this size requires an if conditional inside the kernel to make sure the last block does not access memory outside the m rows of **A**. In Fig. 2 (a) the kernel is shown for a GRIDSIZE_m of 4 as indicated with the red 4×1 mesh.

Since all threads need the same n values of **x** for their dot products it is best to read these into shared memory once per block and then let threads access them from there. This allows for maximum reuse of the data. We therefore divide **x** into chunks of BLOCKSIZE and set up a loop to let the threads collaborate in reading chunks in a coalesced fashion into a shared memory once per block. It requires the allocation of a shared memory array of size BLOCKSIZE for each block. The usage of shared memory is illustrated by red-dotted boxes in Fig. 2.

The one-thread-per-row matrix-vector multiplication kernel is appropriate as a high-performance kernel on the C2050 card for tall and skinny **A** only. This is because the Fermi GPU with 14 SMs supports 1536 active threads per SM [10], so that full occupancy requires $1536 \times 14 = 21504$ rows in **A**. If m is less than this, and **A** is not skinny, then we are not utilizing the hardware to the maximum. SMs might be idle or running at low occupancy during kernel execution, while the running threads might do a lot of work each. If **A** is skinny, e.g., $n < 100$, then dispite the low utilization, the individual threads complete fast enough for this kernel to be the best implementation. In Fig. 1, we indicate the dimensions of **A** for which the one-thread-per-row kernel is designed to perform well.

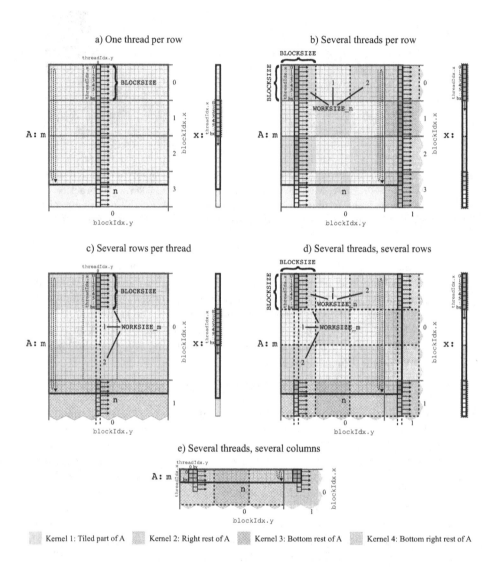

Fig. 2. Schematic illustrations of the matrix-vector multiplications kernels implemented in this work. The transversal of **A** can be conveniently separated into distinct device kernels 1 − 4 as indicated by color in the figures. The red lines show the division of the elements of **A** into work-chunks and the CUDA keywords blockIdx.x and blockIdx.y show how to map these onto a grid of blocks. Vector **x** is read to shared memory for data re-use indicated by the red-dotted boxes. BLOCKSIZE, WORKSIZE_m and WORKSIZE_n are tuning parameters. Memory storage is assumed to be column major.

3.2   Several Threads per Row

The low utilization of hardware for the one-thread-per-row kernel when **A** is not tall and skinny is mainly due to the lack of grid-level parallelism in the kernel design. A Fermi GPU can support up to 8 resident blocks per SM, giving up to 112 blocks for full utilization, which is out of reach for shorter **A** using a reasonable BLOCKSIZE and a 1D grid. The utilization can be improved by allowing several threads per row and thereby introducing a 2D grid for the kernel.

As illustrated in Fig. 2 (b), each thread of each block in this kernel then does part of a row only and adds its partial result to the results of other threads from other blocks in order to produce an element of **y**. We introduce a new parameter WORKSIZE_n to designate how many elements of a row each thread should handle. For simplicity in our implementation this parameter represents multiples of the parameter BLOCKSIZE. The values of **x** are still read into shared memory in chunks of size BLOCKSIZE only once per block and then accessed from here to facilitate reuse of data. We use the CUDA function atomicAdd() [1] for the inter-block reduction of partial results in order to avoid race conditions.

The several-threads-per-row kernel is launched with a 2D grid of dimension (GRIDSIZE_m, GRIDSIZE_n), where

GRIDSIZE_m $= (m + $ BLOCKSIZE $- 1)/$BLOCKSIZE,

GRIDSIZE_n $= (n + $ BLOCKSIZE $*$ WORKSIZE_n $- 1)/($BLOCKSIZE $*$ WORKSIZE_n$)$,

and requires an if conditional in the kernel to make sure the bottom blocks do not access memory outside the m rows of **A**. Since only the right most column of blocks require an if conditional to stay within the columns n of **A**, it is convenient to design this kernel as two device kernels, 1 and 2, that takes care of the left fully tiled part of **A** and the right rest of **A**, respectively. Device kernels in CUDA work similarly to inline functions in C++. Threads in the fully tiled part of **A** add up results for a fixed number of elements BLOCKSIZE $*$ WORKSIZE_n. Threads in the right rest part of **A** possibly do less. In Fig. 2 (b) the case of WORKSIZE_n $= 3$ and grid dimension $(4, 2)$ is shown.

As is illustrated in Fig. 1, the several-threads-per-row design performs well for most shapes of **A**, i.e., those that are close to square or wide. The most significant performance limitation for this kernel is the use of the atomicAdd() function, which reads a 32-bit word in global memory, adds a number to it, and writes the result back to the same address. No other thread can access the address until the operation is complete, so until then those other threads working the same row might be stalled. As a rule of thumb, we find that if **A** has less than the 21504 rows needed for full occupancy of all SMs on the C2050 card and more than $n > 100$ columns, the gain from an increase in grid-level parallelism and hardware utilization significantly outweighs the loss from having stalled threads.

3.3   Several Rows per Thread

If **A** has more than 21504 rows it becomes less beneficial to have more threads per row since all SMs can have the supported 8 active blocks utilized with one-thread-per-row if we use less than 192 threads per block. In fact, for cases where

A is very tall, e.g., having hundreds of thousands of rows, it is a major advantage to let each thread handle several rows. The performance gain from doing this is mainly related to the decrease in shared memory accesses for elements of **x** when each thread handles more rows.

We have implemented a several-rows-per-thread kernel which is illustrated in Fig. 2 (c). In addition to the parameter BLOCKSIZE we introduce the parameter WORKSIZE_n to designate how many rows each thread should handle. The kernel is launched with a 1D grid of dimension

$$\text{GRIDSIZE\_m} = (m + \text{BLOCKSIZE} * \text{WORKSIZE\_m} - 1)/(\text{BLOCKSIZE} * \text{WORKSIZE\_m}),$$

and only the bottom block requires an if conditional to stay within the rows m of **A**. The other blocks assigned to the top fully tiled part of **A** always work on the same fixed number of rows. Again, it is convenient to design this kernel as two device kernels, 1 and 3 (see figure), that takes care of the top fully tiled part of **A** and the bottom rest of **A**, respectively.

3.4 Several Threads, Several Columns

Until now all kernels were designed for 1D blocks having each thread assigned to a different row. However, for matrix-vector multiplication with matrices **A** that have less than BLOCKSIZE rows this can give rise to a large percentage of idle threads. For matrices with very wide and fat shapes, the performance will significantly decrease when some threads are not working. In order to avoid this it is necessary to use either 2D blocks or index the threads of the 1D block differently, e.g., as illustrated in Fig. 2 (e). The new indexing distributes the threads of a block along the column-wise layout of **A** instead of assigning m of them to distinct rows and leaving the rest idle. As long as there are threads within a block to fill an entire additional column of **A**, these threads will be put to work.

The design of this kernel makes it possible to have several-threads-per-row both within a block and between different blocks and all of them are required to add up their partial results to obtain an element of **y**. This can have a considerable cost on performance, which is also seen from the results in Sect. 4.1, but still makes up the best design for wide and fat shapes of **A**. In our implementation, we again use the CUDA function atomicAdd() for the reduction of partial results. Alternatively, one could apply shared memory reduction techniques for the intra-block reduction, e.g., as presented by Harris et. al. [11], but such methods complicates the implementation and does not result in a significant performance boost compared to using atomicAdd() on the C2050 card. As indicated in Fig. 1, this kernel is performing well for wide matrices having less than ~ 50 rows.

3.5 Several Threads, Several Rows

In order to have high-performance for all matrix shapes we combine the designs of the four above kernels into a single versatile kernel. The implementation is

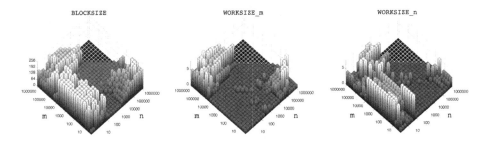

Fig. 3. Result of the auto-tuning process indicating the best values of the tuning parameter BLOCKSIZE, WORKSIZE_m, and WORKSIZE_n at different shapes $m \times n$ of **A**. See the respective kernel for which the parameters are selected in Fig. 1.

illustrated in Fig. 2 (d) and requires three parameters BLOCKSIZE, WORKSIZE_m and WORKSIZE_n. It uses a 2D grid of dimension (GRIDSIZE_m, GRIDSIZE_n), where

$$\text{GRIDSIZE\_m} = (m + \text{BLOCKSIZE} * \text{WORKSIZE\_m} - 1)/(\text{BLOCKSIZE} * \text{WORKSIZE\_m}),$$
$$\text{GRIDSIZE\_n} = (n + \text{BLOCKSIZE} * \text{WORKSIZE\_n} - 1)/(\text{BLOCKSIZE} * \text{WORKSIZE\_n}),$$

and includes as special cases all the previous three kernels.

4 Results

In this section, we present various performance results for the high-performance GPU matrix-vector multiplication kernels developed in this paper. All kernels are implemented for single-precision arithmetic and auto-tuned for optimal performance. We use the Nvidia Tesla C2050 graphics card having 3 GB device memory on a host with a quad-core Intel(R) Core(TM) i7 CPU operating at 2.80 GHz. The GPU has 448 cuda cores with a peak performance of 1.03 GFlops and a theoretical bandwidth peak of 144 GB/s (ECC is on). Note that the performance timings do not include transfer of data between host and GPU.

4.1 Auto-tuner Results

We run the auto-tuner on a 24×24 logarithmic tuning mesh (see Fig. 1) to find the best matrix-vector multiplication kernel (from 3 implementations) and the best parameters from an exhaustive search of the parameter space

$$\text{BLOCKSIZE} \in \{32, 64, 96, 128, 160, 192, 224, 256\},$$
$$\text{WORKSIZE\_m, WORKSIZE\_n} \in \{1, 2, 3, 4, 5, 6, 7, 8\},$$

corresponding to $3 \times 8 \times 8^2 = 1536$ kernels for each particular size of **A**. In order to increase the quality of the kernel selection for this very coarse tuning mesh, the auto-tuner is set up to measure performance on a finer 3×3 logarithmically

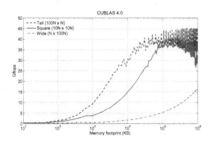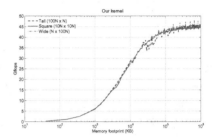

Fig. 4. Performance of matrix-vector multiplication (`SGEMV`) on a Nvidia Tesla C2050 graphics card for matrices having different shapes (tall, square, and wide) as a function of memory footprint. The curves are obtained by calling `cublasSgemv` in the CUBLAS 4.0 library (left) and our auto-tuned kernel (right) and show the average throughput in Gflops from ten subsequent calls. Note the logarithmic memory footprint axis.

spaced grid of points within each mesh tile and take the average. The execution time of the auto-tuner on our test platform is 1.8 hours.

In the right part of Fig. 1 we show the auto-tuner result for finding the best kernel out of the four kernels described in Sect. 3. The black area represents the sizes of **A** that do not fit into memory on the graphics card. We see that the region of best performance for each kernel corresponds reasonably well to their target region, as illustrated in the left part of the figure.

Fig. 3 shows the best values of the tuning parameters `BLOCKSIZE`, `WORKSIZE_m`, and `WORKSIZE_n`, which was determined by the auto-tuner when selecting the best kernel. For all three parameters, we see that the full range of allowed values are used. The best parameters differ distinctively between kernels, however, with no clear pattern otherwise. These results can be seen as a strong advocation for using auto-tuning for matrix-vector multiplication kernels on GPUs.

4.2   Performance Results

In Fig. 4 we plot the performance in Gflops of our matrix-vector multiplication kernel for different shapes of matrices as a function of memory footprint. The shapes are denoted as tall, square, and wide, and given by sizes $100N \times N$, $10N \times 10N$, and $N \times 100N$, respectively, for $N = 10, 20, \ldots$. Regardless of the shape of **A**, we observe that the curves show generally the same behavior for our kernel, which is a significant improvement over the similar performance plots for the SGEMV function of the CUBLAS 4.0 library [2] shown on the left.

We note that there are several drops in the tall shape performance in the region starting around 3×10^4 MB and ending at 2×10^5 MB, which is linked to the coarse granularity of the tuning mesh. In this region, the tuning parameters change rapidly (see Fig. 3). Since the several-rows-per-thread kernel, which is selected as the best in this region, is quite sensitive to these parameter changes, a more fine-grained mesh is needed for the kernel to be optimally auto-tuned.

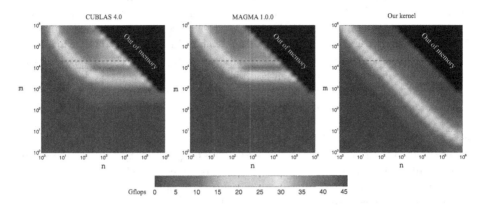

Fig. 5. Performance of matrix-vector multiplication (SGEMV) in color coded form over the 24 × 24 logarithmic auto-tuning mesh of matrix sizes. Dark blue represents low performance, while dark red represent high performance. The figures compare results from the current versions of the most commonly used numerical libraries for GPUs, the Nvidia CUBLAS 4.0 and the MAGMA 1.0.0, to our auto-tuned kernel.

4.3 Performance Comparison

In Fig. 5, we present the performance of our matrix-vector multiplication kernel in color coded form over the 24 × 24 logarithmic auto-tuning mesh of matrix sizes. We also show the corresponding performance of the SGEMV routine from the current versions of the most commonly used numerical libraries for GPUs, the CUBLAS 4.0 [2] and the MAGMA 1.0.0 [3]. The performance measurements displayed correspond to averages over 3 × 3 logarithmically spaced sample points within each mesh tile. We would like to stress that the matrices in these numerical tests are not padded in any way to increase performance.

The figures show that both the CUBLAS 4.0 and MAGMA 1.0.0 matrix-vector multiplication kernels are performing well only above the dashed line (21504 rows), which suggests that they are designed as one-thread-per-row kernels. In particular, the performance for wide matrices, which is problematic for this type of kernel, does not meet the hardware's potential for high-performance. Moreover, the kernels are not auto-tuned, resulting in the several features in the coloring, that indicate lack of performance for certain sizes of matrices.

We see that the figure for our kernel shows good performance for all shapes of matrices, depending primarily on the number of elements in **A**. The figure appears to be almost skew-symmetric, which is a sign of close to optimal shape-dependence behavior. For very wide and fat matrices, the performance is not as good as for comparable tall and skinny matrices. This is related to the necessary use of the CUDA function `atomicAdd()` for the reduction of partial results to the same output address in the several-threads-several-cols kernel.

5   Conclusion

In this paper, we have developed a high-performance matrix-vector multiplication kernel in the CUDA programming model for the latest generation of Nvidia's high-performance computing GPUs. As a starting point, we designed four different matrix-vector multiplication kernels, each aimed for optimal utilization of the fine-grained parallelism of the GPU hardware, but for different matrix shapes. The four kernels were then combined into a single versatile kernel.

We used auto-tuning of the kernel in order to achieve a high-performance for all problem sizes. The auto-tuning consisted of a heuristic search of a tuning space containing the kernel design and key hardware dependent arguments that sets the number of threads per block, the number of rows per thread, and the number of columns per tread, respectively. The proposed auto-tuning procedure then required a total of 1536 different kernels to be compiled and benchmarked on a 24×24 logarithmic tuning mesh over sizes of the matrix $\mathbf{A}$.

The performance of the matrix-vector multiplication kernel was measured in a series of numerical experiments for different problem sizes. The obtained performance increases as the size of $\mathbf{A}$ increases, until the matrix-vector multiplication kernel can fully utilize the many-core hardware of the GPU. There was very little dependence on the shape of the matrix in the performance of our kernel, which is a significant improvement compared to the current GPU libraries for dense linear algebra, CUBLAS 4.0 and MAGMA 1.0.0, which only reach the GPU hardware's potential for tall matrices.

References

1. NVIDIA Corp.: CUDA C Programming Guide Version 4.0 (2011)
2. NVIDIA Corp.: CUDA CUBLAS Library (2011)
3. Tomov, S., Nath, R., Du, P., Dongarra, J.: MAGMA v0.2 Users' Guide (2009)
4. Sørensen, H.H.B.: Auto-tuning Dense Vector and Matrix-Vector Operations for Fermi GPUs (2011) (submitted)
5. Fujimoto, N.: Faster matrix-vector multiplication on GeForce 8800GTX. In: IEEE International Symposium on Parallel and Distributed Processing (2008)
6. Tomov, S., Nath, R., Dongarra, J.: Accelerating the reduction to upper Hessenberg, tridiagonal, and bidiagonal forms through hybrid GPU-based computing. Parallel Computing 36(12) (2010)
7. Anderson, E., Bai, Z., Bischof, C., Blackford, L.S., Demmel, J., Dongarra, J.J., Du Croz, J., Hammarling, S., Greenbaum, A., McKenney, A., Sorensen, D.: LAPACK Users' guide, 3rd edn. SIAM, Philadelphia (1999)
8. Nath, R., Tomov, S., Dongarra, J.: Accelerating GPU kernels for dense linear algebra (2009)
9. Li, Y., Dongarra, J., Tomov, S.: A Note on Auto-tuning GEMM for GPUs (2009)
10. NVIDIA Corp.: Fermi, Whitepaper (2009)
11. Harris, M.: Optimizing Parallel Reduction in CUDA. NVIDIA Dev. Tech. (2008)

Relaxed Synchronization
with Ordered Read-Write Locks

Jens Gustedt and Emmanuel Jeanvoine

INRIA Nancy, Grand Est, France
LORIA, AlGorille
{jens.gustedt,emmanuel.jeanvoine}@inria.fr

Abstract. This paper promotes the first stand-alone implementation of our adaptive tool for synchronization *ordered read-write locks*, ORWL. It provides new synchronization methods for resource oriented parallel or distributed algorithms for which it allows an implicit deadlock-free and equitable control of a protected resource and provides means to couple lock objects and data tightly. A typical application that uses this framework will run a number of loosely coupled tasks that are exclusively regulated by the data flow. We conducted experiments to prove the validity, efficiency and scalability of our implementation.

Keywords: synchronization, iterative algorithms, read-write locks, experiments.

1 Introduction

Lock or token based mechanisms to protect shared resources have a long tradition in parallel distributed computing. They are closely integrated into nowadays operating systems (POSIX mutex, semaphores and read-write locks), run times (OpenMP), and higher level languages (Java). They act on shared objects (POSIX `rwlock`), file ranges, or distributed entities (Corba, Chord, read-write locks [8]).

In contrast to implicit methods such as atomic snapshots or transactional approaches, see [7,1,6], they require an *explicit* action by the programmer or algorithm designer to mark the parts of her/his code that is judged *critical*. This paper is based on the assumption that such a labeling of critical parts will be provided. On a longer time scale the tool presented here might be a good basis to do such annotations automatically, but such an automatic annotation is not the subject of this paper.

Many parallel or distributed computations follow data dependency patterns between their different computation tasks [2]. Usually the output of one task (producer) is taken as input of other tasks (consumers), but write access (of the producer) and read access (of the consumer) to that data cannot be done atomically. This can occur in a shared memory setting where the data is too

M. Alexander et al. (Eds.): Euro-Par 2011 Workshops, Part I, LNCS 7155, pp. 387–397, 2012.
© Springer-Verlag Berlin Heidelberg 2012

large to be accessible in one atomic read or in a distributed setting where data is sent and received in slices.

Algorithmically, the commonly implemented tools that we mention above are unsatisfactory with respect to at least one of the following three properties:

Liveness: Guarantees for liveness can in general not be given easily. Usually it needs supplementary tools such as barriers that come with an important cost whence they inhibit dynamic optimizations by the run time. Sporadic deadlocks are common software bugs that are quite costly to debug.

Equity: In case of contention, tools such as POSIX' reader-writer lock or semaphores voluntarily leave the order of lock acquisition either to the system implementation (in the simplest cases) or to the scheduling policy. If the order of treatment by different subtasks is fixed by the algorithm designer and may even be cyclic, guaranteeing equity and a precise flow of control can be challenging.

Efficiency: Using a lock structure (a mutex in the simplest case) introduces fixed points in the program between which a resource needs to be accessible. It usually gives no explicit indication to the run-time which resource is targeted and also what could be done proactively to represent the resource in the address space of the program. Possibilities of overlapping computation and communication (in a broad sense) are easily lost by that, exploiting such possibilities can become tedious to implement. Again in the simplest case of a mutex, a resource is only fetched and pushed when it is accessed where usually the transfer from one task P_1 to another P_2 could be done as soon as P_1 unlocks the mutex.

To target the three criteria from above, in [3,4] we introduced the framework of *ordered read write locks*, ORWL, that are designed to favor algorithmic control and data consistency. This framework for inter-task synchronization is conceptually independent of the execution context and can be implemented in both shared memory or distributed environments.

A first adhoc implementation of this tool was integrated as part of the PARXXL library and is only fully available for shared memory. This paper here presents a new implementation that is only based on standard languages and interfaces (C and POSIX) and that can be used in shared, distributed or mixed contexts.

The basics of our model and the designs of the underlying tool for iterative parallel algorithms are briefly reviewed in Section 2, in particular we remind the features that guarantee liveness and equity for iterative settings. Then, in Section 3, we present the three different features that distinguish the use of ORWL from other tools: the possibility to announce the future use of a resource, a comfortable interface for iterative computations and a tight binding between control structures and data. In Section 4, we present benchmarks that address the potential overhead that our implementation introduces. Finally, we conclude and discuss our next steps in Section 5.

2   Ordered Read-Write Locks, an Adaptive Tool for Synchronization

We call the building block of our model *Ordered Read-Write Locks* (ORWL), a special kind of read-write locks. All proofs on properties of the model have been presented in [4]. ORWL have the following features:

1. A waiting queue with FIFO-policy.
2. An explicit association of a lock with application data.
3. A distinction between *request* and *acquire* operations that replace a classical one-step *lock* operation. So the typical sequence for an access is *request*, *acquire* and then *release*.
4. A distinction between locks (as opaque objects) and lock-handles (as user interfaces acting on locks).
5. A distinction into exclusive or write locks and inclusive or read locks.

All of these features have been used previously for lock data structures, see *e.g* [5]. But to the best of our knowledge their intentional combination in a single framework is original.

Property 1 and 2 together ensure a controlled access order of the application to its data. For an important class of applications that will iterate over their data, we must be able to control when and what data is accessed. In addition, Property 2 restricts the access to the data to the time that a lock is held, pointers become invalid outside that time window. We thus enforce data consistency: no thread may write to data that it has not locked and if a read is granted to data it is guaranteed to be invariant while the lock is held.

Property 3 allows us to reserve resources pro-actively. At first, this gives the application programmer the possibility to issue some sort of hint (a request operation) that a resource will be used in the future with a require operation. Such a hint is non-blocking and incurs only negligible cost by itself. This is a big advantage for the *programming logic* of iterative algorithms which access data in a cyclical pattern. They may insert their request for the next iteration in the FIFO while holding a lock for the current one. The other advantage lies in *performance* issues. The run time system then may use this information to anticipate the access, e.g by doing a data prefetch.

When doing such a pro-active locking the Property 4 comes into play: a thread or process may define several handles (usually two in our case) on the same lock and thereby newly request a lock by means of one handle while still actively holding a lock via another handle. The type of request in view of Property 5, namely if the access will be just for reading (and thus potentially shared) or for writing must be specified when the lock is requested and that type is kept track via the handle.

Property 5 ensures that we may easily handle the case that the output of a task is read by several others. It allows for important optimizations: buffer space with read-only data can be shared among threads and processes; data that is only presented for reading may be thrown away once the lock is released and thus costly updates (or just checks for consistency) may be avoided.

Recurring Tasks. To model a recurring task of an iterative process we proceed as follows. Whenever all the lock requests that such a task has requested have been acquired, the task is said to be *active* and can perform its job.

After finishing the computation of the job itself, before releasing any of the locks, a second set of lock handles is used to posts copies of its requests for the next iteration, first. These guarantee the reservation of the resources for the next iteration. The task then releases the acquired locks to pass the control over to other tasks that operate on the same data. This procedure guarantees that access to the resources is given in a cyclic pattern and thus that all tasks iteratively get access to the data in an equitable way, see [4]. Ensuring liveness of such system needs an additional effort. It has been shown that for this property the initialization order of the lock handles in the FIFO is crucial. Any initialization that doesn't contain certain types of cyclic dependencies never will run into a deadlock and that such an initialization is always possible.

3   User Interfaces

This section will introduce a handful of data types and functions that compose the user interface of ORWL. There are three data types:

orwl_mirror   a representation of a local or remote resource.
orwl_handle   a lock handle to queue up for that resource, and
orwl_handle2   a pair of lock handles used for recurrent locking requests.

The function interfaces can be classified in three different sets:

- orwl_read_request   (or   orwl_write_request),   orwl_acquire (or orwl_test) and orwl_release that form a lock sequence on the resource.
- orwl_truncate, orwl_write_map and orwl_read_map that allow to control and access the data that is eventually associated to a resource.
- A set of analog functions with a "2" appended to the name that operate on pairs orwl_handle2, such as orwl_read_request2 or orwl_write_map2. They suit particularly the needs for iterative tasks.

3.1   Resource Protection

Simple resource protection that is analogous to a protection of a critical section through a mutex can be implemented in a straight forward manner.

Listing 1.1. Simple exclusive protection of a resource loc through a handle handle

```
orwl_write_request(&loc , &handle );        /* announce future access */
/* some operation without the resource                                */
orwl_acquire(&handle );                      /* Block until granted    */
/* some critical operation with locked resource                       */
orwl_release(&handle );                      /* Free the resource      */
```

Here the first call to `orwl_write_request` binds `handle` to resource `loc` and announces the intent to access it. Until the time we call `orwl_acquire` the system may

- satisfy other demands to the resource that have higher priority,
- route the corresponding data to our host
- allocate space in our address space or
- perform other operations that are needed to satisfy the demand.

During that time the application can perform any type of operation that doesn't need access to the resource.

Then, once the application comes to a point it can't proceed further without the resource, `orwl_acquire` ensures that it is blocked until the request can be fulfilled. The critical section then ends by calling `orwl_release`.

If the application has a variety of tasks to perform before access to the resource can't be avoided further, `orwl_test` can be used to query for the lock acquisition and allows to adapt the application at run time, see Listing 1.2.

Listing 1.2. Adapted protection of a resource `loc` through a handle `handle`

```
orwl_read_request(&loc, &handle);          /*  announce future read */
while (!orwl_test(&handle)) {              /*     check if produced */
    /* Do some operation while the resource is produced            */
}
orwl_acquire(&handle);                      /*   block until granted */
/* Do some operation while the resource is stable                  */
orwl_release(&handle);                      /*    free the resource */
```

3.2 Associating Data

Up to now we have introduced a use of ORWL that only uses its controlling aspect, analogous to POSIX' `pthread_mutex_t` or `pthread_rwlock_t`. In addition to that ORWL allows one to associate data to the resource directly, Listing 1.3.

Listing 1.3. Associate data to `loc` and initialize it properly

```
orwl_write_request(&loc, &handle);      /* reserve the resource for maintenance */
orwl_acquire(&handle);
orwl_resize(&handle, 168 * sizeof(uint64_t));     /* write access is needed to */
size_t size;                                       /* get a pointer to the data */
uint64_t* data = orwl_write_map(&handle, &size);  /*   in our address space */
assert(size == 168 * sizeof(uint64_t));            /*       check the size */
my_special_initialization(data);                   /*    initialized the data */
orwl_release(&handle);                             /*        free the resource */
data = 0;                                          /*   invalidate the pointer */
```

To associate data to a resource we just have to assign a non-zero size to the data (here 168 units for the type `uint64_t`). Per default the data is initialized to all zero values, in the example it is initialized by a special function. Data is viewed as untyped bytes (`void*`) and the size returned by `orwl_write_map` accounts the number of bytes in the data. To ease the underlying communication routines, data sizes are always multiples of `sizeof(uint64_t)`, usually 8 bytes.

Another task or process may then modify the data without changing its size, Listing 1.4, and any number of readers may inspect the results of that modification simultaneously, see Listing 1.5.

Listing 1.4. Modify the data

```
orwl_write_request(&loc, &handle);        /* reserve the resource for modification */
orwl_acquire(&handle);
size_t size;                              /* get a pointer to the data */
uint64_t* data = orwl_write_map(&handle, &size);  /*    in our address space */
size /= sizeof(*data);
for (size_t i = 0; i < size; ++i) {       /*     do some operation with */
  data[i] *= i;                           /*          exclusive access */
}
orwl_release(&handle);                    /*        free the resource */
data = 0;                                 /*     invalidate the pointer */
```

Listing 1.5. Access the associated data

```
orwl_read_request(&loc, &handle);         /* reserve the resource for reading */
orwl_acquire(&handle);
size_t size;                              /* get a pointer to the data */
uint64_t const* data = orwl_read_map(&handle, &size);  /* in our address space */
size /= sizeof(*data);
for (size_t i = 0; i < size; ++i) {       /*    some operation while */
  printf(stderr, "item_%zu_is_%" PRIu64 "\n",  /*     the resource */
    i, data[i]);                          /*           is stable */
}
orwl_release(&handle);                    /*        free the resource */
data = 0;                                 /*     invalidate the pointer */
```

3.3 Recurrent Access to Resources

Iterative computations need to be implemented with a lot of care if we want
to guarantee liveness for all processes and equity among them. As introduced
above ORWL, as an abstract tool can guarantee these properties if we issue a
lock request on a resource for the next iteration before we abandon a current
lock that we hold. This is facilitated by our library with the type orwl_handle2.
It represents a pair of orwl_handle that are used in alternation for even and
odd numbered iterations.

Listing 1.6. A simple iterative procedure with one resource and one orwl_handle2

```
orwl_write_request2(&loc, &handle2);      /*              bind the pair */
while (!done) {                           /*  do until some external event */
  orwl_acquire2(&handle2);                /*     block until our turn comes */
  /* work exclusively with the resource */
                                          /* insert ourselves in the queue */
  orwl_release2(&handle2);                /*        for the next iteration */
                                          /*              free the resource */
                                          /* pass control to somebody else */
}
orwl_cancel2(&handle2);                   /*         withdraw from the queue */
```

Here, before entering into the iteration, we bind the first handle of the pair to
the resource. Then, at the start of each iteration the handle in the pair with
the request pending is acquired and we gain exclusive access to the resource. At
the end of the iteration orwl_release2 first issues a new request on the handle
that is currently inactive and then releases the lock on the resource. When going
out of the iteration, orwl_cancel2 has to be called since otherwise one of the
handles in the pair would be left with a pending lock request.

Listing 1.7. An iterative procedure with two resources and two `orwl_handle2`

```
orwl_write_request2(&hereResource, &here);        /*        bind the two pairs */
orwl_read_request2(&thereResource, &there);
while (!done) {                                   /*     until some external event */
  orwl_acquire2(&here); orwl_acquire2(&there);    /*              block twice */
  size_t size;                                    /*         the data access is */
  uint64_t* hereData = orwl_write_map2(&here, &size);    /* exclusive here */
  uint64_t const* thereData = orwl_read_map2(&there, &size);/* inclusive there */

  size /= sizeof(*thereData);                     /*            application code: */
  for (size_t i=0; i<size; ++i) {                 /*      average componentwise */
    hereData[i]=(hereData[i]+thereData[i])/2;/*      store in hereResource */
  }

                                                  /* insert ourselves in the queues */
  orwl_release2(&here);                           /*          for the next iteration */
  orwl_release2(&there);                          /*           free the resources */
                                                  /* pass control to the others */

}
orwl_cancel2(&here); orwl_cancel2(&there);        /*      withdraw from the queues */
```

Finally, with Listing 1.7, let us look into a more complicated pattern, namely with two resources and two pairs of handles that act on them. This can be seen as each process "owning" one resource (called **hereResource**) that he will update and "inspecting" one resource of a "neighboring" process (**thereResource**). The access pattern between different processes could then be any collection of directed circles or trees. The basic scheme is similar, only that always two calls to `orwl_acquire2` and `orwl_release2` are issued in the iteration, one for each resource. Using the mapping feature of ORWL we see how we easily can implement an iterative vector averaging on the associated data.

4 Experiments

4.1 Benchmark Application

Livermoore Loops Kernel 23. To benchmark the library, we use the Livermoore Loops Kernel 23 (LLK23) benchmark (see `http://www.netlib.org/benchmark/livermorec`).

Listing 1.8. Core computation of the Livermoore Loops Kernel 23 benchmark

```
for (i = 2; i < (N - 1); ++i) {
  for (j = 2; j < (M - 1); ++j) {
    q = data[i-1][j] · zb[i][j] + data[i][j-1] · zv[i][j]
      + data[i][j+1] · zu[i][j] + data[i+1][j] · zr[i][j]
      + zz[i][j] - data[i][j];
    data[i][j] += 0.175 · q;
  }
}
```

The core computation of the benchmark is given in Listing 1.8. To simplify, each element of a matrix called **data** is computed using four neighbors elements (N, S, E and W) and five coefficient matrices (**zb**, **zr**, **zu**, **zv**, **zz**).

This application has significant characteristics to test our approach. It is an iterative computation of which the different parts can be executed asynchronously and where each part shows constant progress. Furthermore, for a parallelization, some data exchange is required between the frontiers. This can be done transparently with ORWL; the nested for loops of Listing 1.8 would go in the place marked "**application code**" in Listing 1.7.

Parallelization with ORWL. An intuitive method to parallelize the problem is to decompose `data` into several blocks. For each block, the inner computation is independent from the other blocks whereas the computation of the edges and the corners depends on some neighboring blocks.

Thus, for each block, we define a main task (MT) that performs the computation and eight sub-tasks (ST) that are used to export the frontier data (edges and corners) to the neighboring MT. Figure 1 shows an example of a simple decomposition into four blocks. The four MT are numbered from 0 to 3 and the associated ST are prefixed with their direction.

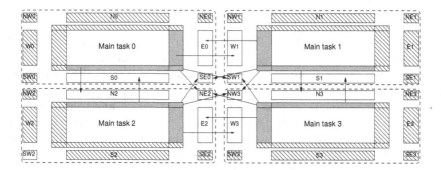

Fig. 1. A four block decomposition example. The gray parts represent the MT parts that require some frontier data to be computed. Hatched parts are constant boundary conditions or unused.

4.2 Experimental Results

The experiments have been conducted on the *graphene* cluster of the Grid'5000 experimental testbed. Each node is composed of 4 cores at 2.53 GHz and 16 GiB of memory, and a Gigabit Ethernet interconnection network. All the following results are obtained after running 100 iterations of the LLK23 computation.

Average Execution Time per Matrix Element. In this experiment, the goal is to evaluate the average execution time per `data` element. First, we divide `data` in 4, 16, 36, 64 and 100 blocks. Then, for each division, we increase the global problem size by varying the size (in number of elements) of a block. One node is reserved for each block, such that we can reach the limit of a maximum block size that fits into RAM.

In Figure 2(a) we see that the computation cost per element decreases when the problem size increases, and that it tends to a lower limit. We note that the times corresponding to the 4 block division are below the others. This is due to the simplified connection pattern (see Figure 1) where half of the block boundaries don't participate in communication. The other running times are not distinguishable, which proves that for subdivisions into more parts this effect is already negligible.

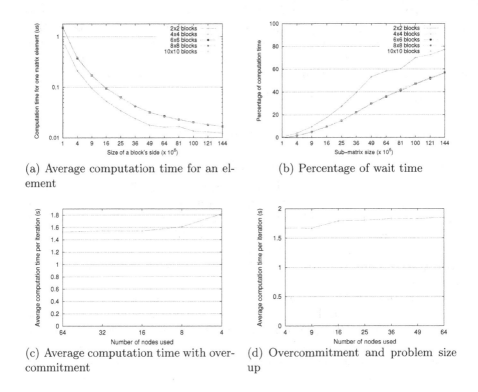

(a) Average computation time for an element

(b) Percentage of wait time

(c) Average computation time with overcommitment

(d) Overcommitment and problem size up

Fig. 2. Experimental results

Computation Efficiency. Because our parallelization of LLK23 requires frontiers of neighboring regions, not all parallel tasks can compute simultaneously. In this experiment, see Figure 2(b), the goal is to relate the time that MT spends either to compute or to wait for some frontier data. The setup is the same as in the previous experiment. We see that for small problems, almost all the time is spent to wait. For larger problems, the computation time increases and finally reaches about 55 % of the total time. Actually, the *absolute* wait time itself (not shown) is basically spent in `orwl_acquire2` and does not vary much, but the computation partially overlaps with these waiting periods.

Overcommitting. In this experiment the global problem size is constant, 4000×4000 elements per blocks with a division into 64 blocks. We launch the computation successively on 64, 32, 16, 8 and 4 nodes; thus commit 1, 2, 4, 8 and 16 MT per quad-core node. The average time to compute an iteration is shown in Figure 2(c). We can see that the overcommitment of several tasks per cores allows to take full advantage of the four cores of each node. The time per iteration only increases slightly when we have much more MT per core.

So, even if the parallelization induces long waiting times for the tasks, ORWL is able to hide this cost: tasks that have received their data autonomously start their execution while other tasks are waiting for theirs.

Scalability. In this last experiment we study the impact of increasing the global problem size. We place 16 MT per quad-core node on 4 to 64 nodes. Each MT computes a 3000x3000 element block. The average time to compute an iteration is shown in Figure 2(d). We see that increasing the problem size does not increase the average computation time much. Thus, ORWL is suitable for the construction of scalable applications.

5   Conclusion and Future Work

In this paper we introduced a new library that implements the ordered read-write lock (ORWL) paradigm to control access to shared or distributed resources. We presented the basic use patterns for that library that ranges from simple implementations of critical sections that allow a pro-active announcement to more involved patterns of alternating resource allocation in iterative computations. Macro-benchmarks show that the library behaves well on multi-core machines and clusters; it realizes almost perfect computation/communication overlap and weak scaling properties.

A forthcoming article will describe the implementation of the library in more detail and present micro-benchmarks of the individual functions and components. Future plans with ORWL include application to other types of applications and architectures. Namely we are currently implementing an application that uses ORWL to control computations on compute cluster equipped with GPU co-processors. Other future work includes improvements to use ORWL as simple and efficient locking features in a shared memory context.

Acknowledgment. Experiments presented in this paper were carried out using the Grid'5000 experimental testbed, being developed under the INRIA ALADDIN development action with support from CNRS, RENATER and several Universities as well as other funding bodies (see https://www.grid5000.fr).

References

1. Afek, Y., Attiya, H., Dolev, D., Gafni, E., Merritt, M., Shavit, N.: Atomic snapshots of shared memory. J. ACM 40(4), 873–890 (1993)
2. Barrett, R., Berry, M., Chan, T.F., Demmel, J., Donato, J., Dongarra, J., Eijkhout, V., Pozo, R., Romine, C., Van der Vorst, H.: Templates for the Solution of Linear Systems: Building Blocks for Iterative Methods. SIAM, Philadelphia (1994)
3. Clauss, P.N., Gustedt, J.: Experimenting Iterative Computations with Ordered Read-Write Locks. In: Danelutto, M., Gross, T., Bourgeois, J. (eds.) 18th Euromicro International Conference on Parallel, Distributed and Network-based Processing, pp. 155–162. IEEE, Pisa (2010), http://hal.inria.fr/inria-00436417/en
4. Clauss, P.N., Gustedt, J.: Iterative Computations with Ordered Read-Write Locks. Journal of Parallel and Distributed Computing 70(5), 496–504 (2010), http://hal.inria.fr/inria-00330024/en

5. Danek, R., Golab, W.M.: Closing the Complexity Gap between FCFS Mutual Exclusion and Mutual Exclusion. In: Taubenfeld, G. (ed.) DISC 2008. LNCS, vol. 5218, pp. 93–108. Springer, Heidelberg (2008)
6. Herlihy, M., Eliot, J., Moss, B.: Transactional memory: Architectural support for lock-free data structures. In: Proceedings of the 20th Annual International Symposium on Computer Architecture, pp. 289–300 (1993)
7. Vitányi, P.M.B., Awerbuch, B.: Atomic shared register access by asynchronous hardware (detailed abstract). In: FOCS, pp. 233–243. IEEE (1986)
8. Wagner, C., Müller, F.: Token-Based Read/Write-Locks for Distributed Mutual Exclusion. In: Bode, A., Ludwig, T., Karl, W.C., Wismüller, R. (eds.) Euro-Par 2000. LNCS, vol. 1900, pp. 1185–1195. Springer, Heidelberg (2000)

The Parallel C++ Statistical Library 'QUESO': Quantification of Uncertainty for Estimation, Simulation and Optimization

Ernesto E. Prudencio* and Karl W. Schulz

Institute for Computational Engineering and Sciences (ICES),
The University of Texas at Austin, USA
{prudenci,karl}@ices.utexas.edu

Abstract. QUESO is a collection of statistical algorithms and programming constructs supporting *research* into the uncertainty quantification (UQ) of models and their predictions. It has been designed with three objectives: it should (a) be *sufficiently abstract* in order to handle a large spectrum of models, (b) be *algorithmically extensible*, allowing an easy insertion of new and improved algorithms, and (c) take advantage of *parallel computing*, in order to handle realistic models. Such objectives demand a combination of an *object-oriented design* with robust software engineering practices. QUESO is written in C++, uses MPI, and leverages libraries already available to the scientific community. We describe some UQ concepts, present QUESO, and list planned enhancements.

Keywords: Software Design, Uncertainty Quantification, Parallel MCMC.

1   Introduction

QUESO stands for Quantification of Uncertainty for Estimation, Simulation and Optimization, and it is a library of statistical algorithms and programming classes for *research* on uncertainty quantification (UQ) of mathematical models and their predictions. We have three main objectives for QUESO. It should (a) be *model agnostic*, i.e., it should be able to handle a large spectrum of models; (b) be *algorithmically flexible*, allowing for easy insertion of new and improved algorithms; and (c) take advantage of *parallel computing*, enabling it to be used on realistic problems. Its design then follows three main principles. The library should (d) be *object-oriented*, naturally mapping into the code the *mathematical concepts* present in the models and algorithms; (e) *leverage* existing libraries and packages (e.g. GSL [7], Trilinos [10], PETSc [17], DAKOTA [6]); and (f) have its algorithms implemented in a way such that they become *independent* of the underlying vectors and matrices. Our decision to implement QUESO with the object oriented programming language C++ and with the message passing interface (MPI) standard is consistent with such objectives and principles. Class

---

* Corresponding author.

M. Alexander et al. (Eds.): Euro-Par 2011 Workshops, Part I, LNCS 7155, pp. 398–407, 2012.

derivation, polymorphism and templating give QUESO the desired levels of abstractness and adaptability, allowing researchers to concentrate their efforts on algorithms rather than spending time on the details of underlying datatypes.

In Section 2 we present some concepts and algorithms supported by QUESO, paving the path for the description, in Section 3, of QUESO's main features and classes. We conclude with a list of planned enhancements in Section 4. Throughout the paper we use boldface letters to denote vector and matrix quantities.

2   Stochastic Models and Algorithms

In order to comprehend an actual phenomenon and to predict the future behavior of the actual system underlying it, one needs to (a) collect experimental data $\mathbf{d}$, and (b) construct a *computational model*, which refers to the combination of a mathematical model with a discretization procedure that enables one to compute an approximate solution using computer algorithms. At its core, a computational model (see Figure 1) is composed of two parts: a vector $\boldsymbol{\theta}$ of n parameters, and a set of governing equations $\mathbf{r}(\boldsymbol{\theta}, \mathbf{u}) = \mathbf{0}$, whose solution $\mathbf{u}$ represents the *state variables*, or model state. By *parameters* we designate various concepts, e.g.,

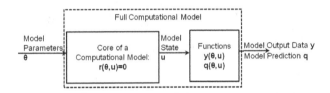

Fig. 1. Computational model: parameters $\boldsymbol{\theta}$, state $\mathbf{u}$, equations $\mathbf{r}$, output $\mathbf{y}$, QoIs $\mathbf{q}$

material properties, coefficients, constitutive parameters, boundary and initial conditions, external forces, parameters for describing the model inadequacy and characteristics of an experimental apparatus. The computational model includes functions for the calculation of *model output data* $\mathbf{y} = \mathbf{y}(\boldsymbol{\theta}, \mathbf{u})$, and the prediction of a vector $\mathbf{q} = \mathbf{q}(\boldsymbol{\theta}, \mathbf{u})$ of m quantities of interest (QoIs). Model output data is compared against experimental data during a model calibration, while QoIs are predicted during a model prediction and might not be directly measurable.

There are many possible sources of uncertainty on procedures (a) and (b) above. First, $\mathbf{d}$ need not be equal to the actual values of observables because of errors in the measurement process. Second, the values of the input parameters to the phenomenon might not be precisely known. Third, the appropriate set of equations governing the phenomenon might not be well understood.

In deterministic models, all parameters are assigned numbers, and no parameter is related to the parametrization of a random variable (RV) or field. As a consequence, a deterministic model assigns a number to each of the components of quantities $\mathbf{u}$, $\mathbf{y}$ and $\mathbf{q}$. In stochastic models, however, at least one parameter is

assigned a probability density function (PDF) or is related to the parametriza-
tion of a RV or field, causing $\mathbf{u}$, $\mathbf{y}$ and $\mathbf{q}$ to become random. Parameters that are
not directly measurable need to be *estimated* through the solution of an *inverse
problem* (IP) [12,14], where $\mathbf{d}$ is given and one estimates the values of $\boldsymbol{\theta}$ that
cause $\mathbf{y}$ to best fit $\mathbf{d}$. A computational model might also be used in a *forward
problem* (FP), where $\boldsymbol{\theta}$ is given and one computes $\mathbf{u}$, $\mathbf{y}$ and/or $\mathbf{q}$.

QUESO supports a Bayesian approach [11,16], i.e., the posterior PDF

$$\pi_{\text{post}}(\boldsymbol{\theta}|\mathbf{d}, M) = \frac{\pi_{\text{like}}(\mathbf{d}|\boldsymbol{\theta}, M) \cdot \pi_{\text{prior}}(\boldsymbol{\theta}|M)}{\pi(\mathbf{d}|M)} \tag{1}$$

is the solution of statistical IPs, combining the prior information $\pi_{\text{prior}}(\boldsymbol{\theta}|M)$
about the parameters with the likelihood $\pi_{\text{like}}(\mathbf{d}|\boldsymbol{\theta}, M)$ of observing the data
$\mathbf{d}$ given parameter values $\boldsymbol{\theta}$. The letter M designates a *model class* [2,4,5] and
represents all the assumptions and mathematical statements that are involved
in the modeling of the system. The choice of a particular $\boldsymbol{\theta} \in \mathbb{R}^n$ specifies a
particular model in the set M of models. The denominator

$$\pi(\mathbf{d}|M) = \int \pi_{\text{like}}(\mathbf{d}|\boldsymbol{\theta}, M) \cdot \pi_{\text{prior}}(\boldsymbol{\theta}|M) \, d\boldsymbol{\theta} \tag{2}$$

is called the *evidence* [3] for M provided by $\mathbf{d}$, and it can be used for ranking
competing candidate model classes that reflect different modeling choices. Given
M, $\mathbf{d}$, and a conditional PDF $\pi(\mathbf{q}|\boldsymbol{\theta}, \mathbf{d}, M_j)$ of $\mathbf{q}$, the predictive PDF of $\mathbf{q}$ is [2]

$$\pi_{\text{predicted}}(\mathbf{q}|\mathbf{d}, M) = \int \pi(\mathbf{q}|\boldsymbol{\theta}, \mathbf{d}, M) \cdot \pi_{\text{post}}(\boldsymbol{\theta}|\mathbf{d}, M) \, d\boldsymbol{\theta}. \tag{3}$$

Stochastic algorithms are used to generate samples from (1). Metropolis Hastings
(MH) [13,9] is one of them. Given (a) the target PDF $\pi_{\text{target}} : B \subset \mathbb{R}^n \to \mathbb{R}_+$, up
to a multiplicative constant, (b) the number $n_{\text{pos}} \geqslant 2$ of positions in the chain,
(c) an initial guess $\boldsymbol{\theta}^{(0)} \in \mathbb{R}^n$, and (d) a symmetric positive definite proposal
covariance matrix $\mathbf{C} \in \mathbb{R}^{n \times n}$. MH runs as follows,

```
01. Do {
02.    Generate candidate z ∈ ℝⁿ by sampling from q(θ⁽ᵏ⁾, z);
03.    If z ∉ supp(π_target) then θ⁽ᵏ⁺¹⁾ = θ⁽ᵏ⁾;
04.    If z ∈ supp(π_target) then {
05.        Compute acceptance probability α(θ⁽ᵏ⁾, z);
06.        Generate sample 0 < τ ⩽ 1 from uniform RV defined over (0, 1];
07.        If α ⩾ τ then θ⁽ᵏ⁺¹⁾ = z; else θ⁽ᵏ⁺¹⁾ = θ⁽ᵏ⁾;
09.    }
10.    Set k = k + 1;
11. } while (k + 1 < n_pos),
```

where $q : \mathbb{R}^n \times \mathbb{R}^n \to \mathbb{R}_+$ is a proposal distribution [8,12], e.g.

$$q(\mathbf{x}, \mathbf{y}) \propto e^{-\frac{1}{2}\left\{[\mathbf{y} - \mathbf{x}]^T \cdot [\mathbf{C}]^{-1} \cdot [\mathbf{y} - \mathbf{x}]\right\}},$$

$supp(\cdot)$ denotes the support of a function, and

$$\alpha(\boldsymbol{\theta}^{(k)}, \mathbf{z}) = \frac{\pi_{\mathrm{target}}(\mathbf{z})}{\pi_{\mathrm{target}}(\boldsymbol{\theta}^{(k)})} \cdot \frac{q(\mathbf{z}, \boldsymbol{\theta}^{(k)})}{q(\boldsymbol{\theta}^{(k)}, \mathbf{z})}.$$

A sample $\mathbf{z}$ is given by $\boldsymbol{\theta}^{(k)} + \mathbf{C}^{1/2}\mathcal{N}(0, I)$, where $\mathcal{N}(0, I)$ designates a Gaussian RV of zero mean and unit covariance matrix. MH can be improved in different ways, e.g. delayed rejection adaptive Metropolis [8] and stochastic Newton.

Stochastic algorithms are also needed to compute high dimensional integrals like (2). One example is the adaptive multilevel sampling [4] that simultaneously generates samples and computes (2) through a sequence of intermediate PDFs

$$\pi_i(\boldsymbol{\theta}|\mathbf{d}, M) \propto \pi_{\mathrm{like}}(\mathbf{d}|\boldsymbol{\theta}, M)^{\alpha_i} \cdot \pi_{\mathrm{prior}}(\boldsymbol{\theta}|M), \ i = 0, 1, \ldots, L,$$

where $0 = \alpha_0 < \alpha_1 < \ldots < \alpha_{L-1} < \alpha_L = 1$ are adaptively selected exponents. A *load balanced* parallel version is proposed in [15].

Many other statistical calculations are also important, e.g. Monte Carlo (MC) for (3), autocorrelation, kernel density estimations, and accuracy assessment.

3   The QUESO Design and Implementation

Section 2 identified many mathematical entities present in the description of statistical problems and in some algorithms used for their solution. As part of the design, QUESO attempts to conceptually implement these entities in order to allow algorithmic researchers to manipulate them at the library level, as well as for algorithm users (the modelers interested in UQ) to manipulate them at the application level. Examples of entities are vector space $\mathbb{R}^n$; vector subset $B \subset \mathbb{R}^n$; vector $\boldsymbol{\theta} \in B$; matrix $\mathbf{C} \in \mathbb{R}^n \times \mathbb{R}^n$; function $\pi : \mathbb{R}^n \to \mathbb{R}_+$, e.g. joint PDF; function $\pi : \mathbb{R} \to \mathbb{R}_+$, e.g. marginal PDF; function $\pi : \mathbb{R} \to [0, 1]$, e.g. cumulative distribution function; realizer function; function $\mathbf{q} : \mathbb{R}^n \to \mathbb{R}^m$; sequences of scalars; and sequences of vectors. QUESO tries to naturally map such entities through an object-oriented design. Indeed, QUESO C++ classes include vector spaces, subsets, scalar sequences, PDFs, and RVs.

An application using QUESO will fall into three categories: a statistical IP, a statistical FP, or combinations of both. In each problem the user might deal with up to five vectors of potentially very different sizes: parameters $\boldsymbol{\theta}$, state $\mathbf{u}$, output $\mathbf{y}$, data $\mathbf{d}$ and QoIs $\mathbf{q}$. Figure 2 shows the software stack of a typical application that uses QUESO. Even though QUESO deals directly with $\boldsymbol{\theta}$ and $\mathbf{q}$ only, it is usually the case the one of the other three vectors ($\mathbf{u}$, $\mathbf{y}$ and $\mathbf{d}$) will have the biggest number of components and will therefore dictate the size of the minimum parallel environment to be used in a problem. So, for example, even though one processor might be sufficient for handling $\boldsymbol{\theta}$, $\mathbf{y}$, $\mathbf{d}$ and $\mathbf{q}$, eight processors at least might be necessary to solve for $\mathbf{u}$. QUESO currently only requires that the amounts n and m can be handled by the memory available to one processor, which allows the analysis of problems with thousands of parameters and QoIs, a large amount even for state of the art UQ algorithms.

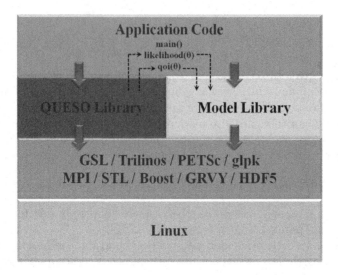

Fig. 2. An application software stack. QUESO requires the input of a likelihood routine $\pi_{\text{like}} : \mathbb{R}^n \to \mathbb{R}_+$ for IPs and of a QoI routine $\mathbf{q} : \mathbb{R}^n \to \mathbb{R}^m$ for FPs. These application level routines provide the bridge between the statistical algorithms in QUESO, physics knowledge in the model library, and relevant calibration and validation data.

QUESO currently supports three modes of parallel execution: an application user may simultaneously run (a) multiple instances of a problem where the physical model requires a single processor, or (b) multiple instances of a problem where the physical model requires multiple processors, or (c) independent sets of types (a) and (b). For example, suppose an user wants to use the MH algorithm to solve a statistical IP, and that 1,024 processors are available. If the physical model is simple enough to be handled efficiently by a single processor, then the user can run 1,024 chains simultaneously, as in case (a). If the model is more complex and requires, say, 16 processors, then the user can run 64 chains simultaneously, as in case (b), with 16 processors per chain. QUESO treats this situation by using only 1 of the 16 processors to handle the chain. When a likelihood evaluation is required, all 16 processors call the likelihood routine simultaneously. Once the likelihood returns its value, QUESO puts 15 processors into idle state until the routine is called again or the chain completes. Case (c) is useful, for instance, in the case of a computational procedure involving two models, where a group of processors can be split into two groups, each handling one model. Once the two model analysis end, the combined model can use the full set of processors. The parallel capabilities of QUESO have been exercised on the Ranger system of the TACC [18] with up to 1,024 processors [5].

Classes in QUESO can be divided in four main groups:

- core: environment (and options), vector, matrix;
- templated basic: vector sets (and subsets, vector spaces), scalar function, vector function, scalar sequence, vector sequence;

- templated statistical: vector realizer, vector RV, statistical IP (and options), MH solver (and options), statistical FP (and options), MC solver (and options), sequence statistical options; and
- miscellaneous: C and FORTRAN interfaces.

The templated basic classes are necessary for the definition and description of other entities, such as RVs, Bayesian solutions of IPs, sampling algorithms and chains. In the following we briefly explain 10 QUESO classes.

Environment Class: This class sets up the environment underlying the use of the QUESO library by an executable. The constructor of the environment class requires a communicator, the name of an options input file, and the eventual prefix of the environment in order for the proper options to be read (multiple environments can coexist, as explained further below). The environment class (a) assigns rank numbers, other than the world rank, to nodes participating in a parallel job, (b) provides MPI communicators for generating a sequence of vectors in a distributed way, (c) provides functionality to read options from the options input file (whose name is passed in the constructor of this environment class), (d) opens output files for messages that would otherwise be written to the screen (one output file per allowed rank is opened and allowed ranks can be specified through the options input file).

Let $S \geqslant 1$ be the number of problems a QUESO environment will be handling at the same time, in parallel. S has default value of 1 and is an option read by QUESO from the input file provided by the user. The QUESO environment class manages five types of communicators, referred to as *world* (MPI_WORLD_COMM); *full* (communicator passed to the environment constructor, of size F and usually equal to the world communicator); *sub* (communicator of size F/S that contains the number of MPI nodes necessary to solve a statistical IP or a statistical FP); *self* (MPI_SELF_COMM, of size 1); and *inter0* (communicator of size S formed by all MPI nodes that have subrank 0 in their respective subcommunicators).

A *subenvironment* in QUESO is the smallest collection of processors necessary for the proper run of the model code. An *environment* in QUESO is the collection of all subenvironments, if there is more than one subenvironment. So, for instance, if the model code requires 16 processors to run and the user decides to run 64 Markov chains in parallel, then the environment will consist of a total of $F = 1024$ processors and $S = 64$ subenvironments, each subenvironment with $F/S = 16$ processors. Any given computing node in a QUESO run has potentially five different ranks. Each subenvironment is assigned a subid varying from 0 (zero) to $S - 1$, and is able to handle a statistical IP and/or a statistical FP. That is, each subenvironment is able to handle a *sub* Markov chain (a sequence) of vectors and/or a *sub* MC sequence of output vectors. The *sub* sequences form an unified sequence in a distributed way. QUESO takes care of the unification of results for the application programming and for output files.

Vector Set Class: The vector set class is fundamental for the proper handling of many mathematical entities. Indeed, the definition of a scalar function like $\pi : \mathbf{B} \subset \mathbb{R}^n \to \mathbb{R}$ requires the specification of the domain $\mathbf{B}$, which is a *subset* of the *vector space* $\mathbb{R}^n$, which is itself a *set*. The relationship among the classes set, subset and vector space is sketched in Figure 3. An attribute of the *subset* class is the *vector space* which it belongs to, and in fact a reference to a vector space is required by the constructor of the subset class. The power of an object-oriented design is clearly featured here. The *intersection* subset derived class is useful for handling a posterior PDF (1), since its domain is the intersection of the domain of the prior PDF with the domain of the likelihood function.

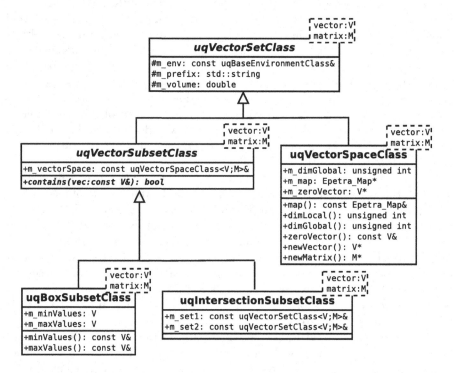

Fig. 3. The class diagram for vector set, vector subset and vector space classes

Scalar Function and Vector Function Classes: PDFs are examples of scalar functions. QUESO currently supports basic PDFs such as uniform and Gaussian. See Diagram 4. The definition of a vector function $\mathbf{q} : \mathbf{B} \subset \mathbb{R}^n \to \mathbb{R}^m$ requires only the extra specification of the image vector space $\mathbb{R}^m$.

Scalar Sequence and Vector Sequence Classes: The scalar sequence class contemplates *scalar* samples generated by an algorithm, as well as operations that can be done over them, e.g., calculation of means, variances, and convergence indices. Similarly, the vector sequence class contemplates *vector* samples and operations such as means, correlation matrices and covariance matrices.

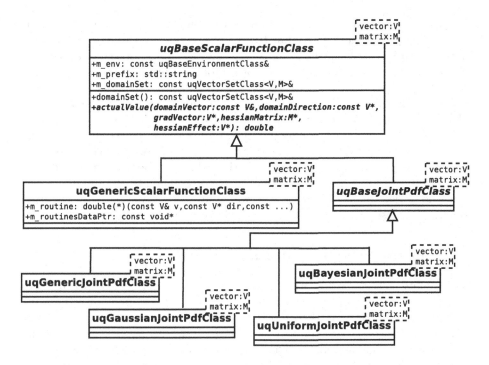

Fig. 4. The class diagram for the scalar function class

Vector Realizer Class: A *realizer* is an object that, simply put, contains a *realization()* operation that returns a sample of a vector RV. QUESO currently supports basic realizers such as uniform and Gaussian. It also contains a *sequence realizer* class for storing samples of a MH algorithm, for instance.

Vector Random Variable Class: Vector RVs are expected to have two basic functionalities: compute the value of its PDF at a point, and generate realizations following such PDF. The joint PDF and vector realizer classes allow a straightforward definition and manipulation of vector RVs. QUESO currently supports basic vector RVs such as uniform and Gaussian. A derived class called *generic vector RV* allows QUESO to store the solution of an statistical IP: a *Bayesian joint PDF* becomes the PDF of the posterior RV, while a *sequence vector realizer* becomes the realizer of the same posterior RV. QUESO also allows users to form new RVs through the concatenation of existing RVs.

Statistical Inverse and Forward Problem Classes: For QUESO, a statistical IP has two input entities, a prior RV and a likelihood routine, and one output entity, the posterior RV. Similarly, a statistical FP has two input entities, an input RV and a QoI routine, and one output entity, the output RV. QUESO differentiates the entities that allow us to define a problem from the entities that allow us to solve it. Indeed, QUESO defines the MH and MC sequence generator classes. The former expects the specification of a target distribution, a proposal covariance matrix, and the initial position in the chain, while the latter expects the specification of an input RV, a QoI function, and an output RV. The proper definition, by QUESO, of more basic entities allows an easy specification of more complex entities such as statistical problems and solvers.

Software Engineering: We utilize various community tools to manage the QUESO development cycle. Source code traceability is provided via subversion and the GNU autotools suite is used to provide a portable, flexible build system, with the standard `configure; make; make check; make install` steps. We employ an active regression testing and utilize the BuildBot system in order to have a continuous integration analysis of source code commits. We also utilize the Redmine project management system, which provides a web-based mechanism to manage milestone developments, issues, bugs, and source code changes.

4   Conclusions and Future Directions

High quality software is essential for developing, analyzing and scaling up new UQ algorithmic ideas involving complex simulation codes running on HPC platforms. QUESO helps researchers to *quickly* prototype new algorithms in a sophisticated computational environment, rather than first coding and testing them with a scripting language and only then recoding in a C++/MPI environment. It also allows them to more naturally translate the mathematical language present in algorithms to a concrete program in the library, and to concentrate their efforts on *algorithmic, load balancing* and *parallel scalability* issues.

Planned features for QUESO include (a) convergence diagnostics and statistical accuracy assessments on the fly, for the optimization of computational effort, (b) more basic distributions (e.g. log-normal), (c) Gaussian random fields, (d) stochastic collocation algorithms [1], (e) parallel vectors for parameters and/or QoIs, (f) graphical user interface, (g) real time interaction capabilities, and (h) robustness (resiliency) w.r.t. node crashing, via the interaction with fault tolerant versions of MPI. *Fault tolerance* is critical for UQ methods due to their greater computational requirements compared to single deterministic simulations. Sampling algorithms, the current focus of QUESO, *need themselves to be fault tolerant*, since they are the drivers, not any of the model simulations. Also, they have the nice property of allowing statistical explorations to continue even if a group of nodes fails. The more nodes are used, the smaller the potential impact of a node failure in the overall sampling mechanism. Also, because checkpoints deal with parameter vectors and QoIs, as opposed to full state vectors, it becomes easier to handle a potential statistical bias due to a node failure.

Acknowledgments. This work has been supported by the National Nuclear Security Administration, U.S D.O.E., under Award Number DE-FC52-08NA28615. The first author was also partially supported by Sandia National Laboratories, under Contracts 1017123 and 1086312, and by King Abdullah University of Science and Technology (KAUST), under the Academic Excellence Alliance program. The authors would also like to thank fruitful discussions with many researchers, including P. Bauman, S. H. Cheung, M. Eldred, O. Ghattas, J. Martin, K. Miki, F. Nobile, T. Oliver, C. Simmons, L. Swiler, R. Tempone, G. Terejanu and L. Wilcox.

References

1. Babuška, I., Nobile, F., Tempone, R.: A stochastic collocation method for elliptic partial differential equations with random input data. SIAM J. Num. Anal. (2007)
2. Beck, J.L., Katafygiotis, L.S.: Updating of a model and its uncertainties utilizing dynamic test data. In: Proc. 1st International Conference on Computational Stochastic Mechanics, pp. 125–136 (1991)
3. Beck, J.L., Yuen, K.V.: Model selection using response measurements: A Bayesian probabilistic approach. ASCE Journal of Eng. Mechanics 130, 192–203 (2004)
4. Cheung, S.H., Beck, J.L.: New Bayesian updating methodology for model validation and robust predictions of a target system based on hierarchical subsystem tests. CMAME (2010) (accepted for publication)
5. Cheung, S.H., Oliver, T.A., Prudencio, E.E., Prudhomme, S., Moser, R.D.: Bayesian uncertainty analysis with applications to turbulence modeling. Reliability Engineering & System Safety (2011) (in press)
6. Eldred, M.S., et al.: DAKOTA, A Multilevel Parallel Object-Oriented Framework for Design Optimization, Parameter Estimation, Uncertainty Quantification, and Sensitivity Analysis (1994-2009), http://www.cs.sandia.gov/DAKOTA/
7. Galassi, M., et al.: GNU Scientific Library (1996-2009), http://www.gnu.org/software/gsl/
8. Haario, H., Laine, M., Mira, A., Saksman, E.: DRAM: Efficient adaptive MCMC. Stat. Comput. 16, 339–354 (2006)
9. Hastings, W.K.: Monte Carlo sampling methods using Markov chains and their applications. Biometrika 57(1), 97–109 (1970)
10. Heroux, M.: Trilinos (2009), http://www.trilinos.gov/
11. Hoeting, J.A., Madigan, D., Raftery, A.E., Volinsky, C.T.: Bayesian model averaging: a tutorial (with discussion). Statistical Science 14, 382–417 (1999)
12. Kaipio, J., Somersalo, E.: Statistical and Computational Inverse Problems, Applied Mathematical Sciences, vol. 160. Springer (2005)
13. Metropolis, N., Rosenbluth, A.W., Rosenbluth, M.N., Teller, A.H., Teller, E.: Equations of state calculations by fast computing machines. Journal of Chemical Physics 21(6), 1087–1092 (1953)
14. Prudencio, E.E., Cai, X.C.: Parallel multilevel restricted Schwarz preconditioners with pollution removing for PDE-constrained optimization. SIAM J. Sci. Comp. 29, 964–985 (2007)
15. Prudencio, E.E., Cheung, S.H.: Parallel adaptive multilevel sampling algorithms for the Bayesian analysis of mathematical models (2011) (submitted)
16. Robert, C.: The Bayesian Choice, 2nd edn. Springer (2004)
17. Smith, B.: PETSc (2009), http://www.mcs.anl.gov/petsc/
18. TACC: Texas advanced computing center (2008), http://www.tacc.utexas.edu/

Use of HPC-Techniques
for Large-Scale Data Migration

Jan Dünnweber, Valentin Mihaylov,
René Glettler, Volker Maiborn, and Holger Wolff

MaibornWolff GmbH, München, Germany
{Jan.Duennweber,Valentin.Mihaylov,Rene.Gletter,
Volker.Maiborn,Holger.Wolff}@mwea.de

Abstract. Any re-design of a distributed legacy system requires a
migration which involves numerous complex data replication and transformation steps. Migration procedures can become quite difficult and
time-consuming, especially when the setup (i. e. , the employed databases,
encodings, formats etc.) of the legacy and the target system fundamen-
tally differ, which is often the case with finance data, grown over decades.
We report on experiences from a real-world project: the recent migration of a customer loyalty system from a COBOL-operated mainframe
to a modern service-oriented architecture. In this context, we present
our easy-to-adopt solution for running most replication steps in a high-
performance manner: the *QuickApply* HPC-software which helps minimizing the replication time, and, thereby, the overall *downtime* of the
migration. Business processes can be kept up and running most of the
time, while pre-extracted data already pass a variety of platforms and
representations toward the target system. We combine the advantages
of traditional migration approaches: transformations, which require the
interruption of business processes are performed with static data only,
they can be made undone in case of a failure and terminate quickly, due
to the use of parallel processing.

1 Introduction

The ongoing re-design of a multi-organization customer loyalty system demands
a fast large-scale data migration. The system, which was originally launched in
the mid-90ies, now holds financial data for over 18 million customers. Whenever a
customer performs a transaction involving a business partner, such as subscribing
to a certain newspaper, using a certain credit card or shopping at a partner mall,
the system credits "bonus points" to the customer. Points can be honored by free
weekend getaways, rental cars, CDs, books or other goodies. For facilitating the
miscellaneous rewards, the loyalty system is connected to multiple distributed
servers and huge databases which must provide high availability. However, until
the end of the last decade, the core customer data still persisted on tapes of a
60ies-style mainframe computer, operated by one monolithic COBOL program
(as it is still quite common in financial software).

M. Alexander et al. (Eds.): Euro-Par 2011 Workshops, Part I, LNCS 7155, pp. 408–415, 2012.
© Springer-Verlag Berlin Heidelberg 2012

The company in charge of the core system recently decided to migrate its software to a state-of-the-art *service-oriented architecture* (SOA), i. e., a scalable network of loosely coupled Web services which can be exchanged or extended on demand. Such a migration scenario is not specific for our loyalty program but very common, whenever IT-landscapes of big financial or actuarial organizations are fused together or modernized. The main difficulties of such a migration are:

1. How to cope with the masses of data which are constantly changing and stored in entirely different formats in the source and in the target system?
2. How to keep the business-critical processes permanently alive, or, at least, absent for only a very short *downtime*, during the data used by these processes is transferred, transformed, re-arranged or re-formatted?

The paper is structured as follows: Section 2 compares popular migration approaches. Section 3 introduces our HPC-software called *QuickApply* and points out where it is superior to traditional migration software, especially in financial applications. Section 4 concludes the paper and summarizes our contributions.

2   Popular Approaches toward Migrating Finance Data

Developing a custom migration software is a challenging task for vendors like us [1], who aim at building efficient and reliable solutions for *single use* (i. e., once the migration is done, the software is no more needed) in time and budget, and, for researchers as well, who face the problem of mapping well-defined, but static models (e. g., graphs or fixed networks [1]) to highly dynamic finance software [2].

Let us review the three most popular approaches to data migration and identify their shortcomings for financial applications. All these approaches have an extract, a transform, and, a load step forming the *ETL process* [3].

2.1   The Big Bang Approach

The big bang approach is illustrated in Fig. 1 [3]. Vertical lines represent boundaries between network sites and horizontal lines represent levels of abstraction: *business level* processes are, e. g., orders and reversals which, on the *tool level*, correspond to work units, i. e., sequences of jointly committed statements, such as INSERT, DELETE and UPDATE, processed record-by-record on the *database level*.

In step ①, the source DB is disconnected from the legacy system which is shut down to extract all its contents. Big bang migration software focuses on transforming static data which changes no more during the migration (see question 1 of the introduction).

In step ②, the data is transformed, whereby the formatting and arranging of data is performed in a *pipeline-parallel* [7] way, for keeping the downtime as

---

[1] MaibornWolff[et al] GmbH - www.mwea.de - is a software and IT-consulting company, based in Munich and Frankfurt serving some of the European leading providers of tourism, telecommunication and finance services.

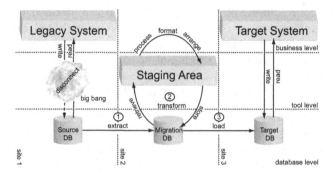

Fig. 1. Big Bang ETL

short as possible (see question 2). Successive transformation steps follow after the data is stored in the migration DB, such that step ② becomes cyclic, as shown in Fig. 1.

In step ③, the extracted data is loaded into the target DB using a mechanism like *batch insert, external tables* or Oracle's *SQL*Loader* (see [8] for a performance comparison of these loading mechanisms for ETL).

Advantages of the big bang approach are: new software must be developed and installed only on the staging area; the correctness of all data can be verified completely, once before and once after the migration; and, the big bang approach is *fault-tolerant*, i.e., a fallback is possible by relaunching the legacy system. Obviously, the big bang approach has the disadvantage of a noticeable downtime of all involved business-level applications.

2.2   The On-The-Fly Approach

The on-the-fly migration [4] is illustrated in Fig. 2. This approach introduces a *data access layer* to the ETL process which has one component on the source side and one component on the target side.

In step ①, the source-side data access layer *captures* δ-data in the source DB. In the δ-data, each record reflects the data that is actually written plus the write statement type (UPDATE, DELETE or INSERT), a timestamp, a sequence number and a work unit identifier. Once the δ-data capturing has started, the source DB's original schema is fully extracted and transferred to the migration DB. In the successive phases, δ-data is extracted analogously.

In step ②, a full dump of source DB is transformed as in the big bang approach and then successively the contents of the δ-data schema, which were captured and extracted during the previous transformation phase are transformed. Provided that the amount of δ-data is reduced in each phase, the migration terminates with a transform phase during which no new δ-data is stored in the source DB (e.g., during a regular system maintenance interval).

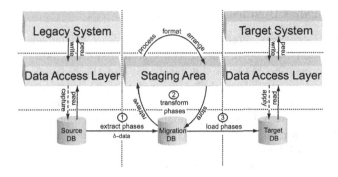

Fig. 2. On-The-Fly ETL

In step ③, the transformed data is loaded. Source-side work units are mapped onto target-side work units which are committed to the target DB. If , e. g. , the δ-data contain a work unit X which corresponds to a reversal and is composed of an UPDATE statement x_1 and a DELETE statement x_2 in the source DB, it is mapped onto the work unit X' for the target system reversal process, composed of the statements $x'_1..x'_n$ which may differ from the source DB statements regarding their types, affected tables and quantity.

The legacy system is never shut down until the target system is launched. This answers question 2 of the introduction even more satisfactorily than above. In trade-off, there is no convincing answer to question 1, since the work unit mapping for different business processes in step ③ is not always combinatorially decidable. Consider, e. g. , a commit sequence that may correspond either to process X or process Y in the source system. Should the target-side data access layer run process X' or process Y'? Moreover, when steps ② and ③ (δ-data apply plus process mapping) are not faster than step ① (δ-data capture), δ-data will not be reduced and the ETL process will never terminate.

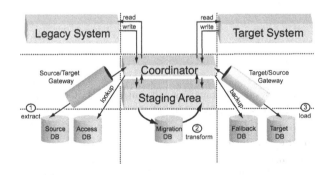

Fig. 3. Parallel Business ETL

2.3 The Parallel Business Approach

In the *parallel business* migration, sketched in Fig. 3, the legacy system is kept in operation even *after* the target system has been launched [5].There is no direct connection between the databases and the business level systems. Any data access in steps ① and ③ is routed through the central *coordinator* which provides the legacy system with target system data and, vice versa, the target system with legacy system data using appropriate *gateways*. The format and location of the most recent version of each record is stored in an *access DB* and before each transformation (step ②) the original data is stored in a *fallback DB*. Downtime is never required, irrespective of the processing load. However, the gateways perform complex but redundant conversions (already performed on the staging area) and any data access is routed across network boundaries, which may result in serious performance drawbacks for this approach.

3 Introducing the QuickApply HPC-Software

For our novel approach to large-scale finance data migration, we developed a parallel software called QuickApply that combines the advantages of the big bang and the on-the-fly migration (Fig. 4).

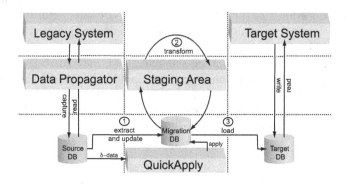

Fig. 4. QuickApply for Parallel ETL

Step ① captures recent changes in the source DB. Contrary to the on-the-fly approach, no target system component depends on the data capturing, and, therefore, a standard tool can be used for this purpose: the *data propagator* [9] for IBM mainframe databases [6].

Step ② makes use of QuickApply to update the migration DB record-by-record until it is in-sync with the source DB. Static data from the source DB is extracted and transferred in advance (i.e., before the downtime) and the downtime (in case that a noticeable period remains) is fully exploited for running transformations.

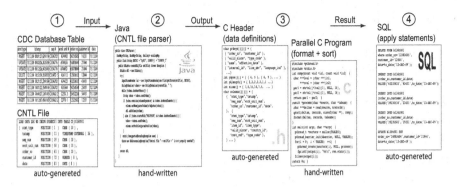

Fig. 5. Overview of the code and data pieces for QuickApply

Step ③ loads the transformed data which, in contrast to the big bang approach, is up-to-date and which, in contrast to the on-the-fly and parallel business migration, must neither be mapped onto processes nor converted.

3.1   The Implementation of QuickApply: Combining Java, C & SQL

QuickApply is a parallel δ-data apply software that is portable across different operating systems, hardware platforms and across SQL-compliant databases as well. As shown in Fig. 5, our implementation makes use of Java, C and multiple input pieces. QuickApply works on the database level and only runs on one network site (the staging area). It processes the change data capture tables (CDC) which IBM's data propagator uses for capturing δ-data in a δ-data schema.

The tiny code and data excerpts in Fig. 5 (not intended to be read) illustrate the relation between auto-generated and hand-written code: In step ①, the input data are CDC tables and CNTL-Files (table structure definitions) which are generated by the data propagator and parsed by a hand-written Java program that also provides the user interface. In step ②, the output generated by the Java program is a C-header file (.h), wherein the CDC-data is encoded in arrays. In step ③ a hand-written C-program sorts and formats the δ-data. In step ④, SQL-statements, which the C-program generates as result, are applied to the migration database. As shown in Fig. 6, for each CDC-table, the C-program explicitly starts a new POSIX thread which sorts the corresponding array, according to the elements' sequence numbers.

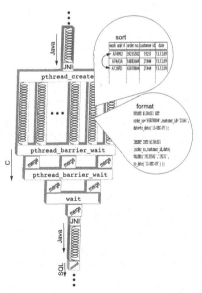

Fig. 6. Execution Model

After sorting the threads join at a barriers where the statements, sorted table-wise, are merged together, such that statements forming a common work unit are committed sequentially (to prevent concurrency anomalies like *lost updates* [11]).

Due to the fact that QuickApply runs below the database level, it is significantly faster than a replication tool which applies work units directly to the database using, e. g. , JDBC.

3.2   Case Study: Time Needs For Migrating the Loyalty Program

Our example data stock is ≈ 3 TB large. Our migration DB (and the target DB) are approximately 400 kilometers away from the legacy system. The periodical updates processed via QuickApply (i. e. , the δ-data volume) vary: Fig. 7 shows the runtimes (in sec.) for the Java-based part and the multithreaded C-segment of Quick-Apply for 906672 (≈ 350 MB of δ-data), 3485068 (≈ 1.4 GB) and 6095741 SQL statements (≈ 4.2 GB).

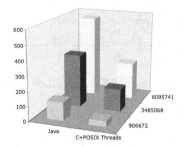

Fig. 7. Java vs. C Part

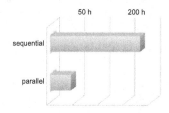

Fig. 8. Full Transform

Our execution platform (the staging area) comprises two 24 CPU Servers with 8 cores per CPU, both running the Java HotSpot^{TM} 64-Bit Server VM under Linux 2.6.18. QuickApply helps saving valuable downtime, which is fully usable for running transformations. Fig. 8 and Fig. 9 show the parallel runtimes for the transform step and the clearance steps, following the replication, each compared to the sequential runtime.

Each bunch of δ-data was captured by running the data propagator for 24h. We use a dedicated line which has an average transfer rate of ≈ 30 MBit/s, i. e. , transferring 2–4 GB δ-data takes only 6–12 minutes. When QuickApply is used, the final transfer carries δ-data, not the full load, and this is the only transfer which we perform during the downtime.

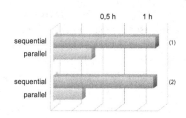

Fig. 9. Data Cleansing (1) & Functional Clearance (2)

In experiments with 1–8 processors, the data replication scaled almost linearly and the transformation speedup ranged from 3 to 5. The average efficiency for was > 50%.

4   Conclusion

Technically, the presented work is in the tradition of component-based *grid computing*, which also combines multiple technologies (and, potentially, multiple programming languages) [12].

Compared to other research in the data migration realm, our HPC-approach has proven to be more efficient than a big bang and, which is especially important in finance, more reliable than on-the-fly or parallel business. Some big bang implementations migrate audit data separately for reducing downtime. Other implementations, additionally, keep the legacy DB running in *read-only* mode permanently. Such optimization can be combined with QuickApply, since the data propagator keeps the source DB always up-to-date and a selection of DB contents is possible via filtering. From our experiences with QuickApply, we conclude that properly implemented HPC-methods, like Pthreads, JNI and partially auto-generated code, are no risky adventure but a tremendous improvement for applications processing finance or other sensitive data.

References

1. Hall, J., Hartline, J., et al.: On Algorithms for Efficient Data Migration. In: Proceedings of ACM Symposium on Discrete Algorithms, Washington, DC, USA (January 2001)
2. Allgaier, M., Heller, M.: Research Challenges for Seamless Service Integration in Enterprise Systems. In: Proceedings of IE4SOC: Workshop on Industrial Experiences for Service-Oriented Computing, Stockholm, Sweden (November 2009)
3. Brodie, M.L., Stonebraker, M.: Migrating Legacy Systems. Morgan Kaufmann, San Francisco (1995) ISBN 9781558603301
4. Wu, B., Lawless, D., et al.: The Butterfly Methodology: A Gateway-Free Approach for Migrating Legacy Information Systems. In: IEEE Conference on Engineering of Complex Computer Systems, Villa Olmo, Como, Italy (September 1997)
5. Pyla, P.S., Tungare, M., Homan, J., Pérez-Quiñones, M.A.: Continuous User Interfaces for Seamless Task Migration. In: Proceedings of HCII: IASTED Conference on Human-Computer Interaction, San Diego, CA, USA (July 2009)
6. Ebbers, M., O'Brien, W., Ogden, B.: Introduction to the New Mainframe: z/OS Basics. Vervanté books, Huntington Beach (2005) ISBN 9780738496740
7. DeWitt, D., Gray, J.: Parallel Database Systems: The Future of High Performance Database Systems. Comm. ACM 35(6), 85–98 (1992)
8. Orlando, S., Orsini, R., Raffaetà, A., Roncato, A.: Trajectory Data Warehouses: Design and Implementation Issues. Journal of Computing Science and Engineering 1(2), 211–232 (2007)
9. Jäntti, J., Kerry, D., Kompalka, A., Long, R., Mitchell, G.: DataPropagator Implementation Guide. IBM Redbooks, Armonk (2002) ISBN 0738426342
10. Liang, S.: Java^{TM} Native Interface: Programmer's Guide and Specification. Prentice Hall, Harlow (1999) ISBN 9780201325775
11. O'Neil, P.: Database: Principles Programming and Performance. Morgan Kaufmann Publishers (June 1994) ISBN 9781558602199
12. Dünnweber, J., Gorlatch, S.: Higher-Order Components for Grid Programming: Making Grids More Usable. Springer, Germany (2009) ISBN 9783642008405

Algorithms, Models and Tools for Parallel Computing on Heterogeneous Platforms (HeteroPar 2011)

Preface

Heterogeneity is emerging as one of the most profound and challenging characteristics of today's parallel environments. From the macro level, where networks of distributed computers, composed by diverse node architectures, are interconnected with potentially heterogeneous networks, to the micro level, where deeper memory hierarchies and various accelerator architectures are increasingly common, the impact of heterogeneity on all computing tasks is increasing rapidly. Traditional parallel algorithms, programming environments and tools, designed for legacy homogeneous multiprocessors, can at best achieve on a small fraction of the efficiency and potential performance we should expect from parallel computing in tomorrow's highly diversified and mixed environments. New ideas, innovative algorithms, and specialized programming environments and tools are needed to efficiently use these new and multifarious parallel architectures. The workshop is intended to be a forum for researchers working on algorithms, programming languages, tools, and theoretical models aimed at efficiently solving problems on heterogeneous networks.

This volume contains the papers presented at HeteroPar'11: Workshop on Algorithms, Models and Tools for Parallel Computing on Heterogeneous Platforms held on August 28, 2011 in Bordeaux.

October 18, 2011   George Bosilca
Knoxville

A Genetic Algorithm with Communication Costs to Schedule Workflows on a SOA-Grid

Jean-Marc Nicod, Laurent Philippe, and Lamiel Toch

LIFC, Laboratory, Université de Franche-Comté, Besançon, France

Abstract. In this paper we study the problem of scheduling a collection of workflows, identical or not, on a SOA (Service Oriented Architecture) grid . A workflow (job) is represented by a directed acyclic graph (DAG) with typed tasks. All of the grid hosts are able to process a set of typed tasks with unrelated processing costs and are able to transmit files through communication links for which the communication times are not negligible. The goal of our study is to minimize the maximum completion time (makespan) of the workflows. To solve this problem we propose a genetic approach. The contributions of this paper are both the design of a Genetic Algorithm taking the communication costs into account and its performance analysis.

1 Introduction

Nowadays, to go further in their research, scientists often need to connect several applications together. Therefore, since few years, workflow systems have been designed to provide tools that support these multi-application simulations. In e-Science [16] many fields as medical image processing, geosciences or astronomy use workflow applications. A workflow is defined as a set of applications that are connected to each other by precedence constraints. An input data set enters the workflow, it is processed by an application which computes an output data set that is, in turn, sent to the next application of the workflow structure. Generally a workflow has the structure of a DAG (Direct Acyclic Graph): a graph whose nodes are tasks and whose edges are precedence constraints.

When the size of the data entering the workflow increases the processing time may become very long and it becomes necessary to use larger computing resources as grids. Because of their heterogeneity these platforms are however difficult to efficiently use for non computer scientists mainly due to the complexity of scheduling the tasks on the hosts. Several research projects have already tackled this problem. The Pegasus framework [8] proposes a convenient way for scientists to compute their workflows onto heterogeneous platforms without learning distributed programming concepts. Other tools, like DIET [2] or NINF-G [15], provide a SOA-Grid (Service Oriented Architecture) that facilitates user accesses to remotely accessible computing applications and make the execution of workflows on a heterogeneous platform easier.

When the number of workflows to be executed in parallel is large, we must efficiently map them onto the heterogeneous resources. Minimizing the execution time (makespan) of a workflow or a set of workflows onto a heterogeneous

M. Alexander et al. (Eds.): Euro-Par 2011 Workshops, Part I, LNCS 7155, pp. 419–428, 2012.

platform is however an optimization problem that is known to be NP-Hard [13]. As a consequence, the problem considered here is also NP-Hard and we can just rely on heuristics to find a solution as good as possible. Classical scheduling algorithms often rely on list-based scheduling algorithms. They use heuristics such as Heterogeneous Earliest Finish Time (HEFT) [17] or Critical Path [11]. In a homogeneous context, [12] gives a survey on the DAG scheduling topic and the study presented in [9] evaluates eleven heuristics, such as Min-min, Max-min or Sufferage. Makespan oriented strategies to schedule workflows onto the grid are presented in [14], with the description of real life medical applications. In [18], the problem of scheduling a set of different DAGs is studied. These approaches compute an off-line schedule considering the whole set of tasks. But, when the number of tasks scales up, the computation time becomes too long because of the complexity of the algorithm. Genetic Algorithms (GA) are known to give good results in several optimization domains and algorithms that schedules tasks are for instance presented in [10] and [5]. They are designed for scheduling tasks of one workflow onto a heterogeneous platform but without taking communication costs into account. Other studies tackle workflow scheduling onto heterogeneous platforms but with other objective functions than the makespan. The Steady-State technique presented in [1] provides an optimal algorithm to schedule a set of identical workflows also for the throughput objective function.

In this study, the general problem we deal with is to schedule a set of workflows (jobs) onto a SOA-grid. Each task of a workflow has a type that corresponds to a service type in the SOA-Grid. We consider the two following cases: (1) the general case where the structure of each workflow differs from one another; (2) the particular case when the structure of the workflow is the same for all jobs. In this paper we focus on researches that we carried out on the design of a Genetic Algorithm and we assess its performance to schedule a set of workflows. The contributions of this paper are both the design of a Genetic Algorithm taking the communication costs into account and the performance analysis. In the general case (1) we compare the performance obtained by a GA approach to the performance obtained by a list-based scheduling algorithm. In the particular case (2) of the scheduling of a collection of identical workflows which structure is limited to intrees, we compare our results to a lower bound and we show that our Genetic Algorithm approach allows us to get a schedule with good performance.

The paper is organized as follows. In Section 2 we detail the framework which defines both the grid and the workflow models. We present in Section 3 a Genetic Algorithm that takes communication costs into account to deal with our problem. Section 5 introduces the simulation setup, the results of the simulations and their analysis for workflows of different shape. Section 6 presents the simulations for workflows with identical structure. Finally, we conclude in Section 7.

2   Framework

In this section we formally define the context of our study.

Applicative Framework. Our problem that is to schedule a collection $\mathcal{B} = \{\mathcal{J}^j, 1 \leq j \leq N\}$ of N workflows. Each workflow $\mathcal{J}^j$ is represented by a DAG $\mathcal{J}^j = (\mathcal{T}^j, \mathcal{D}^j)$ where $\mathcal{T}^j = \{T_1^j, \ldots, T_{n_j}^j\}$ is the set of its tasks and $\mathcal{D}^j$ represents the precedence constraints between the tasks. These precedence constraints are files: $F_{k,i}^j$ is the file sent between T_k^j and T_i^j when $(T_k^j, T_i^j) \in \mathcal{D}^j$. Let $\mathcal{T} = \cup_{j=1}^{N} \mathcal{T}^j = \{T_{i_j}^j, 1 \leq i_j \leq n_j$ and $1 \leq j \leq N\}$ be the set of tasks to schedule. We define $t(i,j)$ as the type of task T_i^j.

Target Platform. The target platform PF is a heterogeneous platform of n machines modeled by an undirected graph $\mathcal{PF} = (\mathcal{P}, \mathcal{L})$ where the vertices in $\mathcal{P} = \{p_1, \ldots, p_n\}$ represent the machines and where the edges of $\mathcal{L}$ are the communication links between machines.

Let τ be the set of all task types available onto the platform. Each machine p_i is able to perform a subset of τ. If the type $t \in \tau$ is available on the machine p_i, $w(t, p_i)$ is the time to perform a task of type t on p_i. Moreover, each link (p_i, p_j) has a bandwidth $bw(p_i, p_j)$ which is the number of data per time unit that can be transferred through that link. We define $a(i,j)$ such that $p_{a(i,j)}$ is the machine on which T_i^j is assigned.

Communication Model. In our study the processors are interconnected by communication links in a point-to-point fashion to model a computation grid. In the literature [1,3], several communication models exist such as the one-port model or the multi-port model. We choose to use the one-port model because of its ease of modeling and of implementation while still being realistic. In this model only one data can be transmitted at the same time over a communication link and a node can do at most one reception and one transmission at the same time. We define $\mathcal{R}(p_k, p_i) = \{(p_j, p_{j'}) \in \mathcal{L}\}$ as a route from p_k to p_i.

3 GA with Communication Costs

For the execution we use the same genome representation as in [5,10], i.e., a chromosome is a two-dimension table with one row per node where the tasks assigned to the node are recorded. Some improvements to take SOA-Grids and collections into account, presented in [7], are added. As these GA coding does not however take communication costs into account, we study their integration in this section.

Communication Integration. The main issue we faced is the step of the genetic algorithm where we should integrate the communications.

The first solution we have studied is to add communications in chromosomes, as for executions. We thus introduce the notion of *"communication task"* to represent file exchanges in the task graph and we map them onto communication links. The chromosome thus becomes a two-dimension table with one row per node and one row per communication link. Tasks are recorded in the node's rows and communication are recorded in the link's rows. This leads however to issues regarding both the crossover and the mutation genetic procedures. As the choice of a communication link depends on the source and sink nodes not every link can be used for a given communication. So these procedures generate inconsistent communication routes and so numerous non feasible schedules that waste a lot of computation time.

A more convenient way to introduce communications is in the fitness evaluation step of the genetic algorithm. Indeed the allocations of the communication tasks depend on the allocations of the computation tasks since the possible routes between two nodes are limited. Choosing a good mapping for the computation tasks intuitively involves finding a valid allocation for the communication tasks. So we use the chromosomes only to map the computation tasks onto the nodes, and in a second step to look for a valid route to send the data according to this mapping. The fitness of each individual is then evaluated by algorithm 1. For each task of the chromosome it computes its start time depending on the processor avalaibility (lines 5-7) and when the used processor will become iddle (lines 8-9). The algorithm then remove the task for the set of remaining tasks (line 10). At the end it returns the fitness of the chromosome.

Algorithm 1. Computing the fitness of a chromosome

Input : PF: the platform and B: collection of workflows
Output: $f(ch)$: the fitness of the task with chromosome ch
Data: $\mathcal{T}_{ToSched}$: the set of remaining tasks to schedule, $C(T_i^j)$: the completion time of T_i^j, $\sigma(T_i^j)$: the start time of T_i^j on $p_{a(i,j)}$, $\delta(p_u)$: the next time p_u is idle, $p_{a(i,j)}$ the machine on which T_i^j is assigned, $w(t,p_i)$: the time to perform a task of type t on p_i, $CT(F_{k,i}^j)$: the communication time to send $F_{k,i}^j$ along route $\mathcal{R}(p_{a(k,j)}, p_{a(i,j)})$

1   $\mathcal{T}_{ToSched} \leftarrow \mathcal{T}$
2   **while** $\mathcal{T}_{ToSched} \neq \emptyset$ **do**
3   choose a free task $T_i^j \in \mathcal{T}_{ToSched}$ (Earliest Finish Time heuristic)
      $\mathcal{T}_{pred} \leftarrow \{T_k^j | (T_k^j, T_i^j) \in \mathcal{D}^j\}$
4      $\sigma(T_i^j) \leftarrow 0$
5   **foreach** *task* $T_k^j \in \mathcal{T}_{pred}$ **do**
6        $\sigma(T_i^j) \leftarrow \max(\sigma(T_i^j), C(T_k^j) + CT(F_{k,i}^j))$
7      $\sigma(T_i^j) \leftarrow \max(\delta(p_{a(i,j)}), \sigma(T_i^j))$
8      $C(T_i^j) \leftarrow \sigma(T_i^j) + w(t(i,j), p_{a(i,j)})$
9      $\delta(p_{a(i,j)}) \leftarrow C(T_i^j)$
10     $\mathcal{T}_{ToSched} \leftarrow \mathcal{T}_{ToSched} \setminus \{T_i^j\}$
11 **return** $f(ch) = 1/C_{max} = 1/max_{T_i^j \in \mathcal{T}}(C(T_i^k))$

---

4 Simulation Setup

To assess the performance of the scheduling algorithm we need to implement it on a heterogeneous platform. The context is indeed too complex to be studied with a formal approach and, to get realistic results, the platforms used must integrate the network contention. On the other hand, the implementation on a computation grid can however not give reproducible results as the experimental conditions, as the network load, may change. So, we use a grid simulator to evaluate the performance of the Genetic Algorithm. The simulator is implemented using SimGrid and its MSG API [4].

All simulations have been made using batch sizes from 1 to 10 000. The platforms and the applications are randomly generated with a uniform distribution. Platforms have between 4 and 10 nodes and are strongly connected. Applications have between 4 and 12 tasks. For the case presented in Section 5, where workflows are different from each other, 200 platforms and 10 000 DAGs are randomly generated. For each couple (platform, batch size) different applications are randomly chosen among the 10 000 ones. So we generate 1 900 simulations of platform/application scenarios. In the case where workflows are identical, we use 10 platforms and 10 applications, so 100 scenarios for each batch size.

We define the *"communication to computation ratio"* (CCR) of a simulation as the average computation time divided by the average communication time. To assess the impact of the communications on the algorithm performance, we run simulations with different CCR, from 1 000 (i.e., communication time is predominant) to $1/1 000$ (i.e., communication time is negligible). The speed of the nodes are unrelated. We also assess the impact of the platform heterogeneity on the performance: execution and communication times fluctuate respectively in a range from 1 to 10 and from 1 to 4.

For the GA, the population is set to 200 individuals and a generation is set to 100 iterations.

5   Results with General DAGs

As the execution time of a collection of workflows cannot be computed in polynomial time, we must compare the performance of the GA to another algorithm: we use a standard list-based scheduling algorithm. The results presented in this section concern fully heterogeneous platforms and $CCR \approx 1$.

Impact of the Communication Model. Choosing the network links for each communication is complex. Always using the shortest (or the fastest) path may lead to a high contention so that we need to take the network load into account. We assess here four communication policies:

- "GA-no-comm": the route between two nodes is statically and arbitrary chosen and the communication costs are not used to compute the fitness.
- "GA static-route": the same as the previous policy but the communication costs are used in the fitness computation.
- "GA 1-route-Bellman-Ford": the static route for each couple of computation nodes is the fastest one by using the Bellman-Ford algorithm.
- "GA 3-routes-Bellman-Ford": for each couple of computation nodes, during the evaluation fitness step, the 3 best routes are tested.

Figures 1a and 1b show the efficiencies of the GA with different communication integrations. The notion of relative measure to optimal (RMO) is introduced in Section 6, however, we just need to know that the higher the curve, the more

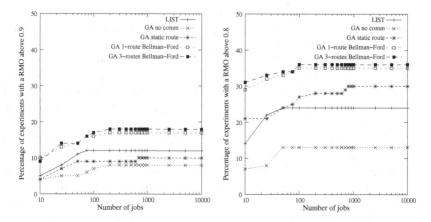

Fig. 1. Communication integrations with a RMO above 0.9 and 0.8

efficient is the algorithm. Comparing these policies to a list-based scheduling (LIST) allows us to remark on one hand that this is mandatory to take communication into account to increase the performance but on the other hand that the use of dynamic information in *GA 3-routes-Bellman-Ford* does not significantly improve the performance. We nevertheless use this implementation, as we get the best results for the performance analysis in the following.

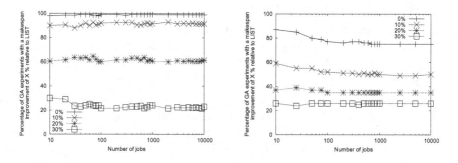

Fig. 2. Improvement for different DAGs   **Fig. 3.** Improvement for identical DAGs

Figure 2 shows the improvement of the makespan for a set of different workflows on a heterogeneous platform. Each curve shows the percentage of GA experiences whose makespan is improved respectively by more than 0%, 10%, 20% and 30% when compared to the list-based scheduling algorithm (LIST). We notice that more than 80% of the GA experiments have a makespan improved by more than 10%. The 0%-curve shows that GA never slows down the performance.

Figure 3 shows the improvement of the makespan for a set of identical workflows. We can notice that GA gives less important improvements relative to LIST in this case. For each 0, 10, 20 and 30%-curve, GA improvements decrease by about 10% compared to experiments obtained when scheduling different work-flows. We can also note that 10% to 20% of the GA schedules are less efficient than the LIST schedules in this case. GA improvements remain however high.

In general, more than 70% of the GA experiments give a makespan with an improvement greater than 10% for almost any size of sets of workflows. The diversity of the workflows promotes the GA algorithm: as GA tries randomly a lot of combinations, it can benefit from different workflows while LIST which is directed by greedy choices, cannot.

6 Results for a Set of Identical Intrees

Comparing two algorithms gives relative information but no absolute informa-tion on the quality of the algorithm. For the particular case of batches of intrees it is possible to compute an optimal throughput by using a Steady-State algo-rithm [1]. In this section we assess how far the GA is from the optimal and we compare it to the list scheduling and to a practical makespan oriented implemen-tation of the Steady-State algorithm [6]. The latter reaches the optimal solution for an infinite number of jobs, as its objective function is the throughput, but limits this study to the particular case of intree-shaped workflows.

Relative Measure to Optimal. The optimal throughput ρ can be computed thanks to the Steady-State algorithm using linear programming. This optimal throughput is used to compute a lower bound L_0 for the optimal makespan as the number of jobs to be processed over the throughput ($L_0 = \frac{N}{\rho}$). Let $makespan_o$ be the optimal makespan, then $makespan_o \geq L_0$. To evaluate the algorithm performance, we introduce the notion of Relative Measure to Optimal (RMO) as the ratio between this lower bound L_o over the makespan $makespan_r$ of the schedule given by the algorithm ($RMO = \frac{L_o}{makespan_r}$). So, the nearer RMO is from 1.0, the more efficient is the scheduling algorithm.

Since we run 100 simulations, for each of the 19 sizes of job sets, we cannot get a simple scalar RMO value for the overall experiments. A mean value would indeed be not meaningful as the longer simulations will weight more than the sorter ones with this metric. So we compute the percentage of experiments that gives a RMO greater than t for each size of batches. In the following we present the distribution of the results depending on this percentage on the 3D curves. Two lines are thickened on the surfaces to highlight the RMO curves for threshold values 0.8 and 0.9. They represent the quality of the schedule.

Fully Homogeneous Platforms. Figures 4a, 4b and 4c give the results for homogeneous platforms (homogeneous nodes and homogeneous communication links) and computation intensive applications ($CCR \approx 0.01$). In that case the GA algorithm give almost optimal results for 85% of the experiments. Figures 5a, 5b and 5c show the results for homogeneous platforms and communication in-tensive applications ($CCR \approx 1$). In that case the GA algorithm gives the best results for batches with less than 2 500 jobs and is overtaken by the Steady-State algorithm for jobs with more that 10 000 jobs. It also reaches the optimality for

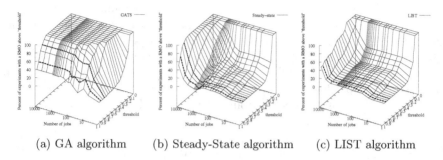

(a) GA algorithm   (b) Steady-State algorithm   (c) LIST algorithm

Fig. 4. Simulation with fully homogeneous platforms, $CCR \approx 0.01$

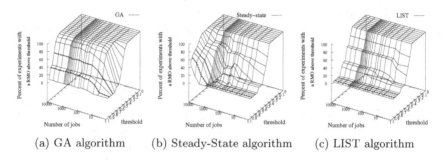

(a) GA algorithm   (b) Steady-State algorithm   (c) LIST algorithm

Fig. 5. Simulation with fully homogeneous platforms, $CCR \approx 1$

almost 70% of the experiments. From these experiments we can conclude that the GA algorithm performs globally well, much better than the simple LIST algorithm. The results are however lowered when we introduce communications because it makes the problem more complex.

Fully Heterogeneous Platforms. Figures 6a, 6b and 6c show the results obtained for a heterogeneous platform with $CCR \approx 0.01$ and Figures 7a and 7c show the results with $CCR \approx 1$. In this communication intensive case, no algorithm gives good results due to the complexity of the problem. The Steady-State tends slowly toward optimality. The GA nevertheless gives the best results for batches with less than 2 000 jobs. In the computation intensive case (i.e., $CCR \approx 0.01$), the GA performs the best compared to the other algorithms and its performance is not far from the homogeneous case.

On the whole set of curves, we can note that the GA globally gives good schedules and it out performs the other algorithms for the studied context. It usually reaches its best performance from a few tens of jobs and stays stable for more jobs. So, in all of the studied cases, GA is a good choice for batches from one to a few thousand jobs. This latter limit depends on the properties of the platform.

Computation Times. The simulations have been run on a 2.8 GHz Intel Xeon bi-processor. The time needed to compute a schedule using the GA varies linearly according to the batch size: about 1 second per DAG. The CPU time needed

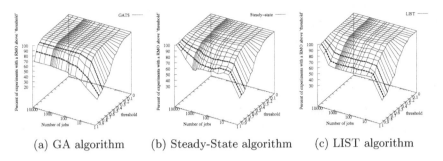

(a) GA algorithm   (b) Steady-State algorithm   (c) LIST algorithm

Fig. 6. $CCR \approx 0.01$, fully heterogeneous platforms

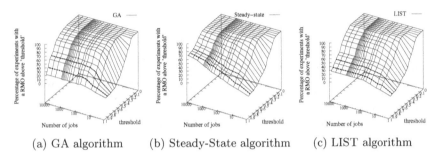

(a) GA algorithm   (b) Steady-State algorithm   (c) LIST algorithm

Fig. 7. Simulation with fully heterogeneous platforms, $CCR \approx 1$

by LIST varies linearly as well. It is about 5 times faster than GA. Finally, for
Steady-State, the CPU time is very low for any batch size : about 75 seconds for
scheduling 1 000 DAGs. So the GA and LIST are very time consuming while the
computation time spent by the Steady-State algorithm is very low. Nevertheless,
for large sizes of batches, the GA computation takes usually less than 20 minutes.

7   Conclusion and Future Work

In this paper, we propose a genetic algorithm that solves the problem of scheduling a collection of workflows on a set of heterogeneous nodes interconnected by
heterogeneous communication links. This GA takes the communication costs into
account. We show that for a collection of different workflows, GA obtains better
execution performance than a classical LIST algorithm. For the case where the
DAGs are identical intrees we are able to compare the GA results to an optimal
lower bound and to show that its results tend towards the optimality for more
than 1 000 jobs. The obtained results are moreover comparable to a practical
implementation of the Steady-State algorithm. The main idea that we keep in
mind is that scheduling with GA by taking communications into account is difficult, as for implementing the practical Steady-State solution. For future work,

other communication models should be implemented in the simulator, like the multi-port models, and other genetic representations could be explored.

The huge amount of simulations have been run on the cluster of the *Mésocentre de Calcul de Franche-Comté* in Besançon, France.

References

1. Beaumont, O., Legrand, A., Marchal, L., Robert, Y.: Assessing the impact and limits of steady-state scheduling for mixed task and data parallelism on heterogeneous platforms. In: HeteroPar 2004, pp. 296–302 (2004)
2. Caron, E., Desprez, F.: Diet: A scalable toolbox to build network enabled servers on the grid. IJHPCA 20(3), 335–352 (2006)
3. Casanova, H.: Modeling large-scale platforms for the analysis and the simulation of scheduling strategies. In: APDCM 2004 (2004)
4. Casanova, H., Legrand, A., Quinson, M.: Simgrid: A generic framework for large-scale distributed experiments. In: UKSIM 2008, pp. 126–131 (2008)
5. Daoud, M., Kharma, N.: GATS 1.0: A Novel GA-based Scheduling Algorithm for Task Scheduling on Heterogeneous Processor Nets. In: Genetic And Evolutionary Computation Conference (2005)
6. Diakité, S., Marchal, L., Nicod, J.-M., Philippe, L.: Steady-State for Batches of Identical Task Trees. In: Sips, H., Epema, D., Lin, H.-X. (eds.) Euro-Par 2009. LNCS, vol. 5704, pp. 203–215. Springer, Heidelberg (2009)
7. Diakité, S., Nicod, J.-M., Philippe, L.: Comparison of batch scheduling for identical multi-tasks jobs on heterogeneous platforms. In: PDP 2008, Toulouse, France, pp. 374–378 (2008)
8. Deelman, E., et al.: Pegasus: a framework for mapping complex scientific workflows onto distributed systems. Scientific Programming Journal 13, 219–237 (2005)
9. Braun, T.-D., et al.: A comparison of eleven static heuristics for mapping a class of independent tasks onto heterogeneous distributed computing systems. JPDC 61, 810–837 (2001)
10. Goh, C.K., Teoh, E.J., Tan, K.C.: A hybrid evolutionary approach for heterogeneous multiprocessor scheduling. Soft Comput. 13, 833–846 (2009)
11. Kwok, Y., Ahmad, I.: Dynamic critical-path scheduling: An effective technique for allocating task graphs to multi-processors. In: PDS, pp. 506 – 521 (1996)
12. Kwok, Y.-K., Ahmad, I.: Static Scheduling Algorithms for Allocating Task Graphs to Multiprocessors. ACM Computing Surveys 31(4), 406–471 (1999)
13. Lenstra, J.K., Rinnooy Kan, A.H.G.: Complexity of scheduling under precedence constraints. Operations Research 26(1), 22–35 (1978)
14. Mandal, A., Kennedy, K., Koelbel, C., Marin, G., Mellor-Crummey, J., Liu, B., Johnsson, L.: Scheduling strategies for mapping application workflows onto the grid. In: HPDC 2005, NC, Triangle Park, USA, pp. 125–134 (July 2005)
15. Tanaka, Y., Takemiya, H., Nakada, H., Sekiguchi, S.: Design, implementation and performance evaluation of gridrpc programming middleware for a large-scale computational grid. In: GRID 2004, pp. 298–305 (2004)
16. Taylor, I.-J., Deelman, E., Gannon, D.-B., Shields, M.: Workflows for e-Science (2007)
17. Topcuouglu, H., Hariri, S., Wu, M.: Performance-effective and low-complexity task scheduling for heterogeneous computing. In: PDS, pp. 260–274 (2002)
18. Zhao, H., Sakellariou, R.: Scheduling multiple DAGs onto heterogeneous systems. In: HCW 2006, Rhodes, Greece (2006)

An Extension of XcalableMP PGAS Lanaguage for Multi-node GPU Clusters

Jinpil Lee[1], Minh Tuan Tran[1], Tetsuya Odajima[1],
Taisuke Boku[1,2], and Mitsuhisa Sato[1,2]

[1] Graduate School of Systems and Information Engineering, University of Tsukuba
[2] Center for Computational Sciences, University of Tsukuba

Abstract. A GPU is a promising device for further increasing computing performance in high performance computing field. Currently, many
programming langauges are proposed for the GPU offloaded from the
host, as well as CUDA. However, parallel programming with a multi-
node GPU cluster, where each node has one or more GPUs, is a hard
work. Users have to describe multi-level parallelism, both between nodes
and within the GPU using MPI and a GPGPU language like CUDA. In
this paper, we will propose a parallel programming language targeting
multi-node GPU clusters. We extend XcalableMP, a parallel PGAS (Partitioned Global Address Space) programming language for PC clusters,
to provide a productive parallel programming model for multi-node GPU
clusters. Our performance evaluation with the N-body problem demonstrated that not only does our model achieve scalable performance, but
it also increases productivity since it only requires small modifications
to the serial code.

1 Introduction

GPGPU is becoming a popular research topic in High Performance Computing
area. GPU vendors provide programming models for GPU computing. For example, NVIDIA provides CUDA, an extension of C, C++ and Fortran, which
provides GPU data and threads management functions. Because CUDA only
provides a primitive interface to control the GPU, GPU parallelization is often
hard and time-consuming work. When using GPU clusters, the problem is getting
worse because the user also needs to consider data distribution and inter-node
communication using MPI, which also provides very primitive user APIs.

In this paper, we are proposing a parallel programming language called
XcalableMP-ACC (XMP-ACC in short, ACC stands for ACCelerator).
Following are the features of XMP-ACC.

- XMP-ACC is a GPGPU extension of XcalableMP[1] (XMP in short), a
  directive-based parallel programming language for PC clusters. It extends
  C language with new directives for GPU computing.
- XMP-ACC is targeting multi-node GPU clusters, where each node has one
  or more GPUs. So it can be used not only for not only a single GPU but
  also multiple GPU environment such as GPU clusters.

M. Alexander et al. (Eds.): Euro-Par 2011 Workshops, Part I, LNCS 7155, pp. 429–439, 2012.
© Springer-Verlag Berlin Heidelberg 2012

```
int array[YMAX][XMAX];

#pragma xmp nodes p(4)
#pragma xmp template t(0:YMAX-1)
#pragma xmp distribute t(BLOCK) onto p
#pragma xmp align array[i][*] with t(i)

main() {
    int i,j,res = 0;
#pragma xmp loop on t(i)
    for(i = 0; i < YMAX; i++) {
        for(j = 0; j < XMAX; j++) {
            array[i][j] = func(i,j);
            res += array[i][j];
        }
    }
#pragma xmp reduction (+:res)
}
```

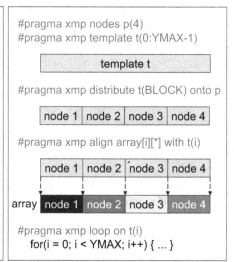

Fig. 1. Data Parallelization in Global View Model

- XMP-ACC provides directives to describe typical processes for GPU computing like data allocation and loop parallelization on GPUs. XMP-ACC's directive-based programming model requires few modifications from a serial code. Users can exploit GPU performance with high productivity.
- Data distribution and inter-node communication for multi-node GPU environment is taken on by XMP directives in XMP-ACC. Users can do hybrid parallel programming on multi-node GPU clusters with little effort using XMP and XMP-ACC directives.

In section 2, we will give a brief overview of XcalableMP. In section 3, we will introduce new directives to describe GPGPU within the XcalableMP framework. Section 4 will show our implementation of the XMP-ACC compiler, and section 5 will shows the performance achieved by the compiler. We will show related work in section 6 and then, conclude the paper in section 7.

2   Overview of XcalableMP

Like OpenMP[2], XMP supports typical parallelization methods based on the data/task parallel paradigm under the **global view** model, and enables parallelizing the original sequential code with minimal modification using simple description. In this section, we will give a brief overview of XMP directives.

2.1   Execution Model

Like MPI, The basic execution model of XMP is the SPMD (Single Program Multiple Data) model. An XMP process begins its execution with a single thread

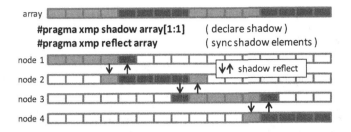

Fig. 2. Shadow Reflection

on each node, which is equivalent to a single-threaded MPI process. Because of its explicit parallelism design, memory access is always local, which means the compiler does not insert any automatic communications. To access the correct data during parallel execution, users should synchronize the local buffer using inter-node communication, which can be described by XMP directives.

2.2 XcalableMP Directives

The global view programming model provides a simple way to describe a parallel program starting from the sequential version: the user parallelizes it by adding directives incrementally. Because these directives can be treated as comments by sequential compilers of the base languages (C and Fortran), an XMP program derived from a sequential program can preserve the integrity of the original program when it is run sequentially.

Figure 1 shows a global view style code segment in XMP. The global view model shares major concepts with High Performance Fortran[3]. The programmer describes the data distribution of data shared among nodes by data distribution directives. The **node** directive declares a node set executing a XMP program, so the sample code would be executed on 4 nodes.

Data Distribution Using Templates. A template, a dummy array indicating data index space, is declared (via the **template** directive) and distributed onto nodes (via the **distribute** directive). In the sample code, a 1-dimensional template, t, is block distributed onto 4 nodes. Array distribution is declared by aligning the array to a template using the **align** directive. In the sample code, array $array[i]$ is aligned to template $t(i)$, that is, $array[i]$ will be allocated on the owner node of $t(i)$.

Work-Sharing. The **loop** directive splits up loop iterations among the executing nodes. The data accessed in a loop statement should be allocated in local memory, because communication is explicit in XMP, that is, work-sharing and data distribution should be done in the same way. A template can be used in the **loop** directive to specify the data allocation. In the sample code, template t is used for parallelizing the loop statement. Consequently, the local part of the distributed array would be processed on each node.

#pragma xmp align [i] with t(i) :: a, b	#pragma xmp acc replicate_sync in (a)
#pragma xmp shadow a[*]	#pragma xmp loop on t(i) acc
int a[N], b[N];	for (i = 0; i < N; i++) {
void main(void){ . . .	b[i] = x;
int i, x = 0;	for (int j = 0; j < N; j++) {
#pragma xmp loop on t(i)	b[i] += a[j];
for (i = 0; i < N; i++)	}
a[i] = i;	}
#pragma xmp reflect a	#pragma xmp acc replicate_sync out (b)
#pragma xmp acc replicate (a, b)	} // #pragma xmp acc replicate
{	} // main()

Fig. 3. Sample Code of XcalableMP-ACC (sample.c)

Directives for Inter-node Communication. The XMP specification guarantees that communication takes place only when communication is explicitly specified. In the global view model, communication directives are used to synchronize and keep the data consistent among the executing nodes.

When an array is distributed, referencing the neighbor elements of the local block is a very typical access pattern that results in inter-node communication. To access the neighbor elements, we need to extend the local block because all memory access is local in XMP. We call the extended area a *shadow* of the array. Fig. 2 shows the shadow area of the array *array*. The **shadow** directive states that the size(the number of elements) of the shadow area on the array is 1 at both the lower and upper sides. A shadow is just a local memory buffer. To get the correct value of the neighbor elements, the data must be synchronized among the executing nodes. The **reflect** directive invokes inter-node communication, copying the original data to the shadow area. XMP also provides communication directives for barrier, reduction and broadcast communication which are commonly used functions in MPI.

3   Language Extension for Multi-node GPU

As shown in the previous section, users can easily write parallel programs using XMP directives. Our goal is to provide a productive and efficient parallel programming model for multi-node GPU clusters. In this section, we will introduce new directives to describe GPGPU within the XcalableMP framework. These directives are used to describe typical processes for GPU computing such as data allocation, data movement between the host memory and the GPU memory and loop parallelization on GPUs. Since XMP directives take on inter-node communication, XMP-ACC can be used not only for a single GPU but also multi-node GPU clusters.

Figure 3 shows some XMP-ACC sample code that calculates the sum of some of an array elements are on GPU. Lines including the keyword **acc** are the new directives/clauses added in XMP-ACC. In XMP-ACC, all actions involving GPUs occur only when the **acc** directives/clauses are used. Typical GPGPU actions including allocation/free data on GPU, data transfer between the host and

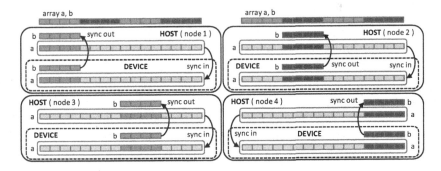

Fig. 4. Memory Image of Data in XcalableMP-ACC

the device and loop work sharing on GPU can be described using the **acc** directives/clauses. Note that there are no directives for inter-node communications (e.g. broadcast, reduction and shadow synchronization) for GPU. In XMP-ACC, the data should be copied to the host memory, then the data should be moved between the hosts using XMP directives (e.g. **bcast**, **reduction** and **reflect**), and then copied from the host to the device.

We assume that each XMP process uses only one GPU, which keeps the language model simple. If there are two or more GPUs in one node, users should assign an XMP process to each GPU (like flat MPI).

3.1   Data Declaration

GPUs have thier own seperate memory, and data should be allocated on the device before being processed. The **acc replicate** directive declares variables to be allocated on the GPU. The following is the syntax of the **acc replicate** directive.

#pragma xmp acc replicate (*list*)
compound-statement

When a variable is declared as **acc replicate**, a copy of the allocated local memory area is also allocated on each node's GPU. Fig. 4 shows the memory image of the arrays a and b declared in Fig. 3 (using 4 nodes). Array b is distributed among the nodes, so the distributed part of the array will be allocated on the GPU. And array a has shadow elements (in this case, full shadow is declared for array a) on both the host and the GPU.

The scope of the **acc replicate** variables is limited to the compound statement following the **acc replicate** directive. The replications will be allocated on the GPU when entering the compound statement and freed at the end of the statement. This helps users to use GPU memory more efficiently. It is also possible to describe the **acc replicate** directive in the global scope (like the **align** directive in Fig.3). Then the replications will be allocated on the GPU when the program starts and freed at the end of the program.

3.2 Data Transfer

Users can describe the data transfer between the host and the GPU using the **acc replicate_sync** directive. The following is the syntax of the **acc replicate_sync** directive and **acc** clause.

#pragma xmp acc replicate_sync *clause*
clause ::= **in** (*list*) | **out** (*list*)

The **acc replicate_sync** directive allows two clauses, **in** and **out**, which indicate the direction of the data transfer. When a process encounters a **acc replicate_sync** directive with the **in** clause, it copies the data from the host to the device. And with the **out** clause, it copies the data from the device to host. Currently, there is no way to indicate the range to be copied, so all of the variable's data is moved between the host and the device. Fig. 4 shows data transfer for arrays *a* and *b*. All the elements of the array *a* including the shadow elements are copied to the device.

3.3 Work Sharing

If every iteration in a loop statement can be processed independently, the loop statement can be parallelized not only among the nodes but also with GPUs. Therefore, the **loop** directive can be exetended to use GPUs. We introduced the **acc** clause for the **loop directive**. The following is the syntax of the **acc** clause for the **loop** directive.

#pragma xmp loop [(*list*)] **on** *on-ref* [**reduction** (*op:list*)] **acc** {*clause*}
loop-statement

clause ::= **private** (*list*) | **firstprivate** (*list*) | **shared** (*list*) |
num_threads (*x*[, *y*[, *z*]])

Variables listed in the **private, firstprivate** and the **shared** clause are declared as private variables on each thread. And the data of **firstprivate** variables is copied from the host to the device before the loop statement. The **private** and the **firstprivate** clause only allow scalar variables. Array variables should be replicated on the device using the **acc replicate** directive. The **shared** clause lists the variables allocated on the GPU. The data will be allocated and synchronized before loop execution. **acc replicate** variables are declared as **shared** variables by default. The **num_threads** clause is used to determine the thread block size. The default value is (16×16) when the clause is omitted.

4   Implementation of XcalableMP-ACC

Compiler Implementation. Our XMP-ACC compiler is based on the Omni XcalableMP Compiler[4]. Fig. 5 shows the compilation process. *sample.c* is written in the C language and XMP/XMP-ACC directives. The compiler creates two files from the source code. *sample.i* is a intermediate file including the host code (executed by the CPU). *sample.cu* includes the device code which is executed by the GPU. We are using CUDA as the GPGPU backend compiler for XMP-ACC. *sample.cu* is compiled by the CUDA compiler. Finally those object files are linked with the runtime library and produce a parallel program. When multiple XMP-ACC processes are assigned to a physical node, the runtime library will assign each XMP process to a GPU in a circular order.

Code Translation. When *sample.c* in Fig. 3 is compiled, it will produce the parallel codes, *sample.i* and *sample.cu* as shown in Fig. 5. *sample.i* shows the host code of the parallel program. _XMP_gpu_init/finalize_data_ALIGNED() initializes/finalizes the data region and the descriptor on the device. _XMP_gpu_sync() transfers the data between the device and the host.

The loop statement parallelized by the **acc** clause is translated into a GPU kernel function in CUDA and added to *sample.cu*. The compiler replaces the loop statement with a GPU function call. The compiler analyzes the loop statement to create the function arguments. If a **acc replicate** array variable appears in the loop statement, the array address on the device will be added to the argument list. And the descriptor address also will be added for calculating parallel parameters. The scalar variables are added to the argument list unless they are described explicitly as thread-private or shared variables.

sample.cu includes the GPU kernel function and its wrapper function which is invoked by the host code. The wrapper function is called from *sample.i*. The thread block size is calculated before invoking the GPU kernel function. The number of threads the compiler creates is equal to the number of iterations allocated to the node. _XMP_GPU_M_BARRIER_KERNEL() waits for the GPU execution to end. Each GPU thread executes the kernel function, and calculates local array indices from its thread ID and the allocated iteration number.

5   Performance Evaluation

We evaluated our compiler using a benchmark that solves the n-body problem, which is often used for evaluating GPGPU performance. Fig. 6 shows our implementation of the XMP-ACC version of the n-body problem. p_x, p_y and p_z contain the x, y, z locations of the particles. The array has shadow elements because every element is needed to calculate the force on a particle. In each time step, the array data is updated. So the shadow elements should be also exchanged each time step. Because those arrays are stored in GPU memory, the data should be exchanged via host memory. The **acc replicate_sync out** directive is used to copy data from the device to the host. Then the **reflect** directive exchanges shadow elements in the host memory. Finally, the **acc replicate_sync in** directive copies the array data from the host to the device.

The force calculation is parallelized on the GPU. The **acc** clause directs the compiler to produce GPU code for the target loop statements. Note that we split the one loop into two seperate loops. This is because the update of p_x, p_y and

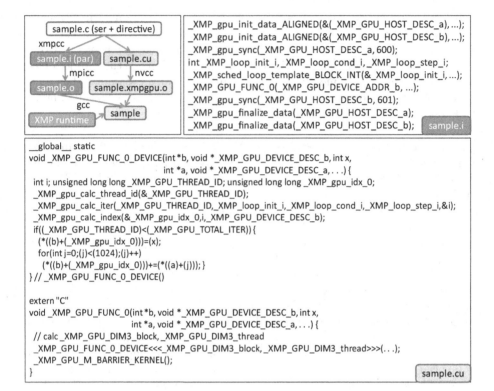

Fig. 5. Compilation Process and Translated Codes

p_z should be done after all threads finish calculating the force on its allocated particle. Because each loop is translated into a GPU function, it is guaranteed that barrier synchronization takes place among all threads. In the future version, we need to implement inter-block barrier synchronization so we only have to use one loop.

Table 1 shows the node configuration of the GPU cluster. We evaluated the performance of 1,2 and 4 XMP processes using 4 physical nodes. Fig. 7 shows the performance of n-body. We compared the performance with the serial version of n-body (1 node, 1 thread, using CPU only). Since most of the execution time is spent on the force calculation which is embarrassingly parallel, XMP-ACC shows scalable performance up to 4 XMP processes. This is especially true as the data size increases since GPU calculation time dwarfs the data transfer and shadow reflection time, which leads to better performance when using GPUs. We added only 10 lines to write the XMP version of n-body (the serial version has 105 lines). Furthermore 4 directives and 2 **acc** clauses were added to write the XMP-ACC version. This shows that XMP-ACC provides a scalable and productive programming model for multi-node GPU clusters.

```
#pragma xmp align [i] with t(i) :: p_x, p_y, p_z, m, v_x, v_y, v_z
#pragma xmp shadow [*] :: p_x, p_y, p_z, m
#pragma xmp acc replicate (p_x, p_y, p_z, m, v_x, v_y, v_z)
{
#pragma xmp acc replicate_sync in (m, v_x, v_y, v_z)
  for (t = 0; t < TIME_STEP; t++) {
#pragma xmp reflect p_x, p_y, p_z
#pragma xmp acc replicate_sync in (p_x, p_y, p_z)
#pragma xmp loop on t(i) acc
    for (i = 0; i < N; i++) {
      double x_i, y_i, z_i, x_j, y_j, z_j, dx, dy, dz, r2, r, a;
      double acc_x = 0, acc_y = 0, acc_z = 0;
      x_i = p_x[i];   y_i = p_y[i];   z_i = p_z[i];
      for (int j = 0; j < N; j++)
        if (i != j) {
          x_j = p_x[j];       y_j = p_y[j];       z_j = p_z[j];
          dx = x_j - x_i;   dy = y_j - y_i;   dz = z_j - z_i;
          r2 = (dx * dx) + (dy * dy) + (dz * dz) + EPSILON;
          r = sqrt(r2);       a = G * m[j] / r2;
          acc_x += a*(x_j-x_i)/r; acc_y += a*(y_j-y_i)/r; acc_z += a*(z_j-z_i)/r; }
      v_x[i] += acc_x * DT;   v_y[i] += acc_y * DT;   v_z[i] += acc_z * DT; }
#pragma xmp loop on t(i) acc
    for (i = 0; i < N; i++) {
      p_x[i] += v_x[i] * DT;   p_y[i] += v_y[i] * DT;   p_z[i] += v_z[i] * DT; }
#pragma xmp acc replicate_sync out (p_x, p_y, p_z)
  } // for (t = 0; t < TIME_STEP; t++)
} // #pragma xmp acc replicate
```

Fig. 6. n-body Code

6   Related Work

OpenMPC[5] and OMPCUDA[6] are the GPGPU extensions for OpenMP. They produce CUDA code from OpenMP directives with few or no modifications. The OpenMP Architecture Review Board[2] itself is also considering a extension of OpenMP targetting many-core processors including GPUs and Digital Signal Processors. PGI Accelerator Compilers[7] provide original directives for GPU computing. Data allocation and loop parallelization can be described more explicitly than in OpenMPC and OMPCUDA which are based on the OpenMP specification. Those models make it easy to program with GPUs in a single node, but they do not work for GPU clusters or even for multiple GPUs in a single node. HMPP Workbench[8] provides directives to describe data transfer between the GPU and the CPU, launching GPU kernel functions (even asynchronously), etc. Because HMPP uses CUDA and OpenCL as a backend compiler, it works on multi-core CPUs and multiple GPUs in a single node. But HMPP is not considersing GPU clusters now. Yili Zheng et al. are working on a GPGPU extension of Unified Parallel C[9] targeting both single and multiple GPU environments.

Table 1. Node Configuration

CPU	AMD Opteron Processor 6134 × 2 (8 cores × 2 sockets)
Memory	DDR3-1333 2GB × 2 (4GB)
GPU	NVIDIA Tesla C2050 (GDDR5 3GB)
Network	InfiniBand (4X QDR)
OS	Linux kernel 2.6.18 x86_64
MPI	OpenMPI 1.4.2
GPU Backend	NVIDIA CUDA Toolkit v3.2

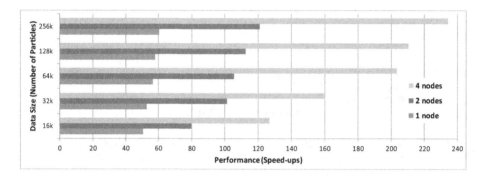

Fig. 7. Performance of n-body

They extended the communication library GASNET to handle one-sided communications for GPUs. It supports unified one-sided communication APIs for GPUs and CPUs. But significant modifications are needed to the serial code in order to parallelize the code.

7 Conclusion

In this paper, we have proposed XcalableMP-ACC, a language extension of XcalableMP for GPU computing. XMP-ACC targets multi-node GPU clusters which has one or more GPUs in each node and provides OpenMP-like directives which allows incremental parallelization from the serial code. XMP-ACC's new directives describe explicit data transfer and loop parallelization for GPU computing, and works naturally with the XMP model used for inter-node communication. Our performance evaluation with n-body problem shows that XMP-ACC achieved scalable performance with few modifications from the serial code.

We are currently improving both the language model and the implementation. We assumed that there is only one GPU per XMP-ACC process to keep the language model simple. However recent platforms feature many more CPU cores than GPUs and thus a variety of execution models exist according to the target applications (e.g. single process using multiple GPUs). So we need to extend the language specification to match various needs. When there are surplus CPU cores, CPU-GPU cooperative computing may be an attractive way to boost the performance. Efficient memory use is one of keys to achieving better performance in GPGPU. Our current implementation only uses the GPU's global memory, so we need to optimize the memory use, for example, using shared memory and coalesced memory access.

Acknowledgment. The specification of XcalableMP is being designed by the XcalableMP Specification Working Group which consists of members from academia, research labs and industries. This research is supported by "Seamless and Highly-productive Parallel Programming Environment for High-performance computing" project funded by Ministry of Education, Culture, Sports, Science and Technology, Japan.

References

1. XcalableMP Official Website, `http://www.xcalablemp.org`
2. OpenMP.org, `http://openmp.org/wp`
3. Rice University. High Performance Fortran Forum, `http://hpff.rice.edu`
4. Lee, J., Sato, M.: Implementation and Performance Evaluation of XcalableMP: A Parallel Programming Language for Distributed Memory Systems. In: 39th International Conference on Parallel Processing Workshops, pp. 413–420 (2010)
5. Lee, S., Eigenmann, R.: OpenMPC: Extended OpenMP Programming and Tuning for GPUs. In: Proceedings of the 2010 ACM/IEEE International Conference for High Performance Computing, Networking, Storage and Analysis, SC 2010, pp. 1–11 (2010)
6. Ohshima, S., Hirasawa, S., Honda, H.: OMPCUDA: OpenMP Execution Framework for CUDA Based on Omni OpenMP Compiler. In: Sato, M., Hanawa, T., Müller, M.S., Chapman, B.M., de Supinski, B.R. (eds.) IWOMP 2010. LNCS, vol. 6132, pp. 161–173. Springer, Heidelberg (2010)
7. PGI Accelerator Compilers, `http://www.pgroup.com/resources/accel.htm`
8. HMPP Workbench, `http://www.caps-entreprise.com/hmpp.html`
9. Hargrove, P.H., Min, S.-J., Zheng, Y., Iancu, C., Yelick, K.: Extending Unified Parallel C for GPU Computing, `http://upc.lbl.gov/publications/UPC_with_GPU-SIAMPP10-Zheng.pdf`

Performance Evaluation of List Based Scheduling on Heterogeneous Systems

Hamid Arabnejad and Jorge G. Barbosa

Universidade do Porto, Faculdade de Engenharia, Dep. de Engenharia Informática,
Laboratório de Intelegência Artificial e Ciência dos Computadores,
Rua Dr. Roberto Frias, s/n, 4200-465 Porto, Portugal
{hamid.arabnejad,jbarbosa}@fe.up.pt

Abstract. This paper addresses the problem of evaluating the schedules produced by list based scheduling algorithms, with metaheuristic algorithms. Task scheduling in heterogeneous systems is a NP-problem, therefore several heuristic approaches were proposed to solve it. These heuristics are categorized into several classes, such as list based, clustering and task duplication scheduling. Here we consider the list scheduling approach. The objective of this study is to assess the solutions obtained by list based algorithms to verify the space of improvement that new heuristics can have considering the solutions obtained with metaheuritcs that are higher time complexity approaches. We concluded that for a low Communication to Computation Ratio (CCR) of 0.1, the schedules given by the list scheduling approach is in average close to metaheuristic solutions. And for CCRs up to 1 the solutions are below 11% worse than the metaheuristic solutions, showing that it may not be worth to use higher complexity approaches and that the space to improve is narrow.

1 Introduction

The problems of task matching and scheduling, in general, are to resolve a composite parallel program into several tasks and assign these tasks to a set of processor elements (PEs) to execute. These tasks have restriction of priority order to execute with each other due to its characteristic of data dependencies. The relationship among the tasks can be represented by a weighted Direct Acyclic Graph (DAG). Also, the processing elements are connected by a high speed communication network. Task matching is to assign a specific task to a suitable processing element to execute; and scheduling is to determine execution priority of each task among the composite parallel program. The general form of the problem has already been proved to be $NP - complete$ [2,11,14,15]. Although it is possible to formulate and search for the optimal solution, the feasible solution space quickly becomes intractable for larger problem instance. To overcome the exponential time complexity, heuristic based scheduling algorithms of been proposed that found a sub-optimal solution in polynomial time. These heuristics are categorized into several classes, mainly list based, clustering and task duplication scheduling. Among these, list scheduling algorithms are generally regarded as having a good cost performance trade-off because of their low

M. Alexander et al. (Eds.): Euro-Par 2011 Workshops, Part I, LNCS 7155, pp. 440–449, 2012.

cost and acceptable results. In list scheduling, tasks are sorted by their priorities and scheduled accordingly [3,6,9,13,17,18]. Although these algorithms can find a feasible solution in polynomial time they are not able to guarantee to find a suitable solution when size of the problem becomes large. In this paper we evaluate the quality of the solutions obtained by two best list scheduling algorithms, namely HEFT and CPOP [18], for heterogeneous systems by comparing with the solutions obtained by metaheuristic algorithms. Once these last algorithms do not guarantee the optimal solution, we obtain for each scheduling the best solution and measure the distance to the list scheduling solution. The metaheuristic algorithms considered in this study are Ant Colony System (ACS), Simulated annealing (SA) and Tabu Search (TA).

At first, we introduce the DAG scheduling problem, then describe two static list scheduling algorithms, HEFT and CPOP. Followed by an introduction to the Ant Colony System, Simulated Annealing and Tabu Search. Further, we describe the design and the implementation on these algorithms with a discussion about the results achieved.

2   DAG Scheduling

A scheduling system model represented by a direct acyclic graph (DAG), $G = (V, E, P, W, data, rate)$, where V is set of v tasks, E is the set of e edges between tasks, and P is the set of processors available in the system. Each $edge(i, j) \in E$ represents the task-dependency constraint such that task n_i should complete its execution before task n_j can be started. A task with no predecessors is called an *entry* task, n_{entry}, and n_{exit} is one with no successors. W is a $v \times p$ computation cost matrix, where v is the number of tasks and p is the number of processors in the system. Figure 1 shows an example of a DAG comprising 12 tasks to illustrate these definitions graphically. It can be seen that the immediate successors of t_3 are t_8, t_9 and t_{11}; the immediate predecessors of t_{10} is t_6. Furthermore, t_1 is an entry task and t_{12} represents a pseudo exit-task.

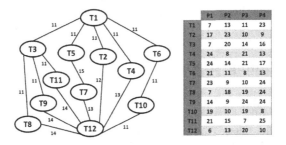

Fig. 1. Example of a DAG and its computation costs matrix [CCR=0.8]

Each $w_{i,j}$ gives the estimated execution time to complete task n_i on processor p_j. The average of execution cost of a node n_i is defined $\overline{w_i} = (\sum_{j \in P} w_{i,j})/p$.

The *data* parameter is a $v \times v$ matrix of communication data, where $data(i, j)$ is the amount of data required to be transmitted from task n_i to task n_j. The *rate* parameter is a $p \times p$ matrix and represent the data transfer rate between processors. The communication cost of $edge(i, j)$, which is for data transfer from task n_i (scheduled on processor p_m) to task n_j (scheduled on processor p_n), is defined by $c_{i,j} = data(n_i, n_j)/rate(p_m, p_n)$. When both n_i and n_j are scheduled on the same processor $(p_m = p_n)$, then $c_{i,j}$ becomes zero. The average communication cost of an edge is defined by $\overline{c_{i,j}} = data(n_i, n_j)/\overline{rate}$, where $\overline{rate}$ is the average transfer rate between the processors in the domain.

The $EST(n_i, p_j)$ and $EFT(n_i, p_j)$ are the *Earliest Execution Start time* and the *Earliest Execution Finish Time* of node n_i on processor p_j. For the entry task $EST(n_{entry}, p_j) = 0$. For other tasks, the EST and EFT values are computed recursively, starting from the entry task as shown by

$$EST(n_i, p_j) = \max\{T_{Available}(p_j), \max_{n_m \in pred(n_i)}\{AFT(n_m) + c_{m,i}\}\}$$

$$EFT(n_i, p_j) = w_{i,j} + EST(n_i, p_j)$$

where $pred(n_i)$ is the set of immediate predecessor tasks of task n_i and $T_{Available}(p_j)$ is the earliest time at which processor p_j is available for task execution. The inner *max* block in the EST equation returns the *ready time*, i.e, the time when all data needed by n_i has arrived at the processor p_j.

The *objective function* of the scheduling problem is to determine the assignment of task of a given application to processors such that the schedule length or *makespan* is minimized. After a task n_i is scheduled on processor p_j, the Actual Start Time of node n_i $(AST(n_i))$ is equal to $EST(n_i)$ and the Actual Finish Time of node n_i $(AFT(n_i))$ is equal to $EFT(n_i)$. After all nodes in the DAG are scheduled, the schedule length will be $makespan = max[AFT(n_{exit})]$, i.e. the Actual Finish Time of exit task.

The *Critial Path (CP)* of a DAG is the longest path from the *entry* node to the *exit* node in the graph. The length of this path $|CP|$ is the sum of the computation cost of the nodes and inter-node communication costs along the path. The $|CP|$ value of a DAG is the lower bound of the schedule length.

3   List Scheduling Algorithms

The list scheduling technique [12] has the following steps: a) determine the available tasks to schedule, b) assign a priorities to them and c) until all tasks are scheduled, select the task with the highest priority and assign it to the processor that allows the earliest start time.

Two attributes frequently used to define the tasks priorities are the *upward* and the *downward* ranks. The *downward rank* of a node n_i $(rank_d)$ is defined as the length of the longest path from an entry node to n_i (excluding n_i). The *upward rank* of a node n_i $(rank_u)$ is the length of the longest path from n_i to an exit node. The nodes of the DAG with higher $rank_u$ values belong to the critical path.

3.1 HEFT Algorithm

The HEFT (Heterogeneous Earliest Finish Time) algorithm [18] is highly competitive in that it generates a comparable schedule length to other scheduling algorithms, with a low time complexity. The HEFT algorithm is an application scheduling algorithm for a bounded number of heterogeneous processors, which has two major phases: a *task prioritizing* phase for computing the priorities of all tasks and a *processor selection* phase for selecting the tasks in the order of their priorities and scheduling each selected task on its best processor, which minimizes the task's finish time. In HEFT algorithm, tasks are ordered by their scheduling priorities that are based on upward ranking ($rank_u$).

Algorithm 1. The HEFT algorithm

Compute $rank_u(n_i)$ for all $n_i \in V$
$ReadyTaskList \leftarrow$ Start Node
while $ReadyTaskList \neq$ Empty **do**
    $n_i \leftarrow$ node with the maximum $rank_u$ in $ReadyTaskList$
    for all $p_j \in P$ **do**
        Compute $EST(n_i, p_j)$
        $EFT(n_i, p_j) \leftarrow w_{i,j} + EST(n_i, p_j)$
    end for
    Map node n_i on processor p_j which provides its least EFT
    Update $T\_Available(p_j)$ and $ReadyTaskList$
end while

3.2 CPOP Algorithm

The critical path (CP)is the longest path in a DAG. The Critical Path on Processor (CPOP) algorithm is a variant of the HEFT algorithm [18]. CPOP adopts a different mapping strategy for the critical path nodes and the non-critical path nodes. A CP processor is defined as the processor that minimizes the overall execution time of the critical path assuming all the critical path nodes are mapped onto it. If the selected node is a critical path node, it is mapped onto the CP processor. Otherwise, it is mapped onto a processor that minimizes its EFT (like in the HEFT algorithm).

Algorithm 2. The CPOP algorithm

Compute $rank_u(n_i)$ and $rank_d(n_i)$ for all $n_i \in V$
Identify the Critical Paths and mark the Critical Path Nodes
$priority(n_i) \leftarrow rank_u(n_i) + rank_d(n_i)$
$ReadyTaskList \leftarrow$ Start Node
while $ReadyTaskList \neq$ Empty **do**
    $n_i \leftarrow$ node with the maximum $rank_u$ in $ReadyTaskList$
    if $n_i \in$ Critical Path **then**
        Map n_i on the CP Processor
    else
        for all p_j in P **do**
            Compute $EST(n_i, p_j)$
            $EFT(n_i, p_j) \leftarrow w_{i,j} + EST(n_i, p_j)$
        end for
        Map node n_i on processor p_j which provides its least EFT
    end if
    Update $T\_Available(p_j)$
    Update $ReadyTaskList$
end while

---

4 Metaheuristic Algorithms

4.1 Ant Colony System

Ant colony system (ACS) is a metaheuristic that was first proposed by Dorigo and Gambardella [4], it is one of the most popular swarm inspired methods in computational intelligence areas. And latter adapted to discrete optimization problems [5]. The basic idea is to imitate the cooperative behaviour of real ants, to solve optimization problems. At first, ants have no clue about which way belongs to the shortest path to nest, so they choose randomly. Once the ants discover a paths from nest to food, they changed pheromone on the path. So another ants can follow the trails to find the food source. The ants that found the shortest path will come back to nest sooner, than ants via longer paths, and that path will have higher traffic. As this process continuous, the shortest paths have a huge amount of pheromone and most of ants tend to choose these paths. ACS includes five steps: (1) ants initialization to positioning (2) for each ant applied a state transition rule to incrementally build a solution and a local pheromone updating rule (3) Global pheromone updating (4) ending test to evaluate the best solution that if it is not acceptable go to step 1.

To apply the ACS meta-heuristic to the task scheduling problem, we need to translate this problem into the structure of ACS so that ants can find solutions. For this purpose, we considered a Graph with two subgraphs G_1 and G_2, where the first represents the set of tasks to schedule and the second denotes the set of processors available. At each iteration, each ant selects a source node and a suitable processor based on a selection rule. Then we add tasks that are ready to schedule, i.e. tasks where their predecessors have been scheduled, and this procedure continues until all task are scheduled.

In ACS (Ant Colony System) the state transition rule provides a direct way to balance between exploration of new edges and exploitation of a priori and accumulated knowledge about the problem. It is defined as follows: an ant positioned on task i chooses the processor u to move to by applying the rule given by

$$
Prob(i,p) = \begin{cases} \max\left[\tau(i,p) \times [\eta(i,p)]^\beta\right] & \text{if } q_0 < q \text{(exploitation)} \\ \dfrac{\tau(i,p) \times [\eta(i,p)]^\beta}{\displaystyle\sum_{q \in P} (\tau(i,q) \times [\eta(i,q)]^\beta)} & \text{otherwise (biased exploration)} \end{cases}
$$

where q is a random number uniformly distributed in $[0..1]$ and q_0 is a parameter ($0 \leq q_0 \leq 1$). Tuning the parameter q_0 allows modulation of the degree of exploration and the choice of whether to concentrate the search of the system around the best-so-far solution or to explore other tours, here $q_0 = 0.7$. And $\eta(n,p) = 1/AFT(n_{i,p})$ is the heuristic function and $\beta = 2$ is a parameter which determine the relative influence of the heuristic information.

The *Global Pheromone Update* Rule is performed only by the best ants that have the shortest path from source to sink. This rule besides the use of the pseudo-random-proportional rule, cause to encourage the ants in next iterations to search in a neighbourhood of the best path found up to current iteration. After all ants finished their tour, we can perform global updating for current iteration. The pheromone level is updated by applying the global updating rule $\tau(i,p) = (1 - \rho) \cdot \tau(i,p) + \rho \cdot \Delta\tau(i,p)$ where $\Delta\tau(i,p)$ for global best tour is $\Delta\tau(i,p) = 1/[AFT_{best\ ant}(n_{exit})]$ and for other nodes is $\Delta\tau(i,p) = 0$. Also, $0 < \rho < 1$ is the pheromone decay parameter and here is $\rho = 0.1$. In addition to the global pheromone trail updating rule, in ACS the ants use a *Local Pheromone Update* rule in each iteration since each ant by choosing a processor p for task i, is applied by $\tau(i,p) = (1 - \xi) \cdot \tau(i,p) + \xi \cdot \tau_0$ where $0 < \xi < 1$ denotes the pheromone decay parameter and $\tau_0 = \frac{1}{|V|}$ is the initial value of pheromone on all edges. Experimentally, a good value for ξ was found to be $\xi = 0.1$.

4.2   Simulated Annealing

Simulated Annealing (SA) is a generic probabilistic meta-algorithm proposed by Kirpatrick, Gelett and Vecchi [10] and Cerny [1] used to find an approximate solution to global optimization problems. It is inspired by annealing in metallurgy which is a technique of controlled cooling of material to reduce defects. In simulated annealing, a cost function to be minimized is defined in terms of the parameters of the problem at hand. The cost minimization process is governed by a cooling temperature which varies from a given high value to a low value slowly. At every temperature, we generate a fixed number of scheduling and calculate cost function(makespan) for each of them. If the cost function is less than the previous cost, the new configuration is accepted. If the cost is more than the previous one, the new configuration is chosen with a probability $r \leq exp(-\Delta C/T_k)$ where $r \in [0,1]$. Probabilistic acceptance of costlier solutions is behind the success of the simulated annealing process. Actually, when $\Delta C \leq 0$, we have a *downhill* step, that means a search for a new solution around a best solution. But if this condition is not satisfied, we can use the new solution instead of the best solution, with higher cost (*uphill* step) and helps the solution process overcome the possibility of getting trapped in a local minimum and move toward the global minimum. The three most important parts are: (1)*Cost Function* that is the schedule length of the solution; (2) *Generating mechanism* to randomly generate a scheduling of a set of tasks; and, (3) *Cooling mechanism* that initializes the temperature to a value T_0, and in each step, it decreases by $T_{k+1} = \alpha \times T_k$ and $\alpha = 0.1$ if we use a higher value for α we will move faster and we would have less exploration of the search space.

In our implementation the length of Markov chain is $|V|$, final temperature is 0.01, initial temperature is $[best_{makespan}(S_i) - worst_{makespan}(S_i)]/\log(0.9)$, where S_i is the initial solution, and the initial value of the cost function C is given by the *makespan*.

Algorithm 3. The Simulated Annealing algorithm

Create an initial(feasible) solution s;
Set an initial temperature T_0 (with $k \leftarrow 0$);
Set number of trials at each temperature level (level-length) α
while termination criterion not satisfied **do**
    for $i = 0 \rightarrow length_{Markov\ chain}$ **do**
        Create new neighbour s' by applying a random move to s;
        Calculate cost difference ΔC between s' and s : $\Delta C = C(s') - C(s)$;
        if $\Delta C \leq 0$ **then**
            Switch over to solution s' (current solution s is replaced by s');
        else
            Create random number $r \in [0, 1]$;
            if $r \leq exp(-\Delta C/T_k)$ **then**
                Switch over to solution s' (current solution s is replaced by s');
            end if
        end if
    end for
    Update best found solution (if necessary);
    Set $k \leftarrow k + 1$ and Set / Update temperature value T_k for next level k;
end while
return Best found solution

4.3   Tabu Search

Tabu search (TS) is one the a heuristic methods proposed by Glover [7] [8]. Unlike other meta-heuristics, in TS, we have an intelligent search to perform a systematic exploration of the solution space. The main idea in TS is to use the information about search history to guide local search approaches to overcome local optimality. In general we examine a path sequence of solutions and moves to the best neighbour of the current solution and, to avoid cycling, solutions that were recently examined are forbidden or tabu. Elements of Tabu Search: 1) *Tabu List* (short term memory): to record solutions to prevent revisiting a visited solution; 2) *Tabu tenure*: number of iterations a tabu move is considered to remain tabu; 3) *Aspiration criteria*: accepting an improved solution even if generated by a tabu move 4) *Long term memory*: to record attributes of elite solutions to be used in: a) Intensification (giving priority to attributes of a set of elite solutions); b) Diversification (Discouraging attributes of elite solutions in selection functions in order to diversify the search to other areas of solution space).

Algorithm 4. The Tabu Search algorithm

$S \leftarrow$ random valuation of variables;
$iter \leftarrow 0$;
initialize randomly the $tabu\_list$
while $(eval(S) > 0)$ and $(iter < Maxiter)$ **do**
    choose a $move < V, v' >$ with the best performance among the non-tabu moves and the moves satisfying the aspiration criteria;
    introduce $< V, v >$ in the $tabu\_list$, where v is the current value of V
    remove the oldest move from the $tabu\_list$
    assign v' to V;
    $iter \leftarrow iter + 1$;
end while
return S

5   Results and Conclusions

In this section, we evaluate and compare the solution performance of the HEFT and CPOP with metaheuristic algorithms for single DAG scheduling using an extensive simulation setup. The metrics used for comparison are the **SLR (schedule length ratio)** and the **Speedup** (used in [18]). In fact, the SLR metric make a normalization on the schedule length to a lower bound.

$$ SLR = \frac{makespan(solution)}{\sum_{n_i \in CP_{MIN}} \min_{p_j \in P} \left(w_{(i,j)} \right)} \qquad Speedup = \frac{\min_{p_j \in P} \left[\sum_{n_i \in V} w_{(i,j)} \right]}{makespan(solution)} $$

The denominator in SLR is the minimum computation of tasks on critical path. With any algorithm, there is no makespan less than the denominator of SLR equation. Therefore, the algorithm with lower SLR is the best algorithm. Average SLR values over several task graphs are used in our results. In $Speedup$, the sequential time is obtained by the sum of the processing time on the processor that minimizes the total computation cost [18]. The DAGs used in this simulation setup were randomly generated using the program in [16] which considers the following parameters: *width* as the number of tasks on the largest level; *regularity* is the uniformity of the number of tasks in each level; *density* is the number of edges between two levels of the DAG. These parameters may vary between 0 and 1. An additional parameter, *jump*, indicates that an edge can go from level l to level $l + jump$. In this paper, we consider DAGs with 10, 20, 30 and 40 tasks; the number of processors equal to 4, 8, 16, and 32; CCR of 0.1, 0.5, 0.8 and 1; width equal to 0.1, 0.2, 0.8; density equal to 0.2, 0.8; and jumps of 1, 2, and 4. These combinations give 1152 different DAG types. Since 5 random DAGs were generate for each combination, the total number of DAGs used in our experiment was 5760. We do not considers CCR above 1 because for a high speed network it would not be a realistic value.

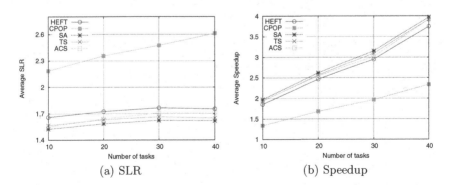

(a) SLR   (b) Speedup

Fig. 2. The SLR and Speedup average values for each size graph and CCR=[0.1 0.5 0.8 1.0]

Figure 2 shows the results of SLR and Speedup for list scheduling algorithms (HEFT and CPOP) and metaheuristic algorithms (ACS, TS and SA). It can be observed that in average there is a consistent gap between the two types of algorithms, being the best solutions obtained by the Simulated Annealing metaheuristic. Also HEFT has always better performance than CPOP, as shown in [18]. Considering the results shown on table 1, it can be concluded that for low CCR (0.1) the HEFT gives near results comparing to metaheuristic approaches. This means that the effort of using a higher time complexity approach may not be worth. For higher CCRs up to 1.0 the improvement is always below 11%, which means that the improvement is not very high in order to compensate the usage of metaheuristic algorithms. For illustrative purpose, in figure 3 we can see an example of the makespan obtained by HEFT, AS, TS and ACS algorithms, for the DAG represented in Figure 1. Task 12 in HEFT is delayed due to communication costs from task 7.

Table 1. SLR improvement observed with metaheuristic algorithms compared to HEFT

CCR	N=10			N=20			N=30			N=40		
	SA	TS	ACS	SA	TS	ACS	SA	TS	ACS	SA	TS	ACS
0.1	0.80%	0.60%	0.53%	1.64%	1.38%	0.62%	3.16%	2.94%	1.35%	4.07%	3.90%	1.79%
0.5	7.03%	5.70%	5.74%	7.09%	5.66%	4.04%	7.97%	6.50%	2.84%	7.93%	6.74%	2.88%
0.8	9.96%	6.91%	8.27%	10.0%	6.80%	6.45%	9.93%	6.49%	4.09%	9.48%	6.61%	1.87%
1.0	10.0%	6.23%	7.74%	10.2%	5.65%	6.14%	9.45%	5.85%	2.98%	10.9%	6.98%	2.51%

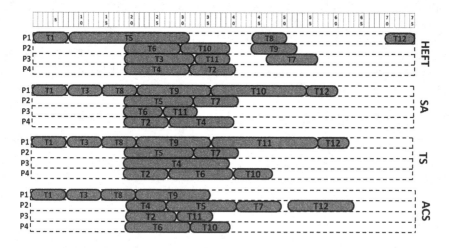

Fig. 3. Scheduling of task graph with HEFT, SA, TS, ACS

In conclusion, we can say that for low CCR (0.1) HEFT produces schedules competitive with metaheuristic approaches, with a lower time complexity. For higher CCRs up to 1, the improvement achieved with SA is below 11%, being also competitive the schedules produced by HEFT. These results show also that new heuristic base algorithms have a narrow space of improvement over HEFT. Regarding the metaheuristic algorithms, SA showed to achieve consistently better scheduling solutions for DAG scheduling in heterogeneous systems.

References

1. Cerny, V.: Thermodynamical approach to the travelling salesman problem: an efficient simulation algorithm. Journal of Optimization Theory and Applications, 41–51 (1985)
2. Coffman, E.G.: Computer and job-shop scheduling theory. Wiley (1976)
3. Dhodhi, M.K., Ahmad, I., Yatama, A., et al.: An integrated technique for task matching and scheduling onto distributed heterogeneous computing system. Journal of Parallel and Distributed Computing 62(9), 1338–1361 (2002)
4. Dorigo, M., Gambardella, L.M.: Ant colony system: A cooperative learning approach to the traveling salesman problem. IEEE Transactions on Evolutionary Computation 1(1), 53–66 (1997)
5. Dorigo, M., Di Caro, G., Gambardella, L.M.: Ant algorithms for discrete optimization. Artifitial Life 5, 137–172 (1999)
6. El-Rewini, H., Lewis, T.G.: Scheduling parallel program tasks onto arbitrary target machines. Journal of Parallel and Distributed Computing 9(2), 138–153 (1990)
7. Glover, F.: Tabu search-part i. ORSA Journal on Computing 1(3), 190–206 (1989)
8. Glover, F.: Tabu search-part ii. ORSA Journal on Computing 2(1), 4–32 (1990)
9. Kim, D., Yi, B.-G.: A two-pass scheduling algorithm for parallel programs. Parallel Computing 20, 869–885 (1994)
10. Kirkpatrick, S., Gelatt Jr., C.D., Vecchi, M.P.: Optimization by simulated annealing. Science 220, 671–680 (1983)
11. Kohler, W.H., Steiglitz, K.: Characterization and theoretical comparison of branch-and-bound algorithms for permutation problems. Journal of ACM 2, 140–156 (1974)
12. Kwok, Y., Ahmad, I.: Static scheduling algorithms for allocating directed task graphs to multiprocessors. ACM Computing Surveys 31(4), 406–471 (1999)
13. Kwok, Y.-K., Ahmad, I.: Dynamic critical-path scheduling: an effective technique for allocating task graphs to multiprocessors. IEEE Transactions on Parallel and Distributed Systems 7(5), 506–521 (1996)
14. Liou, J.-C., Palis, M.A.: A comparison of general approaches to multiprocessor scheduling. In: International Parallel Processing Symposium, pp. 152–156 (1997)
15. Papadimitriou, C., Yannakakis, M.: Scheduling interval ordered tasks. SIAM Journal of Computing 5, 73–82 (1976)
16. DAG Generation Program (2010), http://www.loria.fr/~suter/dags.html
17. Sinnen, O., Sousa, L.: List scheduling: extension for contention awareness and evaluation of node priorities for heterogeneous cluster architectures. Parallel Computing 30, 81–101 (2004)
18. Topcuoglu, H., Hariri, S., Wu, M.-Y.: Performance-effective and low-complexity task scheduling for heterogeneous computing. IEEE Transactions on Parallel and Distributed Systems 13(3), 260–274 (2002)

Column-Based Matrix Partitioning for Parallel Matrix Multiplication on Heterogeneous Processors Based on Functional Performance Models

David Clarke, Alexey Lastovetsky, and Vladimir Rychkov

School of Computer Science and Informatics, University College Dublin,
Belfield, Dublin 4, Ireland
David.Clarke.1@ucdconnect.ie
{Alexey.Lastovetsky,vladimir.rychkov}@ucd.ie

Abstract. In this paper we present a new data partitioning algorithm to improve the performance of parallel matrix multiplication of dense square matrices on heterogeneous clusters. Existing algorithms either use single speed performance models which are too simplistic or they do not attempt to minimise the total volume of communication. The functional performance model (FPM) is more realistic then single speed models because it integrates many important features of heterogeneous processors such as the processor heterogeneity, the heterogeneity of memory structure, and the effects of paging. To load balance the computations the new algorithm uses FPMs to compute the area of the rectangle that is assigned to each processor. The total volume of communication is then minimised by choosing a shape and ordering so that the sum of the half-perimeters is minimised. Experimental results demonstrate that this new algorithm can reduce the total execution time of parallel matrix multiplication in comparison to existing algorithms.

Keywords: Parallel matrix multiplication, functional performance models, heterogeneous platforms, load balance, data partitioning.

1 Introduction

In this paper, we deal with the problem of partitioning matrices across a cluster of heterogeneous processors in order to improve the performance of parallel matrix multiplication. Computation time can be minimised by partitioning the work so that all processors finish their work in the same time. Communication time can be reduced by arranging the partitioning in such a way as to minimise the total volume of communication. Communication time can also be reduced by measuring the interconnect speed between all nodes and choosing a partitioning based on this; however, this approach is beyond the scope of this paper.

Two-dimensional decomposition of matrices yields more efficient parallel algorithms then one-dimensional decomposition. Hence, ScaLAPACK [2], a linear

M. Alexander et al. (Eds.): Euro-Par 2011 Workshops, Part I, LNCS 7155, pp. 450–459, 2012.

algebra library designed for homogeneous platforms, implements the two-dimensional regular grid partitioning in the parallel outer-product routine. In addition, this routine has a blocking factor, b, designed to take advantage of processor cache. Each matrix block contains $b \times b$ elements, and each step of the routine involves updating one block.

To balance the load on heterogeneous platforms, irregular partitioning schemes are used. This approach is based on a concept of the *computational unit*, the smallest amount of work that can be given to a processor. All units require the exact same number of arithmetic calculations and have the same data storage requirements. The computational load is balanced by distributing computational units in proportion to the speeds of processors. In the case of two-dimensional matrix multiplication, the computational unit is the update of a $b \times b$ block. Each processor P_i is responsible for computing a rectangle of $m_i \times n_i$ blocks.

There are no existing algorithms to find the general solution of irregular partitioning. However, there are some algorithms that find sub-optimal solutions under certain restrictions on the arrangements of rectangles. One such algorithm (KL) [7] implements a column-based partitioning. Processors are arranged into columns, and all processors in a column are allocated rectangles of the same width. The widths of all the columns sum to the N dimension of the matrix. The heights of rectangles in a column sum to the M dimension of the matrix. This algorithm does not minimise the total volume of communication and uses a basic partitioning algorithm based on single speed values.

In another column-based algorithm (BR) [1], the area of rectangles is defined by the relative cycle-times of processors. The shape and ordering of rectangles is calculated to minimise the sum of half-perimeters $\sum_{i=1}^{\hat{p}} m_i + n_i$. Therefore, this algorithm partitions a matrix in proportion to processor performance in such a way as to reduce the total volume of communication.

Many traditional data partitioning algorithms use a similar approach for calculating relative processor performance, where processor speed is represented by a single positive number. These algorithms were designed for medium sized problems run on general purpose single core workstations. It has since been demonstrated in [8] that processor speed is not invariant with problem size. Speed represented by a function of problem size has proven to be more realistic than the constant performance models because it integrates many important features of heterogeneous processors such as the architectural heterogeneity, the heterogeneity of memory structure, the effects of paging and so on. A better partitioning can be achieved by using the algorithms based on functional performance models (FPM).

The functional performance model proposed in [8] is one-dimensional and represented by a line in 2D space. In two-dimensional matrix partitioning, the problem size is composed of two parameters, m and n. Hence, the functional performance model becomes a surface in 3D space, where the z axes represents speed. In [11], these surfaces are used as more realistic performance models of processors in order to improve the KL partitioning algorithm. It iteratively slices 2D plains through the 3D space at positions that represent the column width, reducing the problem to a series of one-dimensional partitioning. FPM-based algorithm is used to find optimal partitioning within each column, while the column widths are found using the basic partitioning algorithm based on single values.

This algorithm does find a good partitioning but it has a number of disadvantages: (i) communication cost is not taken into account and any prime number of processors cannot be used efficiently; (ii) convergence is not guaranteed because it uses the basic partitioning algorithm as demonstrated in [3]; (iii) building full 2D models is expensive.

In this paper, we present a modification of the (BR) algorithm. Instead of simplistic performance models of processors, we use more accurate functional performance models. We reduce the complexity of matrix partitioning from two parameters down to one by using the area of rectangles $d = m \times n$. This allows us to build less expensive one-dimensional functional performance models and to solve the partitioning problem in one step with help of the FPM-based algorithm. The result of this partitioning is the areas of rectangles, which are then arranged by the (BR) algorithm so that the total volume of communication is minimised. Therefore, we achieve more optimal data partitioning, which is based on more accurate performance model of processors, while also minimising communication volume.

The rest of the paper is organised as follows. In Section 2, we review existing algorithms for two-dimensional matrix partitioning designed for heterogeneous platforms. In Section 3, we present the main contribution of this paper, namely, the FPM-based modification of the BR algorithm. In Section 4, we present the experimental results for parallel matrix multiplication on a heterogeneous cluster.

2   Related Work

In this section, we summarize existing heterogeneous partitioning algorithms for parallel matrix multiplication. The common features of these algorithms are the following: (i) computational units are mapped to processors in proportion to their speed; (ii) to reduce the space of possible solutions of this mapping, a column-based restriction is applied. These algorithms determine the partitioning for a heterogeneous implementation of the blocked ScaLAPACK outer product [2].

2.1   Column-Based Partitioning (KL)

Column-based partitioning of matrices was first introduced in [7]. This algorithm distributes a unit square between $\hat{p}$ heterogeneous processors arranged into q columns, each of which is made of p_j processors, $j \in [1, ..., q]$:

- Let the relative speed of the i-th processor from the j-th column, P_{ij}, be s_{ij} such that $\sum_{j=1}^{q} \sum_{i=1}^{p_j} s_{ij} = 1$.

- Then, we first partition the unit square into c vertical rectangular slices such that the width of the j-th slice is $n_j = \sum_{i=1}^{p_j} s_{ij}$. This partitioning makes the area of each vertical slice proportional to the sum of the speeds of the processors in the corresponding column.
- Second, each vertical slice is partitioned independently into rectangles in proportion to the speed of the processors in the corresponding processor column.

This algorithm has some drawbacks. Namely, it does not take communication cost into account, and it relies on inaccurate, single-value performance model of the processor speed. These issues are addressed by the algorithms in Section 2.2 and 2.3 respectively.

2.2   Minimising Total Communication Volume (BR)

The BR algorithm [1] minimises the total volume of communication as follows. The objective is to tile the unit square into $\hat{p}$ non-overlapping rectangles, where each rectangle is assigned to a processor, in such a way as to achieve load balancing and minimise communication. Then, this unit square can be scaled to the size of the matrix. The general solution to this problem is NP complete, however, by applying a restriction that all processors in the same column have the same width, the authors of [1] were able to produce an algorithm of polynomial complexity.

First, the relative speed of each processor is calculated from the relative cycle-times t_i: $s_i = \frac{1/t_i}{\sum (1/t_i)}$. This speed gives the area d_i of the rectangle assigned to the processor P_i. However, there are degrees of freedom with regards to the shape and ordering of the rectangles.

In each iteration, the number of elements of matrix **A** that each processor either sends or receives is directly proportional to its height m_i and the number of elements of matrix **B** sent or received is proportional to its width n_i. The total volume of data exchange is proportional to the sum of the half perimeters $H = \sum_{i=0}^{p-1}(m_i + n_i)$. Communication cost can be reduced by minimising H. This is achieved by arranging the rectangles so that they are as square as possible. The optimum number of columns c and the optimum number of processors in each column r_j is calculated by the algorithm. The processors are sorted in order of increasing speed. A table is built to summarise the communication costs for 1 to p columns, i.e. from all processors in the same column to each processor in an individual column. The algorithm then works backwards through the table, selecting values for c and r_j which minimise the half perimeter.

The main disadvantage of this algorithm is that cycle-times is not an accurate measure of the processor performance. This may result in poor performance of parallel matrix multiplication.

2.3   Functional Performance Model-Based Partitioning (FPM-KL)

The assumption that the absolute speed of the processor is independent of the size of the computational task becomes less accurate in the following situations:

- The partitioning of the problem results in some tasks either not fitting into the main memory of the assigned processor and hence causing paging or fully fitting into faster levels of its memory hierarchy.
- Some processing units involved in computations are not traditional general-purpose processors (say, accelerators such as GPUs or specialized cores). In this case, the relative speed of a traditional processor and a non-traditional one may differ for two different sizes of the same computational task even if both sizes fully fit into the main memory.
- Different processors use different codes to solve the same problem locally.

Functional performance models more accurately represent the speed of processors then traditional constant models [8]. The speed of each processor is represented by a continuous positive function of problem size (Fig. 1(a)). These functions are obtained by benchmarking a serial code that is equivalent to one step of the parallel routine. There are two approaches to building the models. If the application is to be run multiple times on a set of machines (or a sub-set of these machines) then an exhaustive full functional performance model can be built for each unique machine. This process is time consuming but needs to be done only once for each routine on each unique machine, it can be done at compile time. An alternative approach, suitable for more dynamic environments, where the available machines change regularly, is to dynamically build only the necessary parts of the models at run-time. This approach has been demonstrated in [10]. Dynamically built models are perfectly applicable to the algorithm proposed in the next section, however for clarity of results, we will use full functional performance models in the remainder of this paper.

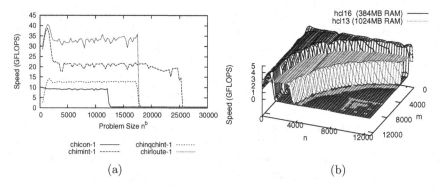

Fig. 1. (a) Functional performance models for 4 nodes from the Grid'5000 Lille site. (b) Two-dimensional models for two nodes from our local heterogeneous cluster, showing hcl16 is a faster node with less memory then hcl13.

The partitioning algorithm based on functional performance models proposed in [8] is designed for partitioning with one parameter. However, the ScaLAPACK outer-product routine requires two partitioning parameters, m_{ij} and n_j, for each processor P_{ij}. An two-dimensional iterative algorithm to overcome this short-coming is proposed in [9]. The strategy is similar to that described in Section 2.1. However, functional performance models are used in place of simplistic single value performance models. The two parameters, m and n, gives two degrees of freedom which leads a model consisting of a surface in 3D space (Fig. 1(b)). The z axes represents processor speed.

Processors are arranged into a $p \times q$ grid. Initially column widths are given by $n_j = N/q \; \forall j$. Iterating:

1. A 2D plane is sliced through the 3D space at positions equal to n_j. This gives one-dimensional functional performance models which can be used by the algorithm in [8] to find the optimum partitioning within each column, m_{ij}. Single value speeds for this partitioning can then be found from the model s_{ij}.
2. If the maximum relative difference between execution times is less then some ϵ the algorithm finishes, otherwise it continues.
3. New column widths n_i are calculated in proportion the single value speed of each column $\sum_{i=1}^{p} s_{ij}$

This algorithm does find a good partitioning but it has a number of disadvantages: (i) it does not take communication cast into account; (ii) the processor grid is fixed and the algorithm is unable to change the ordering of the processors; (iii) it relies on a constant performance model to find the location of the next slice so there is no guarantee of convergence; (iv) building full 2D models requires more time consuming benchmarking (while a 1D model requires x experimental points to achieve a given accuracy, a 2D model requires x^2 points).

2.4   Other Related Work

A matrix partitioning algorithm for a heterogeneous combination of FPGA and general purpose processors is presented in [12]. Their model does consider memory hierarchy, however detailed knowledge of the architecture is requires and each memory level requires a parameter in their partitioning algorithm. Hence, it is not self adaptable to new environments.

The authors of [4] present interesting algorithms for minimising the total volume of communication and for partitioning with respect to both computational power and communication speed. However, these algorithms are targeted for a master-worker platform and so are not directly applicable to our target platform.

A different approach for load balancing is taken in [6]. The problem is broken down into many small processes, each requiring an equal amount of work and data storage. Processes are then mapped to processors in proportion to processor performance. This approach allows for easy adaptation of existing homogeneous algorithms to heterogeneous platforms, however it is unable to achieve fine grained load balancing without incurring an overhead penalty for running a large number of processes per processor.

3 New FPM-BR Two-Dimensional Matrix Partitioning Algorithm

The efficient heterogeneous ScaLAPACK outer-product routine requires two partitioning parameters for each processor. Load balancing with 1D functional performance models only works with problems with one degree of freedom. The existing 2D FPM-KL partitioning algorithm does not take communication cost into account while the BR algorithm minimises communication volume but uses a too simplistic model for processor performance. To overcome these shortcomings, we present a new FPM-BR algorithm that combines the strengths of these algorithms.

The height m_i and width n_i parameters can be combined into one parameter, area $d_i = m_i \times n_i$. Our computational unit is a $b \times b$ block, and benchmarking is done for square areas $m = n = \sqrt{d}$, for $0 < d \le M \times N$. We can then partition using the one-dimensional FPM-based algorithm [8] to determine the areas of the rectangles that should be partitioned to each processor. The BR algorithm is then used to calculate the optimum shape and ordering of the rectangles so that the total volume of communication is minimised.

In the algorithm proposed above we have made the assumption that a benchmark of a square area will give an accurate prediction of computation time of any rectangle of the same area, namely $s(x, x) = s(x/c, c.x)$. However, in general this does not hold true for all c (Fig. 2(a)). Fortunately, in order to minimise the total volume of communication the BR algorithm arranges the rectangles so that they are as square as possible. We have verified this experimentally by partitioning a medium sized square dense matrix using our new algorithm for 1 to 1000 nodes from the Grid'5000 platform (incorporating 20 unique nodes), and plotted the frequency of the ratio $m : n$ in Fig. 2(c). Fig. 2(b), showing a detail of Fig. 2(a), illustrates that if the rectangle is approximately square the assumption holds.

4 Experimental Results

To demonstrate the effectiveness of the new FPM-BR matrix partitioning algorithm we applied it to a heterogeneous MPI implementation of the blocked ScaLAPACK outer product routine [2]. The high performance, cross-platform multi-threaded GotoBLAS2 [5] library was used for the BLAS implementation. Dense square matrices are filled with random numbers. A block size of $b = 16$ was chosen, increasing block size allows the GotoBLAS2 dgemm subroutine to make more efficient use of cache levels, however this reduces the granularity available to the partitioner. The total matrix dimension is given by $N^b = N \times 16$, where N is the dimension used by the partitioner algorithm.

A benchmark to build the functional performance model must be done independently of other nodes. Serial code, which closely resembles one iteration of the parallel code, is timed. Memory is allocated and freed in the same order and MPI point-to-point communications are sent to itself. Statistics are applied so that benchmarks are repeated until a specified confidence interval has been achieved.

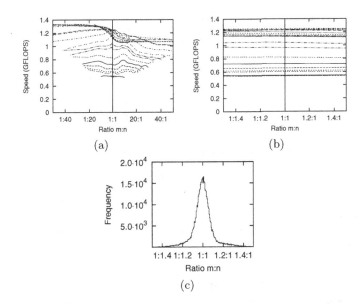

Fig. 2. Showing speed against the ratio of the sides of the partitioned rectangles. Lines connect rectangles of equal area. The centerline at 1 : 1 represents square shape. In general speed is not constant with area (a). However when the ratio is close to 1 : 1, speed is approximately constant (b). (c) Shows the frequency distribution of the ratio of $m : n$ using the new partitioning algorithm for 1 to 1000 machines (incorporating 20 unique hardware configurations).

Table 1. Lille Site Hardware Specifications

Nodes	Processor	Cores	Memory
20	2.6GHz Opteron	4	4
20	2.83GHz Xeon	8	8
19	2.4GHz Xeon	8	16
5	2.4GHz Xeon	8	8

Four partitioning algorithms (even homogeneous, BR, FPM-KL, FPM-BR) are applied to parallel matrix multiplication on 64 nodes from Grid'5000 Lille site. The total execution time for a range of problem sizes was recorded and plotted in Fig. 3. The nodes are from 4 interconnected clusters with 4 unique hardware configurations (Table 1, Fig. 1(a)). Our new FPM-BR algorithm was able to efficiently partition for all problem sizes up a maximum size of $N^b = 160000$ at which point all of the available memory is used. The BR algorithm works successfully for medium sized problems but fails for problems with $N^b > 80000$ because it uses a too simplistic model of processor speed. The FPM-KL algorithm is also able to partition up to the maximum size but performance is lower than FPM-BR because the total volume of communication is not minimised.

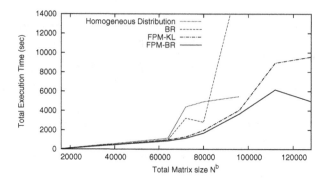

Fig. 3. Total time to execute parallel square dense matrix multiplication for a range of problem sizes using the three algorithms discussed in this paper and an even homogeneous distribution. The experiment is conducted on 64 nodes from Grid'5000 Lille site (incorporating 4 unique hardware configurations).

The speedup for FPM-BR algorithm over FPM-KL algorithm is more pronounced for non-square number of processes, for example 14 as shown in Fig. 4. The total volume of communication is reduced by 17.1% and there is a corresponding 13.6% reduction in total computation time. The difference can be accounted for by an increase, with the FPM-BR algorithm, in the number of point-to-point communications to send matrix **A** horizontally. Namely in the first iteration processor 03 must send to 7 processors (04, 14, 10, 12, 08, 05, 06) (Fig. 4(b)). With the FPM-KL algorithm, processor 03 needs only send horizontally to 3 processors (10, 13, 14) (Fig. 4(a)). Collective communications are used to broadcast elements of matrix **B** vertically.

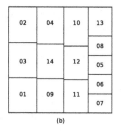

Fig. 4. Matrix partitioning for 14 heterogeneous nodes, with a problem size of $N = 840$. Using: (a) FPM-KL and (b) FPM-BR algorithms. The normalised total volume of communication is 9 and 7.457. Total computation time was 192 sec and 166 sec respectively.

The presented experimental results demonstrate that by combining functional performance models with the BR algorithm we are able to achieve both optimisation goals, namely partitioning the workload in proportion to processor speed and reducing the total volume of communication. This algorithm also allows us to use the simpler one-dimensional models rather then the more complex 2D models to partition for the two-parameter matrix multiplication routine.

Acknowledgments. This publication has emanated from research conducted with the financial support of Science Foundation Ireland under Grant Number 08/IN.1/I2054. Experiments were carried out on Grid'5000 developed under the INRIA ALADDIN development action with support from CNRS, RENATER and several Universities as well as other funding bodies (see https://www.grid5000.fr). We are grateful to Arnaud Legrand who provided sample code for minimising the total volume of communication.

References

1. Beaumont, O., Boudet, V., Rastello, F., Robert, Y.: Matrix Multiplication on Heterogeneous Platforms. IEEE Trans. Parallel Distrib. Syst. 12(10), 1033–1051 (2001)
2. Blackford, L., Choi, J., Cleary, A., et al.: ScaLAPACK: A Portable Linear Algebra Library for Distributed Memory Computers - Design Issues and Performance. In: Supercomputing, p. 5. IEEE (1996)
3. Clarke, D., Lastovetsky, A., Rychkov, V.: Dynamic Load Balancing of Parallel Computational Iterative Routines on Highly Heterogeneous HPC Platforms. Parallel Process. Lett. 21(2), 195–217 (2011)
4. Dongarra, J., Pineau, J.F., Robert, Y., Vivien, F.: Matrix Product on Heterogeneous Master-Worker Platforms. In: PPoPP 2008, pp. 53–62. ACM (2008)
5. Goto, K., van de Geijn, R.A.: Anatomy of high-performance matrix multiplication. ACM Trans. Math. Softw. 34(3), 1–12 (2008)
6. Kalinov, A., Klimov, S.: Optimal Mapping of a Parallel Application Processes onto Heterogeneous Platform. In: Proceedings of 19th IEEE International Parallel and Distributed Processing Symposium, p. 123. IEEE (2005)
7. Kalinov, A., Lastovetsky, A.: Heterogeneous Distribution of Computations While Solving Linear Algebra Problems on Networks of Heterogeneous Computers. In: Sloot, P.M.A., Hoekstra, A.G., Bubak, M., Hertzberger, B. (eds.) HPCN-Europe 1999. LNCS, vol. 1593, pp. 191–200. Springer, Heidelberg (1999)
8. Lastovetsky, A., Reddy, R.: Data Partitioning with a Functional Performance Model of Heterogeneous Processors. Int. J. High Perform. Comput. Appl. 21(1), 76–90 (2007)
9. Lastovetsky, A., Reddy, R., Rychkov, V., Clarke, D.: Design and Implementation of Self-Adaptable Parallel Algorithms for Scientific Computing on Highly Heterogeneous HPC Platforms. [cs.DC] (2011), arXiv:1109.3074v1
10. Lastovetsky, A., Reddy, R.: Distributed Data Partitioning for Heterogeneous Processors Based on Partial Estimation of Their Functional Performance Models. In: Lin, H.-X., Alexander, M., Forsell, M., Knüpfer, A., Prodan, R., Sousa, L., Streit, A. (eds.) Euro-Par 2009. LNCS, vol. 6043, pp. 91–101. Springer, Heidelberg (2010)
11. Lastovetsky, A., Reddy, R.: Two-Dimensional Matrix Partitioning for Parallel Computing on Heterogeneous Processors Based on Their Functional Performance Models. In: Lin, H.-X., Alexander, M., Forsell, M., Knüpfer, A., Prodan, R., Sousa, L., Streit, A. (eds.) Euro-Par 2009. LNCS, vol. 6043, pp. 112–121. Springer, Heidelberg (2010)
12. Zhuo, L., Prasanna, V.K.: Optimizing Matrix Multiplication on Heterogeneous Reconfigurable Systems. In: PARCO 2007, pp. 561–568 (2007)

A Framework for Distributing Agent-Based Simulations

Gennaro Cordasco[2], Rosario De Chiara[1], Ada Mancuso[1], Dario Mazzeo[1],
Vittorio Scarano[1], and Carmine Spagnuolo[1]

[1] ISISLab - Dipartimento di Informatica, Università degli Studi di Salerno
84084 Fisciano (SA) - Italy
{dechiara,vitsca}@di.unisa.it
[2] Dipartimento di Psicologia, Seconda Università degli Studi di Napoli
81100 Caserta - Italy
gennaro.cordasco@unina2.it

Abstract. Agent-based simulation models are an increasingly popular tool for research and management in many, different and diverse fields. In executing such simulations the "speed" is one of the most general and important issues. The traditional answer to this issue is to invest resources in deploying a dedicated installation of dedicated computers. In this paper we present a framework that is a parallel version of the MASON, a library for writing and running Agent-based simulations.

Keywords: Agent-based simulation, Heterogeneous Computing, Distributed Systems , Load-Balancing.

1 Introduction

The traditional answer to the need for HPC is to invest resources in deploying a dedicated installation of dedicated computers. Such solution can provide the computing power surge needed for highly specialized customers. Nonetheless a large amount of computing power is available, unused, in common installations like educational laboratories, accountant department, library PCs.

In this paper we present the architecture and report the performances of D-MASON, a parallel version of the MASON [9] library for writing and running simulations of Agent-based simulation models (ABMs). D-MASON is designed to harness the amount of unused computing power available in the scenarios above described. The intent of D-MASON is to provide an effective and efficient way of parallelizing MASON programs: effective because with D-MASON *you can do more* than what you can do with MASON; efficient because in order to obtain this additional computing power the developer has to do some incremental modifications to the MASON applications he has already written without re-designing them.

As in Condor [17] the purpose of D-MASON is to "harness wasted CPU power from otherwise idle desktop workstations" and to let the developer to look at such PCs as a platform composed by heterogeneous machines and the subdivision of the work among these machines takes into account such heterogeneity.

ABMs are an increasingly popular tool for research and management in many, different and diverse fields such as biology, ecology, economics, political science, sociology, etc.. The computer science community has responded to the need for tools and

M. Alexander et al. (Eds.): Euro-Par 2011 Workshops, Part I, LNCS 7155, pp. 460–470, 2012.

platforms that can help the development and testing of new models in each specific field by providing tools, libraries and frameworks that speed up and make easier the task of (massive) simulations.

Agent-based simulation toolkits are described in [10]. An interesting comparison is presented in [2]. Another interesting tool is Repast [13] with some studies on distributing the workload in [4]. It must be said that, in literature, MASON is recognized as one of the most useful and interesting simulation toolkits.

1.1   A Distributed Framework for Simulations

Among the motivations to our focus on distributing the simulation on a cluster of (homogeneous) machines, we can underline how the need for efficiency among the Agent-Based modeling tools is well recognized in literature: many reviews of state-of-the-art frameworks [2,12,15] place "speed" upfront as one of the most general and important issues. While a consistent work has been done to allow the distribution of agents on several computing nodes (see for recent examples [11,14]), our approach here is to introduce the distribution at the framework level in order to let the user to transparently harness the additional computing power.

This approach allows to hide to the user the most of the details of the implementation and in this way D-MASON requires just a moderate number of modifications into the source code achieving a good backward-compatibility with pre-existing MASON applications.

Because of the very experimental nature of complex social simulations there is always the need for a viable and reliable infrastructure for running (and keeping the records of) several experiments together the entire test settings. The resources needed to run and store results of such amount of experimental runs can be cheaply ensured only by a cluster, since the nature of interactive experiments, led by the social scientists with their multidisciplinary team, requires interaction with the computing infrastructure, which is often extremely expensive and technically demanding to get from supercomputing centers (that may, in principle, provide massive homogeneous environment).

In this scenario, our goal is to offer to such scientists a setting where a traditional MASON program can be run on one desktop, first, but can immediately harness the power of other desktops in the same laboratory by using D-MASON, thereby providing scaling up the size they can handle or significantly reduce the time needed for each iteration. The scientist, then, is able to run extensive tests by enrolling the different machines available, maybe, during off-peak hour.

Of course, it means that the resulting distributed system, collecting hardware from research labs, administration offices, etc. is highly heterogeneous in nature and, then, the challenge is how to use efficiently all the hardware without an impact on the "legitimate" user (i.e., the owner of the desktop) both on performances and on installation/customization of the machine. On the other hand, we would like that the program in MASON should not be very different than the corresponding program in D-MASON so that the scientist can easily modify it to run over an increasing number of hosts.

The rationale: The design of D-MASON is inspired by the need for efficiency, in a setting where computing resources are scarce, heterogeneous, not centrally managed and that are used for other purposes during other periods of the workday. The compromises between efficiency and impact are reached with good results about performances, as witnessed by the tests we report, as well as the impact on the program in D-MASON is minimal, as described later in the paper.

2   MASON

MASON toolkit is a discrete-event simulation core and visualization library written in Java, designed to be used for a wide range of ABMs. The toolkit is written, using the standard Model-View-Controller (MVC) paradigm, in three layers: the *simulation* layer, the *visualization* layer and the *utility* layer. The simulation layer is the core of MASON and is mainly represented by an event scheduler and a variety of fields which hold agents into a given simulation space. MASON is mainly based on step-able agent: a computational entity which may be scheduled to perform some action (step), and which can interact (communicate) with other agents. The visualization layer permits both visualization and manipulation of the model. The simulation layer is independent from the visualization layer, which allows us to treat the model as a self-contained entity.

MASON was written with the aim of creating a flexible and efficient ABM which assures the complete reproducibility of results across heterogeneous hardware. This reproducibility feature is considered as a priority for long simulations (it allows to stop a simulation and move it among computers).

We decided to work on a distributed version of MASON for several reasons: MASON is one of the most expressive and efficient (as reported by many reviews [2,12,15]); MASON structure clearly separates visualization by simulation, making it particularly well suited to the re-engineering into a distributed "shape" of the framework. Another reason is the significant amount of research and simulations already present in the framework, which makes it particularly cost effective for the social scientist. The programmer is asked to use the new distributed version of some classes to transparently transform its already written simulation to a distributed simulation (e.g. extend `DistributedState` instead of `SimState`).

3   D-MASON: Distributed MASON

In the following we view ABMs as step-wise computations; i.e., agents behavior is computed in successive steps named *simulation step*. D-MASON is based on a master/workers paradigm (see Fig. 1): the master assigns a portion of the whole computation (i.e., a set of agents) to each worker. Then for each simulation step, each worker simulates the agents assigned and sends back the result of its computation to each interested worker.

Before presenting the architecture of D-MASON, in the next subsection will present the problems we faced in developing our distributed architecture.

3.1   Issues in D-MASON

Field partitioning. The problem of decomposing a program to a set of heterogeneous processors (workers) has been extensively studied (see [8] for a comprehensive presentation). In the case of ABMs a simple way to partition the whole work into different tasks is to assign a fixed number of agents (proportional to the power of the worker) to each available worker. This approach named agents partitioning allows a balanced workload but introduce a significant communication overhead (since, at each step, agents can interact-with/manipulate other agents, an all–to–all communication is required). By noticing that most ABMs are inspired by natural models, where agents limited visibility allow to bound the range of interaction to a fixed range named agent's Area of Interest (AOI), several space partitioning approaches have been proposed [5,18,19] in order to reduce the communication overhead. In D-MASON, the space to be simulated (D-MASON field) is partitioned into regions. Each region, together with the agents contained are assigned to a worker. Since the AOI radius of an agent is small compared with the size of a region, the communication is limited to local messages (messages between workers, managing neighboring spaces, etc.).

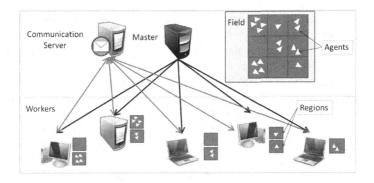

Fig. 1. D-MASON functional blocks

Synchronization. In order to guarantee the consistency of parallel implementation with respect to the sequential one, each worker needs to collect information about the neighboring regions. Each simulation step is formed by two phases: *communication/ synchronization* and *simulation*. First of all the worker sends to its neighbors (i.e., the workers responsible for its neighbor regions) the information about the agents that: are migrating to them; or may fall into the AOI of their agents. This information exchange is locally synchronized in order to let the simulation run consistently. We use a standard approach to achieve a consistent local synchronization of the distributed simulations. Each step is associated with a fixed state of the simulation. Regions are simulated step by step. Since the step i of region r is computed by using the states $i-1$ of r's neighborhood, the step i of a region cannot be executed until the states $i-1$ of its neighborhood have been computed and delivered. In other words, each region is synchronized with its neighborhood before each simulation phase.

Communication. D-MASON uses a well-known mechanism, based on the publish–subscribe design pattern, to propagate agents state information: a multicast channel is assigned to each region; users then simply subscribe to the channels associated with the regions which overlap with their AOI to receive relevant message updates. The current version of D-MASON uses Java Message Service (JMS) for communication between workers. We use a special machine that run an Apache ActiveMQ Server [1] and acts as a JMS provider (i.e., it allows to generate and manage multicast channels and route messages accordingly). D-MASON however, is designed to be used with any Message Oriented Middleware that implements the publish–subscribe pattern. By providing a mapping between the abstract D-MASON's mechanism and the concrete implementation, it is possible, for instance, to use Scribe [3], a fully decentralized application-layer multicast built on top of the DHT Pastry [6]. Of course, also other simpler communication protocols can be used (such as sockets, Remote Method Invocation, etc.) but the effort of the programmer will be more consistent, since a mapping between a semantically rich paradigm, such as the publish–subscribe, and a simpler communication mechanism (stream, remote invocations, etc.) is needed.

Reproducibility. In order to guarantee an easy parallelization and to assure the reproducibility of results, paramount objective of the research areas interested in the ABMs, it is important to design the simulation is such a way that agents evolves simultaneously. Said in other words, during each simulation step, each agent computes its state at step i based on the state of its neighbors at step $i-1$. Thereafter all the agents updates their state simultaneously. Using this approach the simulation become embarrassingly parallelizable (there are no dependencies between agents' state), each simulation step can be executed in parallel overall the agents. Moreover, using this approach the order in which agents are scheduled does not affect the reproducibility of results[1].

Heterogeneity. D-MASON uses a simple but efficient technique to cope with heterogeneity. The idea is to clone the software run by high capable workers so that they could serve as multiple workers; i.e., a worker that is x times more powerful than other workers could execute x virtual workers (that is, simulating, concurrently, x regions).

3.2 Architecture

D-MASON adds a new layer named *D-simulation* which extends the MASON simulation layer. The new layer adds some features to the simulation layer that allows the distribution of the simulation work on multiple, even heterogeneous, machines. Notice that the new layer does not alter in any way the existing layers. Moreover, it has been designed so as to enable the porting of existing applications on distributed platforms in a transparent and easy way.

D-MASON architecture is divided into three functional blocks: *Management,Workers* and *Communication* (see Fig. 1). The Management layer provides a master application which will be used for coordinating the workers, handle the bootstrap and running the simulation. The master is responsible for partitioning the field into regions and assigning them to workers. Currently in D-MASON there are two types of field partitioning:

---

[1] Some simulations, especially those that evolve using a randomized approach, still require a mechanism that allows to schedule agents always in the same order, to obtain the reproducibility of results.

horizontal, where the division is done by splitting the field along one axis and square, where the division is done by using a grid. When all the parameter are set it is possible to start and interact with the entire distributed simulation (e.g. play, pause, stop). The workers are in charge of: simulating the agents that belongs to the assigned regions; handling the migration of agents; managing the synchronization between neighboring regions. Workers communicate by using the communication layer which provides a publish–subscribe mechanism.

D-MASON is available at http://www.isislab.it/projects/dmason/.

4   Testing

We performed a number of tests of D-MASON in order to assess both its ability to run simulations that are impractical or impossible to execute on a single computer (e.g., for CPU or memory requirements), its scalability and its effectiveness on exploiting heterogeneous hardware.

Setting of the Experiments. Simulations were conducted on a scenario consisting of five different type of hosts/workers described in the following table.

	P4	Xeon	Opt	i5	i7
CPU	1 x P4 3.4GHz	2 x Xeon 2.67GHz	2 x Opteron 1.9 MHz	1 x dual core i5 2.53 MHz	1 x quad core i7 2.53 MHz
RAM	2GB	3GB	4GB	4GB	8GB

The DFlockers testbed. We have performed our tests on *DFlockers* (see Fig. 2 right) by considering more than 50 different test settings. *DFlockers* is the distributed version of *Flockers* (see Fig. 2 left) which implements the *boid model* [16]. In the *boid model* each agent, named *boids* (from *birdoid*), gets instilled a range of *behaviors*. The behaviors are, in the most of cases, simply geometric calculations that every boid makes, considering the nearest boids it is flying with: for example the behavior called *pursuit* just let the boid to pursuit a moving target (e.g. another boid). Boids react to their neighbors so they must be able to identify them by filtering nearby boids out of the whole population. The brute force approach to this filtering consists in a $O(n^2)$ proximity screening and for this reason the efficiency of the implementation is yet to be considered an issue.

The boid model is designed for the aggregate motion of a simulated flock of boids as the result of the interactions of the relatively simple behaviors but, for the purposes of the test, this simulation reproduces common problems that must be taken into account in every other simulation: the search for nearest neighbors and a phase during which each agents updates its state. In the following we will use *Flockers* to indicate the MASON version of the simulation and with *DFlockers* we will indicate its D-MASON version.

Each test setting is characterized by the choice of the following parameter: number of agents (the size of the field is updated accordinglyin order to maintain a fixed density); regions-workers configuration, which establishes: the granularity of the field decomposition (i.e., the number of regions), the number of workers and the association between regions and workers.

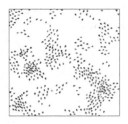 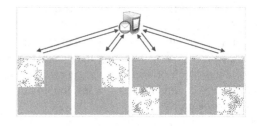

Fig. 2. (left) The *Flockers* testbed application. (right) *DFlockers* with 4 regions.

The configuration of each run of the test is represented by k couples (type of host, # of regions), where k is the number of hosts. For instance, the configuration $\{(\mathbf{P4}, 1), (\mathbf{Xeon}, 2), (\mathbf{Opt}, 2), (\mathbf{i7}, 4), (\mathbf{i7}, 16)\}$ denotes a simulation run with $k = 5$ hosts (a **P4** simulating one region, a **Xeon** simulating two regions, an **Opt** simulating two regions and two **i7** simulating respectively 4 and 16 regions). Overall the field decomposition comprises $1 + 2 + 2 + 4 + 16 = 25$ regions.

In the following tests, each region is simulated by using a dedicated Java Virtual Machine (JVM). D-MASON also allows to simulate several regions on the same JVM by using different threads but the use of this approach requires tuning *each* virtual machine by increasing the amount of heap space accordingly to the number of regions simulated: this would be too burdensome to the heterogeneous setting we are envisioning, where we would like the users of PCs involved only marginally in the configurations. For sake of conciseness we opted for a one-JVM-one-region assignment since this represents also the worst-case for D-MASON (e.g. the overhead of the JVM is paid for each region, even on the same host). This decision also allowed us to uniquely indicate with JDK 1.6.0 update 25 the configuration of the JVM.

The communication is managed by a dedicated host running Apache ActiveMQ Server. Master, Workers and the Communication Server are connected using a standard 100Mbit LAN network (see Fig. 1). Each run is composed by 100 simulation steps and we used the average of each step running time, in our comparisons while the variance of such values was not significant.

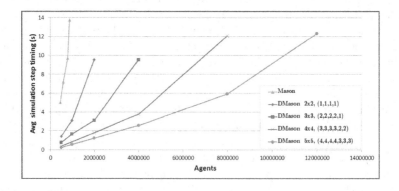

Fig. 3. D-MASON performances

4.1 Beyond MASON Limits

We first tested the limits of *Flockers* on MASON and we found that it is not possible to simulate more than $900{,}000$ agents. Moreover, using our best host (i.e., the **i7**), the simulation with $900{,}000$ agents took about 12 seconds for each simulation step. The purpose of this test is to show that the limits of MASON can easily be overcome by using a small number of workers. We performed a set of simulations with D-MASON on up to 7 homogeneous (**i7**) hosts (see Fig. 3). Results show that: (1) D-MASON is able to simulate far more agents than MASON does. The configuration $\{(\mathbf{i7}, 4), (\mathbf{i7}, 4), (\mathbf{i7}, 4), (\mathbf{i7}, 4), (\mathbf{i7}, 3), (\mathbf{i7}, 3), (\mathbf{i7}, 3)\}$ allows to run a *DFlockers* simulation with $12{,}000{,}000$ agents and an average simulation step timing around 12 seconds; (2) D-MASON scales pretty well, using a fine grained field partitioning, as the number of workers increases we are able to increase D-MASON performances.

We have also analyzed the workload of the communication layer in order to check whether it may represent a bottleneck for the whole system performances. Clearly, we discovered that the communication cost of simulations increases proportionally to the number of regions used. However, our tests report that the workload on the communication server was always reasonably low and, therefore, it would be possible to further increase the granularity of partitioning and thus improve both the degree of parallelism, and load balancing.

4.2 Exploiting Heterogeneity

We performed another test with the aim of assessing D-MASON capability on exploiting heterogeneous platforms. Since the simulation is locally synchronized after each step, the application advances with the same speed provided by the slower worker/region in the system. For this reason it is necessary to configure the system in order to balance the load between the workers. In this test the field partitioning is always 5×5 square (25 regions), while we tested seven different configurations with five hosts and two values of the number of agents ($3{,}000{,}000$ and $5{,}000{,}000$). We decided to use very different hosts with the aim of showing that by adding a set of few old (usually unused) machines to a very powerful machine, one can measure sensibly improved performances (see Fig. 4). We will shortly discuss each of the bar in the figure: (a) D-MASON performances using only one **i7** machine; (b, c) by assigning regions to workers proportionally to each worker computational capability, it is possible to significantly improve performances; (d, e) gave the best performance with both $3{,}000{,}000$ (improvement 24%) and $5{,}000{,}000$ (improvement 28%) of agents; (f) reveals that one of the slowest machines has reached its limits and this badly reflects on overall simulation speed; (g) is the worst case in which the distribution of the region is uniform among machines, the slowest machines slow down the simulation while the fastest machines waste time waiting for synchronization.

The higher is the granularity of the partitioning, the better is the balancing that can be achieved. For instance, running the same simulation with a coarser granularity (e.g., 3×3 partition) would not allow to exploit the computational power of slower machines (each region is too computationally expensive for such machines).

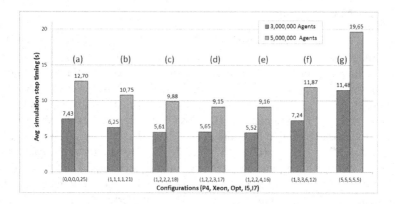

Fig. 4. D-MASON on a heterogeneous system. Seven different configurations are compared on *DFlockers* with $3,000,000$ and $5,000,000$ agents.

4.3   Fixed Timing Analysis

Iso-timing tests are justified by the need of having an interactive tool that allows faster development, debug and analysis of complex simulations. We intend to measure the maximum number of agents at a fixed simulation step pace of one step per second. The test is designed to measure this value on up to 7 homogeneous (**i7**) hosts while the field partitioning is always 5×5 square (25 regions). Regions are distributed uniformly among hosts. Then for each $h \in \{1, 2, 3, 4, 5, 6, 7\}$ we designed a set of simulations with h hosts. With each simulation we iteratively increased the number of agents until the average simulation step duration under 1 second. Under the conditions above in Fig. 5 we represent the performances of D-MASON.

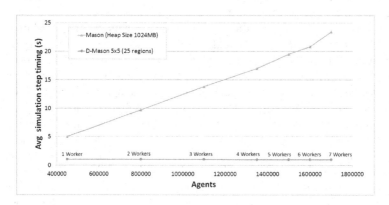

Fig. 5. Isotiming Analysis

In order to have a comparison for these results, we have performed a similar test on MASON. We used the same host (**i7**) and we increased the heap size of the JVM to 1024MB to let the machine to accommodate the increasing number of agents up to $1,700,000$. Obviously the performances of MASON fall down dramatically as along as the number of agents increase. In the slowest configuration the average step completion time was around 25 seconds while, on 7 hosts D-MASON is 24 times faster. While this may reveal a superlinear speed up it is worth noting that each of the i7 machines has a quad-core CPU. Of course D-MASON has been designed to exploit such configurations whose increasing presence seems to be a clear trend in the next years.

5   Conclusion and Future Work

D-MASON is a distributed version of MASON. MASON is a quite widespread framework for ABMs. Commonly to many kind of simulations, ABMs are CPU intensive applications and requires large amount of memory: these two characteristics put some limitations on the number and the complexity of the simulated agents. On the other hand the need for more complex simulations involving a large number of agents is always felt by researchers and practitioners. The rationale of developing D-MASON is to tackle this problem by providing a solution that does not require the user to rewrite his simulations and, nonetheless, pushing the limits of the maximum number of agents. This result is achieved by harvesting the unused CPU power usually largely available in installations like laboratories and by letting the computational work to be distributed among machines by addressing heterogeneity.

This paper reports on an currently undergoing project, and several issues are going to be tackled in the future. About the architectural level, first of all, we will further refine and try to optimize the thread-based version of D-MASON (i.e., when each region is a separate thread and not a separate JVM) by optimizing the thread management and providing short circuit of communication among regions on the same worker. This should further improve the already good results on performances. Then, we are planning to tackle load balancing issues by, first, allowing regions to migrate from particularly loaded workers to unloaded ones, and, then, modify the size and (possibly) the shape of regions on-the-fly.

About the simulation library, we are currently tackling other fields, since different categories (such as 3D, graph-based, etc.) do require suitably tailored approaches for the partitioning in regions. A long-term objective is also an improved management of parallelism, with distributed visualization and monitoring workers.

Finally, the project will be soon released under a Free and Open Software license.

References

1. Apache ActiveMQ, http://activemq.apache.org/
2. Berryman, M.: Review of Software Platforms for Agent Based Models. Technical Report DSTO-GD-0532, Australian Government, Department of Defence (2008)
3. Castro, M., Druschel, P., Kermarrec, A.-M., Rowstron, A.: SCRIBE: A large-scale and decentralized application-level multicast infrastructure. IEEE Journal on Selected Areas in Communications (JSAC) 20, 100–110 (2002)
4. Cicirelli, F., Furfaro, A., Giordano, A., Nigro, L.: Distributed Simulation of RePast Models over HLA/Actors. In: Proceedings of the 2009 13th IEEE/ACM International Symposium on Distributed Simulation and Real Time Applications, DS-RT 2009, pp. 184–191. IEEE Computer Society, Washington, DC (2009)

5. Cosenza, B., Cordasco, G., De Chiara, R., Scarano, V.: Distributed load balancing for parallel agent-based simulations. In: Proc. of the 19th Euromicro Inter. Conf. on Parallel, Distributed and Network-Based Computing, PDP 2011 (2011)
6. Druschel, P., Rowstron, A.: Pastry: Scalable, Decentralized Object Location, and Routing for Large-Scale Peer-to-Peer Systems. In: Proc. of the 18th IFIP/ACM Inter. Conference on Distributed Systems Platforms (Middleware 20), pp. 329–350 (November 2001)
7. Epstein, J.M.: Generative Social Science: Studies in Agent-Based Computational Modeling. Princeton University Press (2007)
8. Hwang, K., Xu, Z.: Scalable Parallel Computing: Technology, Architecture, Programming. McGraw-Hill (1998)
9. Luke, S., Balan, G.C., Panait, L., Cioffi-Revilla, C., Paus, S.: MASON: A Java Multi-Agent Simulation Library. In: Proceedings of the Agent 2003 Conference, Chicago, IL, October 2 - October 4 (2003)
10. Macal, C.M., North, M.J.: Tutorial on agent-based modeling and simulation part 2: how to model with agents. In: Proceedings of the 38th Conference on Winter Simulation, WSC 2006, pp. 73–83 (2006)
11. Mengistu, D., Troger, P., Lundberg, L., Davidsson, P.: Scalability in Distributed Multi-Agent Based Simulations: The JADE Case. In: Proc. Second Int. Conf. Future Generation Communication and Networking Symposia FGCNS 2008, vol. 5, pp. 93–99 (2008)
12. Najlis, R., Janssen, M.A., Parkerx, D.C.: Software tools and communication issues. In: Parker, D.C., Berger, T., Manson, S.M. (eds.) Proc. Agent-Based Models of Land-Use and Land-Cover Change Workshop, pp. 17–30 (2001)
13. North, M.J., Collier, N.T., Vos, J.R.: Experiences creating three implementations of the Repast agent modeling toolkit. ACM Trans. Model. Comput. Simul. 16, 1–25 (2006)
14. Pawlaszczyk, D., Strassburger, S.: Scalability in distributed simulations of agent-based models. In: Proc. Winter Simulation Conf. (WSC) the 2009, pp. 1189–1200 (2009)
15. Railsback, S.F., Lytinen, S.L., Jackson, S.K.: Agent-based simulation platforms: Review and development recommendations. Simulation 82, 609–623 (2006)
16. Reynolds, C.: Steering behaviors for autonomous characters (1999)
17. Thain, D., Tannenbaum, T., Livny, M.: Distributed computing in practice: the Condor experience. Concurr. Comput.: Pract. Exper. 17, 323–356 (2005)
18. Zhang, Y., Mueller, F., Cui, X., Potok, T.: Large-Scale Multi-Dimensional Document Clustering on GPU Clusters. In: IEEE International Parallel and Distributed Processing Symposium (2010)
19. Zhou, B., Zhou, S.: Parallel simulation of group behaviors. In: WSC 2004: Proceedings of the 36th Conference on Winter Simulation, pp. 364–370 (2004)

Parallel Sparse Linear Solver GMRES for GPU Clusters with Compression of Exchanged Data[*]

Jacques M. Bahi, Raphaël Couturier, and Lilia Ziane Khodja

University of Franche-Comte, LIFC laboratory,
Rue Engel-Gros, BP 527, 90016 Belfort Cedex, France
{jacques.bahi,raphael.couturier,lilia.ziane_khodja}@univ-fcomte.fr

Abstract. GPU clusters have become attractive parallel platforms for high performance computing due to their ability to compute faster than the CPU clusters. We use this architecture to accelerate the mathematical operations of the GMRES method for solving large sparse linear systems. However the parallel sparse matrix-vector product of GMRES causes overheads in CPU/CPU and GPU/CPU communications when exchanging large shared vectors of unknowns between GPUs of the cluster. Since a sparse matrix-vector product does not often need all the unknowns of the vector, we propose to use data compression and decompression operations on the shared vectors, in order to exchange only the needed unknowns. In this paper we present a new parallel GMRES algorithm for GPU clusters, using compression vectors. Our experimental results show that the GMRES solver is more efficient when using the data compression technique on large shared vectors.

Keywords: GMRES, GPU cluster, CUDA, MPI, data compression.

1 Introduction

Iterative linear solvers are often more suited than direct ones for solving large sparse linear systems. In fact, an iterative method computes a sequence of approximate solutions converging to the exact solution. In contrast, a direct method determines the exact solution after a finite number of operations which may lead to an expensive consumption in both computation time and memory space, and thus, it is not very well suited for large linear systems. GMRES (Generalized Minimal REsidual method) is one of the most widly used iterative solvers chosen to deal with the sparsity and the large order of linear systems. It was initially developed by Saad and al. [1] to deal with nonsymmetric and non-Hermitian problems, and indefinite symmetric problems too. The convergence of the restarted GMRES with preconditioning is faster and more stable than those of some other iterative solvers. Furthermore, the GMRES algorithm is mainly based on mathematical matrix/vector operations that are easily parallelizable, and therefore, they allow us to exploit the computing power of parallel platforms.

---

[*] This work was supported by Région de Franche-Comté.

M. Alexander et al. (Eds.): Euro-Par 2011 Workshops, Part I, LNCS 7155, pp. 471–480, 2012.
© Springer-Verlag Berlin Heidelberg 2012

For the past few years, GPUs (Graphic Processing Units) have proved their ability to provide better performance than CPUs for many parallel applications, including solving linear systems [2]. They have become high performance accelerators for data-parallel tasks and intensive arithmetic computations. Therefore, several works have proposed the efficient GMRES algorithms using the computing power of GPUs [3][4].

Nowadays, the parallel platforms exploiting the high performances of this architecture are GPU clusters. They are very attractive for high performance computing, given their low cost compared to their computational power and their abilities to compute faster and to consume less energy than their pure CPU counterparts [5].

We have already used GPU clusters to accelerate numerical computations of GMRES method for solving large sparse linear systems [6]. We have tested our parallel GMRES solver on linear systems with banded sparse matrices. We have noticed that GPU clusters are less efficient in case of large matrix bandwidths. Indeed a matrix bandwidth defines the size of the shared vectors that must be exchanged between GPUs in order to perform the full matrix-vector products of the GMRES method. So a large matrix bandwidth leads to the transfer of large vectors between a CPU core and its GPU, whereas a GPU/CPU data transfer is the slowest communication in GPU cluster and it affects greatly the performances of sparse linear system solutions.

In this paper, we propose a new parallel GMRES solver with some improvements to reduce the communication overheads. We use the *compression* and the *decompression* operations on the shared vectors. This technique has already used to speed-up the data transfers between the computing nodes of a cluster. In [7], the author has proposed a dynamic algorithm with the compression/communication overlap which is suited for any data transfer whatever the speed of the network. In our case, this technique allows a GPU to communicate only the shared unknowns required by other GPUs to its CPU core. This paper is organized as follows. In section 2 a general overview of the GPU architecture is given. In section 3 the main key points of our improved parallel GMRES solver for GPU clusters are presented. Section 4 is devoted to the performance evaluation of our solver. Section 5 concludes this paper.

2   GPU Architecture

A GPU architecture is composed of hundreds of processors organized in several streaming multiprocessors. It is also equipped with a memory hierarchy. It has a private read-write *local memory* per processor, a fast *shared memory* and read-only *constant* and *texture* caches per multiprocessor, and a read-write *global memory* shared by all its processors. To exploit the computing power of this architecture, Nvidia has released the CUDA programming language (Compute Unified Device Architecture) [8] allowing us to program GPUs for general purpose computations of graphic and non-graphic applications. In CUDA programming environment, the GPU is viewed as a co-processor to the CPU. All data-parallel operations of a CUDA application running on the CPU are off-loaded onto the GPU. CUDA is C programming language with a minimal set of extensions to define the parallel functions to be executed by the GPU as *kernels*.

At the GPU level, the same kernel is executed by a high number of parallel CUDA threads grouped together as a grid of thread blocks. Each multiprocessor of the GPU executes one or more thread blocks in SIMD fashion (Single Instruction, Multiple Data) and in turn each processor of a GPU multiprocessor runs one or more threads within a block in SIMT fashion (Single Instruction, Multiple threads). In order to avoid the execution dependencies between thread blocks, the number of CUDA threads involved in a kernel execution is computed according to the size of the problem to be solved. In contrast, the block size is restricted by the limited memory resources of a processor. On current GPUs, a thread block may contain up to 1024 concurrent threads.

GPUs only work on data filled in their global memories and the final results of their kernel executions must be communicated to their hosts (CPUs). Hence, the data must be transferred *in* and *out* of the GPU. However, the speed of memory copy between the GPU and the CPU is slower than the memory copy speed of the GPUs. Accordingly, it is necessary to limit data transfers between the GPU and its host during the computations.

3   GMRES Implementation on GPU Clusters

3.1   Parallel GMRES Algorithm for GPU Clusters

Algorithm 1 shows the key points of the parallel GMRES algorithm for GPU clusters that we developed in our previous work [6]. It must be executed in parallel by each pair (CPU core, GPU) of the cluster, such that each CPU core holds one MPI process managing one GPU. GMRES is mainly based on matrix/vector operations: sparse matrix-vector products denoted in Algorithm 1 by $SpMV()$, dot products (line 15), scalar-vector products (lines 8 and 19), Euclidean norms (lines 7, 18 and 27) and AXPI operations (line 16). All parallel and mathematical functions inside the main loop of GMRES are executed as kernels by the GPU. The superscripts *local* and *shared* over solution vector x and vector v respectively denote the local vector and the shared vectors with neighbor processes, required to perform full sparse matrix-vector products.

Besides these local computations, synchronizations between GPUs must be performed to ensure the solving of the complete sparse linear system. Before computing an $SpMV$ product, it is mandatory to construct the global vector x (or v_j) required for the full product. First each GPU copies the entries of vector x^{local} (resp. v_j^{local}) to its host vector h_tmp^{local} (lines 3, 10 and 24), then all MPI processes in the cluster exchange their shared entries of vector h_tmp^{local} (lines 4, 11 and 25) using an $MPI\_Alltoallv()$ function and, finally each MPI process copies entries of the computed shared vector h_tmp^{shared} to its GPU vector x^{shared} (resp. v_j^{shared}) (lines 5, 12 and 26). After each vector operation, as Euclidean norms and dot products, the MPI processes must perform a reduction operation on local scalars computed by their GPUs, by using

---

Algorithm 1. Left-Preconditioned GMRES with Restarts for GPU Clusters

---

1: Set ε the tolerance for the residual norm r, $convergence = false$ and x_0
2: **while** $!convergence$ **do**
3:    $gpu\_to\_cpu(x_0^{local}, h\_tmp^{local})$
4:    $\boldsymbol{DataExchange}(h\_tmp^{local}, h\_tmp^{shared})$
5:    $cpu\_to\_gpu(h\_tmp^{shared}, x_0^{shared})$
6:    $r_0 \leftarrow M^{-1} \times (b - SpMV(A, x_0^{local}, x_0^{shared}))$
7:    $\beta \leftarrow \|r_0\|_2$
8:    $v_1 \leftarrow r_0 / \boldsymbol{Sqrt}(\boldsymbol{AllReduceSum}(\beta^2))$
9:    **for** $j = 1$ to m **do**
10:      $gpu\_to\_cpu(v_j^{local}, h\_tmp^{local})$
11:      $\boldsymbol{DataExchange}(h\_tmp^{local}, h\_tmp^{shared})$
12:      $cpu\_to\_gpu(h\_tmp^{shared}, v_j^{shared})$
13:      $w_j \leftarrow M^{-1} \times SpMV(A, v_j^{local}, v_j^{shared}))$
14:      **for** $i = 1$ to j **do**
15:        $h_{i,j} \leftarrow (w_j, v_i^{local})$
16:        $w_j \leftarrow w_j - \boldsymbol{AllReduceSum}(h_{i,j}) \cdot v_i^{local}$
17:      **end for**
18:      $h_{j+1,j} \leftarrow \|w_j\|_2$
19:      $v_{j+1}^{local} \leftarrow w_j / \boldsymbol{Sqrt}(\boldsymbol{AllReduceSum}(h_{j+1,j}^2))$
20:    **end for**
21:    Set $V_m = \left[v_1^{local}, \ldots, v_m^{local}\right]$ and $\bar{H}_m = (h_{i,j})$
22:    Solve: $min_{y \in \mathbb{R}^m} \|\beta e_1 - \bar{H}_m y\|_2$
23:    $x_m^{local} \leftarrow x_0^{local} + V_m y_m$
24:    $gpu\_to\_cpu(x_m^{local}, h\_tmp^{local})$
25:    $\boldsymbol{DataExchange}(h\_tmp^{local}, h\_tmp^{shared})$
26:    $cpu\_to\_gpu(h\_tmp^{shared}, x_m^{shared})$
27:    $\delta \leftarrow \|M^{-1} \times (b - SpMV(A, x_m^{local}, x_m^{shared}))\|_2$
28:    **if** $\boldsymbol{Sqrt}(\boldsymbol{AllReduceSum}(\delta^2)) < \varepsilon$ **then**
29:      $convergence \leftarrow true$
30:    **end if**
31:    $x_0^{local} \leftarrow x_m^{local}$
32: **end while**

$MPI\_Allreduce()$ function. In Algorithm 1, the function calls written with bold fonts denote the functions to be executed by the MPI process. $\boldsymbol{DataExchange}()$ denotes the $MPI\_Alltoallv()$ function to build the global vectors, $\boldsymbol{AllReduceSum}()$ denotes the $MPI\_Allreduce()$ function using the summation operation and, $\boldsymbol{Sqrt}()$ denotes the square root operation. For more details about our parallel GMRES algorithm, please refer to [6].

3.2 Minimizing Communication Overheads

As we can see from Algorithm 1, our parallel GMRES solver requires data transfers between the different components of the GPU cluster. Indeed before any computing of the $SpMV$ product, we must construct the global vector of unknowns x required for this operation by using the following data transfers:

(1) a memory copy of the local vector from the GPU memory to the host memory, (2) a data exchange of the shared vectors between all MPI processes and, (3) a memory copy of the shared vector from the host memory to the GPU memory.

However, as we mentioned in Section 2, data transfers *from* or *to* the GPU memory are the slowest communications in a GPU cluster. Hence, the GPU/CPU data transfers of large local and/or shared vectors can dramatically reduce the performances of solving sparse linear systems. Nevertheless the sparse matrix-vector products do not often need all the values of the shared vector. So in order to reduce the GPU/CPU and CPU/CPU communication overheads, we propose to perform *compression* and *decompression* operations on the shared vectors of unknowns.

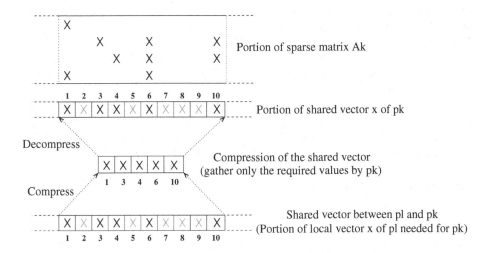

Fig. 1. Compression/decompression of shared vector x between processes p_k and p_l

After the data partitioning, each process p_k sends to its neighbors the indices of global vector of unknowns x_k needed for its full *SpMV* products. As shown in Figure 1, process p_k needs unknowns corresponding to indices 1, 3, 4, 6 and 10 in the local vector of process p_l. So before the GPU→CPU data transfer of local vector x_l^{local}, neighbor process p_l uses these indices (1, 3, 4, 6 and 10) to *compress* x_l^{local}. The *compression* operation allows process p_l to build a small shared vector x^{comp} from its local vector x_l^{local}, consisting of only the shared unknowns needed by process p_k (vector elements drawn with bold fonts X). The CPU↔CPU data exchanges of these shared compressed vectors must be performed between all processes on the cluster. Once the GPU←CPU data transfer of vector x^{comp} is held, process p_k *decompresses* shared vector x^{comp} received from its neighbor p_l such that each value of x^{comp} is copied to the corresponding index of its shared vector x_k^{shared}.

In order to accelerate the computations, the compression/decompression operations must be performed by GPUs. We developed in CUDA two kernels to compress and decompress the exchanged shared vectors of unknowns before *gpu_to_cpu*() and after *cpu_to_gpu*() communications. These operations allow the transfer of small vectors between the MPI processes and between an MPI process and its GPU. Hence they minimize the GPU/CPU and CPU/CPU communication overheads.

4   Performance Evaluation

4.1   Our GPU Cluster

Our GPU cluster is an Infiniband cluster having six Xeon E5530 CPUs. Each CPU is a Quad-Core processor running at 2.4GHz. It provides a RAM memory of 12GB with a memory bandwidth of 25.6GB/s, and it is equipped with two Nvidia Tesla C1060 GPUs. In turn, each GPU contains in total 240 processors running at 1.3GHz. It provides 4GB of global memory with a memory bandwidth of 102GB/s, accessible by all its processors and also by the CPU through the PCI-Express 16x Gen 2.0 interface with a throughput of 8GB/s. Hence, the memory copy operations between the GPU and the CPU is about 12 times slower than those of the Tesla GPU memory.

Linux cluster version 2.6.18 OS is installed on CPUs. C programming language is used for coding the GMRES algorithm on both GPU cluster and CPU cluster. CUDA version 3.1.1 [8] is used for programming GPUs, using CUBLAS 3.1 [9] to deal with vector operations and CUSP library [10] to perform a HYB SpMV product in GPUs, and finally MPI functions of OpenMPI 1.3.3 are used to carry out communications between CPU cores.

4.2   Sparse Matrices of Tests

We chose to work on linear systems having banded sparse matrices, since they arise in many numerical computations, and large sizes exceeding 10 million of unknowns. For that, we developed in C a generator of large sparse matrices which takes one real matrix of the Davis collection [11] as an initial matrix to build large banded matrices. This generator must be executed in parallel by all MPI processes before starting the resolution of the linear system.

In addition to the matrix generation, the generator performs the data partitioning of the generated matrix among all pairs of (MPI process, GPU). According to the desired matrix size n of the sparse linear system and the number of the pairs (MPI process, GPU) p in the cluster, each MPI process k computes the size of its sub-matrix $sizeloc_k$ and its $offset_k$ in the global generated matrix, such that:

$$sizeloc_k = \frac{n}{p}. \tag{1}$$

$$offset_k = \begin{cases} 0 & \text{if } k = 0 \\ offset_{k-1} + sizeloc_{k-1} & \text{otherwise} \end{cases} \tag{2}$$

The offsets and the sizes of the sub-matrices on the cluster allow a process to determine which processes own the needed unknown values.

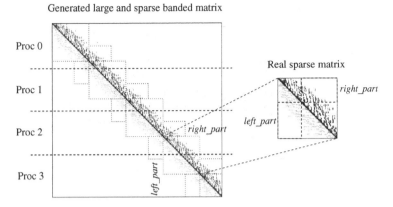

Fig. 2. A large sparse banded matrix generated by four processes from a real matrix of the Davis collection

After that, each MPI process k builds its sub-matrix of size $sizeloc_k$ by performing several copies of the same real matrix of the Davis collection. And all generated sub-matrices in the cluster construct the global sparse matrix of the linear system. In order to generate banded matrices, each MPI process places its copies on its part of the main diagonal of the global matrix as shown in Figure 2. Furthermore, the empty spaces between two consecutive copies on the main diagonal are fulfilled by sub-copies *right_part* and *left_part* of the same initial real matrix.

4.3   Experimental Results

The performance evaluation of our GMRES solver is made in double precision data. All experimental results obtained from our tests are for a residual tolerance threshold $\varepsilon = 10^{-10}$, a restart limit of GMRES method $m = 16$, a right-hand side b filled with 1 and an initial guess x_0 filled with 12. For the sake of simplicity, we took the preconditioning matrix M as the main diagonal of the sparse matrix A of the linear system. Indeed it allows us to easily compute the required inverse matrix M^{-1} and it provides a relatively good preconditioning in most cases.

Table 1 shows the main characteristics of the banded sparse matrices on which we performed our tests. First column gives the type of test matrices: *symmetric* or *unsymmetric*. In the second column, we have the set of real sparse matrices chosen in the Davis collection and from which we generated our sparse matrices of tests. All sparse linear systems solved in our tests are of size 90 million of unknowns. The fourth and fifth columns show respectively the number of nonzero values and the bandwidth of the generated matrices of tests.

In our tests, we compared the performances of the parallel GMRES solver implemented on a cluster of 12 GPUs with those obtained on cluster of 12 CPU cores and those obtained on a cluster of 24 CPU cores. Tables 2 and 3 report respectively the performances of the GMRES solver *without* and *with* the data

Table 1. The main characteristics of the generated sparse banded matrices of tests

Matrix type	Real matrix	Nb. rows	Nb. nonzeros	Bandwidth
Symmetric	ecology2	$90 \cdot 10^6$	449,729,174	1,002
	finan512	$90 \cdot 10^6$	915,824,547	106,017
	G3_circuit	$90 \cdot 10^6$	443,429,071	525,429
	shallow_water2	$90 \cdot 10^6$	360,751,026	23,212
	thermal2	$90 \cdot 10^6$	643,458,527	1,928,223
Unsymmetric	cage14	$90 \cdot 10^6$	1,674,718,790	1,266,626
	language	$90 \cdot 10^6$	276,894,366	398,626
	stomach	$90 \cdot 10^6$	1,277,498,438	22,868
	swang2	$90 \cdot 10^6$	600,518,274	5,801
	torso3	$90 \cdot 10^6$	1,561,856,844	327,737

compression technique. We took into account the speedups of both GMRES solvers implemented on the GPU cluster compared to those implemented on CPU clusters.

The fourth and sixth columns of these tables show respectively the ratio of execution times T_{12cpus} and T_{gpu} and the ratio of execution times T_{24cpus} and T_{gpu}, where T_{gpu} is the execution time obtained on the cluster of 12 GPUs, T_{12cpus} is that obtained on the cluster of 12 CPUs and T_{24CPUs} is that obtained on the cluster of 24 CPUs. The ratios define the relative gains of the GMRES solvers implemented on the GPU cluster compared to those implemented on CPUs clusters, such that:

$$ratio = \frac{T_{cpu}}{T_{gpu}}. \tag{3}$$

Table 2. Performances of GMRES solver *without* data compression on a GPU cluster and CPU clusters

Matrix	T_{gpu}	T_{12cpus}	$ratio_{12cpus}$	T_{24cpus}	$ratio_{24cpus}$	#iter	Prec.	Δ
ecology2	1.68s	14.22s	8.46	9.85s	5.86	22	1.86e-10	2.32e-10
finan512	5.35s	43.03s	8.04	28.97s	5.42	52	1.03e-09	2.66e-15
G3_circuit	2.05s	16.44s	8.02	11.30s	5.50	25	1.44e-09	9.66e-13
shallow_water2	2.45s	22.98s	9.83	15.88s	6.49	33	4.27e-15	1.35e-18
thermal2	3.95s	25.91s	6.56	17.12s	4.34	31	3.15e-09	5.88e-15
cage14	2.95s	20.44s	6.93	15.62s	5.30	21	1.39e-08	1.20e-11
language	9.60s	84.58s	8.81	56.57s	5.89	112	2.61e-08	3.78e-10
stomach	12.66s	107.97s	8.53	74.40s	5.88	125	1.10e-08	2.13e-14
swang2	3.84s	32.42s	8.44	22.10s	5.76	45	5.75e-08	3.41e-13
torso3	15.20s	125.45s	8.25	86.40s	5.68	134	1.93e-08	3.13e-13

From both ratios shown in Table 2 and Table 3, we can see that the GMRES solvers implemented on the GPU cluster are faster than those implemented on the CPU clusters. Moreover, the GMRES solver *with* the data compression technique is faster than that *without* the data compression. Indeed, the GMRES

Table 3. Performances of GMRES solver *with* data compression on a GPU cluster and CPU clusters

Matrix	T_{gpu}	T_{12cpus}	$ratio_{12cpus}$	T_{24cpus}	$ratio_{24cpus}$	#iter	Prec.	Δ
ecology2	1.06s	14.13s	13.33	9.75s	9.18	22	1.86e-10	2.32e-10
finan512	4.27s	42.95s	10.06	29.02s	6.80	52	1.03e-09	2.66e-15
G3_circuit	1.32s	16.33s	12.37	11.24s	8.53	25	1.44e-09	9.66e-13
shallow_water2	1.78s	22.95s	12.89	15.85s	8.92	33	4.27e-15	1.35e-18
thermal2	2.36s	25.26s	10.70	16.64s	7.05	31	3.15e-09	5.88e-15
cage14	2.25s	20.50s	9.11	13.99s	6.21	21	1.39e-08	1.20e-11
language	7.04s	84.02s	11.93	56.63s	8.05	112	2.61e-08	3.78e-10
stomach	10.11s	107.73s	10.66	74.30s	7.35	125	1.10e-08	2.13e-14
swang2	2.95s	32.37s	10.97	22.14s	7.51	45	5.75e-08	3.41e-13
torso3	11.61s	124.70s	10.74	86.24s	7.43	134	1.93e-08	3.13e-13

solver using the data compression on the GPU cluster is about 11 times faster than on the cluster of 12 CPUs and about 7.7 times faster than on the cluster of 24 CPUs. In contrast, the GMRES solver without the data compression on the GPU cluster is about 8 times faster than on the cluster of 12 CPUs and about 5.6 times faster than on the cluster of 24 CPUs. Hence, it is interesting to use the *compression/decompression* operations on the shared vectors of unknowns *before/after* the GPU/CPU data transfers in the GMRES solver on GPU clusters. Indeed it allows us to exchange small shared vectors between the different components of the GPU cluster, and thus, to minimize the communication overheads in solving large sparse linear systems using GMRES solver.

The seventh, eighth and ninth columns of Table 2 and Table 3 give respectively the number of iterations for solving the linear system, the solution precision *Prec* computed on the GPU cluster and the difference Δ between solutions computed on the CPU clusters and the GPU cluster, such that:

$$Prec = max(M^{-1} \cdot (b - AX^{GPU})). \qquad (4)$$
$$\Delta = max|X^{CPU} - X^{GPU}|. \qquad (5)$$

where X^{CPU} and X^{GPU} are respectively the solutions computed on the CPU cluster and the GPU cluster. We can see that the precisions *Prec* of the solutions computed on the GPU cluster are sufficient, varying from 5.75e-8 to 4.27e-15, and the two versions of GMRES solver compute almost the same solutions in both CPU cluster and GPU cluster, with Δ varying from 3.78e-10 to 1.35e-18.

5   Conclusion

In this paper we have presented an efficient parallel GMRES algorithm for solving large sparse linear systems on GPU clusters. We have shown that it is interesting to use compression/decompression techniques on the sub-vectors of unknowns shared between GPUs of the cluster. In fact, the parallelization of GMRES method on a GPU cluster requires CPU/CPU and GPU/CPU data transfers in order to perform full matrix-vector products. And since the parallel sparse matrix-vector product does not often need all values of the vector, the use of the data compression and decompression techniques on the shared vectors before and after the GPU/CPU data transfers allows us to minimize the communication overheads of the parallel GMRES solver on GPU clusters. The experimental results show that the GMRES solver is more efficient when it uses the data compression/decompression techniques on GPU clusters.

Obviously, even if the compression/decompression techniques reduce globally the communication overheads, they do not provide enough gains to the GMRES solver on GPU clusters. In fact, a large matrix bandwidth produces many data dependencies between GPUs of the cluster. It means that each GPU will have many neighbors with which it will share data. Therefore, a large matrix bandwidth increases the number of communications, and thus, it reduces dramatically the performances of solving large sparse linear systems on GPU clusters. In future work, we will study the data partitioning methods required to minimize the data dependencies between the computing nodes of a GPU cluster and to improve the performance of the GMRES solver for GPU clusters.

References

1. Saad, Y., Schultz, M.: GMRES: a Generalized Minimal Residual Algorithm for Solving Nonsymmetric Linear Systems. SIAM J. Sci. Stat. Comput. 7(3), 856–869 (1986)
2. Jost, T., Contassot-Vivier, S., Vialle, S.: An Efficient Multi-algorithms Sparse Linear Solver for GPUs. In: EuroGPU Mini-Symposium of ParCo 2009, Lyon, pp. 546–553 (2009)
3. Wang, M., Klie, H., Parashar, M., Sudan, H.: Solving Sparse Linear Systems on NVIDIA Tesla GPUs. In: Allen, G., Nabrzyski, J., Seidel, E., van Albada, G.D., Dongarra, J., Sloot, P.M.A. (eds.) ICCS 2009. LNCS, vol. 5544, pp. 864–873. Springer, Heidelberg (2009)
4. Ghaemian, N., Abdollahzadeh, A., Heinemann, Z., Harrer, A., Sharifi, M., Heinemann, G.: Accelerating the GMRES Iterative Linear Solver of an Oil Reservoir Simulator using the Multi-Processing Power of Compute Unified Device Architecture of Graphics Cards (2010)
5. Abbas-Turki, L., Vialle, S., Lapeyre, B., Mercier, P.: High Dimensional Pricing of Exotic European Contracts on a GPU Cluster, and Comparison to a CPU Custer. In: IPDPS 2009, pp. 1–8. IEEE Computer Society (2009)
6. Bahi, J., Couturier, R., Ziane Khodja, L.: Parallel GMRES Implementation for Solving Sparse Linear Systems on GPU Clusters. In: HPC Symposium, pp. 23–30. ACM/SIGSIM, Boston (2011)
7. Jeannot, E.: Improving Middleware Performance with AdOC: An Adaptive Online Compression Library for Data Transfer. In: IPDPS, vol. 1, p. 70. IEEE, USA (2005)
8. Nvidia: NVIDIA CUDA C Programming Guide, Version 3.1.1 (2010)
9. Nvidia: Cuda Cublas Library, Version 3.1 (2010)
10. CUSP library, http://code.google.com/p/cusp-library/
11. Davis, T., Hu, Y.: The University of Florida Sparse Matrix Collection (1997), http://www.cise.ufl.edu/research/sparse/matrices/

Two-Dimensional Discrete Wavelet Transform on Large Images for Hybrid Computing Architectures: GPU and CELL

Marek Błażewicz, Miłosz Ciżnicki, Piotr Kopta,
Krzysztof Kurowski, and Paweł Lichocki

Poznan Supercomputing and Networking Center,
Noskowskiego 10, 61-704 Poznań, Poland
{marqs,miloszc,krzysztof.kurowski,pawel.lichocki}@man.poznan.pl

Abstract. The Discrete Wavelet Transform (DWT) has gained the momentum in signal processing and image compression over the last decade bringing the concept up to the level of new image coding standard JPEG2000. Thanks to many added values in DWT, in particular inherent multi-resolution nature, wavelet-coding schemes are suitable for various applications where scalability and tolerable degradation are relevant. Moreover, as we demonstrate in this paper, it can be used as a perfect benchmarking procedure for more sophisticated data compression and multimedia applications using General Purpose Graphical Processor Units (GPGPUs). Thus, in this paper we show and compare experiments performed on reference implementations of DWT on Cell Broadband Engine Architecture (Cell B.E) and nVidia Graphical Processing Units (GPUs). The achieved results show clearly that although both GPU and Cell B.E. are being considered as representatives of the same hybrid architecture devices class they differ greatly in programming style and optimization techniques that need to be taken into account during the development. In order to show the speedup, the parallel algorithm has been compared to sequential computation performed on the x86 architecture.

Keywords: Discrete Wavelet Transform, JPEG200, GPU, CELL.

1   Introduction

1.1   JPEG2000

The Discrete Wavelet Transform (DWT) is a signal processing technique for extracting information. It is based on sub-coding and can represent data by a set of coarse and detail values in different scales. DWT is frequently used in many practical applications including, audio analysis, image compression and video encoding. In image compression DWT decomposes data into the horizontal and vertical characteristics. It is one-dimensional transform in nature, but applying it in the horizontal and vertical directions forms two-dimensional transform.

M. Alexander et al. (Eds.): Euro-Par 2011 Workshops, Part I, LNCS 7155, pp. 481–490, 2012.

This result in four smaller images. DWT process can be repeated a number of times and it is called dyadic decomposition. The Cohen-Daubechies-Feauveau wavelet is one of the most commonly used set of discrete wavelet transforms in image compression. There are two versions of CDF wavelets: reversible integer-to-integer (CDF 53) and non-reversible real-to-real (CDF 97) wavelet transforms. The reversible transform uses only rational filter coefficients during decomposition and no data is lost due to rounding. It is called *lossless* decomposition. The non-reversible transform called *lossy decomposition* uses non-rational filter coefficients, so it allows for some data to be lost. Both of these transforms are implemented in JPEG2000 image compression standard [1], which has better performance compared to JPEG standard [2]. The detailed description of DWT can be found in [3].

DWT can be realized by iteration of filters with rescaling. This kind of implementation has high complexity, needs a lot of memory and computational power. The better way is to use the lifting-based wavelet transform proposed by Swedlens [4]. Lifting-based filtering is done by using four lifting steps, which update alternately odd or even sample values.

One of the most known application of DWT is JPEG2000 standard. JPEG2000 is a standard for picture encoding in digital movies. The movie with 4K (4096x2160) resolution demands very fast real time encoding solution to distribute it for instance via live broadcasts. Although there are some hardware implementations that offers real time encoding, they are costly as specialized hardware is required. Current consumer-level architectures with software implementations can provide low-cost alternative to hardware solutions. Therefore, our main motivation was to use new hybrid computing architectures: GPGPU and CELL B.E. to implement low-cost software base alternative solutions.

1.2   Cell B.E. Architecture

The Cell Architecture [9], [10] grew from a challenge posed by Sony and Toshiba to provide power-efficient and cost-effective high-performance processing for a wide range of applications, including the most demanding consumer appliance: game consoles. Cell-B.E. (CBEA) - is an innovative solution based on the analysis of a broad range of workloads in areas such as cryptography, graphics transform and lighting, physics, fast-Fourier transforms (FFT), matrix operations, and scientific workloads.

1.3   GPGPU Architecture

General-Purpose GPU is a highly parallel, multithreaded, many core processor with a very high computational power and memory bandwidth, e.g. offered by nVidia. In our work we used recent NVIDIA GPUs: Tesla S1070 Computing System consisting of four T10 computing processors and one gamer's card GTX 280. Each of Tesla T10 processors consists of 30 multiprocessors (MP). Multiprocessor is built from 8 Scalar Processors (SP) cores, two special function units, a multithreaded instruction unit, one double precision unit and on-chip shared memory. GTX 280 processor has very similar specification, but only possess 1GB memory.

The rest of this paper is organized as follows. The related work is described in Section 2. Section 3 describes generally sequential and parallel DWT algorithm. The optimizations techniques on Cell B.E. and GPU architectures are presented in Section 4 and 5 respectively. Section 6 summarizes and compares results performance obtained on Cell and GPU. Conclusions are given in Section 7.

2 Related Work

In the context of the DWT algorithm several implementations on GPU has been proposed. In [5], it is presented a CUDA algorithm that performs the one-level 2D DWT algorithm in 45ms (without data transfer to and from GPU) on high resolution image with 4096x4096 pixels using NVIDIA Tesla C870. Another highly optimized algorithm is proposed in [6]. This implementation also adopts CUDA, which performs the three-level 2D Daubechies (9,7) wavelet transform in 2.13ms (without data transfer) on 1920x1080 pixels image using NVIDIA GeForce 8800 GTX.

In the case of Cell architecture the efficient implementation of the DWT algorithm is proposed in [7]. The one-level non-reversible wavelet transform executes in 54ms on 3800x2600 pixels image using the IBM QS20 Cell blade server with Cell/B.E. 3.2 GHz chip.

3 Discrete Wavelet Transform

3.1 Sequential Algorithm

First, in the horizontal transform a source image data rows using lifting procedure are decomposed into a set of low pass samples and a set of high pass samples. Than, samples are exposed to the de-interleaving procedure and the image data is transposed to represent rows as columns. The whole process is repeated to create a 2-dimensionally transformed image data.

Lifting Procedure. The lifting procedure consists, in fact of multiple lifting steps: splitting step, two predicting steps, two updating steps and the last scaling step. The splitting step simply splits image data row into two subsequences. One subsequence consists of odd elements and the second one consists even elements. In the predicting step the odd sample values are updated with a weighted sum of even samples and in updating step the even sample values are updated with a weighted sum of odd samples. In order to avoid errors at boundaries of the input row symmetric extension is used. Symmetric extension adds a mirror image of the signal to the outside of the boundaries, refer to [8]. In the last step all sample values are scaled.

De-interleaving. After the lifting procedure the next procedure is de-interleaving. Two subsequences with even and odd samples are called high-pass samples and low-pass samples respectively. They are mixed together in the input array after the lifting procedure. The high-pass and low-pass results have to be moved to the right half and left half of a output array respectively. The computed base position in the input array is linked with the corresponding output pixel in the output array.

3.2 Parallel Algorithm

In the first our approach the sequential algorithm was parallelized without any major changes. This is called the *base* version, it uses the many-loops approach and it is computed in two steps - first horizontally (on entire rows) and than vertically (on entire columns or transposed rows). Columns are processed after rows, so there is a need to synchronize computations. The *base* algorithm was a starting point for further optimizations. Then, we developed a parallel algorithm so-called *tiled* DWT.

The main difference is the problem decomposition. Whereas the *base* DWT works on an image as a whole, the *tiled* version splits images into rectangles of the same size and invokes DWT on them independently. The *tiled* DWT achieves much better performance than the *base* one. However, please note that the result of DWT processing the image in tiles is not identical to the result obtained when working on an image as whole, because *tiling* may introduce artifacts in the resulting image. In other words running the DWT on a whole image at once gives better resulting image quality, but at a very high cost of algorithm performance.

4 DWT on Cell B.E.

4.1 Basic Optimizations

Assumptions. For simplicity we focus on one-level forward transform, since the inverse one is symmetrical. We used a so-called lifting decomposition scheme, which is a very efficient way of computing discrete wavelet transforms. DWT is computed on one-channel grey image of size 4096 pixels (width) on 2048 pixels (height).

Base Version - Parallelization and Vectorization Using SPEs. Parallelization and vectorization of a sequential DWT algorithm resulted in *base* DWT. It uses the many-loops approach and is computed in two steps - first horizontally (on rows) and than vertically (on columns). Columns are processed after rows, to synchronize the computation, in the following way: each SPE thread is executed two times and the POSIX thread join on PPE is used as a natural barrier. The *base* algorithm is fully vectorized and all computations are done on SPEs. The PPE is used only for thread management. Horizontal DWT works on chunks of 4 rows and before computing DWT itself, it shuffles the float order. Vertical DWT works on chunks of 32 columns and arranges the data in correct order on-the-fly during memory *get/put*.

When the buffer size in Local Store is set to 64kb, this allows to use three of them (to enable double-buffering) and leaves 64kb for the code. One chunk of 4 rows of 4096 pixels (floats) fits ideally into the 64kb's buffer, so horizontal DWT is computed on entire rows at once. This is not the case for vertical DWT, where chunk of 128 columns limits the maximum height to 512 pixels. As the image height is set to 2048, the vertical DWT is computed in 4 steps, successively for every quarter of 128 column's chunk.

The *base* DWT works in place, which means the resulting image is stored in the same place in main memory as the input data. De-interleaving the columns in horizontal DWT is relatively easy, as it works on all rows and might be executed on SPEs before storing the results into the main memory. In case of vertical DWT, rows are deinterleaved on-the-fly while storing to the main memory. A complex scheme of loading and storing data was developed in order to enable double-buffering and not to erase the input data before time.

Tiled Version - Problem Decomposition and Memory Issues. The our analysis of the *base* DWT algorithm shown that it requires costly memory transfers and thread management. To address this issue, we improved the *tiled* DWT algorithm. The main idea is to compute both horizontal and vertical DWT at once on tiles of image, thus reducing the cost of synchronization and minimize the number of memory store/load operations. Therefore the main difference between *base* and *tiled* version is the problem of decomposition.

The optimal size of tile images has been estimated experimentally, assuming the tile should fill in entire 64kb buffer and that both height and width should be a power of 2. This resulted in 512 image tiles of the optimal size of 512 pixels on 32 pixels.

4.2   Advanced Optimizations

First optimization technique is reducing the number of separate loops and merge them into a single one. This included merging two predicts and two updates of DWT values, as well as bytes shuffling and reshuffling in case of horizontal DWT (for vertical DWT bytes are reordered on-the-fly during memory transfer). This significantly reduced the cost of handling loop counters and also allowed to apply next optimization, which was moving most computation into registers. In the final algorithm each pixel is read from an array in Local Store only once, all intermediate values computed during DWT are kept in the registers. Then the final results are written just once back to the array in Local Store. Each pixel was read from and written to Local Store only once, whereas all arithmetic calculations were performed in the registers. Such a approach resulted in a very noticeable increase of algorithm efficiency. Tiling an image and loop merging reduced significantly the execution time. Consequently, the initialization phase started to play a major role in the overall effectiveness, and we decided to apply two additional optimization techniques. The algorithm has been balanced for 6

SPEs for Playstation3 and 8 SPEs for QS21. In case of QS21, balancing threads optimization allowed us to run parallel instances of the application, as QS21 has two PPEs. We applied a simple double buffering. Thus, computation and data transfer steps were overlapped and the execution time was reduced. Further optimizations were pointless, as the actual computational part performed on SPEs dropped below 1ms, whereas the thread management part performed by PPE took approximately 10ms (on QS21).

5 DWT on GPGPU

We implemented two versions of parallel DWT algorithm on GPGU: the base DWT and the tiled DWT. DWT algorithm can be effectively paralleled, as data are separated. Naturally, the algorithm can be divided into a number of completely independent tasks, updated by a block of threads and executed by a separate multiprocessor.

5.1 Basic Optimizations

Base Version. The simplest approach to implement DWT on GPGU is using a sequential algorithm and try to parallelize it. First, the image data is simply saved in the global memory. Then, the image data is divided to data chunks which are loaded to the shared memory, to perform lifting and de-interleaving procedures and finally to store back results in the device memory. The whole process is performed two times, on every column and on every row. Each block of threads process one data chunk from the image. A single thread in a block reads one input pixel and generates one output pixel, so thread corresponds to one pixel form the image.

Every thread loads one pixel to the shared memory. During the lifting process, all the pixels at the edge of the data chunk depend on pixels which were not loaded to the shared memory. Around a data chunk within a thread block, there is a two-sided margin of pixels that is required in order to properly do the calculations. This margin of one data chunk overlaps with adjacent data chunks. In order to avoid idle threads, data from the margin should be loaded by threads within block. To avoid large errors at the boundaries the margins of the blocks on the edges of the image should be symmetrically extended.

Before the vertical(column) and the horizontal(row) processing the image should be transposed to access array elements that are adjacent in the global memory. The image data block was loaded to the shared memory array, transposed and written back to the global memory, to avoid uncoalesced access during lifting process. The image was partitioned into square tiles. We used 16x16 threads in block and every thread transposed one pixel.To do processing on columns and rows there were two separate kernel invocations. Between kernel invocations was a global barrier synchronization. It ensured that after every step the output signal was written back to the global memory. After transposition of the image, we used four lifting loops to calculate the output signal. Firstly, the block of threads was divided into two parts. The left part with threads that referred to even memory cells (low pass samples) and right part with threads that referred to odd memory cells (high pass samples). Therefore only every second thread in a warp was participating in every lifting step. Odd threads were responsible for high resolution pixels and even threads were responsible for low resolution pixels. The margin was updated by few threads that were taken additionally form the left or the right part of threads block. After every lifting step threads were synchronized in order to write back results to the shared memory. However this approach has major disadvantage. During every predict or update step (see Lifting procedure 3.1) the other part of threads in a warp was idle till to synchronization. In order to improve the parallelism, the algorithm was changed and it was used one-loop approach as follows: every thread loaded all necessary data to registers, as it was needed to correctly compute one output pixel. The necessary data were composed of 8 adjacent pixels. Additional improvement was maximizing a number of arithmetic operations by using each thread to load and calculate multiple pixels instead of one.

To sum up every thread read and synchronized two pixels from the global memory to the shared memory. Then, all the threads read adjacent pixels from the shared memory to registers and perform the lifting procedure. When registers were used instead of shared memory, each thread from the block was able to calculate two adjacent output values: high pass and lows pass. It gave us more speedup, as memory transactions were better overlapped by arithmetic operations. After the lifting procedure pixels were scaled and written to the global memory. We restricted our experiment to the shared memory size and a reasonable amount of 2048 pixels. The optimal time we observed was for threads which compute 8 pixels in a block of size 256. The fastest computations run in 11ms.

Tiled Version. A single image can be composed of a single tile or multiple independent tiles. In tiled version of the algorithm the image is divided to multiple tiles and on every tile DWT algorithm is applied. Similar to the base version, the image data chunk was loaded to the shared memory, however the processing on columns and rows was done in one kernel invocation including data transposition. As a result a number of kernel invocations and the global memory calls were reduced. It minimized the amount of global memory transactions.

Data Partition in the Shared Memory. The image was divided into multiple same size data blocks. Every data block was loaded to the shared memory. All the edges of rows and columns in a data block were symmetrically extended. In this case, we did not load pixels from adjacent data blocks. As a result small artifacts on edges were introduced. Each thread within data block loaded one or more pixels, depending on the kernel used in experiments.

Lifting Procedure and Transposition. Algorithm applying the lifting procedure was similar to the algorithm we presented for the base version. If we divided
the image into non-overlapping data blocks we were able to apply another optimization. The margin for the row and the column had the same length. When
the first transposition was done we had to add new margins between rows in
the shared memory in order to do symmetric extension. All performance results
depend on the size of the data blocks. The optimal size for the image tile was
64 pixels on 32 pixels using 256 threads in one block, and the execution time
was 2,4ms.

5.2   Advanced Optimization

In this section we show more advanced techniques and try to reach maximum
efficiency of DWT algorithm on GPU. First optimization is block balancing and
maximizing arithmetic operations. Scaling size of the threads block brings more
speedup. A number of threads per block should be chosen as multiple of the
warp size to avoid wasting computing resources with under-populated warps.
Our tests shown that the number of 256 threads in one block is optimal. Second
optimization is data transposing. One should note that loading data from the
global memory in a column-major fashion is inefficient. Therefore data should
be transposed before loading it form the global memory. The next optimization
approach was to load all necessary data to registers. We used registers for computations and wrote data back to the shared memory only once. Last optimization
was to reduce the data transfer time. The large amount of time was taken by the
data image transfer, between CPU and GPU memory. In order to reduce this
bottleneck we applied double buffering and split images through all available
Tesla modules. Thus, we overlapped a kernel computation with memory copy
from different streams.

6   Performance Analysis

6.1   Cell B.E. - Scalability and Execution Time Analysis

To compare various optimization techniques, first we developed a single processor
version of the DWT algorithm without any optimization. It was run on one PPE
(on Playstation 3 and QS21, with and without Altivec vectorization) and on one
2.16GHz x86 compatible processor.

Each optimization technique helped us to reduce significantly the execution
time. The most efficient version of DWT we obtained on QS21 11.5ms. The
version of the DWT algorithm in which SPE threads immediately quit with
return statement, runs for 10.8ms. This means that both DWT computation
and memory transfer took less than one millisecond and constitute approx. 6%
of the entire computational time.

In order to address the scalability issues we analyzed the algorithm without
double buffering and balancing thread procedure (see Figure 1a and Figure 1b

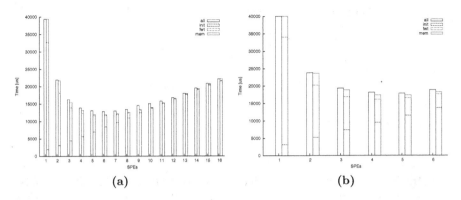

Fig. 1. a) QS21 scalability. b) PS3 scalability.

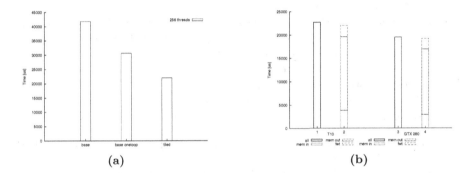

Fig. 2. a) Tesla T10 - best times comparison. b) Tesla T10 and GTX 280.

for details). For both Playstation 3 and QS21 with a rising number of SPEs we discovered that the thread management cost (operations performed on PPE) started to play a major role in the whole execution process.

6.2   GPU - Scalability and Execution Time Analysis

Our program is built on the top of the CUDA 2.1 (Compute Unified Device Architecture). We performed a warm-up computation before of the timed computation to remove the CUDA start up overhead from performance measurements. Figure 2b shows that the best DWT algorithm achieved 19,5ms using gamer's card GTX 280 and 22,7ms using one GPU module on Tesla S1070. The GTX 280 card had higher memory bandwidth and lower computation time than one Tesla S1070 module. According to our tests it has about 16% faster data transfer. The difference in time results between this two device can result from slightly different architectures.

Table 1. Computation time: x86, GPU and CELL

Device	Init.	Mem. copy	Comp.	Speedup
x86	0.0ms	0.0ms	1500ms	1.00x
GTX 280	0.15 ms	16.9ms	2.29ms	76.92x
QS21	10.8ms	0.7ms (double buff.)		130.43x

7   Conclusions

We wish to summarize stressing out the issue which we consider to be the most important difference between Cell B.E. and GPU. Cell B.E. relies on heavy persistent threads, whereas GPU paradigm is to use very light-wighted threads. This has a huge impact on programming style for those architectures, resulting in the development of totally different approaches. Although the concept of parallelization the algorithm for both GPU and Cell B.E. is similar the optimizations details are completely different.

In our opinion the biggest drawback of GPU computing is relatively high cost of memory transfers, which is not a problem in case of Cell B.E. thanks to Element Interconnect Bus that allows the memory transfer and computation to overlap. To some extent this could be addressed by using many GPUs, currently Tesla server consists of four graphical cards.

References

1. ISO/IEC 15444-1: Information technology JPEG 2000 image coding system Part 1: Core coding system (November 2000)
2. ISO/IEC 10918-1: Information technology Digital compression and coding of continuous-tone still images: Requirements and guidelines (1994)
3. Taubman, D., Marcellin, M.: JPEG2000 Image Compression Fundamentals, Standards and Pratice (2002)
4. Sweldens, W.: The lifting scheme: a new philosophy in biorthogonal wavelet constructions. In: Proceedings of the SPIE, Wavelet Applications in Signal and Image Processing III, vol. 2569, pp. 68–79 (September 1995)
5. Franco, J., Bernabé, G., Fernández, J., Acacio, M.: A Parallel Implementation of the 2D Wavelet Transform Using CUDA. In: Proceedings of the 2009 17th Euromicro International Conference on Parallel, Distributed and Network-based Processing (2009)
6. van der Laan, W., Jalba, A., Roerdink, J.: Accelerating Wavelet Lifting on Graphics Hardware Using CUDA. IEEE Trans. Parallel Distrib. Syst. (January 2011)
7. Bader, D., Agarwal, V., Kang, S.: Computing discrete transforms on the Cell Broadband Engine. Parallel Comput. (March 2009)
8. Aboufadel, E., Elzinga, J., Feenstra, K.: JPEG 2000: The Next Compression Standard using wavelet technology (December 2001)
9. IBM Corporation, Cell Broadband Engine Technology,
   http://researchweb.watson.ibm.com/cell/home.html
10. IBM Corporation, Cell Broadband Engine Technology,
    https://www-01.ibm.com/chips/techlib/techlib.nsf/products/
    Cell_Broadband_Engine

Scheduling Divisible Loads on Heterogeneous Desktop Systems with Limited Memory

Aleksandar Ilic and Leonel Sousa

INESC-ID, IST/UTLisbon,
Rua Alves Redol, 9, 1000-029 Lisbon, Portugal
{Aleksandar.Ilic,Leonel.Sousa}@inesc-id.pt

Abstract. This paper addresses the problem of scheduling discretely divisible applications in heterogeneous desktop systems with limited memory by relying on realistic performance models for computation and communication, through bidirectional asymmetric full-duplex buses. We propose an algorithm for multi-installment processing with multi-distributions that allows to efficiently overlap computation and communication at the device level in respect to the supported concurrency. The presented approach was experimentally evaluated for a real application; 2D FFT batch collaboratively executed on a Graphic Processing Unit and a multi-core CPU. The experimental results obtained show the ability of the proposed approach to outperform the optimal implementation for about 4 times, whereas it is not possible with the current state of the art approaches to determine a load balanced distribution.

Keywords: Scheduling, divisible loads, heterogeneous desktop systems, multiple installments, memory constraints.

1 Introduction

Modern desktop systems are already true heterogeneous platforms capable of sustaining remarkable computation power by coalescing the execution space of multi-core CPUs and programmable accelerators, such as Graphics Processing Units (GPUs) [9]. In this paper, we consider the problem of scheduling discretely divisible load (DL) applications on heterogeneous desktop platforms, from the perspective of employing all the available computing devices. The DL model [12] represents parallel computations that can be divided into pieces of arbitrary sizes, where these load fractions can be processed independently with no precedence constraints. In recent years, divisible load theory (DLT) has been widely studied for a wide range of applications in heterogeneous computing, such as image and signal processing, database applications and linear algebra [11,12].

The problem of scheduling DL applications can generally be viewed as two-fold. Firstly, it is decided how many "load units" has to be sent to each device to achieve a balanced load distribution. Secondly, in order to reduce the impact of inevitable delays when distributing and retrieving the load, each individual load (assigned to a device) needs to be sub-partitioned into many smaller chunks,

M. Alexander et al. (Eds.): Euro-Par 2011 Workshops, Part I, LNCS 7155, pp. 491–501, 2012.

in order to: *(i)* overlap computation and communication; *(ii)* efficiently use the communication links in desktop systems typically with bidirectional asymmetric bandwidth; *(iii)* respect the amount of supported concurrency, and *(iv)* fit into the limited device memory. In DLT, this organization is usually referred as *multi-installment (multi-round) processing* [12].

Although several authors have already studied multi-installment divisible load scheduling (DLS) in heterogeneous star networks [2], with limited memory [3,5], and results collection [7], we show in this paper that the considered restrictions and assumptions may be realistic for some particular applications, but certainly not for all of them. These studies considered: an one-port communication model with symmetric bandwidth; when dealing with limited memory, the main focus is on fitting the input load into the finite memory size; they derive the closed-form solutions or optimal DLS algorithms by modeling computation and communication times by linear or affine functions of the number of chunks.

We naturally target a heterogeneous star (master-worker) networks, due to the basic architectural principle of desktop systems, which positions the CPU (host, master) to be responsible for controlling and orchestrating the operation of all the processing devices (workers), namely GPUs. The system heterogeneity is described with different processing speeds for each worker, and different bandwidths of master-worker communication links. Precisely, each link is modeled as an asynchronous bidirectional full-duplex communication channel with asymmetric bandwidth in different transfer directions. In contrast to the previous works dealing with limited memory [3,5], we consider the real application behavior, that generally requires additional memory space to be allocated during the processing. Moreover, we do not make any assumptions, but we rather model computation and communication via continuous functions of the number of chunks, constructed from the real application execution. The works presented in [4,10] also model computation through continuous functions, but do not consider either communication or multi-installment scheduling. To the best of our knowledge there is only one publication dealing with DLS problems in desktop systems [1], but for a specific application and based on affine cost models.

2   System Model and Problem Formulation

Let $\mathcal{D} = (\mathcal{A}, \mathcal{H}, \psi_t, \psi_w, \sigma_\iota, \sigma_o, \mu_\iota, \mu_w, \mu_o)$ be a DLS system, where the divisible load $\mathcal{A}$ is to be distributed and processed on a heterogeneous star network $\mathcal{H} = (P, B, E)$. Due to employment of master cores for execution, a set of $k + m$ processing devices is defined as $P = P_M \cup P_W$, where $P_M = \{p_1, ..., p_k\}$ is a set of k cores on the CPU master (positioned at the center of the star), and $P_W = \{p_{k+1}, ..., p_{m+k}\}$ is a set of m 'distant workers". Unless stated otherwise, we will use the term "distant worker" to designate a processing device, such as GPU, connected to the master via a communication link. $E = \{e_{k+1}, ..., e_{m+k}\}$ is a set of m links that connect the master to the P_W distant workers (locally, to perform load execution on the master cores P_M no extra communication costs are considered). $B = \{b_{k+1}, ..., b_{m+k}\}$ is the set of parameters describing the available memory at each distant worker.

Initially, the total load N of the application $\mathcal{A}$ is stored at the master, which can be split into load fractions of an arbitrary size x. In contrast to the usual DLT practice to model computation/communication time with linear or affine functions of the load size x, we describe these relations with performance functions dynamically built during the application execution. In detail, for each load fraction x processed on a device or communicated over a link for a certain time t, we calculate its relative performance x/t in order to construct the function $f : \mathbb{N} \to \mathbb{R}_+$ which is continuously extended by piece-wise linear approximation to a performance function $g : \mathbb{R}_+ \to \mathbb{R}_+$ ($f(x) = g(x), \forall x \in \mathbb{N}$), such as in [4]. Therefore, those performance models are much more realistic in capturing the behavior of applications and the characteristics of complex heterogeneous systems [10]. Hence, $\psi_w(x)$ models relative computation performance of each P device as a function of the load size x. Bidirectional full-duplex asymmetric bandwidth of each link from E is modeled with $\sigma_\iota(x)$ and $\sigma_o(x)$ functions (where index ι reflects the communication direction from the master to a distant worker, and index o from a distant worker to the master). Dedicated links for each master-distant worker pair allow modeling of total relative performance with $\psi_t(x)$ function, calculated as ratio between the load size x and the total time taken to distribute and process the load and to return the results.

Current research in limited memory DLS [3,5] mainly focuses on fitting the input load into the worker's memory (or input buffer) without considering the additional memory allocated during processing. Although for traditional distributed systems (with CPUs) this requirement is usually neglected, due to possible allocation in virtual memory address space, this can not be assumed for accelerators in desktop systems, such as GPUs. Therefore, we characterize the application by input, output and execution memory requirement functions, $\mu_\iota(x)$, $\mu_o(x)$, and $\mu_w(x, P)$, respectively. We define the execution memory requirement $\mu_w(x, P)$ as a function of load size x and device type P, to express the high level of heterogeneity in modern desktop systems where different implementations of the same problem might have different memory requirements.

The first part of the problem is how to divide the total load N into fractions $\alpha = \{\alpha_1, ..., \alpha_k, \alpha_{k+1}, ...\alpha_{m+k}\}$ to be simultaneously processed on each master core and distant worker $p_1, ..., p_k, p_{k+1}, ..., p_{k+m}$, such that the load distribution α is as balanced as possible. We adopt herein the results of the research conducted in [10] for the case without any communication modeling, to our communication-aware total performance functions $\psi_t(x)$. Hence, the optimal load distribution lies on a straight line that passes through the origin of the coordinating system and intersects $\psi_t(x)$ performance functions, such that:

$$\frac{\alpha_1}{\psi_{t_1}(\alpha_1)} = \cdots = \frac{\alpha_k}{\psi_{t_k}(\alpha_k)} = \cdots = \frac{\alpha_{m+k}}{\psi_{t_{m+k}}(\alpha_{m+k})}; \quad \sum_{i=1}^{m+k} \alpha_i = \text{N} \qquad (1)$$

We tackle herein the second part of the DLS problem: how to sub-partition a given load fraction $\{\alpha_i\}_{i=k+1}^{m+k}$ in terms of number of chunks and number of sub-load distributions at the distant worker p_i according to: *(i)* relative performance

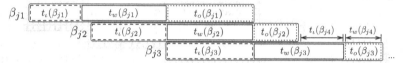

(a) Overlap of a single communication with computation at the time.

(b) Complete concurrency between communication and computation.

Fig. 1. Examples of different amounts of overlapping concurrency

models of computation, ψ_{w_i}, and asymmetric full-duplex network links, $\sigma_{L_i}, \sigma_{o_i}$; (ii) amount of concurrency supported by the p_i; and (iii) limited worker's memory b_i, such that the processing is finished in the shortest time.

3   Algorithm for Device-Level Multi-installment with Multi-distributions

As referred in the previous section, current multi-installment DLS studies [3,5] consider the one-port communication model, where the load fractions are sub-partitioned into smaller chunks to allow earlier activation of workers. Thus, the problem is how to interleave those chunks (in rounds) between the workers to reduce the total application processing time by overlapping computation at·one worker with communication between the master and the next worker. In this paper, we consider asymmetric full-duplex model which allows the master to simultaneously communicate with distant workers. Hence, the problem investigated herein is how to sub-partition the given load α_i to reduce the processing time at a single distant worker level by overlapping worker's sub-partitions. We allow the load α_i to be partitioned into sub-load distributions $\beta = \{\beta_j\}, 1 \leq j \leq |\beta|$, each of them consisting of sub-load fractions $\beta_j = \{\beta_{j,l}\}, 1 \leq l \leq |\beta_j|$, such that the total sum of load fractions is equal to α_i. The DLS procedure requires in-order scheduling of β_j distributions, and overlapped execution of $\beta_{j,l}$ fractions in each of them, which means we define a *single device multi-installment execution space with multi-distributions*. For limited memory systems, each β_j distribution must satisfy an additional requirement that the sum of input, output and execution memory requirements of each sub-fraction $\beta_{j,l}$ must fit into the available memory size b_i of the distant worker p_i. In fact, each sub-distribution may consume the whole amount of available memory, which is released between consecutive and independent β_j distributions.

Fig. 1 depicts the optimal overlap of three load fractions in a single load distribution for examples with different amounts of concurrency. The linear programming formulation of the problem in Fig. 1(a) states the necessary conditions for optimal overlap between subsequent load fractions in a β_j sub-distribution, where $t_\delta(\beta_j)$ represents the total processing time of β_j. We define the sub-distribution maximum relative performance, $\psi_\delta(\beta_j)$, as the optimality criterion, due to ability not only to select the distribution that efficiently uses both computation power of the distant worker p_i, ψ_{w_i}, and asymmetric bandwidth of the e_i network link, σ_{ι_i} and σ_{o_i}, but also to minimize the impact of the intrinsic communication overhead in the first, $\beta_{j,1}/\sigma_{\iota_i}(\beta_{j,1})$, and the last load fraction, $\beta_{j,|\beta_j|}/\sigma_{o_i}(\beta_{j,|\beta_j|})$, to the overall β_j execution time.

$$\text{MAXIMIZE} \quad \psi_\delta(\beta_j) = \frac{\sum_{l=1}^{|\beta_j|}\beta_{j,l}}{t_\delta(\beta_j)} \quad \text{SUBJECT TO:}$$

$$\sum_{l=1}^{|\beta_j|}\beta_{j,l} \le \alpha_i; \quad \sum_{l=1}^{|\beta_j|}\left(\mu_\iota(\beta_{j,l}) + \mu_w(\beta_{j,l},p_i) + \mu_o(\beta_{j,l})\right) \le b_i \tag{2}$$

$$\frac{\beta_{j,1}}{\psi_{w_i}(\beta_{j,1})} \ge \frac{\beta_{j,2}}{\sigma_{\iota_i}(\beta_{j,2})}; \quad \frac{\beta_{j,3}}{\psi_{w_i}(\beta_{j,3})} \ge \frac{\beta_{j,2}}{\sigma_{o_i}(\beta_{j,2})} \tag{3}$$

$$\frac{\beta_{j,2}}{\psi_{w_i}(\beta_{j,2})} \ge \frac{\beta_{j,1}}{\sigma_{o_i}(\beta_{j,1})} + \frac{\beta_{j,3}}{\sigma_{\iota_i}(\beta_{j,3})} \tag{4}$$

$$\frac{\beta_{j,l}}{\sigma_{\iota_i}(\beta_{j,l})} \le \frac{\beta_{j,l-1}}{\psi_{w_i}(\beta_{j,l-1})} - \frac{\beta_{j,l-2}}{\sigma_{o_i}(\beta_{j,l-2})}; \quad \frac{\beta_{j,l}}{\psi_{w_i}(\beta_{j,l})} \ge \frac{\beta_{j,l-1}}{\sigma_{o_i}(\beta_{j,l-1})}; \quad \forall l \in \{4,|\beta_j|\} \tag{5}$$

It can be observed that the number of sub-distributions and load fractions depend not only on the system capabilities and concurrency amount, but also on the application's computation and communication characteristics. In the general case, it may not even be possible to satisfy all the above-mentioned conditions. Hence, we propose herein an algorithm that finds a sub-optimal β distribution from a closed set $\beta^* = \{\beta^{(n)}\}_{n=1}^{|\beta^*|}$, where $\sum_{j=1}^{|\beta^{(n)}|}\sum_{l=1}^{|\beta_j^{(n)}|}\beta_{j,l}^{(n)} = \alpha_i, \forall n \in \{1,|\beta^*|\}$, and $\sum_{l=1}^{|\beta_j^{(n)}|}(\mu_\iota(\beta_{j,l}^{(n)}) + \mu_w(\beta_{j,l}^{(n)},p_i) + \mu_o(\beta_{j,l}^{(n)})) \le b_i, \forall n,j$, such that:

$$\beta = \beta^{(r)}; \quad \psi_\tau(\beta^{(r)}) = \max\{\psi_\tau(\beta^{(n)})\}_{n=1}^{|\beta^*|}; \quad \psi_\tau(\beta^{(n)}) = \alpha_i/t_\tau(\beta^{(n)}), \tag{6}$$

where $t_\tau(\beta^{(n)})$ is the total processing time of a $\beta^{(n)}$ distribution on the distant worker, and $\psi_\tau(\beta^{(n)})$ its total relative performance. Therefore, in order to construct the set β^*, we firstly determine the initial optimal load distribution with three load fractions satisfying (2) and (4). Due to the space limitations, only the main algorithm steps are present herein, more details can be found in [8].

Step 1. *Determination of the initial optimal distribution with three load fractions.* The algorithm firstly determines the optimal solution search space limits by finding minimum and maximum for $\beta_{1,1}^{(1)}$, $\beta_{1,2}^{(1)}$, and $\beta_{1,3}^{(1)}$ [8]. In case of Fig. 1(a), the process of finding the optimal initial solution requires to build interpolated curves from discreet values: *(i)* $\sigma_{\iota_i}^{(x_1)}$ from σ_{ι_i} and $x_1 \in [\beta_{1,1\,min}^{(1)}, \beta_{1,1\,max}^{(1)}]$; *(ii)* $\sigma_{o_i}^{(x_3)}$ from σ_{o_i} and $x_3 \in [\beta_{1,3\,min}^{(1)}, \beta_{1,3\,max}^{(1)}]$. Then, the optimal solution is the maximum relative performance, ψ_δ, solution that satisfies (2) and (4) and lies on a straight line passing through the coordinate system origin, such that:

$$\frac{\beta_{1,1}^{(1)}+\beta_{1,3}^{(1)}}{\sigma_{\iota_i}^{(x_1)}\left(\beta_{1,1}^{(1)}+\beta_{1,3}^{(1)}\right)} = \frac{\beta_{1,2}^{(1)}}{\psi_{w_i}\left(\beta_{1,2}^{(1)}\right)}, \quad \frac{\beta_{1,1}^{(1)}+\beta_{1,3}^{(1)}}{\sigma_{o_i}^{(x_3)}\left(\beta_{1,1}^{(1)}+\beta_{1,3}^{(1)}\right)} = \frac{\beta_{1,2}^{(1)}}{\psi_{w_i}\left(\beta_{1,2}^{(1)}\right)}. \tag{7}$$

If no optimal initial distribution is found, the algorithm continues with **Step 5.**

Step 2. *Generate additional three-fraction distributions.* In order to satisfy (3), at maximum three additional distributions are created with the optimal initial distribution, if permitted by the application characteristics and (2). Initially, $\{\beta_{1,2}^{(n)}\}_{n=2}^{4} = \beta_{1,2}^{(1)}$ ($\beta_{1,3}^{(2)} = \beta_{1,3}^{(1)}$, $\beta_{1,1}^{(3)} = \beta_{1,1}^{(1)}$) values are assigned, and the remaining loads are determined to completely overlap their computation and communication in $\{\beta_{1,2}^{(n)}\}_{n=2}^{4}$. Namely, the values lie on a straight line passing through the coordinate system origin, such that (2), (3), and:

$$\frac{\beta_{1,1}^{(2)}}{\psi_{w_i}\left(\beta_{1,1}^{(2)}\right)} = \frac{\beta_{1,2}^{(1)}}{\sigma_{\iota_i}\left(\beta_{1,2}^{(1)}\right)}, \quad \beta_{1,1}^{(2)} = \beta_{1,1}^{(4)}; \quad \frac{\beta_{1,3}^{(3)}}{\psi_{w_i}\left(\beta_{1,3}^{(3)}\right)} = \frac{\beta_{1,2}^{(1)}}{\sigma_{o_i}\left(\beta_{1,2}^{(1)}\right)}, \quad \beta_{1,3}^{(3)} = \beta_{1,3}^{(4)}. \quad (8)$$

Step 3. *Insert additional load fractions into existing sub-distributions.* Each $\{\beta_{|\beta^{(n)}|}^{(n)}\}_{n=1}^{|\beta^*|}$ sub-distribution is evaluated using the procedure from [8] to determine the possibilities to insert another load fraction into the current sub-distribution schedule, in respect to the amount of supported concurrency. Namely, each sub-distribution is assigned with two real values representing the maximum available time frames that can be allocated to the additional load fraction, i.e., $t_{a_\iota}^{(n)}$ and $t_{a_w}^{(n)}$ ($a = |\beta_{|\beta^{(n)}|}^{(n)}| + 1$), where $t_{a_\iota}^{(n)}$ and $t_{a_w}^{(n)}$ reassemble the notions from (5). Correspondingly, the next load fractions $\beta_{|\beta^{(n)}|,a}^{(n)}$ lie on a straight line passing through the origin of the coordinate system, such that (2), (5), and:

$$\frac{\beta_{|\beta^{(n)}|,a}^{(n)}}{\psi_{w_i}(\beta_{|\beta^{(n)}|,a}^{(n)})} = t_{a_w}^{(n)} \quad \text{or} \quad \frac{\beta_{|\beta^{(n)}|,a}^{(n)}}{\sigma_{\iota_i}(\beta_{|\beta^{(n)}|,a}^{(n)})} = t_{a_\iota}^{(n)}. \quad (9)$$

The obtained values are inserted as the last load-fractions for current sub-distribution and an additionally created sub-distribution by duplicating current $\beta^{(n)}$ schedule. In the case that the calculated load fraction does not satisfy (2), the sub-distribution is marked as examined. This procedure is iterative, until all $\{\beta_{|\beta^{(n)}|}^{(n)}\}_{n=1}^{|\beta^*|}$ sub-distributions are examined.

Step 4. *Generate new sub-distributions by restarting.* After the insertion, in each $\{\beta^{(n)}\}_{n=1}^{|\beta^*|}$ schedule the new sub-distribution is added on which the complete procedure is repeated (from **Step 1**) for the remaining unscheduled load:

$$\alpha_i - \sum_{j=1}^{|\beta^{(n)}|} \sum_{l=1}^{|\beta_j^{(n)}|} \beta_{j,l}^{(n)}, \forall n \in \{1, |\beta^*|\} \quad (10)$$

In case that the amount of remaining load is insufficient to produce the optimal three-fraction sub-distribution, the algorithm proceeds with **Step 5**.

Step 5. *Expand all sub-distributions.* In this step, each schedule $\{\beta^{(n)}\}_{n=1}^{|\beta^*|}$ is expanded with a single sub-distribution containing a single load fraction of the size obtained by (10) in case that (2) is satisfied, or with multiple single-fraction distributions which are iteratively assigned to meet the condition from (2).

Step 6. *Select the schedule with maximum relative performance.* As previously referred, the final schedule β is selected from the β^* set according to (6).

4   Iterative Procedure for Partial Performance Modeling

The proposed approach relies on relative performance models of system resources, which are usually not known a priori. Hence, we propose an iterative procedure with two main phases (*initialization* and *iterative phase*), based on the algorithm presented in Section 3 that, at the same time, builds the models and makes scheduling decisions according to their current partial estimations.

Initialization phase begins by assigning $\alpha_i = N/(m+k)$ load fractions to each p_i device. For each distant worker $\{p_i\}_{i=k+1}^{m+k}$, the initial α_i load is iteratively split into sub-fractions by applying a factoring-by-two strategy. In general, this results in a single sub-distribution β_1^i with sub-fractions calculated as:

$$\beta_{1,l}^i = \left[\left(\frac{1}{2} \right)^l \alpha_i \right] \tag{11}$$

For systems with limited memory, we propose a recursive procedure that sub-partitions load-fractions from the original sub-distribution into additional sub-distributions by applying the factoring-by-two strategy, until β^i satisfies (2). After β^i schedule is processed, the initial performance models are built via piecewise linear approximations on the real execution values [4]. Namely, ψ_{w_i}, σ_{ι_i}, σ_{o_i} and ψ_{t_i} models are constructed from the values obtained from each load-fraction, and ψ_{t_i} is further extended with the values from each sub-distribution execution.

In the *iterative phase*, the new load distribution α is calculated for each p_i device by applying (1) to the total performance models, ψ_t. For each distant worker, sub-distributions and sub-load fractions are further calculated with the algorithm presented in Section 3 by relying on partial estimations of performance models. After load processing, the device execution times are compared and if the relative differences satisfy the given accuracy, the procedure stops by marking α as the load balanced distribution. If not, the performance model estimations are updated with the newly obtained values, and the procedure restarts with the *iterative phase*, until the load balanced distribution is found.

5   Experimental Results

The proposed approach was evaluated in a real heterogeneous desktop system consisting of an Intel Core 2 Quad Q9550@2.83 GHz CPU with 12 MB L2 cache and 4 GB of DDR2 RAM, and an NVIDIA GeForce 285 GTX@1.476 GHz GPU with 1 GB of global memory. The GPU is connected to the CPU with PCI Express 2.0 x16 bus, where only a single transfer can be successfully overlapped with computation at the time. It is considered that the relative performance models were not a priori known, thus the iterative procedure was applied to the collaborative (GPU + 3 CPU Cores) execution of a real DL application performing two

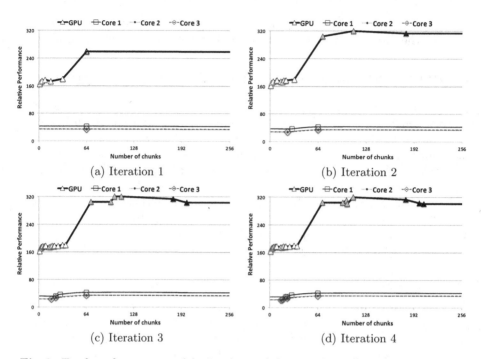

Fig. 2. Total performance models ψ_t obtained for two forward and inverse double complex 2D batch CUFFT kernels of size $x \times 512 \times 512$

forward and inverse 2D batch double floating complex Fast Fourier Transforms (FFT) of size 256 times 512×512, divisible in the first dimension. We used the optimal vendor-provided FFT implementations, i.e., NVIDIA's CUFFT 3.2 for the GPU and Intel MKL 10.3 for the CPU, on Linux OpenSuse 11.3 system.

By applying the proposed algorithm, we achieved the load balanced execution in only 4 iterations, and the obtained relative per-device performance models (after each iteration) are presented in Fig. 2. In the first iteration, the total load is equally partitioned among devices, i.e., $\alpha = \{\alpha_i = 64\}_{i=1}^4$. The GPU load is further sub-partitioned with the factoring-by-two strategy resulting in $\beta_1 = \{32, 16, 8, 4, 2, 1, 1\}$ distribution, which load fractions are executed in overlapped fashion. As shown in Fig. 2(a), we model the GPU total performance with 7 points after a single application run, i.e., 6 points are obtained at the level of each load-faction, and the final point is the performance of a complete β_1 schedule. Repeated load fractions or sub-distributions are considered as accuracy points, which do not contribute to the overall number of points, but improve the model accuracy (in this case, one accuracy point is obtained for the load fraction size of 1). By applying factoring-by-two strategy, we obtained the speed up of about 1.4 comparing to a single-fraction non-overlapped execution of the $\alpha_i = 64$ load.

According to the current ψ_t models, the load distribution for the second integration is calculated as $\alpha = \{181(\text{GPU}), 29(\text{Core 1}), 23(\text{Core 2}), 23(\text{Core 3})\}$. The GPU load is sub-fractioned according to the algorithm presented in Section 3, by

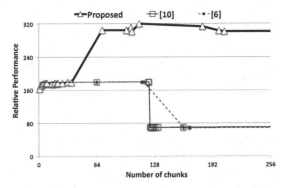

Fig. 3. Comparison of obtained performance models and relative performance

relying onto the initial partial estimations of ψ_w, σ_i and σ_o, resulting in the distribution vector: $\beta = \{\beta_1 = \{8, 14, 18, 20, 9, 1\}, \beta_2 = \{8, 14, 18, 20, 21, 21, 9\}\}$. After the second iteration, we model the GPU performance with 15 approximation points (see Fig. 2(b)), including 3 points obtained for β_1 and β_2 sub-distributions and the overall β schedule. In terms of performance, with our algorithm we outperformed the optimal single load CUFFT execution for about 4.6 times in this iteration. The calculated distributions for the third iteration are: $\alpha = \{199, 23, 17, 17\}$, and $\beta = \{\{14, 26, 36, 16, 7, 3\}, \{14, 26, 36, 16, 5\}\}$ for the GPU. As presented in Fig. 2(c), the GPU performance is modeled with 23 points after the third iteration, resulting in 4.5 speed-up comparing to the CUFFT single load execution. Finally, with the obtained distribution for the fourth iteration ($\alpha = \{205, 21, 15, 15\}$, and $\beta = \{\{14, 26, 36, 16, 7, 3\}, \{14, 26, 36, 16, 7, 3, 1\}\}$ the load balancing is achieved across all 4 devices, outperforming the single load non-overlapped CUFFT execution for about 4.3 times.

In total, by using the proposed approach, the GPU performance is modeled with 53 points in only 4 application runs, i.e., 25 approximation points (see Fig 2(d) and 28 accuracy points. In average, we obtain the speed up of about 4.5 comparing to the direct use of the optimal CUFFT library.

5.1   Comparison with the State of the Art Approaches

In order to provide a better insight on the efficiency of the proposed algorithm, we conducted the comparison with two iterative approaches to achieve load balancing that rely on the functional performance models, [6] and [10]. Albeit those approaches are developed without any communication awareness, they can be straightforwardly applied to our communication-aware total performance curves ψ_t. The performance models in [6] are represented as constants obtained from the last application run, whereas the algorithm from [10] deals with the complete functional performance curves when deciding on load balancing. Figure 3 presents the comparison of obtained ψ_t total GPU performance models when executing the above-mentioned DL application for a situation when the load balancing is achieved (if possible). By using the approach in [10], it takes 10 iterations to converge to a steady load distribution, but even then the obtained distribution is not load balanced, due to the refinement procedure applied to the performance curve with instantaneous change in the relative performance. On the other hand, the algorithm presented in [6] will neither achieve load balancing nor converge to the final distribution, as after 8 iterations it arrives to a state referred as "ping-pong" effect [4], due to its unawareness of a complete shape of the performance curve.

For both approaches, the total number of approximation points obtained for GPU performance is equal to the number of iterations, i.e., 10 for approach in [10], and 8 for approach in [6] (where 6 points are actually contributing, and the last two are repeated), comparing to 53 points obtained with our approach. Considering the time taken to completely perform the iterative procedure, the approach in [10] requires 4.3 times more time to determine the steady state distribution, whereas the algorithm from [6] takes about 3.2 times more time to arrive to a "ping-pong" state. In terms of performance, in the final iteration, our load balanced distribution is capable of achieving more than 2 times better performance comparing to a steady state distribution from [10] (when executing the complete problem in the same execution environment), and about 2.2 times better performance than the best distribution found with [6].

6 Conclusions

This paper proposes, for the first time, an algorithm for scheduling discretely divisible applications in heterogeneous desktop systems with limited memory by considering realistic performance models of computation and bidirectional asymmetric full-duplex communication links. This algorithm achieves device level multi-installment processing with multi-distributions to allow efficient overlap of computation and communication. The presented approach was experimentally evaluated for an FFT computation using optimized libraries on a GPU and 3 CPU cores. The obtained results show its capability to outperform what is thought to be the optimal implementation for about 4 times, whereas the current state of the art approaches were incapable of determining the load balanced distribution. Moreover, by employing the proposed algorithm not only more accurate performance models are constructed significantly faster, but also the overall application performance is improved.

Acknowledgments. This work was supported by FCT (INESC-ID multiannual funding) through the PIDDAC Program funds and a fellowship SFRH/BD/ 44568/2008.

References

1. Barlas, G.D., Hassan, A., Jundi, Y.A.: An Analytical Approach to the Design of Parallel Block Cipher Encryption/Decryption: A CPU/GPU Case Study. In: PDP, pp. 247–251 (2011)

2. Beaumont, O., et al.: Scheduling divisible loads on star and tree networks: results and open problems. IEEE Trans. Parallel Distributed Systems 16, 2005 (2003)
3. Berlińska, J., Drozdowski, M.: Heuristics for multi-round divisible loads scheduling with limited memory. Parallel Comput. 36, 199–211 (2010)
4. Clarke, D., Lastovetsky, A., Rychkov, V.: Dynamic load balancing of parallel computational iterative routines on platforms with memory heterogeneity. In: HeteroPar 2010 (2010)
5. Drozdowski, M., Lawenda, M.: A New Model of Multi-installment Divisible Loads Processing in Systems with Limited Memory. In: Wyrzykowski, R., Dongarra, J., Karczewski, K., Wasniewski, J. (eds.) PPAM 2007. LNCS, vol. 4967, pp. 1009–1018. Springer, Heidelberg (2008)
6. Galindo, I., Almeida, F., Badía-Contelles, J.M.: Dynamic Load Balancing on Dedicated Heterogeneous Systems. In: Lastovetsky, A., Kechadi, T., Dongarra, J. (eds.) EuroPVM/MPI 2008. LNCS, vol. 5205, pp. 64–74. Springer, Heidelberg (2008)
7. Ghatpande, A., Nakazato, H., Watanabe, H., Beaumont, O.: Divisible load scheduling with result collection on heterogeneous systems. In: IPDPS, pp. 1–8 (2008)
8. Ilic, A., Sousa, L.: Algorithm for divisible load scheduling on heterogeneous systems with realistic performance models. Tech. rep., INESC-ID (May 2011)
9. Ilic, A., Sousa, L.: Collaborative execution environment for heterogeneous parallel systems. In: APDCM/IPDPS 2010 (2010)
10. Lastovetsky, A., Reddy, R.: Data partitioning with a functional performance model of heterogeneous processors. Int. J. High Perform. Comput. Appl. 21, 76–90 (2007)
11. Shokripour, A., Othman, M.: Survey on divisible load theory and its applications. In: ICIME 2009, pp. 300–304 (2009)
12. Veeravalli, B., Ghose, D., Robertazzi, T.G.: Divisible load theory: A new paradigm for load scheduling in distributed systems. Cluster Computing 6, 7–17 (2003)

Peer Group and Fuzzy Metric to Remove Noise in Images Using Heterogeneous Computing

Ma. Guadalupe Sánchez[1], Vicente Vidal[2], and Jordi Bataller[2]

[1] Departamento de Sistemas y Computación, Instituto Tecnológico de Cd. Guzmán,
49100, Cd. Guzmán, Jalisco, Mexico
msanchez@dsic.upv.es
[2] Departamento de Sistemas Informáticos y Computación E.P.S. Gandia,
Universidad Politécnica de Valencia, 46730, Grao de Gandia, Valencia, Spain
{vvidal,bataller}@dsic.upv.es

Abstract. In this paper, we report a study on the parallelization of an algorithm for removing impulsive noise in images. The algorithm is based on the concept of peer group and fuzzy metric. We have developed implementations using Open Multi-Processing (OpenMP) and Compute Unified Device Architecture (CUDA) for Graphics Processing Unit (GPU). Many sequential algorithms have been proposed to remove noise, but their computational cost is excessive for real-time processing of large images. We developed implementations for a multi-core CPU, for a multi-GPU (several GPUs) and for a combination of both. These implementations were compared also with different sizes of the image in order to find out the settings with the best performance. A study is made using the shared memory and texture memory to minimize access time to data in GPU global memory. The result shows that when the image is distributed in multi-core and multi-GPU a greater number of Mpixels/second are processed.

Keywords: remove impulsive noise, peer group, fuzzy metric, parallel algorithm, CUDA, OpenMP, multi-core, multi-GPU.

1 Introduction

Image denoising is still an open problem in the field of image processing, because damaged images may affect the performance and accuracy of some processes. Also, images under consideration may be very large and may require a real-time processing and this requires optimal implementations. For instance, noise removal is of paramount importance in emerging applications related to biomedical science, earth science, cultural heritage preservation, video communications, image post-processing, robotic inspection and surveillance. Impulsive noise is commonly found in images caused by the malfunction of sensors during the process of image formation, aging of the storage material or transmission errors due to natural or man-made processes [1]. This type of noise affects individual pixels, changing its original value. The widespread model of impulse noise is the "Salt and Pepper" model, or fixed-value noise. It considers that when a pixel is wrong, its value is an extreme value within the signal range. This is the model that we assume in the present paper.

M. Alexander et al. (Eds.): Euro-Par 2011 Workshops, Part I, LNCS 7155, pp. 502–510, 2012.
© Springer-Verlag Berlin Heidelberg 2012

Many algorithms (filters) to reduce impulsive noise in images have been introduced: [1–13]. These cited works are based on the concept of "peer group". Given a pixel x_i, a peer group is the set of its neighbors that are similar to it, according to a chosen metric, [1] [10]. These filters have recently shown good results in quality but they do not seem to be appropriate for real-time processing.

Resources for real-time processing are easily available. For example, the Graphics Processing Units (GPUs) are currently a very popular platform for developing parallel applications, considering price and speed. It is obvious the convenience to develop parallel filter implementations for them.

In this paper, we introduce a parallel version of filters based on peer group and fuzzy metric in order to keep their best quality results while trying to improve its performance, making them usable for real-time processing. We have tested these algorithms using several GPUs (multi-GPU) in parallel, using also a multi-core CPU, and using the GPUs and the CPU in combination. We have investigated the most convenient distribution of the pixels on the memories and caches for these devices (for instance: shared memory versus texture memory) to take the most advantage of the hardware.

The paper is organized as follows: Section 2 explains the two steps of the denoising algorithm to be parallelized. Section 3 discusses how the algorithm has been implemented in a multi-GPU and in a multi-core CPU. The results of the experimental study are shown in Section 4. Finally, section 5 presents the conclusions reached using heterogeneous computing to eliminate noise in the images.

2   Denoising Algorithm

Our algorithm uses the peer group of a central pixel x_i in a window W according to [1], but with a fuzzy metric instead. The fuzzy distance [12] between pixels x_i and x_j in the color image is given by the following function:

$$M\left(x_i, x_j\right) = \prod_{l=1}^{3} \frac{min\ \{x_i(l), x_j(l)\} + k}{max\ \{x_i(l), x_j(l)\} + k},$$

(1)

where $(x_i(1), x_i(2), x_i(3))$ is the color vector for the pixel x_i in RGB and x_j is a neighbor of x_i. In [6], it was shown that $k = 1024$ is an appropriate setting to maintain the image quality, and this is therefore the value that we use in our study.

The peer group of a pixel x_i is comprised by the pixels of a window centered in x_i whose distance M from x_i exceeds d:

$$P(x_i, d) = \{x_j \in W : M\left(x_i, x_j\right) \geq d\}$$

(2)

where $0 \leq d \leq 1$ is the distance threshold.

The sketch of the denoising algorithm has two main steps. In the first step, *detection*, the pixels are labeled either as *corrupted* or as *uncorrupted*. In the second step, *filtering*, the corrupted pixels are corrected. This is the description of the processing for each pixel x_i.

— Detection: x_i is declared as corrupted if $\# P\ (x_i, d) \leq (q + 1)$, where q is the value defined to decide if the pixel is labeled as corrupted or uncorrupted, and $\# P$ the cardinality of the set P.
— Filtering: if x_i was previously marked as corrupted, it is replaced using the well known arithmetic mean filter (AMF) [2], [3]. This is the new value for x_{ik} (color component k of x_i) is $(\sum x_{ij})/(\#W\text{-}1)$ for all $x_j \in W$ with $j \neq i$.

The algorithm must be divided into two steps because the AMF considers only uncorrupted pixels for the mean computation and, therefore, the second step cannot start until the detection is completely done.

3   Multi-GPU and Multi-core CPU Implementations

We have developed three implementations of the algorithm described in the previous section, for two parallel architectures. The first implementation is based on OpenMP and targets a multi-core CPU. The second implementation is developed in CUDA for a multi-GPU. The third version uses the combination of CPU and GPU.

The first decision to make is which part of the image is to be processed by each computing unit. For instance, figure 1 shows the case of the CPU, in which rows above the line s are assigned to one core, and the rest to a second core, leaving the remaining cores and the GPUs idle. Figure 2 shows an example of dividing an image into two parts, each one to be processed by a different GPU. Finally, figure 3 shows a partition of the image into eight horizontal blocks, to be processed by a combination of GPUs and cores CPU.

The implementations on GPUs have some differential traits. Data to be processed must be transferred from main memory (RAM) to the GPU memory and the results must be copied back to main memory. On the other hand, tasks to be executed by a GPU are coded into functions called kernels. In order to ensure the synchronization of the two steps of the algorithm, we have developed two kernels, one for detection and another for filtering, so that the latter won't start until the first ends. Therefore, before the actual processing starts in a GPU, the CPU control program must select which GPU to be used, to copy data to them, to launch the kernels (with the appropriate scheduling) and to recover the results. It is obvious that the transfers will affect the processing time.

An additional issue is that the GPUs have a stack of memories [16], [14] with different features (size, speed and access). This requires considering where to place and how to access data once they are into the GPU. For instance, figure 4 shows two choices: using shared memory (a) or using texture memory (b).

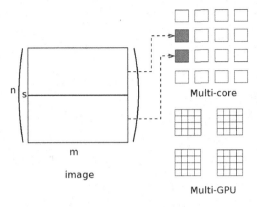

Fig. 1. Image divided in 2 cores, none GPUs used

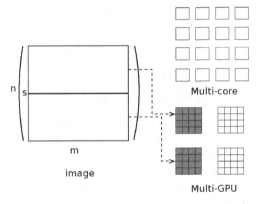

Fig. 2. Image divided in 2 GPUs, none cores used

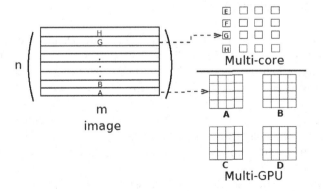

Fig. 3. Image divided in 4 GPUs and 4 cores

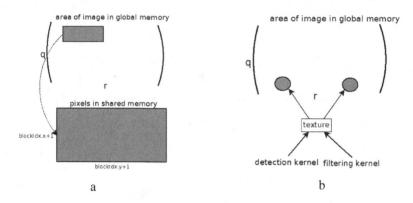

Fig. 4. GPU global memory access with a) shared memory b) texture memory

Fig. 5. Original image of a building

Using shared memory implies that data must be further copied from the GPU global memory to a shared memory block, available only to the set of threads being executed by the same multi-processor in a GPU. Texture memory is used in read-only mode and accessed by the detection and filtering kernels.

4   Experimental Study

We conducted the experimentation on a Mac OS X (Intel Quad-Core Xeon 2 x 2.26 GHz, 8GB of RAM) with 4 NVIDIA GPUs. Each card is a GeForce GT120, 512MB of memory, and 4 multi-processors. The image for the tests is shown in figure 5. This image was taken from the Kodak database ([15]) and it was resized in several sizes.

The first tests performed were to compare the use of shared memory versus texture memory, using 1, 2 and 4 GPUs. Table 1 summarizes the results. This results shows improvements if texture memory is used. Therefore, in the following tests, texture memory is always used.

The following test was the use of the CPU with 16 cores for the noise removal on different sizes of the image. Figure 6 shows the results. For sizes larger than 384x256, we got the best results when all the 16 cores are used. On the contrary, for smaller sizes, it is better using only 8 cores.

Table 1. Results in Mpixels/sec when the image is processed and stored in texture memory and shared memory

Image size	Texture memory	Shared memory	GPU
6144x4096	20.6599	17.3378	1
6144x4096	30.5744	29.4889	2
6144x4096	47.1182	41.3707	4

Now, our study focuses on the effect of using several GPUs. Figure 7 collects the results in function of the number of GPUs used, but only for the execution inside the GPUs, this is, without data transfer RAM-GPU. It is clear that the better outcomes occur when all the GPUs are used (4 in our case). On the other hand, figure 8 shows results for the overall execution, now including the data transfer RAM-GPU. If the image is smaller than 1536x1024 pixels, it is better to use a single GPU because the time used in transfers is not compensated by the use of more GPUs. On the contrary, for larger sizes than 1536x1024, using more GPUs improves the performance despite the memory transfers. Therefore, we conclude the following:

— for image sizes less than 768x512, it's better to use one GPU.
— for image sizes between 768x512 and 3072x2048, it's better to use two GPUs.
— for image sizes greater than 6144x4096, it's better to use four GPUs.

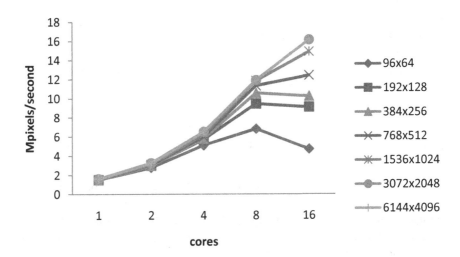

Fig. 6. Parallelizing image with multi-core

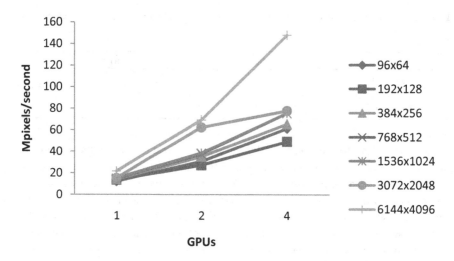

Fig. 7. Mpixels/sec executed by both kernels (no memory transfers accounted)

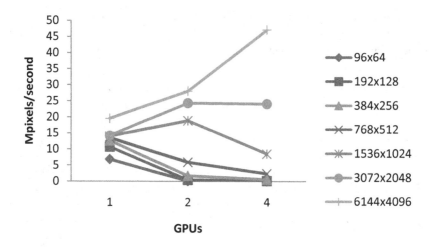

Fig. 8. Mpixels Mpixels/sec executed by both kernels (total processing)

In the last tests, the cores CPU and the GPUs were simultaneously used. Table 2 compares the best results if only the CPU, only the GPU or both are used. For any size of the image, it is better to use the combination of both.

Table 3 shows the combination GPU and CPU, and how many cores and GPUs was used for each size of the image, also the table shows the size of the image assigned to the GPU (the rest is processed by the CPU, obviously). If the image size increases, more processing is done on the GPU and more GPUs are used.

Table 2. Megapixels/sec results for processing using only Multi-core, only Multi-GPU, and both

Image size	Multicore	MultiGPU	Multicore and MultiGPU
96x64	6.8267	6.83	8.3706
192x128	9.4523	10.69	15.5446
384x256	10.5703	12.60	20.0130
768x512	12.4043	13.51	37.1379
1536x1024	14.8805	18.86	42.3953
3072x2048	15.9601	24.34	43.7819
3072x2048	15.9601	24.10	69.9105
6144x4096	16.1206	47.12	68.4600

Table 3. The size of the image assigned to the GPU for processing, the cores and the GPU used

Image size	GPUs	Cores	Size on GPU
96x64	1	16	1/4
192x128	1	11	3/8
384x256	1	7	1/2
768x512	1	9	3/4
1536x1024	2	9	3/4
3072x2048	2	9	3/4
3072x2048	4	11	7/8
6144x4096	4	7	7/8

5   Concluding Remarks

The availability of inexpensive parallel processing hardware provided by graphics processing units has boosted the development of many applications for demanding problems. Image denoising is a problem that fits very well in this scenario because images may be large, the processing is costly, and image pixels, to an extent, can be handled simultaneously.

In this paper we have adapted a denoising algorithm, based on the peer group concept and using a fuzzy metric, to run concurrently. Our implementation was developed to be executed either on a multi-core CPU, on several GPUs, or using the CPU along with the GPUs. The results showed that this latter option (CPU+GPUs) gives the best performance. On the way, we have shown the best settings when using GPUs, because they need a very fine tuning to get the best yield.

The final conclusion is that implementing image denoising algorithms to be run on multi-core CPUs and GPUs are very advisable. This opens the door to use such algorithms for real-time processing. In future works, we plan to test our programs on the last generation GPUs cards and to try other common problems on images, such as edge detection.

Acknowledgments. This work was funded by the Spanish Ministry of Science and Innovation (Project TIN2008-06570-C04-04) and M. Guadalupe would also like to acknowledge DGEST ITCG for the scholarship awarded through the PROMEP program (Mexico).

References

1. Smolka, B.: Peer group switching filter for impulse noise reduction in color images. Pattern Recognition Letters 31, 484–495 (2010)
2. Camarena, J.G., Gregori, V., Morillas, S., Sapena, A.: Fast detection and removal of impulsive noise using peer group and fuzzy metrics. Journal of Visual Communication and Image Representation 19, 20–29 (2008)
3. Toprak, A., Guller, I.: Impulse noise reduction in medical images with the use of switch mode fuzzy adaptive median filter. Digital Signal Processing 17(4), 711–723 (2007)
4. Schulte, S., Nachtegael, M., De Witte, V., Van der Weken, D., Kerre, E.E.: A Fuzzy Impulse Noise Detection and Reduction Method. IEEE Transaction on Image Processing 15, 5 (2006)
5. Shulte, S., Morillas, S., Gregori, V., Kerre, E.E.: A New Fuzzy Color Correlated Impulse Noise Reduction Method. IEEE Transaction on Image Processing 15, 10 (2007)
6. Shulte, S., De Witte, V., Nachtegael, M., Van der Weken, D., Kerre, E.E.: Fuzzy Two Step Filter for Impulse Noise Reduction From Color Images. IEEE Transaction on Image Processing 15, 11 (2006)
7. Shulte, S., De Witte, V., Nachtegael, M., Van der Weken, D., Kerre, E.E.: Fuzzy random impulse noise reduction method. Journal Fuzzy Sets and Systems 158(3) (2007)
8. Mélange, T., Nachtegael, M., Kerre, E.E.: Fuzzy Random Impulse Noise Removal From Colour Image Sequences: IEEE (2010)
9. Morillas, S., Gregori, V., Hervas, A.: Fuzzy Peer Groups for Reducing Mixed Gaussian-Impulse Noise From Color Images. IEEE Transaction on Image Processing 18, 7 (2009)
10. Camarena, J.G., Gregori, V., Morillas, S., Sapena, A.: Some improvements for image filtering using peer group techniques. Image Vis. Comput. 28(1), 188–201 (2010)
11. Morillas, S., Gregori, V., Peris-Fajarnés, G.: Isolating impulsive noise pixels in color images by peer group techniques. Comput. Vis. Image Underst. 110(1), 102–116 (2008)
12. Camarena, J.G., Gregori, V., Morillas, S., Sapena, A.: Two-step fuzzy logic based method for impulse noise detection in colour images. Pattern Recognition Letters 31, 1842–1849 (2010)
13. Smolka, B.: Fast detection and impulsive noise removal in color images. Real-Time Imaging 11, 389–402 (2005)
14. Sánchez, M.G., Vidal, V., Bataller, J., Arnal, J.: Implementing a GPU fuzzy filter for Impulsive Image Noise Correction. In: CMSSE (2010)
15. Kodak, http://r0k.us/graphics/kodak/index.html
16. Nvidia, http://www.nvidia.es/page/home.html

Estimation of MPI Application Performance on Volunteer Environments

Girish Nandagudi[1], Jaspal Subhlok[1], Edgar Gabriel[1], and Judit Gimenez[2]

[1] Department of Computer Science, University of Houston
{jaspal,egabriel}@uh.edu
[2] Barcelona Supercomputing Center
judit@bsc.es

Abstract. Emerging MPI libraries, such as VolpexMPI and P2P MPI, allow message passing parallel programs to execute effectively in heterogeneous volunteer environments despite frequent failures. However, the performance of message passing codes varies widely in a volunteer environment, depending on the application characteristics and the computation and communication characteristics of the nodes and the interconnection network. This paper has the dual goal of developing and validating a tool chain to estimate performance of MPI codes in a volunteer environment and analyzing the suitability of the class of computations represented by NAS benchmarks for volunteer computing. The framework is deployed to estimate performance in a variety of possible volunteer configurations, including some based on the measured parameters of a campus volunteer pool. The results show slowdowns by factors between 2 and 10 for different NAS benchmark codes for execution on a realistic volunteer campus pool as compared to dedicated clusters.

1 Introduction

Most desktop computers and workstations are virtually idle as much as 90% of the time, representing what the volunteer computing community sees as an attractive "free" platform for parallel computations. Idle desktops have been successfully used to run sequential and master-slave task parallel codes, most notably under Condor [1] and BOINC [2]. Extending the classes of application that can be executed in a volunteer environment is challenging, since the compute resources are heterogeneous, have varying compute, memory and network capacity, and become unavailable for computation frequently and without warning. The Volpex project team, that includes the authors of this paper, has developed middleware for executing communicating parallel programs on volunteer nodes with orchestrated use of redundancy and communication logging. Volpex Dataspace API [3] provides a mechanism for applications to communicate through anonymous, asynchronous Put/Get operations. VolpexMPI [4] and P2P MPI [5] are MPI implemetations customized for volunteer environments.

Porting a large scale application to a volunteer environment presents numerous challenges even for MPI, a portable Message Passing Interface, examples of which are as follows:

M. Alexander et al. (Eds.): Euro-Par 2011 Workshops, Part I, LNCS 7155, pp. 511–520, 2012.

- A modest effort and some expertise is necessary to deploy applications in a BOINC or CONDOR execution management environment.
- As volunteer nodes may have limited memory, a memory intensive application may have to be recast, e.g., on a higher number of parallel processes, to run correctly and efficiently.
- Communication intensive applications may require some customization for scheduling, such as limiting execution to nodes on a campus network.
- For applications employing licensed software, arrangements have to be made that the applications can run correctly and legally on volunteer nodes.

The reasons that make parallel computing in a volunteer environment challenging - primarily heterogeneity, variable compute and communication capacity, and high rates of failure - also make performance prediction on such environments challenging. Hence it is often unclear if a parallel message passing code will run effectively in a volunteer environment. Given that porting to a volunteer environment represents a significant investment, it is highly desirable that an estimate of the expected performance in a volunteer environment be available *before* the actual porting. The key objective of this research is to build a framework for estimating the performance of message passing MPI codes on volunteer environments. The paper also specifically characterizes the performance of NAS benchmarks in volunteer environments.

Performance on a volunteer environment depends on the computation and communication characteristics of the volunteer environment. This research employs the Dimemas framework to predict application performance in different types of volunteer environments. The high failure rates in volunteer environments can add an additional overhead, if, e.g., checkpoint restart is used for recovery. This overhead is dependent on a large set of parameters such as failure characteristics, degree of redundancy, and checkpointing frequency and overheads. These are not the subject of this paper and are partially addressed in related work. The main subject of this work is to estimate the performance of a given MPI application under a variety of scenarios including scenarios representing measured characteristics of a campus LAN.

2   Related Work

This work is in the context of fault tolerant MPI libraries. Several MPI libraries incorporate checkpoint-restart for fault-tolerance, with MPICH-V [6] being probably the best known example. This library is based on uncoordinated checkpointing and pessimistic message logging. MPI/FT [7] and P2P-MPI [5] are based on process replication techniques. Volpex MPI [4], which is the context of this work, employs checkpointing as well as replication. The focus of this work is estimating the performance of an MPI library in a volunteer computing environment in general.

Dimemas [8] is a performance analysis tool that allows the user to predict the performance of a parallel application on a simulated target architecture. Dimemas is the basis of of the simulations employed in this work and is discussed in more detail in the following sections. Dimemas has been used in heterogeneous environments to predict the performance of applications for resource selection [9].

SimBOINC [10] is a simulator designed to test new scheduling strategies in BOINC and other desktop and volunteer systems. SimBOINC simulates a client-server platform where multiple clients request work from a central server. The characteristics of the client, the workload and the network connecting the client and server can be specified as simulation inputs. The results provide scheduler performance metrics, such as effective resource shares, and task deadline misses. EmBOINC [11] (Emulator of BOINC Projects) is a trace-driven emulator that models heterogeneous hosts and their interaction with a real BOINC server. EmBOINC uses statistical information obtained from real BOINC traces to characterize volatile, heterogeneous, and error-prone hosts. Both the above tools (SimBOINC and EmBOINC) are focused on scheduling and node selection and do not provide a way to simulate the performance of communicating parallel applications on desktop grids.

3   Simulation Framework

The main goal of this research is to estimate the performance of an MPI application under volunteer environments with different execution characteristics. The simulation framework is based on the *Dimemas* tool chain developed at Barcelona Supercomputing Center. Dimemas [8] simulates the performance of an application on a user-defined virtual architecture. Dimemas has an extensive suite of parameters that can be used to customize a virtual environment to mimic a real-life environment. The following important properties of an execution environment can be defined with Dimemas:

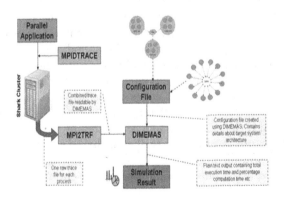

Fig. 1. Dimemas based simulation framework

– *Simulated Node Architecture* including the number of CPUs per node, relative processor speed, memory bandwidth, file system parameters, and number of parallel network links.

– *Simulated Network Architecture* including LAN/WAN configuration, maximum bandwidth on network links, latency on network links, external network traffic model, and network sharing model.

In addition to the the Dimemas simulator, the framework employs tools to record and merge execution traces. *MPIDTRACE* program traces the application execution and generates a trace file (one per process) containing the run time actions of the application including communication calls and computation blocks, along with details such as elapsed times and the source and destination processes for communication calls. *MPI2TRF* program is used to merge the per-process trace files generated by the MPIDTRACE program into a single file that can be read by Dimemas. Estimating the performance of a given application on a volunteer environment consists of the following steps: i) Execute the application linked with MPIDTRACE on a reliable execution platform like a cluster and collect the trace, ii) combine the individual process traces into a single trace with MPI2TRF, iii) configure Dimemas to reflect the desired volunteer computing environment, and iv) perform the simulation with Dimemas to obtain the predicted execution time. The simulation steps are also summarized in Figure 1.

4   Experiments and Results

4.1   Simulation Configuration

The simulation is performed on two types of network configurations. We refer to the first configuration as the *Desktops over Internet (DOI)* configuration, and to the second as the *Collection of Networked Computers (CNC)* configuration. These configurations are illustrated in Figure 2.

The DOI configuration consists of desktop PCs connected with an institutional LAN or Wide Area Network/Internet. This environment is characterized by the latency and bandwidth between individual nodes and the network. There are no shared network resources that would represent a fundamental bottleneck. The assumption is that the switch that connects the PCs in a LAN environment offers full bisection bandwidth. For nodes connected by the Internet, it is implicitly assumed that the PCs in different regions do not share the same route in the Internet, and if they do, the traffic generated by the nodes is negligible as compared to the rest of the Internet traffic on shared routes.

The CNC configuration on the other hand, is a two stage hierarchy of networks of computers. Individual groups of computers, representing separate labs or computation centers physically, are connected to each other over a LAN within the lab. Then these groups/labs communicate with others through WAN/Internet. In contrast to the DOI configuration discussed above, the connections between PCs in one lab communicating to PCs in another lab have to share a single link.

Both configurations apply a *linear* model for access to a shared network implying that only one node accesses a shared LAN/WAN at a given time. In general, DOI has the relative advantage over CNC that no links to the WAN are shared, while CNC has the relative advantage over DOI that there is a reduced possibility of delays at the central WAN as some communication can be completed within the local LANs. The latter is most significant for all-all type communication patterns.

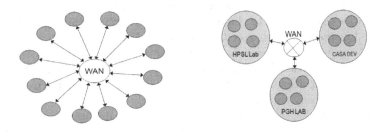

Fig. 2. Graphical representations of the Desktops over Internet configuration (left) and Collection of Networked Computers configuration (right)

All traces for the simulations were generated on the "Shark" cluster at the University of Houston. The Shark is a heterogeneous cluster consisting of 24 Sun X2100 nodes, each with a 2.2 GHz dual core AMD Opteron processor and 2 GB main memory, and 5 Sun X2200 nodes, each with two 2.2 GHz quad core AMD Opteron processors (8 cores total) and 8 GB main memory. The network interconnect of Shark cluster comprises of a 4xInfiniBand network interconnect and a Gigabit Ethernet network. For results presented, the Gigabit Ethernet network has been used. This cluster also serves as a reference cluster for estimating relative performance on volunteer nodes.

Four NAS benchmarks are used for evaluation: The CG, IS, SP, and FT represent diversity in terms of communication volume and communication pattern. The CG and the IS benchmarks are considered communication intensive for different reasons. CG sends a large number of point-to-point messages between processes. IS is dominated by an all-to-all communication pattern with relatively few large messages. The FT benchmark also uses an all-to-all communication pattern, but with smaller messages and more frequent operations. Due to the complexity of the compute operations involved in the FT benchmark the ratio of computation to communication in FT is lower than in IS. The dominant communication pattern of the SP benchmark is a 5-point stencil communication, which leads to a 'localized' communication behavior of the code.

4.2   Desktop over Internet Configuration Results

We report on experiments carried out on the DOI configuration. Execution of NAS Class B benchmarks CG, FT, IS and SP on 16 and 32/36 processes was simulated with a range of (synthetic) bandwidth and latency values for the network. The *reference* execution simulated a cluster with 128MBps bandwidth and 0.05 seconds latency. Simulations were performed for bandwidths {12.5 MBps,

1.25MBps, 0.125 MBps} and latencies {0.1ms, 1 ms and 10 ms} spanning the range from clusters to very slow Internet connected nodes. The goal is to estimate the impact on execution time of reduced bandwidth and increased latency that represent various flavors of volunteer computing environments. The results are plotted in Figure 3.

Figure 3 (a) shows expected increase in execution time for a comprehensive set of scenarios as compared to cluster execution. We omit detailed comments for brevity, and instead focus on specific scenarios in Figure 3 (b) and (c). Figure 3 (b) simulates the expected slowdown when the available bandwidth is reduced from the reference cluster level value of 128MBps while the latency is fixed at .1 msecs. We limit our discussion to the case of 16 nodes as the patterns for 32/36 nodes are qualitatively similar.

We notice that the slowdown for reduction of bandwidth to 12.5 MBps is relatively modest, ranging from a low of 17% for FT to a high of 265% for IS. Reduction of bandwidth to 1.25MBps has a far more dramatic effect: from a roughly 2fold slowdown (190%) for FT and up to a 30fold slowdown (2913%) for IS. The conclusion is that for NAS benchmarks, the impact of reduction in bandwidth is specific to the computation/benchmark in question, and relatively modest (say around or below a factor of 2) in many interesting scenarios.

We now focus on Figure 3(c) that shows the sensitivity of the benchmarks to latency. Here, the bandwidth is fixed at 128 MBps and comparisons are made for various latency values against a reference latency value of 0.1 milliseconds. The graph shows that the impact is very low, below a 15% slowdown, for most scenarios. The notable exception is CG, where the slodown is 43% for a latency of 1 msecs and over 600% for a latency of 10 msecs. The slowdown of SP rises to 190% for a latency of 10 msecs.

4.3   Collection of Networked Computers Configuration Results

Simulations were conducted using the CNC configuration with the same set of benchmarks, problem sizes and number of processors. Selected results are presented in fig. 4. The key difference between DOI and CNC configuration is that in CNC configuration groups of nodes share a link to the backbone network. For this reason, CNC configuration is generally slower for a uniform setting of latency and bandwidth, but can be faster as fewer connections access the central WAN.

Figure 4 (a) simulates the expected slowdown when the available bandwidth is reduced with the same parameters as those for Figure 3 (b) for the DOI configuration. Similarly Figure 4 (b) shows the sensitivity of performance to latency for a fixed bandwidth with parameters same as Figure 3 (c) for the DOI configuration.

The general pattern of results is the same as for the DOI configuration but with generally higher slowdowns due to sharing. An interesting case is the FT benchmark which is far more sensitive to available bandwidth in CNC configuration as compared to its performance in DOI configuration. The probable reason is that the all-all communication in FT saturates the bandwidth of the links

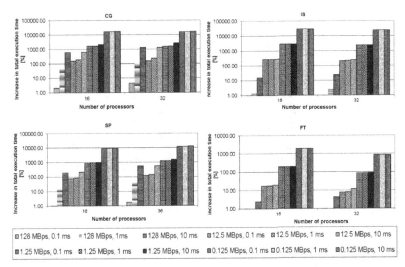

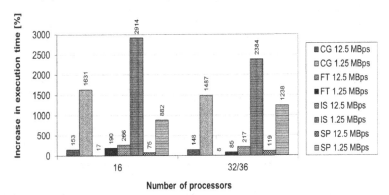

(a) Slowdown for a suite of latency/bandwidth configurations

(b) Slowdown with fixed latency (0.1 msecs) and reduced bandwidth

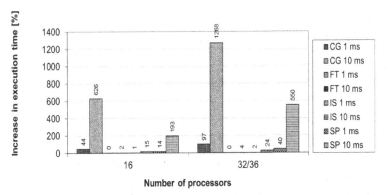

(c) Slowdown with fixed bandwidth (128 Mbps) and increased latency

Fig. 3. Percentage increase in execution time versus a cluster for the DOI configuration

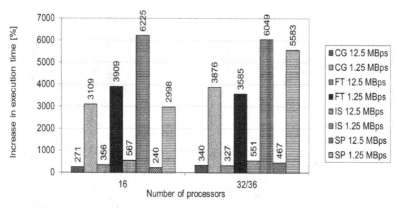

(a) Slowdown with fixed latency (0.1 msecs) and reduced bandwidth

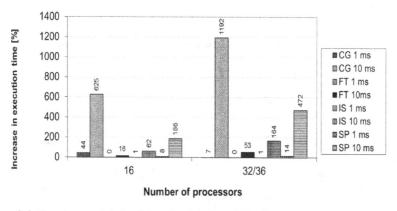

(b) Slowdown with fixed bandwidth (128 Mbps) and increased latency

Fig. 4. Percentage increase in execution time versus a cluster for the CNC configuration

connecting LAN groups to WAN/Internet connection which cannot happen in the DOI configuration. The overall slowdown numbers underline the potential of LAN to WAN bottlenecks to impact performance: for bandwidth reduced to a worst case of 1.25Mbps, the slowdown approximately ranges between 30fold to60 fold for the CNC configuration. In comparison, the DOI configuration exhibited up to a 30fold slowdown.

4.4   Simulation on Real-Life Environments

For this set of experiments, we measured the actual latency and bandwidth in the following scenarios in our computing environment. For the Shark cluster; the measured point to point bandwidth was 95MBps and latency 0.05 milliseconds. Between the desktops in a single lab in our building, the measured point to point bandwidth was 12MBps and latency .4 milliseconds. Between lab desktops connected across a LAN, the measured point to point bandwidth was 7MBps and latency .8 milliseconds.

First this data was used to validate and parameterize simulations as shown in Figure 5(a). While the absolute measured and predicted performance varies up to around 25%, the accuacy was judged sufficient for our purposes as the relative comparison of different configuratios is still meaningful. Next, the performance of the cluster environment was compared with our PC lab environment with 3 groups of nodes; the nodes within a group are connected at measured LAN specs of 12MBps and latency .4 milliseconds, while the WAN latency and bandwidth across the groups of nodes are .8 msecs and 7MBps respectively. The results are presented in Figure 5(b). The results show 2fold to 10fold slowdowns.

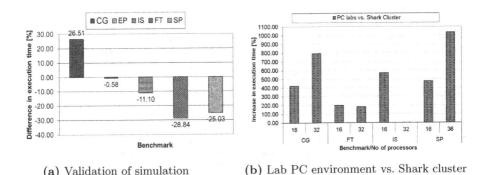

(a) Validation of simulation   (b) Lab PC environment vs. Shark cluster

Fig. 5. Validation and performance in realistic environments

5   Conclusions

This paper has presented a methodology based on Dimemas toolkit that allows the estimation of performance of MPI codes on heterogeneous volunteer nodes. The methodology was employed to estimate the performance of selected NAS benchmarks on a large number of scenarios including those that are typical of a volunteer environment built from idle desktops. The result also provide significant insight into likely performance of NAS benchmarks on realistic desktop PC environment. NAS benchmarks executing on volunteer nodes connected by commodity LAN network is a factor of 2 to 10 slower than a dedicated cluster. While a volunteer environment is not expected to compete with a dedicated cluster in performance for a fixed number of nodes, the results show that it offers a practical 'free' alternative that may be satisfactory for many application scenarios.

Acknowledgments. Partial support for this work was provided by the National Science Foundation's Computer Systems Research program under Award No. CNS-0834750. Any opinions, findings, and conclusions or recommendations expressed in this material are those of the authors and do not necessarily reflect the views of the National Science Foundation.

References

1. Thain, D., Tannenbaum, T., Livny, M.: Distributed computing in practice: the condor experience. Concurrency - Practice and Experience 17(2-4), 323–356 (2005)
2. Anderson, D.: BOINC: a system for public-resource computing and storage. In: Fifth IEEE/ACM International Workshop on Grid Computing (November 2004)
3. Pedamallu, E., Nguyen, H., Kanna, N., Wang, Q., Subhlok, J., Gabriel, E., Cheung, M., Anderson, D.: A robust communication framework for parallel execution on volunteer PC grids. In: CCGrid 2011: The 11th IEEE/ACM International Symposium on Clusters, Cloud and Grid Computing, Newport Beach, CA (May 2011)
4. LeBlanc, T., Anand, R., Gabriel, E., Subhlok, J.: VolpexMPI: An MPI Library for Execution of Parallel Applications on Volatile Nodes. In: Ropo, M., Westerholm, J., Dongarra, J. (eds.) EuroPVM/MPI 2009. LNCS, vol. 5759, pp. 124–133. Springer, Heidelberg (2009)
5. Genaud, S., Rattanapoka, C.: Large-scale experiment of co-allocation strategies for peer-to-peer supercomputing in p2p-mpi. In: IEEE International Symposium on Parallel and Distributed Processing, IPDPS 2008, pp. 1–8 (2008)
6. Bosilca, G., Bouteiller, A., Cappello, F., Djilali, S., Fédak, G., Germain, C., Hérault, T., Lemarinier, P., Lodygensky, O., Magniette, F., Néri, V., Selikhov, A.: MPICH-V: Toward a scalable fault tolerant MPI for volatile nodes. In: Proceedings of the SuperComputing 2002 Conference (November 2002)
7. Batchu, R., Neelamegam, J., Cui, Z., Beddhua, M., Skjellum, A., Dandass, Y., Apte, M.: MPI/FT: architecture and taxonomies for fault-tolerant, message-passing middleware for performance-portable parallel computing. In: Proceedings of the 1 IEEE International Symposium of Cluster Computing and the Grid (2001)
8. Badia, R., Labarta, J., Gimenez, J., Escale, F.: DIMEMAS: Predicting MPI applications behavior in Grid environments. In: Workshop on Grid Applications and Programming Tools, GGF8 (2003)
9. Lindner, P., Gabriel, E., Resch, M.M.: Performance Prediction Based Resource Selection in Grid Environments. In: Perrott, R., Chapman, B.M., Subhlok, J., de Mello, R.F., Yang, L.T. (eds.) HPCC 2007. LNCS, vol. 4782, pp. 228–238. Springer, Heidelberg (2007)
10. Taufer, M., Kerstens, A., Estrada, T., Flores, D., Teller, P.: Simba: a discrete event simulator for performance prediction of volunteer computing projects. In: International Workshop on Principles of Advanced and Distributed Simulation 2007 (March 2007)
11. Estrada, T., Taufer, M., Anderson, D.P.: Performance prediction and analysis of BOINC projects: An empirical study with EmBOINC. Journal of Grid Computing 7(4), 537–554 (2009)

Author Index